FIFTH EDITION

Social Work

An Empowering Profession

Brenda DuBois

St. Ambrose University

Karla Krogsrud Miley

Black Hawk College

PEARSON

Boston New York San Francisco
Mexico City Montreal Toronto London Madrid Munich Paris
Hong Kong Singapore Tokyo Cape Town Sydney

Series Editor: *Patricia Quinlin*
Editorial Assistant: *Annemarie Kennedy*
Marketing Manager: *Kris Ellis-Levy*
Editorial-Production Administrator: *Annette Joseph*
Editorial-Production Service: *Holly Crawford*
Photo Researcher: *Katharine S. Cook*
Composition Buyer: *Linda Cox*
Electronic Composition and Art: *Omegatype Typography, Inc.*
Manufacturing Buyer: *JoAnne Sweeney*
Cover Administrator: *Kristina Mose-Libon*
Cover Designer: *Susan Paradise*

For related titles and support materials, visit our online catalog at www.ablongman.com

Library of Congress Cataloging-in-Publication Data

DuBois, Brenda
Social work : an empowering profession / Brenda DuBois, Karla Krogsrud Miley.—5th ed.
p. cm.
Includes bibliographical references and index.
ISBN 0-205-40180-5
1. Social service. 2. Social service—United States. I. Miley, Karla Krogsrud. II. Title.

HV40.D78 2005
361.3'2—dc22

2003069047

Printed in the United States of America

10 9 8 7 6 5 4 3 2 1 RRD-VA 09 08 07 06 05 04

See page 524 for a continuation of the copyright page.

CONTENTS

PREFACE

Social work is a professional discipline. It is a field of study that has uniquely blended perspectives from other disciplines, particularly the biological and social sciences, with its own values, knowledge, and skills. Education for the profession requires foundational understanding of human needs, social problems, social welfare responses, consumers of social services, and professional interventions. In short, students, early in their educational experience, want to know the who, the what, and the why of social work.

The importance of an introductory textbook is in the way it presents that foundation so that students can develop a mindset, or an approach to thinking about social work. Curriculum frameworks for social work education include content on human behavior and the social environment, social welfare policy and services, social work practice, and research that is soundly built on a liberal arts foundation. Additionally, it is essential to have grounding in a values orientation about people and society, an appreciation of cultural diversity, and an understanding of the unique needs of special populations. A discipline-oriented introductory textbook, we conclude, needs to explore the broad common base of professional values, knowledge, and skills in all these educational components.

What distinguishes this introductory textbook from others is that it takes a discipline-based, empowerment approach rather than a social problems approach to framing the foundation of social work knowledge, values, and skills. To this end, this text provides an overview of the various elements that make up social work. The text covers the historical and philosophical roots of social work; the professional value base; dimensions of human behavior and social problems; perspectives on diversity; the social service delivery network and the consumer populations; and the social work interventions of practice, policy, and research.

The textbook reflects our combined experience as social work educators and our collaborative efforts in developing content for our respective introduction to social work courses. Although we both currently embrace a generalist ecosystems orientation to social work practice, this book juxtaposes contrasts in our early theoretical orientations—generalist and social systems perspectives from the University of Iowa School of Social Work and social group work from the University of Chicago, School of Social Service Administration; our varied practice experiences in public welfare and school and medical social work; and our differing foci of macrolevel and clinical practice. The book reflects the themes of empowerment and a strengths perspective for generalist social work.

This fifth edition continues to feature empowerment-based social work, the strengths perspective, and diversity. Major changes include updating demographic data, statistical information, and citations and providing additional content consistent with the new educational policy and accreditation standards of the Council on Social Work Education. The full text of the code of ethics of the International Federation of Social Workers, *The Ethics of Social Work: Principles and Standards,* has been added as an appendix. This edition includes expanded content on human rights and international social work. A new box feature, Profiles of Social Work, has been added in each chapter. These boxes describe social work activities in various fields of practice. As in previous editions, each chapter also includes two other boxes—Reflections on Empowerment, and Reflections on Diversity—that feature contemporary issues, service delivery examples, or ethical concerns in the context of empowerment and diversity. Most chapters still include Social Work Highlights that provide examples of social service programs, social workers' perspectives on practice, and case material.

Plan of the Book

The book is divided into four parts. Part One, The Profession of Social Work, lays out the who, what, why, and where of social work and the social service delivery system in historical and contemporary perspectives. Chapter 1 defines social work and examines the purpose and objectives of the profession. This chapter presents the relationship of social work and the social welfare institution, and describes the various fields of social work. Chapter 2 surveys the historical roots of the social work profession and details the professional knowledge, skill, and value base. Chapter 3 introduces the social systems and ecological frameworks for practice. Consumers of social services are delineated in a social systems context. Chapter 4 examines the social service delivery network and presents issues related to the settings of service delivery, staffing patterns, and funding parameters.

Part Two, Social Work Perspectives, critically examines the values, the social justice mandate, and issues of diversity that both inform and shape social work practice. Chapter 5 features the values context of social work, including the values of society, social work, and consumer systems. Professional ethics and practice principles are examined. Chapter 6 focuses on the principles of social justice and the realities of social injustice, including the effects of racism, elitism, sexism, heterosexism, ageism, and handicapism. Chapter 7 considers the cultural, racial, and ethnic diversity; the religious orientation and diversity; and the sexual diversity of consumers of social services.

Part Three, Generalist Social Work, introduces social work as an empowering profession and integrates this theme in social work practice interventions, policy formulation, and research. Chapter 8 explores the nature of the partnership between practitioners and clients and briefly describes empowering processes for generalist practice. Chapter 9 presents a framework for generalist social work practice across all social systems levels, describing roles and strategies for each function of social work—consultancy, resource management, and education. Chapter 10 explores the relationships between social work and social policy and presents tools for policy analysis and policy formulation. This chapter also reviews major social welfare policies and services, including Social Security, Temporary Assistance for Needy Families, Medicaid, and Medicare.

Part Four, Contemporary Issues in Fields of Practice, features the opportunities and challenges of social services and population groups within the broad fields of public welfare, health systems, and family services. Content in each of the chapters in Part Four is organized into several stand-alone modules that can be rearranged to fit any number of course designs. Chapter 11 profiles social work services to people in the public domain, including persons who are poor, homeless, or unemployed, or who are criminal offenders. Information includes the incidence, dynamics, and services related to poverty, homelessness, unemployment, and criminal justice. Chapter 12 presents social work services in the fields of health, rehabilitation, and mental health and includes discussions of the unique needs of people with mental and physical disabilities, people who have a mental illness, and people who are chemically dependent. Chapter 13 examines social work services designed for families and youths and includes a compendium of child welfare services. The dynamics of child maltreatment are discussed in the context of family-based services. This chapter also features such fields of social work practice as school social work and adolescent services. Chapter 14 details a range of social work service responses available to adults of all ages and incorporates material on a number of traditional fields of practice, including occupational social work and gerontological social work. The dynamics of violence in families, including intimate partner violence and elder abuse, are included. The section on older adults emphasizes the range of available services that support successful aging.

Acknowledgments

We acknowledge the many colleagues and friends who provided materials and resources, librarian Charlet Key for her helpfulness in locating resource materials, and Jim and David for their ongoing support and encouragement. We are extremely grateful to the social workers who conveyed their passion for the profession and graciously shared their practice stories for the social work profiles: Mary Dubert, Dan Ebener, Cynthia Green, Dana K. Harmon, Judith Holmgren, Janine S. Johnson, Rhonda McInroy, Sandra J. Mills, Lucinda M. Mohr, Phil Piechowski, Wendy Rickman, Julie Seline, and Frank Ware. We are also thankful to reviewers who offered valuable critiques and suggestions as we prepared this fifth edition. Reviewers included David A. Iacono-Harris, Western Illinois University; Linda L. Newell, San Diego State University; Salome Raheim, University of Iowa; and Alice W. Sewell, Millersville University. Finally, we thank Karen Hanson, Vice President, Social Sciences, and other staff at Allyn and Bacon including Patricia Quinlin, Janice Wiggins, and Annemarie Kennedy, and freelancer Holly Crawford for their careful guidance and diligent work during various stages of production.

B. D.
K. K. M.

PART ONE

The Profession of Social Work

Social work emerged as a profession early in the twentieth century and today is the profession charged with fulfilling the social welfare mandate to promote well-being and quality of life. Thus, social work encompasses activities directed at improving human and social conditions and alleviating human distress and social problems. Social workers, as caring professionals, work with people to enhance their competence and functioning, to access social supports and resources, to create humane and responsive social services, and to expand the structures of society that provide opportunities for all citizens.

Part One examines the contemporary purpose of social work, drawing on the historical development of social welfare and the evolution of professional ideology, identity, and interventions. It considers the relationship among society, the social welfare institution, and the social work profession. The chapters in this part describe the person and the environment as the targets of change effected by social work; introduce the professional knowledge, values, and skills base of the social worker; identify consumer systems as individuals, families, groups, organizations, communities, and societies; present case work, group work, and community organization methods; and consider the complexities of the social service delivery network.

CHAPTER

1 Social Work

A Helping Profession

Imagine a society without human suffering. Do you envision a society in which all members have the basic necessities of life and sufficient resources and opportunities to achieve their educational dreams and career aspirations? Are you picturing healthy, competent individuals who have access to needed health care and other social provisions to enhance their lives? Is it a society in which racism and discrimination are absent and in which cultural and racial diversities are celebrated? Can you see a match between society's resources and needs on the one hand and its citizens' resources and needs on the other? If so, then you have imagined a society that doesn't need social workers.

Human societies are not perfect. Social problems emerge that require societal solutions, and human needs arise that must be satisfied. Are you willing to confront the realities of these social problems and human needs? Are you concerned with the plight of the many who endure the strife and hardship of poverty and homelessness and the tears of hunger and pain? Do you question a society in which children have babies and infants are born addicted to drugs? Are you offended when illness and disease go untreated because health care is not affordable? Are you intolerant of the pervasive violence that touches familial and intergroup relationships? Do you challenge the inequity of personal and institutional discrimination that denies certain populations, based only on their skin color or disability, the realization of their fullest potential and their right to participate in mainstream life? Do you want to be involved in shaping a society that strives to ensure a high quality of life and social justice for all societal members? Welcome to the social work profession!

All citizens of a society should enjoy the full benefits that society offers. A society, in turn, flourishes when its citizens contribute their fullest potential. Interrupting normal developmental processes by personal crises, poverty, unemployment, poor health, and inadequate education jeopardizes the well-being of citizens. The prevalence of inequity, discrimination, and other forms of social injustice compromises the well-being of society.

Social workers respond to both the demands of living in a changing society and the call for social justice to promote citizens' rights. In practice, social workers address social concerns that threaten the structures of society and redress social conditions that adversely affect the well-being of people and society. The new international definition of social work, adopted by the International Federation of Social Workers (IFSW) and endorsed by the National Association of Social Workers (NASW) in 2000, indicates:

> The social work profession promotes social change, problem solving in human relationships and the empowerment and liberation of people to enhance well-being. Utilising theories of human behaviour and social systems, social work intervenes at the points where people interact with their environments. Principles of human rights and social justice are fundamental to social work. (IFSW, 2000, Definition section, ¶ 1)

In essence, social work activities empower client systems to enhance their competence and enable social structures to relieve human suffering and remedy social problems. According to the IFSW, "the holistic focus of social work is universal, but the priorities of social work practice will vary from country to country and from time to time depending on cultural, historical, and socio-economic conditions" (Practice section, ¶ 1).

This chapter addresses several questions that provide an orientation to social work, including:

- Who are social workers?
- What do they do in their day-to-day social work activities?
- What is the purpose of social work?
- How are social work and social welfare related?
- How is social work an empowering profession?

Who Are Social Workers?

What leads you to think about choosing social work as your profession? If you're like most social workers, you want to work with people, you want to do something that counts, you want to have a career that makes a difference. Which of your personal qualities lend themselves to working closely with other people? If you're like most social workers, you possess personal qualities that will enhance your competence as a professional.

Caring Professionals

People enter helping professions such as social work for many different reasons. For many, their motivation is an unselfish regard for others. Others want to make a difference by bettering the human condition and promoting social justice. Yet others enter the field to reciprocate for help they themselves once received. Even considering these different reasons for entering the profession, almost without exception, social work professionals demonstrate caring.

Often, social workers describe themselves as professional "helpers"—helping others resolve problems and obtain resources, providing support during crises, and facilitating social responses to needs. They are professionals to the degree that they have mastered the requisite knowledge base, developed competencies in the required skills, and adhere to the values and ethics of the social work profession.

Social work professionals share similar orientations toward values. They hold others in positive regard and demonstrate a genuine concern about the well-being of others. Altruism, or an unselfish regard for others, energizes their other-directedness. Moreover, effective helping professionals are optimistic about the potential for change and about life in general. Realistic hopefulness motivates change processes. Above all, they have a vision of the future based on the ideal of social justice.

Valuable Personal Qualities. With whom do you choose to work? What are they like? Most likely you'll list characteristics such as friendly, respectful of others' feelings, honest, a good listener, cooperative, and genuinely interested. You may also note the positive effect of those who appreciate you, support your efforts, and express confidence in your capacity to accomplish tasks. Our personal qualities make a difference in our ability to work effectively with others.

Likewise, social workers' personal characteristics enhance their abilities to function professionally. Among these essential personal qualities are warmth, honesty, genuineness, openness, courage, hopefulness, humility, concern, and sensitivity. In his book *Learning from Clients,* Maluccio (1979) indicates that clients respond more to social workers' human qualities than to their technical skills. These qualities are indispensable for establishing rapport and building relationships with colleagues and clients alike.

Working in Partnerships. Under what circumstances do you put forth your best effort? It's not likely that you'll do your best when you feel like you're a cog in a wheel, wondering if what you're doing truly matters. It's not likely that you'll contribute fully when you feel subservient, wondering if what you're doing will be judged to be inferior. It's more likely that you'll do your best when you feel appreciated and supported by those with whom you work. It's more likely that you'll participate actively when you feel as though you're a part of the process, making a valuable contribution. It's more likely that you'll commit to a project when you view yourself as a partner in the process.

Social workers value working in partnerships with both their clients and their colleagues. Social work practice involves facilitating change—in other words, working *with* others, not doing something *to* them or *for* them. Empowering practitioners appreciate differences, celebrate diversity, and value people for their own uniqueness. Effective social workers are trustworthy, act responsibly, demonstrate sound judgment, and are accountable for their actions.

What Do Social Workers Do?

Social work provides opportunities to work in many different settings with people whose problems, issues, and needs are diverse. As you will note in the examples that follow, there are common threads as well as distinguishing characteristics in what social workers do in their day-to-day practice of social work.

Voices from the Field

Professor George Johnston invited several graduates of the social work program to participate in a panel presentation for introductory social work students. He asked the practitioners to describe something about what they do in their day-to-day social work activities. Participating social workers include Joannie Devereaux, from the Nursing and Retirement Center; Karen Ostlund, a legislative caseworker with the local congressional office; Mike Nicolas, a social worker with County General Hospital's hospice unit; and Mary Ann Grant, a social worker with a rape crisis program.

Joannie Devereaux describes her practice in a nursing home:

> *The Nursing and Retirement Center is a long-term care facility. We currently have over 200 residents. Most of the residents are older adults. However, recently the center has added a program for younger persons who have disabili-*

ties that interfere with their living independently. One wing of the center houses a program for residents with Alzheimer's disease.

As one of three social workers at the center, I work mainly with the older adults in our program. One of the things I really like about my job is its variety. I am involved in a lot of different activities, such as admitting new residents, counseling with residents and their families, preparing social histories, participating at the interdisciplinary team care-plan review, and leading staff development in-service workshops. Recently we've begun a support group for family members of our residents with Alzheimer's disease. I cofacilitate the meetings along with the family member who has participated in the planning process for the group.

I'm also involved in professional activities in the community. I chair a professional group of nursing home social workers that meets monthly to review issues that are critical to long-term care. But our group does more than comment on the issues. We try to find ways to take action. For example, we're concerned about the fate of public-pay residents in nursing homes. State programs pay a fraction of the actual cost. Even more problematic, payments are usually six to nine months behind. Currently we're consulting with area legislators about this pressing need.

Professor Johnston, you'll be pleased to know that I have found the information from the research class quite helpful. Right now I'm involved in evaluating a new technique that increases residents' participation in deciding to live at the center. We hope to be able to demonstrate that residents who are more actively involved in making their own decisions will make a more positive transition to living in a nursing home.

Karen Ostlund describes her role as a legislative caseworker in a congressional office:

I certainly didn't realize that social work practitioners worked in legislative offices before I started school here. In fact, the first I heard of this kind of a job for a social worker was at a panel presentation like the one we're doing today. But when I heard Elaina Conteros talk about her work, I liked what I heard. Now I'm her colleague as a legislative caseworker.

Many of my daily activities involve advocacy for constituents. People call with questions about various federal agencies. Often I am able to refer them to appropriate local and regional resources. Frequently a crisis of some kind precipitates their calls. In my opinion, bureaucracy magnifies the crisis all too often. Using response techniques that calm people down and clarify their situations, I am able to help them find some solutions. Actually, I find that good communication skills are essential, whether I'm talking with clients or I'm trying to find my way through the bureaucratic maze.

Those constituents who seek congressional assistance include a large number of veterans. I serve as the office liaison with a consortium of agencies that provide services for these veterans and their families. This means that I attend monthly meetings with representatives from the various agencies. This gives us an opportunity to keep up-to-date about programs and services, and it provides a forum for working out any difficulties in service delivery that we encounter.

I, too, draw on research skills, but I use research somewhat differently from Joannie. Elaina and I often gather background information for proposing new legislation. I am currently conducting research in the congressional district on the impact of welfare reform.

Mike Nicolas talks about his work as a social worker with County General Hospital's hospice unit:

Thanks for inviting me to speak on this panel. It gives me a chance to talk about something that means a lot to me—my work as a medical social worker.

Hospice Care is an interdisciplinary health care program at County General Hospital. Members of our interdisciplinary team include a doctor, nurse, physical therapist, dietician, chaplain, and me—the social worker. Our hospice program coordinates medical, emotional, social, and spiritual services for people who are terminally ill and their families. Its purpose is to make it possible for people to exercise the option of living and dying among family and friends. Our program provides various health care, social, and psychological supports.

As a social worker in the hospice program, I work with participants and their families in a lot of different ways. For example, they participate in planning activities as team members. I provide counseling services and coordinate the services participants select. Family members often continue to use the support services of our program after their loved one has died. I facilitate the bereavement group that our hospice program sponsors. Grief counseling before and after the death of a participant is a very important part of our program.

We at the hospice are aware of the impact of AIDS. I am the social work representative on the community force on AIDS. We have two projects right now. One is a community education effort. You'll see the publicity soon about the AIDS quilt display that will be at the community center next month. We hope that the display itself and the related media attention will heighten awareness to the needs we have in our own community. We're also instituting a volunteer befriender program. Currently I'm also on the committee that's collecting demographic information and other data to prepare the statistical portion of a grant request to get funds for this program.

The holistic approach of the hospice means that I have opportunities to work with professionals from other disciplines to provide an alternative approach to caring for people who are terminally ill. A lot of people ask me, "How can you immerse yourself in death?" You may be asking that question, too. Paradoxically, working with issues of death, I've immersed myself in life. I've learned a lot about living from people who are dying! And I have come to appreciate the significance of working in an atmosphere of collegial support.

Mary Ann Grant, a rape crisis worker, summarizes her social work practice:

> *I work at the Rape Crisis Counseling Center. Our program provides support for people who have been sexually assaulted. The sexual assault treatment program has three components, and I participate in all of them. First, I provide counseling services to rape survivors and their families or significant others. Up until last year, all of our counseling services were offered individually. Now we've added group sessions and find them very helpful.*
>
> *My responsibilities also include advocacy for clients at hospitals and police stations and during various legal procedures. Advocacy certainly takes on different forms, depending on the situation. Often I help clients anticipate medical procedures and legal processes. Advocacy also involves reviewing options and accompanying clients as they proceed through legal channels.*
>
> *Third, there's the community education component of our program. My colleagues and I provide a lot of community education programs on sexual assault and rape prevention. We make presentations to schools, hospitals, law enforcement personnel, and other interested groups. We realize that we need to extend our services among African American, Hispanic, and Asian American members of our community. Currently we're expanding ethnic representation on our advisory board and in our pool of volunteers. We also are making plans to translate informational material into Spanish and concurrently ensure that bilingual staff will be available.*
>
> *One of the types of rape we often read about is date rape. Currently, very few of our clients indicate their assault was an acquaintance rape. However, our hunch is that this is more widespread than our program data indicate. At present we are participating in a university study on date rape. As part of the initial stages of the project, we are field testing a questionnaire that focuses on the incidence and dynamics of date rape.*

Generalist Social Work

Joannie Devereaux, Karen Ostlund, Mike Nicolas, and Mary Ann Grant all work in very different practice settings: a nursing home, a legislative office, a community-based hospice, and a rape crisis advocacy program. Each setting offers distinctive programs and services, serves a dissimilar clientele, and faces unique issues. Yet, as these social workers describe their daily activities, there are similarities in what they do. They facilitate clients' resolution of problems, help clients obtain tangible resources, provide education, and influence the development of social policy. They work with clients individually and in groups. They use their professional skills as members of community groups and professional teams. They fine-tune their knowledge of community resources. They also conduct practice evaluation and research.

These examples describe professionals who are *generalist* social workers. As generalists, they draw on a common process for working with clients as well as on specialized knowledge and skills to address unique characteristics of each situation. Generalist practitioners

> acknowledge the interplay of personal and collective issues, prompting them to work with a variety of human systems—societies, communities, neighborhoods, complex organizations,

> formal groups, families, and individuals—to create changes which maximize human system functioning. This means that generalist social workers work directly with client systems at all levels, connect clients to available resources, intervene with organizations to enhance the responsiveness of resource systems, advocate just social policies to ensure the equitable distribution of resources, and research all aspects of social work practice. (Miley, O'Melia, & DuBois, 2004, p. 10)

Generalist social work practice

- Utilizes generic practice processes to organize work with client systems
- Recognizes the potential for change at multiple system levels—within human systems, between systems, and among environmental systems
- Views human behavior in the context of the social environment
- Integrates direct practice with social policy and social work research activities

What Is the Purpose of Social Work?

As social workers, Joannie Devereaux, Karen Ostlund, Mike Nicolas, and Mary Ann Grant share more than the commonalities of their generalist perspective. In fact, the purpose of social work lends vision to their work and provides the direction for their professional goals and objectives. The purpose of social work orients their activities as they work with clients to develop solutions in the context of a continuum of strengths and needs.

Social Work's Purpose

The National Association of Social Workers' "Working Statement on Purpose" (1981) defines the unifying purpose or mission of social work as "promot[ing] or restor[ing] a mutually beneficial interaction between individuals and society in order to improve the quality of life for everyone" (p. 6). Social work is known for its integrated view, which focuses on persons in the context of their physical and social environments.

In response to the mission of the profession, social workers strengthen human functioning and enhance the effectiveness of the structures in society that provide resources and opportunities for citizens. Social workers strive to release human power so that individuals can actualize their potential and contribute to the well-being of society. Moreover, social workers initiate activities that release the social power that creates changes in society that in turn create changes in social policies, social institutions, and other social structures in society (Smalley, 1967).

Personal Troubles and Public Issues. The dual focus of social work on people and their social environment raises questions about the interconnections between private troubles and public issues. C. Wright Mills (1959) first distinguished between the personal troubles of milieu and the public issues of social structures. His seminal work, *The*

Sociological Imagination, provides a critical view about the location of problems and their solutions. He suggests that

> Troubles occur within the character of the individual and within the range of his [or her] immediate relations with others; they have to do with his self and with those limited areas of social life of which he is directly and personally aware. Accordingly, the statement and the resolution of troubles properly lie within the individual as a biographical entity and within the scope of his immediate milieu—the social setting that is directly open to his personal experience and to some extent his willful activity. A trouble is a private matter: values cherished by an individual are felt by him to be threatened.
>
> Issues have to do with matters that transcend these local environments of the individual and the range of his inner life. They have to do with the organization of many such milieu into the institutions of an historical society as a whole, with the ways in which various milieu overlap and interpenetrate to form the larger structure of social and historical life. An issue is a public matter: some value cherished by publics is felt to be threatened. (p. 8)

Mills's perspective separates private troubles from public issues and suggests that the solutions for each focus on separate realms. In contrast, the social work perspective holds that private troubles and public issues intersect. The cumulative effects of personal troubles are public issues. Likewise, individuals feel the repercussions of public issues personally as private troubles. Moreover, in today's world, the global dimensions of personal troubles and public issues echo around the world. Not only do private troubles translate into public issues, but international issues translate into personal problems as well (Staub-Berasconi, 1991).

Social Work's Goals

The goals of the social work profession translate its general purpose into more specific directions for action (Figure 1.1). These goals and objectives lead social workers to enhance clients' sense of competence, link them with resources, and foster changes that make

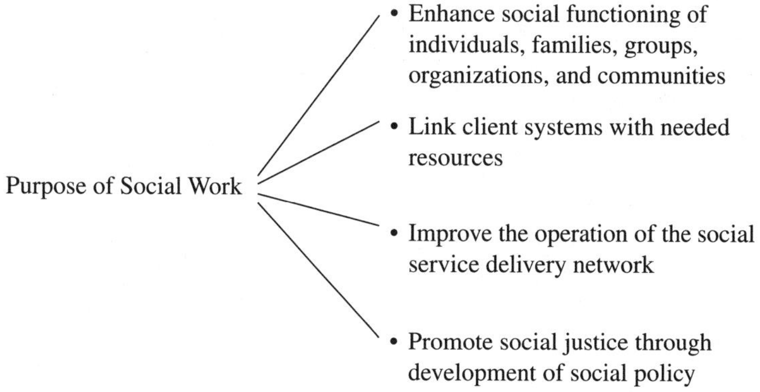

FIGURE 1.1 Goals of Social Work

organizations and social institutions more responsive to citizens' needs (NASW, 1981). Specifically, social work's goals and related activities include the following:

1. *Enhancing people's capacities to resolve problems, cope, and function effectively.* To accomplish this goal, practitioners assess obstacles to clients' ability to function. They also identify resources and strengths, enhance skills for dealing with problems in living, develop plans for solutions, and support clients' efforts to create changes in their lives and situations.

2. *Linking clients with needed resources.* On one level, achieving this goal means helping clients locate the resources they need to deal more effectively with their situations. On another level, this means that social workers advocate policies and services that provide optimal benefits, improve communication among human service professionals who represent various programs and services, and identify gaps and barriers in social services that need to be addressed.

3. *Improving the social service delivery network.* This goal means that social workers must ensure that the system that delivers social services is humane and adequately provides resources and services for participants. To accomplish this, social workers advocate planning that centers on clients, demonstrates effectiveness and efficiency, and incorporates measures of accountability.

4. *Promoting social justice through the development of social policy.* With respect to developing social policies, social workers examine social issues for policy implications. They make suggestions for new policies and recommendations for eliminating policies that are no longer productive. Additionally, social workers translate general policies into programs and services that respond effectively to participants' needs.

Consider the professional activities that Joannie Devereaux, Karen Ostlund, Mike Nicolas, and Mary Ann Grant describe to the introductory social work class. How do their activities reflect the goals of the profession?

Joannie's work at the nursing home involves activities that enhance the developmental capacity of people. Her counseling with residents and their families aims to aid residents' transitions to living in the nursing home. Through her association with a community group, she advocates changes in state policies and procedures for funding nursing home care.

Karen's description of her work as a legislative caseworker emphasizes linking clients with needed resources and finding ways to untangle the bureaucratic maze in order to improve social service delivery. She also uses her research skills to gather background data for developing new social policies.

Mike is making a difference in many ways, but especially through his work with the task force on AIDS. This group is finding ways to create programs and services that address pressing issues in their community—promoting community education about AIDS, gaining community backing, and developing networks of support for people in their community who have AIDS.

Finally, Mary Ann's presentation about her work in the rape crisis program reveals ways in which her activities reflect the goals of the social work profession. Crisis intervention, by definition, supports people during crises in their lives. In the rape crisis program,

Mary Ann counsels rape survivors individually and in small groups. She supports them through the aftermath of their assault through her advocacy in hospital emergency rooms, police stations, and court hearings. She and her colleagues are also seeking ways to make their services more ethnically sensitive.

Strengths and Needs

The mission of the social work profession as well as the statements of its goals and objectives implicitly concern human needs and human strengths. Human needs are the substance of the social work profession—the impetus for social work activities. Human strengths are the building blocks of social work practice—the source of energy for developing solutions. The following review of sources of strengths and needs provides a context for understanding the dimensions of social work that focus on the interactions between people and their physical and social environments.

Universal Basic Needs. Universal basic needs are those needs that all people share, including needs for physical, intellectual, emotional, social, and spiritual growth (Brill & Levine, 2002). *Physical needs* encompass basic life supplies such as food, shelter, and clothing; opportunities for physical development; and essential health care. *Intellectual development* thrives when opportunities synchronize with individual capacity. Relationships with significant others and self-acceptance nurture *emotional development. Social growth* includes socialization needs and developing meaningful relationships with others. Finally, *spiritual growth* centers on discovering a meaning for life that provides purpose and transcends everyday experience.

Experts make several assumptions about these universal basic needs (Brill & Levine, 2002). First, they assume that all people have needs for security and dependency as well as for growth and independence. Furthermore, they assume that all people are unique and possess the potential to develop competence in every aspect of their lives. Finally, they believe that people realize their potential for physical, intellectual, emotional, social, and spiritual growth only through dynamic interaction of these growth areas. No single aspect of growth occurs in isolation from the others.

Basic needs are met differentially. For some people, personal strengths and environmental resources allow them to achieve optimal functioning. For others, their abilities and environmental constraints are limiting, and they experience deprivation.

Motivational Needs. Abraham Maslow's hierarchical schema (1970) depicts these motivational needs, which underlie all human behavior. Maslow contends that people must fulfill their fundamental basic needs before they begin to pursue higher-level growth needs. The most basic needs revolve around *physiological necessities* such as the need for food, water, and sleep. The second level entails the need for *security,* which is satisfied by a safe, secure physical and psychological environment. The next level involves fulfilling needs for *belongingness* and love through intimacy and satisfying relationships. *Esteem needs* follow, including feelings of competence and a sense of personal worth derived from recognition of accomplishments. Finally, *self-actualization* is at the pinnacle of the hierarchy. Self-actualization is the process of realizing one's maximal potential, marked by a vision that encompasses the whole of humankind. In Maslow's perspective, deficits denote need and growth relates to self-actualization.

Personal Development. Biological, psychological, interpersonal, social, and cultural factors influence personal development. Charlotte Towle, an early leader in social work education, provides a schema for understanding developmental needs in her classic book, *Common Human Needs,* first published in 1945. According to Towle (1957), developmental needs include those related to physical welfare, psychological well-being, intellectual development, interpersonal relationships, and spiritual growth. All of these factors influence personal adjustment. A unique configuration of developmental needs emerges at each stage of the human life span. Each of these developmental needs interacts with the others to provide resources that contribute to developmental growth and adaptation.

Life Tasks. People must confront the demands of various situations—some predictable, some not—throughout their lives. These life tasks have significant implications for personal functioning and for developing social relationships. The concept of life task relates to "daily living, such as growing up in the family, learning in school, entering the world of work, marrying and rearing a family, and also with the common traumatic situations of life such as bereavement, separation, illness, or financial difficulties" (Bartlett, 1970, p. 96). Life tasks confront everyone. Although people's responses may differ, everyone must find ways to deal with the challenges of these tasks.

Identity Development. Many developmental theorists, including Erikson (1963), Kohlberg (1973), and Levinson (1978), presume that men and women share similar developmental needs. However, these theorists use "masculine" traits such as autonomy, independence, and achievement as the standard for normal development (Gilligan, 1982). They equate mature identity with autonomous functioning, work achievement, and individuation or separation from others. In contrast, "concern about relationships has been seen as a weakness of women (and men) rather than as a human strength" (McGoldrick, 1989, p. 203).

This perspective creates a void for both men and women. For men, relationship needs are submerged in the expectations of masculine roles. Prominent masculine qualities are those "qualities deemed necessary for adulthood—the capacity for autonomous thinking, clear decision-making, and responsible action" (Gilligan, 1982, p. 17). According to Gilligan, developmental theorists have defined women's development in terms of women's place in the male life cycle, rather than considering the uniqueness of the female experience.

To understand more fully women's development of identity, one must understand the intimate and generative relationships that are so much a part of female development. In the context of human relationships, women's roles reflect nurturing, caregiving, and helping. For women, the context of relationships defines their identity. Women define themselves in the web of their relationships with others. For women, interdependence and attachment are prominent throughout their developmental life cycle. Gilligan's perspective challenges us to understand the differences in identity development between women and men.

Cultural Strengths. The values, customs, and symbols associated with each society reflect diversity in cultural heritage and define cultural identity. Many people treasure the cultural patterns of their ancestors. Ethnic groups share particular traits, customs, values, and symbols. As a source of pride and esteem, cultural identity offers a sense of belonging to ethnic and racial groups.

Ethnicity influences all of the tasks related to the various stages of the life cycle. For example, the socialization patterns of children and adults differ because of social class, ethnicity, and minority group status (Devore & Schlesinger, 1999). Cultural identity determines the parental roles in child care and prescribes norms for parental authority in child rearing. Cultural assumptions about the independence or dependence of children and the sex-specific experiences and role assignments of family members affect the socialization of family members.

Other important cultural factors include the effects of bilingualism and biculturalism. Depending on their ethnic origin, families experience differences in intergenerational kinship networks and cultural strengths. People also vary in the degree to which they identify with an ethnic group and in their responses to stereotyping. The effects of racism, discrimination, and segregation may impede the completion of developmental tasks.

BOX 1.1
Reflections on Diversity

Everyone's Diverse . . . in Different Ways

Social workers need to understand and appreciate human diversity, recognizing differences and similarities in the characteristics, life experiences, and belief systems of all people. People are diverse in race, ethnic and cultural heritage, age, sex, religious affiliation, sexual orientation, class, and physical and mental abilities. By definition everyone falls within one or more of these categories of diversity at any given point in their lives. Simply put, the answer to the question "Who is diverse?" is "Everyone."

The issue of diversity in social work is not so much that practitioners work with people who are diverse, but that they work with diverse populations who also suffer the consequences of discrimination, economic deprivation, and oppression. Populations defined as at risk for experiencing these consequences include women, minorities of color, homosexuals, people with disabilities, the elderly, and the poor. These are all populations that experience disenfranchisement in many ways—their civil rights are abrogated, they lack political redress, and their access to opportunities and resources is limited.

Understanding the issues and needs of culturally and ethnically diverse populations is a prominent theme in social work education. Practitioners must critically evaluate theoretical constructs for their cultural and ethnic relevance as well as their application to populations at risk. They must select practice theories that value diversity and incorporate the strengths and resources of diversity. Culturally competent social workers utilize assessment, intervention, and evaluation skills that take into consideration the dynamics of culture, race, age, sex, and sexual orientation as well as the consequences of discrimination, oppression, and degradation.

Culturally competent helping professionals value cultural differences. Additionally, they are aware of their own cultural identity, including how culture influences their values and perspectives; can adapt their general base of knowledge about other cultures to the situations of specific clients; and have "the ability to identify and articulate the power and privilege differentials that characterize intercultural relationships" (Miley, O'Melia, & DuBois, 2004, p. 68).

Physical Environment. The physical environment, including the natural and human-constructed world and its temporal and spatial arrangements, affects how people view possibilities, meet goals, and fulfill needs (Germain, 1981). Physical components of the human environment include such things as ecological needs (clean water, uncontaminated soil, and pure air), space for living, housing arrangements, and transportation provisions. Human survival depends on abating widespread environmental pollution and conserving natural resources. Space defines identity. In Western culture, overcrowding and lack of privacy hinder personal development. Cultural interpretations influence how people perceive their interaction with the physical environment.

Environmental competence derives from the congruence between provisions and needs and from people's perception that they are able to effect environmental changes (Germain, 1981). Environmental competence increases when the configuration of the physical environment is pleasing, stimulating, and protecting. In contrast, the physical environment is disabling when it debilitates one's sense of self, heightens the fear of danger, and interferes with meeting life cycle needs.

Social Justice. Ideally, all members of a society share the same rights to participation in the society, protection by the law, opportunities for development, responsibility for social order, and access to social benefits. Social justice prevails when all members of a society share equally in the social order, secure an equitable consideration of resources and opportunities, and enjoy their full benefit of civil liberties.

Social problems result when societies do not accord citizens equity and equality and when they violate their citizens' human and civil rights. Prejudicial attitudes, discriminatory practices, oppression, and exclusion of some citizens from full participation in the society deny people equal access to the opportunities and resources necessary for optimal social functioning. The construction of human and civil rights in any society prescribes the societally defined limits to justice. For example, although laws in some countries constrain personal liberties, some defend these laws as necessary to the social order; however, other members of the global community criticize these practices and deem them violations of human rights.

World Living. We live in an interdependent global society. Thus we must be concerned with world issues and needs and with how solutions generated within one society affect the well-being of other societies. Needs created by food shortages, economic problems, political upheavals, natural disasters, pollution, and wars threaten the functioning of societies and have repercussions for all world citizens.

Mutual dependence on energy resources, food supplies, and medical and scientific technologies requires intersocietal cooperation. In order to eliminate the threat of war and achieve world harmony and peace, world citizens must appreciate diverse cultures, recognize the viability of many different social structures, and develop solutions for social problems that consider the world context.

Interactions of Strengths and Needs

We all share common biological, developmental, social, and cultural needs. At the same time, each of us develops a unique spectrum of strengths and needs influenced by our own particular physical, cognitive, psychosocial, and cultural development. Also, our interaction with the social environment influences our ability to get along. Ordinarily, we draw upon the resources of our everyday environment to meet our personal social needs. To the extent that the demands and resources of our environment match our requirements, we experience a "goodness of fit and sense of competence." To the extent that a mismatch occurs, we experience problems in living.

How Are Social Work and Social Welfare Related?

What comes to mind when you hear the term *social welfare?* Does your view only equate social welfare with public assistance programs, or does it recognize social welfare as one of society's social institutions? This section clarifies the interconnections between social work and social welfare. To do so, it defines social welfare in the context of social institutions, examines the functions of social welfare, surveys fields of social work practice, and explores the relationship between social work and society.

Social Institutions

Social institutions that address the physical, economic, educational, religious, and political needs of citizens fulfill human needs and resolve social problems. Social institutions such as the family, education, government, religion, the economy, and social welfare evolve in response to individual and collective needs in society (Table 1.1). *Families* nurture their children's health, growth, and development; provide food, shelter, and clothing; and socialize children for effective living. Through the *educational institution,* people formally acquire the knowledge, skills, beliefs, attitudes, and norms of a society. The *economic institution* provides a vehicle for the production and distribution of goods and services. *Political institutions* function as structures that exercise power and protect law and order. Direction and meaning for humankind in understanding the ultimate concerns of life is the central

TABLE 1.1 The Functions of Social Institutions

Social Institution	Function
Family institution	Primary personal care and mutual assistance system between children and parents and between the family unit and society
Educational institution	Socialization and preparation for productive, participatory citizenship
Economic institution	Allocation and distribution of resources
Political institution	Authoritative allocation of public social goals and values
Religious institution	Promotion of personal meaning and understanding of ultimate concerns
Social welfare institution	Provision of supports to sustain or attain social functioning

concern of *religious institutions.* Finally, the *social welfare institution* provides services needed by all people at some time or another to sustain or attain their roles as socially productive members of society.

The Social Welfare Institution

The social welfare institution responds to the needs of society and its members for health, education, and economic and social well-being. Some view social welfare as a "first-line support to enable individuals to cope successfully with a changing economic and social environment and to assure the stability and development of social institutions" (Romanyshyn & Romanyshyn, 1971, p. 34). Ideally, societies use the institution of social welfare to provide all citizens with opportunities to participate fully in society and to achieve their maximum potential.

Social welfare addresses the "general well-being" needs of individuals and meets the universal needs of the population:

> Social welfare includes those provisions and processes directly concerned with the treatment and prevention of social problems, the development of human resources, and the improvement of the quality of life. It involves social services to individuals and families as well as efforts to strengthen or modify social institutions . . . social welfare functions to maintain the social system and to adapt it to changing social reality. (Romanyshyn & Romanyshyn, 1971, p. 3)

Social welfare provisions encompass diverse public and private social services. For example, the social welfare system provides family and child welfare services, medical and health provisions, legal services, criminal justice activities, and income supports. Social welfare may provide these services as social utilities that are available to all people and groups as citizens' rights. Or, social welfare services may meet specialized needs or address the unique problems of particular groups of people.

Functions of Social Welfare

Opinions differ on the function of social welfare. On the one hand, people who hold a *residual view* believe that welfare applies only when family, economic, or political structures break down. Many criticize the residual view of social welfare as a stopgap measure or "bandage approach" to the provision of services. On the other hand, people who subscribe to an *institutional view* recognize welfare as an integrated function of a modern industrial society that provides services as a citizen's right (Wilensky & Lebeaux, 1965). Although the institutional form of social welfare in the United States derives its legitimacy from the constitutional mandate to promote well-being, many criticize it for usurping the legitimate functions of other institutions. Ideally, social welfare responds promptly to shared social needs by providing adequate income, housing, education, health care, and personal safety.

The beneficiaries of social welfare are not any one group of people. In actuality, social welfare includes diverse provisions that benefit the total population. Some suggest that social welfare services are an integral part of the societal infrastructure that provides public utility services, such as transportation and education. This frame of reference suggests that users of public utility services, including social welfare, are citizens with rights rather than people who are deviant, helpless, and stigmatized.

Typically, social needs are not identified until they become critical, complex social problems requiring large-scale interventions through social planning. With fragmentation and/or the absence of social planning, the magnitude of the challenge can be catastrophic.

Further fragmentation occurs as a consequence of the social welfare institution's failure to meet the needs of all people equally. First, people experience various degrees of need. When demands are greater, social resources may be inadequate. Also, those accorded status and power are in a position to define which needs are pressing and how needs will be addressed. Those without power—that is, individuals differentiated by socioeconomic status, age, gender, sexual orientation, or racial or ethnic diversity—have less influence and often experience gaps and barriers in institutional provisions.

Ironically, instead of explaining these gaps and barriers in terms of the structural factors that create needs, individuals are often stigmatized, judged, and blamed for the shortcomings of institutional structures. As Pierce (1989) reflects:

> To be bothered by the question of who receives social welfare is to miss the point of a social institution. The needs a social institution meets and the people who exhibit those needs are neither good nor bad. The needs and the institution that develops to meet those needs are an outcome of the interactions of all parts and people within a given society. To blame those who are in need and to put a stigma on them is to hold them accountable for the outcome of a social process to which they alone did not have input. The part social work plays in meeting the needs of people within the institution of social welfare is a natural and useful one within society. Such meanings and values associated with social welfare should be carefully examined. Social workers must constantly deal with people who are devalued by society and deal with a society which devalues social workers. (p. 47)

Social workers have been summarily described as "professional helpers designated by society to aid people who are distressed, disadvantaged, disabled, deviant, defeated, or dependent. They also are charged to help people lessen their chances of being poor, inept, neglected, abused, divorced, delinquent, criminal, alienated, or mad" (Siporin, 1975, p. 4). Indeed, a chief mandate of the social work profession is to work with people who are disenfranchised and oppressed. Rather than applying labels that denote pathology, empowerment-based social workers focus on the strengths of human systems, thereby promoting personal and societal competence.

Fields of Social Work Practice

Social workers confront problems such as child abuse and neglect, homelessness, poverty, health care needs, neighborhood decline, community apathy, drug abuse, and domestic violence. Generalists work with community organizations, neighborhood groups, families, and individuals who are elderly, delinquent, unemployed, or chronically mentally ill, or who have disabilities. Fields of practice organize the types of services social workers provide. Services are grouped within numerous fields of practice as they relate to addressing specific social problems, meeting the needs of client population groups, or reflecting particular settings.

Traditional fields of practice include family and child welfare services, health and rehabilitation, mental health, occupational social work, housing, community development, information and referral, income maintenance, aging or gerontological services, education or school social work, and social work in corrections (Table 1.2):

- *Family Services.* Social workers provide support services for families to enhance family functioning. Examples of services include counseling, family therapy, and family life education.

- *Child Protection Services.* Typically provided by state departments of child welfare, these services address issues of child abuse and neglect. Services include child protection services; child abuse investigation, prevention, and intervention; and family preservation and reunification services.

- *Health Care.* In the health care field, practitioners work in medical settings such as hospitals, nursing homes, public health agencies, and hospice programs. They also provide rehabilitation counseling.

- *Occupational Social Work.* Usually under the auspices of an employee assistance program, occupational social workers provide counseling, referral, and educational services for employees and their families. Issues may be work-related, such as job stress, or personal, such as family crises or addictions.

- *Gerontological Social Work.* Gerontological social workers offer services to older adults and their caregivers. Comprehensive and specialized services for the elderly typically fall within the auspices of service agencies for older adults. However, services for older adults also may be a component of a multifaceted community agency.

- *School Social Work.* Social workers in schools are part of an interdisciplinary team that often includes guidance counselors, school psychologists, and teachers. School social work services are available to school-age children and their families to resolve school-related educational and behavioral problems.

- *Criminal Justice.* Social workers have a presence in both juvenile and adult corrections. They monitor clients on probation or parole, provide counseling in prisons and juvenile detention facilities, and work in victim restitution programs.

- *Information and Referral.* Information and referral (I & R) specialists play a key role in offering service delivery information, making referrals to community resources, and initiating community outreach programs. Many agencies include an I & R component in their spectrum of services.

- *Community Organizing.* Social workers employed by community-action programs engage in community and neighborhood development, social planning, and direct-action organizing. Organizers mobilize community members or constituent populations in reform activities.

- *Mental Health.* Case management, therapy, drug and alcohol treatment, and mental health advocacy are a few of the activities of social workers employed in mental health settings. Mental health settings include, for example, community mental health centers, state hospitals, day treatment programs, and residential facilities for people with mental disorders.

TABLE 1.2 Fields of Social Work Practice

Field	Examples of Services
Family and children's services	Family preservation Family counseling Foster care and adoption Day care Prevention of child abuse and neglect Prevention of domestic violence
Health and rehabilitation	Hospital social work Public health work Maternal health work Vocational rehabilitation Hospice care
Mental health	Mental health clinics Day treatment for drug and alcohol addiction Community integration
Information and referral	Provision of information on resources Publication of community directories First-call services Emergency relief Crisis management
Occupational social work	Employee assistance programs Treatment for work-related stresses Job relocation programs Retirement planning
Juvenile and adult corrections	Probation and parole services Police social work Work in detention facilities and training schools Prison work Deferment programs
Gerontological services	In-home support Respite help for family caregivers Adult day care Long-term care Nursing home services
School social work	School adjustment counseling Educational testing Family counseling Behavior management
Housing	Subsidized rents Homeless shelters Handicap accessibility programs
Income maintenance	Social insurance programs Public assistance programs Food stamps
Community development	Social planning Community organizing Neighborhood revitalization

Sometimes social workers develop specialties in a field of practice, such as adoption, substance abuse, planning, juvenile probation, or hospital social work. Additional specialties are grouped according to practice roles, such as direct service practitioners, community organizers, policy analysts, foster care specialists, family life educators, and administrators. However, even when social workers develop specialties, the wide-angle lens of the generalist is still applicable, as problems must be understood in their context and interventions developed with an eye on their implications at all system levels.

Employment Outlook. The professional ranks of social workers are expanding. Occupational outlook estimates indicate the workforce of about 468,000 social workers in 2000 will increase faster than the average rate for other occupations through 2010 (Bureau of Labor Statistics, 2002a). Recent trends in service delivery reveal that the number of social work positions is increasing in the areas of home health, aging services, mental health, criminal justice, rehabilitation, and school-linked services. Additional areas for future growth include forensic social work, corporate-based employee assistance, international practice, and political social work (Clark, 2003). Neighborhood-based, multidisciplinary service centers as "one-stop shops" ease access to a constellation of services including public assistance, employment services, literacy programs, family-centered services, juvenile court services, and health care. Social workers bridge these services as family service consultants through case management activities.

Social Work, Social Welfare, and Society

To fulfill its social welfare mandate, social work assumes different roles in relation to society. These roles reflect different models of society and corresponding social work activities. The exact nature of the social problem and the way in which society defines the social welfare arrangements influences the role of social work.

Consensus and Conflict Models. Two models of society, the consensus and the conflict models, reflect different sociological perspectives, the structural functionalist perspective and the conflict perspective (Leonard, 1976).

A consensus or structural functionalist model of society values maintaining equilibrium in the relationships between the society and its members. In this model, social work's role is to resolve conflicts and tensions, to socialize people labeled "deviant," and to create harmony between people and their social environment through their mutual adaptation. In other words, social workers' roles are to control disruptive citizens and to reform dysfunctional social structures.

In contrast, the conflict model focuses on power issues and holds that social problems result from inequitable distributions of power and authority. From the point of view of the conflict model, social workers play a more direct role in confronting injustice and advocating the interests of oppressed and vulnerable groups. Social work's goal is to change the power and authority in social arrangements.

Social Work and Society: Four Possible Relationships. The relationship between social work and society can be understood in terms of four possible patterns:

- Social work as an agent of social control on behalf of society
- Social work as a reformer of society
- Social work as separate from society
- Social work as an intermediary between individuals and society (Cowger, 1977)

As agents of society, social workers resocialize clients by exercising social control. Clients are likely to be involuntary—that is, compelled or required to seek or accept services. Examples of involuntary clients include court-adjudicated delinquents, parolees, and some institutionalized populations. As agents of society, social workers seek to reform individuals on society's behalf.

When social work is viewed as being in opposition to or in conflict with society, social work's role is to advocate social change that reforms political, economic, and social institutional structures. People who hold this perspective believe that problems result from malformed social structures. Social workers respond to problems by improving or reforming social conditions through strategies such as social action and political reform.

When social work is seen as separate from society, there is little or no interactive relationship between social workers and society. An example of this perspective is clinical practice that focuses on individual treatment rather than on social change. If they adopt this neutral stance toward society, social workers do not employ strategies of social reform or social change.

The final possible relationship places social work in an intermediary position between client systems and the social environment. This viewpoint emphasizes the context of social functioning. As intermediaries, social workers mediate between client systems and their social environment.

Each of these positions views the relationship between social work and society differently. Each brings a different meaning to the practice of social work. Social work as a socialization instrument of society emphasizes social control. This suggests that the public good takes precedence over the needs of individuals. On the other hand, while social reformers have often forced the social work profession to respond to problems by taking action to improve social conditions, a radical stance may alienate potential allies and block social change efforts. Further, while some social workers may engage solely in therapeutic intervention and take a "neutral stance" in relation to society, this position does not seem consistent with the social justice mandate of the profession. The intermediary role seems to approximate most closely the idea of social work as an empowering process that works in partnership with clients to create change, change that can occur in both individuals and their environments. Furthermore, an understanding of these underlying principles of partnership and empowerment can transform the way social workers implement strategies related to social control and social change.

How Is Social Work an Empowering Profession?

What happens when you decide to make a change and set your plan in motion? What leads you to decide to take action in the first place? What gives you the courage to believe in your ability to carry out your plan? How do you translate the personal into the political?

If you believe the task is impossible, think your actions won't make a difference, or conclude your abilities and resources are inconsequential, will you even do anything at all? Probably not! It's more likely that you will feel incapable, helpless, and powerless. When people feel powerless, they acquiesce, feel defeated, and lose their sense of control over their lives (Kieffer, 1984).

To initiate changes, you must believe that your actions are possible and that your efforts will make a difference. You must believe that you are capable of taking action and garnering resources to augment your own. Your perspective of hopefulness complements the benefits of your resources to energize your response. In these circumstances, you are likely to experience empowerment. When people experience empowerment, they feel effective, conclude that they are competent, and perceive that they have power and control over the course of their lives. They recognize the interconnections among the personal, interpersonal, organizational, and community arenas of empowerment.

BOX 1.2
Reflections on Empowerment

How We Think Determines What We Do
Empowerment-oriented social workers apply abstract ideas about empowerment in their everyday practice. Empowerment has implications for how social workers view clients, build relationships, and align personal and political resources.

A number of assumptions underlie the process of empowerment in social work:

- Empowerment is a collaborative process, with clients and practitioners working together as partners.
- The empowering process views client systems as competent and capable, given access to resources and opportunities.
- Clients must perceive themselves as causal agents, able to effect change.
- Competence is acquired or refined through life experiences, particularly experiences affirming efficacy, rather than from circumstances in which one is told what to do.
- Multiple factors contribute to any given situation, and therefore effective solutions are necessarily diverse in their approach.
- Informal social networks are a significant source of support for mediating stress and increasing one's competence and sense of control.
- People must participate in their own empowerment; goals, means, and outcomes must be self-defined.
- Level of awareness is a key issue in empowerment; information is necessary for change to occur.
- Empowerment involves access to resources and the capacity to use those resources effectively.
- The empowering process is dynamic, synergistic, ever-changing, and evolutionary.
- Empowerment is achieved through the parallel structures of personal, political, and socioeconomic development.

Empowerment Defined

Empowerment is the "process of increasing personal, interpersonal, or political power so that individuals, families, and communities can take action to improve their situations" (Gutiérrez, 1994, p. 202). The roots of empowerment lie in the political and philosophical foundations of our culture as "the concept of democracy and its embodiment in our political institutions are based on the principle of empowering citizens to participate in decisions affecting their welfare" (Swift, 1984, p. xiii). As Rappaport (1987) says, empowerment

> suggests both individual determination over one's own life and democratic participation in the life of one's community, often through mediating structures such as schools, neighborhoods, churches, and other voluntary organizations. Empowerment conveys both a psychological sense of personal control or influence and a concern with actual social influence, political power, and legal rights. It is a multilevel construct applicable to individual citizens as well as to organizations and neighborhoods; it suggests the study of people in context. (p. 121)

As an outcome, empowerment defines the end state of achieving power. Empowerment refers to a *state of mind,* such as feeling worthy and competent or perceiving power and control; it also refers to a *reallocation of power* that results from modifying social structures (Swift & Levin, 1987). In other words, empowerment involves subjective elements of perception as well as more objective elements of resources of power within social structures. Empowerment implies exercising psychological control over personal affairs, as well as exerting influence over the course of events in the sociopolitical arena (Gutiérrez, 1990; 1994).

Access to Resources

Presuming that people will be able to experience empowerment without having options simply makes a mockery of empowerment (Breton, 1993; 1994; 2002). Empowerment hinges on having access to resources. This means that people know about their choices and have opportunities to select their courses of action from among options. "Empowerment implies that many competencies are already present or at least possible, given niches and opportunities . . . [and] that what you see as poor functioning is a result of social structure and lack of resources which make it impossible for the existing competencies to operate" (Rappaport, 1981, p. 16). In other words, the personal, interpersonal, and political-structural dimensions of empowerment are interrelated. Accessing resources in one dimension leads to developing resources in others.

Individuals, groups, organizations, and communities alike all may strive for empowerment. As Anderson (1992) says:

> The empowerment concept links individual strengths and competencies, natural mutual aid systems, and proactive behaviors to social action, social policy, social change, and community development. It can be applied at all levels of generalist practice. For example, organizations can be empowering because they influence policy decisions or because they provide contexts for individuals to feel in control of their own lives. A community can be empowered

> because citizens engage in activities that maintain or improve the quality of life and respond to community needs. (p. 7)

While empowerment implies that people increase their control or power over the course of their lives, empowerment does not necessarily result in a power struggle or relinquishment of power by one group to another, as "there is nothing in the definition of empowerment that requires that increasing the power of one person or group means decreasing the power of another person or group" (Swift & Levin, 1987, p. 75).

Implications for Social Work

The values of the social work profession support an empowerment base for practice. Social work adopts a view that suggests that humans are "striving, active organisms who are capable of organizing their lives and developing their potentialities as long as they have appropriate environmental supports" (Maluccio, 1983, p. 136). Note how this view emphasizes humans' capacity for adaptation and opportunities for growth throughout the entire life cycle. The view links with the purpose of social work as a way of releasing human and social power to promote personal, interpersonal, and structural competence.

People achieve empowerment through experiences that are empowering. However, social workers will not find a how-to manual to use to empower clients, nor will they find a recipe with exact measurements of ingredients that combine to achieve empowerment. Empowering processes are multifaceted and multidimensional (Rappaport, 1984). The combinations and permutations of psycho-social-cultural factors, persons, situations, resources, and solutions are countless. Because each circumstance, set of actors, or combination of influencing factors is unique, the process that leads to empowerment is highly individualized and nonreplicable. Clients and social workers generate solutions that they uniquely tailor to the dynamics of each situation. There are, however, common elements that characterize these processes.

Focusing on Strengths. An orientation toward strengths and competence contrasts with the inclination to focus on deficits and maladaptive functioning. The professional literature abounds with information on functional problems, maladaptation, victimization, and powerlessness. All too often professionals identify deficits, incompetencies, and maladaptive functioning, yet seem unable to notice clients' strengths. The helping process doesn't facilitate change when we describe problems in terms of deficits, incompetencies, or maladaptation in clients; when experts render the sole definition of problems; or when social workers direct plans of action as a way to overcome clients' deficiencies. In fact, "this triumvirate helps ensure that the helping encounter remains an emergency room, where wounded people come to be patched up" (Weick, Rapp, Sullivan, & Kisthardt, 1989, p. 352). Focusing on strengths considers the multidimensional nature of personal and environmental resources (Cowger & Snively, 2002; Miley, O'Melia, & DuBois, 2004; Saleebey, 2003).

Certainly social workers must consider the dynamics of victimization and powerlessness; however, characterizing clients as poor, needy, impotent victims who are unable to find solutions to their problems is counterproductive to change. "Empowerment of clients and changing their victim status means giving up our position as benefactors" (Pinderhughes, 1983, p. 337).

Working Collaboratively. Empowerment-oriented social workers work collaboratively with their clients. They focus on clients' strengths and adaptive skills as well as clients' competencies and potential. Believing in human potential is central, as empowerment is

> tied to the notion that people have untapped, undetermined reservoirs of mental, physical, emotional, social and spiritual abilities that can be expressed. The presence of this capacity for continued growth and heightened well-being means that people must be accorded the respect that this power deserves. This capacity acknowledges both the being and the becoming aspects of life. (Weick, Rapp, Sullivan, & Kisthardt, 1989, p. 352)

Moreover, empowerment presumes that people themselves should be integrally involved in change processes—from defining their situations to determining goals, selecting their courses of action, and evaluating the results. Collegiality between the practitioner and the client is requisite to empowerment-oriented practice (Breton, 1993; 1994). Likewise, Bricker-Jenkins (1990) emphasizes the importance of regarding clients as primary experts and consultants for developing models for social work practice.

The embedded patriarcal organizational culture of social service delivery thwarts collaborative work with clients. To counter this influence, social workers address power imbalances that favor professional expertise and client dependency, denounce jargon and labels that exploit clients and escalate social control, and incorporate taxonomies of inclusiveness and collaboration (Holmes & Saleebey, 1993). Human service organizations that apply empowerment principles to their own organizational structures and processes support workers' efforts to engage collaboratively with clients (Shera & Page, 1995).

Critically Reflecting on Structural Arrangements. Responding to the core values of human dignity and social justice, social workers who incorporate critical reflection into their practice engage in a continuous process of thinking, doing, and reflecting—a process that gathers feedback to refine perspectives and actions. Empowerment-oriented social workers critically examine the sociopolitical arrangements that delimit access to resources and opportunities. "Critical reflection seeks to challenge the prevailing social, political, and structural conditions which promote the interests of some and oppress others" (Ruch, 2002, p. 205). By analyzing the consequences of discrimination, oppression, and other violations of human rights, critical reflection questions the status quo of structural arrangements, the distribution of power and authority, and access to resources and opportunities. "With respect to critiquing the status quo, one cannot critically examine what one takes for granted" (Miley, O'Melia, & DuBois, 2004, p. 29).

Linking Personal and Political Power. Empowerment links two main sources of power—personal power and political power. Personal power involves an individual's ability to control his or her destiny and influence his or her surroundings. Political power is the ability to alter systems, redistribute resources, open up opportunity structures, and reorganize society (Lee, 2001).

The process of social work practice provides the context for empowering individuals, families, and other human systems by increasing their social competence. Participating in the formulation of social policy is an avenue for exercising political power for constructive social change. The integration of social work practice and policy efforts creates a dynamic synergistic effect for promoting adaptive functioning and creating just societal conditions. Empowerment for personal and family development fosters self-sufficiency, and empowerment for social and economic development reduces anomie and alienation (Hartman, 1990). Essentially, the goal of empowerment-oriented social work is not merely adapting to problems; rather, empowerment requires systemic change.

Looking Forward

Social work is just one of several occupations in the social welfare arena; historically, however, social work has been identified as the primary profession that carries out the social welfare mandate. Differentiating social work from other occupations is complicated by the tendency to identify anyone working in the broad area of social welfare with social work. Thus, with respect to human services, the general public tends to identify individuals with a variety of educational backgrounds, training, and levels of competence as social workers. These human service employees may also identify themselves as "doing social work." In fact, social work requires a particular education to acquire the knowledge, skills, and value base fundamental to professional social work practice.

Preparation for professional practice requires understanding human and societal needs, developing skills to facilitate change, and assimilating a social work value orientation. Clients touched by personal and social problems engage with social workers to enhance the clients' social functioning through a partnership of planned change. Society authorizes professional social workers to implement social welfare. The purpose, mission, goals, and objectives of the social work profession prescribe the behaviors, attitudes, and skills that are required to effect change. Chapter 2 explores the history of social work; the common base of practice; and the base of values, knowledge, and skills of professional social workers.

CHAPTER

2 An Evolving Profession

Social work is a profession that has historically maintained a partisan commitment to working with people who are poor or otherwise disenfranchized. However, social workers' views of their clients and their preferences with respect to courses of action have differed. Many have viewed disenfranchized populations as victims of social disorder, social injustice, and social change. As social reformers, they confronted the root causes of problems, modified societal structures, and engaged in advocating policy and legislative changes to improve environmental conditions and create opportunities. Others viewed disadvantaged populations as supplicants—unworthy, powerless, and in need of personal reform. As charity workers, they applied measures to improve individuals' moral and social acceptability.

This chapter examines the perspectives on reforming society and reforming individuals that have shaped the evolving profession of social work. This chapter also does the following:

- Traces the emergence of social work as a profession
- Profiles social work's quest for professional status, the rise of professional organizations, and the development of social work education
- Describes the common base of social work's values, knowledge base, and skills
- Explicates tenets that guide the profession

The Emergence of Social Work as a Profession

Social work emerged as a professional activity during the late nineteenth century. Its roots lie in early social welfare activities, the charity organization movement, and the settlement house movement.

Early Social Welfare Organizations

Numerous social welfare organizations sprang up in the United States during the nineteenth century to address concerns about social issues. Some examples include the New York Society for the Prevention of Pauperism (1818); Associations for Improving the Conditions of the Poor (the 1840s); various child saving agencies; and the American Social Science Association (1865), from which some members interested in practice withdrew to form the Conference of Charities in 1874 (which became the National Conference on Charities and Correction in 1879). Many of these organizations sponsored publications and journals to inform their membership. Examples of early journals include the *Lend-A-Hand* (1886), *Charities Review* (1891), *Social Casework* (1920), *Child Welfare* (1922), *Social Service Review* (1927), and *Public Welfare* (1943).

The National Conference of Charities and Correction was formed in 1879 to address social problems such as poverty, crime, and dependency. The membership of the National Conference, composed primarily of public officials and volunteer members of the State Boards of Charities and Correction, was concerned with the effective administration of welfare programs and the humanitarian reform of welfare institutions.

Although the National Conference of Charities and Correction predates social work as a professional field by nearly three decades, themes from its annual proceedings reflect the roots of social work. The care of the poor, the disabled, the mentally disturbed, and orphans in almshouses, reformatories, and asylums was of central interest in the last decades of the nineteenth century. As a fundamental institution for American poor relief, almshouses "contained the insane, the paupers, the feebleminded, the illegitimate and dependent children, the prostitutes and unmarried mothers, or such of them as were 'abjectly destitute, not otherwise provided for'" (Van Waters, 1931, p. 4). This "era of big buildings" focused on providing for society's dependents within the confines of custodial care. The special needs of dependent children and delinquent youth, as well as the new humanitarian approach to the treatment of the mentally ill, led the membership of the National Conference to examine institutionalized care with a critical eye and to develop practical methods for dealing with the insane, paupers, dependent and neglected children, and criminals.

Charity Organization Societies

S. Humphreys Gurteen founded the first U.S. Charity Organization Society (COS) in 1877 in Buffalo, New York. An English Episcopal priest, Gurteen was impressed with the work of the London Society for Organizing Charitable Relief and Repressing Mendicancy. He recommended adopting this society's organizational structure to deal with the chaos and indiscriminate charity relief practices prevalent in Buffalo, which Gurteen believed perpetuated pauperism (Lubove, 1965). Within a few years, 25 branches of the COS had been established in eastern and midwestern areas of the United States to deal with the economic crisis of the aftermath of the Civil War. By 1892, the number of branches of the COS in the United States had increased to 92 (Brieland, 1995).

Efforts of the charity organization movement were directed chiefly at administrating social services through private charities. The COS used neighborhood district committees composed of local residents and agency representatives to organize communities' welfare services (Lubove, 1965). It popularized the techniques of investigation and registration of the poor to eradicate pauperism. Its method of scientific philanthropy based charity on thorough investigations of applicants and efficient procedures.

Based on the belief that receiving charity corrupted individuals' character and motivation, a "paid agent" directed "friendly visitors" to meet with applicants regularly. Friendly visitors provided encouragement and served as models of moral character (Germain & Gitterman, 1980). Charity organization workers tried to locate resources within families' own situations, providing charity relief as a last resort (Austin, 1985). Vocational preparation for charity work was deemed necessary as casework methods evolved. The demand for trained workers led to the gradual replacement of volunteers with professional staff.

Mary Richmond (1861–1928), an influential leader in the COS, was first involved with charity work as a staff member for the Baltimore COS. She was appointed general secretary of the Philadelphia COS in 1900 and later worked for the Russell Sage Foundation. As a prominent leader in charity organization activities, Richmond was instrumental in shaping the course of the social work profession. Her book *Social Diagnosis* (1917) outlined assessment techniques, and her work *What Is Social Case Work?* (1922) provided a definition of the casework method (Brieland, 1995).

The history of the COS shows that services were provided almost exclusively to White families. "It was the general feeling among COS staff members that it was wiser to concentrate on problems of poverty among the whites, leaving problems among the colored for the future" (Solomon, 1976, p. 75). However, the Memphis COS operated the Colored Federated Charities, a Black auxiliary to the organization, which had its own Black board of directors, operated with its own workers, and conducted its own fundraising activities.

Charity Organization Society work also included community organizing activities (Dunham, 1970). For example, networks for the cooperative approach to dealing with the problems of the poor were developed, and many of the societies instituted community activities aimed at preventing tuberculosis, addressing housing problems, and curtailing child labor. As a case in point, the New York COS began its own publication, founded the first school of social work (now the Columbia University School of Social Work), and conducted field research (Warner, Queen, & Harper, 1930, cited in Dunham, 1970).

Many identify the COS's responses to individuals' needs as the genesis of social casework. Interest in understanding family relationships, utilization of "natural helping networks," emphasis on personal responsibility (which could translate to self-determination), and concern for accountability in service delivery are some of the COS's enduring contributions to social work (Leiby, 1984).

Settlement House Movement

The settlement house movement began in London in the late nineteenth century when Samuel Barnett founded Toynbee Hall. An Anglican priest in one of the most rundown areas of London, Barnett converted the rectory of his parish into a neighborhood center. He recruited university students to live at the center and work with families in the neighborhood.

Based on his own experience at Toynbee Hall, Stanton Coit established the first settlement house in the United States, the Neighborhood Guild of New York City. Coit characterized the purpose of settlement houses in this way:

> The fundamental idea which the settlement embodies is this: that, irrespective of religious belief or non-belief, all the people, men, women, and children, in any one street, on any small number of streets in every working-class district...shall be organized into a set of clubs which are by themselves, or in alliance with those of other neighborhoods, to carry out, or induce others to carry out, the reforms—domestic, industrial, educational, provident or recreative—which the social ideal demands. It is an expression of the family idea of co-operation. (Trattner, 1999, p. 170)

Many other settlement houses were established in cities across the country, including Chicago's Hull House, started by Jane Addams and Ellen Gates Starr in 1889; the Chicago Commons, begun by Graham Taylor in 1894; Boston's Andover House, founded by Robert Woods in 1891; and New York's Henry Street Settlement, established by Lillian Wald in 1893.

The settlement house movement combined social advocacy and social services to respond to the social disorganization that resulted from widespread industrialization and urbanization and the large influx of immigrants to America at the turn of the century. Activists in the movement were concerned with the deplorable social conditions under which individuals lived, and they defined problems environmentally, looking after the social and economic needs of the individual (Franklin, 1986). Through group work and neighborhood organizing strategies, the settlement house workers established neighborhood centers and offered services such as citizenship training, adult education, counseling, recreation, intercultural exchanges, and day care. Through research and political advocacy, settlement house workers supported legislative reforms in child welfare, tenement housing, labor laws, and public health and sanitation.

Typically, settlement house workers were young, idealistic college graduates from civic-minded, wealthy families. For the most part they were volunteers and community leaders and were not employed as social work professionals. These well-intentioned volunteers lived among the poor as "settlers" and viewed their involvement as good neighboring by offering goodwill and creating opportunities for immigrants to adapt to their new environment and for the poor and working classes to improve their quality of life (Germain & Gitterman, 1980). White women ranked high among their numbers, including women such

BOX 2.1
Reflections on Empowerment

Roots of Empowerment

The roots of empowerment in social work are found in the settlement house movement of the late nineteenth and early twentieth centuries. In the United States, settlement house workers were keenly aware of community conditions that adversely affected their neighborhoods. Inadequate public health and sanitation, lack of concern for occupational safety, deplorable housing conditions, and the clash of cultures among immigrants were of concern during this period of industrialization and urbanization. Settlement house workers employed empowerment strategies as they worked in partnership with their neighbors to address these social conditions.

For example, in 1902, Chicago experienced a typhoid epidemic, and the mortality in the Hull House Settlement ward was very high. Hull House residents and their neighbors were all at risk. Seeking to locate the cause of this tragedy, the Hull House residents studied the situation and drew two conclusions: "(1) that the uncovered privy vault, supposedly outlawed in 1897, was the source of the malady, the infection being carried by the common housefly; and (2) that the Health Department was either criminally inefficient or actually corrupt" (Breckinridge, 1936, p. 63).

Changes that resulted from the research and actions of the residents improved the living conditions in the neighborhood. Their efforts led to new plumbing codes, stricter building ordinances, sanitation inspections, and more enforcement efforts. The Chicago Civil Service Commission's subsequent investigation into allegations about the health department eventually led to censure of the head of the health department and secured the indictment of a number of inspectors in the sanitation bureau.

Social work was emerging as a profession concerned with both individual functioning and environmental conditions. Settlement house workers recognized the need for both individual adaptation and social reform. The messages inherent in settlement house work were "do with" their neighbors to effect changes in environmental conditions and broaden opportunities for individuals. These messages clearly reflect an orientation of empowerment for social work.

as Edith Abbott, Jane Addams, Sophonisba Breckinridge, Mary Follett, Julia Lathrop, and Lillian Wald. They gained national prominence for furthering social causes and shaping humanitarian legislation.

Of particular interest in the settlement house movement, *Jane Addams (1860–1935)* was noted for her social activism and social reform. She and Ellen Starr began Hull House in an old mansion on Chicago's South Halstead Street. Settlement house programs expanded to include a young women's boarding club, day care, a community kitchen, a book bindery, and numerous educational programs and activities that promoted the arts. An outspoken activist, Addams led the charge for social change through political reform. In 1912, she was elected the first woman president of the National Conference of Charities and Correction. Her position of leadership in both political and social work circles declined as a result of her pacifist activities during World War I. Addams was awarded the Nobel peace prize in 1931 (Hoover, 1986; Lundblad, 1995).

Settlement houses also developed in predominantly Black neighborhoods, founded by African American settlement workers such as Janie Porter Barrett of the Locust Street Settlement in Hampton, Virginia; Lugenia Burns Hop of the Neighborhood Union in Atlanta, Georgia; and Margaret Murray Washington of the Elizabeth Russell Settlement in Tuskegee, Alabama. Speaking of the African American helping tradition, Berman-Rossi and Miller (1994) comment:

> Strengthened by their own helping tradition and fueled by their systematic exclusion from white philanthropy and only limited access to public social service, African-Americans used their mutual aid societies to organize: hospitals, educational programs, economic assistance, aid to the sick, to widows and orphans, employment and rehabilitative services, and residential programs, such as homes for children, the aged and sick and for homeless women. (p. 88)

After earning her master's degree in social work from New York University, *Sarah Fernandis (1863–1951)* established the first Black settlement house in the United States, in Washington, D.C.; she also established another in Rhode Island. She taught school in Baltimore before she initiated her career in social welfare activities. Fernandis initiated the Women's Cooperative Civic League, a group that advocated changes in conditions, such as inadequate sanitation, in Black neighborhoods. Later in her career she was employed by the Baltimore Health Department's Venereal Disease Clinic. Her social work activities focused on improving health conditions in Baltimore's Black community (Peebles-Wilkins, 1995a).

Defining Social Work as a Profession

Many definitions of social work found throughout the professional literature reiterate the themes of helping individuals and changing social conditions. Some definitions emphasize people, whereas others incorporate the reciprocal interactions between people and their social environment. Among those historical trends that influenced the definition of practice are the emergence of social casework as a methodology in the early 1900s, the prominence of the psychoanalytic movement in the 1920s, the public welfare movement in the 1930s, the acceptance of group work and community organizing methodologies in the 1940s and 1950s, social reform activities in the 1960s, and the popularity of the social systems and ecological perspectives in the 1970s and 1980s (Table 2.1).

TABLE 2.1 Influential Activities and Publications

1915	Flexner evaluates social work's professional status Flexner, A. (1916). Is social work a profession? In *Proceedings of the National Conference of Charities and Correction, 1915* (pp. 576–590). Chicago, IL: The Hildmann Printing Co.
1929	Milford Conference considers social work's generic nature American Association of Social Workers (1929). *Social casework: Generic and specific: A report of the Milford Conference* (reprinted 1974). Washington DC: National Association of Social Workers.
1951	Hollis-Taylor Report examines social work's role in professional practice Hollis, E. V., & Taylor, A. L. (1951). *Social work education in the United States.* New York: Columbia University Press.
1957	Greenwood reexamines the professional status of social work Greenwood, E. (1957). Attributes of a profession. *Social Work, 2,* 45–55.
1958	Social workers form a definition of social work practice Working definition of social work practice. (1958). *Social Work, 3*(2), 5–9.
1961	Bartlett analyzes social work by fields of practice Bartlett, H. M. (1961). *Analyzing social work practice by fields.* Silver Spring, MD: National Association of Social Workers.
1969	Social workers apply general systems theory to social work Hearn, G. (Ed.), (1969). *The general systems approach: Contributions toward an holistic conception of social work.* New York: Council on Social Work Education.
1970	Bartlett explicates the common base of social work practice Bartlett, H. M. (1970). *The common base of social work practice.* New York: National Association of Social Workers.
1977	Professionals examine social work's purpose and objectives Special issue on conceptual frameworks. (1977). *Social Work, 22*(5).
1981	NASW develops a working statement on social work's purpose Conceptual frameworks II: Second special issue on conceptual frameworks. (1981). *Social Work, 26*(1).
2000	New international definition of social work Adopted by the International Federation of Social Workers. www.ifsw.org/Publications/4.6e.pub.html

Social Casework

In *Social Diagnosis* (1917) and *What Is Social Case Work?* (1922), Mary Richmond identified the first principles, theories, and methods of social casework, or work with individuals:

> Richmond explicated a tentative but concrete and comprehensive process of assessment of social functioning. She addressed the many dimensions of social interaction that contribute to adequate or inadequate social functioning, the caseworker's state of mind as a factor in assessment, the importance of context in understanding behavior, the impact of family and

> other social roles on mental well-being, and essentials of the interviewing process, including objectivity, empathy, utilization of the individual's strengths, and the interaction of personality and the social environment. . . . The first guide to social casework practice reflected the territory that social work was pioneering—the interaction between the individual and society. (Watkins, 1983, p. 46)

According to Richmond, social casework incorporated four processes: "insight into the individual, insight into the social environment, 'direct action mind upon mind,' and 'indirect action through the social environment'" (Lubove, 1965, p. 48). Edith Abbott offers an interesting remark attributed to Richmond that clarifies her position: "The good social worker, says Miss Richmond, doesn't go on mechanically helping people out of a ditch. Pretty soon, she begins to find out what ought to be done to get rid of the ditch" (Abbott, 1919, p. 313). Although the central focus was individual change—"helping people out of the ditch," Richmond did not ignore the impact of the "ditch"—the environment—on individual functioning.

One formative social work perspective, set forth in the Milford Conference Report (American Association of Social Workers, 1929), reflected a resolve to cultivate the generic nature of social work identity (Lubove, 1965) and, in this process, placed greater emphasis on adaptation by the individual. The Milford Conference Report spurred professional social work education to focus on how to make adjustments in impaired or deviant individuals.

Psychoanalytic Movement

This focus on individuals, which considered internal factors such as personal failure and maladjustment, was no doubt also influenced by the psychoanalytic movement, a movement that had gained popularity in the 1920s. Sigmund Freud's psychodynamic perspective stressed people's intrapsychic dynamics rather than the influence of environmental conditions on social functioning. Trattner (1999) suggests that, "Once alerted to the effects of the unconscious on motivation, psychiatric caseworkers felt that environmentalism, based upon the assumption that people are rational, had no relation to the dynamic factors in human behavior" (p. 261).

Mary Cromwell Jarrett (1877–1961) initiated a specialty in psychiatric social work, developed a psychiatric training curriculum, and founded the American Association of Psychiatric Social Workers. Her emphasis on psychiatry shifted social work's focus from environmental concerns to internal, personal distress. Jarrett contended that internal mental processes were the primary determinants of behavior (Hartman, 1986a).

Two additional factors fostered the emphasis on treating individuals: the prominence of the mental hygiene movement and the mental health services provided by professionals with the American Red Cross at the time of World War I. Professionals and lay people involved in the mental hygiene movement pressed for improved conditions in mental hospitals. "The early advocacy movement focused public attention on care and treatment in the hospital setting and hospital-based programs were expanded to include specialized hospital care and psychiatric units in general hospitals" (Lin, 1995, p. 1705). The American Red Cross provided casework services for World War I veterans and their families to address the psychological aftermath of the war (Schriver, 1987). This work with

BOX **2.2**

Reflections on Diversity

It Is Time to Update Social Work History

The contributions of minority social workers are overlooked in most historical accounts of the development of the social work profession. In general, minorities were excluded from mainstream social work services. Therefore, parallel structures of civic organizations, social services, and philanthropies developed to serve minority populations (Peebles-Wilkins, 1989). "Individual and collective forms of empowerment built private social institutions to address the needs of the African American community" (Carlton-LeNey & Alexander, 2001, p. 69).

For example, African Americans developed a structure of service clubs, benevolent societies, civic organizations, and self-help and welfare services to address needs within the Black community. Some functioned as "Negro auxiliaries" of organizations such as the COS. Other direct social work services included Black settlement houses, orphanages, residential schools, and child placement activities. African Americans at the forefront of these movements included Janie Porter Barrett (1865–1948), one of the founders of the Virginia Federation of Colored Women's Clubs; Sarah Fernandis (1863–1951), founder of the first Black social settlement in the United States, located in the District of Columbia; and Fredericka Douglass Sprague Perry (1872–1943), a pioneer in child welfare services for Black children. Targeting policy at both the local and national levels, the political activities of these African American leaders in social welfare foreshadow the integration of policy practice into contemporary social work (Carlton-LeNey & Alexander, 2001).

In the early twentieth century, African American professionals provided leadership in Black schools of social work as well as in politically oriented groups such as the Urban League and the National Association for the Advancement of Colored People (NAACP). Lester Granger (1896–1976) is known for his long-standing leadership of the Urban League. Militant civil rights activist W. E. B. DuBois (1868–1963) was professor of history and economics at Atlanta University and served on the Board of Directors of the NAACP from 1910 to 1934. Edward Franklin Frazier (1894–1962) is noted for his research on Black families and for his leadership role in the social work program at Howard University. Mary Eliza Church Terrell (1863–1954), noted social activist and international lecturer on race relations and women's rights, demonstrated unrelentingly against segregation. Civil rights leader Whitney Moore Young (1921–1971) was the director of the National Urban League from 1961 to 1971 and served as president of the NASW in 1966.

World War I veterans represented pioneering efforts of social workers in the area of mental health (Austin, 1985). With these movements, Richmond's earlier diagnostic foundation of social work was tempered to reflect a more individual focus at the cost of deemphasizing social reform.

Public Welfare Movement

The public welfare movement of the 1930s emphasized the sociocultural, political, and economic dimensions of social functioning. This emphasis grew out of the aftermath of the Great Depression. Widespread unemployment and poverty pointed to a structural cause of social problems. However, the trend toward environmental intervention was overshadowed by the conservative psychoanalytic movement, with its emphasis on individual maladjustment and a medical model of psychological change.

Two social workers, Harry Hopkins and Frances Perkins, are among those who provided leadership in the public welfare movement. *Harry Hopkins (1890–1946),* a social worker from Iowa who moved to New York to work in the settlement house movement, played a significant role in the development of social policy during the era of the Depression. As the administrator of New York State's Temporary Emergency Relief Administration, he developed a system of providing public relief for people who were unemployed. In 1933, he joined Roosevelt's federal program to supplement state and local relief efforts, advocated the formation of work relief programs, and engineered the development of the Social Security Act of 1935 (Bremer, 1986).

A social worker and social reformer, *Frances Perkins (1880–1965),* was the first woman to be a member of a U.S. president's cabinet. Prior to her appointment as secretary of labor in Franklin D. Roosevelt's administration, she advocated legislative reform in New York State to improve hazardous working conditions. Perkins gained administrative experience as the statewide industrial commissioner in New York. In her position in Roosevelt's cabinet, she played a key role in developing the national social security policy. As a result of Perkins's influence, stipulations for maternal and child health, crippled children, child welfare services, vocational rehabilitation, public health, aid to dependent children, and assistance to the blind were included in this legislation (Cohen, 1986).

Social Group Work and Community Organization

Social group work and community organization methodologies gained formal acceptance and recognition as social work interventions in the 1940s and 1950s. Both emphasize the situational context of behavioral change. The inclusion of group work and community organization as acceptable social work methods marked a significant transformation in the social work profession. Previously, social work had tended to be seen as identical to casework (Goldstein, 1973).

Group Work. Group work uses small-group interaction as a vehicle for social change. Early in its history, group work focused on educational, recreational, and character-building activities through organizations such as the YMCA and YWCA, scouting, neighborhood centers, the settlements, Jewish centers, and the Salvation Army. Social group work's focus included enrichment, education, and social reform. As a social work method, social group work uses the interplay of personalities in group processes to achieve cooperative group action that addresses common goals.

Grace Coyle (1892–1962) was an early leader in social group work. After graduating from Wellesley College, she earned a certificate from the New York School of Philanthropy, a master's degree in economics, and a doctorate in sociology from Columbia University. She initially worked in a settlement house and then worked for the YWCA, and eventually she became a faculty member of Case Western Reserve University. With the publication of her book, *Social Process in Organized Groups,* she began to develop social work's social science base for work with individuals and groups. Coyle emphasized using creative group experiences as a vehicle for change and stressed group members' participation and democratic control (Reid, 1986).

Community Organization. Community organization creates changes in larger groups and organizational units. The efforts of community organization, by their very nature, create change in situations or in the environment, which in turn affects personal well-being. For example, early community organization efforts addressed community problems stemming from World War II, such as the need for a network of services for military families and day care services for children whose mothers were filling gaps in the work force.

One community organization leader, *Eduard Lindeman (1885–1953),* taught at the New York School of Social Work from 1924 to 1950. His vision for social work looked beyond the factional techniques of the psychoanalytic method and incorporated a philosophy that emphasized the social context of social work: "He developed an integrated, holistic, interdisciplinary perspective on human behavior and social problems at a time when social workers were dividing into warring camps along ideological, philosophical, and theoretical lines" (Davenport & Davenport, 1986, p. 500).

Dual Perspective

The definitions of social work in the 1950s began to recapture the dual perspective of the individual and the social environment that was so much a part of the early history of the profession. Among the contributors to this perspective are the ideas of Bertha Capen Reynolds, the Hollis-Taylor report, the *Working Definition of Social Work Practice,* and Hollis's notion of "person-in-situation."

Reynolds's Contribution. *Bertha Capen Reynolds (1885–1978)* was a noteworthy social advocate for working-class and oppressed groups. After receiving her certificates in social work and advanced psychiatric training, Reynolds worked at a state hospital in Massachusetts. Her opposition to the popular medical model and its explicit notion of expert cure was evident in her emphasis on mobilizing environmental changes and her regard for clients' strengths. Later in her career, she worked for the National Maritime Union in a program that served as a model for social work in unions. Reynolds's emphasis on consumers' involvement in directing social services distinguished her philosophy of social service delivery (Freedberg & Goldstein, 1986; Hartman, 1986b).

Reynolds wrote extensively about the need for social workers to demonstrate concern for social justice and civil rights issues through political activity. Reynolds (1951) described social casework as helping "people to test and understand their reality, physical, social and emotional, and to mobilize resources within themselves and in their social environment to meet their reality or change it" (p. 131). She was "troubled that the profession was losing sight of its commitments to the whole person, to the community, and to reform" (Goldstein, 1990, p. 34). The individual's responsibility for change is evident, yet the elements of change are located in both people and their environments.

The Hollis-Taylor Report. The Hollis-Taylor report on social work education (1951) portrays social work as a helping activity, a social activity, and a liaison activity. Drawing extensively on a United Nations statement about the international dimensions of social work practice, the report describes social work as follows:

> 1. It is a "helping" activity, designed to give assistance in respect to problems that prevent individuals, families, and groups from achieving a minimum desirable standard of social and economic well-being.
> 2. It is a "social" activity, carried on not for personal profit by private practitioners but under the auspices of organizations, governmental or non-governmental or both, established for the benefit of members of the community regarded as requiring assistance.
> 3. It is a "liaison" activity, through which disadvantaged individuals, families, and groups may tap all the resources in the community available to meet their unsatisfied need. (pp. 58–59)

The Working Definition of Social Work Practice. The *Working Definition of Social Work Practice* (1958), a product of the National Association of Social Workers Commission on Practice, chaired by Harriet Bartlett, also emphasized this dual focus:

> The social work method is the responsible, conscious, disciplined use of self in a relationship with an individual or group. Through this relationship the practitioner facilitates interaction between the individual and his social environment with a continuing awareness of the reciprocal effects of one upon the other. It facilitates change: (1) within the individual in relation to his social environment; (2) of the social environment in its effect upon the individual; (3) of both the individual and the social environment in their interaction. (p. 7)

This definition expands the focus of social work from working with individuals to working with both individuals and groups. It also delineates the interactional dimension of the reciprocal relationship between individuals and their environment as a target of change.

Hollis's Perspective on "Person-in-Situation." Florence Hollis (1964), a prominent social work educator, coined the phrase "the person-in-his-situation" to describe the threefold interaction of the "configuration consisting of the person, the situation, and the interaction between them" (p. 10). Hollis's psychosocial method stresses the person's physical, social, and psychological realities, as well as the outer social components in an individual's development and functioning (Grinnell, 1973). Hollis indicated that social work needed to give "weight to both the personality and the social situation" (p. 266). Her point of view further suggested that intervention occurs primarily at the individual level; she focused on environmental intervention as a way to improve individuals' functioning.

Social Reform

The 1960s represented another turning point for the profession. In many ways, the turmoil of the 1960s touched all societal institutions, including social work and social welfare. One social activist of this period, *Whitney Young (1921–1971),* began his professional career with the Minnesota Urban League after earning his MSW from the University of Minnesota. At the time of his death, he was the executive director of the National Urban League. As a social work educator, he taught at the University of Nebraska and at Creigh-

Social worker and civil rights activist Whitney Young received the Medal of Freedom in 1968.

ton University, and was dean of the Atlanta University School of Social Work. As a leader in the social work profession, Young was president of the National Conference of Social Welfare (1965) and the NASW (1966). He received national recognition for his exemplary civil rights activities when President Lyndon Johnson awarded him the Medal of Freedom in 1969 (Peebles-Wilkins, 1995b). Young told practitioners at the National Conference on Social Welfare that social work had lost its zeal for social reform in its press to achieve professional status. He challenged "the profession to reclaim the lost heritage of its founders" (Trattner, 1999, p. 311).

An examination of professional activities in this decade testifies that in the

> expansion and refinement of services in both public and private sectors, social work services, traditional and innovative, proliferated. The Economic Opportunity Act, the broadening of social insurance and public welfare services, the expansion in the type and quantity of family services, the increasing availability of mental hygiene clinics and day treatment centers, community action, and poverty programs were a few of the projects and settings in which the profession assumed a major role. (Goldstein, 1973, p. 47)

Nonetheless, the "war on poverty" activities, emanating from a federal program intended to address social problems at a grassroots level, were in many ways critical of the social work profession and even antiprofessional in orientation. Policymakers raised questions about the effectiveness of traditional casework and group work approaches. Once again, the profession was challenged to reexamine its focus (Brieland, 1995).

That challenge was met by those who transformed the sequencing of process and method. Instead of beginning with method and then examining the person-in-situation, they suggested that the *starting* point ought to be the person-in-situation. In other words, clients' problems, issues, and needs should dictate the selection of intervention methods. Thus a generic base of practice foundational to all social work activities gained attention. The generalist perspective, emphasizing the social systems and ecological perspectives, provided a unified approach to problem-oriented social work practice.

Ecosystems Approach

In the 1970s and 1980s, the social work profession was receptive to definitions of social work that introduced the language of the ecosystems approach. These definitions focused on both the ecological and the systems elements that were being crystallized by Meyer (1970; 1983; 1988) in the ecosystems approach; Germain and Gitterman (1980; 1996) in the ecological life model; and Maluccio (1981) in the client competency model.

Meyer's (1988) paradigm on ecosystems "considers environmental variables as interrelated and reciprocal with the person variables, and therefore environmental intervention must be included among the treatments of choice" (p. 287).

Germain (1979) describes the transactional nature of the person-in-situation approach of social work. "In an ecological view, [social work] practice is directed at improving the transactions between people and environments in order to enhance adaptive capacities and improve environments for all who function within them" (pp. 7–8).

Maluccio's (1981) competence-oriented practice addresses the need to consider capacities and skills, motivational aspects, and environmental qualities as components of ecological competence for transactions between people and their physical and social environments. In other words, "the essence of competence-oriented social work practice consists of changing the person-environment transaction so as to support and/or enhance the competence of individuals, families and groups to deal effectively with the environment" (p. 11).

The Evolving Definition of Social Work

In the last hundred years, definitions of social work have reflected evolving professionalism, changing theoretical perspectives, and the emerging practice trends. Although the definitions are similar in their descriptions of the mission and purpose of social work, they show some remarkable differences in how they delineate the nature of professional activities. All definitions focus on the problems, issues, and needs that arise in the transactions of people within social systems. The trend toward identifying a dual focus that includes both individual treatment and social reform, rather than viewing individuals as the primary point of intervention with some limited attention to the environment, is noteworthy.

Traditionally, social workers have dealt with personal problems presented by individual clients. Yet the private troubles of individuals must be viewed within the context of larger social issues. "Treating" people through counseling and psychotherapeutic intervention may enhance their coping and adaptive capacities, but it does not resolve the complex social problems that bear on individuals' situations. Widespread societal problems, deleterious societal attitudes, and limited opportunities and resources, in themselves, require corrective action in order for people to maximize their potentials. Current definitions of social work incorporate two simultaneous activities for social workers: problem solving in human relationships and engaging in social reform.

The Quest for Professional Status

The question of whether social work is in fact a profession has challenged social workers for nearly a century and parallels the evolving definition of the profession. The history of social work reflects the systematic efforts by early pioneers to acquire professional status, unify professional organizations, and develop standards for education.

"Is Social Work a Profession?"

Social work's professional status was evaluated by Abraham Flexner in 1915, and his conclusion has reverberated among social workers ever since. In 1957, Ernest Greenwood applied criteria to assert social work's standing as a profession. Today, the social work profession continues to confront issues related to maintaining its professional legitimacy.

Flexner's Assessment. Flexner's speech, "Is Social Work a Profession?" delivered at the 1915 meeting of the Baltimore Conference on Charities and Correction, was an event of utmost significance in the process of developing the foundational rationale for social work as an organized profession (Austin, 1983). Flexner (1916), a noted expert on professional education, delineated six attributes that he called "earmarks of a profession." According to Flexner, "Professions involve essentially intellectual operations with large individual responsibility, derive their raw material from science and learning, this material they work up to a practical and definite end, possess an educationally communicable technique, tend to self-organization, and are becoming increasingly altruistic in motivation" (p. 580). These characteristics provided a framework for assessing social work's professional status.

Flexner acknowledged the rapid evolution of a "professional self-consciousness," recognized that social work was in the beginning stages of professionalization, and praised the altruistic motivation of social workers and their devotion to "well-doing." However, he concluded that, as of 1915, social work was not yet a profession. Because social work mediated between other professions, it did not have the responsibility or power of a true profession.

Educational efforts were apparent, but the lack of specificity in the aim of social work was not conducive to an orderly and highly specialized educational discipline. Flexner observed that, although social work drew its body of knowledge, facts, and ideas from both the laboratory and seminars, it was not founded on a purposefully organized educational discipline.

Additionally, because of the broad scope that characterized social work practice at that time, social work did not possess the high degree of specialized competency required for professional status. In other words, Flexner didn't discern any single practice method common to the wide array of fields of social work. Considering all these factors, Flexner concluded that social work had not yet attained professional status.

Since the time Flexner publicly proclaimed that social work did not fulfill the criteria of a true profession, there has been a preoccupation with and a zealous quest for achieving professional status (Greenwood, 1957; Hodson, 1925). Using Flexner's framework as a model, social workers set out to prove that social work was indeed a profession (Austin, 1983). Their activity focused on addressing the identified deficiencies in order to claim professional status. The subsequent flurry of activity included expanding the number of schools of social work, forming a professional accreditation body, standardizing educational curricula, advocating training for all social workers, and holding a series of conferences to testify to the singular, generic nature of social work skills applicable in any setting (Popple, 1985). After considerable advances in developing methodologies for practice, enhancing the educational preparation of social workers, expanding social work's empirical knowledge base, and consolidating and solidifying professional associations, social workers asserted that social work had in fact attained professional status.

Greenwood's Reevaluation. Ernest Greenwood's (1957) classic article, "Attributes of a Profession," provides another landmark in the evaluation of the professional status of social work. Greenwood's continuum, noting differences between professional and nonprofessional status, includes the following indicators of professional standing:

- A profession has fundamental knowledge and develops a systematic body of theory that directs the skills of practice; educational preparation must be intellectual as well as practical.
- Professional authority and credibility in the client-professional relationship are based on the use of professional judgment and competence.
- A profession is empowered to regulate and control its own membership, professional practice, education, and performance standards. The community sanctions regulatory powers and professional privilege.
- A profession has an enforceable, explicit, systematic, and binding regulatory code of ethics that compels ethical behavior by its members.
- A profession is guided by a culture of values, norms, and symbols within an organizational network of formal and informal groups, through which the profession functions and performs its services.

Using these indicators to evaluate the professional status of social work, Greenwood contended that "social work is already a profession; it has too many points of congruence with the model to be classifiable otherwise" (p. 438). Additionally, he pointed out that social work was attempting to gain status in "the professional hierarchy, so that it, too, might enjoy maximum prestige, authority, and monopoly which presently belong to a few top professions" (p. 438).

Professional Status Today. In more recent years, social work's professional status has been scrutinized by evaluating whether social work has the "monopoly" in the provision of the social work services to which Greenwood refers. Some assert, however, that it is neces-

BOX 2.3
Social Work Profile

Family Services

My passion for social work developed when I enrolled in an Introduction to Social Work course as an undergraduate. Learning about the history of social work and social workers' roles in furthering the social justice agenda with respect to oppressed population groups touched me in ways that I incorporate in my practice today. I'm not offended when people think I'm a "bleeding heart liberal." After all, social work and social justice is where my heart is.

Although my practice beliefs derive from various historic social work figures, two stand out: Jane Addams and Abraham Flexner. The settlement house movement, as exemplified by Jane Addams and her colleagues, placed social workers in the trenches so to speak. Settlement workers practiced *in* the community *with* their neighbors. I never want to lose sight of how the profession developed; I always want to include this interaction with clients at the front line in my practice of social work. I think also about the arguments that Flexner raised—arguments concerning whether social work was really a profession and whether we had standards that define us as a profession. I believe Flexner's questions remain relevant today. As social work professionals, we need to continually examine the nature of our professional identity and the effectiveness of what we do as professionals.

In my current job at a family service agency, I provide counseling to individuals and families, facilitate groups for adolescents with first-time substance abuse offenses, and conduct groups focusing on divorce, anger management, and domestic violence. All of my clients have been court ordered for treatment services. I am challenged daily to think on a deeper level about who my clients are. All of them bring their own history, their own cultural traditions, and their own worldviews. I find myself needing to be open-minded and responsive to people whose values, life experiences, and cultures are very different from my own. As an African American social worker, I now acknowledge that I have been practicing social work from the Eurocentric perspective that I was taught and am now incorporating more Afrocentric perspectives in my practice. However, I also recognize that the Eurocentric perspective applies to more than a social work exchange between Black and White persons. For me to be effective in a counseling position, I need to know about the history, culture, and experiences of many different ethnic groups, including Hispanic Americans, Asian Americans, and Native Americans. Not only do I not want to impose my own value system on clients, but I also need to hold other practitioners accountable for what they do and how their actions are perceived as oppressive or racist by others.

Finally, I believe that agencies need to ensure they do not lose the focus of the social work purpose with the press for managed care and the adoption of business management models in not-for-profit agencies. Since I began practicing as a social worker in the field of child welfare, I've noted the detrimental influence on the quality and effectiveness of services by the administrative press for billable service hours, clients' lack of insurance coverage for mental health and social work services, and social workers' burgeoning number of cases and workload requirements. Clearly, social workers will continue to be challenged to balance the financial ledgers without losing the vision of being caring helpers who are committed to our reason for being—our clients.

---

sary to go beyond either an attribute or a process assessment of professional status in order to examine the presence of power and control, which includes factors such as legitimate professional authority, membership solidarity, and a sanctioned monopoly in the provision of services (Lowe, Zimmerman, & Reid, 1989). Some argue that increased licensure and regulation will limit those who can legally define themselves as social workers. But licensure fails to address the critical issue of securing a unique domain of activity for social work, that is, services that can be provided exclusively by professionally prepared social workers. In fact, some argue that the current preoccupation with licensure subverts the issue of defining a professional domain of practice expertise: Before the social work profession can achieve the necessary occupational control, social workers must assert the parameters of their own professional domain.

The Rise of Professional Organizations

To expedite job placement for their graduates, in 1911, several women's colleges established a professional organization called the Intercollegiate Bureau of Occupations in New York City. One department, the National Social Worker's Exchange, which was particularly interested in professional standards, led the movement to establish a comprehensive organization, the American Association of Social Workers, in 1921 (Austin, 1983). A further impetus for forming professional associations came from social work educators attempting to gain acceptance in the academic community: "To have social work recognized as a legitimate professional degree program, and social work faculty as legitimate members of the academy, it was essential that the professional status of social work be asserted" (p. 361). As specialty areas emerged, other professional associations were formed, including the American Association of Medical Social Workers (1918), the National Association of School Social Workers (1919), the American Association of Psychiatric Social Workers (1926), the American Association of Group Workers (1936), the Association for the Study of Community Organization (1946), and the Social Work Research Group (1949).

National Association of Social Workers. In a quest for professional unity, various social work organizations merged in 1955 to form the National Association of Social Workers (NASW). With a membership of nearly 150,000, NASW is currently the largest social work organization in the world (NASW, 2003). Full membership in NASW is available to graduates of social work programs accredited by the Council on Social Work Education. Students enrolled in these baccalaureate and master's degree programs are also eligible for membership. Associate membership in NASW is available to other human service practitioners. In addition to the national organization, there are chapters in each state and in the District of Columbia, New York City, Puerto Rico, the Virgin Islands, Guam, and Europe (primarily for Americans working on military bases). As a membership association, NASW provides support and resources to social work practitioners, promotes professional development, establishes practice standards and a code of ethics, and promotes the humanitarian ideals and values of social work.

Other Professional Organizations. In addition to the NASW, a number of special-interest professional associations have been formed, representing, for example, particular groups of professionals, special interests, advocacy issues, and areas of expertise. Examples include the Association for Community Organization and Social Administration, Canadian Association of Social Workers, International Federation of Social Workers, National Association of Black

Social Workers, National Organization of Forensic Social Work, and Society for Social Work Leadership in Health Care. These specialty associations influence both change and stability. They are also important sources of professional identity and renewal.

The Development of Professional Education

Early leaders in both the Charity Organization Society and the settlement house movement realized that formal education was a requisite for the success of the emerging profession. There was, however, considerable debate about whether the focus should be on "training" or on university-based education (Pumphrey & Pumphrey, 1961).

Mary Richmond advocated establishing training schools directly affiliated with philanthropic agencies, training programs that emphasized practicalities rather than academic theories (Costin, 1983). The first such program was a six-week training course initiated in the summer of 1898 for the New York Charity Organization Society. It was formalized into a year-long training program through the New York School of Philanthropy in 1904.

In response to the demand for trained workers, social work programs developed in other cities. In Chicago, leadership for early education efforts came from Graham Taylor of the Chicago Commons settlement house and Julia Lathrop from Hull House. When the Chicago School of Civics and Philanthropy became the School of Social Service Administration, affiliated with the University of Chicago, this educational venture became the first in which social work education was included in a major coeducational university structure (Costin, 1983). The university programs emphasized both theoretical understanding and practice experience.

Council on Social Work Education. Recognition that common standards should apply to educational programs has paralleled the development of curricula. Initially, the American Association of Schools of Social Work, organized in 1919, guided the curriculum policy (Lowy, Bloksberg, & Walberg, 1971). In 1952, this association, which focused on professional education at the graduate level, merged with the National Association of Schools of Social Administration, which promoted undergraduate social work education, to form the Council on Social Work Education (CSWE). The CSWE became the standard-setting organization for social work education. Although initially charged with accrediting master's degree programs, since 1974 the CSWE has been concerned with all levels of social work education, including the baccalaureate degree in social work.

The purpose of the CSWE is to promote high-quality social work education. It achieves its purpose by accrediting programs, holding conferences for educators, spearheading professional development activities, initiating task forces on educational programming, and publishing journals (Beless, 1995). Accreditation—certifying that certain minimum standards have been met—is a means of quality assurance. Many states require that candidates possess a degree from an approved program in order to take a qualifying examination for licensure or certification. Also, a degree from an accredited baccalaureate social work program often affords advanced standing in a master's degree program, a practice that recognizes that accredited undergraduate-level social work programs provide the professional foundation core of practice, policy, research, and human behavior. The Hollis-Taylor (1951) report concluded that study of the arts and sciences, basic to professional preparation, and of the foundational concepts of social work, the cornerstones for advanced social work education, can be achieved in the undergraduate college.

Social Work Today

Both NASW and CSWE have played vital roles in defining the purpose and objectives of the social work profession and in refining the appropriateness of professional activities at various levels of practice. Change has not occurred without controversy, however. The recognition of the professional status of baccalaureate social workers by NASW in 1970 and the subsequent accreditation of baccalaureate programs by the CSWE in 1974 came about only after considerable debate. In fact, the acceptance of graduates of baccalaureate social work programs as full members in NASW was met with open resistance and even charges that recognizing BSW social workers as professionals was deprofessionalizing the practice of social work.

Acceptance of the BSW degree and BSW practitioners required the social work profession to develop a differential classification of professional tasks and activities and to explicate the baseline of practice competencies—knowledge, skills, and values—that all social workers should have. According to the CSWE (2001), students who graduate from baccalaureate CSWE-accredited programs and MSW students after the foundation year should be able to do the following:

1. Apply critical thinking skills within the context of professional social work practice.
2. Understand the value base of the profession and its ethical standards and principles, and practice accordingly.
3. Practice without discrimination and with respect, knowledge, and skills related to clients' age, class, color, culture, disability, ethnicity, family structure, gender, marital status, national origin, race, religion, sex, and sexual orientation.
4. Understand the forms and mechanisms of oppression and discrimination and apply strategies of advocacy and social change that advance social and economic justice.
5. Understand and interpret the history of the social work profession and its contemporary structures and issues.
6. Apply the knowledge and skills of generalist social work practice with systems of all sizes (Baccalaureate level). Apply the knowledge and skills of a generalist social work perspective to practice with systems of all sizes (Master's level).
7. Use theoretical frameworks supported by empirical evidence to understand individual development and behavior across the life span and the interactions among individuals and between individuals and families, groups, organizations, and communities.
8. Analyze, formulate, and influence social policies.
9. Evaluate research studies, apply research findings to practice, and evaluate their own practice interventions.
10. Use communication skills differentially across client populations, colleagues, and communities.
11. Use supervision and consultation appropriate to social work practice.
12. Function within the structure of organizations and service delivery systems and seek necessary organizational change. (p. 9)

The objectives outlined by the CSWE ensure that baccalaureate-level social workers develop competencies in a uniform foundation of knowledge, values, and skills.

The Common Base of Social Work Practice

The common base of practice delineated by Harriet Bartlett (1970) was formative in the conceptualization of generalist social work practice. Bartlett described the central focus of social work as helping people cope with life situations and helping them balance the demands of their social environments. According to Bartlett, social workers have a particular orientation that reflects their concern for individuals in the context of their situations. To act on this orientation, social workers draw their attitudes toward people from a body of professional values and base their understanding of human behavior and environmental responses on a body of knowledge. The techniques and methods of practice derive from this value and knowledge base.

The foundation for generalist practice as specified by the CSWE (2001), thus, has a generic or common base of purpose, values, knowledge, and skills shared by all social workers. This common base unifies the profession even though social work practitioners utilize a variety of methods, work in different settings, have diverse groups as clients, and practice with clients at different system levels. The values-knowledge-skills complex of the profession describes the *why,* the *what,* and the *how* of social work (Table 2.2).

TABLE 2.2 Social Work Values, Knowledge, and Skills

Fundamental Values and Principles	
Respect for diversity	Nonjudgmentalism
Confidentiality	Ethical conduct
Professional comportment	Access to resources
Dignity and worth	Self-determination
Social justice	
Foundational Knowledge	
Philosophy of social work	Human systems
Theories of human behavior	Social welfare policy
Cultural diversity	Fields of practice
Social welfare history	Self-knowledge
Family dynamics	Organizational theory
Group dynamics	Community theory
Service delivery system	
Requisite Skills	
Thinking critically	Cultural competence
Building relationships	Computer literacy
Empowering processes	Research
Practice methods	Social planning
Analyzing policies	Crisis intervention
Effective communication	Time management

Professional Values

To achieve the objectives of the profession, social workers must be responsible partners in the change process. Their professional activities should be permeated with the values of the profession, founded on the purpose of social work, and guided by professional standards of ethical practice. Social work values focus on three general areas: values about people, values about social work in relation to society, and values that inform professional behavior.

Values about People. The common values of the profession reflect social workers' fundamental ideas about the nature of humankind and the nature of change—"core values of service, social justice, dignity and worth of the person, importance of human relationships, integrity, and competence" (NASW, 1999a, p. 5). Valuing the dignity and worth of all people regardless of their stations in life, cultural heritage, life-styles, or beliefs is essential to practicing social work. Professional social workers maintain an unconditional positive regard for others by respecting diversity and accepting variations in personal life-styles. Social workers advocate clients' rights to access services and participate in decision making. They integrate the principles of self-determination, nonjudgmentalism, and confidentiality into their interactions with clients.

Values about Society. Social workers champion social justice and value the democratic process. Social workers assume responsibility for confronting inequities and social injustice. They are professionally committed to making social institutions more humane and responsive to human needs. Improving social programs and refining social policies reflect practitioners' commitment to improving societal conditions in ways that actualize social justice.

Values about Professional Behavior. Values guide the professional activities of social workers in their efforts with client systems. Social workers value client systems' strengths and competencies and work in partnership with clients to develop creative solutions. Social workers also value quality in their practice and continually examine their own practice effectiveness. Additionally, they take responsibility for ethical conduct and continual professional development.

The Knowledge Base of Social Work

The knowledge base of social work includes the ways of thinking about and means for understanding human behavior and the social environment. To this end, social work education includes both a liberal arts perspective and a professional foundation. Liberal arts courses prepare students with broad knowledge from the humanities and sciences and equip students with tools for critical thinking and analysis. The professional foundation includes coursework about the history and philosophy of social work, fields of social work practice, theoretical constructs and practice models, legislation and social policy, cultural influences, research, and self-awareness.

Liberal Arts Foundation. Education for the professional practice of social work is university based and includes a broad spectrum of liberal arts courses. A background in various social sciences, such as psychology, sociology, anthropology, economics, political science, and history, is essential for understanding societal circumstances and human behavior. Studying fine arts and literature encourages appreciation of aesthetics and creativity. Philosophy affords an opportunity to examine methods of thought and the structure of knowledge. Science courses provide insight into the biological characteristics of humans and the physical characteristics of the environment. A strong liberal arts foundation is central to social work education at both the undergraduate and graduate levels.

Philosophy and History of Social Work. The philosophical and historical bases of social work and social welfare form the backbone of the profession. Social workers must understand trends in contemporary practice in the context of the history of social work practice. A historical perspective provides insight into conflicting attitudes about social service clients and the ways in which social workers have provided social services.

Fields of Practice. Although social workers practice in particular settings, they need to have a comprehensive understanding of all the major fields of social work practice—the public and private sectors of social welfare such as income maintenance, family and children's services, health care facilities, mental health settings, business and industry, schools, and corrections. They need to be knowledgeable about social service resources, as they often make referrals and link clients with other services. Understanding various fields of practice also enhances social workers' ability to participate in social planning activities.

Theoretical Constructs and Practice Models. The formal knowledge base of social work includes theories about human behavior and the social environment and theories about practice methods and models. Social workers practice from a theoretical base that provides an understanding of how biological, social, psychological, and cultural systems affect and are affected by human behavior. Many social work perspectives derive from social science theories.

Theories about human behavior, interpersonal communication, and social systems as well as theories about social, organizational, community, group, and individual processes of change inform social work practice. Theoretical perspectives influence how social workers view clients and communicate with them. These perspectives also influence how social workers make assessments, design interventions, develop solutions, access resources, and evaluate outcomes. Social workers draw on many different approaches in their work with clients at various system levels.

Legislation and Social Policies. A significant number of health and human service programs derive from federal, state, and local legislative mandates. Social workers therefore need to be familiar with the provisions of the Social Security Act of 1935 and its subsequent amendments as well as with social welfare legislation concerning housing, transportation, mental health, disabilities, child welfare, and health care. Additionally, to effect policy changes that promote social and economic justice, practitioners must have a working knowledge of policymaking processes at the local, regional, state, and national levels.

Cultural Influences. To prepare for ethnically sensitive practice, social workers must understand the impact of culture on human behavior. They must recognize that the dynamics of ethnic, social, and cultural diversity account for the unique ways in which people deal with the myriad of challenges in their daily lives.

Social workers need to recognize the total impact of an ethnic reality on day-to-day life (Devore & Schlesinger, 1999). Understanding the roles and status of women, ethnic groups, racial minorities, people with disabilities, gay men and lesbians, and others who suffer discrimination and oppression is critical to effective social work practice. This understanding should include an ability to identify differences between various groups as well as individual differences within groups. Ethnically sensitive social workers experience a process of recognizing and understanding how their own ethnicity affects their perception of themselves and others (Devore & Schlesinger, 1999; Pinderhughes, 1995b; 1997). Social workers ensure that service resources are allocated to meet the unique needs of special population groups. They also address the inherent inequities in the delivery of social services and in social welfare policy development for those groups, including minorities, women, older adults, and homosexuals.

Research. Research findings inform social workers' understanding of human needs, social functioning, and adaptation processes. In addition, knowledge about research methods is a requisite for evaluating the effectiveness of practice methods and programs. Social workers also need to understand basic research design and statistical analysis so that they can read reports intelligently, draw appropriate conclusions, and integrate findings into their practice.

Knowledge of Self. To function effectively as professionals, social workers need to know themselves. Thus, social workers explore their own life-styles, ethical perspectives, moral codes, values, and cultural backgrounds. They strive to increase their awareness of their own learning styles; attitudes toward change; and responses to various situations, biases, and stereotypes. Acquiring self-knowledge is a lifelong process: "It is a lifelong journey toward self-knowledge and self-acceptance. It is also a necessary journey if the helping person is to be able to use a major tool—the self—skillfully, fully, and with maximal results" (Johnson, 1998, p. 110).

The Skill Base of Social Work

In addition to professional values and knowledge, social work practice requires skills that range from applying theories to practice to utilizing technology and managing time effectively.

Applying Theory to Practice. Throughout their work with clients—from building relationships to framing solutions to ending professional relationships—social workers must be able to apply a theoretical understanding of human behavior, human diversity, and social functioning to their day-to-day practice of social work. Skillful social workers consciously apply theory to practice and evaluate their practice using the social work profession's ethical standards.

Planned Change. In the initial stages of intervention processes, social workers must demonstrate skill in identifying challenges and incorporating clients' perceptions of their problems into their plans, assessing clients' abilities, setting realistic goals, framing solutions, and collecting relevant information. In formulating and implementing intervention plans, social workers must be able to generate a range of plans, engage client systems in collaborative partnerships, and develop goals and objectives, as well as locate and assess community resources, expedite referrals, and establish other linkages between clients and needed resources. Finally, to conclude their work with clients, social workers need skills that facilitate effective endings and expedite evaluating intervention methods and outcomes.

Intervention at All System Levels. Generalist social workers develop practice skills for working with clients at various system levels—individuals, families, formal groups, complex organizations, and communities. Specific skills in working with individuals, group work, interdisciplinary teamwork, organizational development, community practice, and social reform enhance social workers' ability to work with a variety of clients.

Relationship Skills. Professional relationships between clients and social workers are the heart of social work practice. Social workers' ability to develop working relationships hinges on their interpersonal effectiveness and self-awareness. Social workers must be skillful in communicating empathy, genuineness, trustworthiness, respect, and support.

Communication Skills. Good oral and written communication skills are absolutely essential. Interviewing skills are vital, since the basic processes of social work are exchanges of information. Social workers must be able to listen with understanding and respond with purpose. Competency in making oral presentations bolsters practitioners' ability to work with groups, organizations, and communities. Being able to write clearly and concisely enhances social workers' effectiveness in keeping records, writing reports, and applying for grants.

Cultural Competence. Social workers employ cross-cultural skills to make their interactions with clients more culturally relevant. Social workers must possess ethnographic interviewing skills, or skills that elicit minorities' views of problems and situational contexts from their cultural perspective. Social workers should demonstrate sensitivity and awareness of cultural implications and influences in all aspects of their work with clients (Green, 1999).

Policy Analysis. Social workers need skills to be able to analyze social policies and contribute to policymaking in their personal practice and at the agency, local, state, regional, and national levels. Social workers need to be able to provide public testimony, advocate legislative positions that improve clients' situations, and participate in policymaking processes. Social workers must be skillful advocates to influence the development of social policies that address issues faced by oppressed population groups in society—for example, the poor, elderly, gays and lesbians, and people with disabilities.

Research Skills. Social workers need to be proficient as research consumers and research practitioners. Social workers use their research skills to conduct literature reviews, formulate research designs, direct research projects, analyze policies, and evaluate their practice. Research skills include the ability to collect and analyze data, present findings, apply statistical analysis, and use computers. Ethical standards, including informed consent and the right to privacy, should guide research activities.

Computer Literacy. Contemporary social workers need to be computer literate. Computers have become an essential technological support in the delivery of social services. Essential skills include the ability to do word processing and data entry, and to follow menu-driven instructions. Computer technology enhances data analysis in research, program planning, and even direct work with clients.

Time Management. The rigorous demands of social work practice require orderliness and organization. Time-management skills include being able to use time effectively, schedule events realistically, keep appointments, meet deadlines, and follow through on assigned tasks.

Tenets for the Social Work Profession

How do the purpose, values, knowledge, and skills of the profession translate into the practice of social work? We differentiate 12 professional tenets that reflect the essence of the social work purpose and the core of the common base of practice. These tenets guide generalist practitioners in carrying out the purpose of social work through their respective modes of intervention. They are as follows:

1. *Empower people, individually and collectively, to utilize their own problem-solving and coping capabilities more effectively.* Social work involves a partnership between client systems and social workers. *Partnership* suggests that all consumer systems have strengths on which to build solutions. *Empowerment* is the process of releasing the potential and strengths of social systems and discovering and creating resources and opportunities for promoting effective social functioning in clients' resolutions of problems, issues, and needs.

2. *Support a proactive position in regard to social and economic policy development, to prevent problems for individuals and society from occurring.* Social workers need to anticipate challenges and to create and implement policies that prevent difficulties from emerging. Proactive involvement is directed toward developing equitable social and economic policy, thereby promoting social justice.

3. *Uphold the integrity of the profession in all aspects of social work practice.* The values and ethics of the profession are foundational for professional practice. In fact, the ethical code provides a general guide for professional activity in relation to client systems, social work employers, colleagues, the social work profession, and society as a whole. Becoming a member of the profession means making a commitment to uphold the integrity of the profession and fulfilling professional mandates for enhancing quality of life, justice, and equality.

4. *Establish linkages between people and societal resources to further social functioning and enhance the quality of life.* Social workers ensure linkages between consumer systems and the resources and opportunities of community and societal institutions. Knowledgeable about services available within the social welfare structure, the social worker serves as a "resource directory," providing information and referral, and acts as a "resource advocate," confronting barriers to utilizing and accessing appropriate resources.

5. *Develop cooperative networks within the institutional resource system.* Human resources, including social service programs, that are designed to promote the well-being of all societal members are provided within social (i.e., economic, political, health, social welfare, educational) institutions. Having a cohesive, nondiscriminatory, and comprehensive system for the delivery of social services that benefits diverse members of society requires careful planning and a commitment to cooperation among service providers.

6. *Facilitate the responsiveness of the institutional resource systems to meet health and human service needs.* Supported by the mandate in the U.S. Constitution "to provide for the general welfare," social service provisions are available citizens' rights. Social workers are charged to address quality-of-life issues through educational activities and to redress institutional discrimination and other injustices through social reform activities.

7. *Promote social justice and equality of all people in regard to full participation in society.* Ideally, social justice is the social condition that enables all members of a society to share equally in the rights and opportunities afforded by that society and in the responsibilities and obligations incurred by their membership in that society. Full participation in society means that individuals have access to the social benefits of society in order to realize their own life aspirations, and, in turn, that they contribute to societal well-being.

8. *Contribute to the development of knowledge for the social work profession through research and evaluation.* Practice knowledge evolves and practice methodologies are refined through social workers' empirical research efforts and their evaluation of practice effectiveness. Social workers use research findings to enhance social functioning and to effect social change. The profession draws upon its own members to contribute to the professional knowledge base, the skill dimensions of practice, and the foundation of values.

9. *Encourage an information exchange in those institutional systems in which both problems and resource opportunities are produced.* All social institutions have the potential to both create and resolve problems. Although a social structure may be blamed for causing problems, it is within that same structure that social workers and clients find solutions. Social workers use an empowering process to encourage social institutions to recognize their part in creating stressors and to participate in developing solutions.

10. *Enhance communication through an appreciation of diversity and through ethnically sensitive, nonsexist social work practice.* An understanding of the person:environment transaction is founded on an understanding of the impact of diversity. Practitioners working for social justice are sensitive to the implications of diversity. Sensitivity to ethnicity, emanating from the purpose and values of the profession, should be reflected in all aspects of social work, from the application of a method of intervention to the construction of the social service delivery network.

11. *Employ educational strategies for the prevention and resolution of problems.* As a social work function, education is a vital process that, in the long term, contributes to the prevention of social problems. Education provides opportunities for learning that may serve as catalysts for change and as bases for generalization for future problem-solving efforts. Education is a process whereby the learner and the educator collaborate to acquire information, develop new skills, and heighten awareness of some characteristic or situation, all of which contribute to adaptive social functioning.

12. *Embrace a worldview of human issues and solutions to problems.* We live and interact in a global society. Although the problems experienced in industrialized and agrarian societies may differ in character and scope, they reflect similarities. There are common human needs that transcend the political and geographical boundaries of continents and countries. In addition, world problems require world solutions. We must recognize the ripple effect of a single society's problems, issues, and needs and its impact on the rest of the world in the social systems context. This view supports achieving social justice in a global context and protecting human rights in all societies.

These tenets are formulated from the expanding definition and evolving position of social work in society today. Some social workers may take offense at their language, claiming that it is too idealistic, too lofty, or too radical. However, phrases such as "empowering people," "assuming a proactive stance," "embracing a worldview," "engaging in collaborative partnerships," and "promoting social justice" are not new. They are embodied in the historic purpose of social work and evidenced in our professional heritage.

Looking Forward

Tracing the historical roots of practice provides an understanding of our professional heritage and gives us a glimpse of the legacy left by early pioneers. Social work has always been driven by the purpose of improving the quality of life for all people through promoting and restoring a mutually beneficial interaction between individuals and society.

The relationship between individuals and the institutions of society continues to be a central concern for social work. Social workers deal in those situations in which the transactions between people and their social environment disrupt social functioning, impair ability, limit opportunity, create stress, or hinder the realization of individual and societal goals.

Contemporary social workers recognize that problems in living have a number of dimensions and that many alternative solutions are possible. These solutions include individual change, interpersonal adaptation, and social reform. Recognizing that the sources of problems and their solutions are located at all levels of the social system, practitioners reasonably consider the interactions between social structures in their interventions. Chapter 3 explores the social systems construct and the ecological perspective, which have recently gained prominence in social work, and examines the consumer systems with which social work deals.

CHAPTER

3 Social Work and Social Systems

Alanda Morrison's story sounds all too familiar to Helen Washington, the part-time school social worker at Township Heights Elementary School. The Morrison family moved to Woodland Township a year ago, when Alanda's father was hired at the meat-processing plant. Things had been going fairly well for the family until three months ago. Mr. Morrison left the family then, leaving Alanda's mother with no money and four children. When her mother couldn't pay the rent, they lost their rental home. For the past several weeks, the Morrison children and their mother have been staying "here and there" with friends because low-cost housing and shelter facilities for families are not available in this nonmetropolitan community.

Helen Washington reflects on the initial referral by Alanda's teacher. Her teacher reported that Alanda wasn't completing her schoolwork, seemed listless and sometimes tearful, and was withdrawing from group activities. How different Alanda's school problems seem in the context of the family issues that she described.

As Ms. Washington leaves to visit Alanda's mother, she resolves to call Bob Peters at the Family Welfare Planning Council to encourage his efforts on behalf of persons who are homeless. The council is attempting to respond to the housing needs in the community. Professionals with the council are pressing for municipal funding of low-cost rental units. The council has plans to apply for a demonstration grant to develop support services for homeless families in rural communities.

Helen Washington and Bob Peters have similar concerns about homelessness. Helen spends the bulk of her time in direct service, working with schoolchildren and families in need. Direct services are social work activities provided to client systems and include counseling, providing resources, education, information and referral, and advocacy. For Alanda's family, Helen will provide crisis counseling and link them with resources they need immediately. As a generalist, Helen voices her concern about the dearth of available housing options and recognizes that the problem of homelessness is a public issue.

Bob Peters engages primarily in social work activities that affect individuals and families indirectly. His professional activities concentrate at the community problem-solving level and include policy formulation, social planning, grant writing, and research. Bob Peters knows that economic conditions, family policy, and the provision of services or lack thereof affect the private troubles of Alanda Morrison and her family. While Helen's and Bob's social work activities focus primarily on different aspects of social work—the micro and macro arenas, respectively—many social workers have overlapping responsibilities for both direct and indirect services.

The locus or context of practice for both Helen Washington and Bob Peters includes the township community, the Morrison family, and Alanda herself. Their primary focuses, however, differ. Helen's client is Alanda and her family; Bob's focus is on Woodland Township.

This example dramatizes the social systems perspective that generalist social workers commonly use to visualize the contextual nature of social problems, the transactions between social systems, and the breadth of potential social work interventions. To further explore these issues, this chapter

- Summarizes the ecosystems perspective
- Explores social functioning
- Examines human systems as social work clients
- Highlights the social work practice methods including casework, group work, community organization, and generalist social work

The Ecosystems Perspective

Many social workers draw upon the ecosystems perspective to understand the interrelationships between people and their physical and social environments (Germain, 1979; Siporin, 1980; Germain, 1983; Germain & Gitterman, 1995). As its name suggests, the ecosystems perspective incorporates ideas from general systems theory and ecology.

General systems theory provides a universal framework to help us understand the complexities and the diversity of human behavior and the social environment (Shafer, 1969). It offers principles that describe how human systems operate and interact with one another. In contrast, ecology "focuses specifically on how things fit together, how they adapt to one another" (Greif, 1986, p. 225). In ecological terms, adaptation is "a dynamic process between people and their environments as people grow, achieve competence, and make contributions to others" (p. 225). Together, general systems theory and ecology describe how human systems interact in their social and physical environments.

The Social Systems View

Social work practitioners work with human systems such as individuals, families, work groups, play groups, organizations, neighborhoods, and communities. They focus on the relationships that exist among members of human systems and between these systems and their impinging environments. The social systems perspective provides a way to visualize the interrelationships among people and various social structures as webs of interrelated networks.

Social System Defined. A social system is "an organized whole made up of components that interact in a way distinct from their interaction with other entities and which endures over some period of time" (Anderson, Carter, & Lowe, 1999, p. 294). In simple terms, social systems are structures of interdependent people (Greene, 1999). Systems theory is

> based on the assumption that matter, in all of its forms, living and non-living, can be regarded as systems and that systems, as systems, have certain discrete properties that are capable of being studied. Individuals, small groups—including families and organizations—and other complex human organizations such as neighborhoods and communities—in short, the entities with which social work is usually involved—can all be regarded as systems, with certain common properties. (Hearn, 1969, p. 2)

Systems come in all shapes and sizes. Families, teams, work groups, community organizations, service clubs, street gangs, neighborhoods, communities, and corporations are all systems. Characteristics that distinguish one system from another include their patterns of relationships, their purposes, and attributes their members have in common.

Subsystems and Environments. All systems are parts of larger systems and, at the same time, are made up of smaller systems (Anderson, Carter, & Lowe, 1999). This means that systems are subsystems of other systems while simultaneously having component parts or subsystems. Human systems are nested within each other: The larger the system, the more component parts it has. Each system, itself composed of smaller units, is a part of a larger network of systems.

Whether we identify a system as a subsystem or an environment depends on our frame of reference. So, in the opening example, the Morrison family is both an environment and a subsystem. When we focus on Alanda, her family is one aspect of her social environment. When we focus on the Morrison family, we recognize that it exists as a subsystem in the environmental context of the community, and that Alanda herself is a subsystem within the Morrison family.

Highly organized systems, such as most family systems, have extremely interdependent component parts. Less-structured systems, such as a neighborhood system, have characteristically independent and autonomous components or subparts (Anderson, Carter, & Lowe, 1999). In any system, the whole working together achieves or means more than the subparts functioning independently. In other words, the whole is greater than the sum of the parts.

Structurally, systems are separated from one another by boundaries or points that differentiate one system from another. Boundaries may be open or closed—that is, receptive or nonreceptive—to exchanges of resources. When systems exchange energy, the process actually multiplies the energy available to each system. Without an influx of energy, systems may deplete their own energy reserves and ultimately lose their ability to function.

Transactions. Human systems are always interacting with other systems and exchanging resources. Through give and take, systems borrow and share, consume and dispose, and accept and reject their own resources and the resources of other systems. For example, exchanges between a child and its family, an employee and the workplace, a neighborhood block and the city, or a social service consumer and an agency provide the energy for both maintenance and change.

These exchanges of resources are called *transactions,* or the processes through which systems exchange information and energy (Figure 3.1). Energy is sent and received within

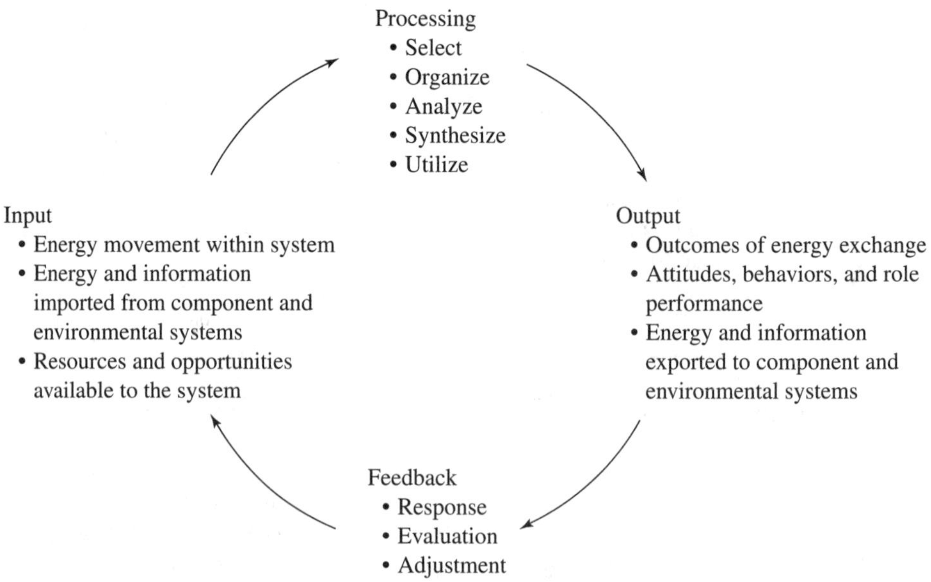

FIGURE 3.1 Information and Energy Exchange

one human system or between one human system and another. This give and take involves input, processing, output, and feedback.

Inputs are the resources available within systems and their environments. Examples include material resources, systems interpersonal associations, communication, traumatic experiences, defense mechanisms, and felt social pressures. Inputs ultimately sustain or change systems. *Processing* refers to the system's reponse to the energy or information it receives. It involves selecting, analyzing, synthesizing, and utilizing resources within systems and their environments. This processing produces responses or outputs. Resulting *outputs* include both products and ways in which systems act on their environments. Note that a system's actual output may differ from the output it desires or others expect. *Feedback* transmits further information. As a transactional process, feedback helps systems evaluate their situations and make modifications or take corrective actions. Feedback dramatizes the reciprocal effect of one system on another. It also completes the loop of information and energy exchange.

As reciprocal interactions, transactions are "the processes by which people continually shape their environments and are shaped by them, over time" (Germain, 1983, p. 115). In other words, people are active participants in influencing the world around them. People are also products of their environment. The phrase *person:environment* symbolizes this mutual, interactive relationship (Germain & Gitterman, 1987).

Implications for Social Work. The general systems approach is a useful framework for social workers, given that their professional focus is on relationships that exist between persons and their social environment. From the social systems perspective, social work activities focus

> at the interface between or the meeting place of person and environment—at the point where there is or is not matching with all its good and bad consequences for person and environment. The phenomenon of concern at this interface is the *transaction* between person and environment. Transaction is *exchange in the context of action or activity.* This action or activity is a blend of person-activity and impinging environment-activity. (Gordon, 1969, p. 7)

Although client systems usually fall within the boundaries of a discrete system level—for example, family, neighborhood, organization, or community—social workers practicing from a generalist orientation examine clients' situations in the context of the entire social milieu. In this way, social workers and clients consider the potential problems and effects of intervention on the client system, its subunits, and the units of which it is a part.

Although a change initially occurs at one system level, it affects the entire network of interrelated systems. For instance, in the example at the beginning of this chapter, Helen Washington's work with Alanda and her family can ultimately affect the larger social structure of the school. Bob Peters's work in advocacy and community planning will also have a ripple effect on individuals and families in his constituency.

Understanding the relationships between people and society and the interrelationships between various social systems is critical for understanding the social work interface with clients. The psychosocial dimension of the systems approach emphasizes examining the "person in situation," recognizing the impact of environmental influences on human

BOX 3.1
Reflections on Diversity

My Culture, Myself

All members of a society experience the cultural ethos of their society. The culture of a society reflects the dominant values, beliefs, traditions, language, and institutions of society. In addition, members of defined groups identify with the culture of their particular race, ethnic origin, profession, gender, age cohort, organization, religious affiliation, socioeconomic class, geographic location, and sexual orientation. Consider, for example, the culture that accompanies being a midwesterner, a Hispanic, a member of a labor union, a farmer, a Mason, a homosexual, an adolescent, an athlete, a socialist, or a social worker. People are simultaneously products of and reflections of their culture.

Culture engulfs us and exerts a powerful influence on all aspects of our existence. Our cultural memberships give us personal identity, but they also affect the way others treat us. The cultural category to which one belongs determines the status and privileges society grants. A person whose cultural identity includes being male, White, and heterosexual has more opportunities than an individual whose cultural group membership includes being female, African American, and lesbian. Cultural group membership also forms the basis for stereotyping and discrimination.

When social workers examine a human system, they explore what's inside that system, what's outside that system, and how the two relate (Miley, O'Melia, & DuBois, 2004). In their analysis of ecosystems, social workers identify cultural variables and consider how culture influences the actions, reactions, and interactions of the system under study. Empowerment-oriented social workers recognize cultural identity as a source of strength and cultural heritage as a resource.

---

behavior. Furthermore, this generalist perspective recognizes the multicausal nature of problems and fosters the development of multiple solutions. A systems perspective embraces the notion of partnership in the transactions between practitioners and client systems. Social workers enter client systems' environments as resources, all the while recognizing clients' inherent strengths and potential.

The Ecological Perspective

These ideas from the systems perspective complement the ecological perspective for generalist social work practice. The term *ecology* originated in the biological sciences. It refers to the interrelationships between living organisms and their physical and biological environments. Translating the principles of ecology to the relationships between people and their social environments, social scientists emphasize the environmental context of human functioning and the transactional relationships that occur (Holahan, Wilcox, Spearly, & Campbell, 1979).

Life Model. The ecological perspective provides a basis for Germain and Gitterman's life model of social work (1980; 1996). This model suggests that the nature of the transactions between people and their environments is the source of human needs and social problems. Humans affect and are affected by their physical and social environments through a process of continuous, reciprocal adaptations. The purpose of social work is to enhance those transactions that maximize growth and development by matching people's adaptive capacities with environmental properties.

In this view, stress results from discrepancies between individuals' needs and capacities on the one hand and environmental qualities on the other. In other words, the "fit" between individuals and their environments is inadequate. According to Germain and Gitterman (1980; 1996), stress arises from three interrelated phenomena: life transitions, environmental pressures, and interpersonal processes. Social workers and clients assess the objective and subjective facts, and, through a helping process, clients work on developing skills to function more effectively.

The Ecosystems View

A combination of general systems theory and the ecological perspective forms the basis for a number of practice models that emerged in the 1970s and that gained professional acceptance in the 1980s (Bartlett, 1970; Goldstein, 1973; Meyer, 1983; Pincus & Minahan, 1973; Siporin, 1975). The ecosystems perspective offers

> a lens for viewing case phenomenon; it is an orientation to practice, but does not provide practice principles to focus intervention.
>
> Through the use of ecological concepts, it [the ecosystems perspective] identifies adaptive possibilities between persons and their environment. Using general systems theory, it highlights the way the actors and their situational variables are connected. It attempts to examine the environmental context in which people live, thereby addressing the essential focus of social work practice, that of the person in the environment. In the interests of organizing complexity and placing appropriate boundaries around practice situation, it favors a systemic or circular construct as contrasted with a linear view. The perspective simply is a way of noticing; of using professional vision to encompass the client's complex reality. (Meyer, 1987, p. 414)

In empowerment-based social work practice, workers and clients don't simply help people adapt to their environment. They also consider actions that will create favorable changes in clients' social and physical environments in order to enhance clients' abilities to function more effectively. In the opening example, Bob Peters's work with the Family Welfare Planning Council exemplifies this concept of environmental change. Improving the availability of public housing in the community helps families like the Morrisons secure adequate and affordable housing and reduces the risks of homelessness.

Social Functioning

Although people all have basic needs in common, they also develop their own unique needs. Likewise, there is considerable variation in their abilities and their access to opportunities to meet these needs. Why is there this variation? Psychologists argue that the variation is due to individual differences. Sociologists examine social structure and its effect on individuals.

Social work theory suggests that the answer lies in the interface and transactions between individuals and their environment.

In the social work view, social functioning relates to

> living up to the expectations that are made of an individual by that person's own self, by the immediate social environment, and by society at large. These expectations, or functions, include meeting one's own basic needs and the needs of one's dependents and making positive contributions to society. Human needs include physical aspects (food, shelter, safety, health care, and protection), personal fulfillment (education, recreation, values, aesthetics, religion, and accomplishment), emotional needs (a sense of belonging, mutual caring, and companionship), and an adequate self-concept (self-confidence, self-esteem, and identity). (Barker, 2003, p. 403)

For individuals, social functioning encompasses striving toward a life-style that meets basic needs, establishing positive relationships, and accentuating personal growth and adjustment. Many individuals seek supportive assistance from the social service delivery system to enhance their social functioning.

Other human systems, such as groups, organizations, and communities, enhance their capacity for social functioning by developing resources, promoting harmony among members, and creating dynamic opportunities for growth and change. For all human systems, the source of improvement of social functioning may be within the system itself, or it may lie in creating changes in other social structures.

Alanda Morrison's mother possesses personal talents that can be activated to improve her employment status and her interpersonal resources, such as supportive friends. The Woodland Township officials' commitment to community development is evident in their support of a program that will provide housing vouchers for homeless families.

Types of Social Functioning

Different types of social functioning—effective, at-risk, and difficult—result from the interaction between people and their social and physical environments. The different types call for different social service responses.

Effective Social Functioning. Understandably, competent systems activate personal, interpersonal, and institutional resources to deal with problems, issues, and needs. Also, these resources are relatively available and accessible to these systems in the social structure. Adaptive systems recognize their problems and take the necessary steps to resolve them—for example, individuals who are able to adjust successfully to stresses resulting from life transitions such as marriage and divorce, parenting, the death of a loved one, or retirement. When concerns arise, these people are able to cope with the stresses associated with the problem, adapt to change, and make adjustments in their immediate environment. They may or may not access social work services, depending upon whether they identify a need and whether resources are available.

At-Risk Social Functioning. Some populations or social systems are at risk of difficulties in social functioning. This means that they are vulnerable to specific problems, although such problems have yet to surface. In other words, identifiable conditions exist that could have a negative impact on social functioning. For example, research indicates that certain conditions, such as unemployment, alcohol and drug abuse, and illness, place children at risk for abuse and neglect. People with disabilities are at risk of underemployment. The elderly are vulnerable to early and unnecessary institutionalization. Some inner-city neighborhoods may be at risk of declining educational and economic opportunities.

Through case finding, the social service delivery network attempts to identify those groups that are at risk of difficulties and proffer services to them before the onset of actual problems. Professionals develop outreach services as measures of prevention. Prevention activities are usually informational, supportive, and educational. Also, social work efforts may be directed at those systems that create at-risk conditions. However, identifying a population group as at-risk raises an ethical dilemma. This labeling process, in and of itself, may create problems that stigmatize adaptive individuals within those groups identified as at-risk.

Difficulties in Social Functioning. Finally, in some human systems, problems become so exacerbated that the ability to cope is diminished or the system is immobilized and unable to initiate a change process. In some situations, systems may themselves recognize serious problems that inhibit their ability to function. Individuals may experience depression and loneliness, families may identify communication problems or intrafamilial conflict, or an industry may recognize high levels of worker stress that threaten productivity.

In other situations, society may label the behavior of the system as aberrant or dysfunctional. Such is the case with criminal offenders, perpetrators of child abuse, and institutions that violate civil rights. Society imposes sanctions on all types of systems for the violation of laws and other social norms.

Environmental Press

The concept of environmental press (Lawton, 1980; Lawton & Nahemow, 1973) expands our understanding of social functioning and illustrates the implication of the transactional relationships between persons and their environment for generalist social work. Environmental forces exert pressure on individuals that affects them either negatively or positively. Environmental stressors—such as poverty, poor health care, inadequate education, unemployment, discrimination, erosion of civil rights, lack of quality education, architectural barriers, and overcrowded housing, among other things—press on individuals and create barriers, problems, or difficulties in functioning. When systems' competence levels are lowered for any reason, the systems' thresholds for experiencing adversity from environmental press are also lowered. For example, consider the impact of the environment on an adult who has a significant visual loss. A disorganized environment can be disabling—the source of considerable environmental press that results in internal stress.

On the other hand, enrichments—such as having access to health care, securing civil rights and civil liberties, creating job opportunities, providing adequate housing, and modifying buildings so that they become accessible—are resources on which individuals can draw to improve their social functioning and enhance their well-being. For example, consider the positive impact of a patterned, orderly, and predictable physical environment that offers auditory signals, hand rails, and signs in braille for people with visual losses. An enriched environment is "abling" rather than disabling.

The press of environmental conditions affects the competence of individuals and their levels of social functioning; however, people react differently to environmental press and stress in their lives. Press may hinder, enhance, or have no noticeable effect. When press has a negative effect, people often experience internal distress or stress. One factor that influences their different reactions is their current level of stress, as stress tends to be cumulative. Thus, reactions will depend on the combinations of stressors that individuals experience. In addition, certain factors may have a double jeopardy effect. For example, to be female elicits particular societal pressures; to be a Black female adds a potentially compounding dimension.

Furthermore, what is described as problematic by one person or community may be overlooked by another, and what is minimized by one may be overwhelming to another. If clients describe a situation as problematic, they are inclined to resolve it; on the other hand, if clients don't perceive a condition as a problem, they tend to live with it. The starting point for understanding the effects of environmental stressors is necessarily the client's perspective.

Press creates stress. In response to this stress, people may adapt individually or they may respond collectively, exerting pressure for change back on their environment. In response to pressure from its members, society modifies, refines, and creates resources and opportunities. For example, in social work and social welfare, this means that society provides medical benefits for the health care needs of its citizens, offers family and children's services in response to family problems and child abuse, expands educational opportunities for a changing technology, and develops public awareness activities to reduce stigma and structural discrimination.

Social Problems and Social Functioning

Social problems affect social functioning in a number of aspects of individuals' lives, including physical and mental health, employment and education, financial security, housing, recreation, and family and community integrity:

> A social welfare problem is an *alteration in the status of functioning (movement toward dysfunction) of individuals, groups, or institutions, in one or more domains of living, brought about or made worse by any one of several obstacles to optimum functioning.* Furthermore, these problems rarely occur in isolation or in just one domain. For example, deficiencies in education generally result in occupational vulnerability. This vulnerability, when it reaches crisis (unemployment), will lead to crisis in financial resources and housing. Eventually, the integrity of family life is threatened and this has implications for the physical and mental well-being of the family and ultimately the community. (Teare & McPheeters, 1970, pp. 16–17)

Social workers direct their interventions concurrently toward restoring client systems' social functioning and toward realigning opportunities by reforming social conditions. Generalist social workers consider social functioning in the context of the larger social structure, as both problems and solutions may be located there. Too often, victims of social problems are blamed and held accountable for both the problems and their solutions. However, what people label as maladaptive in one human system may actually be a response to a social problem in the larger social structure:

> Victims of social problems are those targeted as the "deviants" in U.S. society. They are the drinkers in the social problem of alcoholism. They are the abusers in the social problem of child abuse. They are depressed or angry women and minorities in the social problems of sexism and racism. They are the most accessible and easily labeled participants in social problems, and society is more willing for social workers to work with these victims than with other components of social probelms. (Parsons, Hernández, & Jorgensen, 1988, p. 417)

Helen Washington and Bob Peters both work to restore the Morrison family's ability to function effectively. Yet their approaches differ. Helen works directly with the Morrison family, and Bob works on behalf of all families in Woodland Township. Helen assists Mrs. Morrison in accessing financial aid and counsels Alanda at school. Bob Peters advocates for community economic development to ensure job opportunities and the availability of housing.

Environmental Context of Generalist Social Work

Because of the long tradition of focusing social work practice on individual clients, social workers may direct their efforts toward individual change, adapting people to environments rather than modifying environments to better meet the needs of people. Social workers are

BOX 3.2

Reflections on Empowerment

Save Your Labels for Jars, Not People

How practitioners refer to clients—that is, the labels they assign to clients—may empower or disempower clients. Labels influence our perceptions of ourselves and others. Labels shape behavior, influence response to others, and, indeed, define professional roles for interaction and strategies for intervention.

At one time in social welfare history, clients were referred to as "supplicants" who received charitable help and moral advice from friendly visitors. As the psychoanalytic approach and medical model came into vogue, clients were typically called "patients," who were treated in therapy. More recently, the term "receiving help" has described the social worker-client relationship. This nomenclature tends to characterize the client as impotent, or someone in need of fixing. The labels imply that the professional has all the knowledge, power, and authority necessary to supply, heal, or treat, and that the receiver of services is a have-not who passively acquires supplies, healing, or treatment.

In today's thinking, social work clients are considered consumers of social services. Consumers select services and contract for or purchase products through fees, vouchers, or citizens' rights. Social service consumers seek information, make choices, and contract for what they need from public and private organizations or corporations. "Consumer" conveys the idea of a person or other social system seeking services perceived as needed to improve the quality of life. Usually we think of a consumer as one who voluntarily chooses to consume; however, even those who are mandated to seek services, who are in protective situations, or for whom services in the social service delivery system are initiated involuntarily or without their consent are also considered consumers (Tracy & DuBois, 1987). The concept of the client as a consumer promotes a sense of partnership with the social worker for the purposes of solving problems, accessing resources, and learning.

less knowledgeable about environmental dynamics and, hence, environmental change (Kemp, 2001; Kemp, Whittaker, & Tracy, 2002). This predisposes social workers to view the social environment as the context of individuals' lives, rather than as a target of change in and of itself.

Social workers consider any system as containing options for change and recognize that change in one system results in changes in other systems. In some situations, generalist social workers might focus on individually oriented solutions that promote individuals' competence in dealing with environmental constraints or press. In other situations, generalists plan environmentally oriented interventions that require environmental modifications or reforms (Holahan, Wilcox, Spearly, & Campbell, 1979).

Generalist social work intervention encompasses a full range of levels of intervention that parallel the ecological model for understanding the person:environment construct. In other words, generalist social work, thoroughly founded in the knowledge and value base of the profession, utilizes the full interventive repertoire of social work. Generalist social work focuses on intervention at all system levels. The definition of the problem, issue, or need, *not the method alone,* determines the strategies that social workers and clients select.

Client Systems in Social Work

Generalist social workers define client systems' difficulties in the context of person: environment transactions. Likewise, plans of action potentially create changes at a variety of system levels. Social work clients may be at any level in the social systems continuum—at the microlevel, individuals, families, and groups; at the midlevel, formal groups and organizations; at the macrolevel, community, society, or even the world community; and even the professional system of social work (Figure 3.2).

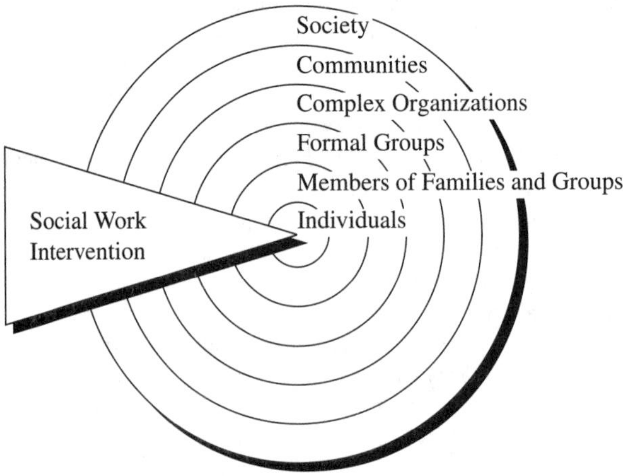

FIGURE 3.2 Systems-Level Intervention

Microlevel Intervention

Microlevel intervention involves working with individuals—separately, in families, or in small groups—to facilitate changes in individual behavior or in relationships. Individuals often seek social work services because they experience difficulties with personal adjustment, interpersonal relationships, or environmental stresses (Table 3.1).

Changes at this level focus on creating changes in individuals' functioning. However, considering the dynamics of change in the context of systems theory, social workers and microlevel clients have numerous options. They also may make plans to initiate modifications in clients' social and physical environments to achieve changes at the microlevel.

To work with microlevel clients, social workers need to know about individual, interpersonal, family, and group dynamics as well as human development, social psychology, and the individual effects of environmental influences. Work at this level requires facility with clinical techniques such as crisis intervention and counseling.

Social Work Highlights. Lucinda, having experienced spouse abuse, may be involved in individual counseling, family counseling with both spouses and children, or group counseling with other victims of domestic violence. Through such counseling, Lucinda may come to understand the cyclical nature of domestic violence in her own life and to view violence as a pervasive social problem. With such an understanding, Lucinda can be empowered to confront her situation, enhance her self-esteem, and take control of her life.

Midlevel Intervention

The midlevel of social work intervention represents interactions with formal groups and complex organizations. Examples of complex organizations include social service agencies, health care organizations, educational systems, and correctional facilities. Practice with formal groups includes work with teams, work groups, interdisciplinary task forces, task-oriented groups, community service clubs, and self-help groups.

TABLE 3.1 Determinants of Social Functioning for Individuals, Families, and Small Groups

Personal		Families and Small Groups	
Genetics	Prenatal health	Size	Composition
Nutrition	Developmental disability	Unity	Communication
Mental health	Disabling condition	Rules	Roles
Health	Personality	Values	Relationship patterns
Coping capacity	Life experience	Natural support systems	Socioeconomic level
Income/assets	Self-concept	Functional capacity	Kinship networks
Life-style	Age	Multigenerational patterns	
Ethnicity	Cultural heritage		
Motivation	Developmental stage		
Cognitive level			

With midlevel intervention, the focus of change is on the groups or organizations themselves. Factors such as group or organizational functions, structures, roles, patterns of decision making, and styles of interaction influence the process of change. In midlevel intervention, the client system is literally the group or organization. Working at the midlevel necessitates understanding the dynamics of formal groups and organizational structures. Effective midlevel work requires skills in organizational planning, decision making, and conflict negotiation (Table 3.2).

Social Work Highlights. Dave Perkins, a social worker employed at the Rescue Mission, is asked to facilitate the goal-setting activities of a coalition formed to address the needs of the homeless. Dave works with this task group, which includes both providers of human services and consumers, to identify needs and set goals and priorities for community action.

Bureaucratic structures characterize complex organizations. They include public and private organizations whose purpose is to coordinate people and resources in order to provide products and services. How a complex organization utilizes information depends on the organization's size, structure, and style of authority. How organizational managers perceive employees' motivation and needs, as well as how they perceive the nature of work itself, are influenced by their particular organizational perspectives. Social workers provide resources such as consulting services for organizational development, education, human resource development, and evaluation to complex organizations. Since social workers typically work in organizational settings, knowing how to facilitate midlevel change is crucial for developing quality programs and services.

Social Work Highlights. A change in the reporting law for child abuse and neglect prompts the director of Kiddie Land Day Care to ask Lee Wong, a child welfare specialist from the

TABLE 3.2 Determinants of Social Functioning for Formal Groups and Complex Organizations

Groups	Organizations
Size	Bureaucracy
Focus/purpose	Personnel management
Past history together	Membership roles
Developmental stage	Governance
Characteristics of individual members	Organizational behavior
Communication patterns	Administrative functions
Decision-making style	Day-to-day operations
Manner of managing conflicts	Decision-making processes
Overt/covert goals	Conflict resolution style
Divergence in individual goals and group goals	Group cohesion
Interpersonal relationships	Socialization
Norms/values of the group	Committee structure
Leadership roles	Mission or purpose
Length of time group will meet	
Setting of group meetings	

State Division of Children's Services, to provide in-service training for the day care staff. Lee reviews the law and instructs the staff on the proper procedures for reporting suspected child abuse or neglect.

Macrolevel Intervention

Macrolevel intervention includes working with neighborhoods, communities, and societies to achieve social change. Macrosystems practice reflects social work's heritage of social reform—the pursuit of social change to improve the quality of life.

Traditionally, social workers participated in social reform to work on behalf of people who were oppressed, disenfranchised, or powerless. With the profession's renewed emphasis on poverty and the social movements of the 1960s for open housing, civil rights, and peace, social workers again became activists. This renewal of activism reflected a new approach: working in partnerships with those who are oppressed and disenfranchised.

Social planning theorists used the label *citizen participation* to describe this new approach—helping others to know, to choose, and to participate in making decisions about issues that touched their lives. Additionally, movements such as those related to product-safety concerns emphasized citizens' involvement. Consumer protection initiatives led to the formation of various consumer rights organizations that provided information, protection, and legal representation concerning the safety of products (Tracy & DuBois, 1987).

The historical thrust for social advocacy continues to energize efforts to promote social justice through community and societal change. At this level of intervention, the client system is the community or society. Examples of macrolevel clients include neighborhoods; cities; rural areas; bistate communities; and local, state, and national governments. The primary target of change is the community or society itself; however, because of the transactional nature of change, changes at the macrolevel also effect changes at all other system levels.

In their work at the macrolevel, social workers help resolve intergroup tensions and community problems by initiating social action and social change. Their work includes activities such as community organizing, economic development, legislative action, and policy formulation.

Macrolevel practice requires knowledge of community standards and values, and skills in mobilizing the community are needed for problem-solving initiatives. With regard to interventions at the societal level, social work is "society's conscience in action." Social workers strive to eliminate social problems that affect the social functioning of citizens, erode the quality of life, or weaken the structure of society. Social workers need to have a sociological and cultural understanding of primary and secondary societal institutions, and of vulnerable and oppressed populations in society. They must possess skills in taking corrective actions to ensure legal, civil, and human rights.

An international perspective is emerging in social work with the growing recognition that problems transcend societal boundaries. Shared concerns about human rights, health, world poverty, social and economic development, the environment, and population expansion require international cooperation through international federations in both industrialized and developing countries. To expand their knowledge base for a worldview approach, social workers need information about international health and service organizations, world affairs, politics, and cultural diversity, or perhaps, even more fundamentally, world geography. See Table 3.3.

TABLE 3.3 Determinants of Social Functioning for Communities, Societies, and the World Community

Community	Society	World Community
Housing	Technology	World poverty
Transportation	Social values	Hunger
Economy	Social class	Food storage
Availability of jobs	Stratification	Ecology
Educational resources	Institutions	World health
Standard of living	Alienation	Space exploration
Urban/rural natures	Economic cycles	Human rights
Cultural diversity	Social policy	Population base
Diversity of life-style	Government	Political climate
Environmental stress	The "isms"	Energy
Availability of resources	Prejudice	Power and authority base
Support networks	Pop culture	Threat of war
Relative social class	Demographic trends	International law
	Laws and legislation	

Social Work Highlights. Penny Sherman serves as a member of a community forum that plans employment programming services for people with chronic mental illness. The traditional orientation of supportive employment programs for people with disabilities involves training and teaching skills that are transferable to job placement. The staff at Transitions, an agency for people with chronic mental illness, has determined that individuals with mental illness are more likely to succeed if they are trained on the job. Currently, the forum is pressing for a policy change in the state's funding of supportive employment services for the chronically mentally ill so that programming will better reflect the unique needs of this population group.

Working with the Social Work Profession

Finally, social work practitioners work for change within the system of the social work profession. Social workers attain their professional identity through their association with the social work profession, and, in turn, they contribute to the evolving identity and actions of the profession. Ethical social workers commit themselves to participating in professional activities that will renew and refine the social work profession.

There are a number of reasons why it is important to consider the social work profession and its membership organizations as targets for change. The social work profession educates practitioners, provides the foundation for professional performance in accordance with ethical principles, sets standards for practice in various fields, supervises practitioners at all levels, monitors and evaluates individual and group behavior, and contributes to the knowledge and skill base of practice (Tracy & DuBois, 1987). Historically, social work has maintained a dual commitment: to improve the quality of social work practice and, of equal importance, to work for social justice and promote the general welfare.

BOX 3.3
Social Work Profile

Mental Health

I am a social worker and the director of a regional mental health center located in a large urban area. The center serves 4,000 consumers each year, many of whom have serious mental illnesses. In many ways, the center is in the right downtown location for serving our consumer population. Neighboring the mental health center are the county jail, the city bus terminal, and the largest homeless mission in our area. Statistics tell us that one-third of the persons who are homeless and one-third of the persons in the criminal justice system have serious mental illness. In addition to providing medication and rehabilitative services, the center has a case management program, a housing component, and job placement and support services. Had our agency not expanded its continuum of services over the past decade to include housing development and job locaters, I would say that it would be just a huge crisis center.

I favor a "recovery" model rather than a "casualty" model for the delivery of mental health services. The casualty model, derived from the medical model, views mental illness as a problem that needs to be treated. The stigmatizing effects of mental illness compound matters by leading some to conclude that the casualties of mental illness either cannot or should not be involved in making decisions about their care or their lives. In contrast, the recovery model, which incorporates the strengths and empowerment perspectives, supports full participation in community life by people who have mental illness. The recovery model validates the consumers' beliefs that mental health practitioners are *most* helpful when they do not regard their consumers as "patients" who need treatment. Our center surveyed agency consumers about what aspects of services make a difference for them. Inevitably, the consumers indicated that they believe that the personal qualities of the agency staff have influenced their outcomes. Characteristics like warmth, being genuine, communicating effectively and respectfully, and focusing on strengths are noted. When I hire new staff members, I look for people who will be able to genuinely care about the persons with whom they will work.

I believe, in general, that social workers today, in all fields of practice, have retreated from involvement in public policy issues. Now, more than ever, there is an urgent need for mental health practitioners to have a voice in public policy. The major service delivery issue with respect to mental health services is that we have a disjointed approach to providing services to persons with severe and persistent mental illness. Current policies separate state services into discrete divisions or departments—for example, mental health, public aid, education, public housing, substance abuse programs, and disabilities services. The current fragmented system of care in mental health and other related social welfare services is so complex that consumers have difficulty finding their way through the system. There is a need for a comprehensive service delivery approach so that consumers can easily access the supports that they need. For this to happen, I believe the system needs to be remade, not reformed.

I am also a vocal advocate for public policies that fund prevention and early intervention services. I am particularly concerned about the lack of services for children who have mental health issues. We see children who did not receive mental health services until they became "casualties." I also see young adults who have serious mental illnesses warehoused in nursing homes when at their stage in life they should have friends and jobs. There are no simple answers to any of the issues I've raised. But one thing is clear to me: We social workers need to be involved!

Professional acculturation is central to the education and development of the professional social worker. Professional acculturation is a process that results in social work practitioners who maintain personal and professional integrity in relationships with clients and who treat colleagues with respect. A process of peer review ensures quality. Social workers have an ethical responsibility to enhance community service. This responsibility can be fulfilled by working to eliminate discrimination, being concerned with equality in the provision of resources and opportunities, assisting the oppressed, and promoting understanding and acceptance of the diversity of a global society. The responsibility entails bringing professional knowledge and experience to bear on social and economic policies and related legislation. In addition, planned change efforts require respectful relationships with professionals from other disciplines.

The strength and viability of the social work profession are related to its ability to engage in meaningful research and to make contributions to the knowledge base of the profession and society. Knowledge building is not the province of only a few. By applying the scientific method, every social worker can contribute needed research. Every social worker can also compile and communicate practice wisdom. Guided by the logic of scholarship and research, collective efforts will improve the quality of practice and the image of social work with its active and potential consumers.

Social Work Highlights. Esther Mayfield and Carlos Ramirez responded to a call for papers to be presented at the regional NASW symposium, a professional forum for exchanging techniques and strategies for informed practice. Esther and Carlos have written a report on their findings concerning a demonstration project integrating a generational approach to working with Hispanic teenage parents.

Social Work Methods

Traditionally, social workers have conceptualized the change process as the mutual adaptation of people and their social environment. Utilizing the traditional strategies of casework, group work, and community organization, social workers undertook change efforts aimed at developing clients' personal competence, strengthening families, organizing neighborhoods and communities, humanizing bureaucratic organizations, and creating responsive social institutions. The particular method employed by the worker—casework, group work, or community organization—directed the process of change. Currently, a generalist perspective that integrates work with individuals and families, groups and organizations, and communities has gained prominence.

Casework

Casework was the predominant method of social work up to and through the 1960s. Casework emphasizes direct work with individuals. Five influential orientations—traditional psychosocial, functional, problem solving, psychobehavioral, and crisis intervention—characterize casework intervention (Pinderhughes, 1995a). Each of these models focuses on individual adaptation. They differ in that some place greater emphasis on reforming individuals, whereas others place greater emphasis on changing transactions between individuals and their environments. In the decades of the 1960s and 1970s, specific approaches to brief intervention, crisis intervention, task-centered, and eclectic models emerged.

Social work with families became an identifiable field of social work practice in the 1960s, drawing from interdisciplinary theoretical perspectives, including social science systems theory (Pinderhughes, 1995a). The family systems approach provides a framework for dealing with the dynamic interactions between persons and their environments. With the emergence of family interventions, practitioners recognized the influence of family on individual development, role expectations, and communication patterns. Initially, family treatment dealt with the pathology of individuals in the context of their families; however, early family theorists also began to focus on the pathology of families.

Group Work

Group work methods were introduced into professional social work in the 1930s, and group work theories developed in the late 1940s. Group work is a social work method that uses group process and interactions to promote growth and change. The group itself is a vehicle for change, and change occurs at several levels. In other words, social workers use the group structure and process to facilitate change. Small groups are significant resources for persons who need to develop social competencies, especially those experiencing "powerlessness, alienation, and hopelessness; being victimized; not feeling understood in their current human relations; and/or feeling inadequate in changing systems of which they are part" (Anderson, 1979, p. 291). As a social work method, group work is an empowerment-oriented strategy for working collaboratively for change with individuals and extends its applications to working with organizational and community groups.

Teams. Teams are gaining prominence in the delivery of social services. Social workers are often called on to work with interdisciplinary colleagues in a teamwork effort. Brill (1998) states that:

> a team is a group of people each of whom possesses particular expertise; each of whom is responsible for individual decisions and actions; team members share a common purpose; and meet together to pool knowledge, ideas, and meanings from which interaction plans are determined and future plans influenced. (p. 193)

In other words, characteristics of teams reflect the dynamics of other small groups. Team members, with their own specialized knowledge and patterns of work and relationships influence team processes. Research indicates that respectful interactions, clear communication, and agency support all contribute to effective team functioning (Lewandowski & Glenmaye, 2002). The purpose set by the team provides the direction and focus of its work.

Community Organization

Community practice involves a range of activities, including community organizing, organizational development, and social reform. Macrosystems practice includes models for community organization, neighborhood development, work in organizational contexts, and formulating and administering social policy. Although community practice can trace its roots to the reform efforts of the settlement house and the community coordinating efforts of the charity organization societies in the early twentieth century, it gained prominence as a method of professional social work practice in the United States in the 1960s during the War on Poverty.

Community problem-solving initiatives require the involvement of community leaders, including governmental units; corporation boards; unions; foundations and other funding bodies; ethnic and religious organizations; and professional, consumer, and civic groups. Those people who participate in community change vary from community to community, depending on the particular problem that the community action addresses.

The Integrated Generalist Model

A professional desire to unify the three social work methods—casework, group work, and community organization—precipitated the search for a common base of practice. The multimethod or combined practice approach increased in popularity after the publication of the Hollis-Taylor report in 1951. In the decades of the 1970s and 1980s, the generalist approach to practice gained recognition and acceptance. The early works of Meyer (1970), Goldstein (1973), Pincus and Minahan (1973), Middleman and Goldberg (1974), and Siporin (1975) focused on a unifying perspective, one that was not bound by methods, but rather was shaped by situational or environmental parameters.

The contemporary generalist approach integrates the traditional intervention methodologies into a unified framework. It expands the concept of clients to include all those social systems in the environmental arena. Clients—that is, human systems that consult with social workers—can be communities, neighborhoods, corporations, groups, or individuals. People make up all these social systems. Accordingly, to make systemic changes requires changing the attitudes and behaviors of the members of a system.

Some may argue that the effectiveness of the specialized methods—casework, group work, and community organization—is lost in a generic orientation. However, proponents of the generalist approach believe that the unified perspective fosters breadth in potential interventions. The generalist approach to social work practice is oriented toward finding solutions to problems and challenges. Presenting issues, rather than a particular method, direct generalists' practice activities. This is not to say that generalists are jacks-(or jills-)of-all-trades and masters of none; rather, generalists are masters of resolving problems. Social workers seek solutions in many social structures. Thus, even in generalist practice, social work intervention occurs at the individual, family, group, organizational, community, and societal system levels—often simultaneously.

From this unified perspective, Goldstein (1973) defines change as a process of adaptations to life circumstances manifested in the individual's behavior. Change requires the accommodation of others in the social milieu. In other words, change in one system is likely to precipitate change in other systems. This view of change asserts that change

> takes place in *persons,* as the major or minor adaptations made to life situations that are ultimately manifested in behavioral forms. . . . Change also impinges on and has implications for others in one's social milieu, for it calls upon these others to make certain accommodations to new actions.

> The assertion that change is ultimately lodged in persons is not incongruent with more sweeping or expansive emendations of larger systems—for instance, social legislation, economic innovations, racial integration, or modifications in a community's structures and institutions. We tend to abstract these phenomena, to see them in nonhuman, institutional, or societal terms as if they were occurring in a self-enclosed sphere. They are, in reality, human endeavors brought about *by* persons who are committed to the need for change, reform, or modification. They are, in the final analysis, change events only as they have some significant meanings *for* the life patterns of certain persons, individually or in concert. (p. 159)

Generalist Practitioners. Typically, at the foundation or entry level of the profession, social workers today are generalist practitioners. Generalists work directly with client systems that present diverse problems and needs, practice in a wide range of social service settings, and apply a variety of models and methods. As generalists, social workers possess an integrated view of the interaction between people and resources within networks of relationships that make up the human environment. Therefore generalists also intervene indirectly, or on behalf of clients, in legislative advocacy and policy formation activities.

Looking Forward

The conceptualization of generalist social work along a continuum of intervention levels provides a tool for examining practice in a creative manner. Instead of being limited and constrained by a narrow focus of intervention, a generalist social worker is energized by a holistic conception of practice. Intervention from an ecological perspective is guided by the values and ethics of the profession and the purpose of social work.

Social services are offered in the context of a delivery system. Ideally, the delivery system is constructed to respond to personal needs and social problems at all levels. In reality, some inherent weakness in the structure of the delivery system thwarts the ability of social work to respond promptly to problems, delimits those who can receive services, and fragments the actual provision of services. Chapter 4 critically examines the dimensions of the social service delivery system—its settings, personnel, service provisions, and sources of funding—and raises a number of issues that significantly affect both contemporary social work practice and the consumers of social services.

CHAPTER

4 The Social Service Delivery System

Chris Atwood automatically reaches for the computer switch as she hangs up her coat. The computer that once seemed like an unnecessary albatross is now an absolute necessity. It displays Chris's appointment calendar, provides access to a network Directory of Social Services, assists in record keeping, and makes evaluation-research projects a reality.

This morning Chris is on call at Resource and Referral, the information and referral agency where she works. When she is on call, Chris is responsible for fielding phone calls and meeting with clients who drop in without appointments. Being on call challenges Chris, as she must work with diverse clients to assess a wide range of problems, determine possible resources, develop plans of action, and process referrals. If this is a usual day, Chris can expect inquiries about services for senior citizens, family counseling, resources for single parents, day care, food pantries, and emergency relief. Some requests are fairly routine, while others require fine-tuned crisis-intervention skills.

Chris looks forward to her late-afternoon meeting with Charles Greene from Family Opportunities. Charles is going to preview details about his agency's new "Reach Out to Families" program. Since Chris needs up-to-date information about service delivery options, she meets regularly with other social workers in her community. Knowing that two-way sharing of information builds collegiality and interagency cooperation, Chris plans to give Charles a copy of Resource and Referral's new trends study. This research about economic trends in her community represents a cooperative venture by Chris and her colleagues at Research and Referral.

Chris Atwood's practice in an information and referral setting illustrates the work of a generalist social worker. Being technologically up-to-date and knowing about the available resources in the social service delivery system is absolutely essential. Chris is also in a position to identify gaps in and barriers to the delivery of social services. She joins with others in her agency and in the community's network of services to make plans to remedy inadequacies.

Knowledge about service delivery is a requirement in all types of settings. All social workers must understand the general features of social service delivery systems and the unique characteristics of their own community's network of services. To provide background about social service delivery systems, this chapter

- Describes different types and characteristics of social service settings
- Surveys sources of funding
- Profiles staffing patterns and the role of technology in the delivery of social services
- Highlights the resources of self-help groups
- Explores criteria for a comprehensive social service delivery network

Social Service Settings

Social work practitioners work in many different types of practice settings, including organizations such as agencies and associations. These settings can be public or private, primary or host, sectarian or nonsectarian, nonprofit or for-profit settings, or independent practice. Geographic jurisdiction and geographic location characterize settings, as well.

Public and Private Auspices

Social services are classified as either public or private depending on their sources of policy and funding (Table 4.1).

Public Social Services. In the United States, federal, state, and local governments create public social service agencies through legislative statutes. Legislation defines, guides, funds, and sanctions public social services. Allocations of tax funds provide income for these government-sponsored programs. State human resource departments are examples of state-based public programs. Mandated by state law, these agencies provide programs for income maintenance, child protection and family welfare, and rehabilitation, as well as structures for federal programs that in turn provide services for older adults, persons with disabilities, and veterans (Table 4.2). Sometimes agencies and organizations in the public sector are called *code agencies* or *commonweal organizations.*

Private Social Services. Community, national, or international special-interest groups establish organizations that provide private-sector social services. Boards of directors develop policy. Articles of incorporation or the organization's constitution and bylaws codify these policies. Typically, private agencies receive income from multiple sources, including private donations, contributions from affiliates, endowments, foundation grants, allocations from unified fund drives, contractual arrangements, and fees-for-service. Social workers practice in diverse private-sector settings, including family service centers, advocacy agencies, health care facilities, business and industry, and private practice.

Agencies in the private sector are voluntary. As it applies to agencies, the term *voluntary* does not mean that professional staff members volunteer their services. In fact, voluntary agencies pay their staff. By definition, *voluntary* means that a voluntary initiative

TABLE 4.1 Contrasts between Public and Private Social Services

	Public Services	Private Services
Authority	Local, state, and federal laws	Articles of incorporation and bylaws
Scope	Laws specify exact intent and scope of programs	Agency mission provides direction for flexible programming
Affiliation	Part of local, state, or national government	Relatively autonomous, although agencies may affiliate with regional or national organizations
Structure	Bureaucratic hierarchies	Varies according to size from hierarchical to shared management
Income sources	Taxes	Contributions, fees, grants, and other private sources of income
Hiring practices	Typically, civil service	Agency standards and practices

TABLE 4.2 Examples of Public and Private Social Services in Resource and Referral's Service Area

Public Social Services	Private Social Services
Social Security	Resource and Referral
Township Youth Services	Family Opportunities
Veterans' Administration Social Work Department	Jewish Federation Multipurpose Senior Center
County Nursing Home and Home Health Social Services	United Ecumenical Food Pantry
State Department of Children's Services	Clinical Social Work Services, Inc.
Regional Planning for Child Welfare Services	Local hospital's social work department

founds the agency. The formation of private-sector agencies is independent of governmental mandates. For example, denominational groups; fraternal orders; and labor, cultural, social, or civic organizations form voluntary agencies. Some voluntary agencies provide traditional services, such as family service agencies. Others orient their programs toward advocacy efforts that respond to emerging issues of special-interest groups, such as gay men and lesbians, refugees, and immigrants.

By definition, private and public social services are separate; however, current trends blur this distinction. For example, government programs often contract with private agencies for specific services. Although this arrangement expands services in the private sector, it also subjects private agencies to government rules and regulations. Government agencies also set the standards for, or otherwise regulate, private-sector services. For example, government agencies regulate adoption agencies, day care centers, and drug rehabilitation programs. Cooperative working arrangements for interagency involvement in cases, in-service programs, and planning create further links between public- and private-sector agencies.

Agencies and Associations

Two types of organizations in social services are agencies and associations. *Agencies* are organizations that actually deliver social services. *Associations* are groups of people that come together to advance the common purposes of their members.

Of the two, agencies are by far the more common workplace for social workers. Agency mission statements envision directions for programs and services. Structured procedures supply guidelines for implementing them. Typically, larger agencies offer a greater range of service options within particular fields of service. Personnel in larger agencies frequently develop specialties. In the opening example, Charles Greene works at Family Opportunities. This large, multipurpose agency offers a broad spectrum of family-based services ranging from counseling, family-life education programs, and adoption to foster care and specialized residential programs. Smaller agencies often focus on single programs. Resource and Referral, where Chris Atwood works, is a relatively small agency that currently employs three other professionals besides Chris, including a coordinator for volunteers. Of necessity, social workers in small agencies perform a variety of functions within the parameters of their programs. In all agencies, large or small, social workers must perform their duties creatively within bureaucratic structures to achieve their clients' goals.

Associations primarily provide services for their members. Agencies, professionals, and special-interest groups often join associations such as professional organizations, federated efforts, alliances, and community councils (Table 4.3). The collective efforts of associations include forging the identity, cohesiveness, and culture of social work professionals, implementing standards, advocating just public social policies, and spearheading social work research (Tourse, 1995). Associations hire professional staff to carry out their constituencies' directives.

Primary and Host Settings

The main objective of some employment settings is to provide social work services; in other settings this is not the case. *Primary settings* principally offer social services. In primary settings, social work services directly relate to the organizational mission. In the chapter example, both Resource and Referral and Family Opportunities are primary settings. While the services each offers differ, each has as its primary purpose some facet of social service.

Host settings offer social work services as adjuncts to their organizational purposes. In host settings, social service components complement, support, or enhance the mission of host institutions. Social workers have a long tradition of working in host settings such as schools, hospitals, court services, and business and industry. Currently, opportunities for social work services in health maintenance organizations (HMOs), home health care agencies, schools, and employee assistance programs (EAPs) are expanding.

Social Work Highlights. Chris Atwood, in her role as a community resource specialist, confers with social workers employed in a variety of host settings. For example, she responds to calls from Rose Hernandez, a medical social worker at the local hospital; Helen Washington, a school social worker; Clarke Stewart, a juvenile court officer; and Kim Lee, the social worker with Agricompany's employee assistance program. The calls she receives from practitioners in these settings often relate to requests for information about referral sources, reports of gaps and barriers in service delivery, and help in seeking sources of funding for innovative community-based programming in these agencies and organizations.

TABLE 4.3 Examples of Associations

Alliance for Children and Families
American Public Human Service Organization
Association of Community Organization and Social Administration (ACOSA)
Canadian Association of Social Workers (CASW)
Child Welfare League of America (CWLA)
Council on Social Work Education (CSWE)
International Federation of Social Workers (IFSW)
National Association of Social Workers (NASW)

Typically, because of their centralized nature, information and referral agencies link social workers in host settings with the broader social work community.

Sectarian and Nonsectarian Affiliations

Sectarian and nonsectarian classifications further distinguish agencies, organizations, and associations. *Sectarian* designates a religious affiliation; *nonsectarian* indicates secular sponsorship.

Because of the constitutional separation of church and state, all public domain organizations in the United States are nonsectarian. Some private organizations are also nonsectarian. In the chapter example, Resource and Referral, Family Opportunities, the local hospital's social work department, Clinical Social Work Services, Inc., and all of the public agencies fall into the nonsectarian classification.

Sectarian agencies have always played a significant role in the delivery of social services (Cnaan, Wineburg, & Boddie, 1999). Congregations may sponsor local programs, such as meal sites, gardening projects, after school programs, and adult day centers. Larger-scale sectarian organizations often include hospitals; child care facilities; child welfare and family services agencies; community centers; and programs for older adults such as meal sites, day centers, and residential facilities. Examples of large sectarian organizations in the United States that offer a range of services include the Jewish Federation, Catholic Charities, and Lutheran Social Services. Prominent sectarian social service providers also include ecumenical ventures such as Church World Services' international efforts to address issues such as hunger, poverty, human rights, and social and economic development, and the Illinois Conference of Churches' refugee resettlement and domestic violence programs. Two examples of sectarian agencies in this chapter are the Jewish Federation's Multipurpose Senior Center and the United Ecumenical Food Pantry. Although the religious orientations of sectarian agencies undoubtedly influence their missions and programs, these programs usually serve clients from diverse religious and cultural backgrounds.

Nonprofit or For-Profit Status

Social service agencies in the private sector may be either nonprofit or for-profit. *Nonprofit* means that the agency has a service motive rather than a profit motive. However, the term *nonprofit* is misleading (Ostrander, 1985). Nonprofit refers to a tax status and does not preclude generating income and accumulating investments. What agencies do with their income determines whether they have a nonprofit or for-profit status. Generally, nonprofit agencies use their earnings for their programs and services. In our chapter example, Family Opportunities and Resource and Referral are both nonprofit agencies.

Some organizations in the private sector are profit-oriented. In *for-profit* corporations, a portion of earned income is returned to investors or shareholders or used to increase organizational fund balances. Profit-oriented businesses delivering social services include for-profit agencies and practitioners in private practice. Chris Atwood, the resource specialist in the chapter example, interacts with social service personnel at the local hospital and Clinical Social Work Services, Inc., both for-profit organizations.

The origins of business ventures in social service delivery date back to the 1960s, when Medicare and Medicaid instituted payments of funds to proprietary businesses for the delivery of social welfare service. Prominent entrepreneurial endeavors include nursing homes, hospital management, mental health maintenance, child care, home care, life care, and juvenile and adult corrections. In 1995, 27.1 percent of the NASW membership reported working in the for-profit sector of social services (Gibelman & Schervish, 1997).

The expansion of for-profit corporations in the social service delivery network is remarkable. Their market share grew from less than 1 percent in 1973 to 23 percent in 1984 (Frumkin & Andre-Clark, 1999). By 1992, for-profit firms dominated the market in day care and home health care services and, more recently, they have expanded their activities in job-training and welfare case management services. Such corporations as Maximus, Inc., Lockheed Martin, Electronic Data Systems, and Anderson Consulting maintain a strong corporate presence in welfare reform activities (Frumkin & Andre-Clark, 1999). Moreover, these large corporations have the distinct competitive advantages of their large-scale operations, investment resources, and freedom to lobby. The record is clear: For-profit corporations are expanding their multimillion dollar enterprises into many arenas served by traditional not-for-profit human service organizations. In assessing the impact of the changing venue for many types of social services, Frumkin and Andre-Clark caution that the bottom line for business is profit; whereas, non-profit organizations have usually "focused squarely on meeting the needs of clients."

Independent Practice

The *independent practice* of social work is another expanding entrepreneurial venture. Social workers in private practice work independently of governmental or agency organizations, take responsibility for the business of their practice, and arrange for their own contracts for services (Barker, 1991). The NASW formally authorized independent practice in 1958 and defined practice standards in 1962 (Wallace, 1982).

The scope of independent practice has increased with the expansion of state licensure, regulation, and lobbying efforts to establish privileges for vendors of social services. Private-practice opportunities include solo practice; partnerships with other social workers or interdisciplinary colleagues; and contracts for services in host settings such as medical clinics, industrial employee assistance, health maintenance organizations, and insurance companies.

Social workers in private practice must be duly licensed, certified, or registered in accordance with state laws that regulate independent practice. The option of private social work practice is available only for properly credentialed professionals with appropriate experience beyond their master's-degree education.

Independent social work practice requires attention to a number of business details. Private practitioners must arrange for office space, acquire referrals, and contract for consultants. They must plan for handling crises, such as clients who threaten to harm themselves or others, or who require hospitalization for mental illness. Additionally, private practitioners must consider the potential of malpractice litigation.

Independent practitioners must develop their own measures of practice effectiveness and networks of collegial support. Private practitioners do not have access to the support networks and "safety nets" provided under agency auspices, within collegial relationships, and through the guidance of supervisors. Isolation from other professionals or overscheduling their time increases practitioners' risks for burnout. Perceptive practitioners plan for collegial consultation, professional development, and sufficient restorative activities (Barker, 1991).

The independent practice of social work encompasses both proprietary and clinical interventions (Barker, 1991). *Proprietary practice* includes nonclinical activities such as providing consultation, leading workshops, contracting for research, and other nonclinical professional services. Therapeutically oriented *clinical social work* is most often associated with mental health. In this chapter's example, social workers at Clinical Social Work Services, Inc., offer both proprietary and clinical services. They lead workshops, consult on grants and research, and apply a solution-focused approach in their work with families.

Arguments in favor of and against private practice abound. Proponents argue that private practice increases consumers' options, offers flexible hours, and ensures greater autonomy for professionals as well as economic advancement. Critics characterize private practice as elitist, micro-focused, and available only to those who can pay a fee.

Geographic Location

The social work service delivery network includes services in a variety of geographic areas and jurisdictions. Recently, increased attention has been focused on the contrasts between urban and rural settings.

BOX 4.1

Reflections on Diversity

Agency Welcome Mats—What Do They Really Say?

Clients' initial impressions make a difference. How staff members greet clients, the general appearance of the waiting room, brochures, and even routine forms convey acceptance and respect or rejection and disapproval. Culturally competent agencies extend their welcome to diverse clients by ensuring that cultural responsiveness extends to such features as agency settings, orientations to practice, decision-making structures, policies, and links to community resources (Miley, O'Melia, & DuBois, 2004). Questions for evaluating agency-level cultural competence include:

- Are multilingual signs, brochures, and forms available?
- Are offices, meeting areas, and restroom facilities accessible?
- Is the agency conveniently located on public transportation routes or are programs and services offered in participants' neighborhoods?
- Do agency policies demonstrate sensitivity to diverse cultures?
- Does staff membership reflect the range of diversity represented in the community?
- Does the agency provide staff development training on diversity issues?
- Does the agency's orientation to practice consider social and cultural contexts?
- Does agency policy support activities leading to environmental change and social action?
- Are consumers involved in program evaluation, policy development, and decision-making activities?
- Has the agency formed links with indigenous resources in the community? for social change?
- Does the agency participate in community coalitions that press for social change?

Jurisdictions. Geographic and political *jurisdictions* define the boundaries of service delivery. The social service delivery network includes services at the local (including city, township, and county jurisdictions), state, regional, national, and international levels. Other types of jurisdictions include metropolitan areas, multicity and intercounty districts, and interstate or regional territories. Typically, general policy and funding filter down through the bureaucratic jurisdictional systems. In the United States, this often means that federal jurisdictions shape the design and implementation of public social services at the state and local levels.

Geographic boundaries are necessary for efficient planning and effective funding, yet they may present drawbacks too. For example, living in a particular city, county, township, state, or region often establishes clients' qualifications for services. However, boundaries limit accessibility for clients who live close to but outside of service areas. They also create accounting problems for agencies that provide programs and services in multiple administrative areas.

Social Work Highlights. Chris Atwood of our chapter example often refers families to Township Youth Services (TYS). TYS provides free counseling services for youth and their families who live within the township boundaries of the service area. Chris faces dilemmas when she recognizes families who could benefit from TYS services but fall outside the agency's catchment area. While Chris acknowledges that boundaries are necessary for determining eligibility, she also knows that boundaries restrict clients' choices of service providers.

Urban Settings. The magnitude of the need presented by a large population base undoubtedly affects the delivery of urban social services. Common issues caused by a heterogeneous population, overcrowding, deteriorating physical conditions, visible unemployment, obvious poverty, and an ever-changing population base challenge typical urban communities. Because of the magnitude of the social problems and the geometric expansion of service needs, a wide range of service responses emerges in metropolitan areas.

Designing coordinated, comprehensive social service delivery systems in urban areas requires effective planning efforts. Social planning activities were highly visible as a specialization in social work in the 1960s and early 1970s, as social workers systematically waged a war on poverty. The demand for planners increased because of a requirement that planning be integrated with community mental health services; maternal and child health services; and the programs of the Economic Opportunity Act (EOA), Comprehensive Employment and Training Act (CETA), and Job Training and Partnership Act (JTPA).

Community action agencies in metropolitan areas addressed the root causes of poverty, such as inadequate education, unemployment and underemployment, poor health, and lack of affordable housing. However, even considering the mandate to deal with these areas, planning efforts were focused on limited populations or service areas and were not necessarily related to the needs of total communities. Categorical funding led to categorical planning for service delivery. Furthermore, employment of planning specialists declined as the War on Poverty waned in the late 1960s and the effects of federal reductions in funds for social services in the 1980s were felt. Decreased federal support for public planning initiatives eliminated many social planning activities and specialized planning positions.

Lack of financial support for planning weakens the delivery of social services and reduces the likelihood of coordinated, comprehensive services. Without a comprehensive planning process, social service providers are ill equipped to respond systematically to emerging needs and take responsibility for community problem solving. Without funding and a legislative mandate for social planning, communities must rely on individual practitioners' commitments to cooperative planning and coordinated leadership. Social work professionals must continue to assume responsibilities for building coalitions and working collaboratively regardless of the status of public funding for planning.

Rural Settings. Social workers in nonmetropolitan areas face a set of demands different from that faced by their colleagues in urban areas. Both the unique characteristics of rural settings and the fact that professionals are usually members of the communities in which they work create challenges (Martinez-Brawley, 1990; NASW, 2002a).

Distinctive physical and economic features, face-to-face social relationships, and integral roles for local organizations such as schools and churches characterize rural communities (Martinez-Brawley, 1993). Rural life-styles and the prevalence of natural helping networks further distinguish nonmetropolitan areas. Social workers report that such characteristics as "the cultural norms of slower pace of life, the importance of informal communication, suspicion of governmental control and outsiders, and the value of independence" influence their practice in rural communities (Gumpert, Saltman, & Sauer-Jones, 2000, p. 31). While more visible in cities because of their sheer volume, social problems such as poverty, inadequate health care, gentrification, shortages of affordable housing, and an unstable agribusiness economy continue to plague small towns and rural communities. Furthermore, diversity is an important concern, as rural areas include such groups as the "Missouri Amish, Louisiana Cajun, Wyoming Basque, New Mexico Pueblo, Alaska Aleute, North Carolina Hmong, [and] Utah Mormon" (Davenport & Davenport, 1995, p. 2081).

Examining social service delivery networks in rural areas reveals gaps in the availability and accessibility of services. Services in rural areas tend to cluster in one location, such as a county seat. Since rural populations are often widely scattered and public transportation systems in rural areas are virtually nonexistent, services are often inaccessible. Moreover, the scope of services may be limited, and the service delivery organizations are staffed by fewer professionals. These limitations do "not allow for the division of labor among practitioners around specific areas of expertise that is afforded in urban settings" (Gumpert, Saltman, & Sauer-Jones, 2000).

Social work practice in rural areas presents its own unique challenges. Social work professionals in rural areas acknowledge burnout associated with geographic isolation, the limited number of professional colleagues, and the scarcity of formal resources. Social workers who live in the same community in which they work must seek ways to establish collegial networks, protect their personal time, and separate personal from professional relationships.

Josephine Brown and Eduard Lindeman, pre–World War II rural social work leaders, pointed out the importance of community-based involvement—rural planning for rural needs. In *The Rural Community and Social Work,* Brown (1933) notes that:

> the specialized and complicated organization of city social work can never be successfully transplanted to rural communities. Perhaps the outstanding problem which leaders in rural social work are facing at present is that of freeing the "creative processes" of socialization within the rural community in such a way that the peculiarly urban characteristics of

social work may be avoided and only those essentials used which may be truly assimilated. (pp. 24–25)

Brown furthermore emphasized the need for rural social workers to develop partnerships with rural communities by identifying needs collaboratively, cultivating community leadership, using volunteers, and working with county administrative units.

The charge issued by Brown over 50 years ago is still relevant today. In *Social Work in Rural Communities,* Leon Ginsberg (1976; 1993) pointed to the need for rural social

BOX 4.2

Reflections on Empowerment

Burned Out or Fried Up?

The workplace can either be a source of burnout or promote empowerment. Burnout refers to the emotional exhaustion caused by work-related stress. Burnout is often precipitated or exacerbated by working conditions. When this occurs, burnout results from workers being "fried" by organizational practices that drain their energy and undermine their sense of professional well-being.

Workers are more likely to experience job stress and burnout in settings that limit their opportunities for influencing decisions, devalue accomplishments, and fail to authorize any latitude for collaborative work with either colleagues or clients (Chenoweth, 2002; Gabassi et al., 2002; Leon, Altholz, & Dziegielewski, 1999; Maslach, 2003; Maslach, Schaufeli, & Leiter, 2001; Wharton, 1999). When demands spiral, the possibility of experiencing the physical and emotional effects of burnout increases exponentially. Professionals who are burned out are more negative and cynical, project blame on others, and distance themselves from others. In essence, burnout can result in workers' "loss of idealism, feelings of hopelessness, lowered morale, lack of initiative, absenteeism, alcohol and drug use, and physical and emotional exhaustion" (Dressel, 1992, p. 216). In contrast, settings that are oriented toward empowerment emphasize strengths, incorporate collaborative styles into decision-making processes and program development, affirm employee achievements, and promote feelings of competence. Social workers must themselves experience being empowered to employ empowering processes in their work with clients.

On an organizational level, supervisors can lessen the stress and burnout experienced by social workers when they consciously assign manageable workloads, promote interpersonal relations, ensure participatory processes for decision making, and create less stressful work environments (Acker, 1999; Bednar, 2003; Brotheridge & Lee, 2002; Shera & Page, 1995). Workplaces that promote resiliency incorporate elements of social support, promote participatory decision making, build a sense of organizational community, and establish clear channels of communication (Zunz & Chernesky, 2000). On an individual level, workers can apply stress management techniques, reframe their perceptions of stressful events, and maintain an optimistic outlook and a sense of humor. Research indicates that factors such as feelings of personal efficacy, access to social support, a sense of purpose, and recognition for accomplishments also promote resiliency and counter the effects of burnout (Zunz, 1998). "Agencies managed with an eye toward enhancing protective strategies like worker empowerment, functional communication systems, and a positive 'corporate' culture with a strong sense of community, develop competencies that will stand them in good stead in the face of any challenging current or future environment" (Zunz & Chernesky, 2000, p. 171).

work education and practice. Also *The West Virginia 1990: Trends Study* found that social planning in rural areas differs from that in urban areas (Locke, Lohmann, & Meehan, 1985). For example, in one rural area, social workers used a planning process to help localities define their own distinct concerns and promote rural social change by using local experts, facilitating democratic decision making, and building consensus. Community forums are an effective way of bringing human service providers together with local leaders to develop rural social services. Culturally sensitive social workers in rural areas "emphasize supportive and collaborative roles with community-based systems" (Gumpert, Saltman, & Sauer-Jones, 2000, p. 31).

Two facts point to the significance of preparing for rural social work experiences. In the United States, social workers play prominent roles in rural social services, but staff are primarily baccalaureate-prepared social workers assisted by a cadre of paraprofessionals (NASW, 2002a). Internationally, social workers are more likely than not to work in rural settings. These factors make investigating both the particular needs of rural communities and the unique contributions of social work in rural settings imperative. Contemporary social work professionals need to prepare for effective social work practice in rural areas. "Rural practitioners and advocates need to remember their unique resources, their special strengths and those of their communities and clients. They need the flexibility to be creative" (Cooper, 2000, Summary Section, ¶ 2).

The Funding of Services

The social service delivery network derives funds from a number of sources. Federal and state funds supply both public- and private-sector social services. Local communities contribute through taxes and fund-raising efforts such as united fund drives. Individual agencies have their own sources of income, which include contributions, fees, insurance reimbursements, purchase of service contracts, and grants (Table 4.4).

TABLE 4.4 Resource and Referral's Sources of Income

Income Sources	Description
Community Chest	Annual allocation application New programs allocation
Emergency Flood Relief	Special one-year funds
Williams Foundation	Response to RFP (two-year funding)
Computer Technology, Inc.	In-kind computer hardware and software
Mollie Barker Trust	Capital improvement project
Travelers' Aid Society	Annual allocation
Community Block Grant	Annual grant request
Riverboat Authority Grant	Start-up funds—demonstration project
Friends of Resource and Referral	Annual solicitation—fund-raising events
Henley's Department Store	Incentive match for fund drive
Gifts and memorials	Donor contributions

Federal and State Funding

Federal and state legislative mandates earmark appropriations for social services from both general taxes and social security contributions. Often the federal government channels allocations through state and local governments. Agencies may access these funds by applying for grants and responding to requests for proposals (RFPs). Many federal provisions call for grants-in-aid to states. For example, states match funds for public welfare entitlement programs such as Temporary Assistance for Needy Families (TANF) and Supplemental Security Income (SSI).

There are a number of other legislative mandates and executive orders for the funding of social services that fall under different federal administrative bodies. The Social Security Act is an excellent example of legislation that prescribes different types of programs administered at a variety of governmental levels and funded from multiple sources. Other examples of major federal programs include the Food Stamp Program administered by the United States Department of Agriculture (USDA), funds for housing subsidies through Housing and Urban Development (HUD), and Project Head Start in the Department of Education.

Funding Reductions. Reductions in financial commitments by federal and state governments occur in two principal ways: through fiscal retrenchment and social policy retrenchment. Fiscal retrenchment efforts to reduce the national budget deficit—particularly the Gramm-Rudman-Hollings Bill of 1986—significantly diminished the funding stability for human services. These budget cutbacks overtly reduce fiscal allocations. In contrast, social policy retrenchment or *bureaucratic disentitlement* (Lipsky, 1984) covertly reduces programs and services. Lipsky says:

> Bureaucratic disentitlement consists of structural imperatives in public agencies that narrow the range of resources available to lower-status members of society. It permits the expression of structural biases against the interests of social welfare clients while maximizing the likelihood that potential opponents of these biases will remain quiescent, and that separate costly community cleavages will be avoided. The problem is not that bureaucratic disentitlement contributes to a declining social welfare sector. It is that its contribution to the decline is unheralded and unavailable for public inspection. (p. 22)

Lipsky identifies eight forms of bureaucratic disentitlement:

- Imposing regulations that restrict access to services
- Limiting resources
- Postponing decisions so as to avoid expanding programs
- Increasing bureaucratic accountability to reduce line workers' discretion
- Imposing sanctions in fair hearings and appeals
- Failing to heed the suggestions of citizens' advisory boards
- Fragmenting the delivery of services
- Co-opting providers of services that are dependent on government funds

Naturally, elected officials are reluctant to support obvious slashing of budgets for "quality-of-life" services. In many instances, the same reductions can be achieved covertly through policy retrenchment at the programmatic level. These policy retrenchments "erode the position of relatively powerless groups without arousing them or their watchdog allies" (Lipsky, 1984, p. 20).

Social Work Highlights. Chris Atwood took her eighth call this week from individuals caught in an administrative rule change by the State Division of Aging Services. Resulting from statewide budget reconciliation strategies, this rule change placed greater restrictions on financial assets for client eligibility, thus restricting the pool of potential clients and reducing program costs. The calls to Chris were from former clients of the local agency on aging who were no longer eligible for services under the new guidelines. Chris intends to network with other Information and Referral social workers in her state to find out how other communities are responding to these newly legislated gaps and barriers in services for older adults.

Grants

Grants are sums of money awarded to social service organizations that submit applications to fund particular programs and services. Grant evaluators subject applications to competitive review processes. Social service organizations secure grants from numerous outside resources, including national and local foundations, corporations, and government agencies. Grants are usually available for either capital improvements or program operations. Venture grants are one-time-only grants. These grants often provide start-up costs for new programs or pilot demonstration projects. Sometimes funding appropriations stipulate *matching dollar challenges.* This means that grant applicants must make in-kind contributions and/or financial commitments to programs in order to be eligible for grant funding.

Applicants for funding submit grant proposals. These proposals usually include documentation of the problem and assessment of needs, measurable program objectives, program activities and methods, evaluation procedures, plans for continuation of funding, and budget details (Wolk, 1994). Often agencies respond to *requests for proposals* (RFPs) issued by the granting organization. RFPs specify guidelines for proposals and indicate restrictions on the availability of funding, time limits, and goals for service delivery. In essence, the funding body defines the parameters for programs and services. Typically, funding bodies hold grant recipients accountable for specific program outcomes and press agencies to incorporate specific plans for outcomes assessment into their grant proposals.

Community Funds

Taxes and donors' contributions constitute two primary sources of funds for social services within local communities. Local governing units such as counties, cities, and townships channel *tax dollars* into the social service delivery network. For example, local governing bodies appropriate funds for general assistance, a program for people who do not qualify for the categorical assistance programs that are funded by the states and the federal government. General assistance often serves special population groups, such as people who are indigent or homeless; transients; and people with mental retardation, developmental disabilities, or chronic mental illness. In addition, some localities assess special taxes for nursing homes, youth service programs, and public health services. Recently stipulations for community participation have increased local responsibility for making decisions about distributing funds that are channeled into local communities from regional, state, and national resources.

Local United Way organizations conduct *community fund raising* for social services in 1,400 communities in the United States (United Way of America, 2001). These organizations typically hold one annual, comprehensive community campaign that responds to identified needs in the community. The United Way then distributes funds to affiliated agencies or the agencies contributors designate. In some communities, collective health appeals solicit contributions to distribute to health-specific agencies and organizations.

Endowments and Special Funds

Endowments consist of income-producing monetary or property investments. Some agencies obtain funds for endowments through bequests, gifts by individual contributors, or special fund drives sponsored by service leagues. Agencies use income generated from endowments to further their mission by funding specific activities. Sometimes social service organizations solicit financial and programmatic support from individuals who are "friends" of the agency or "sustaining members." These annual membership drives provide supplementary funds to agencies.

Fees-for-Service

Another way agencies derive income is through *fees-for-service.* Clients pay for services rendered, often based on their ability to pay. Typically, fees-for-services are calculated and charged by a "unit of service." For individuals, units of service include such things as an hour of counseling or a day of day care. An example of a charge for a unit of service at an organizational level is the per-employee rate a provider agency charges a private industry for employee assistance services.

Many debate the utility of charging fees for social services. Those favoring the fee arrangement argue that personally paying for services increases clients' commitment in social work relationships. Those who argue against a fees-for-services system suggest that fees create a two-class system of service—one level for those who can pay and a different level for those who cannot pay.

Insurance Reimbursement

At the insistence of many traditional funding sources, nonprofit organizations have had to seek ways to become more financially self-sustaining. Agencies' survival often depends on expanding service options that generate income through alternative payment systems such as *insurance reimbursement* and health maintenance organizations (HMOs). In fact, "current research suggests that as government funding becomes less reliable, the established agencies will put more emphasis on income generating programs that service the middle classes and weaken services to those most in need" (Ostrander, 1985, p. 443).

Providers feel pressure to design services that reach beyond the poor and marginally dependent to the medically insured and members of HMOs. Through third-party payment mechanisms, insurance companies provide coverage for social work services in medical and mental health settings. Third-party payments are expanding to other clinically oriented services in agencies and private practice as well. Rules about insurance provisions vary from state to state. Generally, practitioners who receive insurance reimbursements must possess appropriate credentials. Because many insurance carriers and HMOs have cost-containment goals, service providers must reconcile professional decisions about interventions with the managed-care systems' cost containment goals.

Purchase of Service Contracting

Many public welfare agencies contract with nonprofit and for-profit private agencies to fulfill service mandates through the *purchase of service contracts* (POSCs). Purchase of service contracts specify contractual agreements whereby governmental sponsors purchase specific services from private contractors for a set fee. Currently, in the United States, POSCs are the main source of funding for personal social services (Kramer, 1994; Kettner & Martin, 1996). POSCs and privatization go hand in hand, as POSCs represent one means to accomplish governmental divestiture of public social services (Gibelman, 1995).

In essence, in POSCs, one service provider purchases the services of other professionals in order to fulfill legislative mandates to respond to clients' needs. The contractual arrangement specifies types of service, units of service, eligibility criteria for receiving services, and expected outcomes. Typically, contracts specify fixed prices for predetermined numbers of service units. Alternatively, POSCs may incorporate cost-sharing arrangements. In *cost sharing,* agencies that receive POSCs match costs for services with their own funds. Another alternative, *performance-based contracting,* is a relatively new concept in the purchase of service arrangements. Performance-based contracts specify incentives for the performance of service objectives at specified achievement levels (Kettner & Martin, 1993; 1998; Wedel, 1995).

Among the factors affecting the decision to purchase a service contract are cost effectiveness, the volume of services required, the capabilities of government agencies and private contractors, the potential of contracts to improve services, the applicable legal mandates, and community relations (Kettner & Martin, 1994; 1998).

Issues in Funding

The preceding discussion raises numerous questions about funding for social services, such as: Should the base of funds be public or private? How do the distinctions between public and private services blur with grants, POSCs, vendor payments, and loan subsidies? Does the increased reliance on insurance payments expand or contract options for clients? Specific issues, such as privatization, the effects of competition for funding, and triage decision making, emerge.

Privatization. *Privatization* results when governments support private nonprofit and for-profit social services rather than expanding their own government-based public services. Through the purchase of service contracts, income maintenance vendor payments, and low-cost loans, various levels of government add to the financial support base for voluntary and for-profit agencies. These financial incentives have ushered private business and industry into the social service delivery network as mainstream providers of social services. Policymakers who favor privatization argue that profit-oriented businesses can provide more cost-effective social services than the government can. They see privatization as a way to shrink what they call "the burgeoning welfare state."

Trends toward privatization are as common worldwide as in the United States (Demone, 1998). With increasing emphasis on decreasing federal involvement in social services, privatization is occurring in numerous fields of practice, including child protection services, foster care, adoption services, mental health services, residential homes for youths, aging services, and various types of programs and services in the area of criminal justice (Gibelman, 1998). Privatization "results in a preference among many welfare professionals for working in voluntary agencies and is used to justify citizen opposition of the welfare state" (Ostrander, 1985, p. 445).

Social work professionals give privatization mixed reviews. Some social workers embrace privatization. They see possibilities for new employment opportunities, higher salaries, sanitized working conditions, more attractive clients, and prestige. Others view privatization as yet another policy that undercuts social work's mandate to provide services to the needy. They believe that social work professionals ought to recognize the fallacy of the premise that "cheaper is better" when it comes to the well-being of societal members.

Competitive Funding. Competition rather than cooperation among agencies results when agencies vie for funds. Several issues arise with *competitive funding* (Miller, 1988). Sometimes only those agency programs that turn a profit receive adequate funding, leaving scant resources for less affluent agencies. Furthermore, the competition for dollars directly relates to competition for professional staff. Agencies with greater resources can attract qualified professionals at more competitive salaries. The net effect is that services for the poor may suffer both in their ability to obtain grants for innovative programs and in their ability to hire experienced practitioners.

Agency Turf. Protection of agency self-interest, or *agency turf,* is often at the bottom of disputes about which agency should gain funds to provide certain types of services or work with particular types of clients. While some agencies have broadly stated missions and offer comprehensive services, others use single-focus approaches that limit the types of services they provide or the clientele they serve. In reality, agencies may develop new programs only because funds are available, not because these programs match their mission. Conscientious social workers who recognize that the financial pie can be sliced in several ways often suffer ethical dilemmas when advocating a bigger piece for one program to the detriment of others.

Social Triage. *Social triage* is a process for classifying clients as "treatable" or "untreatable," or "worthy" or "unworthy." Based on a concept that guides emergency room personnel's decision making during crises, social workers use triage criteria to screen clients for services. In its best construction, social triage is a response to the constraints of limited

BOX 4.3
Social Work Profile

Public Social Services

I am a good example of how someone can transfer the core social work knowledge, values, and skills from one field of practice to another. Over the course of my social work career, I have worked in juvenile justice, child welfare, family services, school social work, public health, and, now, in community welfare services. Any one of these fields of practice is a total career path, but my experience of this combination has led to my current position as director of a county community service agency. This position, which I've held for the past 15 years, provides the variety of service arenas that drew me into social work in the first place and now sustains my interest.

I am involved in the work of the local government by developing and administering the county-funded managed-care plan for people with mental retardation and developmental disabilities and for mental health services. Under the service-umbrella of community public welfare, I oversee the general assistance, veterans' assistance, and protective payee programs. My position also provides opportunities to work in collaborative alliances around service delivery reforms in many fields of practice, including child welfare, mental health, and housing and homeless services.

My social work education provided the foundation of knowledge of human systems and a broad understanding of contextual influences on human behavior; core values of human dignity and social justice that translate into respect for people and just social policies and provisions of services; and skills such as effective communication and critical thinking. Social work education gave me the philosophical and professional base that transcended all the fields of practice in which I've worked. The on-the-job training enabled me to learn the agency jargon and the requirements of the particular field of practice.

I would emphasize to new social workers, the reality that social workers practice in a political and fiscal environment. I have learned that every public policy that is formulated has been guided down the hallway by fiscal concerns. Unless social workers want to work in systems that are managed by accountants, they will need to know about management issues, fiscal realities, policy development, and budgeting skills, and have some expertise in finance and funding. Certainly the current crises in state budgets impact on the funding available at the county level and in turn, affect the types of services available to persons served by the local public sector safety net for long-term needs—persons who are poor, have disabilities, are homeless, or are otherwise at risk.

I became a social worker because I wanted to be on the side of doing the right thing. Doing the right thing, to me, means being involved in formulating and developing social policies. In this process, I am challenged daily to acknowledge that what is politically feasible oftentimes differs from what is actually advantageous. I have learned that in terms of public policy "one size often does not fit all." Policies designed at the larger system level, such as the federal- and state-level, need to have built-in flexibility for application to local levels. If the policy is too specific in its administrative directives, the result is mediocrity at the community level of service delivery. What I find most exciting about public policy development today results from the increased consumer involvement over the past 10 years. Active participation by consumers and other community stakeholders leads to more humane and responsive social policies.

resources and represents a way to do more with those who have some chance at success. Jenkins (1983) pointedly describes the unintended effects of social triage:

> Thus, in giving priority to clients with the greatest chance of success, in helping those most able to accept help, we ignore what happens to the others. We differ from the medical model, however, in that our neglected clients—"the unworkable," "hard to reach," "unworthy," or "resistive"—do not die like unattended critically injured patients. The nonclients are not in the orbit of the social service delivery system, but they comprise a growing number of untreated and currently unreachable people on or off welfare rolls, in or out of psychiatric institutions or training schools, [with a] deficit in social functioning or social contribution. . . . Help will not "filter down," and the generational aspects of failure mean there can be a geometric progression of problems as more children are born into troubled and dependent families. (p. 823)

Social triage reinforces feelings of helplessness on the part of clients whom workers dismiss with the rejection, "There's nothing we can do!" and of whom the delivery system says, "There's nothing to do!" Social workers have a social responsibility to use social triage for continuing to "help those who can be helped, but directing a greater effort to those most in need, including the search for more effective and appropriate modalities of service" (Jenkins, 1983, p. 824).

Staffing Patterns

Staffing patterns combine various levels of professional practice, paraprofessionals, and volunteers in order to deliver programs and services. Staff members are differentiated by levels of professional competence, education, and experience. Technological expertise enhances the delivery of social services by professional, paraprofessional, and volunteer staff.

Social Work Professionals

The social work profession differentiates levels of practice and regulates its members by setting standards for credentials. Recognized social work practitioners receive education and training through CSWE-accredited undergraduate and graduate programs. NASW determines criteria for various levels of practice among its members. State regulatory boards define the legal requirements for social work practice in their respective states.

Levels of Professional Practice. The NASW (1981) *Standards for the Classification of Social Work Practice* describes four levels of social work practice. Ascending levels of professional autonomy and practice specialization differentiate each level of professional practice:

- *Basic Professional Level* practice requires a bachelor's degree from a program accredited by the CSWE. Preparation at the first level of professional practice includes competence in foundational skills, theoretical knowledge, and social work values.

- *Specialized Professional Level* practice requires a master's degree in social work from a social work program accredited by the CSWE. Social work specialists have mastery of therapeutic techniques related to at least one practice method; in-depth knowledge of human behavior and the social environment; and competence in research, supervision, administration, or planning methodologies.

- *Independent Professional Level* practice requires a master's degree from an accredited school of social work plus at least two years of supervised post-master's experience. Through appropriate specialized training, practitioners at the independent level demonstrate the knowledge and skills necessary for autonomous practice.

- *Advanced Professional Level* practice usually requires a doctoral degree in social work or a closely related discipline. At this level, practitioners assume responsibility for furthering the development of the profession, theory building, social work education, research, or social welfare policy implementation.

Credentials for Social Work Practice. Credentials establish social work as a distinct profession and provide a basis for its regulation and protection of its clients. Both private and public organizations issue credentials to social work practitioners.

Several private organizations deal with credentialing, including the CSWE and NASW. The CSWE evaluates social work programs at the baccalaureate and master's degree levels. It grants accreditation to those educational programs that meet CSWE's guidelines. Graduating from an accredited program qualifies people for membership in the NASW and, in many states, is a prerequisite for licensure.

The NASW certifies qualified members with credentials such as membership in the Academy of Certified Social Workers or inclusion in a register of social workers qualified for clinical practice. These certifications require holding membership in the NASW, meeting criteria for supervised clinical practice, and passing a standardized examination. The NASW ensures quality by requiring its members to adhere to practice standards prescribed in the NASW (1999a) *Code of Ethics*. More broadly, courts use the standard of this code for NASW members and other practicing social workers alike to adjudicate lawsuits involving professional social work ethics.

Credentials offered by other private organizations regulate specific areas of social work, such as marriage and family counseling or school social work. Private credentials do not constitute a legally binding public authority; nonetheless, they set professional standards for social work practice.

Laws in all states in the United States and its territories authorize and regulate professional social work practice. State laws vary in the type of legal regulation they stipulate:

State licensing laws set education, training, experience, examination, and supervision requirements for the practice of social work. Licensure is the highest form of legal regulation. As measures that protect the general public, these laws grant states the right to sanction professionals who violate the legally binding professional standards set in licensing laws. Social workers establish their competence through their performance on licensing examinations and through documenting that they meet continuing education requirements.

Two other forms of regulation include voluntary certification and registration for social workers who wish to use a particular title (Biggerstaff, 1995). State *certification* furnishes certificates to those persons who document that they satisfy the qualifications for the certificate. States may sanction professionals who claim to be certified when they are not.

Similarly, state *registration* provides a register of social workers, and states may discipline practitioners who claim to be registered when they are not.

States differ in their requirements for registration, certification, or licensure. Some states regulate the practices of social workers with either baccalaureate or master's degrees. Some states offer additional credentials for clinical specialists. Designations of titles also differ from state to state. For example, depending on the particular state law, titles include:

- Registered social worker (RSW)
- Certified social worker (CSW)
- Licensed social worker (LSW)
- Licensed clinical social worker (LCSW)
- Licensed independent social worker (LISW)

State laws governing licensure specify parameters for types of social worker services authorized at each level of practice.

Legal regulation establishes a measure of credibility for professional social workers and offers legal protection for consumers (Saltzman & Furman, 1999; Barker & Branson, 2000). These practice regulation acts specify minimal educational and practice competency requirements and grant title protection to professionally educated social workers. The laws that regulate the profession of social work stipulate processes for pressing charges of professional malpractice and conditions for revoking licenses.

Paraprofessionals

Paraprofessionals have some specialized knowledge and technical training but do not have the formal education required for professional status. Current estimates indicate that, by 2008, the number of paraprofessionals employed in human services will increase by nearly 77 percent, making this among the fastest growing occupations in the United States (Bureau of Labor Statistics, 2002b; 2002c). Paraprofessionals work in various fields of practice in positions such as case management aides, caseworker aides, residential counselors, social service designees, community outreach workers, and mental health aides.

The use of paraprofessionals in social services acquired prominence in the 1960s. The community action component of the Economic Opportunity Act of 1964 stressed "maximum feasible participation" by people who were poor in planning social service programs. "Neighborhood store fronts moved services out of the Establishment into their clientele; eventually, services were afforded by their number. The era of consumer participation in the design and delivery of human services was begun" (Vidaver, 1975, p. 435).

The 1966 "new careers" amendment to the Economic Opportunity Act was an effective strategy for increasing indigenous, grassroots involvement in the War on Poverty. New careers started as a demonstration initiative, providing opportunities to persons who were disadvantaged to secure entry-level paraprofessional jobs in health and human services. Building on grassroots strengths, provisions for remedial education and job training ensured maximum opportunities for advancement.

Several issues emerge with respect to paraprofessionals' roles in social service delivery (Khinduka, 1987). First, policymakers hoped the paraprofessional movement would transform the delivery of social services so that it was more effective and relevant to the needs of the people. However, quite often paraprofessionals reverted to traditional methods rather than providing innovative grassroots services as originally intended. A second issue relates to differentiating professional from paraprofessional roles. Declassification of professional social work positions and the seeming overlap of functions between social workers and paraprofessionals creates tensions about their respective domains of activity. On one hand, paraprofessionals resent being controlled by social workers. On the other hand, professionally trained social workers resist encroachment on their roles by paraprofessionals.

Volunteers

Historically, *volunteers,* or unsalaried people who provide services, played a significant role in the delivery of social services. In the early twentieth century, friendly visitors from the Charity Organization Society and social reformers with the settlement house movement were central figures in the emergence of the social work profession. The use of volunteers declined significantly when public-sector agencies became more involved in providing social services.

Currently, with funding cutbacks by the federal and state governments, volunteers are again becoming increasingly important for the delivery of social services. Traditionally, women have been the backbone of the volunteer force; arguably, these women have constituted an unpaid female work force. With more women employed outside the home, however, the resource pool for volunteers is shrinking, although the demand for volunteers continues to expand.

Volunteer Activities. Volunteers offer many different kinds of support. Types of volunteers include the following:

- *Policy-making volunteers* serve on task forces, review panels, committees, and boards of directors.
- *Administrative volunteers* provide office support through activities such as word processing, coordinating schedules, and mailings.
- *Advocacy volunteers* provide support through fund-raising efforts, writing letters to and calling legislators, providing testimony at public hearings, organizing community support, and working on public relations.
- *Direct service volunteers* may be involved in activities such as counseling, recreation, crisis lines, and tutoring. The trend is to link clients, especially those who lack supportive social networks, with trained volunteers. (Mitchell, 1986)

In addition to these roles, agency volunteers make community presentations and lead workshops and study groups. Volunteers also provide transportation, child care, and respite services for clients of social services. Research suggests that agencies involve volunteers in more than direct service roles (Perlmutter & Cnaan, 1993). Based on a sample of nearly 500 volunteers from 105 human service organizations, over two-thirds incorporated administrative and advocacy activities in their volunteer roles.

Effective volunteer programs actively recruit and train volunteers, clearly define their tasks, coordinate the activities of volunteers, and provide them with supervisory support, and honor their contributions. Thorough reviews of references, including fingerprint checks, may be required for certain types of volunteer positions. Carefully designed screening processes match volunteers' talents with agencies' needs.

Social Work Highlights. Chris Atwood serves on an advisory committee for a local initiative to implement the Healthy Families America program. This program utilizes a combination of lay volunteers and professional nurses and social workers to provide in-home support and educational programs for new parents. Chris values the contributions of volunteers in child welfare prevention programs. These programs are designed to strengthen family relationships, increase participation in well-baby clinics, and educate parents about child development. The volunteers follow a regular schedule for visiting with new parents. As a part of the provider team, the volunteers work hand in hand with professionals to promote healthy functioning in families.

Computers and Technology in Service Delivery

The partnership between computers and social work is natural, as computers serve as technological supports that augment social workers' efforts in program development and service delivery. Services providers have come to rely on computer technology in many facets of their work, including day-to-day business operations, assessment activities, educational programs, advocacy, and program evaluation and research. Electronic networking offers numerous possibilities for enhancing inter- and intra-agency communication. E-mail, web-based discussion groups and other electronic bulletin board services literally network social service professionals around the world. The Internet provides links to a phenomenal range of information, including demographic data, fact sheets, laws, reference lists, on-line journals, and organizational resources.

Computer-Related Issues. Incorporating computer technology into service delivery raises numerous issues. For example, in this age of information, access to technology widens the gap between those who are rich and those who are poor. It may also widen the divide between those agencies that can afford technology and those that cannot, creating more difficulties for resource-poor operations and potentially narrowing the range of consumer choice. Second, for those clients who are unfamiliar with computers, using a computer to fill out forms may be intimidating and demoralizing. Finally, another issue centers on loopholes in information security. For example, breaches of confidentiality can easily occur in using database systems, electronic file transfers, and e-mail communication. In sum, social workers face the challenge of drawing on computer technology in ways that are consistent with the values and ethics of the social work profession.

Social Work Highlights. Self-help groups are now taking advantage of electronic technology to develop networks of computer-based mutual aid. Finn and Lavitt (1994) report on social support groups for sexual abuse survivors using "echo conferences." Participants post e-mail messages in response to general discussion topics or individual members' specific concerns. These groups offer a broad base of support from any location that has a phone and to any member who has a computer modem. Their versatility makes this medium of support beneficial for people "on the road" with their jobs or for those who live in remote areas. Interestingly, members often preserve their anonymity by using pseudonyms. They also communicate emotional support through innovative typing. For example ":)" and "<g>" both represent smiling. Participants indicate a high level of satisfaction with the support they receive through these computer-based groups.

Self-Help Groups as Resources

As a venue for mutual aid, self-help groups provide valuable community resources both separate from and in addition to professional services for a significant number of people. They are influential resources in the social welfare delivery network in terms of the magnitude of participation, the types of issues addressed, and the kinds of assistance offered.

Based on a national random sample survey, Kessler, Mickelson, and Zhao (1997) concluded that over 25 million people in the United States have participated in a self-help group at one time in their lives. They estimate that at least 10 million people are involved in self-help initiatives each year. About one-third of the respondents who reported involvement in self-help activities indicated they participated in substance use groups. They, as well as participants in groups for people with disabilities and parent support groups, were most likely to indicate long-term commitments to self-help organizations. Findings also revealed that individuals reporting lower levels of family support were more likely to become involved in self-help groups.

The number and variety of self-help or mutual-aid groups is increasing dramatically, particularly with the proliferation of self-help activities available on-line. In general, groups deal with issues related to challenges, such as substance use, life transitions, bereavement, disability and illness, caregiver support, life-style differences, and parenting. *The Self-Help Sourcebook* (White & Madara, 2002), also available on-line through the American Self-Help Clearinghouse at http://mentalhelp.net/selfhelp/, lists thousands of self-help groups. Many nationally and locally based groups now sponsor websites that detail information about the purposes and activities of their groups.

The format of self-help groups varies considerably from one group to another. While initially self-help groups tend to be informal, more formal organizational structures may eventually develop. Some may be like a club or association. Others form coalitions, federations, or even national organizational structures. And some, disdainful of professionalism and bureaucracy, avoid hierarchical structures of any kind.

The basis for self-help groups include "principles of empowerment, inclusion, nonhierarchical decision-making, shared responsibility, and a holistic approach to people's cultural, economic, and social needs" (Finn, 2000). Exchanges of information and sharing among peers who have much in common reduce isolation and provide potent experience of mutual support. Self-help focuses on strengths, emphasizes participating by both giving and receiving help, provides social support through a shared community, and exponentially multiplies available resources. Mutual aid often involves activities such as one-on-one conversations, educational programs, social activities, group discussions and personal sharing, hot lines, outreach activities, and legislative advocacy (Powell, 1995).

Numerous studies report that traditional self-help groups are effective sources of support for participants (Ben-Ari, 2002; Humphreys & Moos, 1996; Kyrouz & Humphreys, n.d.; McCallion & Toseland, 1995; Telfair & Gardner, 2000). A recent study of an on-line self-help group for people with disabilities indicates the helping processes present in on-line interactions were similar to those found in face-to-face groups (Finn, 2000). To date, no studies have evaluated the effectiveness of on-line self-help. On the one hand, according to Finn, on-line self-help groups increase accessibility, can ensure anonymity, allow for variations in communication response time, and hold the potential for networking with similar others from around the world. On the other hand, participants may be harmed by malicious interchanges, inundated with misinformation, and lured into participating in potentially addictive activities.

Further research is needed to identify differential benefits of professionally led groups and self-help groups. By clearly defining their relationships, mutual aid groups and professionals can complement rather than compete with each other in the delivery of services. To maximize benefits, social workers can take steps to identify local self-help resources; maintain an up-to-date file of contact information, meeting times, and meeting locations; and understand the potential of self-help for providing culturally sensitive support. Simply put, building alliances with self-help groups broadens the base of available resources.

Service Delivery Issues

There are two views of the social service delivery system. In one view, the system is a collection of discrete program options that are available to eligible clients. The other view pictures the social service delivery system as a coordinated system of services that addresses quality-of-life issues and flexibly responds to the needs of clients. User involvement is emerging as an important addition to service delivery. Whether to redress inequities and fragmentation in service delivery or to incorporate consumer involvement into planning and evaluating coordinated programs, empowerment-oriented social workers advocate user involvement to ensure respectful and responsive services.

Fragmented Services

The first view more than likely represents the social service delivery system now in place in most communities. This system, fraught with fragmented and limited service options, is a smorgasbord of programs constrained by categorized funding and rigid eligibility requirements. Ultimately clients must accept available, often limited, services to relieve their immediate problems. Available services are frequently restrictive or so overburdened that clients must place their names on waiting lists to participate in appropriate service options. Clients fall through the service delivery cracks.

A number of factors lead to fragmented, restrictive social service delivery systems:

- Workers make subjective judgments about clients' eligibility based on clients' "worthiness" or "motivation," rather than on objective and equitable guidelines, leading to unfair and discriminatory practices.

- The press for bureaucratic accountability ties funding to categorically based programs. Discounting social effectiveness, cost-effectiveness stresses the number of clients served in relation to the cost per unit of service.

■ In response to gaps in the service delivery system, well-intentioned advocates focus on the unmet needs of particular social groups or particular problems rather than promoting general responses to human needs. They add a vast number of programs that target specific needs of particular client groups to a system that is already fragmented. Consequently, more and more services limit eligibility to particular groups rather than provide services as social utilities.

■ Funding bodies often demand that agencies eliminate or reduce duplication of services. As sources of funding change, agencies compete with one another for funds, clients, and exclusive rights to provide services. The total effect is to limit clients' choices.

■ Because of changing political and economic climates, programs or social issues literally are in vogue one year and then decline in popularity the next. These social welfare reforms result in expanding or contracting services, which ultimately affects programs' stability.

■ Comprehensive, coordinated arrangements among social service providers suffer when policymakers fail to support social planning either financially nor in principle.

■ Clients experience reductions in their access to services as the cost accountability emphasis of managed care has shifted over time from cost-consciousness to cost-effectiveness to cost-containment to providing the least costly services.

Each of these factors addresses legitimate concerns, yet leads to fragmented services.

Coordinated Services

In contrast, an ideal social service system features coordinated services that address the quality of life for everyone. It includes flexible eligibility standards and creative adaptations of services in order to address clients' unique needs. A comprehensive service delivery model provides immediate responses at appropriate levels of intervention. It also includes provisions to enhance social functioning and create avenues for social policy change. Ideally, social service provisions:

- Are comprehensive and universal
- Incorporate clients' participation, choice, and decision making
- Involve a broad base of representation including consumers, providers, and the community-at-large in making policies
- Evaluate outcomes to ensure both the quality and effectiveness of services to all constituencies including consumers, funders, administrators, and policymakers
- Afford procedural simplicity to ensure efficiency and effectiveness
- Allocate adequate financing (NASW, 2002b)

User Involvement

Members of the service-user movement hold that consumer involvement is absolutely essential for redressing power inequalities in service delivery and for ensuring that empowerment saturates all facets of social work practice. For example, the main objective of the empowerment-oriented service-user movement—including such groups as mental health system survivors, older adults, persons with learning difficulties, and persons with disabilities—is to ensure service-user autonomy in decision making (Barnes & Bennett, 1998; Barnes & Shardlow, 1997; Beresford, 1999; Morris, 1997; Oliver, 1997). Although much of their energy is devoted to enhancing possibilities for personal control, they also advocate user participation through changes in service delivery and social policies and user involvement in research (Beresford & Evans, 1999; Evans & Fisher, 1999).

The title of a recent book, *Nothing About Us Without Us* (Charlton, 1998), captures a phrase that has become the mantra of the disability rights movement. Practice research also supports "establishing an active and prominent role for users in policy and practice development" (Fisher, 1994, p. 289). This unmistakable demand for involvement underlies the service-user movement and underscores the practice significance of collaborative partnerships. Moreover, service-user involvement must include more than ensuring self-determination. It is essential to extend user participation into a full range of activities, including theory building, research, program evaluation, staff development training, and policy development.

Service Delivery Reform

Communities need comprehensive and coordinated service delivery systems that respond to human needs holistically. Recent trends in allocating funds for service delivery reform and in coordinating efforts of existing programs make this possible. Premier service delivery systems are client-driven, have flexible funding parameters, expand eligibility, focus on prevention, and respond to human and social needs by providing services as social utilities.

Looking Forward

On what basis are decisions made, priorities set, and resources utilized in the social service delivery network? Ultimately, responses are shaped by our beliefs about the nature of humankind in relation to society. Are viewpoints informed by individualism? Cooperation or competition? The work ethic? Humanism? Social Darwinism? Self-determination? How do "isms"—ageism, sexism, racism, elitism—inform views of worthiness? Are people politically liberal or conservative? How do we view economic arrangements, technological development, and even social change? When social justice is defined, is the explanation global and inclusive or local and exclusive? Is the purpose of the social service delivery network to maintain the status quo, or is it a vehicle for social change? Answers to these questions inform viewpoints about how the components of the social service delivery network should be configured. Policy, which provides the framework for the social service delivery network, emerges from the collective response to these questions. The following part addresses these salient questions. Chapter 5 examines the philosophy, ideology, and values of the profession; Chapter 6 considers social justice issues; and Chapter 7 offers perspectives on diversity.

PART TWO

Social Work Perspectives

Social work may aptly be described as society's conscience. Our professional conscience derives from an affirmation of the inherent dignity and worth of people, a belief in the tenets of social justice, and an appreciation and celebration of diversity. Because people are not perfect, nor do they live in perfect societies, we must continually strive for harmony throughout our lives. Social workers are in a pivotal position to reconcile the challenges of living and provide a vision for social betterment.

Part Two is devoted to critically examining social work values and ethics, social justice issues, and cultural and social diversity. Professional values and ethical codes of conduct for social workers are explicated to provide practice direction and socialization to the norms and expectations of the profession. Social justice is defined, and the implications of social injustice—discrimination, victimization, and oppression—for social work are explored. Cultural, life-style, and religious differences are affirmed from a perspective of competence or strengths.

CHAPTER

5 Values and Ethics in Social Work

The discharge planning referral form received by Rose Hernandez, a social worker at the hospital, indicated that Dr. Brown wanted her to arrange a transfer to a skilled-care facility for 80-year-old Irma Douglas, who recently broke her hip. According to the information on the referral form, Miss Douglas was refusing to "comply" with her doctor's order. She had changed from a "sweet old lady" to a person the staff described as angry, aggressive, noncompliant, and uncooperative. When Rose met with Miss Douglas for the first time, she fielded a barrage of comments.

"I suppose you're here to tell me what to do—like everyone else. Well, save your breath! I have decided to go home. I do not want to be herded into a nursing home for those old people! It's bad enough to be held captive in this hospital so long."

Rose asked, "Since you broke your hip, everything seems out of control, Miss Douglas?"

"That's exactly right," the diminutive woman resounded, "I feel like shouting, 'Stop! I want to get off of this crazy merry-go-round.' "

Rose responded, "You're wanting to get back in charge of your life."

Miss Douglas replied, "I'm so tired of hospitals and their 'Do this and do that!' routines. Then some of my so-called friends tell me I should be grateful. Huh! Others come in and you can see it in their eyes. 'Poor Irma, what a pity.' And someone even had the nerve to say I was at fault. 'You and your scatter rugs,' she said. 'The only person you have to blame is yourself.' I pretended to fall asleep so she would leave. But maybe they're right. Maybe I am just an old lady who expects too much."

Miss Douglas continued, "I just want to feel the warmth of my home, rather than cold sterile hospital sheets. I want to smell the flowers blooming in my garden, instead of medicine in the air. I want to taste my homemade bread and preserves and not the bland stuff they peddle as food here. I just want to go home! I feel like I will never get home unless I go home now!"

The conversation continued for some time, leading to Rose's question, "How will you know when you feel hope again?"

Miss Douglas paused, "When I can walk . . . when I can make decisions for myself." Then Miss Douglas reached out and took the social worker's hand and said, "I've got some planning to do, some tough decisions to make. And I'm just tough enough to do it!"

This example raises a series of questions involving values and ethics, such as: What are the consequences of society's views about older adults? How do Miss Douglas's values affect her views of herself and others, her alternatives, and her resolve? How does ageism affect how professionals interact with older adults? How might the outcome have been different if the social worker believed that elderly persons were incapable of making decisions for themselves? Would the discussion have been directed differently if Miss Douglas were younger? What conflicts would Rose face if Miss Douglas insisted on going home even though that decision could put her safety at risk? These questions point to the centrality of values and ethical considerations in day-to-day social work practice.

To communicate the base of values and ethics of the social work profession, this chapter

- Differentiates values from ethics
- Details social work values

- Delineates principles that guide social work practice
- Examines the stipulations of ethical codes
- Analyzes the value context of social work

Values and Ethics

Values are foundational to social work practice. Thus, social work is a value-based profession that incorporates "a constellation of preferences concerning what merits doing and how it should be done" (Levy, 1976, p. 234). In fact, there are value and ethical dimensions to almost every aspect of social work (Reamer, 1999).

Values Defined

Values are the implicit and explicit ideas about what we cherish as ideal or preferable. Consequently, values determine which goals and actions we evaluate as "good." Our values shape our beliefs and attitudes, and, in turn, our beliefs and attitudes shape our values. Values define norms or guidelines for behavior. Our values are also laden with emotions. As such, values influence our evaluations of situations and motivate the actions we take (Day, 2003).

Think back for a moment to the example of Miss Douglas. What does she value, and how do her values affect her behavior? It's apparent that Miss Douglas values her independence. Her accident interrupted her usual ways of taking charge, but it didn't change her desire for independence. In fact, her behavior, which staff members labeled "noncompliant and uncooperative," really allows her to maintain control. Her priority of independence translates into emotionally charged actions.

Value systems are complex networks of values that people develop either individually or collectively. Ideally, the values within these systems are congruent, or internally consistent. However, more likely than not, some conflicts exist within these systems of values. For example, when people believe that "all people are equal" and simultaneously believe that "only people who work productively are worthwhile," their values reveal inconsistencies.

Translating Values into Actions. People's orientations toward values provide both the motivation and the direction for their behavior. Within a system of values, individual values are most likely to be arranged hierarchically. Depending on the situation, one value is likely to take precedence over another.

On one level, people state their values in rather abstract terms. On another level, however, they transform their values into concrete actions. Generally, people tend to agree on abstract values and disagree about the implications of those values for concrete actions. For example, almost everyone agrees on the sanctity of life. However, upholding the sanctity of life translates into different actions with respect to abortion: Both those who favor and those who oppose legal abortion believe their actions support their values for life. In this instance, people hold a value in common yet translate that value into opposing directions for action.

Ethics Defined

While values are the implicit or explicit beliefs about what people consider good, ethics relates to what people consider correct or right. Ethics generates standards that direct one's conduct. With respect to professional ethics and values, ethics represents "values in action" (Levy, 1976, p. 233). Specifically, "social work ethics represents behavioral expectations or preferences that are associated with social work responsibility" (p. 79). Ethics embodies

> preferences not to the extent that they have *proven* worthy of realization but because they have been *deemed* worthy of realization. These preferences continue to be compiled, modified, and crystallized in response to accumulating knowledge and technology and in response to social change. Despite their evolving nature, however, they rest on a fairly constant and fundamental value base with which social workers have been identified since the advent of their professionalization. (pp. 79–80)

Microethics and Macroethics. *Microethics* deals with those standards and principles that direct practice. *Macroethics,* or social ethics, is "concerned with organizational arrangements and values as well as ethical principles that underlie and guide social policies" (Conrad, 1988, p. 604). Microethics guides Rose's work with Miss Douglas. Questions that the micro perspective on ethics raises include: Does self-determination take precedence over safety issues? Does sharing information about Miss Douglas with the rest of the medical team constitute a breach of confidentiality? If Miss Douglas has family members, should they be included in the process of decision making? On the other hand, macroethics concerns the organizational context of the hospital that employs Rose and the social policies about health care. Issues that macroethics raises include how to distribute limited health care resources equitably, how to extend health care coverage to all citizens, and how and when to honor the instructions of advanced directives and living wills.

Ethical Behavior. Ethical behavior comprises actions that uphold moral obligations and comply with standards for practice as prescribed by ethical codes. Ethical codes derive from the profession's base of values. In discussing Max Weber's ethics of responsibility, Levy (1973) indicates that social workers should be accountable for all of the foreseeable results of their actions. However, ethical social work practice is not measured by practice outcomes; instead it "transcends the requisites of competence" (p. 81). Ethical behavior is based on an interpretation of the application of values. Because people interpret abstract imperatives differently, they often disagree about what constitutes ethical behavior or "appropriate actions."

The Foundation of Professional Social Work Values

Values infuse the historical roots as well as the contemporary practice of social work. Understanding the shifts in values that have occurred brings the common values of contemporary social work into sharper focus. Over the years, the focus of social work values has shifted from concerns about the morality of individual clients to concerns about the morality of professional behavior (Reamer, 1990; 1994).

Focus on Individual Morality

In late-nineteenth-century England, attitudes toward the poor reflected the belief that

> people were poor because they refused to profit by the abundant opportunities to improve their condition. Thrift and virtue, thriftlessness and immorality were synonymous. To be destitute to the point of having to ask for relief was to be guilty of a defect in character—in short, to be in need of "reform." (de Schweinitz, 1961, p. 143)

Late-nineteenth-century social welfare activities in the United States reveal similar attitudes. For example, Robert M. Hartley, a charity organization leader with the Association for Improving the Condition of the Poor, suggested that the poor required guidance if they were to escape the evils of intemperance, laziness, and idleness (Lubove, 1965).

An overview of the activities of a district agent with the Boston Associated Charities reveals that time was spent on investigating, listening to troubles, and advising families of their options. Agents focused on reforming individuals rather than addressing social injustices through social reform:

> The day of one such agent began with a refusal of aid for a sick woman in the district because of alleged intemperance. The appeal for fifteen cents from an "undoubted tramp" was denied and the supplicant advised to earn his keep at Stephen's Lodging-house. Learning from a visitor that a woman "known to be good and industrious" was ill, the agent authorized a fifty-cent contribution for food. Referrals from the Children's Aid Society and a dispensary physician were brought to the attention of the agent who also sent two cases of her own to the officers in charge of vagrancy: a boy of eight found selling newspapers, and a woman with a baby caught begging. She turned down a request from a young woman for money to help pay the rent, claiming that the applicant was one of a family of six, only one of whom was willing to work. . . . A prescription was filled for a family, sewing obtained for a needy client, and an extension of time procured for a woman and child who had been placed in the Temporary House for Working Women. The day ended with an examination of a report which had been requested from the police and a dispensary, and a consultation with a lawyer concerning a man unjustly deprived of his wages. (Lubove, 1965, p. 12)

These references illustrate social welfare's focus on the morality of individuals at the turn of the century. This point of view emphasizes the character and morality of clients and clearly distinguishes between the "worthy" and "unworthy" poor.

The Moral Imperatives for the Profession

Today, concern with morality has shifted from a focus on the morality of clients to a focus on the morality of social work, the behavior of practitioners and actions of the social work profession (Reamer, 1990). The early-twentieth-century American settlement house movement provided an impetus for this shift with its emphasis on social rather than individual reform. The experience of the Great Depression of the 1930s provides further evidence of the ways in which social and economic problems contribute to human needs (Reamer, 1995).

Held in the 1920s to identify commonalities in social work practice, the Milford Conference delineated a philosophy for social work and raised numerous value-oriented questions. An excerpt from the conference proceedings notes the centrality of values in conference participants' concerns:

> The social case worker has need of a thought-out system of social values not only to clarify his general purpose and orient him in relation to theories of social progress, but also to guide him in every professional contact. Such practical questions as the following illustrate the need of a philosophy:
>
> - What are the client's rights as an individual?
> - What are his obligations to his family?
> - Under what circumstances is it good to try to maintain a family as such unbroken?
> - Under what circumstances is it good to try to break up a family? (i.e., What values are involved for individuals, groups, society?)
> - Is coercion justified in any given case?
> - How far and when is individual dependency a public responsibility, how far and when a private responsibility?
> - What individual social needs other than subsistence are public responsibility: education; health examination; mental test; vocational guidance; recreation; etc.?
> - How far should social environment be altered in the interest of the sick or unadjusted person?
> - In what circumstances, if any, should the client's confidence be violated by the social caseworker?
> - Is the social caseworker responsible for law enforcement? (American Association of Social Workers, 1929, p. 28)

The Milford Conference played a pivotal role in bringing together diverse factions within the social work profession and in raising questions about the profession's value base. Essentially, the Milford Conference focused on the morality of the profession. While formulated over 50 years ago, these questions remain critical for understanding the role of values in social work practice today.

Common Values of Social Work

The value base of the social work profession reflects fundamental beliefs about the nature of humankind, change, and qualities that have intrinsic worth:

> Since its central concern is humanness and the development of humanity, social work values must be radically humane—they must render up and strike at the roots of the human condition. At the very least, the values must include equality, social justice, freeing of life styles, rightful access to social resources, and liberation of self-powers. These values require social workers to stand as liberators of human beings from constricting, obsolete, and oppressive social situations. (Hunter & Saleeby, 1977, p. 62)

The key elements of the social work value base have endured changes within social work as a developing profession. The social work profession's commitment to quality of life, social justice, and human dignity and worth, evident in the earliest years of the profession, persists today (Reamer, 1995; 1999).

Core Values. The Council on Social Work Education identifies several core values as central to all levels of social work education. Its statement is consistent with social work values listed by other professional organizations such as the NASW and the International Federation of Social Workers (IFSW). According to the CSWE (2001)

> The profession of social work is based on the values of service, social and economic justice, dignity and worth of the person, importance of human relationships, and integrity and competence in practice. With these values as defining principles, the purposes of social work are:
>
> - To enhance human well-being and alleviate poverty, oppression, and other forms of social injustice.
> - To enhance the social functioning and interactions of individuals, families, groups, organizations, and communities by involving them in accomplishing goals, developing resources, and preventing and alleviating distress.
> - To formulate and implement social policies, services, and programs that meet basic human needs and support the development of human capacities.
> - To pursue policies, services, and resources through advocacy and social or political actions that promote social and economic justice.
> - To develop and use research, knowledge, and skills that advance social work practice.
> - To develop and apply practice in the context of diverse cultures. (p. 6)

Continuum of Professional Values. The social work profession expresses its values along a continuum from general to specific (Compton & Galaway, 1999). In general terms, value statements express the abstract ideals usually accepted by all members of the profession. In concrete terms, actions operationalize values. For example, if social workers believe in the dignity and worth of all people, how do their beliefs shape their actions? If social workers believe people should have access to resources, what are the implications of their beliefs for advocacy? If social workers believe people have the right to self-determination, how does this change their approach to practice? One of the challenges of becoming a professional social worker is identifying with the values of the profession and incorporating them in actions. In fact, Perlman (1976) says that "a value has small worth, except as it is moved, or is moveable, from believing into doing, from verbal affirmation into action" (p. 381). More likely than not, specific choices of actions represent a variety of interpretations of how social workers should translate values into actions.

The Value Context of Social Work

Many systems, each with its own unique value orientation, converge in social work practice, creating tension. Among these systems are the sociocultural milieu, agency settings, clients, and social workers. As systems intertwine, their interactive mix creates a unique hierarchy of competing values and conflicting loyalties (Figure 5.1). For instance, approaches to resolving social problems may reflect opposing community and professional priorities; the appropriateness of intervention methods prescribed by agency policy could conflict with the social worker's professional opinion about which intervention strategies are appropriate

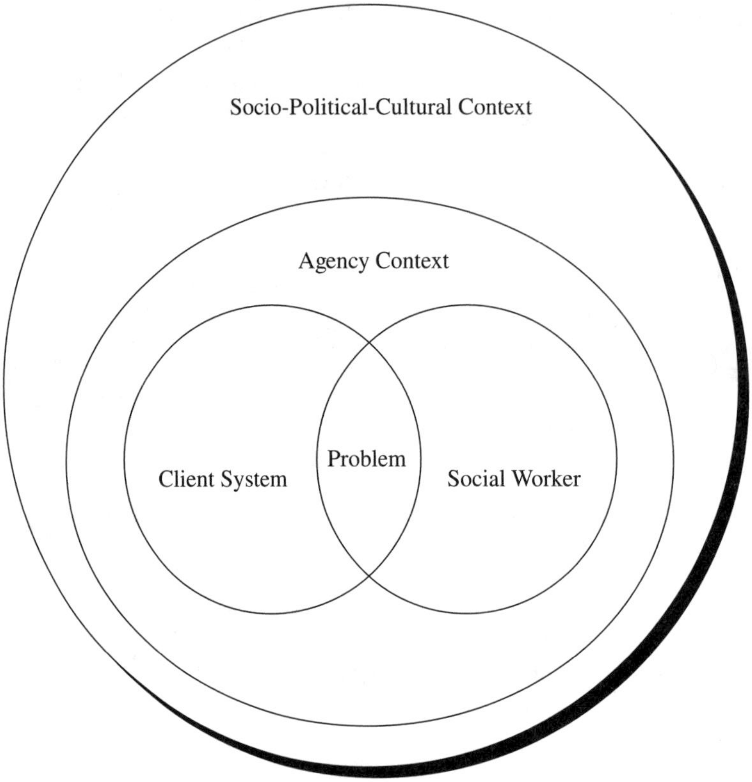

FIGURE 5.1 Values Context of Social Work

for a given client; and family members' disagreement about the "right" solution may place social workers in a quandary when balancing issues of self-determination.

Society and Values

At the most macrolevel of analysis, social and cultural values provide the broad context for understanding the interactions among client systems and social workers. Social and cultural values become apparent in commonly held beliefs and traditions. For example, with regard to dominant values in the society of the United States, we can identify in the Judeo-Christian religious tradition; we identify a sense of human dignity and worth and communal responsibility "for one's neighbors." In the puritan ethic, we see the emphasis on the morality of work and the evaluation of people by the products of their labor. And in the individualistic interpretation of democratic ideals, we realize the significance placed on individual pursuits, competition, and autonomy. In any society, dominant values become the benchmark for measuring citizens' worth. Those who do not meet the mark experience the deleterious effects of denigrating comments as well as prejudicial attitudes and discriminatory behaviors. Centermost in the United States are institutionalized racism, sexism, ageism, heterosexism, regionalism, and ethnocentrism, among others. All of these dominant value imperatives—and all of the other

BOX 5.1

Reflections on Diversity

Minority Values: A Valued Strength

Individualism and the democratic ideals of self-determination, free choice, and social responsibility form the basis for social work values. Lum (1996) challenges social workers to examine these professional values in the light of minorities' values—to focus on family, spirituality, and ethnic identity in the context of collective entities such as the family, church, and nature.

Lum indicates that the following social work values link with values of minorities:

- Social work values family unification, parental leadership, respect for the elderly, and collective family decision-making.
- Social work encourages the healthy application of religious and spiritual beliefs and practices, which join the individual and family to collective institutions and cosmic forces in the universe, resulting in harmony, unity, and wholeness.
- Social work seeks to use family kinship and community networks as supportive means of treatment for persons who are able to benefit from collective helping.
- Social work values the rediscovery of ethnic language and cultural identity, which strengthen a person's relationship to his or her heritage. (p. 62)

Clearly, social work values are compatible with many minority values. Translating social work values into action with clients who are ethnically and racially diverse requires sensitivity to and appreciation of their belief systems and life experiences. Ethnically sensitive practitioners account for diverse value orientations in all aspects of their practice.

---

values that are a part of our own particular heritage—influence how we view social work and social welfare, configure personal and social problems, and envision solutions.

Societal Values and Social Welfare. In his now classic work, *The Giving and Taking of Help,* Alan Keith-Lucas (1972) describes three predominant societal values that undergird society's mandate for social welfare. First, the capitalist-puritan belief system popularizes the American creed. As such, it is the most powerful of the belief systems. With its emphasis on material achievement and success, this belief system is more puritan than capitalist. It links God's favor with success so that "the successful are thought of as 'good' and the unsuccessful as 'bad' or inferior. . . . Those who do not exercise sufficient ambition or will are shamed, exhorted, punished, or left to the workings of the economic system" (p. 138). Basic assumptions of the capitalist-puritan belief system include:

1. Man is responsible for his own success or failure.
2. Human nature is basically evil, but can be overcome by an act of will.
3. Man's primary purpose is the acquisition of material prosperity, which he achieves through hard work.
4. The primary purpose of society is the maintenance of law and order in which this acquisition is possible.

5. The unsuccessful, or deviant, person is not deserving of help, although efforts should be made, up to a point, to rehabilitate him or to spur him to greater efforts on his own behalf.
6. The primary incentives to change are to be found in economic or physical rewards and punishments. (p. 138)

In general, the capitalist-puritan position is not likely to lead people to help each other. This position holds individuals responsible for their own actions. Threats of punishments and promises of rewards induce change: "Helping becomes a simple matter of us arranging the appropriate rewards and punishments. There is no room for relationship, or concern for another, except in a highly condescending or judgmental way" (p. 142).

Most social scientists and many liberals adopt a second view, the humanist-positivist-utopian belief system. Underlying assumptions include the ideas "that all human suffering is undesirable, and should be prevented, or at least alleviated, that all human behavior is the result of interrelationship between the biological organism and its environment and that the scientific method is basic to an understanding of man" (p. 143). The assumptions of this position include:

1. The primary purpose of society is to fulfill man's needs both material and emotional.
2. If man's needs were fulfilled, then he would attain a state that is variously described . . . as that of goodness, maturity, adjustment, or productivity, in which most of his and society's problems would be solved.
3. What hampers him from attaining this state is external circumstance, not in general under his individual control. This . . . has been ascribed to lack of education, economic circumstance, his childhood relationships, and his social environment.
4. These circumstances are subject to manipulation by those possessed of sufficient technical and scientific knowledge, using, in general, what is known as "the scientific method," and consequently
5. Man, and society, are ultimately perfectible. (pp. 139–140)

People who adopt this view differ in how they envision ways to create ideal societies. For example, "Dewey saw education as the answer; Marx, reform of the economic system; and Freud, the early Freud at least, the removal of repressions" (p. 140).

Finally, the Judeo-Christian traditions form the basis for the third belief system. Biblical scriptures reveal this view's assumptions about humankind and the universe. Judeo-Christian concepts include nonjudgmentalism, self-determination, equality of opportunity, and the ultimate worth and dignity of all of humankind. Its basic assumptions include:

1. man is a created being one of whose major problems is that he acts as if he were not and tries to be autonomous;
2. man is fallible, but at the same time capable of acts of great courage or unselfishness;
3. the difference between men, in terms of good and bad, is insignificant compared with the standard demand by their creator, and, as a consequence, man cannot judge his fellow in such terms;
4. man's greatest good lies in terms of his relationship with his fellows and with his creator;
5. man is capable of choice, in the "active and willing" sense, but may need help in making this choice;
6. love is always the ultimate victor over force. (p. 141)

This view contrasts with the capitalist-puritan and humanist-positivist-utopian belief systems. In the Judeo-Christian tradition, people "are neither the evil beings of capitalist-puritan belief, nor [are they] as good as many humanist-positivist-utopians believe" (p. 148). The Judeo-Christian view recognizes humans as fallible, but also sees them as having capabilities. This view holds that people can recognize problems, make choices, and seek solutions in ways that transcend fallibility.

All these sources relate to the relationship between society and individuals and the attitudes of society toward various constituencies that make up the society. Values operate explicitly and implicitly. Ageism, sexism, classism, racism, and colonialism are intertwined in the institutional structure and interpersonal networks of U.S. society.

Social ideologies affect the attitudes held toward those who receive services and the stipulations for service provisions. Two predominant themes pervade social work history in this respect—humanitarian and punitive approaches to service delivery. Humanitarian ideals recognize that societal conditions impinge on individuals' abilities to meet their own needs. The humanitarian approach supports humankind through services that are citizens' rights and through seeking social and economic reform. The punitive approach places blame directly on individuals and makes the receiving of services as unbearable and intolerable as possible.

Values and the Social Work Profession

The discussion so far has examined the influence that society has on social work. Societal values influence individuals, groups and communities, agencies, social workers, and the social work profession; however, these elements also influence the values espoused by society. Bertha Capen Reynolds (1951) describes the inseparable relationship between social work and society:

> Our practice has its roots and finds its opportunity in the kind of concern for the well-being of people which society really has. What we social workers believe about people, then, cannot be uninfluenced by what society wants of us. Neither can the philosophy we hold and the practice of social work in our hands fail to make an imprint upon the society of our time. (p. 163)

Historically, the relationship between society and social work is envisioned as reciprocal. Yet, exploring the potential relationship between society and social work can lead to interesting speculations. We might conclude that society commissions social worker professionals to work with people who are oppressed, poor, and disenfranchised to make right the wrongs of social ills. Or is it more accurate to conclude that society commissions social workers to be the "dirty workers" to do what others won't?

Critical areas for exploration include the impact of the puritan work ethic, democratic ideas, the implications of individualism, and the various "isms" on social welfare policy and program development, on the attitudes of clients themselves and others, and on the evolution of social work values. Among the challenges facing social workers are balancing client's rights with social control issues and working toward social reform and social change through education and advocacy.

Societal Authorization. Societies sanction professions, that is, give professionals the authority to function in the context of legitimate professions. In essence, society, through its sanction, recognizes a profession and allows and encourages it to function in the society. The authority any society grants the social work profession is predicated on the willingness of that society to continue to authorize and fund professional activities. At a recent conference of the International Federation of Social Workers, social workers from a number of countries reported the dangers of adopting an empowerment-oriented approach to social work in nondemocratic countries. In these circumstances, promoting social action and social change can lead to serious consequences. Social workers may lose not only their positions in social service delivery systems, but also their freedom and their lives!

The Agency and Values

A whole spectrum of values influences social work processes, including the value system of the organization in which social work transactions take place. Organizational value systems include such factors as the organization's philosophy and mission, policies and procedures, and eligibility priorities.

The agency mission statement implicitly reflects the values upon which the agency is founded and explicitly states the purpose of the organization. Values are one standard against which we can measure the success of the day-to-day operation of programs and services. If an agency subscribes to the importance of human dignity and worth, communication in intra- and interagency relationships and in relationships with clients should demonstrate respect. If agency values include valuing diversity, staffing patterns, programs and services, and organizational style should reflect multiculturalism. If agency values emphasize empowerment, then a focus on strengths, collaborative partnerships, support for social action activities, and consumer involvement in planning, policy development, staff development, program evaluation, and research should all be apparent. Effective agencies continuously strive to match the realities of the day-to-day delivery of services with the ideal of their vision of values.

Furthermore, a social work agency is obliged to uphold the values of the profession. Agencies foster ethical practice by establishing systems of accountability, initiating peer review processes, sponsoring in-service training and consultation that focuses on ethical issues in social work practice, instituting appeals procedures, and organizing a committee on ethics in social work for consultation on "thorny" dilemmas (Loewenberg, Dolgoff, & Harrington, 2000). The NASW has developed professional standards for personnel practice, including personnel selection, staff development, evaluation, promotion, benefits, and termination. Standards for specific settings include those for health care, long-term care facilities, child protection, clinical social work, case management, and school social work. When agencies do not uphold the prescribed standards of the profession, they are subject to adjudication processes and reprimands by the ethics committee of the NASW.

Critical areas include priorities for programs and program development, decisions about who will be served and who will not, and the consonance of the policy and practice of the agency with the values and ethical code of the profession. Challenges are directed toward creating a work milieu that empowers social workers as well as clients and toward grassroots or client involvement in policy and program development. Challenges may also focus on trying to determine "the greater good" or the "lesser evil" as value-conscious boards of directors and legislators struggle with policy issues.

The Client System and Values

All people have their own unique sets of values. Factors that influence values include racial or ethnic heritage, gender, educational level, and socioeconomic status. We may be tempted to generalize about the value preferences of ethnic and cultural groups; however, it is important to remember that inevitably large variations exist within each group. Solomon (1983) emphasizes within group differences in her discussion of people who are oppressed:

> [T]he evidence that oppressed minority groups tend to place higher value on kinship structures, religion, or primary-group relationships than the majority group should not lead one to directly infer that an individual who belongs to the oppressed minority group will have the same value priorities. For example, if 40 percent of the members of the oppressed minority group hold traditional religious values as compared with only 10 percent of the majority group, the difference will be significant. Yet, in each instance most members do not hold those values. (p. 868)

On the surface, some ethnic and cultural groups seem similar. Upon closer inspection, we discover that how members of each group prioritize values differs considerably. For example, although all women may share some characteristics, women are not all alike. Although people with similar educational levels may share particular perspectives on values, their values may also be quite different. Although communities may have similar structures and political organizations in common, their priorities and expectations may differ. In a global context, generalizations that indicate similarities among all industrialized or developing nations ignore individual differences created by factors such as courses of history, availability of natural resources, views of humanity, and political ideologies.

Moreover, comparisons between groups create a false sense of division. For example, research identifies statistically significant differences between males and females with respect to visual-spatial reasoning and language abilities. A closer inspection of the data reveals a continuum of abilities present in both men and women that when characterizing individual men or women makes these group distinctions meaningless. Group differences may be statistically significant; however, even given these differences, the characteristics of group members may be similar. Social workers draw on generalizations; however, they individualize clients' situations to understand particular systems in their specific circumstances.

Effective social work practice considers each client system's unique base of values. Sometimes social workers and clients seek solutions within clients' existing frameworks of values. Other times, social workers change clients' values. However, clients' values should become targets for change only when these values conflict with the welfare of others or interfere with the achievement of the clients' own goals (Solomon, 1983).

The Presenting Problem and Values

Often, clients' problems are value-laden. Clients' problems are by nature moral or ethical, infused with value conflicts and ethical dilemmas. Clients also exhibit behaviors that have harmed themselves and others (Siporin, 1985). In fact, even "difficulties in social functioning are more understood as disorders of moral action and relationships" (p. 230). Value issues, including feelings about the problem, the moral decision-making nature of many problems, and society's judgment that a particular behavior is immoral, abound in the problems clients present.

Questions such as "What should I do?" signal the presence of a moral dilemma. Sometimes clients' difficulties involve *intersystem conflicts,* or conflicts between themselves and others (Goldstein, 1987). For example, parents may disagree on what behavioral expectations for their children should be. Staff groups may disagree on funding priorities. Communities may argue about how to approach a social problem they have in common.

Other times, people experience *intrasystem conflicts,* or moral dilemmas within themselves (Goldstein, 1987). For example, an individual partner may struggle with whether he or she should remain committed to the marriage union, or a group may experience disagreement within its membership about which program options are "right."

In either type of conflict, clients' decisions are complicated and ambiguous, rather than simple, clear-cut choices. Their quandaries may be that they find themselves between what they perceive as two "right options" or two "wrong options." Clients may also experience a complicated combination of rights and wrongs. Intervention often involves "helping people to choose their ways of life in light of ethical principles, so as to do good and to act rightly and justly" (Siporin, 1985, p. 210). Value-conscious social workers understand the potential value-laden nature of presenting problems and work in partnerships with clients rather than imposing values on them.

Social Workers' Personal Values

Social workers enter their profession as individuals with established networks of values. Although often subtle, factors such as family, peers, spirituality, cultural background, and personal experiences influence personal values.

Becoming professionals requires social workers to explore their values and confront their biases. However, becoming a professional does not mean giving up all values. Rather, social workers need to develop an understanding of how their personal viewpoints impinge on their professional functioning. The critical question is whether personal values create barriers. When social workers are preoccupied with their own values or impose their values on clients, they are less likely to notice the role of clients' values (Levy, 1976). When values are similar, social workers may presume congruence between their views and clients' and miss both subtle and unmistakable differences. Likewise, when the values of clients and social workers are dissimilar, social workers may interpret clients' views from the bias of their own points of view rather than in the context of the clients' own unique circumstances.

Self-Awareness and Values. Becoming self-aware is an important element of becoming effective professionals. Some people may try to fool themselves into thinking that they can be a "blank slate" when it comes to values—that they can somehow be value-neutral mediators when ethical choices are made. Effective workers must be aware of themselves as walking value systems, be conscious of what those values are, evaluate them rationally, and change those that require changing. If people are free enough to acknowledge particular biases, they are in a position to overcome those biases. Good social workers "always return to the need to be self-aware and self-knowing, for authentic dialogue with and true understanding of our clients, as well as for effective helping" (Siporin, 1985, p. 214).

Generally speaking, those who enter the field of social work agree with the abstract values of the profession. However, even though social work professionals may espouse the same general values, they may differ greatly in their interpretations of how to apply professional values to their practice (Freud & Krug, 2002; Linzer, 1999; Reamer, 1994; 1999).

Social Work Codes of Ethics

Codes of ethics are written in general terms, reflecting the philosophy of the profession and prescribing expectations for proper conduct. As such, codes guide decision making, regulate professional behavior, and set a standard by which to evaluate the profession. Ethical codes

1. Provide practitioners with guidance when faced by practice dilemmas that include ethical issues.
2. Protect the public from charlatans and incompetent practitioners.
3. Protect the profession from governmental control; self-regulation is preferable to state regulation.
4. Enable professional colleagues to live in harmony with each other by preventing the self-destruction that results from internal bickering.
5. Protect professionals from litigation; practitioners who follow the code are offered some protection if sued for malpractice. (Loewenberg & Dolgoff, 1992, p. 34)

Codes of ethics tend to be written in general terms in order to reflect the philosophy of the profession and present a model for professional behavior. Codes provide the clearest guidance for professionals when the situation at hand represents a choice between a good and a bad decision. Codes are less definitive when selecting a course of action that rests on a choice between two good decisions or two bad decisions (Loewenberg, Dolgoff, & Harrington, 2000).

The NASW Code of Ethics

The NASW (1999a) *Code of Ethics* provides guidelines for ethical practice. See Appendix A. These ethical guidelines derive from a set of ethical principles, which are, in turn, based on the core values of the social work profession. Social work's core values include service, social justice, dignity and worth of the person, importance of human relationships, integrity, and competence. Corollary ethical principles include the following:

- Social workers' primary goal is to help people in need and to address social problems. . . .
- Social workers challenge social injustice. . . .
- Social workers respect the inherent dignity and worth of the person. . . .
- Social workers recognize the central importance of human relationships. . . .
- Social workers behave in a trustworthy manner. . . .
- Social workers practice within their areas of competence and develop and enhance their professional expertise. (pp. 5–6)

The *Code of Ethics* guides social workers' professional conduct and serves as a basis for the adjudication of ethical issues if someone alleges that a social worker's conduct has deviated

BOX 5.2
Reflections on Empowerment

Ethical Issues in Working with Older Adults Who Are Frail

Aligning home health supports is a strategy of case managers in aging services to empower older adults to remain in their own homes. Community resources such as home-delivered meals, visiting nurses, homemaker assistance, and adult day care provide elderly clients with a comfortable and safe home environment. Well-planned and coordinated at-home care reduces unnecessary nursing home placements.

Empowerment-oriented case managers face ethical dilemmas in decisions regarding at-home care for older adults who are frail. Ethical issues arise in those situations when case managers question whether their decisions are right and proper. Ethical questions emerge in conflicts between the client's interest and the interest of family members, between the client's wishes and the case manager's professional opinion about the client's needs, and between the client's preferences for certain services and the affordability of these services (Kane & Caplan, 1992).

Ethical questions that case managers who work with adults who are frail grapple with include the following:

- When is the client's right to self-determination and decision making countered by health risks and safety issues?
- At what point is advocacy for independent living at odds with the necessity of nursing home placement?
- How do case managers balance issues of client autonomy versus client protection?
- Who ultimately makes placement decisions?
- What limits are placed in the client's choice in risk situations even though the client has the capacity to make his or her decisions?

Answering these ethical questions is not easy. Individual circumstances, clients' preferences, and competency criteria must be considered. Nonetheless, the ethical principle of autonomy is closely related to the social work principle of client-self-determination. A client's rights to make decisions for him- or herself may conflict with what practitioners believe is in the best interest of the client. To the extent that the client is competent to make decisions and is fully informed of risks associated with those decisions, self-determination should prevail. Case managers may rely on supervisory input and case reviews by agency ethics committees in developing appropriate care plans.

---

from professional standards. The *Code of Ethics* explicates general principles for exercising ethical judgments and fulfilling professional responsibilities to clients and colleagues, in practice settings, as professionals, to the social work profession, and to the broader society. The NASW *Code of Ethics* serves six purposes:

1. The *Code* identifies core values on which social work's mission is based.
2. The *Code* summarizes broad ethical principles that reflect the profession's core values and establishes a set of specific ethical standards that should be used to guide social work practice.

3. The *Code* is designed to help social workers identify relevant considerations when professional obligations conflict or ethical uncertainties arise.
4. The *Code* provides ethical standards to which the general public can hold the social work profession accountable.
5. The *Code* socializes practitioners new to the field to social work's mission, values, ethical principles, and ethical standards.
6. The *Code* articulates standards that the social work profession itself can use to assess whether social workers have engaged in unethical conduct. (p. 2)

The International Code of Ethics

The International Federation of Social Workers (IFSW) identifies values and ethical behaviors common to social work practice throughout the world. The International Federation is an organization representing colleagues and professional associations from 77 countries. This organization identifies several professional values that it claims transcend cultural differences. The preamble of the *International Code of Ethics* (see Appendix B) summarizes these universal values:

> Social work originates variously from humanitarian, religious and democratic ideals and philosophies and has universal application to meet human needs arising from personal-societal interactions and to develop human potential. Professional social workers are dedicated to service for the welfare and self-fulfillment of human beings; to the development and disciplined use of validated knowledge regarding human and societal behavior; to the development of resources to meet individual, group, national and international needs and aspirations; and to the achievement of social justice. (IFSW, 1994, Sec. 3.1)

The Radical Code of Ethics

Arguably, social activism and the social justice commitments of social work make social work a radical profession. Proponents of the radical perspective, Bertha Reynolds and Jeffrey Galper, saw "social work values and ideals as very compatible with political radicalism, and even revolutionary zeal, since they place the concerns of people above profits, and seek to empower the poor, the downtrodden, and the discriminated against to fight for social change" (Wagner, 1990, p. 7).

Radical social work activities that sought progressive change in the social environment paralleled the mass protest movements in the 1930s and the social movements of the 1960s, including the civil rights, antiwar, women's, and welfare rights movements. Although radical social work activities surged and declined with the flow and ebb of these movements, the radical perspective has significantly affected the social work profession. Social work moved leftward in the 1970s and 1980s, incorporating an egalitarian posture with consumers of social services and embracing a consciousness about social class, race relations, and sexual discrimination (Wagner, 1990).

Jeffrey Galper (1975) developed the *Code of Ethics for Radical Social Service* to respond to the conservative bias he perceived in the conventional goals of practice reflected in the NASW *Code of Ethics.* Galper's *Code* captures the goals and ideologies of radical social service workers. The radical perspective reflects the call for a transformation of social welfare along socialist lines and a revolutionary change in society to create a noncapitalistic welfare state. Among the planks Galper proposes in the radical code of ethics are the following:

- I regard as my primary obligation the welfare of all human kind.
- I will work toward the development of a society that is committed to the dictum, "from each according to his or her ability, to each according to his or her need."
- I will struggle for the realization of a society in which my personal interests and my personal actions are consistent with my interests and actions as a worker.
- I will consider myself accountable to all who join in the struggle for social change and will consider them accountable to me for the quality and extent of the work we perform and the society we create.
- I will work to achieve the kind of world in which all people can be free and open with one another in all matters.
- I will use information gained from my work to facilitate humanistic, revolutionary change in the society.
- I will treat the findings, views, and actions of colleagues with the respect due them.
- I will use all the knowledge and skill available to me in bringing about a radically transformed society.
- I recognize my responsibility to add my ideas and findings to our society's knowledge and practice.
- I accept my responsibility to help protect the community against unethical practice by any individuals or organizations in the society.
- I commit myself to use myself fully in the struggle for revolutionary change.
- I support the principle that all persons can and must contribute to the realization of a humanized society.
- I accept responsibility for working toward the creation and maintenance of conditions in society that enable all people to live by this Code.
- I contribute my knowledge, skills, and support to the accomplishment of a humanistic, democratic, communal socialist society. (pp. 224–227)

The Significance of Ethical Codes

Knowing, understanding, and applying a professional code of ethics is important to practitioners for several reasons. Most states now require licensure to practice social work. Licensure examinations typically contain a number of pertinent questions about the professional code of ethics. Obviously, professionals must conduct themselves appropriately by integrating their professional behavior with their personal behavior.

Ethical Principles for Social Work

Social workers transform the abstract values of the profession into principles for practice. Then they translate these principles into concrete actions in specific situations. Values abstractly shape social workers' ways of thinking and concretely direct their actions through principles for social work practice (Biestek, 1957; Goldstein, 1973; Levy, 1976; Perlman, 1976; Siporin, 1975). Among these are the common principles of acceptance, individualization, purposeful expression of feelings, nonjudgmental attitudes, objectivity, controlled emotional involvement, self-determination, access to resources, confidentiality, and accountability. When social workers fail to operationalize these principles, they victimize clients and disempower them. Conversely, upholding these practice principles facilitates empowerment (Table 5.1).

TABLE 5.1 Effects of Social Work Values and Principles in Action

Empowerment			*Victimization*	
Potential Effect	*Positive Manifestation*	**Social Work Values and Principles**	*Barriers*	*Potential Effect*
Affirm personhood	Affirm individuality Appreciate diversity	**Uphold uniqueness and worth**	Stereotyping Denigration Labeling	Impotence Self-fulfilling prophecy
Efficacy Competence Partnership	Develop alternatives Delineate roles	**Promote self-determination**	Control Advice Manipulation Paternalism	Incompetence Failure to change Dependency
Openness Lowered defenses	Strength perspective Active listening Empathy	**Communicate nonjudgmentally and with acceptance**	Blame Pity and sympathy Focus on deficits	Defensiveness Helplessness
Affirm rationality	Gaining perspective	**Attain objectivity**	Overidentification Coldness Distancing	Bias Distortion
Trust	Respecting privacy	**Ensure confidentiality**	Inappropriate communication	Breach of confidence Mistrust
Increased opportunities	Building linkages Developing policies and programs Coordination of services	**Provide access to resources**	Red tape Rules and regulations Discrimination	Stigma Lack of opportunities
Sanction Theory building	Process evaluation Research Follow-up	**Achieve accountability**	Lack of evaluation Burnout	Dropping out No felt responsibility

Acceptance

Social workers who accept clients treat them humanely and considerately and afford them dignity and worth (Biestek, 1957). Social workers convey acceptance by expressing genuine concern, listening receptively, acknowledging others' points of view, and creating climates of mutual respect. Acceptance implies that social workers understand clients' perspectives and welcome their views (Plant, 1970). Acceptance also suggests building on clients' strengths and recognizing the potential they each have for growth and change.

A variety of factors block social workers' communication of acceptance. These factors include lack of self-awareness, insufficient knowledge of human behavior, projection of personal perspectives onto clients' situations, prejudicial attitudes, unwarranted reassurances, and the confusion of acceptance with approval (Biestek, 1957). Acceptance may also threaten some people. Acceptance stirs apprehension in people who have histories of poor relationships or experiences of alienation in their backgrounds (Goldstein, 1973).

Tillich (1962), an existentialist theologian, commented on the roots of acceptance in his writings about the philosophy of social work. Tillich relates the roots of acceptance to love—in Greek, *agape,* and in Latin, *caritas*—a "love which descends to misery and ugliness and guilt in order to elevate. This love is critical as well as accepting, and it is able to transform what it loves" (p. 15). However, this love is not charity, which simply contributes to causes and provides an escape from the demands of critical love. In Tillich's view, the transformative action of acceptance participates in the inner selves of others and affirms their humanity.

Individualization

All people are unique and possess distinctive capabilities. When social workers affirm clients' individuality, they recognize and appreciate their unique qualities and individual differences. They treat clients as persons with rights and needs rather than as objects, "cases," or "yet another appointment." Social workers who individualize clients free themselves from bias and prejudice, avoid labeling and stereotyping, and recognize the potential of diversity. They demonstrate that clients have a right "to be individuals and to be treated not just as *a* human being but as *this* human being with personal differences" (Biestek, 1957, p. 25).

Social workers necessarily draw on generalized information about people's situations. However, they acknowledge that each client's circumstances require adaptations of these general schemes. Social work practitioners work with *this* particular client in *this* particular situation. The principle of individualization translates into actions that "begin where the client is."

Purposeful Expression of Feelings

Emotions are an integral part of human life, and people experience a range of feelings. Clients need to have opportunities to express their feelings freely (Biestek, 1957). Although it is not particularly prudent to encourage clients to gush unabashedly with sentiment or be uncontrollably tied up with anger or negative feelings, social workers need to direct clients to express their feelings purposefully. Social workers have to go beyond the content of "just the facts" to uncover feelings that underlie these facts. By listening attentively, asking relevant questions, and demonstrating tolerance and nonjudgmentalism, social workers encourage clients to share both facts and feelings.

Although expressing feelings is desirable, a client's expression of feelings must be purposeful—it must serve a purpose in the process of discovering solutions. The purpose may be to relieve pressure or tension in a way that releases the client for positive or constructive actions. Feelings also reveal the depth of the client's understanding of problems, or feelings themselves may even be the problem. For some clients, expressing their feelings to a concerned listener is a cathartic, or cleansing, experience that enables them to put their situations in perspective.

Expressing feelings solidifies relationships. The purposeful expression of feelings brings feelings into the open so that they can be dealt with constructively, allows for a more accurate understanding of the affective or emotional elements of the situation, and provides opportunities for demonstrating psychological support.

Nonjudgmental Attitudes

Nonjudgmental attitudes are foundational to effective working relationships. The premise that all humans have dignity and worth forms the basis for nonjudgmental attitudes; nonjudgmentalism presumes acceptance.

Frequently, clients are in positions where they must critically examine themselves and their situations. This requires taking risks, something they are not likely to do when they feel judged (Keith-Lucas, 1972). Nonjudgmental social work "excludes assigning guilt or innocence, or degree of client responsibility for causation of the problems or needs, but does include making evaluative judgments about the attitudes, standards, or actions of the client" (Biestek, 1957, p. 90).

Nonjudgment applies to all social work processes. However, certain circumstances—such as occasions when clients feel demoralized, stigmatized, or blame-worthy—require especially sensitive nonjudgmentalism. When clients' own feelings of blame and judgment have heightened availability, they will likely interpret others' actions through that filter of blame and judgment. For example, a couple seeking services to develop skills in resolving conflicts with their children are probably aware of the worker's attitudes toward them. However, if the problem is the sexual abuse of their children, they would be keenly aware of the slightest suggestion of judgmentalism by the social worker.

The term *nonjudgmental* may be confusing. Nonjudgmentalism signifies social workers' nonblaming attitudes and behaviors. Social workers do not judge others as good or bad, or worthy or unworthy. However, social workers do make professional judgments or decisions every day about alternative approaches and appropriate solutions, among other issues.

While nonjudgmentalism is important throughout the helping process, it is especially crucial in the initial stages. First impressions do count! And first impressions have a lasting effect, and they act as a screen through which people filter subsequent interactions. Nonjudgmental attitudes during initial contacts set the stage for developing ongoing, effective working relationships.

Nonjudgmentalism is a principle that should be applied universally, yet the personal biases of practitioners may interfere. Social workers need to recognize in themselves those circumstances that trigger judgment and blame. Professional standards oblige social workers to confront personal values and beliefs that can have detrimental effects on interactions with clients.

Objectivity

The practice principle of objectivity, or examining situations without bias, is closely related to nonjudgmentalism. To be objective, practitioners avoid injecting their personal feelings and prejudices into their relationships with clients. A highly personalized or unreasoned judgment affects practitioners' assessments of clients and their situations. Slanted judgments may cause social workers to select or to encourage one outcome over another inappropriately. Practitioners' educational experiences, understanding of the social world, life experiences, beliefs, varying positions of privilege, values, and physical predispositions all affect their objectivity.

Controlled Emotional Involvement

Social workers who control their emotional involvements with clients gain perspective from their understanding of human behavior, seek direction for relationships from the general purpose of the social work profession, and respond to clients' feelings with sensitivity (Biestek, 1957). Uncontrolled emotional responses range from a lack of investment in clients to an overidentification with clients' points of view.

Social workers who lack investment detach themselves from clients and fail to care about clients and their situations. Coldly objective social workers deal with clients as objects—people to study, manipulate, or make to change (Keith-Lucas, 1972). Professionals' detachment often leads to clients quitting their work prematurely. It may also signal to clients that workers lack concern, and it can add layers to clients' feelings of despair, worthlessness, and anger.

Overidentifying with clients means that social workers are unable to differentiate their own responsibilities from clients' responsibilities in resolving problems or that social workers confuse their own perspectives with clients' situations. Overidentification impedes objectivity and neutrality. Workers may overidentify with clients when they perceive clients as either quite similar to or quite different from themselves. There are perils in too much similarity. Help may occur initially; however, "there is no more harmful a helper than the person who has successfully solved a problem, taken credit for it, and has forgotten what it cost him to overcome it" (Keith-Lucas, 1972, p. 60). When clients' situations seem extremely sad, desolate, or bleak, charitable do-gooding can override professional judgment. Or when clients seem repugnant or their problems are extremely unbelievable or deviant, it may be difficult to control judgmentalism.

Learning to control emotional responses develops with continued practice experience. "Subjectivity diminishes with experiences. . . . This is in no sense a 'hardening' process. It is rather a mellowing process in which knowledge and acceptance of the differences among human beings, including ourselves, and security as to our professional purposes and capacities serve to steady and temper our emotional responses" (Perlman, 1957, p. 83).

BOX 5.3

Social Work Profile

Home Health and Hospice

I do think I have always been a social worker at heart, although I earned my advanced degree in social work relatively recently. As an undergraduate, I majored in anthropology—a discipline that provides an understanding of people and their context. From there, I worked in several human service settings—child welfare, the juvenile court system, and mental health. My work experiences in child welfare motivated me to complete a master's degree in social work. Subsequently, I worked in mental health services and then became a hospital-based social worker and case manager before transferring into my present position in a home health-hospice agency.

In my present position, I work with people who have a terminal illness or who have experienced an illness requiring extensive rehabilitation or supportive care. All of my clients face issues related to personal meaning and hope. Some social workers might shy away from this field of practice because they expect it would be depressing. However, that has not been my experience. Professionally, I believe I make a significant contribution to my clients' quality of life; personally, I have learned a great deal of courage. To work in home health and hospice services, professionals do have to be willing to face their own mortality and genuinely care about others. I judge my emotional health by my reactions to difficult situations. In other words, if I find I don't care, then I conclude I need to find a way to recharge.

Unlike the hospital setting where I worked with bed-bound patients in their hospital rooms, I now make home visits. I am amazed at what a difference the home setting makes to the distribution of power within the social worker–client relationship. In the hospital, even when I attempted to level the playing field, patients lying in bed dressed in hospital gowns deferred to medical authorities, including me, the social worker. Now, when I go into clients' homes as an invited guest, they are more likely to take charge, even when they are lying down.

I have always been drawn to variety, so I thrive on the fact that, in my job, no two days are alike. I work with people of all ages and life circumstances—peoples whose lives are complicated by illness and rehabilitation. My job involves doing intake assessments; counseling; facilitating nursing home placements, referrals to community based-services, and arrangements for respite care; providing emotional support and grief counseling; and working with families and groups. Since I work in a bi-state area, I have had to learn about the idiosyncrasies of service delivery in two states as well as the differences in program eligibility requirements and restrictions. Also, I have opportunities to collaborate with other community professionals on such projects as a multidisciplinary elder abuse review team.

There are many changes afoot in health care. The press to expand the base of managed care to limit expenditures, yet maintain access and affordability causes all medical professionals to reexamine systems of delivery. At the same time, we must find ways to address the health care needs of all community members—those who have health insurance and those who don't. Even with reforms, some things are not likely to change. Patients will still need someone to listen to them and hear what *they* are saying. They will still need information about their options, opportunities to think through the consequences of their choices, and support for the choices they make. They will still need someone who will provide links to resources, guide them through the medical and social service bureaucracies, and advocate their causes. In other words, even with changes, medical social workers will have a vital role to play in health care.

Social workers achieve controlled emotional involvement through their expression of empathy. They "feel with" others—that is, they sense and respond to others' feelings. "Empathy is being able to finish a [client's] sentence. Being empathic, though, is *not* finishing that sentence" (Book, 1988, p. 423). Empathy is antithetical to "blame"; empathy is the healing balm for blame.

Empathy provides a dynamic that differs from either sympathy or pity. If the worker's response is flavored with pity, it suggests that the client system is impoverished and has no way to find constructive solutions. Pity flaws self-determination, as clients who feel pitied often conclude that they are incapable of working toward change. If the worker's response is flavored with sympathy, it reflects "feeling like" the client system or identifying with the client, and fails to individualize the client's uniqueness. Effective social workers maintain a balance between accepting clients and confronting inappropriate behavior. Empathy is an "act of loving imagination" that empowers clients to work toward goals and make plans for change without absolving them from taking responsibility for their actions (Keith-Lucas, 1972).

Self-Determination

With the principle of self-determination, social workers recognize the "right and need of clients to freedom in making their own choices and decisions" (Biestek, 1957, p. 103). Self-determination acknowledges that sound growth emanates from within, or, as Hollis (1967) says:

> [F]or this growth from within to occur there must be freedom—freedom to think, freedom to choose, freedom from condemnation, freedom from coercion, freedom to make mistakes as well as to act wisely. Strength to understand and to act upon one's understanding comes only as one actually experiences and exercises the freedom to direct one's own thoughts and behaviors—and that is what we mean by self-determination. (p. 26)

Stated one way, self-determination means not being coerced or manipulated. Stated another way, self-determination means having the freedom or liberty to make choices. Choices depend on alternatives. There are limits to self-determination, however. According to Biestek (1957), legal restrictions, agency rules, standards, eligibility requirements, and a client's ability to make decisions limit the range of choices.

Responsible social workers create working relationships in which clients exercise choice. Imposing solutions, treating clients as subordinates, and manipulating clients' decisions are all coercive behaviors that limit clients' self-determination. In fact, Keith-Lucas (1972) says that the primary purpose of the helping relationship is to enable a client's active and willing choice. Social workers guide the helping processes, rather than maneuver clients. Clients need travel guides, not directive travel agents! Reynolds (1951) describes this eloquently: "Help must be connected with increase, not diminution, of self-respect, and it must imply the possibility of a reciprocal relationship of sharing, within a group to which both giver and recipient belong" (pp. 162–163).

Access to Resources

Having access to resources is prerequisite for developing solutions. Limited resources reduce options for solutions, and without options, people cannot choose among alternatives. All people rely on resources to meet their challenges and realize their potential.

The NASW (1999a) *Code of Ethics* is very specific in prescribing social workers' obligation to advocate the development of resources. The code implores social workers to ensure that everyone has the resources, services, and opportunities they require; to expand choices and opportunities for people who are oppressed and disadvantaged; and to improve social conditions and promote social justice by advocating legislative reforms.

Confidentiality

Confidentiality, or the right to privacy, means that clients must give express consent to disclose information such as their identity, their discussions with professionals, professional opinions about them, or their records (Barker, 2003). Since clients often share sensitive, personal material with social workers, preserving confidentiality or privacy is essential for developing trust, a key ingredient of any effective working relationship.

The status of confidentiality and privileged communication for social workers varies from state to state, as do the specific circumstances that demand disclosure of information. Circumstances surrounding suspected problems, such as child abuse or threats of violence, may be ambiguous and lead to an ethical quandary about disclosing the information. Rarely is confidentiality absolute; rather, it is relative to the particular conditions of the situation. Good practice dictates that social workers openly discuss the limits of confidentiality with their clients.

Threats to confidentiality are inherent in record keeping. Social workers can protect the privacy of recorded information about clients only up to a given point, subject to agency policy and state law. Questions of confidentiality also arise when discussions take place among multiple providers, at team conferences, or about several clients. Social workers may also be tempted to breech confidentiality by sharing stories about anxiety-provoking or particularly dramatic situations. Social workers need to be familiar with the statutes governing confidentiality and the implication of the law for practice situations, as well as their own legal obligations and constraints concerning confidentiality.

Accountability

The NASW (1999a) *Code of Ethics* holds professional social workers accountable for their personal and professional conduct and comportment. Accountability means that social workers must be competent in the methods and techniques they employ in their professional practice. It means that workers take seriously their obligation to redress discriminatory and inhumane practices, act with unquestionable professional integrity, and implement sound practice and research protocols. Accountability extends to social workers' ethical responsibilities to their clients, their colleagues and employing organizations, society, and the social work profession.

Looking Forward

The professional values and principles discussed in this chapter should be universally applied to all client systems in social work practice. Furthermore, when practice activities demonstrate these fundamental beliefs and postures about people, personal and systems efficacy and competence develop. Yet social workers are frequently challenged throughout their careers by values and ethical dilemmas. In some situations, it is difficult not to judge or to be without bias. Social workers are, after all, human, but they are also professionals and must be committed to internalizing social work values into their very beings. These same values need to be reflected in a just society. The professional mandate to promote social justice embodies the ideals of our profession. Quite often we are called upon to deal with the consequences of injustice, victimization, and oppression. To further our understanding of the effects of social injustice and the call for social justice, these issues will be explored in Chapter 6.

CHAPTER

6 Social Work and Social Justice

This particular Monday is a banner day for Mary Beth Canon. She smiles wryly at her mirrored image as she touches her name badge, with "Miss Mary B. Canon" etched on a blue-colored pin. She notices how nice her new blue smock looks. Others might comment that she is well groomed and that she dresses with careful attention to detail, but that isn't what Mary Beth is thinking about as she considers the smock. Today Mary Beth is wearing the uniform not of a probationary trainee, but of a full-fledged employee in the photocopy center at the regional office of Heartland Insurance.

Two months ago Mary Beth successfully completed a job-readiness program at a sheltered workshop site. She worked hard to learn good work habits and how to relate to coworkers and supervisors. The staff complimented her achievements and recognized her dependability. After Mary Beth completed the training program, the Heartland manager hired her to run the photocopy machine in their print shop. She had the help of a job coach, who worked alongside her as she learned the job requirements. Today Mary Beth runs copies, adds paper to the machine, and changes paper sizes with confidence. However, when the paper jams the machine, her supervisor is always available to help her get it working again.

At Heartland, the secretaries and sales staff bring papers to the print shop for photocopying. They give Mary Beth work order forms on which they indicate the number of copies they need and other requests for collating, stapling, and/or folding by circling small color-coded pictures on the form that correspond to the colored keypad of the copy machine. The form has these pictorial prompts because Mary Beth cannot read—Mary Beth has a mental retardation. When she completes each work order, Mary Beth returns the copies to the originator of the request. That person invariably smiles and says, "Thank you, Miss Canon."

From her living-room window, Mary Beth can see Pauley waiting for her outside. Pauley, who is also retarded, lives in the same supervised apartment building as Mary Beth and works in the mail room at Heartland. They ride the bus together to and from work. Pauley is Mary Beth's boyfriend. Pauley waves at Mary Beth, indicating that he has their city bus passes. She smiles and thinks, "He likes me. Maybe someday Pauley and I will get married!"

Mary Beth is gainfully employed, pays taxes, maintains her own apartment, and enjoys socializing with her friends. She is gaining mastery over the direction of her life. However, achieving this self-sufficiency and independence has been an uphill struggle. Like many people with disabilities, Mary Beth has endured the stigma associated with her mental retardation. Fortunately, Mary Beth was able to access the supports needed to open up the opportunity structures in employment and housing.

The social workers involved in Mary Beth's progress at the job-readiness program, the on-the-job training, the supervised residential apartments, and the community adjustment program treated Mary Beth as a capable and worthwhile person. While the services she received required individualized support throughout this empowering process, Mary Beth succeeded in maximizing her self-sufficiency and integration into the community. Mary Beth feels good about herself; she is proud of her accomplishments.

Mary Beth participates fully in all aspects of community life and contributes her own resources to the community. She meets the definition of a competent human system. Societal responses that maximize the full potential of people with mental retardation or other disabilities are based on the social justice principle.

Equality and justice ensure that all members of society share in the benefits that the society offers and have opportunities to reciprocate with their own contributions. A just social order accords every societal member the same basic rights, opportunities, and benefits.

Social workers share responsibility for championing the general welfare of societal members and achieving social justice. To detail the relationship between social work and social justice, this chapter

- Examines the concept of human rights, including civil rights, civil liberties, and the right to social welfare
- Presents social injustices such as racism, sexism, elitism, ageism, heterosexism, and handicapism
- Surveys the philosophical, sociological, and psychological bases of social injustice
- Describes the effects of social injustice, including oppression, dehumanization, and victimization
- Explores the interrelationships among opportunities, obstacles, and empowerment
- Discusses the implications of injustice for social work

Human Rights in Society

Human rights, civil rights, and citizens' rights to social welfare promote social justice. *Human rights* are those intrinsic rights that protect human life, ensure freedom, and secure personal liberty. *Civil rights* protect citizens from oppression by society or from subjugation by societal groups. *Citizens' rights* promote quality of life through citizens' rightful access to the resources of society.

Universal Human Rights

International laws and agreements that recognize the equal and inalienable rights of all people reflect the international consensus about protecting human rights. Examples of international human rights policies include several United Nations' agreements:

1948 *Universal Declaration of Human Rights*
1965 *International Convention on the Elimination of All Forms of Racial Discrimination*
1966 *International Covenant on Civil and Political Rights*
1966 *International Covenant on Economic, Social and Cultural Rights*
1979 *Convention on the Elimination of All Forms of Discrimination Against Women*
1984 *Convention Against Torture and Other Cruel Inhumane or Degrading Treatment or Punishment*
1989 *Convention on the Rights of the Child*
1990 *International Convention on the Protection of the Rights of All Migrant Workers and Members of Their Families* (United Nations, 1994, pp. 15–17)

These documents proclaim the primacy of human rights and delineate sanctions that condemn human rights violations.

These internationally binding agreements consider societies' similarities with respect to human needs and human rights along with societies' unique characteristics, such as geographical locations, historical developments, sociocultural characteristics, economic resources, political philosophies, and governmental structures (Tracy, 1990). For example, the United Nations' *Universal Declaration of Human Rights* (1948) deals with personal, civil, and political rights:

- The right to life, liberty, and security of persons
- The right to equality before the law
- The right to privacy in one's home and secrecy of correspondence
- The right to freedom of movement

The declaration recognizes the family as the basic societal unit, which is thereby entitled to protection by the state. In addition, the declaration supports freedom of thought, conscience, and religion and freedom of opinion and expression. Finally, it emphasizes the right to social and international order governed by law and based on mutual respect wherein each person has duties to the community.

Human rights are fundamental entitlements that are necessary for personal development and human potential (NASW, 1999b). Basic human rights are the rights to self-determination and the freedoms of life, liberty, thought, and speech; and to security of person without distinction by birth, sex, sexual orientation, race, color, language, national or social origin, property, intellect, ideology, or political conditions. Actions that deny fundamental entitlements violate human rights. Human rights includes social justice, "but transcends civil and political customs, in consideration of the basic life-sustaining needs of all human beings, without distinction" (p. 215).

Civil Rights and Civil Liberties

Civil rights and civil liberties provide citizens protection from discrimination and oppression. Founded on English law, civil rights and liberties have been refined in the U.S. legal system over the last two centuries. In the last half of the twentieth century, reform activities culminated in the passage of civil rights legislation. Laws governing employment practices, access to education and housing, and other critical equal opportunity issues give further guarantees for rights and specify sanctions against discriminatory practices (Pollard, 1995).

Civil rights provide for fair, just, and equitable dealings between governments and individual citizens and among citizens themselves. Civil liberty is "a sword with which the citizen can probe, fashion, and alter government and the conditions of society" (Schroeder, 1987, p. 280). Together, civil rights and civil liberties ensure harmony and order in society and dignity and freedom for individual citizens. Discrimination is a civil rights issue that segregates people and limits their access to societies' opportunities and resources.

Social workers have been in the vanguard of the civil rights movement for decades, advocating antidiscrimination legislation and ensuring that civil rights are central concerns of social work. Hogan and Siu (1988) define "the differential treatment received by minority children in the child welfare system . . . as a civil rights issue" (p. 496). Practices that discriminate include

- Responding more slowly to crises in minority families
- Providing less comprehensive service plans for minority families
- Removing a higher proportion of minority children from their families

People who have been historically discriminated against by society should not have to suffer further indignity from the profession whose purpose is to protect and promote their social well-being! Among the efforts to redress the infringement on the rights of these families are attempts at reducing problems that necessitate entry into the system and at "ensuring equal access, appropriateness of services, and equal treatment" (p. 497). The social work profession challenges its members to ensure civil rights by improving program delivery and supporting policies that are sensitive to the unique needs of diverse populations.

The Right to Social Welfare

The development of social welfare paralleled industrialization in the United States. The technological innovations of the Industrial Revolution created a social and economic revolution. These changes had significant implications for economic conditions, family life, and personal well-being and health. Consequently, the government responded to these changes by initiating social welfare programs to redress economic insecurity.

Principles of equal rights in education, work, and health guide social work. The United Nations' *Universal Declaration of Human Rights* (1948) incorporates these rights as follows:

> ***Article 22.***
> Everyone, as a member of society, has the right to social security and is entitled to realization, through national effort and international co-operation and in accordance with the organization and resources of each State, of the economic, social and cultural rights indispensable for his dignity and the free development of his personality.
>
> ***Article 23.***
> (1) Everyone has the right to work, to free choice of employment, to just and favourable conditions of work and to protection against unemployment.
> (2) Everyone, without any discrimination, has the right to equal pay for equal work.
> (3) Everyone who works has the right to just and favourable remuneration ensuring for himself and his family an existence worthy of human dignity, and supplemented, if necessary, by other means of social protection.
> (4) Everyone has the right to form and to join trade unions for the protection of his interests.
>
> ***Article 24.***
> Everyone has the right to rest and leisure, including reasonable limitation of working hours and periodic holidays with pay.
>
> ***Article 25.***
> (1) Everyone has the right to a standard of living adequate for the health and well-being of himself and of his family, including food, clothing, housing and medical care and necessary social services, and the right to security in the event of unemployment, sickness, disability, widowhood, old age or other lack of livelihood in circumstances beyond his control.
> (2) Motherhood and childhood are entitled to special care and assistance. All children, whether born in or out of wedlock, shall enjoy the same social protection.

Article 26.
(1) Everyone has the right to education. Education shall be free, at least in the elementary and fundamental stages. Elementary education shall be compulsory. Technical and professional education shall be made generally available and higher education shall be equally accessible to all on the basis of merit.
(2) Education shall be directed to the full development of the human personality and to the strengthening of respect for human rights and fundamental freedoms. It shall promote understanding, tolerance and friendship among all nations, racial or religious groups, and shall further the activities of the United Nations for the maintenance of peace.
(3) Parents have a prior right to choose the kind of education that shall be given to their children.

With respect to citizens' rights to social welfare, the social work profession supports rights to adequate housing, food, clothing, health care, employment, education, and any special protection required as a result of race, age, sex, sexual orientation, and physical or mental limitations (Tracy, 1990).

The Mandate for Social Justice

Social work practitioners often work with people whose rights have been violated or threatened, whose privacy has been invaded, or whose basic needs are not being met. Among the practice strategies that address these social justice issues are

- Social advocacy
- Legislation and lobbying
- Court actions
- Community education
- Resource development
- Fiscal reallocation (Tracy, 1990)

Social workers are likely to deal with conflicts between individual rights and governmental regulations and responsibilities (Schroeder, 1987). Protecting clients' civil rights to access governmental subsidies and programs such as unemployment benefits, disability payments, family assistance, and veteran's benefits and programs may require advocacy.

Social Injustice: The "Isms"

Universal human rights, civil rights, and citizens' rights to social welfare contribute to the vision of social justice. Yet the ideals of these societal rights often contrast with the realities of citizens' day-to-day experiences. People experience negative effects of racism, elitism, sexism, heterosexism, ageism, and handicapism. Populations differentiated by race, social class, sex, sexual orientation, age, and ability often experience exploitation (Table 6.1).

Societal *isms* are the prejudicial attitudes directed against groups that society identifies as "lesser"—less capable, less productive, and less normal. The isms provide rationalizations for stratified social structures that provide fewer prospects—fewer opportunities, fewer possibilities, and fewer resources—for those with lower status. Stratified structural arrange-

TABLE 6.1 The Isms

Racism	Ideology that perpetuates the social domination of one racial group by another
Elitism	Prejudice against those in lower economic classes
Sexism	Belief that one sex is superior to the other
Heterosexism	Prejudice against people whose sexual orientation differs from that of heterosexuals
Ageism	Belief that one age group is inferior to another
Handicapism	Prejudice against people who have mental or physical disabilities

ments perpetuate exploitation and dominance of some segments of society by others. Some groups of people have access to power, prestige, and resources, and others do not.

Racism

Racism is an ideology that perpetuates the social domination of one racial group by another. To legitimize their position, proponents of racism often claim that the races they label subordinate are genetically or culturally inferior. Numerous racial groups in the United States continuously struggle with the deleterious effects of racial discrimination and inequality. Although many efforts have been made to eradicate discrimination and racial inequality, racist beliefs remain deeply entrenched. Discrimination also persists because of society's tendency to maintain social structures that benefit the self-interests of powerful groups and institutions. In other words, racial group memberships in racially discriminating societies form the basis for social positions. In sum, dominant racial groups limit the mobility of others.

Racial discrimination manifests itself on three different levels: individually, organizationally, and structurally (Tidwell, 1987). *Individuals* reveal discrimination through their prejudicial attitudes and behaviors. For example, landlords discriminate racially when they screen tenant applications on the basis of race. *Organizations* that enforce policies, rules, and regulations in ways that adversely affect certain groups exhibit discrimination. For example, personnel practices that do not follow affirmative action guidelines may result in preferential hiring. Finally, at the *structural* level, discriminatory practices in one social institution limit opportunities in others. For example, denying access to educational opportunities limits employment options, which, in turn, limits choice in housing or access to health care. Discriminatory practices result in unequal distributions of opportunities and rewards.

The ideals of freedom and justice for all citizens make the struggle to achieve equality especially ironic. When people expect "justice for all," injustice is all the more profound. Throughout its history, U.S. society has denied racial groups access to societal benefits that derive from the democratic values of American society. Racial groups assigned minority status have been exploited politically and economically. They have been relegated to low-status positions—a status ascribed to individuals in the group at birth by virtue of their race. Even today, many racial and ethnic groups continue their struggle to achieve justice and freedom. Institutional discrimination, entrenched in social customs, maintains the status differential between the majority population and the racial minorities.

BOX 6.1
Reflections on Diversity

Getting to Know You
Ronee Wilson is facilitating a day-long workshop entitled "Cultural Sensitivity in Social Service Delivery" for community social workers. Ronee selected an exercise that would lead practitioners to examine their own diversity:

"People describe themselves in many different ways. They describe themselves by age, sex, race, ethnicity, sexual orientation, economic status, political views, religious affiliation, family roles, marital status, and type of employment, among other ways. For example, using these general categories, I would describe myself as a middle-class, married, African American woman, mother of two, liberal democrat, daughter, sister, and all around good friend."

"Now, using these general categories as a framework, describe yourself and consider the following questions:

- What resources and opportunities result from your identity
  ...in your personal life?
  ...in your family?
  ...in your interpersonal relationships?
  ...in your place of work?
  ...in your neighborhood?
  ...in the 'majority' community?
  ...in minority communities?
- What obstacles and consequences result from your identity
  ...in your personal life?
  ...in your family?
  ...in your interpersonal relationships?
  ...in your place of work?
  ...in your neighborhood?
  ...in the 'majority' community?
  ...in minority communities?"

Ronee used this exercise as a way for social work practitioners to understand the implications of diversity in many different aspects of life. Her probing questions challenged participants to examine and analyze how these factors shape their responses to racism, sexism, elitism, ageism, and heterosexism, and how their responses influence their practice with diverse populations.

In the 1960s, social activists brought the plight of racial groups to national attention and pressed for the passage of civil rights legislation. Their press for changes in U.S. policy resulted in legislation for school desegregation, antidiscrimination laws, a rejection of the doctrine of separate but equal facilities, and affirmative action in the workplace. To confront institutional discrimination, the civil rights movement supported equal opportunity in education and employment for minority groups. However, civil rights legislation in and of itself neither redresses discrimination nor deals with the restraints that exist in employment and educational advancement because of oppression and deprivation (Tidwell, 1987). What is required in addition to structural changes cannot be legislated—a social conscience that will not tolerate prejudicial attitudes that lead to discrimination and oppression.

Elitism

Elitism, or classism, refers to prejudicial attitudes that presume people in lower socioeconomic classes are "slackers" who are less worthy and less competent than those in upper classes. While the U.S. ideal states that all people are created equal, in actuality, U.S. society views some people as more equal than others. Ironically, the ideas of equality and charity reinforce elitism and inequality. Sennett and Cobb (1972) elaborate on this theme:

> The idea of potential equality of power has been given a form peculiarly fitted to a competitive society where inequality of power is the rule and expectation. If all [people] start on some basis of equal potential ability, then the inequalities they experience in their lives are *not* arbitrary, they are the logical consequence of different personal drives to use those powers—in other words, social differences can now appear as questions of character, of moral resolve, will, and competence. (p. 256)

Class structure clearly does not imply a stratification of people in which people who are good are above those who are bad. Yet the elite often characterize people in the lower strata as ignorant and incapable.

Social stratification results from inequality related to wealth, power, and prestige. A social hierarchy develops that clusters people within strata or layerlike divisions. This stratification distinguishes the "haves" from the "have-nots." The haves in society are those people who not only have social and economic resources, but also have control over the social and economic opportunities of society. On the other hand, the have-nots have few resources and limited access to opportunities. People's positions in this hierarchy then determine their potential for either accessing resources or experiencing barriers in attempting to acquire the advantages society offers.

Our preoccupation with designer labels on clothing, disposable goods, and other consumer-related items that reflect people's abilities to pay reveals elitist attitudes. The great American dream is that people by their own initiative can alter their social class status. This dream has nightmarish qualities for the underemployed and the poor. Society challenges them to "pull themselves up by their own bootstraps" and berates them when they cannot. When their efforts fail, society members often blame individuals rather than the structural inequalities that create barriers to achievement.

Poor people's movements, particularly welfare rights organizations, recognize these systemic barriers and attempt to remedy them through social reform. Expanding educational and economic opportunities and taking necessary legal actions are among these reform efforts. Reform groups recognize social inequality as a political issue instead of a private trouble and acknowledge classism as a public-domain issue instead of a personal problem.

Elitism extends beyond the boundaries of a society to the international arena, where highly industrialized nations take advantage of other countries. Here again, relationships that take advantage of economic needs develop between the power elite and the underprivileged. For example, in response to local communities' refusals to allow waste disposal within their own jurisdictions, United States–based disposal companies contract with individuals to dump medical, chemical, and nuclear wastes in economically impovershed parts of Africa. In fact, the money offered may literally buy space in a family's backyard. Families trade the use of their land for income to meet their immediate needs. This trade-off exposes them and their children to contaminated waste and jeopardizes their long-range health.

Sexism

Sexism is the belief that one sex is superior to the other. Sexism most frequently manifests as prejudicial attitudes toward and discriminatory actions against females, giving gender privilege to men. People exhibiting sexism make assumptions about the capabilities of men and women solely on the basis of gender, without considering individual characteristics. Institutionalized sexism dominates all aspects of society, including the family as well as the economic, political, welfare, and religious structures (Day, 2003).

Sexism has roots in gender socialization. Parents teach their children from infancy how to behave as males or females. Gender socialization shapes how we perceive our roles and define our self-identity. This socialization also prescribes "gender-appropriate" choices for men and women. Some people cite Biblical scripture and theological writing to justify traditional sex-role definitions.

Sexist attitudes and practices favor men and preferentially regard masculine traits and behavior. This view confers power and authority on men and relegates women to a second-class status. Sexist social structures devalue women, discriminate against them economically, and discourage their full participation in society. Discrimination based on sex, coupled with the already-mentioned discrimination based on race or class, has a double jeopardy effect on minority and poor women (McGoldrick, Garcia-Preto, Hines, & Lee, 1989). Furthermore, the feminization of poverty defines the "new poor" as women and children. Breaking the cycle of poverty becomes more difficult because of the inherent inequalities in the social structure pitted against women.

Since 1900, women have been actively advocating equal rights. They directed their early efforts at attaining voting rights and participating in the political process. More recently, the women's rights movement has centered on economic equity. The Equal Rights Amendment (ERA), which twice failed to pass as a constitutional amendment, simply asked for equal protection for persons under the law, regardless of sex. Those in favor of the ERA sought constitutional protection against sexual discrimination in a 24-word statement: "Equality of rights under the law shall not be denied or abridged by the United States or by any State on account of sex." Opponents of the amendment believed that its passage would disrupt the "natural order." In part, the failure of the constitutional amendment reflects sexism that is firmly entrenched in U.S. society.

Heterosexism

Heterosexism presumes a heterosexual orientation, whereas *homophobia* is a strongly felt prejudice against people whose sexual orientation differs from the heterosexual. Homosexuals represent about 6 percent of the population. Except for sexual orientation, they are similar to heterosexuals. Yet, because of their sexual orientation, gay men and lesbians experience institutional discrimination, defamation of character, belittlement, and stigma.

People's irrational fears of homosexuals form the basis for *homophobic behaviors.* "Homophobia has assumed the proportions of a social pathology in our culture. It is codified in law, social policy, religious beliefs, and child rearing practices" (Sullivan, 1994, p. 294). A study of the attitudes of social work practitioners found that almost 90 percent of the respondents were not homophobic; however, a majority of the respondents evidenced heterosexist bias (Berkman & Zinberg, 1997).

Homophobia has escalated in recent years, after male homosexuals became one of the first populations in the United States identified as being at risk for contracting HIV/AIDS. The general public quickly attributed the cause of HIV/AIDS to a different life-style on the part of homosexual males. Gay men feel the double impact of stigma marked by what some call a "deviant life-style" and the reality of a transmittable, life-threatening disease. Because the connection between HIV/AIDS and homosexuality is so entrenched in the public's perception, all people with HIV/AIDS endure a homophobic stigma at some level.

Whereas heterosexual identity incorporates sexuality as one aspect of personal identity, people often narrowly define homosexual identity as a deviant sex act. In the public's mind, the personal identity of homosexuals becomes secondary to their sexuality. Self-righteous justifications based on interpretations of religious tenets and moral imperatives fuel the public's outrage against homosexuals. As a result, homosexuals often experience depersonalization in addition to social stigma.

Because many people think of homosexuals as troubled or deviant individuals, they are not as likely to identify homosexuals as an oppressed social group. However, "there should be little question that homosexuals constitute a social group, and one which is oppressed" (Berger, 1986, p. 170). Oppression ranges from social ostracism to overt antigay violence and hate crimes. Same-sex couples generally do not share the same benefits in housing laws, insurance coverage, or legal protection of inheritance and investment as do heterosexual couples. As of July 1, 2000, Vermont's Civil Union Law grants the same legal benefits, protections, and responsiblities to partners in a civil union as are accorded spouses in a marriage. Gays and lesbians experience estrangement from their families and friends, loss of jobs, discrimination in housing, exclusion from religious organizations, discrimination in life and medical insurance, prohibition of same-sex marriage, and public humiliation.

Gay and lesbian community organizations and the gay rights movement provide channels for social support and social activism. The National Gay Task Force and the Gay Rights National Lobby are political advocacy groups that monitor public issues, represent gay concerns, evaluate media portrayals of homosexuals, and lobby for legislative protection of gay rights. Within the profession of social work, both the NASW and the CSWE have task forces on gay and lesbian issues.

Ageism

Robert Butler (1969) first used the phrase "Age-ism" to describe the negative attitudes prevalent in the United States toward aging. Although ageism typically refers to prejudicial attitudes about older adults, age prejudice can be directed at any age group. For example, hurrying children to grow up too soon and glorifying adult styles, sexuality, and behavior ultimately devalues childhood and children (Elkind, 1984; 1988). An adultcentric bias evaluates children by adult standards and fails to recognize the differences in children's points of view: "the negative consequences of adultcentrism can be the same as those of ethnocentrism: miscommunication (with children), inaccurate judgments (about children's intents and motivations), misuse of power (to limit children's self-determination), and undermining strengths and competencies" (Petr, 1992, pp. 408–409).

Ageism is particularly blatant as a response to people who are older. Directed at the older generation, it reduces their ability to contribute to the community at large, fosters stereotyping that makes it difficult to view older adults as individual people, encourages older adults to devalue themselves, and perpetuates a fear of aging.

Many misconceptions and stereotypes foster ageism. Exalting youthfulness; equating aging with death; and segregating people by age, thereby limiting contact between the generations, all perpetuate negativism. People are likely to associate age with decay and disability. For example, if our car breaks down, we may complain that it's getting old. So "the jump from broken old cars to broken old people seems quite natural" (Bodily, 1991, p. 257).

Many assume that "all old people are alike." They presume that age is the most prominent factor in predicting characteristics. However, gerontologists contend that, as a cohort group, older adults are more heterogenous than any other age group. Simply put, as people grow older, they are more likely to be dissimilar.

Another misconception suggests that "senility" is a part of aging. This belief associates declines in intellect, memory, and problem solving with aging. Although some older individuals do experience mental deterioration, the crucial factor appears to be health status, not age (Berk, 2004). If social workers believe the misconception that "old people are senile," they may not believe that older adults are worth their effort. The label "senile" masks our ability to identify older adults' potential.

Finally, people may stereotype older adults as rigid, inflexible, and unable to change. When professionals view older adults as people who have already developed rather than as people who are developing, they are unlikely to invest their time and effort in dealing with the problems of older people. The prevailing attitude toward aging determines what is or is not done to address the issues of aging. As Brody (1976) says:

> Ageism—on the macro-level determines such matters as priorities in the allocation of resources for income, the provision of health and social services, and attention to housing and neighborhood environments. On the micro-level, attitudes creep insidiously into incorrect psycho-dynamic cliches such as "parent-child role reversal" and "second childhood." (p. 2)

Change itself is much more likely to be related to past experience and individual traits than to chronological age. People can and do change throughout their life spans.

Age-related issues present a challenge to all of society and raise significant questions about social justice. Maggie Kuhn, founder of the Gray Panthers, an activist organization that promotes the interests and rights of older persons, recommends education to sensitize Americans to the social consequences of ageism, and urges political and economic reform and the overhauling of the U.S. health care system (Kuhn, 1987).

Handicapism

The World Health Organization (WHO) distinguishes among impairment, disability, and handicap. *Impairments* are physical afflictions, limitations, or losses in any body structure

Job coaches enable people with mental retardation to develop skills in the workplace.

or function. *Disabilities* are the consequences of impairments that restrict or prevent people from undertaking activities that are within the range for people without impairments. *Handicaps* are the social disadvantages that result from impairments or disabilities. A handicap "reflects the *social* consequences of that disability" (Scheer & Groce, 1988, p. 24).

Handicapism is the prejudice and discrimination directed against people who have mental or physical disabilities. People often regard those with disabilities as "different" and unable to perform as well as the "able bodied." They treat people with disabilities as if they were disabled in every way. For example, people may conclude that someone who has a physical disability is mentally incompetent or socially immature. Likewise, people sometimes regard those who are retarded as having no feelings, interests, or ideas.

Malicious parodies of people with disabilities provide further evidence of handicapism. Unfortunately, disparaging remarks, belittling slurs, and ridicule directed against people with disabilities do not seem to carry the same personal or social sanction as similar remarks against other groups. For people with disabilities, handicapism leads to social isolation and social marginality.

Disability, like any other characteristic, is a consequence of the interaction between people and their environments. Disabling environments further discourage people with disabilities from participating in the mainstream of society. Barriers in architecture, transportation, communication methods, sociability, economics, and legal rights confront people with disabilities and impose serious limitations within their environments. Although laws guarantee people with disabilities protection from discrimination, there are prejudicial attitudes, building-design limitations, medical coverage liability, and requirements of adaptive devices that obstruct their employment. If people with disabilities are employed, they hold

BOX 6.2

Reflections on Empowerment

The Living Theater—Learning Life's Lessons

The Living Stage Theater Company in Washington, D.C., utilizes creative drama and improvisation as empowering techniques (Nelson, 1993). Participants in the theater reenact historical events, experience cultural traditions, and role-play nonviolent solutions. The scenarios used in the improvisational activities address relevant social issues such as drug abuse, AIDS, and suicide. The improvisational theater incorporates traditional African American culture and values by exploring Kwanzaa, an African American holiday in December. Through drumming, dance, and rituals associated with Kwanzaa, participants deepen their understanding of their African roots.

The *Teen Mothers of Today,* a program designed for young mothers between the ages of 13 and 16, adopts a philosophy of "empowerment through creativity" to effect changes in the lives of these young moms and in the ways in which they interact with their children and within their community. The theater program builds on the strengths these young women bring—tenacity, determination, vivid imaginations, and concern for their children. By role-playing characters other than themselves, the young women found ways to deal with hypothetical situations without resorting to violence.

> One such scene featured two branches of an extended family. One group lived on family-owned land, while the other lived miles away in a city. The drug-related death of a young man in the city required that the family gather together in the country for a funeral. The workshop participants and the company portrayed clan members who had to overcome personal differences as well as handle the repercussions of the young man's death.
>
> As they dealt with the details of these fictitious situations, the teens allowed their characters to undergo transformations in their emotional lives. This was the beginning of a profound learning experience, for young people with a limited knowledge of life generally view the world as composed of immutable forces over which they have no control. They do not understand or believe that people can change, and that they can have an impact upon their own destinies. (Nelson, 1993, p. 25)

Combining performance with social justice themes empowers participants to find new ways of overcoming obstacles in their lives. Theater activities reinforce participants' beliefs that their actions and reactions have an impact on the course of their lives.

the worst jobs (Roth, 1987). Their employment status does not reflect their willingness to work or lack of productivity, however. It reflects the disabling nature of environments.

The limited and often negative ways in which members of the general public perceive people with disabilities deny their competence. In fact, some may make those with visible disabilities objects of their pity. Being perceived as helpless, dependent, and passive denies people with disabilities a functional role in society (Frank, 1988). Research does not support the belief that a disability is "central to the disabled person's self-concept, self-definition, social comparisons, and reference groups" (Fine & Asch, 1988, p. 11). Neither does research support the assumption that "having a disability is synonymous with needing help and social support" (p. 12).

People with disabilities represent the largest disenfranchised group in the United States—19.3 percent of the population or about 50 million with some level of disability

(U.S. Census Bureau, 2003). A number of organizations represent the particular interests of constituency groups with similar conditions, such as the National Association of the Deaf, the American Diabetes Association, Disabled American Veterans, and the Epilepsy Association.

Since the 1960s, the disability rights movement has actively pressed for federal civil rights legislation. Disability activists formed their first national coalition in 1976. The American Coalition of Citizens with Disabilities (ACCD) linked "several local and single-disability organizations while retaining the autonomy of each constituent organization" (Scotch, 1988, p. 165). It is only through these collective political actions that public policy will protect the civil rights of people with disabilities and create abling environments in education, employment, and social settings. The recent passage of the Americans with Disabilities Act of 1990 attests to the policy struggle for equal consideration in all aspects of life. It points the way to understanding that "life with a disability can be as worthwhile as life without a disability and that those with disabilities should be entitled to means that enable them to participate in society" (Asch & Mudrick, 1995, p. 759).

The Collective Isms

Although each of these isms reflects the attitudes and behaviors about particular groups, a common theme unifies them. The population groups that are discriminated against are those perceived as less productive, and hence disruptors of the economic order; those deemed culturally deviant, and thus perils to the cultural order; and those labeled psychologically and socially aberrant, and therefore threats to personal security. The isms clearly dramatize social injustice.

The Bases of Social Injustice

There are many explanations of why social injustice persists. The ideology of social Darwinism provides a rationale. One sociological viewpoint suggests that injustice serves a function in the social order, while another sociological theory views injustice as a result of differential access to power and authority. Psychological theories about attribution, ego-defenses, and information processing offer explanations as well. Other explanations from sociology and psychology include those about blaming victims, belief in a just world, and discriminatory behaviors.

Social Darwinism

Ideologies such as social Darwinism shape our understanding of justice. Social Darwinism originated with Herbert Spencer, an English philosopher, who applied evolutionary theory to society, drawing on Darwin's theory of evolution and Lamarck's theory of inherited characteristics. He described evolution as the "survival of the fittest" and believed that eventually an ideal society of the "fit" would evolve. Because his writing was published in the English language, Spencer had a broad audience in the United States.

William Graham Sumner, the leading proponent of social Darwinism in the United States in the late nineteenth century, combined Spencer's view, laissez-faire economics, and the Protestant work ethic in his theory. According to Sumner, the constant law of nature is competition. Nature is a neutral force that rewards those who are most fit: "Economic life was construed as a set of arrangements that offered inducements to men of good character, while it punished those who were in Sumner's words, 'negligent, shiftless, inefficient, silly and imprudent' " (Hofstadter, 1955, p. 10). In his essay "The Abolition of Poverty," Sumner (1887) correlated poverty with ignorance, vice, and misfortune. Moreover, Sumner argued that giving money to the poor granted capital to ineffective members of society who would not use it productively. Instead, people should invest their capital in labor that would give them a return on their investment.

Sumner viewed changes in society as evolutionary processes, governed by the principles of competition and survival of the fittest. Society achieved these goals by reforming individuals' morality rather than by legislating change. He cautioned that government interventions upset the balance of nature, altered the struggle for existence, and tipped the balance in favor of the unfit. According to Sumner (1903), people should accept poverty as a societal ill that would be abolished by their own industriousness and prudence. Although Sumner questioned the role of public charity, he thought private charity developed altruism and did not interfere with the course of evolution.

Although it is difficult to assess its exact impact, historians suggest that early-twentieth-century America was "social Darwin country" (Hofstadter, 1955). In his book *Social Work in the American Tradition,* Cohen (1958) contends that the general public accepted a social Darwinist view of social welfare. Social Darwinism also left its mark on the early development of the social work profession.

Records of late-nineteenth- and early-twentieth-century charity work reveal the influence of social Darwinism (Krogsrud, 1965). For example, the work of Reverend S. Humphreys Gurteen (1882), the founder of the Charity Organization Society of Buffalo, New York, provides evidence of the social Darwinist leanings of charity organizations. Gurteen indicated that the principles of charity organization sprang up on the basis of certain relevant laws of nature. He pointed out that two principles—the idea that there is variety in the human race and the idea that struggle for existence takes place—combine to make up the law of the survival of the fittest. Gurteen believed that, unlike animals, humans are social and can combine to defeat the law of natural selection. When humans defend the unfit, the unfit survive and societies deteriorate. This, he said, is the scientific origin of poverty.

Records from the Brooklyn Association for Improving the Condition of the Poor (1878; 1885) reveal an individualistic, social-Darwin-like interpretation of poverty:

> It [the Association] does not invite the ideal, the dissolute, or improvident to partake of a bounty that leaves them as helpless as it finds them. It offers no premium for indolence and thriftlessness by supplying the bread which might be fairly earned. Its extended hand is one of help, and is shown by the fact that so large a proportion of those it assists are lifted beyond the need of further aid. (1885, p. 9)

More specifically, late-nineteeth-century charity organization leaders believed that the causes of poverty were ignorance; incompetence; idleness; thriftlessness; imprudent hasty marriages; and intemperance, gambling, and other vices (Schneider & Deutsch, 1941). Still other investigations cited ancestry, drink, blind charity, idleness, a loathing of honest work, and the desire to live off the good will of others (Wayland, 1894). Each of these causes of poverty reflects "individual defects either of nature or character" (Hyslop, 1898, p. 385). These characteristics sharply contrast with industriousness and thrift, identified by social Darwinists as characteristics that lead to fitness.

In the heyday of social Darwinist thought, Charity Organization Society leaders distinguished the "worthy poor" from the "unworthy paupers":

> We cannot think that there is any room in this busy world of ours for those social drones who prey upon the industry of others, and prefer to beg rather than to work. The very existence of the pauper is a disgrace of the civilization. For the "poor" there is ample room in the great heart of humanity, but the very word "pauper" is a blot upon our language. (Gurteen, 1882, pp. 188–189)

This distinction between the poor and paupers suggests that paupers were considered the unfit, whereas the poor were worthy of carefully scrutinized charity. Charity organization leaders believed that their methods of scientific philanthropy would reform the poor so that they would help themselves.

Social Darwinist proponents believed that scientific private charity was more appropriate than the unsystematized methods of public relief. They believed that public relief demoralized recipients (Pellew, 1878). They concluded that charity organizations could use humans' proclivity to band together to combat poverty scientifically by supplementing or correcting the unfit character of the poor.

Today, people do not overtly support social Darwinism as a legitimate viewpoint; however, the general public's attitudes toward welfare provide evidence of its continued existence. The general public often hold people on public assistance in low esteem and even loathe them, particularly those who are "able to work if they were only motivated."

Sociological Theories

Two major perspectives of sociology, the structural functional perspective and the conflict perspective, offer differing views about the origins of social injustice.

Structural Functionalist Perspective. The structural functional perspective of sociology views society as an organism with interrelated parts integral to the functioning of the whole. In this view, even social injustice has a function in the overall balance in society. For example, Herbert Gans (1972) provides a satirical yet incisive structural functional analysis of poverty, one product of social injustice. He speculates about the potential functions of poverty for society as a whole.

According to Gans, poverty serves economic, social, cultural, and political functions. The economic function is to provide a group of people—the poor—who are willing to do society's dirty work—literally dirty, dangerous, dead-end, menial, and undignified work. Likewise, Gans says the poor themselves serve certain social functions. The poor become a handy label for deviance to validate dominant societal norms. The worthy poor provide gratification to the upper class as an outlet for altruism, pity, and charity. The poor also provide causes to which the elite and middle class, who have spare time, respond with volunteerism and charitable fund-raising activities. The cultural function of poverty is to provide labor for the cultural arts and art forms, such as jazz, that are enjoyed by people in higher social strata. Politically, the poor serve as a rallying point for political groups. They carry the burden for "progress" and stabilize the political process by their lack of potent activity. Although Gans does not condone poverty, his satirical analysis clearly describes functions the poor perform to maintain a structural balance in society. From this perspective, recognizing and accounting for the role poverty plays is necessary when analyzing alternatives in order to effect societal change.

Conflict Perspective. According to the conflict perspective of sociology, differential access to power and status perpetuates injustice. Conflict occurs when one group challenges the power inequities other groups maintain (DeVos, 1971). The social order is a product of the coercive power of those in high status positions in the social hierarchy.

Furthermore, competition for scarce resources can generate prejudicial attitudes. The dominant group may be exploitive or derogatory in order to gain an advantage or assert control over less powerful groups. For example, while affirmative action employment practices have been influential in effecting change, they have not entirely eradicated inequitable employment practices. Competition for jobs, especially when jobs are scarce, often evokes negative attitudes and conflict.

Psychological Theories

Social psychologists suggest that there may be additional reasons that people blame victims. People assign blame to victims so that they can assure themselves that they will be able to avoid similar disasters. In other words, if they attribute the problems of others to personal causes, they can stipulate that these individuals likewise personally control their solutions. Thus, they feel secure in knowing that if others can control outcomes, so can they.

Attribution theory focuses on the way people infer causes of behavior. This theory suggests that people draw different conclusions about cause depending on their own perspectives or points of view. In general, people attribute the causes of their own blunders to external situations. They also attribute other people's blunders to their lack of ability or character defects.

Another psychological theory suggests that some people may blame victims in order to protect themselves or even mask their anger. One ego-defensive attitude results when people see specks of sawdust in the eyes of others, yet ignore the logs in their own. Ego-defenses develop from internal conflicts and relate more to personal needs than to the actual character of the "victim" who is blamed:

> In other words, the maintenance of a personal rage or resentment may actually be the unwillingness to release, or even personally confront, a deep fear of what the object of the anger represents to the enraged person. Moreover, it may also be an attempt to protectively deflect an unrealized, "negative" aspect of the self onto another person or group. In the context of the systems metaphor, both persons, the projecting and the receiving person, are reflections of each other, engaged in a shared space, and reacting to mirrorings which the

> other is emitting. In order for the one to protect against an unrecognized, sensitive aspect of the self, for example, a fear, the defense may assume the form of anger and even suspicion. (Booth, 1990, p. 3)

Like all beliefs, prejudicial attitudes are difficult to change, and they even perpetuate themselves. Research in cognitive psychology indicates that the information people tend to process and store in long-term memory is information that is consistent with expectations (Macrae & Bodenhausen, 2000). In other words, information that fits into our own frames of reference is more readily perceived and remembered than information that does not. "Beliefs tend to modify what we look for, what we recognize, how we interpret, and how we respond to these interpretations" (Walsh, 1989, p. 160). If we believe we are victims of our situation with no way out, we may take this self-limiting assumption as truth. This leads us to conclude that there is nothing we can do to help ourselves. Similar vicious cycles occur when our beliefs ascribe blame, inferiority, and dehumanization to others. "Once set in motion, such behaviors tend to 'prove' the apparent validity of the beliefs that created them as well as the 'wisdom' and 'foresight' of those who held them, thereby once again demonstrating the self-prophetic power of beliefs" (p. 160). Belief systems exert a powerful influence on how we process information.

Blaming the Victim

In contemporary society, blaming the victim is an ideology that emphasizes environmental causation rather than one that regards victims as inferior, genetically defective, or morally unfit from birth (Ryan, 1976). Although this new interpretation considers environmental influences, sympathetic social scientists and liberal politicians explain that the forces of circumstance have made people inferior. Thus, even when people consider the social circumstances of poverty, they blame victims for their lower status.

Although problems and the resulting social stigma originate in external forces, people attribute causes to some defect in victims. For example, social change agents condemn the environmental effects of poverty, injustice, and discrimination, and, yet, they ironically direct their efforts at changing victims. Ryan concludes that this theory "is a brilliant ideology for justifying a perverse form of social action designed to change, not society, as one might expect, but rather society's victim" (Ryan, 1976, p. 8). The ideological shift changes the focus from reforming society to reforming victims, all the while cloaked in humanitarian "do-goodism." Although helpers acknowledge social problems, they scrutinize those who "have the problem"; define them as a group that is different from the general population; and view them as incapable, unskilled, ignorant, and subhuman. Ryan concludes that those who hold this view believe that to address poverty or any other social problem requires changes in "those people." Ryan says:

> All of this happens so smoothly that it seems downright rational. First, identify a social problem. Second, study those affected by the problem and discover in what ways they are different from the rest of us as a consequence of deprivation and injustice. Third, define the differences as the cause of the social problem itself. Finally, of course, assign a government bureaucrat to invent a humanitarian action program to correct the differences. (pp. 8–9)

Just World Beliefs

Social psychologists further suggest that beliefs in a just world legitimize blaming the victims. Research indicates that many people believe that there is a positive correlation between individual worth and fate—a connection between virtue and reward (Rubin & Peplau, 1975). Similarly, they perceive a relationship between wickedness and suffering. When people observe suffering, they often conclude that the suffering is an illusion, that it is exaggerated, or that the victim alone is to blame. Interestingly, suffering is more likely to be seen as "just" when the person drawing this conclusion is not the one who is suffering. Janis and Rodin (1980) hypothesize that nearly everyone needs to believe that people actually get what they deserve.

Studies cite evidence that belief in a just world is associated with the tendency to derogate victims of social injustice—especially women, Blacks, and the poor (Lerner, 1965; Lerner & Simmons, 1966). In a series of studies done in England, statistically significant relationships appeared between scores on the belief in a just world and scores related to the disparagement of victims, including negative attitudes toward the poor (Wagstaff, 1983). Research that suggests that belief in a just world is negatively correlated with degree of social activism: More strongly held beliefs in a just world predict lower reported levels of social activism. Belief in a just world seemingly contributes "to the perpetuation of social injustice" (Rubin & Peplau, 1975, p. 83).

Behavioral Aspects of Discrimination

The creed set forth in both the Declaration of Independence and the U.S. Constitution declares that all people are created equal and asserts "the indefeasible principle of the human right to full equity—the right of equitable access to justice, freedom, and opportunity irrespective of race or religion or ethnic origin" (Merton, 1949, p. 100). Merton suggests that people may conform to the creed or deviate from it either in attitudes (being prejudicial or nonprejudicial) or in behavior (being discriminatory or nondiscriminatory). By its name, prejudice implies a prejudgment, an attitude often derived from stereotyping and viewing others as inferior. Discrimination is prejudice in action, that is, an often overt set of behaviors that places others in subordinate positions. "Discriminatory actions reinforce existing ethnic relationships by denying out-group members equal access to jobs, homes, neighborhoods, education, income, political power, influence, and status" (Kivisto, 1995, p. 65).

According to Merton (1949), there are four major types of people who discriminate, differentiated by their belief in the democratic creed and their personal conduct:

1. *Type I: The unprejudiced nondiscriminator (all-weather liberal).* These individuals both believe and practice the democratic creed. Their behavior is congruent with their attitude regardless of the particular situation. Racial and ethnic liberals, they are logical leaders for pursuing social action. However, they must take the initiative to influence others, recognize that not all persons are indeed alike, and work toward collective efforts rather than private solutions.

2. *Type II: The unprejudiced discriminator (fair-weather liberal).* Although these individuals believe in the creed, they may find themselves inadvertently supporting discriminatory practices because of their silence, timidity, or failure to act. When discrimination occurs, they are likely to feel guilty about their level of participation in it.

3. *Type III: The prejudiced nondiscriminator (fair-weather illiberal).* The implicit threat of sanctions for nonconformity to the creed controls the behavior of prejudiced nondiscriminators. They do not believe in the ethnic equality upheld by the creed, but they are timid bigots, fearful of punishment for discriminatory practice.

4. *Type IV: The prejudiced discriminator (all-weather illiberal).* An unashamedly pure bigot, the all-weather illiberal holds firm to his or her prejudicial convictions and discriminatory behaviors, often proclaiming the right or duty to discriminate.

Merton's now-classic sociological typology provides a framework for understanding patterns of ethnic prejudice and discrimination.

Effects of Social Injustice

Social injustice results in discrimination, oppression, and victimization. Oppression is the collective injustice perpetrated by those who dominate by controlling resources and opportunities. Dehumanization is considering people as less than human, stripping them of their individuality and potential. Victimization represents the personal response of those who are oppressed by injustice (Table 6.2).

Oppression through Discrimination

The potential for discrimination, subjugation, and oppression of groups with minority status is inherent in the unbalanced power relationship between dominant and minority groups. Oppression involves political, economic, social, and psychological domination of one group by another—from the microlevel of individuals to the macrolevel of social groups, organizations, and nation-states (Gil, 1994; 2002).

TABLE 6.2 The Effects of Injustice

Oppression	Resulting from an imbalance of power between the identified majority population and groups with minority status, oppression denies minority groups access to opportunities and resources and limits their rightful participation in society.
Dehumanization	By regarding others with cold detachment and showing indifference to human misery, dehumanization obscures the inherent worth and dignity of personhood.
Victimization	Ascribing blame and victim status confers perceptions of helplessness, powerlessness, and alienation.

Frequently dominant groups target minority groups for acts of social injustice. Note that the basis for dominant-minority relationships is differential power. Dominant-minority relationships do not relate to the size of the respective groups. Specific ethnic, religious, or racial groups may, in fact, be society's majority in number but experience minority status. Limited in power, authority, and control, minority groups are often socially submerged, excluded, and considered the out-groups of mainstream society. On the other hand,

> [the] *dominant* group is the one that has established its way of life (culture) or physiognomy as superior to others in the society and that treats differently or unequally other groups in the society who have other life-styles or physical characteristics. The reason for this differential treatment is to preserve the dominant group's status and protect its vested interest.
>
> The dominant group is superordinate. It controls enough economic and political power to advance its various interests over the interests of other groups. Dominant group members share a common value system, language, and history. Their idea of what is "right," "desirable," or "good," is historically rooted. Their preeminence is established and maintained by custom, law, influence, and, ultimately, coercion. They restrict all groups that do not share dominant traits and values from full participation in the society. (Marden, Meyer, & Engel, 1992, p. 29)

Stereotyping reinforces prejudicial attitudes toward minority groups, and ethnocentrism fuels oppressive behavior by the dominant. A stereotype is an overstated characterization and simplified generalization of a minority group based on selected traits. Ethnocentrism is the dominant group's belief in its superiority that leads to self-righteousness and contempt for other groups. According to Gil (1994):

> Societies and work systems are oppressive when people are not considered and treated as equals, and therefore do not have equal rights and responsibilities concerning the key dimensions of social life. Under such inherently undemocratic conditions, different people, and different groups and classes, are entitled to different levels of liberty, and are subject to different levels of constraints and expectations concerning work. Establishing and maintaining unequal levels of rights and responsibilities concerning stewardship of resources and production, and unequal levels of liberty, constraints, and expectations concerning work, is usually not possible without overt and covert coercion, i.e., "societal violence." (p. 235)

Interpersonal Dehumanization

Dehumanization results from being perceived as an inanimate object. "Dehumanization as a defense against painful or overwhelming emotions entails a decrease in a person's sense of his own individuality and in his perception of the humanness of people" (Bernard, Ottenberg, & Redl, 1971, p. 102). As such, dehumanization simultaneously directs itself inward and at others. Whereas self-directed dehumanization diminishes one's own humanness, object-directed dehumanization fails "to recognize in others their full complement of human qualities" (p. 105).

Caught up in ordinarily repulsive attitudes and actions, individuals strive to maintain their self-image and use dehumanization as a psychological defense to protect themselves emotionally. In the extreme, people use this wanton detachment or dissociation to separate themselves from and complacently accept hideous acts against humanity. For example, the general public's apathetic response to the Nazi atrocities and civilian massacres in wartime documents that dehumanization occurs (Opton, 1971). This reaction predisposes people to regard others as somehow deserving of pain and suffering.

Regarding others as subhuman, bad humans, or nonhuman provides a rationalization that legitimizes antisocial acts, justifies maltreatment, and removes guilt and shame:

> There is a tendency toward trivializing the humanness of "undesirable" groups within our society. It is well known, for example, that one of the most effective means of scapegoating a subgroup is to convince the members of the major culture and, if possible, the subordinated group itself of the absence of true humanness in the victimized group. The use of suggestive, derogatory terminology assists this process and the pejorative language leads to the positive sanctioning of certain cognitive schemata, or categories, which then assist in forming perceptual sets, the "eyes" with which we come to view a given group or member of a group. (Booth, 1990, p. 2)

Obtuse labels such as "the boat people," "casualties of war," "cases," and other generalized descriptions reduce individuals' emotional connections to the suffering and injustice victims endure.

Depicting social problems and the consequences of human suffering as mere statistics further obscures the humanness of others. The scope of the problems may be represented statistically, but the figures actually conceal the plight of the individuals counted, their unique situations, and the personal ramifications of suffering in their lives. Indifference to human misery may result from such an objective tally, as it causes people to view others as merely statistics or inanimate objects.

Bernard, Ottenberg, and Redl (1971) describe a number of overlapping aspects of maladaptive dehumanization. Emotional separation and distancing oneself from the human qualities of others, in any extreme, defeats the purpose of caring and helping among professionals. Such detachment creates conditions in which practitioners coldly confront the illness, the poverty, or the problems of clients without feeling concern for their humanness. This diminishes the mutuality of social worker–client relationships. Other offensive responses for dealing with painful feelings occur through the denial of personal responsibility for the consequences of decisions and behaviors and through a preoccupation with procedural details, rules and regulations, and the bureaucratic structure. Pat responses such as "I'm just following orders" and "This is standard procedure" reflect a shirking of "ability or willingness to personalize one's actions in the interests of individual human needs or special differences" (p. 114). Some people may not protest against injustice, even when they know about it, because of pressure to conform exerted by the dominant group. Or they may feel pressed to cover up their own feelings of helplessness. Conscious inaction ensures anonymity and masks feelings of impotence and powerlessness. Silence, in effect, condones dehumanizing actions.

Personal Victimization

People who experience stigma incorporate its negative connotations into their self-images (Patten, Gatz, Jones, & Thomas, 1989). One early study of the effect of labels and self-fulfilling prophecies suggests that people have a tendency to live up to the labels assigned to

BOX **6.3**

Social Work Profile

Social Action and Community Organizing

Early in my adult life, I had a wonderful opportunity to organize for an international interfaith peace organization. The purpose of that group was to bring peace and justice initiatives to local churches. Through participating in this interfaith organization, I learned about Buddhist, Hindu, Muslim, Jewish, and Christian perspectives to name a few. This foundation of understanding led to subsequent involvements in religious peace and justice activism, community organizing, and church-based organizing. Those activities clearly complemented my vocational call and gift to serve others.

In my present position as the social action director for a local diocese, I work in both direct services and in social justice policy arenas including immigration, agriculture, and housing. The philosophy that I bring to my activities strikes a balance between charity and justice, bridging the personal and the political and combining social ministry and social action.

I believe the central value of community organizing is democratic participation. Organizing has more to do with the process than the product. Participants, rather than the organizer, should determine the destination achieved through the process. This process of democratic participation gives members a sense of power. A recent experience that I had in Africa at a farewell ritual dance illustrates this process. Watching and becoming caught up by the rhythm and motion of this expressive dance, I began to imitate our African hosts' rhythmic steps. The dance group quickly stepped behind me, inviting me to lead the dance. As I reflect on this, I realize that my African friends modeled the dance steps. Once I caught on, they stepped aside and let me lead the way. This is a metaphor for what I do in my organizing work. I model the process and quickly let the natural leaders emerge. I believe that the purpose of organizing is to develop leadership among grassroots membership, turn the key functions over to them, and get behind them to support the direction they set for themselves.

I'm very passionate about the public policy regarding immigration. I advocate for legislative positions that allow immigrants to access services regardless of their documented status. For example, because of their fear of deportation, people who are undocumented immigrants feel that they are at the mercy of unethical employers. Because of their need to "stay under the radar," issues like domestic violence, substance abuse, and mental health difficulties often go untreated. The initial goal of my work in immigration services is to work with immigrants to help them become "legalized," which is the first avenue for them to become involved and become leaders. Legalization empowers immigrants to realize the democratic ideal of full participation and, for those who become citizens, to exercise their voice through voting rights.

Community organizing is a good fit for me. For one thing, it requires lifelong learning. Education for social work, particularly for community organizing is not just a "four-year sprint." I have learned an incredible amount through my day-to-day community-organizing experiences and from the participants and activists with whom I've worked. Community organizers are spirited people, willing to take risks and even to make mistakes in order to be catalysts for change. I prefer being on the cutting edge of what goes on in the community. Community organizing as a field of social work practice places practitioners at the edge of change.

---

them by others (Rosenthal & Jacobson, 1968). When people blame themselves, feelings of inferiority, dependency, and rejection result (Janis & Rodin, 1980). The earlier-mentioned beliefs in a just world, which suggest that people somehow deserve the effects of oppression as a retribution for wrongdoing or immorality, may actually compound their situations. Ironically, people who feel victimized may even identify with oppressors and apply the pejorative labels to themselves. This behavior suggests that they have internalized the norms of their oppressors (Gochros, Gochros, & Fischer, 1986).

Typically, people who are victimized feel powerless. Oppressors exaggerate their power and control over others, thereby exacerbating the degree of powerlessness felt by the people they treat as subservient. Powerlessness results in low self-esteem, a sense of impotency, and an inability to muster effective responses to oppression. Individuals who are stigmatized and discriminated against may also feel alienated or estranged from their social environment.

Learned Helplessness. Seligman (1975) describes a type of powerlessness in his studies on helplessness. These studies indicate that perceiving events as uncontrollable undermines motivation to initiate responses. Both personal experiences and beliefs contribute to one's sense of control. Telling ourselves or being told by others that we have no control leads to feelings of helplessness. People do not just experience helplessness; they come to expect a lack of control (Shupe, 1985).

Seligman (1975) contends that poverty can create conditions of helplessness. He says, "I suggest that among its effects, poverty brings about frequent and intense experiences of uncontrollability; uncontrollability produces helplessness, which causes the depression, passivity, and defeatism so often associated with poverty" (p. 161). Seligman concludes that poverty is more than a financial problem. It is also a "problem of individual mastery, dignity, and self-esteem" (p. 161). Deglau (1985) challenges Seligman's position and urges professionals to reexamine the concept of learned helplessness. Helping professionals need to involve people more directly in changing the structures that bring about their distress rather than merely adjusting people to their situations.

Appraisals Influence Responses. Exactly how people respond to discrimination, dehumanization, and victimization hinges on their appraisals of the circumstances that surround them. It is not just the events, but also people's appraisals of the events and the availability of resources for coping with the stress associated with stigma and discrimination (Miller & Kaiser, 2001). Albert Bandura's social learning perspective illuminates the "crucial role of the person as the processor, or meaning-maker, who translates experience into a form of behavior" (Newberger & DeVos, 1988, p. 507). People's interpretations of events are crucial in determining their behavioral responses. In relation to stress, for example, Bandura found a strong positive correlation between personal convictions of effectiveness and actual coping behaviors. These personal feelings of efficacy are associated with an increased capacity for adaptive functioning.

Opportunities, Obstacles, and Empowerment

Responsive environments provide resources that enrich citizens' social functioning. Social policies that promote access to health care, education, technical training, child care, civil rights, job opportunities, transportation, and comprehensive community-based services support individual citizens and contribute to a society's general well-being. Resource-rich environments contribute to people's bases of power. Empowerment-based professionals create resources in social support systems and influence social change in political and economic institutions and social welfare policies that enhance citizens' access to societal resources (Zimmerman & Rappaport, 1988).

Not all population groups enjoy equal opportunities for accessing environmental opportunities. Oppression, discrimination, dehumanization, and victimization prevent full participation in society by some groups. According to Gil (1994):

> The conditions that cause people to seek help from social workers and social services are invariably consequences of oppression and injustice. While these links are fairly obvious in situations such as unemployment, poverty, hunger, homelessness, and educational and occupational marginality, they may be less obvious in situations involving delinquency and crime, developmental defects, substance abuse, mental and physical ills, emotional and relational difficulties, and domestic violence. However, in-depth study of these situations and of individuals and groups of people involved typically reveals direct or indirect links to the dynamics of oppression and injustice. (p. 257)

Environmental risks such as shortages of resources, barriers created by social inequities, and lack of opportunities kindle social problems and create *environmental obstacles* (Garbarino, 1983). These environmental risks work against the well-being of society as a whole as well as against individual citizens. For example, some national economic policies increase the rate of poverty for segments of society, and some social policies aggravate patterns that intensify racism, sexism, or other forms of discrimination. Social workers facilitate empowerment by taking steps to overcome environmental obstacles and expand environmental opportunities.

In the context of empowerment, expanding opportunities means activating strategies that enhance clients' participation in the social and political structures of society and redress social injustices. In relation to social service delivery, this encompasses activities that promote clients' access to social services, maximize their rights, and reduce obstacles to services. In the context of the implementation of social programs, workers and clients work in partnerships to enhance public services such as transportation, housing, and job-training programs. With respect to social policies, social workers forthrightly advocate changes that expand opportunity structures that have otherwise denied citizens' access to institutional supports in the sociopolitical environment. "Expanding opportunities means creating new resources for client systems in their social and physical environments" (Miley, O'Melia, & DuBois, 2004, p. 378).

Social Work's Mandate for Social Justice

Social work's ethical codes mandate that professionals promote social and economic justice; protect the rights and freedom of individuals; and create societal conditions that uphold the values of worth, dignity, and uniqueness of all persons. General principles in the NASW (1999a) *Code of Ethics* delineate social workers' responsibilities with respect to society. According to the *Code,* social workers should strive to do the following:

- Promote the general welfare of society and the realization of social justice
- Facilitate public participation in democratic processes
- Respond to public emergencies with appropriate social services
- Ensure access for all persons to needed resources and opportunities
- Expand options and opportunities for everyone, but especially for persons who are disadvantaged or disenfranchised
- Prevent and eliminate all forms of exploitation and discrimination

The preamble of the *International Code of Ethics* of the International Federation of Social Workers (1994) describes a set of ideals to guide social workers in meeting human needs. Social workers in the international arena respect the unique value of every human being regardless of individual differences, cultural variations, or contributions to society. Likewise, the *Code* dictates the responsibility of all societies to provide maximum benefits for their members.

Looking Forward

Inequality, inequity, and injustice affect all aspects of personal and societal functioning. When social justice prevails, both individuals and the society benefit from the full participation of societal members in the social order. An optimal level of functioning is possible only when social justice prevails. The social work mandate encompasses the complementary processes of social functioning and social justice. Chapter 7 examines the implications of diversity for maximizing social functioning and promoting social justice in social work practice. The chapter offers perspectives on diversity—racial, cultural, religious, and life-style.

CHAPTER

7 Diversity and Social Work

Pat, T. J., and Marty assembled in the Campus Counseling and Resource Center for their regular 2 P.M. staff meeting. They structure their workdays so that the social workers are available to university students in the morning, late afternoon, and evening. With a full-time professional staff of three and several part-time social workers, the center maintains flexible hours so that it can respond promptly to requests for services. Because the center uses an on-call, rotating staff schedule to provide maximum coverage, it is likely that one worker will take an initial call and another will provide follow-up services.

Today Pat, T. J., and Marty are discussing assignments and making suggestions for follow-up responses. Several situations present unique challenges with respect to diversity:

Carmen H., a recipient of an educational grant for children of migrant workers, inquired about the community support available for her family when they eventually relocate in this community. Since Carmen's family does not speak English, bilingual services will be necessary.

Delilah S.'s crisis results from marital difficulties. Her educational experience is beginning to foster her independence. Now her husband is accusing her of abandoning her "God-given" role. Her husband does not want to come to the campus resource center for marriage counseling; however, he will agree to go to a "Christian" counselor.

Rajem B., an international student, requested information about community resources. Now that his wife is pregnant, they have many questions about well-baby clinics, food supplements, and other community resources.

Bill O.'s call was about his relationship with Steve. Bill's concern is about "coming out," or publicly revealing that he is gay. Steve is encouraging Bill to be more open about being gay, but Bill is apprehensive.

Pat, T. J., and Marty always orient their work toward clients' perspectives. However, in situations that involve cultural, ethnic, life-style, or religious differences, they pay particular attention to issues of diversity.

Shifting demographics, cultural pluralism, and variations of life-style in U.S. society magnify the need for social workers to be ethnically sensitive and nonsexist in their professional practice. Social workers practice with people of different races, cultural backgrounds, ethnic heritage, religious preferences, and sexual identifications. To work effectively and with sensitivity to cultural differences, practitioners must understand diversity and its implications for social work practice (Anderson, 1990). This chapter provides background information about

- Diversity and minority status
- Racial and ethnic diversity, including Blacks or African Americans, Asian Americans, Native Americans, and Hispanic Americans, and the implications of this diversity for social work practice
- Religious diversity
- Sexual diversity
- Social work in the context of diversity

Diversity and Minority Status

Cultural diversity is a broad concept that includes racial, ethnic, and social diversity. *Race* is a classification that emphasizes biological or physiological differences. In the United States, racial minorities include African Americans, Native Americans, Asian Americans, and Hispanic Americans.

The phrase *people of color* distinguishes those who must deal with oppression and vulnerability based on racial discrimination. There is no discrimination "so deeply rooted, persistent, and intractable as that based on color" (Hopps, 1982, p. 3). Color creates barriers to African Americans, Latino Americans, Asian Americans, and Native Americans in ways not experienced by ethnic groups who are able to blend into the white-dominated society (Lum, 2004). People of color are especially vulnerable to economic, political, and social conditions that reflect the climate of racism and discrimination.

Ethnicity refers to distinct population groups bound by common traits and customs. Among such groups are immigrants, refugees, and those associated by common religious affiliations. Ethnicity involves cultural differences and emphasizes a cultural ethos—the values, expectations, and symbols of a group. Factors that bring ethnic groups together include the social ties of a common origin, a distinct ethnic identity, and shared values, beliefs, and behaviors (Lum, 2004).

Cultural differences identify groups and distinguish them from one another by the way behavior is guided, structured, and ascribed with meaning. Differences among groups emerge in relation to world views and in perspectives on the nature of humankind and values conveyed in language, socialization, art forms, and artifacts (Devore & Schlesinger, 1999). The particular culture of minorities defines family support systems, confers self-identity and self-esteem, and imparts an ethnic philosophy and outlook on life. All of these factors are potential resources in times of crisis and stress (Lum, 2004).

For many years, professionals used the terms *minority group* and *ethnic group* interchangeably. According to sociology's conflict perspective, minority status affects socioeconomic well-being and cultural and social acceptance (Devore & Schlesinger, 1999). In this way, the term *minority* can refer to those groups, including women, older adults, people with disabilities, and homosexuals, that have less access to power than the dominant group. Those populations that have minority status conferred on them because of social stratification, poverty, disability, life-style, age, and sex are socially diverse. The dominant population often takes advantage of the disadvantaged status of minorities to oppress people who are socially diverse.

Responses to Dominance

Minorities respond to dominance in a variety of ways, including acculturation, assimilation, accommodation, rejection, and marginality. Each response represents an adaptive relationship between the majority's position of dominance and the minority's position of subordination.

Through *acculturation,* minorities incorporate themselves into the dominant culture by adopting its attitudes, values, and norms. Externally, minorities adopt the acceptable normative behaviors and social patterns of the dominant group, but they also retain behavioral patterns unique to their own group (Marden, Meyer, & Engel, 1992). In the process, they may forsake their own cultural heritage. *Assimilation* occurs when a minority group integrates itself into the dominant group. Disparate groups fuse, so that people cannot distinguish one group from another by their cultural characteristics. For this process "to be complete, assimilation must entail an active effort by the minority-group individual to shed all distinguishing actions and beliefs and the total, unqualified acceptance of that individual by the dominant society" (Schaefer, 1998, p. 24). Assimilation represents the Americanization of immigrants, a process some call *Anglo-conformity.* This characterizes the experience of many immigrant groups, especially European immigrants and White ethnic groups, who are similar to the dominant group in cultural and physical characteristics.

Accommodation results in a stable coexistence, with each group taking the other for granted and both groups accepting the same rationalizations for the existing dominant–minority patterns. The mutual accommodation of minority and majority groups results from the acculturation of minorities to the dominant culture, coupled with their assimilation into that culture.

Sometimes, rather than attempting to integrate with the dominant culture, minority groups resist efforts to be enfolded by it. A steadfast holding on to ethnic culture characterizes their *rejection* of the dominant culture. Conflicts may ensue when they openly reject the patterns of the dominant group.

Finally, minority people may experience *marginality* when they strive to be accepted by another group, even emulate that group, yet remain peripheral to it. Although the minority group shares the normative goals of the dominant group, it remains outside of the dominant group, coexisting between two cultures. Conflicts of values, expectations, and loyalties characterize struggles of marginality (Schaefer, 1998).

Ethnic Identity

Today, minority populations often try to maintain their ethnic identities while they seek inclusion in the societal mainstream. Among the factors forming ethnic identity are skin color, name, language, common religious beliefs, common ancestry, and place of origin (Lum, 2004). Individuals' cultural heritage influences their socialization by shaping beliefs and prescribing behaviors. Many people rediscover their ethnic identities by tracing their roots, studying their genealogies and family histories.

Negative social attitudes and devaluations by the dominant group often spur the development of ethnic identity among minority groups. Achieving an ethnic identity promotes self-determination and group cohesion and provides protection from a hostile environment (Washington, 1982). Ethnicity is a powerful force that forges a sense of belonging and community among ethnic group members (Lum, 2004).

Cultural Pluralism

Cultural pluralism is an alternative to a majority–minority relationship that subordinates minority culture. "Pluralism implies that various groups in a society have mutual respect for one

BOX 7.1

Reflections on Empowerment

Empowerment through Macrolevel Change

Empowerment derives from activating both personal and political power. Personal power is achieved through a sense of competence and affirming experiences. Political power reflects access to opportunities and the ability to influence decision making. For cultural minorities and minorities of color, ethnic discrimination and institutional racism diminish political power by closing opportunity structures of society (De Hoyos, De Hoyos, & Anderson, 1986).

According to Solomon (1976), minorities experience indirect and direct barriers to empowerment. Indirect barriers include bias, stereotyping, discrimination, and stigmatization. Direct barriers include underdeveloped skills and personal resources as a result of discrimination; structures that restrict funding or apply political sanctions, thereby constraining the allocation of resources; and discriminatory practices such as limiting the sale of homes in certain neighborhoods to certain people or denying mortgages to certain groups of applicants. Effective empowerment activities identify barriers to power and implement strategies to reduce their effects.

Empowerment-oriented social workers intervene at the sociocultural level, addressing the adverse effects of societal institutions that impair or hinder social functioning or even create barriers to legal and civil rights for minorities. Washington (1982) agrees that any social work effort that deals with problems of ethnic minorities must focus on the macrolevel practice. Macrolevel work, particularly public policy development and income redistribution, is important for dealing with sociocultural factors such as racism, poverty, and victimization. "These change-oriented strategies must be directed toward both individual betterment and social change, and they must emphasize social equality, social justice, new institutional structures, and the redistribution of wealth and resources" (p. 104).

another's culture, a respect that allows minorities to express their own culture without suffering prejudice or hostility" (Schaefer, 1998, p. 26). Rather than seeking to eliminate ethnic character, cultural pluralism strives to maintain the cultural integrity of ethnic groups.

For social work practice, the ideology of cultural pluralism promotes an orientation toward strengths. It requires that social workers understand "the history, diverse traditions, roles, family patterns, cultural symbols, and relations among ethnic and cultural groups. The understanding, sensitivity, and skills developed should help avoid the tendency to impose oneself and one's culture in efforts to help people of a different ethnic or cultural group" (Sanders, 1975, p. 98). Deeply held values and long-standing traditions of ethnic and cultural groups are a source of strength for adaptive social functioning.

Sociocultural Dissonance

Many ethnic minorities who live in the context of a pluralistic society experience sociocultural dissonance or "the stress, strain, and incongruence caused by belonging to two cultures—the ethnic culture and the dominant culture" (Chau, 1989, p. 224). Using Norton's dual perspective of a sustaining and nurturing environment, Chau suggests that ethnic minorities live within the context of a sustaining environment wherein institutional structures of the dominant society provide goods and services necessary for survival. At the same time, ethnic minorities draw upon the resources of their nurturing environment. The nurturing environment is the "immediate ethnic community that has shaped the individual's psychocultural identity in childhood and that continues to provide affective and nurturing supports" (p. 225). Dissonance occurs when people experience a mismatch between the nurturing environment of personal ethnic culture and the sustaining environment of the dominant culture.

Sociocultural dissonance is particularly stressful for ethnic minorities. Differences in status and culture, prejudice directed toward them, unfamiliarity with the environment, and restricted access to needed resources in social and political structures exacerbate their stress and conflict. Stress, disorientation, and other personal reactions may be normal responses "to a transcultural move or to the uprooting of one's customary network of resources and support" (Chau, 1989, p. 227). While dissonance often creates stress, it can also be a source of change and growth. The particular effect of dissonance—conformity, deviance, growth, or change—depends on individuals' perceptions of dissonance and how others regard and react to their cultural differences. The dissonance experienced by a minority population may, in fact, lead the dominant culture to reevaluate its values and institutional structures in light of its regard for all societal members.

Social group work is a vehicle for confronting sociocultural dissonance and strengthening ethnic identity (Chau, 1989). Intervention techniques include normative training, values clarification, empowerment, and advocacy. The particular intervention selected depends on the nature of the sociocultural dissonance experienced by the ethnic minority and the group's goals for intervention. Some group members may seek ethnic adaptation, while others strive to respond to cultural insensitivity, increase ethnic identity and valuation, or confront macrostructural issues (Table 7.1).

Racial and Ethnic Diversity

Census Bureau projections indicate that, by the year 2050, minority groups will comprise about half of the total population in the United States. Immigration accounts for much of the diversification of the population, particularly among the Asian and Hispanic population. At present, more than half of the members of minority populations in the United States live in five states: California, Texas, New York, Florida, and Illinois (Population Reference Bureau, 2003a).

Already the demographic shifts in many urban counties have created such diverse populations that no single ethnic or racial group predominates in number. The migratory patterns of racial and ethnic populations result in a highly diverse mix of African Americans, Hispanic Americans, Asian Americans, Native Americans, and Euro-Americans in large urban areas and in rural counties in the southeast. In contrast, "the least diverse region of the U.S. is a broad swath stretching from northern New England through the Midwest and into Montana" (Allen & Turner, 1990, p. 38).

TABLE 7.1 Sociocultural Dissonance: Four Loci of Concern for Group Work Practice

Locus of Concern	Nature of Sociocultural Dissonance	Underlying Ideology	Goals of Intervention	Strategies of Intervention
Ethnic adaptation	Problems of transition, dislocation, uprootedness; cultural strain and stress; lack resource and support networks; social, personal, vocational skills incongruent with mainstream expectations	Cultural sensitivity; flexibility in service delivery; preferential opportunities	Develop personal, social, and vocational competencies; enhance knowledge of resources; establish new social support network	Normative training, educating, socializing, remediation, counseling
Interethnic integration	Interactional and socially induced; distorted attitudes or misinformation; cultural insensitivity; minority overreaction	Correct information prerequisite for interethnic understanding, harmony, acceptance, and integration	Promote understanding and acceptance of ethnocultural differences; social integration of groups	Reeducative: clarification of values; develop cultural awareness and cultural sensitivity; foster collaborative projects
Ethnic consciousness raising	Low ethnic self-image; low group cohesion; lack power bases; social, political, and economic vulnerability	Interest-group perspective; domination-subordination; power realignment	Raise ethnic consciousness; enhance ethnic identity; overcome subordination; create new power bases	Empowerment: self-help, mutual help, leadership training and development; organization building; political process
Ethnic rights	Inequality in services and policies; few opportunities; discriminatory practices	Social institutions and practices are by nature culture-bound, but do respond to democratic pressures for change	Promote equality of opportunity; facilitate changes in policies, procedures, and service delivery	Advocacy: internal/external, social/legal, administrative compliance; political channels, demonstration projects, action research

Source: "Sociocultural Dissonance among Ethnic Minority Populations" by Kenneth L. Chau, April 1989, *Social Casework,* p. 226. Reprinted by permission of the publisher, Families International, Inc.

Black Americans

Black Americans are the largest minority group in the United States, numbering 36 million in 2002, or about 13 percent of the total population (McKinnon, 2003). Most Blacks in the United States are descendants of slaves, although some are more recent immigrants. The term *Afro-American* refers to both cultural and racial aspects of Black identity. It differentiates descendants of American slaves from African descendants in other places, such as South America and the Caribbean (Pinderhughes, 1982).

Although Blacks in this country are a heterogeneous group (there is no such thing as "*the* Black family"), they share cultural similarities that distinguish them from other ethnic groups. Among the factors that influence the culture of African Americans are a legacy of African customs, the disruptive effects of slavery on family life, the lasting effects of discrimination and racism, and the formulation of a circular victim system that threatens self-esteem and reinforces negative environmental responses (Boyd-Franklin, 2003).

The group's heritage of African values, its identity with mainstream Euro-American values, and its adaptation to victimization and oppression are the sources of African American cultural and ethnic identity:

> American values emphasize individualism, independence, autonomy, ownership of material goods, achievement, mastery, progress, youth, future orientation, efficiency, and planning. African values stress collectivity, sharing, affiliation, obedience to authority, belief in spirituality, and respect for the elderly and the past. Victim system values that are consequences of adaptation to oppression emphasize cooperation to combat powerlessness; strict obedience to authority in the context of felt oppression; strength; toughness of character; present-time orientation (since the past is painful and there is no future); suppression and channeling of feelings into music, art, and other creative activities; and belief in luck, magic, and spirituality. (Pinderhughes, 1982, pp. 109–110)

An African American family celebrates Kwanzaa, a Black American tradition based on African harvest festivals.

These value systems influence all African American families and distinguish them as a cultural group. They also explain the tremendous diversity in the family structures, life-styles, behavior, and values of African American families.

Cultural Duality. By virtue of their oppressed experience in the United States, Black African Americans live in two worlds (Chestang, 1976). Their cultural duality derives from the simultaneous influences of their personal immediate culture and the White-dominant societal culture. Both the nutritive world of family, friends, and the Black community and the sustentative world of employment, education, and status shape personality and social character:

> The sustaining environment consists of the survival needs of man: goods and services, political power, economic resources. It is largely through this environment that status is conferred and power exercised. It is the world of the larger society. The black individual is propelled toward it by the need for survival, and, because he is denied full participation in it, he makes an instrumental adaptation to it.
>
> The nurturing environment, the black community, differs from the sustaining environment in two ways: First, it affords the individual emotional support, cultural values, family relationships, and supportive institutions. His relationship to this world is expressive. This is to say that within this environment, the individual experiences a sense of wholeness and identification. And second, the black individual is pulled toward this world by the force that has been called "being." This latter term suggests that the pull is toward self-realization and dignity. (pp. 70–71)

"When the society admits an individual to full participation in its culture, the sustentative and nutritive aspects are merged" (Chestang, 1976, p. 69). However, when institutions, customs, and codes constrain the societal rights of equality, justice, and freedom, these rights become symbols rather than reality for Black Americans. Black Americans have experienced restricted access to educational and employment opportunities as well as limited availability of health care resources. These limitations in the sustaining environment make some Blacks more vulnerable to impaired physical and psychological functioning (Barbarin, 1983). In spite of widespread discrimination in the sustaining societal environment, however, the nurturing environment of family and Black community promotes competence.

Race and Power. The racial variable is a significant feature of the problems that affect people of color. However, many hold that race in and of itself is not the problem. Rather, the problem is being rendered powerless in society by virtue of racial characteristics. A series of questions help social workers explore the effect of powerlessness:

1. How has the client's family perceived the fact of being black in its life experiences (for example, quality of education, job opportunities, and marital relationships)?
2. What has been the interaction of social class and race in the formation of attitudes, beliefs, values, and behavior patterns?
3. How have formal and informal support systems within the black community been utilized by the individual and/or family?
4. To what extent does the individual consider it possible to change the outcome of his or her interactions with white-dominated social institutions? (Solomon, 1989, pp. 580–581)

When institutional structures are sources of stress to families, modifications of social institutions may be warranted. "Afro-Americans have made it clear that social workers' old preoccupations with finding the source of problems in the individual psyche and in helping clients to 'adjust' to inadequate social supplies are unacceptable" (Solomon, 1989, p. 568).

Several defensive postures emerge from the Black experience in the United States. These adaptive reactions characterize Blacks' normative behavioral responses to the contempt and hatred exhibited by White society:

- *Cultural paranoia* is a survival mode in which the actions and motivations of all Whites and the institutional structures are questioned and presumed to be antagonistic to Blacks.
- *Cultural depression* (or cultural masochism) is a consequence of the long history of Blacks' societal subordination and the internalization of self-deprecating attitudes.
- *Cultural antisocialism* is a posture of disregard and disrespect for laws and legal processes that protect Whites and exclude and denigrate Blacks. (Grier & Cobbs, 1968)

These psychological devices are potentially adaptive and appropriate responses rather than pathological and maladaptive.

Social Support. A strengths perspective emphasizes "the capacity of black families to survive past oppression, current racial discrimination, and economic deprivation to cope with life stress" (Barbarin, 1983, p. 309). To cope with stressful life transitions, Black Americans have relied on informal social support networks to resolve their problems. Characteristics of the Black culture that mediate the pressures of an oppressive society include the adaptive strengths of loyal and strong kinship bonds; flexible family roles; deep religious faith; and orientations toward work, education, and achievement (Hines & Boyd-Franklin, 1996).

The extended family, church organizations, and self-help groups are predominant sources of strength for Black African Americans. For example, the extended family structures and strong sibling relationships among Blacks mediate the single-parent status of one-third of Black families. The multigenerational nature of Black families, shared parental responsibility for child rearing, flexible family roles, and the high value Blacks place on work and educational achievement strengthen Black families.

The socialization of Black children often instills a positive racial identity. This enables Black children to maintain positive self-esteem. This socialization teaches survival skills related to being Black in a White society. Black parents share a concern for their children's welfare, even giving precedence to child-related issues over spousal relationships: "This unique complementary accommodation between spouses and between parents and children characterizes a unique strength of the Black American family structure" (Ho, 1987, p. 196). However, clear role expectations, delegation of authority, and assignment of responsibility are still necessary for effective family functioning in Black families. Shared child-rearing responsibilities are characteristic of Black families. Older siblings and other significant adult family members sometimes take on this role. Ho cautions social workers not to confuse this role flexibility with role confusion and family disorganization.

Social Work Intervention. Black families usually respond positively to short-term, action-oriented intervention processes directed toward concrete behavioral changes (Ho,

1987). In their work with Black African Americans, social workers must select culturally relevant techniques. For example, affirming their strength in seeking services is critical for forming partnerships with Black clients. Considering how Black culture influences clients' developmental transitions and experiences is required in assessment. Through an ecosystems perspective, clients and practitioners examine the resources available to manage the realities of problems posed by the social environment (Figure 7.1).

Asian Americans

Estimates indicate that Asian Americans and Pacific Islanders make up about 4.4 percent of the U.S. population, representing more than a 100 percent increase since the 1980 census (Reeves & Bennett, 2003). About half of the Asian American and Pacific Islander population live in the western part of the United States. Eighteen percent live in the Northwest, 19 percent in the South, and 12 percent in the Midwest (Reeves & Bennett, 2003). Most live in three states—California, New York, and Hawaii. Asian Americans are one of the most

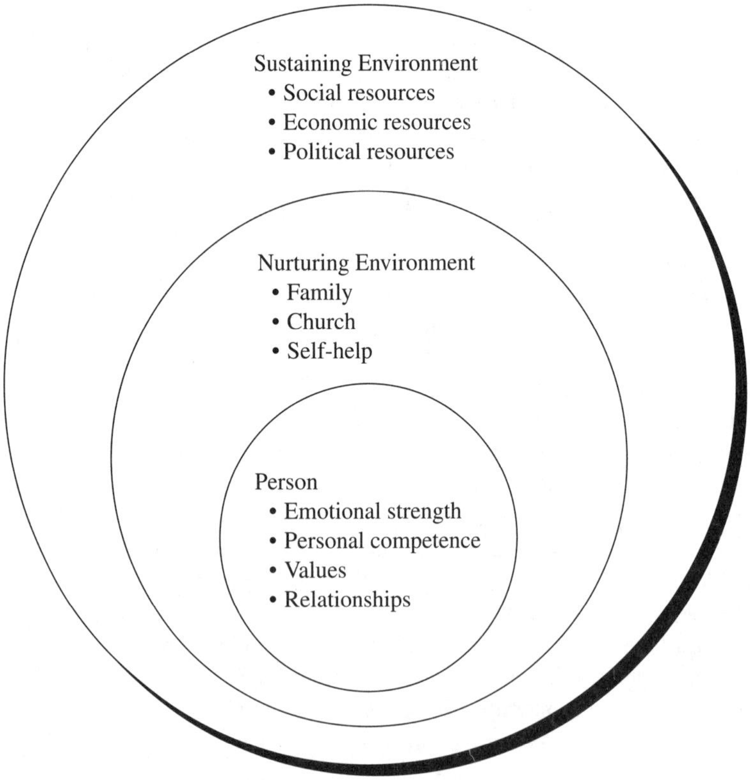

FIGURE 7.1 Ecosystems Analysis

diverse and least understood minority groups in North America (Balgopal, 1995). For example, the economic situation of Asian Americans varies greatly. One the one hand, "Asian and Pacific Islander families are more likely than non-Hispanic White families to have incomes of $75,000 or more, they are also more likely to have incomes less than $25,000" (Reeves & Bennett, 2003, p. 6).

Asian Americans represent diverse ethnic goups from more than 16 countries of origin and 20 Pacific Island cultures. For example, Asian Americans originate from Japan, China, Korea, India, Vietnam, Cambodia, Laos, Thailand, the Philippines, Samoa, and Hawaii (Balgopal, 1995). Within each country of origin, further distinctions include differences in language, religion, art forms, folkways, and other features of everyday life. Two families from the same country can actually have very little in common.

Other factors, such as social class, the influence of other cultures, diversity of socioeconomic and religious backgrounds, the number of generations removed from immigration, and the circumstances of immigration and the resettlement process, further differentiate Asian Americans. For example, one would expect considerable difference between those who planned to immigrate and those who had to emigrate because of war, political persecution, or famine.

Early Immigration Experiences. Asians began settling in the geographically isolated West Coast region and in Hawaii during the middle of the nineteenth century (Balgopal,

Asian Americans are one of the most diverse minority groups in North America.

BOX **7.2**

Reflections on Diversity

Social Work with Immigrants and Refugees

Early settlement house leaders, including Jane Addams, "have left a legacy of dedicated and committed work with new immigrants" (Balgopal, 2000a, p. 15). Their efforts helped immigrant groups adapt to life in the United States through citizenship classes, English lessons, and cultural activities that emphasized the "American ways of life." Today, social workers' activities continue the tradition of providing supports for making the transition to living in a new country. However, today's emphasis is on supporting cultural pluralism, rather than on encouraging the "melting pot mentality" of the past. "Social workers must learn skills that will allow them to maximize the uniqueness of the immigrants' culture while assisting them with their needs in the American society" (p. 23).

Among those considered immigrants are legal immigrants, undocumented immigrants, refugees, and asylees. As defined by the Immigration Act of 1990, immigrants are persons who are lawfully admitted to the United States for permanent residence. Undocumented immigrants enter the United States without proper documentation. This group includes migrant workers who remain after their employment ends. Refugees are those who flee from their countries in fear of persecution and oppression because of their political or religions beliefs, ethnicity, or membership in particular social groups (Balgopal, 2000a). Finally, asylees are those persons filing for protection in a country in which they have sought refuge. U.S. immigration law places limits on the number of asylees who can be accepted as legal residents each year.

Worldwide in 2003, there were 13 million refugees and asylum seekers (U.S. Committee for Refugees [USCR], 2003a). About one-half of these refugees are from Afghanistan and the former Palestine (USCR, 2003b). In addition, nearly 22 million people have been displaced within their own countries. The plight of refugees is sobering as "millions of people on this earth, particularly refugees and displaced persons in Africa, have begun the new millennium living in conditions that are in some ways similar to those that existed a full millennium earlier: In huts or exposed to the elements, without adequate clothing, sanitation, or health care, preyed upon by their fellow men, and effectively unprotected by rule of law" (USCR, 2000).

Numerous opportunities exist for social workers who are interested in working with immigrants and refugees. Social workers in all fields of practice in larger urban areas, particularly in such states as New York, California, Florida, Texas, and New Jersey, and such areas in the Midwest as Illinois, Minnesota, Michigan, and Ohio are likely to encounter immigrants and refugees among their clientele. The International Federation of Social Workers (1998) promotes the following:

> A partnership model of practice, with refugees fully involved at all stages of problem resolution and prevention; ethnically sensitive social work education and training, including special references to the experiences and needs of refugees, recruitment of people from minority groups, including refugees, into the professional, paraprofessional training for members of ethnic groups, including refugees, and co-operation with ethnic support systems, relevant in-service training, refugee advocacy by social workers, aiming to educate the public, influence government, and the policies of other agencies; effective interagency co-operation, nationally and internationally, and systematic research and programme evaluation. (Policy Statement section, ¶ 12)

Where there are concentrations of immigrants and refugees, culturally appropriate services, such as neighborhood centers, case management services, and refugee resettlement programs, develop. Social workers are employed in many international settings. From work with programs sponsored by the United Nations to employment in various nongovernmental organizations (NGOs), opportunities abound. In any setting, "the role of the social worker is to learn how to assess immigrants' situations, advocate for their rights and needs, determine which community resources they need, help them adapt to their new country without leaving behind their cultural customs and traditions, and monitor their progress" (Balgopal, 2000b, pp. 238–239).

1995). The first groups of Asians kept a relatively low profile to avoid racial conflicts during the period of western expansion in the United States. Motivated by economic and educational opportunities, their reason for immigration was very similar to that of other immigrant groups. However, unlike European immigrants, Asian Americans were subjected by U.S. policies to harsh discriminatory legislation that restricted immigration quotas, assigned a legal status of "alien ineligible for citizenship," and forbade interracial marriages.

Further humiliation and oppression occurred during World War II when federal agents removed the *Nisei,* or second-generation Japanese Americans, from their homes to internment camps, ostensibly for their own protection. Many believe that the U.S. policy to detain Japanese Americans manifested deeply rooted prejudice and discrimination against Asian Americans.

Asian American Values. In general, Eastern philosophy and religions such as Confucianism, Hinduism, Islam, and Buddhism influence the value systems of Asian Americans (Chung, 1992). These beliefs differ from the Western world view. Ho (1989) describes values salient to Asian culture:

- *Filial piety,* an unquestioning veneration and respect for and deference to authority, permeates relationships between generations. For example, patriarchy, parental dominance, and the expectation of children's unquestioning obedience characterize parent–child relationships.
- Asian *parents expect their children to comply,* even to the point of sacrificing their personal ambitions. They reinforce compliance through their use of shame and threats of losing face and, thus, family and community support.
- Asians highly value *self-control.* "The value 'enryo' requires a Japanese individual to maintain modesty in behavior, be humble in expectations, and show appropriate hesitation and unwillingness to intrude on another's time, energy, or resources" (p. 529).
- *Middle position virtue* is a norm that fosters communal belonging rather than individual pride. Asians are particularly aware of the group influence of the social milieu. They subordinate individuality to the group and internalize problems.
- *Fatalism* or detached acceptance of situations pervades Asians' response patterns.

These values produce a traditional Asian worldview and inform the way Asian Americans understand problems and select solutions, and even the ways they seek help. For example, Asian Americans hesitate to seek professional intervention because of their deference to parental authority, internalization of problems, tendency toward nondisclosure of problems, and avoidance of shame (Mokuau, 1987). Even Westernized Asian Americans "feel stigma, and shame in talking about problems" (Ho, 1989, p. 533).

However, we must be careful not to overgeneralize, as there are many individual differences among Asian Americans. Some Asian Americans fully incorporate a Western world view. Some combine Eastern and Western views. The views of some reflect their culture of origin. In families, members are likely to express different worldviews, particularly when generational differences are a factor.

Some problems that Asian American minorities experience include those associated with immigration, acculturation, cross-cultural misunderstandings, caregiving relationships, and cultural identity:

■ *Immigration* places strains on families. Reasons for these strains include separation from their country of origin, the experience of refugee resettlement, and the experience of family reunification.

■ For Asian Americans, *acculturation to mainstream values and life-styles* is challenging. Traditional Asian values revered by elders conflict with the dominant societal values that younger generations may express.

■ The transition to a mainstream life-style often requires *adaptation to newly defined roles* and practices. Even such things as child abuse, spouse abuse, and mental illness carry cultural meanings.

■ *Cultural expectations about providing care* for children, elders, and dependent adults often place Asian Americans in a bind. The demands imposed by the need for a dual income make fulfilling the filial duty difficult.

■ Asian Americans' *non-Anglo physical characteristics,* stereotypes of their behavior, and their diverse worldviews complicate issues of identity and finding a place in U.S. culture. (Kitano, 1987)

Native Americans

Native Americans are culturally and linguistically diverse. Based on census data gathered in 2000, population estimates indicate an American Indian and Alaska Native population of about 2.5 million, although another 1.6 million people indicate American Indian and at least one other race (Ogunwole, 2002). Distinct tribal heritage as well as differences in the tribe members' degrees of assimilation creates diversity. Americans Indians are divided among 562 tribes and Alaska Native groups. The largest tribal groupings include the Cherokee, Navajo, Latin American, Choctaw, Sioux, and Chippewa. At present, most reside outside reservation boundaries. About 25 percent of the total American Indian population resides in two states—California and Oklahoma. Other states with large American Indian populations include Arizona, Texas, New Mexico, New York, Washington, North Carolina, Michigan, and Alaska.

Life both on and off reservation is harsh. Poverty is rampant, unemployment is high, and health problems abound. Based on averages from 1999 to 2001, the poverty rate for American Indians and Alaska Natives was 24.5 percent (U.S. Census Bureau, 2002e). The dropout rate from school is inordinately high, and alcoholism, mental health problems, and suicide plague Native American families. The infant mortality rate among American Indians and Alaska Natives is 9.7 per 1,000 live births compared to 5.7 for Whites (Mathews, Menacker, & MacDorman, 2003). Finally, there is a disproportionate rate of Native American children in out-of-home or substitute care arrangements, 3.6 times higher than the rate for other groups (Dobrec, 1990).

Social work intervention with Native Americans has met with little success because of a lack of understanding of and sensitivity to Native American culture, failure to acknowledge the legacy of trauma and unresolved grief resulting from physical and cultural genocide, overriding stereotypes, and the application of standard rather than culturally sensitive intervention techniques (Lewis & Ho, 1989; Weaver, 1998). Parallel social service structures, including tribal welfare councils, the Bureau of Indian Affairs (BIA), and state and federal health and

Distinct tribal heritage and degree of assimilation heighten the diversity among Native Americans.

human services, complicate the social service delivery system for Native Americans. The recent debate over Indian Federalism centers on continuing federal monetary support and governmental intervention through the BIA, thus redefining Native Americans' relationship with the federal government. Indian Federalism is not an effort to dismantle the BIA, but rather to give tribes opportunities to operate more independently of the federal government.

Based on a study that examined the beliefs of indigenous social workers about how best to work with Native Americans, Weaver (1999) recommends that to provide culturally competent services to Native American clients, social workers need to do the following:

- understand and appreciate diversity among and within Native American populations
- know the history, culture, and contemporary realities of specific Native American clients
- have good general social work skills and strong skills in patience, listening, and tolerance of silence
- be aware of his or her own biases and need for wellness
- display humility and a willingness to learn
- be respectful, nonjudgmental, and open-minded
- value social justice and decolonize his or her own thought processes (Conclusion section, ¶ 1)

Social Work Highlights. Working effectively with Native Americans requires an understanding of the role of Native American family networks. Traditional White families operate within single households. In contrast, Native American families are structurally open, and include cousins as brothers and sisters, and aunts and uncles as grandfathers and grandmothers (Sutton & Broken Nose, 1996). Family is extended vertically and horizontally to include numerous relatives, often as far as second cousins (Sue & Sue, 2002). Red Horse, Lewis, Feit, and Decker (1978) provide an interesting illustration of this family characteristic:

> A young probationer was under court supervision and had strict orders to remain with responsible adults. His counselor became concerned because the youth appeared to ignore this order. The client moved around frequently and, according to the counselor, stayed overnight with several different young women. The counselor presented this case at a formal staff meeting, and fellow professionals stated their suspicion that the client was either a pusher or a pimp. The frustrating element to the counselor was that the young women knew each other and appeared to enjoy each other's company. Moreover, they were not ashamed to be seen together in public with the client. This behavior prompted the counselor to initiate violation proceedings. (p. 68)

A Native American professional provided an alternative explanation. The boy's family network consisted of over 200 people representing three generations. He was staying with various members of his extended family. Adults were taking responsibility for him and the girls were like his sisters. A misunderstanding of the family structure led to inappropriate recommendations.

Hispanic Americans

The United States Census Bureau reports indicate that, in 2002, 13.3 percent of the population, or 37.4 million are Hispanic (Ramirez & de la Cruz, 2003). Hispanic Americans comprise several nationalities including Mexican Americans (66.9 percent), Central and South Americans (14.3 percent), Cubans (13.7 percent), and Puerto Ricans (8.6 percent). The Hispanic population will double by the year 2050.

Hispanic is an adjective describing several nationalities that share a common language, religion, history, set of surnames, and cultural heritage and have differences in geographic origin, folkways, and local environment (Castex, 1994). People of Mexican and Puerto Rican descent make up the largest part of the Hispanic population in the United States. A large proportion of Hispanic Americans live in urban areas. Demographic data indicate that Hispanic Americans are less educated, have higher rates of poverty, and are more likely to live in inner-city neighborhoods. Language barriers are particularly problematic. In 2002, about 40 percent of the Hispanic population was foreign born; about half of this population immigrated to the United States since 1990 (Ramirez & de la Cruz, 2003).

Poverty rates for the Hispanic population have risen steadily since 1970. A significant proportion of Hispanic Americans—21.4 percent—live in poverty (Ramirez & de la Cruz, 2003). This is due in part to immigration patterns of Hispanics whose earning capacity is affected adversely by low levels of education and unfamiliarity with the English language

The Hispanic American population will double by the year 2050.

(Council of Economic Advisors, 1998). Poverty rates are especially high among Hispanic American children. Reports indicate that 28 percent of all Hispanic children live in poverty, about three times the number of non-Hispanic White children living in poverty in the United States (Ramirez & de la Cruz, 2003). More specifically, "Hispanic children represented 17.7 percent of all children in the United States but constituted 30.4 percent of all children in poverty" (p. 6).

Mexican Americans constitute a large proportion of migrant laborers (Curiel, 1995). Frequently, migrant laborers find employment in agriculture, food processing plants, fishing, and fishing-related industries; their employment tends to be seasonal. They often work as family groups, with everyone, even young children, working in the fields. Working conditions are often hazardous, exacerbating health problems such as high rates of miscarriage and infant mortality. Mexican American migrant laborers face low socioeconomic status, inadequate physical and mental health care, and lack of consistent education (Ramos, 1995).

Cultural Values. A number of nuances of Hispanic culture have implications for the delivery of social services. Hispanic culture emphasizes *personalismo,* or trust in persons rather than in impersonal institutions or structures. Warmth and sharing characterize personal relationships. *Personalismo* suggests that Hispanic clients are receptive to individualized attention. *Personalismo* also directs Hispanic clients to personalize their relationships with social workers. Hispanic clients prefer having contact with the same social worker throughout the helping process. Responding to "small talk" signals acceptance of clients and builds *confianza,* or trust (Congress, 1990; Morales & Reyes, 2000). Within families, obligations for respect depend on age, role, and gender. This *respecto* is constant and doesn't change with circumstances. For example, Hispanic women who have been abused often proclaim that they "still respect their husbands as they [the abusers] are the fathers of their children or unfaithful husbands claiming they respect their wives as they never brought any of their girlfriends home" (p. 23). Because of its importance, social workers should not underestimate the influence of *respecto.* Finally, *si Dios quiere* (if God wills it) expresses spiritual values and an acceptance of fate. Protection in the form of charms, rituals, herbal water, and prayers of appeal to saints and the Virgin Mary are all efforts to cope with fate. This fatalism is particularly significant for medical social workers. When Hispanic clients believe in *si Dios quiere,* they may not follow through consistently on medical treatments. Effective practitioners creatively incorporate client systems' cultural values into their work together.

Social Work Highlights. The MADRE parent education program demonstrates culturally sensitive practice (Herrerias, 1989). MADRE is an acronym for *Madres Avanzando y Desarollando vil Rol Educativo,* which means Mothers Advancing and Developing an Educational Role. This prevention program targets women who are at risk for child abuse and neglect. To avoid an association with being *loca,* or crazy, workers call themselves "educators" rather than "counselors." They emphasize developing warm, personal relationships with the participants. The program uses bicultural, bilingual staff to provide in-home education to build *personalismo.* They adapted the curriculum to make it linguistically and culturally relevant to their Hispanic clients. Recognizing the value placed on children in the Hispanic family, they motivate participants *por los niños,* for the sake of the children. The in-home educator links clients with additional services, such as group training sessions, supplemental programs for emergency needs, job training, education, and family counseling.

Cultural Competence

The terms *cultural competence* and *ethnic competence* refer to the provision of culturally relevant services that are sensitive to the requirements of cross-cultural situations (Green & Leigh, 1985). Cross-cultural practice requires practitioners' commitment to provide culturally competent services. Culturally competent practitioners have a foundation of knowledge and skills that demonstrates their acceptance of cultural diversity. They recognize the dynamics of ethnic reality in their clients' lives and refine interventions in light of cultural differences. Ethnically sensitive practitioners are aware of the impact of their own cultural and ethnic values during intervention.

Ethnic competence is not just empathic concern, nor does it consist only of interpersonal communication skills. Ethnically competent social workers can do the following:

- Elicit personal values systems of persons who are different from [them]
- Articulate personal and professional values and the manner in which they may conflict or accommodate the needs of people who are culturally different from [them]
- Use practice technologies reflective of self-understanding of the role of language in ethnically distinctive communities. (Green & Leigh, 1985, p. 2)

Our cultural lens modifies our perception of experiences, including stress and crises. Listening to clients' stories in the context of their cultural perspectives enables social workers to form effective partnerships with clients (Green & Leigh, 1985; Leung, Cheung, & Stevenson, 1994). "The task of the ethnically competent social worker is to acquire an awareness of the common sense of another culture and to utilize that awareness in the delivery of a service" (Green & Leigh, p. 11).

Self-Awareness. Personally examining their own ethnic background, identity, and values provides the foundation for social workers to practice with ethnic sensitivity. Social workers can examine their perceptions and feelings about their cultural identity critically by asking themselves the following questions:

1. What is your ethnic background? What has it meant to belong to your ethnic group? How has it felt to belong to your ethnic group? What do you like about your ethnic identity? What do you dislike?
2. Where did you grow up, and what other ethnic groups resided there?
3. What are the values of your ethnic group?
4. How did your family see itself, as similar to or different from other ethnic groups?
5. What was your first experience with feeling different?
6. What are your earliest images of race or color? What information were you given about how to deal with racial issues?
7. What are your feelings about being White or a person-of-color? To Whites: How do you think people-of-color feel about their color identity? To people-of-color: How do you think Whites feel about their color identity?
8. Discuss your experiences as a person having or lacking power in relation to the following: ethnic identity; racial identity; within the family; class identity; sexual identity; professional identity. (Pinderhughes, 1989, p. 217)

Several basic assumptions guide ethnically sensitive practice (Devore & Schlesinger, 1999). Clients' experiences, collective ethnic histories, and responses to oppression bear on how they perceive problems and select solutions: "Personality and life history serve as filters and determine which facets of ethnic history and identity remain an integral part of a person's functioning, which are forgotten, and which are consciously rejected" (p. 157). Although clients' current problems are the central focus, social workers and clients recognize the power of the past in shaping the present. Ethnic heritage influences how people develop their self-identity. It nurtures a sense of belonging and provides historical continuity. The components of ethnic reality—including the family, traditions, ethnic schools,

BOX 7.3
Social Work Profile

Community College

I didn't realize it at the time, but working as a custodian for six years after high school was a good learning experience, and losing that job was the best thing that ever happened to me! I learned the meaning of hard work, and I also learned what it felt like to be invisible, to have people walk by without looking at you, without talking to you, without acknowledging your presence. There was one professional employee, however, who always stopped to talk with me. One day he said, "You're clearly bright, articulate, and have a lot of potential. Why don't you think about going to college!" I thought to myself, "Who me? Nobody from my family's finished college. This job pays the bills, why should I take a chance." However, I remembered his words of encouragement. When the company downsized, I thought, "Why not try a class or two." So here I am many years later, with a master's degree working at a community college where the mission is lifelong learning and the values emphasize diversity. I started out with my undergraduate social work degree as a case manager, acting as a liaison between the college and the public assistance agency. Now I am a master's degree–prepared counselor with a faculty appointment in Adult Education. I often wonder if I would have ended up in the same place if someone hadn't planted the seed of hope that gave me the courage to pursue a dream.

My job is all about believing in people, carefully listening to them, helping them discover solutions to their problems, and encouraging them to pursue their own dreams. Their dreams range from completing a GED to finding a job to earning a college degree. Ages vary, too. I believe the youngest person I've worked with was 16 and the oldest, 84. The students with whom I work come from all walks of life, but most have encountered difficulties that have interrupted their education, their employability, and their lives. We work together to resolve child care issues, housing problems, and job-related stress. More than half of my clients are in the process of getting a divorce or are newly divorced and often struggle with issues of self-esteem and communicating assertively.

Recently, English as a Second Language (ESL) students have added to the diversity of the persons with whom I work daily. They're from all over the world—Bosnia, Iran, Afghanistan, Russia, and many different countries in Africa and Asia. Many are confused by what we might consider simple everyday tasks—things like arranging for a phone or a bank account, navigating public transportation, sorting out junk mail and telemarketing offers, or following various bureaucratic rules and procedures. Many encounter racism and discrimination for the first time in their lives. It's like they had seen the United States as the land of opportunity and freedom and are stunned that the resources in the "land of plenty" aren't equally available to everyone.

My social work background gives me a unique perspective on students. I see both problems and potential solutions holistically in a context of persons within families within their communities and society. I've learned to ask a lot of questions, as I need to paint a picture in my mind of clients' situations and their points of view. I consider the social work value of human dignity and worth—acceptance of all people, no matter who they are—fundamental to my day-to-day practice. Perhaps my being a minority gives me an advantage with clients. Some will say to me when speaking of their own experiences of racism and discrimination, "Well, of course, *you* know where I'm coming from." But, of course, unless I listen carefully and ask questions, I really don't know, because everyone's experience is so unique. I love having the opportunity to help others. Working in this setting gives me a chance to make a difference!

and language—"serve as a source of cohesion, identity, and strength, as well as a source of strain, discord, and strife" (p. 160). Ethnically sensitive practice requires workers to focus their attention "on individual problems at the same time that [they recognize] the systemic source of and possible solution of the difficulty" (p. 165). Finally, ethnically sensitive social workers adapt their techniques to the demands of cultural differences.

Religious Diversity

Varying religious orientations further diversify people. Since a holistic understanding of persons is fundamental to social work practice, an understanding of religion is essential. In fact, religious diversity is central to clients and social workers alike (Canda & Furman, 1999; Gilbert, 2000; Gotterer, 2001; Hodge, 2000; Ortiz, Villereal, & Engel, 2000). To further understand religious diversity and its relationship with social work, this section explores the role of religion in today's world, describes the nature of spirituality, and examines the relationship between religious diversity and social work practice.

Religion in Today's World

Based on the results of large-scale surveys of adults in the United States, experts at the Princeton Religion Research Center report that 9 in 10 people say they pray and three in four say they pray daily (Pew Research Center, 2001). A recent national longitudinal survey of adolescents reports that of those adolescents surveyed, 80 percent pray—40 percent daily and 22 percent weekly (National Study of Youth and Religion, 2002). Current Gallup poll survey findings indicate that 68 percent report holding membership in a religious group and 88 percent say that religion is very important to them (Religion, 2000). About 80 percent of people in the United States identify themselves as Christian (Kosmin, Mayer, & Keysar, 2001). Church attendance in the United States has changed little in the past half century. In 1950, 39 percent of Americans polled by the Gallup organization reported that they attended church in a typical week. A recent survey found that 43 percent of those surveyed attended services weekly (Barna, 2003).

The impact of religion throughout the world may be witnessed in the Islamic resistance in Afghanistan, the establishment and continued support of Israel by Judaism, the part Christianity played in the upheavals of Eastern Europe, the interest of the West in Buddhism and Eastern spirituality, and the rapid growth of Christianity and Islam in Africa. As these examples suggest, we live in an age of religious pluralism. There are more Muslims than Episcopalians in the United States. Those traveling through America's heartland will pass a Hindu temple west of Chicago in Aurora, Illinois.

Religion and Ethnic and Racial Minorities. Religion has strong cohesive power, as evidenced by the Roman Catholic immigrants to the United States during the late nineteenth and early twentieth centuries. Although the Roman Catholic Church of that era held worship services in the common language of Latin, Catholic parishes formed on the basis of ethnicity. Italian, German, Irish, and Polish immigrants maintained their own distinctive piety and practice. Thomas and Znaniecki's classic 1920 study showed that the Polish parish in America reorganized and concentrated the coherent village-group of the immigrants' homeland (Marty, 1986). For Polish immigrants, as for many other ethnic groups, religion provided familiar social structures in their new life in America.

Religion plays a particularly significant role for ethnic minorities. Persecuted because of their religion, Jews have maintained a sense of cultural and religious identity in spite of anti-Semitism throughout history. For many ethnic groups, religion was a haven of support in the new society (Cnaan, Wineburg, & Boddie, 1999).

Historically, the Black church has provided for both the social and psychological needs of its members, giving "hope for a better day" and providing a sense of belonging. Empirical studies indicate that religious involvement is a strong predictor of self-esteem among Black Americans (Hughes & Demo, 1989). The Black church experience in America demonstrates the power that religion has in shaping society. When the dark night of slavery ended, the church provided the structure of society, much as it did in Europe after the fall of the Roman Empire. Dr. Martin Luther King Jr. was a product of a community in which religion permeated every aspect of life. King and his followers could not separate the ethical and political aspects of the civil rights movements from the theological.

Religion in Community

Common beliefs and shared experiences are the basis for a community. The religious community preserves and transmits beliefs, symbols, rituals, and literature that it deems significant. Common beliefs and traditions lead to a wealth of cultural norms within a religious community regarding diet, holy days, art, music, politics, and marriage, among other things.

People within a religious community share common folkways, stories, and vocabulary. For example, a Haitian folkway underscores the centrality of faith healers in their culture, the Exodus story is formative for both Jews and Black Christians, and particular norms of religious traditions influence the words selected for prayers. Therefore clients' words may contain communal and personal meanings or references that social workers do not share. For instance, if a client begins talking about the devil, the social worker needs to explore what the word *devil* means for the client, rather than to infer what the client means on the basis of the social worker's personal worldview. Moreover, in our pluralistic world, some people support the teachings of their own community of faith, yet hold personal beliefs that are entirely different from that faith or even contradictory to it. Again, social workers must explore clients' personal meanings of religious terms.

Religion and Spirituality

Spirituality is "the general human experience of developing a sense of meaning, purpose, and morality" (Canda, 1989, p. 39). In contrast, an organized religion encompasses formal beliefs and practices held in common with others. Often religious beliefs evolve within a particular religious denomination and may involve affiliation with a religious body such as a church, synagogue, or mosque. However, while formal religion and spirituality are related, they are also separate phenomena (Canda). People can and do raise spiritual questions or questions about meaning in their lives outside the purview of organized religion.

Ultimate Concern. Protestant theologian and philosopher Paul Tillich (1959) presents a concept of religion that encompasses both the pluralism of religions and the spirituality of agnostics. Tillich believes that religion is the dimension of depth in all life's functions rather than a special function of a person's spiritual life. He uses the metaphor of *depth* to mean "that the religious aspect points to that which is ultimate, infinite, [and] unconditional in [a person's] spiritual life. Religion, in the largest and most basic sense of the word, is ultimate concern" (p. 7).

For Tillich, religion is neither a system of beliefs nor an institution. Instead, religion points to the presence of the infinite in every finite expression of human life. In the moral sphere, Tillich holds that religion as ultimate concern is the unconditional seriousness of the moral demand. For example, the Roman Catholic social activist Dorothy Day was religious not only because she was Catholic, but also, from Tillich's point of view, because of her passionate commitment to serving the poor. Ultimate concern is the spiritual dimension in people's lives.

Jane Addams, an inspiration to many social workers, was brought up in the Quaker faith and was later influenced by British thinkers Thomas Carlyle and John Ruskin. She spoke of needing to be in harmony with nature and deity. Although she claimed to be an agnostic, she joined a Congregational church near Hull House. Church historian Martin Marty (1986) writes, "Addams had a gift for combining apparently contradictory elements and philosophies, including a passionate highly personal faith with skeptical styles, and treated the combination religiously" (p. 83). Jane Addams may not have been religious by some definitions, but from Tillich's perspective of religion as ultimate concern, she was without doubt spiritual.

Spirituality and Personal Identity. Fundamental spiritual questions include those about the meaning and purpose of life, understanding death in the context of life, and how we *should* act. Our answers to these spiritual questions affect whether we feel hopeful or hopeless, determine the directions we take when we reach turning points in our lives, permeate our relationships with others, inform our moral choices, and connect us to all of humanity. Spirituality shapes how we view ourselves and other people, how we perceive dilemmas, and how we define available solutions. It defines our sense of responsibility, guilt, obligations to others, and interpretations of social justice.

Implications of Religious Diversity

It is within this context of spirituality and religious community that we can discover the significance of religious diversity for social work. Loewenberg (1988) points to the relationship between religion and social work when he says: "No social worker has suggested that religious experiences are a panacea for every problem or for every person, but there is increasing recognition that, for believers, religion is a resource that should not be overlooked" (p. 133). Social workers need to understand the dynamics of value issues and develop a nonjudgmental perspective.

Value Issues. Religious values represent one of several sets of values that influence social work practice. Which value set is most influential in any given circumstance depends on the strength and clarity of the values as well as the demands of the situation. There are "specific practice areas (including abortion, homosexuality, and euthanasia) where religious values do make a difference, especially when these involve practitioner or client behaviors that seem to violate these values and beliefs" (Loewenberg, 1988, p. 84).

Often the problems that clients present focus on moral dilemmas. The question "What *should* I do?" or otherwise searching for personal identity, meaning, and purpose signals the presence of a value issue. Social workers need to assess the role religion plays for clients by asking, "How does religion affect family roles and interactions?" "What role does religion play for the client?" Solutions need to be compatible with clients' belief systems.

The religious or spiritual dimension has increased relevance and heightened meaning in crises. M. Vincetta Joseph's (1988) study of the role of religion and social work reports data that "clearly reflect the prominence of God and religion in times of illness and crises" (p. 448). She contends that "such phenomena can hardly be overlooked in social work practice" (p. 448). In fact, when social workers ignore religious factors, this avoidance inevitably results in a breakdown in their ability to work effectively with clients (Loewenberg, 1988).

Soifer (1991), discussing culturally sensitive interventions with people who are Jewish, suggests that social workers also need to explore their own ethnic and religious backgrounds to gain a deeper appreciation of diverse perspectives in society. It is imperative that social workers examine their own belief systems to understand how their personal definitions of spirituality shape their own beliefs and views of others, as well as their outlooks on problems and solutions.

Several questions help social workers examine their personal feelings toward clients and religion:

- Am I able to accept the client's religious beliefs as part of that client system and attempt to understand that system, no matter how removed it may seem from greater society?
- Am I willing to accept that the client's religious doctrine has great implications for success in treatment?
- Am I willing to concede that efforts to change the client's belief system will be detrimental to the helping relationship and could be detrimental to the client's well-being? (York, 1987, p. 42)

Nonjudgmental Perspective. As a reflection of acceptance and nonjudgmentalism, religious toleration is a given for social workers! This means that social workers should not counsel people to perform actions that are against their personal moral, spiritual, or religious codes. Nor should social workers proselytize their own belief systems or demean others' spirituality. The ethic of self-determination encourages an ecumenical spirit of tolerance and appreciation of religious differences (Canda, 1988).

A quandary about self-determination occurs when clients' value systems are at odds with predominant norms or with the law. Religious tolerance does not imply condoning illegal actions that people rationalize on the basis of religion, such as the ritualistic abuse of children by a cult. Clearly, in such cases, social work practitioners must deal with the reality of child endangerment and their professional, moral, and legal obligations to protect children from harm.

The Resources of the Religious Community

In their search for relevant community resources, clients and social workers may identify those resources available through the religious community. For example, church or temple membership links people with a broad spectrum of resources that can provide social support and concrete assistance (Maton & Pargament, 1986).

Social Support. A participant observation study identified factors that provided empowerment for members of a nondenominational religious community: "The particular religious setting studied appears to provide an adaptive niche for members, one which provides meaning, identity, opportunities for interpersonal development, and access to a network of support and resources" (Maton & Rappaport, 1984, p. 70). Relationships within the religious community appear to be among the reservoir of resources that people draw upon in the course of everyday life as well as in times of crisis. The religious community may therefore be one of the natural helping networks that empower clients.

Concrete Services. The religious community may in fact provide the concrete services that clients need to access. Religious denominations and ecumenical organizations have a long history of providing social services under sectarian auspices. For example, congregations may

- Employ social workers, parish nurses, and other professional staff
- Support neighborhood outreach programs that provide a forum for community action
- Sponsor self-help groups
- Advocate local, national, and international social justice concerns
- Develop a variety of programs, such as community centers, health clinics, youth programs, services for older adults, food pantries, information and referral services, community development initiatives, literacy programs, after-school tutoring, transitional housing, recreation and sports activities, and latchkey and other day care services

Referrals. Clients may access religious resources themselves; however, sometimes social workers need to expedite referrals to religious professionals. For clients who belong to a particular religious congregation, it is appropriate to ask first whether they would like to talk to their own minister, priest, rabbi, or indigenous spiritual leader. If clients desire contact with clergy other than their own, social workers would do well to refer them to religious counselors or chaplains not connected with any particular congregation.

Social workers and religious professionals need to recognize the unique, complementary functions they each offer. The importance of this mutual relationship is underscored by the fact that, although social workers may link clients with clergy, clients often seek initial guidance from religious professionals. Clergy are significant sources of referrals to social workers.

Religion and Social Work

Religion has certainly played a central role in the development of social work as a profession (Cnaan, Wineburg, & Boddie, 1999). Historically, the Charity Organization Society and the settlement house movement originated through the work of clergy. Later, the American social gospel movement played a key role in supporting the development of public social services and a legislative remedy for social problems. Furthermore, the tenets of most major religions—Christianity, Judaism, Shamanism, and Buddhism, among others—are compatible with social work (Canda & Furman, 1999).

Social workers need to be aware of the effects that religion and spirituality have on their own viewpoints and choices. Likewise, they need to be aware of how clients' religious views and spirituality affect the problems, issues, and needs they present. Ultimately, social workers should do the following:

- Increase their awareness of spirituality in themselves and their clients
- Respect differences resulting from religious diversity
- Clarify points of religious bias and the implication of this bias for practice
- Appreciate the significance and meaning of religious metaphors
- Identify the resources of other professionals who have sensitivity and skill for working with particular aspects of religious diversity
- Develop partnerships with members of various religious communities (Miley, 1992)

In sum, religion and spirituality are integral to social work practice. Many people enter the social work profession because of their spirituality—their zeal to "help their neighbors," "feed the hungry," provide for the "least of these," and work for justice. Spirituality provides the vision of and hope for a just society and refuge when we need to revitalize our energy base. Spiritual imperatives are not unlike the humanitarian imperatives of the *Code of Ethics* (NASW, 1999a) that implore social work practitioners to uphold the dignity and worth of individuals and to work for justice.

Sexual Diversity

One of the most diverse groups in the United States is the group defined by their sexual minority status. Gay men and lesbian women are found in all social and economic strata, are members of all racial and ethnic groups, affiliate with various political parties and organizations, and work in all professional fields and career positions. Yet, the general public often characterizes homoseuxals as having a single identity. Previously, the typical stated or unstated agenda of practitioners working with gay men and lesbians was

> "conversion" to heterosexuality. Whether through confrontation, subtle persuasion, exploration of childhood trauma, or even electro shock, the goal was to reclaim the homosexual from the ranks of social misfits. Not surprisingly, gays and lesbians were, at best, reluctant consumers of the therapies of that era. (Markowitz, 1991, p. 27)

The prominence of psychological explanations of homosexuality as a personality or neurotic behavior disorder branded homosexuality as a pathology and exposed gay men and lesbians to overt hostility and demeaning stereotypes. Research in the 1960s challenged these psychiatric assumptions about "homosexual deviance" when studies reported that "homosexually oriented individuals are generally well adjusted and free from gross personality disorders or neuroses" (Gramick, 1983, p. 137). In 1973, the American Psychiatric Association removed homosexuality as a diagnostic category from the *Diagnostic and Statistical Manual for Mental Disorders.* This began to change the professional view of homosexuality from its being a mental disorder. Research indicates that the rate of mental disorders for gay men and lesbians is no greater than it is for heterosexuals (Markowitz, 1991). Many conclude that the prejudice and oppression gay men and lesbians encounter in the social environment represent their most serious sources of stress (DeLois, 1998; Tully, 2000).

Currently we refer to male homosexuals as *gay men* and female homosexuals as *lesbians.* "To many politically active people, *gay* seems more positive than *homosexual,* in the same way that *black* or *African-American* is more positive than Negro and *woman* is more positive than *lady*" (Wade & Cirese, 1991, p. 524). Since homosexual men and women are not alike just because they are homosexual, using the designations *gay men* and *lesbians* differentiates their identities as distinctly *male* and *female.*

Sex and Gender

Sexual identity is complex, including components of both sex and gender. The terms *gender* and *sex* are often used interchangeably; however, *sex* and *gender* have distinctive meanings (Green, 2000). *Sex* refers to "a person's biological or anatomical identity as male or female" (p. 2). In contrast, *gender* refers to "the collection of characteristics that are culturally associated with maleness or femaleness" (p. 2). The precise specifications of masculinity and femininity vary from culture to culture. Not an outwardly visible characteristic, *gender identity,* is a perspective that indicates one's "internal, deeply felt sense of being either male or female, or something other or in between" (p. 3). Evident to others, *gender expression* encompasses "all of the external characteristics and behaviors that are socially defined as either masculine or feminine, such as dress, mannerisms, speech patterns and social interactions" (p. 3).

Transgender refers to all those "whose identity or behavior falls outside of stereotypical gender norms. This includes people who do not self-identify as transgender, but who are perceived as such by others and thus are subject to the same social oppressions and physical violence as those who actually identify with any of these categories" (Green, 2000, p. 4). Often misunderstood and rejected by others, transgendered people have experienced countless instances of oppression, as they "are regularly denied employment, fired from their jobs, denied housing and public accommodations at hotels and restaurants, even harassed, beaten or murdered because of hatred of their gender nonconformity. On average one transgendered person is murdered in the United States each month; 60% of all transgender people have been victimized by hate violence" (Cahill, 2000, p. iii).

Neither homosexuality nor heterosexuality eliminates the possibility of a range of sexual relationships. In fact, there is little evidence to support "the belief that strict heterosexuality and homosexuality are essential and fundamental attributes of human nature, inevitably reflected in lifelong patterns of sexual behavior and life-style" (Hersch, 1991, p. 40). Human sexuality must be understood in a *both-and* context rather than an *either-or* approach. "A more complete understanding of sexual orientation, then, must incorporate what appears to be a quite flexible cluster of human sexual possibilities" (Booth, 1990, pp. 1–2).

Identity Formation for Gay Men. For gay men, homosexual identity emerges in the context of individual and environmental factors, including the sexual encounter task, the social reaction task, and the identity task (Berger, 1983; Berger & Kelly, 1995). The sexual encounter task involves intimate contacts in same-sex relationships. The social reaction task occurs when others label individuals as homosexuals. Complications and confusions result when assigned labels are incongruent with self-perceptions. Finally, the task of forming a homosexual identity often begins with feelings of confusion, involves self-labeling, and then moves to managing homosexual identity. Peer support plays a key role as people move toward accepting themselves. Identity formation for gay men involves personal choices—*not* about homosexual feelings *per se,* but rather with respect to "how these feelings will shape [their lives]" (Berger, 1986, p. 68).

Identity Issues for Lesbians. Although there is a well-documented lesbian subculture, there is great diversity among its members. Those who are not young, white, middle-class, or able-bodied must face the multiple oppressions of ageism, racism, classism, and ableism. Given the presumptions of heterosexism, lesbians face challenges in developing a positive identity: "The process of self-definition as a lesbian arises out of awareness of a physical or emotional attraction to women and may or may not be sexually expressed" (Tully, 1995, p. 1592). For some, the process of identity discovery begins in adolescence; for others, the process begins after years of marriage, raising families, or living alone outside of sexual relationships.

Coming Out. For lesbian women and gay men, *coming out* means recognizing and accepting their homosexual identity and publicly revealing their homosexual identity to their nongay peers and family members. In other words, coming out has both personal and public ramifications. "Not all of us are out. And for many of us who are, the cost has been high: loss of family, loss of job, loss of child custody, retreat into depression and alcoholism; and the constant threat of verbal and physical assault. The fear of being truthful about oneself is not irrational when the potential risks are so high. Of course, one risk of not coming out is being found out" (DeLois, 1998, p. 69). Coming out is a lifelong process, often beginning in adolescence, but for others beginning in later in life (Hunter & Schaecher, 1995). For everyone, the pattern of coming out is unique.

Homophobia

Homophobia is an irrational fear of and negative emotional reaction to homosexuality that manifests itself in contempt, condemnation, and malice toward gay men and lesbians:

> Ignorance, insensitivity, stereotyped thinking, outright prejudice, discrimination, and a host of negative attitudes all can be loosely grouped under the umbrella of homophobia. At its most blatant, homophobia takes the form of outrage that enables gay-bashers to feel justified in striking out against those they consider traitors to the natural order of human relationships. Most of us experience a quieter, more subtle type of homophobia when we encounter homosexuality—it is startling to have our unthinking assumptions about our sexual identities jostled. We may not go on the attack when we feel these uncomfortable stirrings, but despite our best intentions, our hostility, fear, and fumbling self-consciousness may spew out. (Markowitz, 1991, pp. 29, 31)

The dominant societal culture affects all people, including gays and lesbians. Everyone experiences homophobic socialization processes. So all people, to some extent, internalize their fear and rejection of homosexuality. Individuals experience varying degrees of homophobic feelings. These feelings result in various behavioral reactions:

- *Abhorrence and hostility.* Individuals feel contempt, loathing, and revulsion toward homosexuality and react with overt hostility, antigay violence, and gay bashing.

- *Prejudice and rejection.* Fueled by feelings of fear and disgust, individuals respond to homosexuality with ignorance, name calling, and demeaning stereotyping.

- *Uneasiness and defensive bigotry.* People who feel internal discomfort as a result of self-consciousness about sexuality, curiosity about sexual differences, and ambivalence about homosexuality respond with casual joking, story telling and gossiping, and parodying homosexuals. Their reactions are defensive, but, nonetheless, they depersonalize gay men and lesbians.

- *Toleration and subtle stereotyping.* People may resign themselves to accepting sexual diversity in the public realm, yet privately continue to make generalizations and stereotype gays and lesbians without intending animosity.

- *Conscious acceptance and unconscious bias.* People may consciously accept homosexuality, yet still be influenced by societal homophobia, ignorance, and a language base that reflects heterosexuality as the norm. In this case, they are unknowingly insensitive to the effect of these cultural messages on gays and lesbians.

- *Respect and affirmation.* Finally, people may come to regard homosexuals as people and affirm their difference. Their position respects human dignity and worth and regards sexual orientation openly and positively as one dimension of human life.

Homophobia, and in addition, biphobia and transphobia, have serious implications for the delivery of social services. Social workers must know themselves—their values, life-styles, and sexuality—in order to be accepting of others whose values, life-styles, and sexuality may differ. In social work, ignorance and prejudice lead to the inaccurate identification of problems (erroneously assuming that homosexuality is the problem), inappropriate treatment goals (falsely targeting a cure for "sexual deviance"), and improper delivery of services (lacking sensitivity to the pervasiveness of homophobia in the delivery of services).

Work-Related Issues for Gays and Lesbians

Social workers in business and industry need to address gay and lesbian work-related issues (Poverny, 2000). Education and advocacy can address

- Job discrimination
- Fear of HIV/AIDS and resulting vulnerability of gays and lesbians to discrimination in the workplace
- Denial of work-related benefits for same-sex partners that are available to heterosexual partners
- Development of policies and procedures, including nondiscriminatory benefit plans, that are sensitive to gay and lesbian concerns

Social Work with Gay and Lesbian Adolescents

While many youth-oriented social services deal with adolescent developmental issues and teenage problems, traditional social service agencies are ill-equipped to deal with the concerns surrounding sexual orientation and the pressures experienced by teens who identify themselves as homosexuals. Problems at home, rejection by family members, harassment by peers, violence and hate crimes, running away from home, substance abuse, loneliness and isolation, and depression resulting in attempts at suicide are common among gay and lesbian adolescents (Hunter & Schaecher, 1995; Tully, 2000). Mirroring negative social attitudes about homosexuality, two potentially valuable support systems for lesbian and gay adolescents—their family and peer group—are likely to respond with disapproval and rejection. In addition, gay and lesbian youth hesitate to discuss their feelings and longings openly with school counselors in order to avoid suspicion, scorn, and exposure. Lesbian and gay youth underutilize community services and youth groups at a time when they could benefit from services that provide support. These youths need, but are unable to get, accurate nonjudgmental information about their sexuality and its expression. They want, but are often unable to get, guidance as they deal with the disclosure of their sexual orientations. Recently, grassroots organizations and innovative social service programs have been developing drop-in centers and support services for these youths.

Issues for Social Work

Since lesbian women and gay men comprise about 6 to 7 percent of the population of the United States, social workers in all fields of practice—family and child welfare, health and mental health, gerontological social work, social work in business and industry, social work in schools, criminal justice, and public welfare—are likely to find gay men and lesbians among their clientele. Homosexuals may live in heterosexual relationships, as same-sex couples, or alone. They may have children living with them or separately. They, like all others, experience a range of difficulties, including unemployment, depression, chronic mental illness, intimate partner violence, developmental disabilities, chronic illness and bereavement, and issues related to aging. Unlike all others, their experiences are complicated by the context of a heterosexist and homophobic society that creates barriers of oppression, dehumanization, and discrimination. Additionally, those who are not young, white, middle-class, or able-bodied must face the multiple oppressions of ageism, racism, classism, and ableism. The issues of lesbian women and gay men are unique in that they live as a defined oppressed group in a heterosexual society. Ingrained heterosexism and homophobia affect the lives of homosexuals in countless ways.

A number of practice issues emerge with respect to social work with gay and lesbian clients. For example, social workers need to identify community resources for lesbian women and gay men so they can link clients with religious supports, legal assistance, medical care, professional organizations, and life insurance companies that will deal sensitively with them (Tully, 2000). Social workers also need to develop social history forms and other assessment tools that take into account the concerns of gay men and lesbians. For example, substituting the term "partner" for "husband," "wife," or "spouse" begins to address the heterosexist nature of many agency forms.

Addiction services should consider the perspectives of sexual orientation and life-style, as alcoholism rates and drug use are reportedly higher among lesbians and gay men (Shernoff, 1995). Finally, more attention needs to be focused on older gays and lesbians, a group which has been characterized as a misunderstood and underestimated minority (Tully, 2000). Particular concerns include bereavement counseling and the policies and practices of long-term care institutions and other health care facilities with respect to living arrangements, visiting rights, and health care decision-making.

Working with Gays and Lesbians. Practitioners themselves need to examine their assumptions about homosexuality. Some practitioners' mistaken assumptions can be seen as opposing ends of a continuum. At one extreme, practitioners falsely assume that homosexuality itself is the overriding problem, regardless of the issue presented by the client. At the other extreme, practitioners offhandedly dismiss homosexual preference, believing that it makes no difference at all. They ignore the impact of the social environment, make false presumptions, and superimpose heterosexual views on the client. Practitioners' level of comfort or discomfort, receptiveness or defensiveness, and knowledge or ignorance concerning the life-styles will determine their view of homosexuality. Questions to identify remnants of heterosexism and homophobia include the following:

- Do I assume everyone is heterosexual unless they tell me otherwise?
- In what ways do I benefit from heterosexist assumptions?
- Am I comfortable talking about sexual orientation?
- Do I challenge heterosexist/homophobic jokes or remarks?
- Do I assume that lesbians and gays all have the same beliefs, problems, and agenda? (DeLois, 1998, p. 69)

Because sexual orientation is central to personhood, social workers must understand and affirm the sexual orientation of each their clients. To do this, practitioners must understand their own sexuality and their values with respect to sexual expression. If social workers are to be helpful to others, they must be honestly aware of their own motives and vulnerabilities as well as of the pertinent issues that may contribute to misunderstandings and inappropriate interventions (Booth, 1990). From an empowerment perspective, several considerations guide social work practice (DeLois, 1998):

- The issues for gays and lesbians are profoundly political, given the institutionalized history of homophobia and heterosexism.
- The issues for gays and lesbians are profoundly personal because of their risks for "depression, substance abuse, suicide, homelessness, and injury or death from perpetrators of hate crimes" (p. 71).
- Freedom from heterosexism and homophobia has implications for all people as this threatens "the sexist, classist, racist power arrangements under which everyone lives" (p. 71).
- The resources of the gay and lesbian community are abundant, including "refuge, support, and strength to women, men, and youth who seek a place to be themselves while joining with others to create change" (p. 71).

The major focus of social work is not integrating gays and lesbians into mainstream culture as that denies the reality of their identity; rather, the focus must be on creating "an environment in which all people are valued as complete human beings and are encouraged to 'find and live authentic lives' " (DeLois, 1998, p. 71). "The guiding principles for social workers who want to work effectively with gay and lesbian clients are the same principles followed in working with heterosexual clients: accept the client as a total human being, accept his or her sexual orientation, and do not pretend to have all the answers" (Dulaney & Kelly, 1982 p. 180).

Social Work with Diverse Populations

Social work education about diverse populations tends to emphasize demographic data, characteristic traits, historical backgrounds, intergroup relations, and societal responses to diversity. Social workers need more than information about the descriptive aspects of diverse populations, however. Social work practitioners need to understand those practice dynamics and skills that allow them to relate affectively and, therefore, effectively to the minority group experience. Ifill (1989) charges social work to go beyond merely describing minorities to developing effective practice with minorities.

Doman Lum (2004) explicates a social work practice model for intervention with people of color that also applies to intervention with those who are culturally and religiously diverse, oppressed for their differences in life-style, or otherwise relegated to a minority status. Lum details five thematic problems and associated principles for social work practice. The polarities characterizing the problem are oppression versus liberation, powerlessness versus empowerment, exploitation versus parity, acculturation versus maintenance of culture, and stereotyping versus unique personhood:

- *Oppression* is the action and behavior that prevents others from accessing resources and opportunities. The hierarchical arrangement created through oppressive actions places others in lower ranks of society. Oppression calls for *liberation,* which is a process that releases individuals and, through the dynamics of environmental change, frees them from personal and social restraints.

- *Powerlessness* results in feelings of impotency and lack of control. People feel that they have no control when they are continually denied access to the benefits of society, lack information about resources and rights, are labeled inferior, and are relegated to a lower status. Through *empowerment,* minorities can exert interpersonal influence, assert their abilities, and affect their social environment both individually and collectively. Empowerment counteracts powerlessness.

- *Exploitation* is the unjust manipulation of people of minority status for the benefit of the majority in society. Exploitation may occur in economic, political, or social situations. In response to exploitation, *parity* promotes and advances equality in power, value, status, and rank through corrective action.

- Various degrees of *acculturation* can occur as minority people adopt aspects of the dominant culture. Through acculturation, they, in some ways, give up a part of their own cultural beliefs, values, and customs. *Maintenance of culture* is a purposeful effort to use the cultural ethos or ethnic identity as a source of strength and renewal, thus countering acculturation.

■ *Stereotyping* is a negative and often narrow depiction of others that denigrates them, both individually and as members of a group. Emphasizing the *unique personhood* of clients is the opposite of stereotyping.

Looking Forward

Recognizing individuality and ethnic worth is a fundamental social work value. Social workers must appreciate ethnic identification, religious and cultural differences, and personal choices of life-style in the same way that they understand and appreciate individual differences (Washington, 1982). Social work practice with all consumers of social services is understood in the context of perspectives about values, social justice, and diversity. What social workers do in professional intervention is informed by a value orientation held about people, inspired by the social justice mandate, and guided by an understanding of diversity in the populations served.

Affirming a client's dignity and worth and recognizing the client's strength in his or her diversity are central to fostering empowerment in practice activities. Part Three of the text describes the dynamics of social work intervention. Chapter 8 summarizes empowering processes for change, and Chapter 9 examines the roles and strategies of generalist practice at all social system levels. Chapter 10 explores the relationship between social work and social policy and details the emergence of public welfare policies in the twentieth century, including current public welfare programs.

PART THREE

Generalist Social Work

Generalist social workers possess an integrated view of people-and-environments and can use appropriate interventions to empower consumers at all social system levels. Generalists regard clients in relation to the social milieu, view problems in the context of the situation, and seek solutions within both personal and environmental structures.

Part Three presents a generalist model that incorporates empowering processes for carrying out the functions of social work. Empowering processes explicated include forming partnerships, articulating challenges, defining directions, identifying strengths, analyzing resource capabilities, framing solutions, activating resources, creating alliances, expanding opportunities, recognizing success, and integrating gains. The functions of social work—consultancy, resource management, and education—are described in terms of roles and strategies for working with individuals and families, groups and organizations, and communities. Finally, the relationship between social work and social policy is explored.

CHAPTER

8 Empowering Processes for Social Work Practice

Beth Larson, the coordinator of the child welfare reform project, reads her year-end report with great enthusiasm and professional satisfaction. New family services had been implemented, and existing programs had been expanded. In this second year of the project, a new community-based day treatment facility had already served 17 youths, diverting them from residential placements. An early-intervention programming component—front-loading prevention services—had been added to the family-centered program. Support services for foster families had been expanded to provide an allotment for day care expenses, enabling foster parents to be employed outside the home. Several agencies had responded to a request for proposal (RFP) to develop therapeutic foster care components. An emergency fund for families was established that could be accessed at the discretion of caseworkers. Nearly 70 community child welfare practitioners had attended a workshop on designing a new case management system. Finally, a full-time researcher had been hired to evaluate the efforts and outcomes of the demonstration project.

Community leaders had initiated the child welfare reform project to address the problems of a child welfare delivery system that was encumbered by restrictive eligibility requirements and inflexible funding parameters. The project had evolved into a major initiative to provide more accessible, effective, and appropriate services to children and families in the child welfare, mental health, and juvenile court systems.

Beth reflects on the impetus for this reform effort. The project was founded on the assumption that services to families were too often restricted by categorical funding and services and that, if funding and services were decategorized, families could be served better. Guided by a philosophy of family preservation, a decision to provide services locally, and a commitment to strengthening less-intrusive resource options, child welfare practitioners rallied around this innovative concept to redesign the child welfare service delivery system. This restructuring and the new services that resulted did not just happen; they involved the tireless efforts, time, commitment, and vision of many service administrators, providers, and consumers who engaged in systematic planning. They approached their work using an orderly process for resolving service delivery problems in the child welfare field.

In her role as project coordinator, Beth provides direction and staff support to those people involved in the various aspects of the project. Agency administrators and community planners support her work by coordinating the overall efforts of the project. Clients and direct-service practitioners representing diverse fields of practice envisioned an ideal service delivery system. Special-interest groups studied existing barriers. These study groups recommended changes in mental health services, foster care, and day treatment programs. Ad hoc task forces prepared RFPs, established procedures, developed surveys, and planned educational retreats.

All of these groups approached their activities from a solution-seeking perspective. They relied on an organized process that led them through a series of steps. They clarified their purposes, set goals, considered alternatives, agreed on timelines, implemented actions, and evaluated their efforts throughout the planning process.

This chapter introduces empowerment-oriented processes for generalist social work practice. Specifically, it presents

- An empowerment base for social work practice
- An overview of each generic process

An Empowerment-Based Generic Process of Social Work Practice

Words are powerful. Words shape our thinking, inform our interpretations, and predispose our conclusions. It stands to reason that if social work is to be an empowering profession, then the words, labels, and metaphors that social workers draw on to describe their work must promote strengths and facilitate empowerment. The generic approach to social work practice presented in this chapter translates the traditional steps for solving problems into processes that reflect the language of empowerment-based practice (Table 8.1). One transition—the transition from expert professional to collaborative partner—is particularly vital.

From Expert Professional to Collaborative Partner

Both professionals and clients suffer when they have an unrealistic reverence for professional expertise. This view saddles professionals with a false sense of their own omnipotence

TABLE 8.1 An Empowering Approach to Generalist Practice

Forming Partnerships	Building empowering social worker–client relationships that acknowledge clients' privileges and respect their uniqueness
Articulating Situations	Assessing challenging situations by responding to validate clients' experiences, add transactional dimensions, and look toward goals
Defining Directions	Determining a preliminary purpose for the relationship to activate motivation and guide the exploration for relevant resources
Identifying Strengths	Searching for strengths in general functioning, coping with challenging situations, cultural identities, and overcoming adversity
Assessing Resources	Exploring resource capabilities in transactions with the environment including connections to family, social groups, organizations, and community institutions
Framing Solutions	Constructing a plan of action that utilizes client and environmental resources and leads toward desired goals
Activating Resources	Implementing the action plan by mobilizing available resources
Creating Alliances	Forging alliances among clients, within clients' natural support networks, and within the service delivery system
Expanding Opportunities	Developing new opportunities and resources through program development, community organizing, and social action
Recognizing Success	Evaluating the success of the change efforts to recognize achievements and inform continuing actions
Integrating Gains	Ending change process in ways that celebrate success, stabilize positive changes, and provide a platform for future change

and traps clients into a culture of dependency on experts (Rappaport, 1985; Holmes & Saleebey, 1993). Essentially, this creates a hierarchy of "information haves and have-nots." Masterful, expert professionals take charge of and act upon ineffectual, passive client systems. Elevating professional expertise diminishes clients' potential and limits their roles. In sum, it disempowers.

Empowerment presumes active, collaborative roles for client–partners. Paradoxically, "empowering another system" or paternalistically bestowing power on others disempowers those "touched by the star-tipped wand." Giving power away generates hierarchies of power and powerlessness. Professionals foster empowerment only "by providing a climate, a relationship, resources, and procedural means through which people can enhance their own lives" (Simon, 1990, p. 32). In empowerment-based social work practice, social workers and clients approach their work together as collaborative partners (Miley, O'Melia, & DuBois, 2004). For clients, collaboration actualizes empowerment (Table 8.2).

A Generic Approach

Generalist social worker practitioners address problems through policy formulation at the institutional and community levels, resolve issues concerning the delivery of services in agencies and organizations, and work with individual and family client systems to develop solutions for individual and family problems. In fact, the process that social workers use with clients at all system levels and in each field of practice is similar. The processes outline an orderly, empowering approach to working with clients at all system levels. The following sections briefly describe these generic empowering processes.

TABLE 8.2 Clients' Rights from an Empowerment Perspective on Practice

Clients have rights to expect that professionals will

- Show respect
- Communicate nonjudgmentally
- Demonstrate cultural competence
- Appraise clients of options
- Hold themselves accountable for their actions
- Promote social justice
- Uphold professional codes of ethics
- Facilitate rather than direct processes

Clients have rights to expect that processes will

- Support collaborative partnerships
- Provide opportunities to tell their stories from their points of view
- Involve them in determining goals and objectives and developing action strategies
- Provide opportunities to evaluate outcomes

Clients have rights to expect that, as service users, they will be involved in

- Program evaluation, research, and planning
- Organizational policy review and development activities
- Staff education and training
- Social policy advocacy and coalition building

Through dialogue, clients and social workers form their partnership relationships, address power differentials, and establish the tone for client-driven services. In the discovery processes, they contextualize personal troubles to include relevant sociopolitical dimensions and expand the arena of potential solutions beyond personal adaptation to include macrolevel change. Finally, processes in the development phase hold opportunities for developing a critical consciousness by reflecting on social injustices and working toward resolutions that include community, organizational, and sociopolitical change. The following sections briefly describe the empowering generic processes associated with dialogue, discovery, and development.

Forming Partnerships

The process of forming professional relationships sets the tone for the entire interaction between clients and practitioners:

> The core skill of social work is the ability to form a helping relationship. The hallmarks of this relationship are shaped by two radical values: an active belief in the person's, family's, or community's ability to know and choose what is best for them and the belief that the relationship is a collaboration, where both client and worker bring distinctive but essential knowledge necessary for constructive work. These beliefs in discovering, affirming, and building on people's strengths as important resources in accomplishing the work run directly counter to the view of many other practitioners who see themselves as having the knowledge, and therefore the power, to define the nature of the problem and its treatment. (Weick, 1999, p. 331)

Empowerment-oriented social workers respect clients' perspectives and recognize the positive contribution of working collaboratively. Factors that influence building relationships include their professional purpose, the nature of clients' participation, and workers' use of effective interpersonal skills.

Professional Relationships

Professional relationships differ from personal relationships in that the purpose of the social work profession ultimately defines the relationship's purpose. So, the fundamental purpose of social work—"to promote or restore a mutually beneficial interaction between individuals and society in order to improve the quality of life for everyone" (Working Statement, 1981)—sets the tone for professional relationships. Furthermore, the *Code of Ethics* (NASW, 1999a) defines ethical standards for professional relationships that distinguish them from friendships or casual business ventures.

Clients do not approach social workers to seek helping relationships, but rather to address problems. Relationships result from concern, caring, and respect for others through words, actions, and a willingness to listen. A relationship "cannot be manufactured. It begins at the moment that any two people meet. It grows as they work together, but it cannot be forced or hurried" (Keith-Lucas, 1972, p. 48). Professional relationships unfold as the work of clients and practitioners proceeds.

The Nature of Clients' Participation

Some clients seek social work services voluntarily, others accept the proffered services of outreach efforts, and still others are mandated to participate. These variations have implications for clients' motivations and for their readiness to participate.

Social workers recognize that at the point of engaging services the self-esteem of some clients is low, and that social stigma associated with the giving and taking of help complicates clients' responses. Bertha Reynolds (1951) suggested that one obvious answer to the question of why the taking and giving of help is difficult "is that we have a hang-over from the bad old days of a harsh and degrading charity. People who took help should be made to feel outside the normal group, or they would be endlessly demanding. They should not have a status as desirable as that of people who gave—or at least were able to meet their own needs" (p. 25).

Reynolds further distinguishes the status of people who *must* ask for services because of their dire need from that of people who have the choice of either asking or not. Some endure hardships and want rather than face feelings of stigma. However, when survival needs are at stake, people's degree of choice or voluntary participation in social services diminishes.

The term *involuntary* refers to individuals who are mandated or required, sometimes against their will, to participate in social work services. Involuntary clients often experience negative feelings about coercion that social workers must deal with directly. Clients labeled "unmotivated" or "hard to reach" may act indifferently and resist social workers' attempts to work with them.

Social workers must use professional relationships to enhance clients' motivation and instill feelings of hopefulness. Regardless of the circumstances that bring clients and practitioners together, empowerment-based social workers strive to establish productive working relationships that reflect partnerships with client systems from the very beginning.

Interpersonal Skills

By attending to clients' emotional, physical, and interactional needs, social workers enhance the development of effective professional relationships. Mutual trust and confidence are essential ingredients in professional relationships. Among the interpersonal skills necessary for developing professional relationships are accurate empathy, nonpossessive warmth, genuineness, and cultural sensitivity.

Empathy. Practitioners demonstrate empathy by perceiving and responding to clients' feelings with sensitivity and understanding. Drawing on the definitive works of Truax, Mitchell, Carkhuff, and Rogers, Fischer (1978) asserts:

> Being empathic means more than simply understanding another's world (stepping into his or her shoes); it means understanding and *communicating* that understanding. Thus, being empathic implies being an active responder rather than a passive listener. In this way, the helping person is a *participant* in the process, beginning with intense focusing on the verbal and nonverbal cues presented by the client and a continuous sharing with the client of the worker's understanding of what the client has communicated. (p. 192)

Warmth. Social workers communicate warmth to clients through their caring commitment and their unconditional positive regard for clients. Fischer (1978) indicates that nonpossessive warmth

> refers to the worker's communication of respect, acceptance, loving, caring and concern for the client in a nondominating way. . . . Thus, the client is accepted as a person with human potentialities: nonpossessive warmth involves valuing the client as a person, separate from any evaluation of his or her behavior and thoughts. (p. 196)

Genuineness. Social workers convey genuineness by being spontaneous, unpretentious, and authentic. Fischer (1978) believes that genuineness facilitates helping relationships. Genuineness refers to social workers'

> "being themselves," being "real." This means, simply, that at any given moment, workers really are whatever their responses denote. . . . In fact, genuineness may be best understood as the absence of phoniness, as nondefensiveness, as congruence, and as spontaneity. (p. 199)

Cultural Competence. The racial or ethnic identities of workers and clients, as well as the predominant culture reflected in the service delivery system, affect the development of relationships and, ultimately, the success or failure of interventions:

> When people feel predominantly negative about their cultural background their sense of themselves as worthwhile is threatened; when they experience pain, anger, shame, guilt, and other uncomfortable reactions in relation to who they are, these problematic reactions are apt to be mobilized whenever they are in contact with culturally different others. They then become so preoccupied with managing their discomfort that they are not free to interact with others in ways which promote comfortable relationships and respectful interaction. (Pinderhughes, 1997, p. 326)

Positive professional relationships are foundational to the helping process. It is the social worker's responsibility to initiate and maintain respectful interactions with clients that reflect empathy, warmth, genuineness, and cultural sensitivity.

Social Work Highlights. Jodie Princeton, the social worker with the New Parents Outreach Program, and Helen Miles, a perinatal home health aide with the program, visit with Gene and Kendra Bridges. They're discussing home-based services that will be available when the Bridges' baby goes home from the hospital. Born prematurely, baby Lisa requires a heart monitor as well as other special medical care.

Jodie and Helen listened closely as the Bridges shared their concerns about dealing with the baby's medical needs at home. Jodie complimented the Bridges on their attentiveness to the baby during her hospitalization and their decision to seek assistance. The Bridges felt somewhat uncomfortable admitting their nervousness about taking their baby home with the heart monitor. Kendra sobbed, "I feel so inept. It's so hard to feed the baby. A mother should be able to do this."

Both Jodie and Helen were reassuring. Jodie commented that requesting help is a positive action that shows the Bridges' commitment to being good parents. Helen indicated that her role as a home health aide was to support their efforts with the baby, not to take over. The partnership with the Bridges resulted from Jodie's and Helen's ability to communicate effectively with the Bridges, showing their respect and understanding.

BOX **8.1**

Reflections on Diversity

Cross-Cultural Communication

Communication in all cultures encompasses verbal and nonverbal interactions. Cultures vary as to the prominence given to each. Even in Western cultures, where verbal components may seem to predominate, research suggests that nonverbal components dominate communication processes (Mehrabian, 1981).

Some aspects of nonverbal communication reflect universal expression and understanding; other aspects are culture bound. Studies by Ekman and Friesen (1975), Izard (1977), and others suggest that certain facial expressions of emotion, including those indicating surprise, disgust, anger, fear, sadness, and happiness, are universally expressed and understood. However, the bulk of the information in the nonverbal communication channel, such as the meaning of gestures, eye contact, posture, and even the prosodic qualities of voice, is related to the particular culture. For example, looking directly into the eyes of the person with whom you are communicating affords dignity and respect and communicates caring in the context of North American White culture; Native Americans interpret looking straight into the eyes of another as rude and intimidating (Lewis & Ho, 1975). People from Asian cultures especially view nonverbal communication, including silence, as an extremely important means of communicating overt messages: The Japanese term *ishin-denshin* means communicating with the mind through the mind (Crystal, 1989).

Cultural differences also temper verbal communication. For example, in the United States, Euro-American clients usually reveal sensitive, personal information rather quickly in the helping process. Social workers often conclude that a client's failure to reveal such information signals resistance. By contrast, Native Americans avoid the immediate disclosure of inner feelings about personal sensitive issues, so confrontation is contraindicated. Social workers should focus on restating, clarifying, reflecting, or other techniques of active listening that create a climate of trust (Lewis & Ho, 1975). White Euro-Americans expect professional helpers to separate their personal from their professional lives. In contrast, Asians expect social workers to share personal information for the relationship to flourish. Understanding the nuances of both verbal and nonverbal communication when there are cultural differences is a challenge for both senders and receivers!

Articulating Situations

A client engages social work services for a reason. This reason often relates to a problem, issue, or need that the client wants to remedy. Articulating challenges is a process workers employ in their dialogue with clients about the reasons clients seek assistance.

To identify their situations accurately, clients describe the facts, events, reactions, and their previous attempts to deal with the problem. Encouraging clients to express their feelings about their situations and their previous efforts to deal with those situations helps to determine the overall impact of the problem. Empowering social workers frame clients' concerns as challenges, as challenges imply the potential for overcoming obstacles. Social workers necessarily begin their discussion of situations as clients define them. They examine factors that clients know about and believe are related from their own personal experiences, and what social workers know and believe to be related from their professional experience. Clients and social workers may discover interrelated sets of issues that they need to consider in the broader context of the social milieu. Different sorts of challenges are likely to emerge at each system level (Table 8.3).

Cultural Context

To understand clients' situations, social workers explore the nature and scope of needs, identify other relevant information, and examine requirements for services and resources.

TABLE 8.3 Typical Concerns at Various System Levels

Individual, Family, and Small-Group Concerns	
Intrapersonal adjustment	Interpersonal conflict
Marital and family problems	Life transitions
Victimization	Inadequate role performance
Stress	Access to services
Advocacy needs	Need for protective services
Lack of resources	Lack of opportunities
Violation of legal or civil rights	Need for information and referral
Need for developing living skills	Need for developing parenting skills
Need for developing socialization skills	
Formal Group and Organizational Concerns	
Employee relations	Staff burnout
Affirmative action	Employee productivity
Employee counseling needs	Job placement
Administrative policy changes	Membership participation
Strategic planning	Utilization of resources
Coordinating efforts	Grants management
Development of volunteers	Staff development needs
Public relations campaign	Program analysis
Management decision making	
Community and Society Concerns	
Economic development	Lack of affordable housing
Employment	Public health issues
Intergroup tension	Health and human service reform
Reallocation of resources	Legislative needs
Coalition building	Community education
Social policy change	Legislative reform
Conflict of interest	Erosion of legal or civil rights
Social Work Profession Concerns	
Professionalism	Interdisciplinary relations
Professional monitoring	Needs of oppressed client populations
Peer review	Social work image
Gaps and barriers in services	Theory development
Social service delivery network	Communicating results of research

Taking cultural variations as well as historical, physical, developmental, emotional, demographic, and organizational factors into consideration, social workers consider the uniqueness of expressed concerns as well as their common characteristics. To this end, although drawing upon generalized knowledge, effective social workers maintain their perspective about the uniqueness of specific persons or social structures in particular situations.

Cultural contexts are particularly significant, as culture uniquely defines the transactions between people and their social and physical environments. Cultural diversity can be a source of both personal strengths and environmental resources and barriers. Cultural factors social workers and clients might consider include such characteristics as cultural beliefs and traditions, definitions of roles and authority, and construction of social support networks. Additionally, clients and social workers need to analyze environmental issues related to power and powerlessness in personal, interpersonal, and sociopolitical domains (Gutiérrez & Lewis, 1999; Solomon, 1976). For example, they might explore how factors such as prejudicial attitudes, social stratification, unequal access to resources and opportunity structures, and other discriminatory behaviors affect clients' personally, interpersonally, and in the context of their transactions with their social and physical environments.

Social Work Highlights. Jim Brown serves as chairperson of the Homeless Coalition, a representative group of agencies that offer shelter facilities, work with clients who are homeless, and deal with housing issues. The group is surveying area shelters to determine their capacity and to gather statistics on daily usage. Members of the Homeless Coalition assert that the needs of the homeless population outstrip the capacity of the local shelters. After the information is gathered, Jim will analyze it and organize it according to clients' demographic profile, type of shelter, eligibility restrictions, and waiting-list information. The coalition will examine the data for patterns and trends and use the data to inform donors about gaps and barriers. The data will be useful in establishing priorities for the future work of the coalition.

Defining Directions

Social workers and clients need to have some direction for their work together. In the process of defining directions, social workers and clients clarify the preliminary purposes for their working relationship and respond forthrightly to preemptive crises.

Defining directions provides a purpose for social workers' and clients' activities. A purpose orients social workers and clients to the clients' situations, as challenges and strengths are more evident in the context of goals. Practitioners can frame their responses in ways that are directed toward goals, focus their attention on discovering resources that will facilitate reaching goals, and use clients' goals as guides in their quest for relevant information. Research has pointed to a relationship between setting goals, believing it's possible to attain these goals, and gains in performance (Bandura & Cervone, 1983). Determining goals and believing in their possibility energizes behavior.

At this point in their work together, the directions social workers and clients define are preliminary. Preliminary goals frame assessment activities, whereas specific goals and measurable objectives are integral components of a subsequent element in the process—the plan of action. Initial agreements focus on the general purpose of the work rather than specific plans for action.

Preemptive Actions

Sometimes clients' circumstances or behaviors require immediate, preemptive actions. For example, issues of safety, lack of food or shelter, immobilizing emotional crises, threats of suicide, and evidence of abuse or neglect all call for immediate actions on the part of social workers. Agency protocol, supervisors' recommendations, and legal advice provide direction for preemptive actions.

Social workers act to ensure clients' safety and well-being without demolishing clients' sense of power and control. Even in the context of preemptive actions, practitioners work with clients as partners.

Referrals

In talking with clients about their goals, social workers evaluate how well clients' situations match the purpose of the agency, the resources that are available, and criteria for eligibility. Sometimes referrals to other service providers are necessary when clients' needs extend beyond the scope of the agency's programs or the expertise of the social worker or require resources in addition to what the initial agency can supply (Table 8.4).

Social Work Highlights. Marvella Crawford, the social worker at Run and Play Day Care Center, was called to the prekindergarten classroom by the teacher's aide to talk with four-year-old Guy Smith about the bruises on his forehead and cheek. When Marvella commented softly to Guy, "Oh, you have some bruises on your face," Guy immediately responded, "My mother didn't do it!" Marvella then asks, "So, tell me, how did it happen?" Guy told Marvella that he didn't remember getting hurt yesterday. Taking note of Guy's first response, Marvella, a mandated reporter for child abuse and neglect, follows agency policy and reports her suspicions about these unexplained bruises to the state child protection agency.

TABLE 8.4 Elements of Referrals

Practitioners refer clients to other professionals and agencies when

- The service needs of the client system exceed the scope of the agency mission
- Clients require specialized services that go beyond the skill repertoire of the social worker
- Organizational restrictions and eligibility requirements limit service access

Social workers initiate effective referral processes by

- Discussing the need and reasons for the referral with the client system
- Screening services for the best referral fit
- Following agency referral protocols
- Making the actual referral
- Transferring the client's records
- Arranging for follow-up

Identifying Strengths

Empowerment-oriented social workers reorient the way they respond to clients to make strengths the cornerstone of their work. Narrowly focusing on clients' problems excludes from view the resources of their strengths. Emphasizing what clients are doing wrong decreases their sense of competence and heightens their defensiveness and vulnerability. This, in turn, cuts off exchanges of information and curtails clients' resourcefulness. Focusing on strengths provides clients with a reservoir of resources for generating solutions and enhances their participation in the social work process (Table 8.5).

The strengths perspective is "more responsive to the humanistic, ethical, and political considerations that characterize the helping process" (Goldstein, 1990, p. 267). Identifying clients' strengths and resources activates their potential for change. Among the possible strengths clients and social workers consider are the client system's

- Outstanding qualities
- Demonstrations of power
- Alliances
- Distinctive characteristics
- Relationship with environmental systems
- Available resources
- Contributions to the social and physical environments
- Adaptability to change
- Cultural strengths (Miley, O'Melia, & DuBois, 2004)

TABLE 8.5 Principles for Promoting Client Strengths and Competence

Social workers should foster relationships that
- Reflect empathy
- Affirm clients' choices and self-determination
- Value individual differences
- Emphasize collaboration

Social workers should promote communication that
- Respects dignity and worth
- Considers individual differences
- Remains client-focused
- Upholds confidentiality

Social workers sould seek solutions that
- Encourage clients' participation
- Apprise clients of their legal rights
- Reframe challenges as opportunities for learning
- Involve clients in decision making and evaluation

Social workers should reflect standards of the social work profession in actions that
- Adhere to the profession's code of ethics
- Involve them in professional development, research, and policy formulation
- Redress discrimination, inequality, and social justice issues

Social Work Highlights. Billy Maxwell smiled coyly at Jack Reed, the school social worker, as Jack entered his office. Billy, perched on the edge of Jack's chair, announced that he was social worker for the day. Looking directly at Jack, without missing a beat and sounding just like the principal, Billy said, "I think we need to have a serious talk today, young man." Billy waved his hand to a chair, indicating that Jack should take a seat. Seating himself, Jack asked, "Well, what am I in trouble for this time?" Billy rolled his eyes and exclaimed, "Oh, brother!" A sarcastic, "Oh, brother!" is Billy's all-too-frequent trademark expression of disgust with his teacher, classmates, or the principal.

Billy's classmates like him, except when they're the target of his sometimes unkind wisecracks. His teacher describes him as an impulsive, interruptive influence in the classroom. The principal has Billy pegged as a troublemaker. His parents see him as "all boy." In his work with Billy, Jack does not discount Billy's inappropriate actions in the classroom, nor does he take lightly Billy's troublesome behavior on the playground. Jack's approach to working with Billy takes into account the difficulties Billy presents at school, acknowledges those times when Billy is doing things right, and builds on the strengths of this gifted, creative, articulate, likable seven-year-old.

Assessing Resource Capabilities

Assessing resource capabilities, or assessment, is the dynamic process of gathering information in order to understand clients' challenges. Together, practitioners and clients explore the particulars of the situation, the potential effects, and the resources necessary for implementing solutions. The purpose of assessment is to understand the problem and ascertain ways to reduce its impact. Empowerment-based social work practice reframes assessment from a process that gathers information to detect problems to one that focuses on gathering information to discover resources that will strengthen solutions.

Competence Clarification

Competence generally refers to the abilities and potential of human systems to negotiate favorably with their environment. In other words, competent human systems are able to care for their members, interact effectively with other systems, and contribute to the resources of their social and physical environments (Miley, O'Melia, & DuBois, 2004). In successful systems, members contribute to the well-being and overall functioning of the system and benefit from membership in that system. Likewise, competent systems share a similar relationship with their environments; they supply and access resources through reciprocal exchanges.

Competence clarification can extend to all system levels. For example, in assessing the competence of a community, practitioners look for evidence that the community responds to the needs of its members, draws on the resources of its members, distributes community resources equitably among its members, ensures an overall sense of security and well-being for its citizens, and contributes to the larger region of which it is a part.

As such, competence clarification views environmental resources as instruments of help rather than as merely influences on help (Maluccio, 1999). Maluccio's guidelines for competence clarification include (1) clarifying the competence of the client system, including capabilities, strengths, resiliency, and resources; (2) clarifying the environment, including the availability of resources and supports, and the presence of barriers, risks, and obstacles; and (3) clarifying the goodness of fit or balance between the requirements for and the actual availability of resources.

Social Studies

Social studies help to define the pertinent problems, issues, and needs inherent in the situation and to heighten one's awareness of clients' strengths (Table 8.6). Concerns raised by client systems, whether at the micro-, mid-, or macrolevel, must be examined in the context of the larger system of which the client system is a part and the smaller, internal structures that make up the social system. The problem an individual presents (private trouble) may be the result of a larger community situation (public issue). Likewise, a community or organizational problem affects the individual members of the community or organization. The challenge for social work is to merge the "twin images of individual and social need into one" (Schwartz, 1969, p. 357).

At all system levels, social studies individualize information about clients in order to identify problems. Examples of social studies include case histories, social histories, situational analyses, social surveys, community surveys, policy or program analyses, and social research.

Cultural Considerations in Assessments. As clients and social workers gather information for social studies, they explore the cultural context. Culturally competent practitioners form questions from general information about cultural values and patterns to ask about specific aspects of culturally based traditions, values, and beliefs (Congress, 1994). People identify with their cultural or ethnic group to different degrees and ascribe various levels of importance to their cultural heritage. Factors to consider include length of residence in the community; circumstances of immigration; traditions about holidays, religious rituals, and health practices; and values about community, family, work, education, and help-seeking.

TABLE 8.6 Social Studies

Among the questions in a social study are the following:

- How does the client system define the problem?
- What are the boundaries of the problem?
- What is the client system's perception of the intensity of the problem?
- What is the client system's perception of the duration of the problem (long-term, short-term, crisis)?
- What attempted solutions have been forged?
- Who else is affected by the problem?
- How does the problem affect the social functioning of the system that it impinges upon?
- What environmental opportunities, barriers, or constraints affect social functioning and the resolution of the problem?
- What value issues are involved?
- What client strengths or competencies can be directed toward change?
- What resources are available?
- What is the client's perception of social work intervention and the helping process?
- What has the client's past experience with the social service delivery system been like?
- Does the client believe that there is hope for resolution of the problem?
- How motivated is the client to change?

Social Work Highlights. Carmen Molina is a social worker at Pleasant Valley Nursing and Retirement Center. She is preparing to complete a social history and a mental status assessment with a new resident at the facility, Olivia Smith. Carmen reads the resident's chart, which includes background information and medical information. The face sheet of the resident's chart highlights intake data such as admission date, reason for admission, names of family members, and church affiliation. Carmen will use this information as a basis for framing her questions to complete the social history. Carmen likes having some background information available to prompt the resident's recall and to focus the interview. She also knows that residents' social networks are treasure troves of strengths. She often works out eco-maps or genograms with residents (see Figures 8.1 and 8.2).

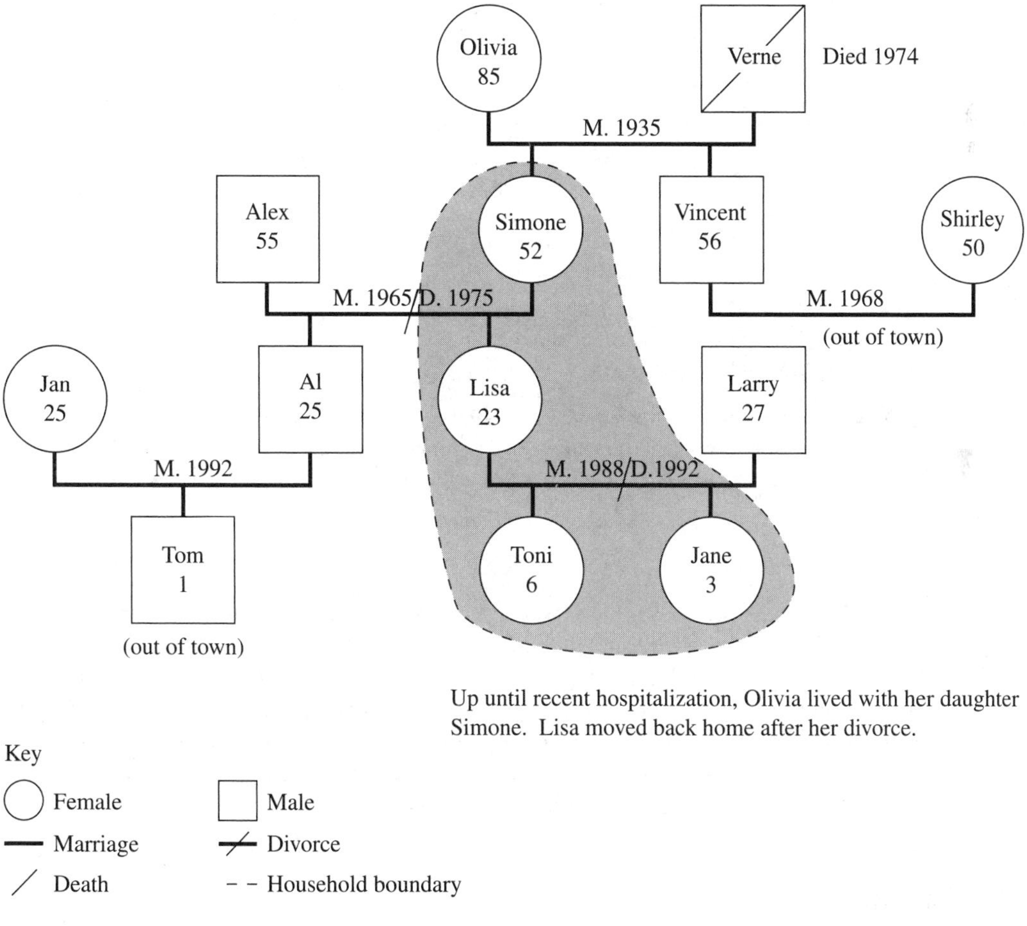

A genogram illustrates the structure and interrelationships within a family. Genograms incorporate information from at least two generations, including names, ages, and dates of marriages, divorces, and deaths. Sometimes workers and clients annotate genograms with other descriptive information, as well.

FIGURE 8.1 Genogram for Olivia Smith

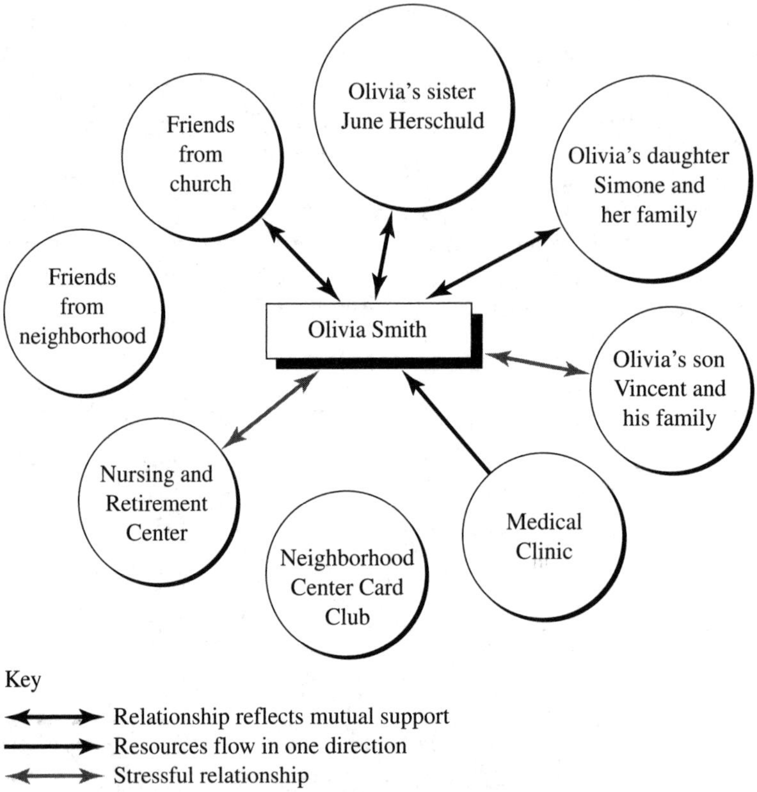

Eco-map for Olivia Smith. An eco-map is a tool that helps workers and clients visualize clients' environmental resources and constraints. Eco-maps picture significant relationships between client systems and their environmental systems.

FIGURE 8.2 Eco-map for Olivia Smith

The nursing home uses the social history and the mental status assessment to formulate care plans with residents and their families. The social history chronicles the resident's life. Questions relate to significant life experiences, family history, educational background, employment experiences, hobbies, and personal preferences. The mental status assessment apprises the staff of the client's level of cognitive functioning and awareness as to time and place. Carmen shares the information from these psychosocial assessments at interdisciplinary team meetings to inform staff about residents' needs.

Framing Solutions

Social work practitioners and clients work together to develop solutions. They draw upon each other's knowledge, skills, and resources. Social workers bring to the relationship professional knowledge and skills pertaining to human behavior, the social environment, the service delivery system, and practice methodologies. Clients systems—whether they are individuals and families, formal groups and organizations, or communities and societies—bring their own experiences and resources, such as personal life experiences, familial relationship patterns, organizational leadership styles, community initiatives, and societal orientations toward values. Framing possible solutions is a process through which social workers and clients draw upon their mutual resources to transform goals and objectives into plans of action.

Goals and Objectives

Clients' goals are statements that specify what the clients hope to achieve through the helping relationship. Typically, the overall purpose forms the long-range, or outcome, goal. Short-term objectives specify steps that will lead to accomplishing the long-range goal. Goals and objectives are the index by which clients and social workers measure change and evaluate success.

Social workers and clients use a technique called *partializing* to separate the overall goal into workable, manageable parts. This technique enables workers and clients to focus on specific aspects of difficulties that they can address, rather than feeling overwhelmed by seemingly insurmountable tasks. In other words, taking small steps leads to the resolution of the more comprehensive goal. "A partialized problem is quite often one one can do something about when one is helpless before the whole. If one can start work on even a little bit of the whole, one may gain courage to tackle a little more" (Keith-Lucas, 1972, p. 58).

Clients' Roles in Setting Goals. Social workers and clients work together to specify goals to achieve solutions to the defined problems, issues, and needs. Very likely, clients have ideas about how their problems should be solved or what services they need. Frequently they are accurate; sometimes they're not. The goal-setting process involves negotiating agreements about the course of action. Empowering social workers fully consider the clients' perspectives. If the resulting goals differ from clients' initial plans, the differences need to be accounted for and mediated.

Accomplishing tasks and attaining goals serve as mileposts of achievement. As clients achieve accomplishments, their sense of competence increases, as do their motivation levels. However, clients must "own" the definition of their difficulties and the goals and assume responsibility for activities that lead to achieving their goals if they are to view themselves as responsible for changing and, thus, competent.

Plans of Action

Plans of action translate goals into strategies that work toward solutions. The following guidelines for formulating action plans ensure that these plans reflect social work values from an empowerment perspective:

- Maximize clients' involvement in all aspects of developing and implementing the plan of action.
- Recognize the interrelationships among social systems in selecting change strategies.
- Build on clients' strengths and promote clients' competence.

- Foster a critical awareness of the interconnectedness between the personal and political, and identify strategies that promote social justice.
- Create feedback loops for continuous assessment of progress and outcomes.

Plans of action often include ways to access the formal provisions of the social service delivery system as well as the informal resources in clients' social networks. Formal provisions involve the myriad of services available to the client in the social service delivery system itself. Plans of action also incorporate informal helpers such as clergy, teachers, family, friends, and neighbors. Formal and informal helping networks play distinct roles, and each is essential for its own unique contribution.

Social workers and clients select from a variety of roles and strategies that facilitate addressing issues at multiple system levels. Table 8.7 highlights these roles within the context of social work functions—consultancy, resource management, and education. Chapter 9 presents them in detail.

Cultural Considerations. Ethnically sensitive social workers consider cultural aspects when determining alternative solutions with ethnic minorities. Culture may be a positive reinforcement and resource for coping during times of stress or crises. At the same time, one's cultural past could be a negative source of conflict (Lum, 2004). In other words, the client's cultural background may be a strength or a limitation depending on the impact of the client's cultural differences on the particular situation. Social workers explore issues of that diversity with their clients to determine how cultural diversity affects problems and their various potential solutions.

Social Work Highlights. Parents United is a support group for family members of children who have autism. At the group's third meeting, social worker Marcia Ostrander from

TABLE 8.7 Social Work Roles

Role	Actions
Consultancy for Problem Solving	
Enabler	Empowers clients to resolve problems
Facilitator	Fosters organizational development
Planner	Coordinates program and policy development
Colleague/monitor	Acts as mentor and guide for support and professional acculturation
Resource Management	
Broker/advocate	Acts as intermediary between individuals and resources
Convener/mediator	Assembles groups and organizations for resource development
Activist	Stimulates and energizes social change
Catalyst	Stimulates interdisciplinary cooperation for resource development
Education	
Teacher	Identifies vulnerable populations and provides education
Trainer	Instructs or educates through staff development
Outreach worker	Conveys public information about social issues and social services
Research/scholar	Engages in discovery for knowledge development

Child Development Services reviewed the goals group members had agreed on at their last meeting. The group had selected three broad goals: to educate the community about autism, to advocate for educational resources in the school system, and to form a local chapter affiliated with the national autism organization. At this meeting, the parents will begin to formulate concrete objectives and identify tasks and activities.

As a starting point, Marcia suggested working on their community education goal. Group members shared a lot of ideas for a media blitz, including getting the message out through public service announcements, seminars and workshops, feature articles in the local newspaper, and radio and television talk shows. The group agreed that the objective—"the Parents United group will arrange for five media exposures within the next three months"—was indeed attainable and realistic. Members identified what needed to be done to make this possible. To start with, Gina Stand will contact the national autism society to obtain literature and brochures. Nora and John West will prepare a press package. Alan Bates will construct a list of contact people in the local media. The members of the Parents United group are framing solutions. They identify desired outcomes, consider alternatives for achieving their goals, and detail a plan of action.

Implementing Action Plans

To implement action plans, practitioners work with client systems and with other systems related to clients' situations. In general, implementation processes fall into three categories: activating resources, creating alliances, and expanding opportunities.

Activating Resources

After social workers and clients determine their overall course of action, it's time to place their plans in motion. The process of activating resources does just that. Activating means initiating actions that will lead to achieving the outcome goals.

Although activating resources is a process that initiates plans of action, this does not imply that social workers direct or control these activities, or that social workers initiate activities that "do to" or "do for" clients. Although social workers may act as catalysts for change, activating resources is a cooperative venture in which both social workers and clients participate.

Ways to Activate Resources. Activating resources includes intervention activities to empower client systems with their own personal resources and increase their access to the resources that already exist in their social environments. In activating resources, clients make connections with necessary interpersonal and institutional resources, and social workers consult on strategies and work with clients to manage resources. Possible strategies and techniques include

- Enhancing personal efficacy
- Fostering interpersonal competence
- Promoting consciousness-raising
- Building on strengths
- Motivating change

- Drawing upon cultural resources
- Exercising personal power (Miley & DuBois, 1999, p. 7)

An enhanced sense of competence and personal self-efficacy is certainly a significant component of empowerment. However, a singular focus on individual competence falls short of the concept of empowerment as both personal *and* political. Limiting activities to the personal arena of efficacy and adaptation disregards the transactional nature of empowerment. Some even argue that narrowly focusing on the personal domain misses the point of empowerment entirely (Breton, 1994).

Emphasizing the development of a critical consciousness ensures that the interconnections between the personal and the political are made (Breton, 1994; 2002; Gutiérrez, 1994; Lee, 2001; Simon, 1994). Consciousness-raising contextualizes experiences, reduces self-blame, and "helps group members to take account of the nature and impact of their own choices and actions and to take responsibility for them" (Simon, 1990, p. 35). Critical reflection leads to an understanding of the social origins of personal actions and the recognition that institutional structures and policies can be altered. Moreover, dialogue within a group context forms a base of solidarity among group members that can result in collective actions that lead to changes in social policies and social structures.

Creating Alliances

Alliances are powerful resources that can energize change. Through the process of creating alliances, social workers and clients add to clients' resource pool of connections with social support networks and community resources. They also draw upon the benefits of social workers' associations with other professionals.

Ways to Create Alliances. By creating alliances, social workers and clients align the efforts of clients in empowerment groups, strengthen the functioning of clients within their natural support networks, and organize the service delivery network. These alliances bring emotional support to clients and build bases of power. Key techniques include

- Forming empowerment groups
- Developing a critical consciousness
- Aligning natural support networks
- Creating responsive social service delivery systems
- Constructing client-service alliances
- Maximizing interpersonal power (Miley & DuBois, 1999, p. 8)

Many practitioners conclude that working with clients in groups enhances their experiences of empowerment (Breton, 1994; 2002; Gutiérrez, 1994; Lee, 2001; Simon, 1994). Work in small groups "is the perfect environment for raising consciousness, engaging in mutual aid, developing skills, problem solving, and experiencing one's own effectiveness in influencing others" (Dodd & Gutiérrez, 1990, p. 71).

Creating alliances also extends to community coalitions, interagency networks, and case management teams. Composed of professionals, client advocates, and service consumers, these alliances have the potential to form a base of power to engage in collective

BOX 8.2
Social Work Profile

Community Action

After completing a practicum in special education as an undergraduate, I considered becoming either a special education teacher or a social worker. After my summer job experience at a state hospital school, I knew exactly what direction my career would take. I wanted to be more than a classroom educator; I wanted to be in a position where I could change systems. As a reform-minded social worker, I believe I have made a difference in the lives of the people with whom I have worked in several fields of practice—mental health, disabilities services, domestic violence and sexual assault advocacy, and, now, in a community action agency. As a master's level social worker, I have been able to combine direct practice work with supervisory and management experiences in each of these positions.

The lessons I have learned about organizational restructuring, fund raising, and public relations carry over to my job as a director of a community action agency that serves a multicounty area, employs over 250 persons, and serves more than 20,000 clients a year. Our agency is a "one-stop-shop" for implementing the state mandate to work with people who are poor. This community-based agency is an original Community Action Program (CAP) agency initiated by the antipoverty programs of the 1960s. The agency's mission is linked very closely to breaking the cycle of poverty. However, whereas antipoverty programs should be preventive, in reality, they are reactive to the conditions of poverty. The programs and services our agency offers include early childhood education, energy assistance, medical assistance, transitional housing, congregate meals, programming for older adults, economic development, food pantry, furniture and appliance replacement, and housing weatherization to name a few. Although these services help our clients out with the increasing costs of living, they are designed to lift people out of poverty.

Our small professional staff is complemented by a large number of paraprofessionals. As an agency, we have an assertive staff development program that emphasizes training in service delivery and ethics. The service delivery and ethical issues faced by our largely paraprofessional staff are no different from those faced by credentialed and licensed practitioners—boundary issues, confidentiality, nonjudgmentalism, acceptance of clients, and client self-determination. Through a variety of staff development opportunities, we educate workers about empowerment and strengths, the perspectives that are foundational to our agency mission and philosophy of service delivery.

As an agency director, I am challenged by a dual role. One role is to ensure that the agency is fiscally solvent. Because our agency is largely funded by state and federal grants, I am involved in grant writing. I have found that as a social work administrator I need to be grounded in budgeting and accounting principles so I can work with the agency's fiscal director to understand and direct how funding flows through the agency. My other role as an administrator is to be involved in changing social policies that impact the clients served by our agency. Public policy issues affect every client with whom we work and pervade every program that we offer. For example, because many of the families we serve are eligible for TANF, they face economic uncertainty now and in their future. The opportunities and resources available to them hinge on the outcomes of the TANF reauthorization and state-level decisions about implementation. In addition, the recent discussions on changing the funding base of the now federally funded Head Start programs to block grants to states will inevitably impact the families and children currently served by the Head Start programs that we administer in our multicounty catchment area.

social action, advocate for policy change, and realign fragmented service delivery. Involving clients in these service delivery alliances ensures their representation and safeguards their rights.

Expanding Opportunities

Whereas activating resources taps resources that are currently available, expanding opportunities creates additional resources, particularly in the social and physical environment. "Practitioners should become experts in methods of environmental modification, use of existing community resources and natural helping networks, [and] creating of new resources that may be needed by their clients" (Maluccio & Whittaker, 1989, p. 176). Empowerment-oriented social workers develop strategies related to service delivery, social policy, and economic development to redress the injustice of limited opportunities.

Many suggest that by seeking ways to redress the injustice of inadequate opportunity structures, social workers are restoring the original intent of the profession. For example, Specht and Courtney (1994) charge social workers to remain faithful to the purpose of the social work profession by reinstating their social function of linking clients with resources; renovating the delivery of services; and participating in activities that involve advocacy, social action, community education, and social change. The NASW (1999a) *Code of Ethics* summons social workers to seek social changes that extend opportunities and resources to all citizens, particularly those who are disenfranchised and oppressed.

Empowerment-based social workers define their role as one "to open up options, to help clients expand their choices, or to help them become free to consider multiple paths" (Hartman, 1993, p. 504). Nevertheless, Hartman suggests that clients face many obstacles in their search for resources and options, including limitations in social institutions, economic policies, political practices, ideologies, and the traditions of history. Pursuing ways to enhance clients' access to resources and environmental opportunities is imperative.

Ways to Expand Opportunities. Expanding opportunities fulfills the professional mandate to ensure a just distribution of societal resources by creating needed resources through social reform, policy development, legislative advocacy, and community change. Social workers join with clients to expand societal resources and develop new opportunities. Practitioners and clients work to redress social injustice and to develop just social policy. Potential techniques and strategies include

- Recognizing environmental opportunities and risks
- Engaging in community empowerment and development
- Promoting social activism and social advocacy
- Championing social justice
- Exercising sociopolitical power (Miley & DuBois, 1999, p. 8)

Social action operationalizes sociopolitical empowerment. Social workers have long favored collective action as a strategy to reallocate power and resources, to redress social inequities, and to benefit disenfranchised and oppressed populations. In empowerment-based social work practice, social action should not be construed as the exclusive domain of the macro-practitioner. Social workers who work primarily with microlevel clients serve as advocates to speak on behalf of clients to influence changes in social policies and work in collaboration with clients so that they themselves may speak in their own voices to effect social and political change. Clients, in this regard, are both subjects and claimants (Simon, 1994; Weil, 1996).

Social Work Highlights. Paul Ware reviewed his notes for the public testimony he was about to present at the legislators' forum on homelessness. Paul works at a large urban shelter for homeless and displaced families. Paul will address the group about the unique school issues experienced by children who live in shelters. The transient nature of their lives complicates the continuity of their education. The local school principals are bickering among themselves about which schools these children should attend. Paul's experience with children whose education is disrupted by constant moves and shelter stays shows that their school records are often incomplete and the documentation of their academic progress is fragmented. Too often, this results in children's being placed inappropriately in classes below their academic level when they change schools.

Paul is speaking as a representative of parents at the shelter who want their children to be able to remain in the neighborhood schools they attended before they were displaced from their homes. Parents see the need for their children to have continuity in their education and stability in that part of their lives. They seek legislative action to create exceptions to residency requirements of school districts. Paul testifies and advocates to expand his clients' opportunities.

Recognizing Success

Have clients achieved their goals? Has the action plan made a difference? Have social workers and clients focused on strengths, and have their activities empowered change? Are strategies effective and efficient? These questions, as well as others, focus attention on evaluating social work practice and participating in research.

In the context of empowerment-based social work, research and evaluation strategies are not merely mechanical techniques for measuring outcomes. Evaluation and research validate clients' achievements and substantiate the usefulness of social service strategies, programs, and policies. Naming these facets of the process for social work practice *recognizing success* emphasizes the motivating effect of crediting participants for the outcomes of their actions.

Practice evaluation and research occurs in many ways at several different levels. Evaluation plays an integral role in practitioners' day-to-day work with each client system. Specifications of grants as well as program planning processes necessitate social workers' involvement in broad-based program evaluation processes. Social workers who develop expertise as research specialists use the tools of formal research to evaluate theories, practice methods, and particular strategies to strengthen the social work profession's scientific knowledge base. Competent professionals hone their skills in the methodologies of evaluation and research.

Types of Practice Evaluation

Through evaluations of their practice, social workers assess outcomes and measure the effectiveness of strategies. Empowerment-based practice evaluation emphasizes progress,

BOX 8.3
Reflections on Empowerment

Action Research

An exclusive domain of professional knowledge undermines the legitimacy of clients' views on their own situations and their opinions about the effectiveness of programs and services. Having expert knowledge gives voice to professionals and silences consumers. In short, theoretical prescriptions create hierarchies that leave professionals in charge and relegate clients to one-down positions. "An ethic of inclusion guides empowerment-oriented [social workers] to redress issues of exclusivity" in their research endeavors (Miley, O'Melia, & DuBois, 2004, p. 412).

Action research, also known as participatory action research, community action research, and collaborative research, involves clients as full participants in research processes and theory development (DePoy, Hartman, & Haslett, 1999; Fleming & Ward, 1999; Healy, 2001; Reitsma-Street & Brown, 2002). Egalitarian by definition, service user groups identify action research as a means to realizing empowerment (Beresford & Evans, 1999; Evans & Fisher, 1999). According to Brown (1994), "participatory research is an empowering experience for participants, a process that validates their realities and their rights as people to be heard, respected and recorded as a part of history" (p. 295). As such, action research is particularly applicable to population groups whose power has been diminished by discrimination and oppression (Parsons, East, & Boesen, 1994; Sohng, 1999).

Elements of action research include dialogue, investigation of contexts, opportunity for dialogue and critical reflection, and collective actions for organizational and social change (Brown, 1994). Consumers are involved in all aspects of action research—from defining the problem, to involving stakeholders, to designing and conducting the inquiry, to analyzing and reporting results, and to taking action.

Action research is helpful for creating organizational and community change. For example, continuous cycles of action research have been applied to assess changes in social work practice that accrue from education on working in partnerships with service users (Fisher, 1994). In another example, a collaborative research team of stakeholders and university personnel identified problems with helping adolescents with special health care needs make transitions to adulthood, developed a strategy to research the issues, gathered information through focus groups and surveys, analyzed the data, and recommended actions for implementation in programs and services (DePoy, Hartman, & Haslett, 1999). Implementing social action research is complex; however, its base of grassroots involvement holds opportunities for active participation by clients or stakeholders in building a base of knowledge and refining programs and services.

---

achievement, and accomplishments. Rather than laying blame and pronouncing failure, empowerment-based practice evaluation examines obstacles as a way of learning what else needs to be done—or what needs to be done differently—to accomplish the agreed-upon goals. Progress evaluation, outcome assessment, and program evaluation are three main types of social work practice evaluation (Table 8.8).

Progress Evaluation. Action plans are blueprints for action that specify strategies and activities for accomplishing clients' goals. However, given the dynamic nature of humans and their social environment, no plan can forecast the accomplishment of outcomes un-

TABLE 8.8 Types of Practice Evaluation

Progress evaluation	Monitoring the effectiveness of the ongoing work of social workers and their clients
Outcome assessment	Measuring clients' achievement of goals and social work methods' effectiveness
Program evaluation	Investigating the effectiveness of specific services in achieving the overall goals of programs, expectations of grant requirements, or the agency's mission

equivocally. In many ways, when social workers and clients implement their plans of action, they are really experimenting with potential solutions. It stands to reason, then, that social workers and clients need to determine what's working and what's not so that they will know how to continue their work together.

As they implement plans, social workers can ask several questions that evaluate progress:

- Are they following the plan?
- Are clients and social workers fulfilling their parts of the agreement?
- Is the plan working? Are some parts of the plan working better than others? Are some parts at an impasse?
- What actions have the most positive effects? The least?
- What actions require maximum input, yet realize minimal results?
- Does the plan meet or fall short of expectations?
- Are clients playing an active role? What factors enhance or limit clients' participation?
- In what ways have clients' goals changed? What are the implications of these changes for the overall plan? (Miley, O'Melia, & DuBois, 2004)

Evaluating progress provides information that allows social workers and clients to monitor their progress and update their plans.

Client Outcome Assessment. Through client outcome assessments, workers evaluate the degree to which clients achieve their stated goals and the effectiveness of the strategies employed. Two evaluative questions are "Did the client system reach its goals?" and "Did the social work strategies produce the change?" Outcome assessment evaluations also provide information about the degree of change and its stability, unintended or unanticipated consequences, and the efficiency of the change activities. Effective client outcome assessments hinge on plans that incorporate measurable objectives. Questions that gather client outcome assessment information include

- To what degree did the client system achieve its goals?
- Did the intervention cause the change?
- What other factors may have affected the level of change?
- What factors could enhance sustaining these gains?
- Do results call for additional interventions?
- How should social workers modify their strategies?

- How do these particular results apply to future work?
- In what ways did the client system participate in the evaluation process? (Miley, O'Melia, & DuBois, 2004)

Social workers rely on information from outcome assessment to refine their practice. Final evaluations involve a systematic review of both what worked and what didn't. Outcomes may have been intended or unintended, anticipated or unanticipated, and positive or negative.

Program Evaluation. Through program evaluation, social workers attempt to address the question: Is this program accomplishing its goals? They may use several different strategies to evaluate programs. For example, they might compile outcomes for each client in a program to determine whether the program met its goals. *Consumer satisfaction surveys* ascertain clients' perspectives about workers as well as about particular programs and services. *Surveys* of former clients and referral agencies yield important information about the effectiveness and reputation of the program. In *reviewing case files,* social workers examine clients' progress in relation to program goals and the agency's mission. Finally, *formalized internal reviews* by peers and supervisors evaluate agency effectiveness. Combining several types of program evaluations provides a more comprehensive view of program effectiveness.

Program evaluations assess the effects of programs on clients, agencies, and the general public. Researchable questions that social workers might ask in evaluating programs include

- Did the program result in the anticipated change?
- Does the program demonstrate cultural sensitivity?
- Has the program achieved the objectives set by funding organizations?
- Are the program objectives consistent with the agency's mission?
- Is this program feasible?
- What are the program's strengths and weaknesses?
- Is there an adequate number of staff?
- Is the program accessible to potential clients?
- Have public attitudes or awareness changed as a result of the program?
- Does the program respond adequately to a community need? (Miley, O'Melia, & DuBois, 2004)

Program evaluation data assist professionals in refining agency policies, allocating resources, planning for programs and services, and reformulating program priorities. Evaluation research identifies programs that require modification and strategies that merit replication.

Social Work Highlights. Social worker Deanne Rivers-Bell reviews goal attainment scales with her clients. Deanne works at an after-school day treatment program for preadolescent boys with conduct disorders. Her six clients identify problematic behaviors and thinking errors associated with those behaviors. Their goals reflect increasing their effectiveness in interpersonal relationships and communication, managing impulses, and channeling their anger in socially appropriate ways. Each youth defines specific objectives along with observable behaviors that will indicate progress.

Deanne and her clients continually monitor improvement throughout their participation in the program. Daily recordings maintained by the boys log their activities and behaviors. Deanne plots this information on a graph for each boy. At weekly group meetings, her clients review the scales to recognize their successes and identify areas for continued improvement.

Integrating Gains

Describing the ending of the social work process as one of integrating gains underscores the fact that change is an ongoing process that continues after the professional relationship between client and social worker ends. In fact, the success of the whole process hinges on the nature of its ending. Effective endings provide springboards to the future by recognizing achievements, consolidating gains, and building a sense of competence.

A number of factors influence the process of ending social workers' and clients' work together. Agency purpose, parameters of programs and services, and reimbursement policies are among these factors. For example, inpatient hospitalization is limited in time and mandates short-term crisis intervention and discharge-oriented services. On the other hand, child protective services often involve long-term, open-ended provisions for service, given by a succession of providers because of staff turnover. Sometimes program services specify a time frame—for instance, a 28-day drug treatment program or an 8-session parenting class. The cost-containment policies of some insurance vendors may limit the number of contacts, thus defining the parameters of the intervention plan. Additionally, in working toward constructive endings, social workers consider such factors as the reasons for ending services; the client's and their own reactions to separations, loss, and transitions; evaluation outcomes; and ways to sustain gains in the future.

Endings are also beginnings! Considering the reciprocal nature of transactions, both clients and social workers have opportunities to benefit by integrating what they have learned into their bases of knowledge and storehouse of strategies for future actions.

Social Work Highlights. Social service providers, law enforcement officials, representatives of civic organizations, community leaders, and concerned neighbors recognized a need for a neighborhood youth center on the lower east side of the city. Youth in this particular neighborhood did not have organized community activities and were at risk of gang participation and delinquency. Juan Rameriz, a community action organizer and social worker at the Neighborhood Development Corporation, served as the chairperson of the committee that was raising funds to secure facilities and hire program staff for a neighborhood youth center. The program was based on a national neighborhood club model.

After ten months of intensive planning, organizing, and fund raising, the committee announces the acquisition of a building for the youth center and a commitment of start-up funds from community donations and a local foundation to hire a program coordinator. A ribbon-cutting celebration brings closure to this aspect of the project. All the people associated with this project, including city officials, police officers, volunteers, agency representatives, and neighborhood families and youth, will participate in a ceremony to celebrate the success of this endeavor and to launch the next phase, refurbishing the building and implementing the programming components. Juan acknowledges that to bring closure to this part of the work is important because accomplishments fuel commitment. Some of the original committee members will continue with the project, although new volunteers will be needed as well.

Looking Forward

In competence-centered social work, practitioners focus on the capabilities and strengths of client systems throughout the intervention process. The generalist orientation is well suited to this approach. A focus on competence necessitates that practice interventions consider the person in the situation—and, specifically, barriers to social functioning—and that the interventions be driven by client needs rather than by a particular practice methodology. Generalist social workers are proficient in assessing problems for micro and macro implications and in utilizing system-level intervention methods for work with individuals, groups, organizations, and communities.

Chapter 9 presents a framework for generalist social work practice based on three functions of social work: consultancy, resource management, and education. Building on the tenets of empowerment and competence, the chapter presents social work roles and describes practice strategies for social work with individuals and families, groups and organizations, and communities.

CHAPTER

9 Social Work Functions and Roles

Julie Glass, a social worker with Community Housing Development, greeted the assembly of social service practitioners:

> *Thank you for your interest in participating in further planning efforts to coordinate the delivery of housing services for individuals and families in our community who are homeless. After the announcement about the planning meeting appeared in the news bulletin last week, I received a telephone call from a woman who urged me to tell you her story today. Linda hopes that her story will point out the many challenges facing our housing services planning network.*
>
> *Linda, who has a persistent mental illness, participates in the behavior health and community support programs offered by our local mental health center. The meager financial benefits she receives through SSI have limited her ability to find safe and affordable housing. Through the rental assistance program of Community Housing Development, the mental health center was awarded a grant to provide rent subsidies to its clients. Linda is now one of a dozen mental health center clients who have moved into one-bedroom townhouses through these rent subsidy agreements. Linda is thrilled with the difference that this permanent housing has made in her life—she feels safe and is reassured by the permanency of her housing arrangement.*
>
> *Linda applauds our efforts to coordinate housing supports for other persons and families, as they too experience the need for crisis shelter and transitional and permanent housing. The shortage of shelter space, transitional housing programs, and affordable permanent housing arrangements presents a challenge for which our community needs to plan. We identify a wide range of homeless population groups who are in need of such housing—persons with low incomes, families displaced by domestic violence, and those who have chronic mental illnesses, to name a few. All this seems like a gargantuan task, but we can address this enormous challenge if we work collaboratively and develop a cooperative plan.*

Julie Glass and her colleagues must address multidimensional problems, issues, and needs. As a group, the members of the housing planning network consider forming two task forces—one to coordinate a system of lease agreements and housing subsidies, and a second to plan grant-writing activities for securing ongoing funding to respond to the increased need for housing services. They consider several issues in the broader context of their community—the press for immediate responses to the families in crises who need housing assistance, the potential drain on existing limited shelter resources, and the need to advocate policy initiatives that support adequate funding for quality services for persons who experience homelessness. As members of the community, social work practitioners are in key positions to identify needs for services and sources of funding. The collective efforts of social workers can also address broader social issues, including poverty and social and economic development.

The problem that Julie Glass poses to her colleagues and that Linda's story dramatizes, like most challenges social workers and clients confront, requires the vision of generalist social work to address multilevel needs. This chapter presents an organizing framework for generalist social work by exploring the following:

- Characteristics of the multilevel approach to generalist social work
- The consultancy function of social work
- Resource management as a function of social work
- Education as a social work function
- Generalist practice as it integrates practice, policy, and research

A Generalist Approach

Generalist social work fosters a comprehensive, "wide-angle lens" view of the problem. This approach incorporates the needs of individuals, organizations, and communities, as well as issues pertaining to service delivery and social policies. As such, generalist practice offers a broad range of potential interventions.

Basically, generalist social work can be organized into three functional areas: consulting with client systems regarding the resolution of problems, managing the resources of client systems and the social environment, and offering information to clients and systems in their impinging environment. To fulfill these functions, social workers assume various practice roles and employ numerous practice strategies.

Functions of Social Work

If you ask Julie Glass and her colleagues what social workers do, you're likely to get an impressive list of activities—counseling with individuals, facilitating groups, working with families, refining agency procedures, initiating new programs, lobbying for legislative changes, organizing community action, educating the public, conducting needs assessments, and evaluating practice and programs. These activities involve various system levels and different targets of change. Essentially, these activities involve seeking solutions to problems and challenges, acquiring and modifying resources, and providing new information. Generalist social work offers a framework for organizing the work of practitioners to accomplish these tasks.

The social work activities and corollary roles of generalist practitioners fall into three broad functions: consultancy, resource management, and education (Tracy & DuBois, 1987). The focus of consultancy is resolving problems. Resource management involves utilizing and coordinating the social service delivery system, as well as linking consumer systems with formal and informal resources. The third function, education, requires some type of instruction or learning processes. Of course, in actual practice, the functions overlap. For example, the resource management strategy of linking clients with needed resources may also be an aspect of consultancy. Education is also involved in many aspects of consultancy and resource management.

Social Work Roles and Strategies

Roles and correlated strategies are associated with each social work function. Social workers' roles are expected patterns of professional behavior. Roles assign certain behaviors and prescribe appropriate responses to particular situations. Three interrelated components make up each role: a *role concept,* or how people believe they should act in a particular situation; *role expectations,* or how others believe people should act when they occupy a particular status; and *role performance,* or how people really do act (Goldstein, 1973). In other words, roles have psychological components, including perceptions and feelings; social components, including behaviors and the expectations of others; and behavioral components.

Social work roles provide direction for professional activities. Roles define the nature of the transactions between practitioners and clients. Roles also define the nature of transactions among professional colleagues. Social work roles and their associated strategies suggest general ways to achieve goals.

Social work roles have been defined by several authors (McPheeters, 1971; Pincus & Minahan, 1973; Teare & McPheeters, 1970; 1982) and variously presented as helping roles (Siporin, 1975), interventive roles (Compton & Galaway, 1999), and role sets (Connaway & Gentry, 1988). This presentation of social work roles accentuates the exchanges of information inherent in each role. Thus, clients' and social workers' tasks emphasize accessing, processing, utilizing, and communicating information. The schema organizes these social work roles in the context of types of client systems—from the microlevel to the midlevel to the macrolevel—and includes roles related to interactions with professional colleagues as well.

Strategies and tasks activate social work roles (Table 9.1). A strategy is a plan that systematizes action, provides a "blueprint" guide, or is the way intent is carried out in practice (Siporin, 1975). Strategies involve the dimensions of planning and action. As strategies

TABLE 9.1 Social Work Roles and Strategies

	Consumers			
Function	*Individuals and Families*	*Formal Groups and Organizations*	*Community and Society*	*Social Work Profession*
Consultancy				
Role	Enabler	Facilitator	Planner	Colleague/monitor
Strategy	Finding solutions	Organizational development	Research and planning	Professional acculturation
Resource management				
Role	Broker/advocate	Convener/mediator	Activist	Catalyst
Strategy	Case management	Networking	Social action	Community service
Education				
Role	Teacher	Trainer	Outreach	Researcher/scholar
Strategy	Information processing	Professional training	Community education	Knowledge development

Source: Adapted with permission of the authors from *Information Model for Generalist Social Work Practice,* p. 2 by B. C. Tracy and B. DuBois, 1987.

become actions, transactions take place in the person:environment context. Others react within these transactions and provide feedback or exchanges of information.

Rather than the social worker's starting with roles or strategies and then determining plans of action, the nature of the situation should drive the selection of roles and strategies. Client systems' challenges, rather than the preferred methods of practitioners, generate strategies. Generalist social workers frame situations in the context of intervention at all system levels. This approach offers numerous possibilities for linking micro-, mid- and macrolevel plans of action. To clarify the social work functions and their associated roles, the rest of this chapter defines each role and provides illustrative examples.

Consultancy

Consultancy refers to the professional activities through which social workers and clients initiate change by clarifying clients' issues, discovering options, and developing plans of action. Consultancy relies on the expertise of clients and social workers alike. Social workers bring formally acquired knowledge, values, and skills; clients bring knowledge, values, and skills based on their personal, organizational, and community life experiences.

In adopting this orientation to collaborative work with clients, empowerment-based social workers need to examine the bias inherent in traditional notions about client–worker relationships. For example, Maluccio (1979), in his comparison of clients' and social workers' perceptions, found that "while workers tend to look upon them [clients] as reactive participants in interaction with the environment, clients emerge as *active* organisms, who view themselves as capable of autonomous functioning, change, and growth" (p. 188).

According to Hepworth, Rooney, and Larsen (1997), "although social workers fervently espouse the belief that human beings have the right and opportunity to develop their potentialities, their tendency to focus on pathology has the effect of undermining that very value commitment" (p. 194). Even a subtle indication that social workers regard clients negatively can damage clients' self-respect and confidence. For those clients who approach helping relationships with an already impaired self-esteem, an unbalanced focus on weakness and pathology escalates their feelings of hopelessness and helplessness. Social workers' images of dysfunction, disorganization, and pathology compound clients' feelings of self-doubt, inadequacy, and worthlessness. If clients are to regard themselves as competent, social workers must so regard them (Hepworth, Rooney, & Larsen). By establishing collaborative partnerships with clients, empowerment-oriented social workers recognize, affirm, and build on clients' strengths and potential for change.

Through roles and strategies associated with consultancy, clients and social workers address personal, family, organizational, community, or societal problems with clients at all system levels (Figure 9.1). With microlevel clients—individuals, families, and small groups—the enabler role incorporates counseling strategies that generate change. At the midlevel, the role of facilitator focuses on organizational development. The macrosystem role of social planner comprises strategies for research and planning to initiate macrolevel change. Finally, with the system of the social work profession, the colleague/monitor role provides collegial support and peer review to improve the competence of practitioners and to strengthen the profession as a whole.

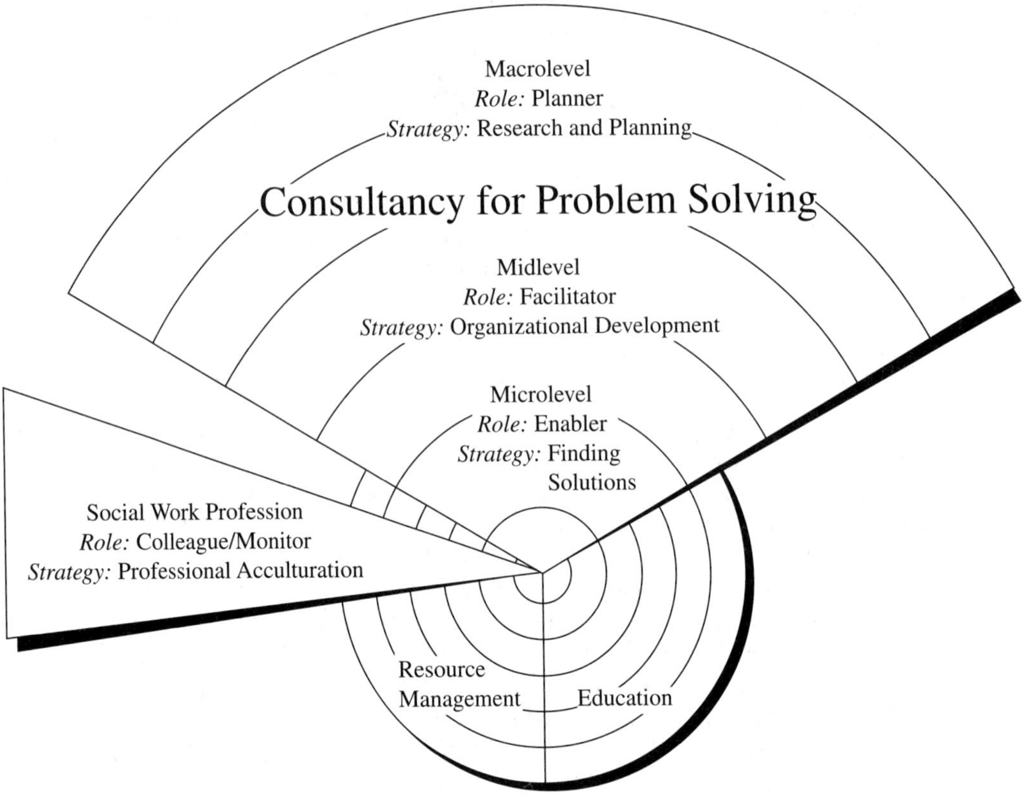

FIGURE 9.1 Consultancy for Problem Solving

Microlevel: Enabler Role

In the enabler role, practitioners work with microlevel clients to resolve challenges in social functioning. Counseling strategies complement the enabler role.

As enablers, social worker practitioners work *with* individual, family, and small-group client systems to improve individual social functioning. Counseling strategies facilitate clients' discovery of solutions. Social workers and clients create changes by refining behavior, altering patterns of relationships, and modifying factors in the social and physical environments. The enabler role is consistent with the professional objective of helping people enhance their competencies and expand their abilities to solve problems and cope (Working statement, 1981).

Empowerment-oriented social workers begin by recognizing clients' strengths and then build on clients' potential for change. Carl Rogers (1961) describes the strengths-focused nature of helping relationships as relationships

> in which at least one of the parties has the intent of promoting the growth, development, maturity, improved functioning, improved coping with life of the other. The other, in this sense, may be one individual or a group. To put it another way, a helping relationship might

> be defined as one in which one of the participants intends that there should come about, in one or both parties, more appreciation of, more expression of, more functional use of the latent inner resources of the individual. (pp. 39–40)

As enablers, practitioners work with clients to identify their needs, clarify their situations, and develop their capacity to deal effectively with their challenges. Practitioners "use varying approaches in order to provide the conditions necessary for clients to achieve their purposes, meet life challenges, engage in their natural life development processes, and carry out their tasks" (Maluccio, 1981, p. 19). The conditions of change lie within individuals and in their transactions with other social systems.

Social Work Highlights. Rita Costello is a social worker with Family Services, a multipurpose agency that offers social services to youth and their families. Currently, Rita's job is with the agency's teen parents program, a program initiative that provides a variety of social services for young parents.

Sally is one of Rita's new clients. Fifteen-year-old Sally recently discovered that she is pregnant. The nurse at the maternal health center suggested that Sally contact Family Services' teen parents program.

Initially, Rita counsels Sally individually. Sally's immediate question is, "Should I place my baby for adoption?" As an enabler, Rita helps Sally examine her alternatives and evaluate potential outcomes, rather than directing her to a single option. With information about options, Sally is better able to determine her course of action.

Rita knows that there are other service options available to pregnant teens like Sally. For example, many of the teens in the program attend a group for new parents. This group provides teen parents with a forum for dealing with the stresses of being a single parent. Members share their experiences and feelings and discover that others experience similar difficulties. Often, in the context of their discussions, group members discover ideas for solutions. By facilitating the group process, Rita enables individual group members to resolve their difficulties.

Sometimes Rita and her clients discover that the source of difficulty is in communication among multigenerational family members. In these instances, Rita and her clients may decide to invite all of the family members to work on communication issues together. For example, Rita is meeting with the Smiths, a four-generation family that includes great-grandmother Rose, grandmother LaVerne, and Tiffany and her one-year-old son Dan. The Smiths are struggling with questions such as "Who takes charge of Dan?" "What is Tiffany's financial responsibility?" "Should Rose do all the work, since LaVerne works and Tiffany is a college student?" Rita's work with the Smiths also reflects the social work enabler role. The Smith family's work with Rita empowers them to redefine their rights, roles, and responsibilities.

Midlevel: Facilitator Role

The facilitator role describes work with formal groups, organizations, or bureaucratic structures that promote more effective functioning in these multiperson systems. Organizational development strategies elaborate this role.

The facilitator role describes work with midlevel client systems—such as formal groups or organizations—that enhances their social functioning. When formal groups or organizations identify problems they are having with their internal processes, structures, or functions, they may consult with social workers to help them pinpoint the difficulties and develop solutions. Their initial task is to clarify mutual expectations and perspectives (Ingalls, 1973). As facilitators, social workers "can support helpful behaviors of other group members, model useful behaviors, ask appropriate questions, or provide appropriate observations and feelings about the group. They can teach other group members information about group process and functioning" (Johnson, 1998, p. 219). After implementing plans, participants need to stabilize changes and integrate gains.

Social work practitioners work collaboratively with midlevel client systems to improve organizational planning, intraorganizational patterns of communication, decision-making processes, and administrative structures. They often act as facilitators within their own agency settings to enhance the cooperation of staff and increase the effectiveness of programs and services.

As another aspect of organizational development, social workers play a key role in shaping organizational policy. Answers to questions such as "Are we reaching the targeted population?" "Are services delivered effectively and efficiently?" and "Are monitoring and evaluation tools measuring success and uncovering unexpected results?" evaluate program effectiveness. Indeed, the ultimate test of a policy is in its actual implementation in a program and its impact on the lives of consumers.

Social Work Highlights. It's time again for Community Service Club members to determine their annual project. In the past, this task has led to heated discussions and conflicts among faction groups. This year the steering committee recommended hiring a social worker, Indera Jones, to work with service club members. Specifically, Indera will facilitate a process for selecting a range of issues and determining the focal issue for the club project. To maximize participation and minimize dissention, Indera conducts a group process that involves a broad base of group membership. By using an objective technique for prioritizing issues, Indera helps the group reach consensus about the club's goals for the coming year. Specifically, Indera's work with this organization reflects the social work facilitator role.

Social workers also use the facilitator role in their work with formal organizations. Again, this work aims to create organizational rather than individual change. For example, the management team at a large industrial plant was concerned about alcoholism, absenteeism, and other personal issues that result in low motivation and reduced productivity. They hired Jose Monteago, a social worker with expertise in business and industry, to evaluate workers' needs in the context of the organizational structure. After gathering information from labor and management, Jose recommends implementing an employee assistance program. He presents several options for employee assistance programs to the newly formed labor–management council for consideration. Jose's work reflects the organizational development strategies of the facilitator role.

Macrolevel: Planner Role

Working with community or societal structures to assess unmet needs, generalist social workers assume the role of planner to set goals, develop policies, and initiate programs. Strategies associated with the planner role include research and planning.

Social planners assist communities in planning to resolve community problems and provide health and human services. The macrolevel focus of social workers as planners and community organizers necessarily requires knowledge of social problems and social policies, community change theories, and macrolevel change processes. Using specialized knowledge and skills in the areas of planning and research, practitioners involve community leaders and social service personnel in addressing community needs and developing community resources.

Social planners' activities include coordinating services, developing programs, evaluating policies' effectiveness, and advocating social welfare reform. Social planners use research techniques such as needs assessments, service inventories, community profiles, environmental scans, and field research to further their understanding of social problems and discover potential solutions.

Social planners serve in an essentially neutral capacity in the planning process; they approach research and analysis objectively to propose a rational course of action. Social planning requires a visionary orientation toward the future. Visionary perspectives motivate, whereas realistic appraisals of environmental factors and constraints define the parameters for change. Releasing potential, and perhaps even stretching communities' resource capabilities, promotes change.

To facilitate planning, social workers, along with macrolevel clients, assess both resource capabilities and environmental constraints in order to define the nature and scope of planning. Table 9.2 depicts the elements involved in planning processes. Planning activities can initiate limited changes through incremental steps or achieve comprehensive changes through widespread systemic reform.

TABLE 9.2 Fundamental Aspects of Planning

Elements	Description
Vision	Ideals Future Desired outcomes
Environmental Considerations	Demographics Economics Legislation Social policies
Resource Capability	Opportunities Staff Budget
Planning Processes	Involvement of stakeholders Assessment of recommendations
Implementation	Evaluation Revisions

Social Work Highlights. Community block grant dollars are available to agencies in Central City to establish neighborhood programs. The Central City Neighborhood Development Corporation hires Ben Cohen, a social worker with grant-writing experience, to assess the needs of the Central City neighborhood and prepare a proposal for developing a comprehensive neighborhood improvement project.

Ben forms a neighborhood advisory committee made up of a broad spectrum of neighborhood residents, city officials, and social service providers. Ben and the advisory committee work together to identify priorities, set goals, and develop a plan of action. Initially, they decided to conduct a needs assessment of the neighborhood and develop a strategy for writing the grant. Based on the findings of the needs assessment, the advisory counsel is considering programmatic and policy initiatives in the areas of crime prevention, beautification, a congregate meal site, and an after-school latchkey day care program. Ben's work illustrates the collaborative style of the planning and research strategy of the social work planner role.

Mary Brown's macrolevel work in her position as a legislative caseworker also represents the planner role. At the request of the district's representative, Mary surveyed the needs of the district's veterans. She designed a survey questionnaire and interviewed 100 veterans to identify gaps and barriers in veterans' benefits, education, economic, health, and social service resources available to veterans in the district. Overwhelmingly, the respondents expressed dissatisfaction with the availability of regional health care services for veterans. They noted that they had to drive over two hours to receive health care services at the nearest VA hospital. Many veterans reported that they and their families have residual health care problems related to their military service. The legislator will use Mary's research findings to press for federal funds to locate a comprehensive health clinic in the district. Mary's macrolevel work in her position as a legislative caseworker represents the planner role.

Professional System: Colleague and Monitor Roles

Professional interactions provide the context for the colleague and monitor roles. Through these roles, practitioners maintain the integrity of the social work profession, uphold ethical standards, and offer support to colleagues.

The role of colleague presumes an atmosphere of partnership, mutual respect, and support among members of the social work profession. Establishing working relationships with other professionals and maintaining membership in national professional organizations such as the NASW and CSWE, and local professional groups express the colleague role.

Maintaining collegial relationships with other professionals is essential for effective social work practice. Colleagues monitor the professional practice of peers to ensure quality and to uphold professional standards. The standards of the NASW (1999a) *Code of Ethics* outline social work professionals' obligations and responsibilities in monitoring the activities of the social work profession and other social work professionals. Monitoring includes advising, informing, mentoring, and providing colleagues with a general orientation to the profession.

Through their acculturation to the profession, social workers identify with the professional values, standards, and ethics of social work. Acculturation orients practitioners to the culture of the social work profession, including its language, methodologies, responsibilities, and obligations. It involves an ongoing process of education, practice experience, and professional development. Acculturation culminates in an integration of social workers' personal and professional selves.

Social Work Highlights. Members of the local NASW chapter are concerned about what they perceive as a lack of identification with the profession by new social workers in the area. The executive committee decides on a twofold approach—increasing social contacts among area social workers and enhancing new social workers' acculturation to the profession. They form two subcommittees to work out the details.

Bonnie Greene chairs the social events committee. This committee will plan bimonthly activities for area practitioners and their families. They will also prepare an agenda of special functions for national social work month in March. Marvin Hedberg's committee plans to launch a mentoring program during that month. The mentoring program will pair seasoned practitioners with prospective social work graduates of the local college. During the month, the students will participate in planned activities with their mentors. Bonnie and Marvin's activities in the local NASW chapter reflect the acculturation strategies of the social work colleague role.

Consider another facet of the colleague and monitor roles. The NASW recently developed a policy statement on professional impairment and colleague assistance programs (NASW, 1999c; Reamer, 1999). According to national statistics, at least 20 percent of social work practitioners are impaired by some type of substance use. The NASW lends support to local chapters' colleague assistance programs. These programs offer a network of services and peer support to help impaired social workers resume effective practice. Peers encourage social workers struggling with addiction to obtain treatment to aid in their recovery from chemical dependency. Social workers face ethical dilemmas when they balance their responsibility to protect the public with their obligation to support professional colleagues. Colleague assistance programs exemplify the profession's colleague and monitor roles.

Resource Management

Frequently, clients seek social work services to access resources that are not found within their personal reservoir of resources or in their informal networks of social support. So, social workers often help clients access resources, coordinate the delivery of services, and initiate new policies and programs. These varied activities all reflect the social work function of resource management.

Rather than controlling or directing clients' decisions and choices, resource management involves coordinating, systematizing, and integrating resources and services. Empowerment-based resource management involves working collaboratively with clients. It reflects Solomon's (1976) contention that social work "involves linking clients to resources in a manner that enhances their self-esteem as well as their problem-solving capacities" (p. 347). Being actively involved in decision making empowers clients to access and utilize resources more effectively.

Resources are available assets or assets held in reserve that support social functioning, meet needs, or resolve problems (Siporin, 1975). While problems and needs emerge in the transactions between persons and their environment, these transactions are also the context in which social workers and clients discover resources that activate solutions. For example,

BOX 9.1

Reflections on Empowerment

Resources Are Power

Resources are located in people, in interactions with others, and within social institutions. *Personal resources* are qualities within individuals, such as resiliency, capabilities, sense of worth, hopefulness, self-esteem, intellectual abilities, motivation for change, perseverance, tenacity, courage, and life experiences (Lawton, 1980; Siporin, 1975). *Interpersonal resources* encompass support systems that emerge from natural helping networks such as family members, friends, neighbors, and coworkers. Members of natural helping networks often link people with others who have had similar experiences and with the resources that employers, clergy, physicians, attorneys, and social service professionals provide (Gottlieb, 1985). *Societal resources* constitute the responses of social institutions that promote the well-being of societal members.

Resources connote power, and power depends on knowledge. In his book *Power Transformed,* MacIver (1964) clarifies the relationship among resources, power, and knowledge. According to MacIver, knowledge is a source of power:

> Power, on the human level, means capacity for effective action, and the quality and scale of action depend on the utilization of resources through the requisite skill or art, the knowing that includes know-how, know-what, know-when, and know-where. The knowing is primary, for that knowing itself can sooner or later possess itself of the resources it needs. (p. 110)

People who have information about resources and are able to mobilize these resources are resourceful (Siporin, 1975). Being resourceful fosters competence. People need resources to accomplish tasks, achieve goals, and master life's challenges. They promote effective social functioning, growth, adaptation, realization of potential, and general human welfare (Siporin, 1975). Conversely, social problems emerge from gaps and barriers in the provision of resources or from the lack of opportunity to access available resources.

---

personal, interpersonal, community, and societal resource systems mediate stress. These resource systems enhance clients' social functioning and promote their full participation in society.

Social work practitioners work at all system levels in their resource management roles (Figure 9.2). At the microsystem level, social workers use case management strategies to carry out their broker and advocate roles. With midlevel clients, the convener and mediator roles network elements of social service delivery. As mobilizers who activate change at the macrosystem level, social workers seek to reallocate societal resources through structural and institutional change in the sociopolitical arena. Finally, the catalyst role reflects the commitment of members of the social work profession to work together and with other professionals as catalysts to eliminate oppression and social injustice.

Microlevel: Broker and Advocate Roles

Through the broker and advocate roles, social workers link clients with available resources or serve as intermediaries to advance clients' causes. Social workers use case management strategies to coordinate the services of multiple providers.

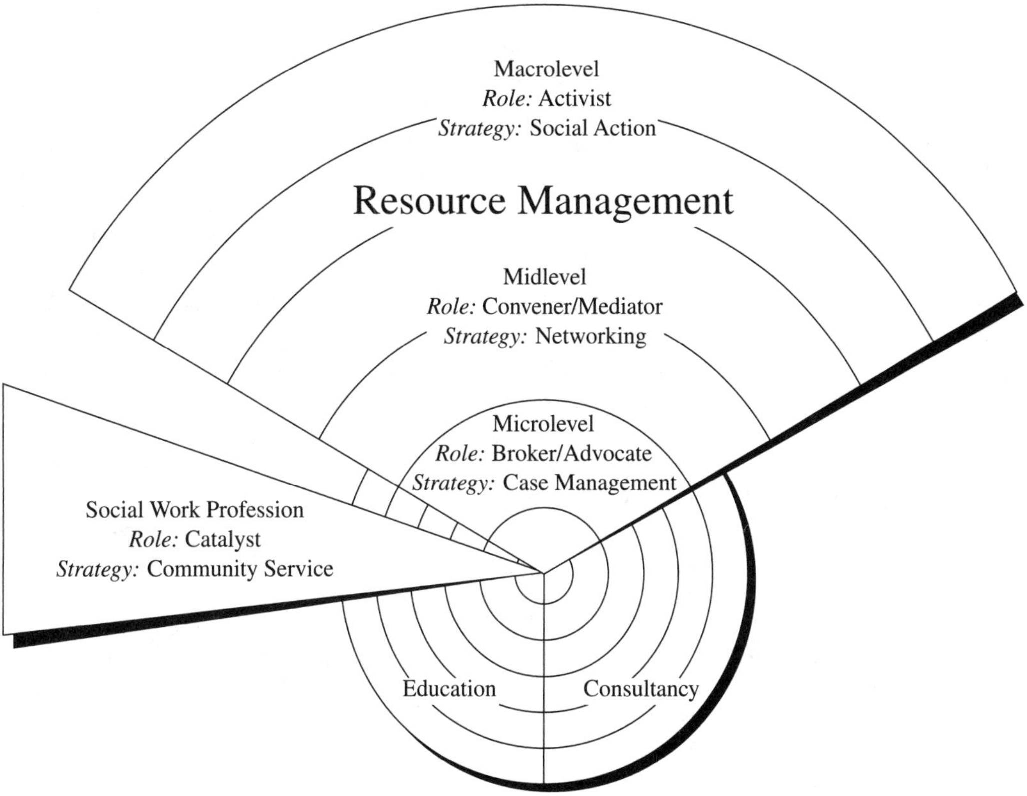

FIGURE 9.2 Resource Management

As brokers, social workers provide valuable information about available resources so that clients can access resources appropriately and expediently. In short, they link clients with resources (McPheeters, 1971). They work collaboratively with clients to achieve the following:

- Assess the client's particular situation
- Facilitate the client's choice from among alternative resources
- Expedite the client's contact with other agencies
- Evaluate the process

Effective brokers comprehend the details of their community's social service delivery system. Brokers should do the following:

- Construct an up-to-date inventory of formal and informal community resources
- Log the locations, parameters of services, eligibility criteria, and contact people for the community resources
- Understand the policies, requirements, procedures, and appeal processes for these community resources
- Maintain working relationships with key professionals in the community (Grinnell, Kyte, & Bostwick, 1981)

Of the two types of advocacy roles—social broker advocate and community organizing advocate (Terrell, 1974)—the social broker advocate role applies to work with microlevel clients. In their work with clients, social workers often become aware of unmet needs, social inequalities, and the erosion of clients' civil or legal rights. Case advocacy redresses these inequalities. Ultimately, case advocacy seeks changes, reinterpretations, or exceptions to policies in relation to a particular client's situation. When social workers aggregate clients' needs into policy issues, they transfer their activities from case to cause advocacy, a shift that illustrates the interrelationships among social work activities at various system levels.

The broker and advocate roles fulfill one of the primary purposes of social work—to help people obtain resources. Using the broker and advocate roles, social workers arrange services that address clients' specific needs or remedy complaints stemming from adverse actions by public bodies or other individuals or organizations. Throughout social welfare history, potentially eligible clients have been denied services under cover of moral excuses. Social workers, as advocates, ensure that clients have access to the services for which they qualify. In other words, brokers and advocates traverse the bureaucratic mazes of governmental structures and protect clients' rights.

Empowerment-oriented resource managers work collaboratively with clients throughout broker or advocacy efforts. To empower clients, Lenrow and Burch (1981) recommend coaching or

> encouragement and information about how clients can approach other professionals and service agencies in ways that enhance the clients' self-respect rather than leaving them feeling defeated or degraded. It includes adding to their information about how to find resources that will be useful in making good decisions and resources that will be useful in implementing them. And it includes providing them with information about what contributes to healthy bodily and psychological functioning. (p. 248)

Social Work Highlights. Carla North works in the child care resource and referral program at the community center. As people require information about child care providers, Carla uses her CHILD LINK computer data bank to compose a list of licensed day care providers and child care centers. Today she's talking with Carmen and Pedro Mendez. Because they both work outside the home and take night courses at the local community college, their child care needs for their three preschool children are substantial. Carla's computer program allows her to tailor this list to the specific requirements of her clients. Licensed babysitters and day care centers pay a nominal fee to list their services in CHILD LINK. Through her broker role, Carla links clients with service providers.

Another example highlights the role of social worker as advocate. Roger Osborn's application and claim for disability assistance was denied. He contacted Jim Young, a social work advocate with the Welfare Rights Association, for help in preparing his appeal. Jim offers several options to Roger. The first is to seek a reconsideration of the eligibility determination. Another alternative is to have legal representation at the appeal hearing. A third option is to request an independent review of Roger's medical history. As Roger decides on a course of action, Jim will continue to advocate his case through the correct procedural channels.

BOX 9.2
Reflections on Diversity

Social Work Roles and Cultural Sensitivity
Culturally sensitive social workers recognize that diversity affects the implementation of practice roles in the helping process. Social work roles define purposeful activities that empower client systems to seek solutions to their challenges, access needed resources, and gain new knowledge and skills. To implement these roles with culturally diverse clients, practitioners must consider how roles are construed and implemented.

For example, Solomon (1976) believes that the traditional interpretations of broker and advocate roles contradict empowerment with minority clients. Such an interpretation of the advocacy role presumes that clients are powerless to the extent that their situations require someone to work on their behalf. Solomon suggests that working "on behalf" of others leads to a self-fulfilling prophecy: "In some instances, advocacy for a client may increase powerlessness by reinforcing the client's feelings of ineptitude or by generating more repressive repercussions from the opposing system" (p. 346). Likewise, the broker role presumes expert knowledge that "can denigrate into such a paternalistic operation that the client becomes a lowly supplicant to the social worker's Lady Bountiful routine" (p. 346). Solomon's position points out that how social workers interpret and enact roles is critical for those roles to be empowering with minorities.

Likewise, according to Fong (1994), effective social workers consider the implications of the cultural concepts of filial piety and loss of face when implementing social work roles with Asian families who hold traditional cultural values. Since filial piety emphasizes patriarchal authority and respect for the elderly, social workers defer to these members of Asian families. Asian families also protect themselves from any public disclosure of their behavior in order to prevent shame and stigma in their ethnic community. Therefore, in their roles that link Asian families with resources outside the family system, culturally sensitive social workers carefully guard confidentiality and their clients' privacy.

Case Management Strategies. Case management is a strategy for coordinating services and ensuring the accountability of service providers. "In essence, [case management] is a series of actions and a process to ensure that clients of human services systems receive the services, treatment, care, and opportunities to which they are entitled" (Weil & Karls, 1989, p. 1). The purposes of case management include coordinating services and achieving continuity, while simultaneously balancing accountability issues such as program costs and service effectiveness.

Social workers are most likely to draw on case management strategies when clients have multiple needs. In these instances, clients must negotiate with many different providers and make plans to sustain services or benefits over time. Case managers assist clients by working with them to take care of the following:

- Appraise their needs
- Identify relevant services, opportunities, or benefits
- Develop comprehensive plans
- Advocate clients' rights to services
- Monitor the actual delivery of services (Moxley, 1989)

Human service professionals in mental health, disability rehabilitation, family welfare, and services for older adults all employ case management strategies extensively. Clients using services in these fields often need help accessing a variety of resources, such as housing, transportation, mental health and medical care, income maintenance, and educational and employment services.

Case management ensures comprehensive programs that meet clients' needs by coordinating services, linking the components of the service delivery system, and advocating clients' rights. Frequently one agency does not provide the types of services or programs that are necessary to achieve clients' goals. Since case managers coordinate services, they facilitate using service options from multiple providers as well as interdisciplinary teamwork approaches. Effective case managers access only required services rather than create a maze of providers and services, which would result in compounding problems rather than enhancing solutions.

Social Work Highlights. Herman and Beatrice Webster's physician refers them to Joyce Phillips, a case manager with At Home. This community-based support program offers case management as well as in-home health care, home-delivered meals, and chore services as alternatives to nursing home placements. The Websters, a frail elderly couple with limited financial resources, require multiple services to remain in their own home. Joyce completes a psychosocial inventory to assess the Websters' physical, cognitive, and social functioning. Based on their scores, financial assets, and personal preferences, Joyce prepares a care plan for the Websters' consideration and approval. Using case management strategies, Joyce will make the necessary arrangements with the care providers the Websters select and coordinate the total plan of care.

Midlevel: Convener and Mediator Roles

As conveners and mediators, social workers serve as intermediaries among representatives of groups or organizations when they gather to identify common problems, formulate goals, discuss potential solutions, mobilize resources, and implement and evaluate plans of action. Social workers use networking strategies to coordinate and develop services.

Through the convener and mediator roles, social workers and midlevel clients address gaps and barriers in the delivery of services and advocate policies that extend social provisions and provide necessary funding. For example, practitioners may work with community task groups, agency committees, or United Way panels to evaluate the delivery of services and recommend necessary policy changes. Conveners and mediators create linkages between systems, improve interaction among organizations, and mobilize organizational resources. Social workers serve in this role through their work with interdisciplinary teams and interagency ventures.

When conflicts arise among participants, social workers use mediation skills to resolve differences. Effective mediators do the following:

- Survey the unique perspectives and special interests of each party.
- Discover the common ground of the conflicting parties.
- Assist each party in ways that promote cooperation among all factions.
- Define, confront, and deal with communication barriers.
- Identify the potential benefits of working together.

- Facilitate an open exchange of information among all parties involved.
- Remain neutral, yet, at the same time, confident and hopeful about the benefits of working together. (Grinnell, Kyte, & Bostwick, 1981)

Social Work Highlights. As a routine part of its periodic assessment of social service delivery, the Community Services Council conducted a services inventory and consumer perception poll. The research identified an unmet need for additional agency counseling hours during the evenings and weekends. Kay Maxwell, a social worker with the Community Services Council, convenes a meeting of key administrators from family service agencies, mental health centers, and psychology clinics to discuss ways in which their organizations can provide these after-hours services. Not all of the agencies represented at the meeting received funds through the Community Services Council. Agency providers expressed concern about the costs associated with expanded hours and often disagreed as to which agencies should have to assume responsibility for making these schedule changes. Kay's group work with these community leaders and her facility with mediating conflicts represent the convener and mediator roles.

Networking Strategies. Social workers as conveners and mediators use networking strategies to develop coalitions among diverse groups and organizations around common purposes or shared goals. Social workers develop networks with human service organizations, other social structures such as business and industry, and influential community leaders. Through coalitions, interagency organizations can work cooperatively to identify service gaps and barriers and to plan ways to address unmet service delivery needs. Collaborative planning enhances the effectiveness of networking strategies. Working collaboratively empowers participants to generate midlevel change.

Social Work Highlights. Vin Phong uses networking strategies in his position as businesses liaison with the Community Service Council. At the request of the labor council, Vin convened a meeting of leaders from business, industry, and labor to explore models for employer-sponsored day care. Some participating businesses are interested in developing on-site day care centers, while others are interested in joining together to sponsor off-site programs. The networking strategy Vin employs not only links the businesses to one another, but also links the businesses to informational and financial resources in the community.

Macrolevel: Activist Role

As activists, social workers bring together key social and economic leaders at the community or society level to initiate social change. Strategies of social action or social advocacy promote social justice by influencing the allocation of resources, lobbying for legislative change, and initiating court actions.

Social activists raise the public's consciousness about social problems and injustice. They mobilize available resources to change these adverse conditions (Barker, 2003). In social activism, social work activities range from garnering resources to enacting social reform. Mobilization implies working with community groups to frame a shared agenda, clarify goals, and design and implement strategies for the purpose of acquiring a broader base of support for the intended action.

In his article "From Service to Advocacy to Empowerment," O'Connell (1978) describes the characteristics that social workers must possess for effective social action. Social workers should

- Focus on a worthy *cause.*
- Feel a *genuine* commitment to the cause.
- Sustain their *focus.*
- Value *activism* as an effective way to create social change.
- Remain *tenacious,* as social change is known to require stamina.
- *Understand* the organizational structures of government bureaucracies and social service agencies.
- Develop a *base of support and influence.*
- Maintain *independence* from other pressure groups.

The goal of advocacy and activism is social reform. Social reform involves "fighting for changes in laws, regulations, etc., on behalf of a whole class of persons or segment of the society. Therefore, advocacy aims at removing the obstacles or barriers that prevent people from exercising their rights or receiving the benefits and using the resources they need" (McPheeters, 1971, p. 18). Through cause advocacy, social workers build coalitions, work for reallocations of funds, and lobby for legislation to provide appropriate social policy and funding to support their priorities for social reform.

As a strategy of activism, social action involves coordinated efforts to achieve institutional change in meeting needs, resolving social problems, remedying social injustices, or enhancing citizens' quality of life (Barker, 2003). In social action efforts, social workers takes sides to pursue social reform and social change.

When activists advocate radical causes, they maintain a partisan commitment to represent economically disadvantaged and politically disenfranchised populations and target the establishment as the adversary (Terrell, 1974). Cause advocates direct their attention to humanizing institutions. They concern themselves with reforming social institutions rather than with adjusting individuals.

Social Work Highlights. A nationwide survey identifies a serious problem with respect to inadequate funding for AIDS services in a number of states. To increase state expenditures for AIDS services, social workers testify before legislators to support increased appropriations. Political action demonstrates a direct link between participating in the formulation of social policy and practicing social work.

In another example, Jeff Miles's role as an activist responds to a community need by mobilizing the action of community members. Because of mass layoffs and plant closings, food staples at Mountain Gap Food Bank are in short supply. This regional food bank supplies community food pantries with nonperishable items and canned foods. Jeff Miles launches a comprehensive emergency food drive. He mobilizes leaders of various civic groups, fraternal organizations, businesses, and churches to spearhead campaign efforts among their members. He engages several local youth groups to participate in neighborhood solicitations. Local media personalities feature newsspots in their programs to heighten community awareness about the food bank crisis.

Professional System: Catalyst Role

As catalysts, social workers organize professional endeavors with social work colleagues and through interdisciplinary relationships to develop an optimal system of social services. Through community service strategies, social workers act on their ethical commitment to serve as volunteers.

In the catalyst role, social workers press for innovation and change. Social workers have an ethical commitment to modify the delivery of services so that services are more humane, to influence social and environmental policies in order to champion social justice and equality, and to urge the adoption of a worldview that embraces global interdependence. For example, the NASW lobbies, provides expert testimony, and builds coalitions with other professional groups to address policy formulation related to pressing social needs identified by its membership. Among the NASW's activities are defining problems, monitoring the progress of legislation, and evaluating the effectiveness of policies and programs.

In addition, professional organizations may be called upon to serve in the role of amicus curiae, or friend of the court. In this role, representatives of the professional organization provide expert information relevant to particular court decisions.

Social workers as catalysts initiate interdisciplinary cooperation to address local, national, and international issues. Political pressure from coalitions of professional organizations can result in substantive changes in policies and funding. For example, as a result of lobbying by a coalition of social workers, other professionals, and concerned citizens, state-based children's trust funds have been established. Supported through surcharges and tax checkoffs, this option is now available in many states and Washington, DC. The Children's Trust provides funding for specialized programs to prevent child abuse and neglect.

Social Work Highlights. At their bimonthly meeting two months ago, the members of the Hill and Dell Consortium of Medical Social Workers learned of the increase in the number of people seeking genetic counseling. These individuals must drive more than 150 miles to a larger metropolitan community, where specialized genetic counseling services are available. The membership charged a task force to study this issue and submit their recommendations. At the meeting today, the task force proposes that the local maternal health center seek grant funding to employ a specialist in the field to meet this identified gap in services. The consortium members serve as catalysts for initiating changes in service delivery.

Community Service Strategies. Professional social workers provide community service through their volunteer work in professional organizations and through their membership on community planning task forces, advisory boards, coalitions, review panels, or boards of directors. Social workers often serve as resource people for community education, volunteering to provide educational programs for community, church, and civic groups. Social workers readily give of their time to community efforts in response to a genuine commitment to social responsibility as prescribed by the NASW (1999a) *Code of Ethics.*

BOX 9.3

Social Work Profile

School Social Work

Like many new social service practitioners, my career began working in a residential treatment facility. Unlike many new social workers, my undergraduate degree was in political science. The residential treatment work experience led me to enroll in an MSW program. My background in political science directed that graduate education toward a specialty in social development. Over time, I have learned that social workers in any organization need to be politically astute. As a school social work administrator, I have come to realize that schools are *very* political. Understanding the social systems perspective is essential for discerning the various elements of the connections among families, schools, and communities.

Early on, I recognized that if children from poverty or chaotic life circumstances have the influence of one stable adult in their lives, they have a chance for success. Because of the nature of school social work and the luxury of working with children over the course of several years, the school social worker can have opportunities to be that stable adult. School social workers can witness children's progress over time in both their academic improvement and social skills. I believe the most important role of school social work is to make those healthy connections with children. As such, being able to convey respect, build relationships, and develop trust are the most important skills of school social workers. I believe that, in many ways, the "helping techniques" of social work practice are secondary to relationship building.

Clearly, school social work takes place in a host setting, a reality that creates its own challenges. In schools, professional staff who are not educators all start at the lowest rung of the hierarchal ladder. Social workers can contribute a valuable dimension of the holistic view of children necessary to supporting children's success in school. To be heard and, thus, to influence the perspectives of educators and school administrators, school social workers need to find creative ways to fit into the school setting. The old adage "Start where the client is" becomes "Start where the school is." School social workers can expect that it will take at least three years to become part of the system and to achieve a level of influence in it.

Over time, school social work has become more bureaucratic. The influence of the "No Child Left Behind" legislation and its press for accountability through increased standardized testing lessens the amount of time available for students to meet with social workers in one-to-one interaction. As social workers' roles adapt to these structural changes, their roles shift from direct service to coordination, with less time dedicated to counseling with children.

I like to approach the press for outcomes by asking a reflective question, "What are we *all* doing to ultimately increase student performance?" Today, more than ever, school social workers are research based in their approach, as they must show evidence that school social work services contribute to students' success. The interdependence of various disciplines in school settings heightens the need for social workers to enhance their social work expertise with cross-training in such areas as educational theory and practice and child development.

School social work is an exciting field of practice as it offers a chance to work with a wide range of youths, from birth to age 21, who are at all developmental ages and stages of life. School social work and school-based services provide opportunities for practitioners to make a difference in the lives of children who are at risk or have special educational needs.

Education

Since knowledge is power, education is a central force in empowerment-oriented practice (Kemp, Whittaker, & Tracy, 1997). Social workers often interact with clients "as teachers, mentors, coaches, and guides" (p. 55). Through their education function, they provide clients with much needed information. Such exchanges provide resources that facilitate decision making and enhance competencies. Practitioners also work together with clients "to develop knowledge about client system issues, resources, and challenges" (p. 56) through such collaborative activities as participatory action research. "The capacities gained through such participation become a resource for action and thus are a critical component of the process of emancipatory change" (p. 56). Finally, social workers may teach a variety of skills that enhance clients' abilities to access opportunities and resources.

In empowerment-based social work, learning processes begin with the capabilities of the learner (Freud, 1987). At all system levels, education is a partnership between co-learners and co-teachers. This view credits learners with having resources to enhance learning (Libassi & Maluccio, 1986). Learners' experiences are the core of empowerment-based education (Kieffer, 1984). Freire (1990) favors dialogue as the most productive educational technique.

Models of adult learning influence educational exchanges. One such model, *andragogy* (from the Greek noun *agoge* meaning the activity of learning, and the stem *andr,* adult) "envisions [individuals] as capable of directing [their] own destiny . . . affirms that learning takes place from experience that is partly external and partly internal . . . and affirms the necessity for continuous creative exploration and discovery" (Ingalls, 1973, p. 91). A number of assumptions about adult learning guide social workers: Adult learners are self-directing, have a reservoir of experiences and resources for learning, demonstrate an interest in immediate applications, and shift their orientation from "subject-centeredness" to "problem-centeredness" (Knowles, 1980).

Considering these principles, learning experiences for adult clients should purposefully engage them in identifying learning objectives that build upon their experiences and apply directly to meeting their identified educational needs and resolving their problems. Social workers who approach their clients as partners in educational relationships value the active contributions of clients and, in fact, "encourage clients to be confident that it is *appropriate* for them to expect to participate as an active collaborator with a professional and that it *benefits both* the professional and the client for them to participate as equals" (Lenrow & Burch, 1981, p. 253).

Prevention, heralded as an important initiative to address issues in the twenty-first century, comprises a set of complex activities to develop personal and social competencies and modify social systems so that people's needs will be met more effectively. Prevention activities are primarily educational in nature, generally targeting large groups of people prior to the occurrence of problems in social functioning (Adam, 1981; Caplan, 1964; Gesten & Jason, 1987; Gullotta, 1987; Hall & Torres, 2002; Monahan, 2002). Prevention includes "practices aimed at simultaneously preventing predictable problems in individuals or populations at risk; protecting or maintaining current strengths, competencies, or levels of health and healthy functioning; and promoting desired goals and enhancing human potential" (Bloom, 1995, p. 1895). Prevention assumes a proactive stance for addressing personal and social problems. It incorporates a continuum of activities that promote optimal conditions for personal and social competence or that eradicate problematic conditions that block optimal functioning.

Education roles encompass social work activities at all system levels (Figure 9.3). The teaching role expands microlevel clients' base of information through learning strategies.

At the midlevel, the trainer role facilitates staff development. At the macrolevel, the outreach role uses community education strategies to provide information to the general public. Finally, with respect to the professional system, social workers as researchers and scholars share their research findings and practice wisdom with other professionals.

Microlevel: Teacher Role

Social workers as teachers use learning strategies to promote clients' development of skills and enhance their base of information.

By expanding clients' base of information, education empowers individuals, families, and small groups. In this regard, education provides "progress in [the] effective mastery of life tasks, role performance and control over one's life" (Freud, 1987, p. 115). Armed with the power of information, clients are in a position of strength to make informed decisions.

The information-processing strategy is a communication process that involves acquiring information (accessing), understanding or giving meaning to the information (processing), then acting on the information in some way (utilizing) and sharing the information (communicating). This exchange of information may occur in structured client–worker conferences, formalized instructional settings, or experiential exercises such as role plays.

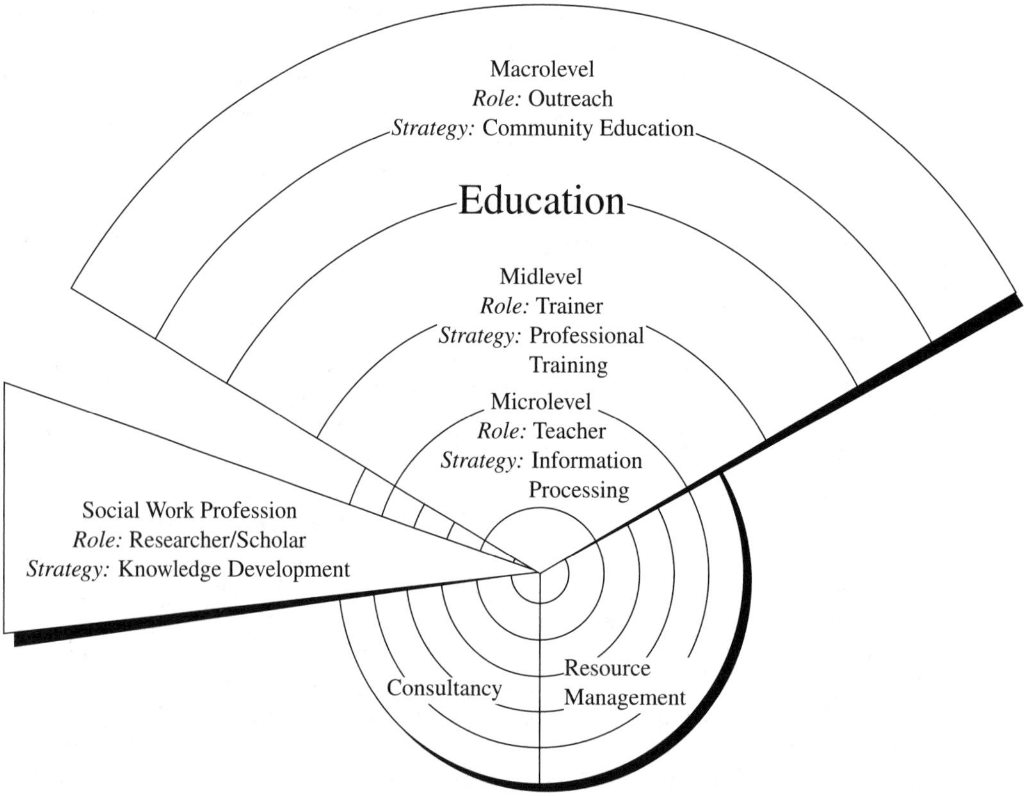

FIGURE 9.3 Education

Clients benefit from information that will strengthen their interpersonal effectiveness, increase their ability to access resources, and establish a base on which to make informed decisions. These educational experiences help clients develop skills related to becoming more assertive, resolving conflicts constructively, parenting, planning for retirement, and providing care for elderly relatives.

Guided by an orientation toward collaborative partnerships and the goal of empowering clients, social workers, as educators, provide opportunities for clients to understand the connection between social policy and their own situations and to discover ways to affect policy issues individually and collectively. For example, if a support group for single parents identifies inadequate day care as a significant source of stress, learning to address the issue as a matter of policy has the potential for increasing the group's sense of personal control and competence as well as influencing policy changes.

Social Work Highlights. Brian Mattson is a medical social worker in the rehabilitation unit of the local hospital. Currently one of his clients is recovering from a stroke. Brian facilitates the educational group for rehabilitation patients and their families. He offers information about the psychosocial aspects of rehabilitation and draws on the expertise of former patients in providing these learning experiences. Brian's facilitation of educational groups exemplifies social workers' teaching role with microlevel clients.

Midlevel: Trainer Role

Through the trainer role, social workers provide instruction to members of midlevel systems such as formal groups and organizations. Among the training strategies that social workers use are workshops, staff development, in-service experiences, and other types of continuing education.

Trainers are educational resource specialists for formal groups and organizations. They make presentations, serve as panelists, conduct public forums, and facilitate workshop sessions. Sometimes organizations employ full-time trainers. In other instances, organizations hire social workers to provide specific training experiences. Competent trainers base their sessions on research concerning staff development, adult education, changing attitudes, and learning processes. Effective trainers employ staff-development strategies to assess organizational goals, define learners' objectives, investigate the subject matter, determine formats for educational experiences, and develop processes for evaluation.

Providing effective training requires knowledge about the subject matter, group process skills, and technical competence. Of course, trainers need a base of expertise about the training topic. They should be able to convey information through appropriate training formats. Finally, effective trainers need to be able to use a variety of media equipment to enhance their presentations.

Organizations may contract with social workers to conduct staff-development workshops in such areas as stress-management techniques, skills for interpersonal effectiveness, assertiveness training, and supervisory relationships. In fact, training experiences often prepare participants for transitions that they anticipate. For example, social workers conduct preretirement planning sessions for corporate employees and skill-development training with family caregivers so that the caregivers' actions with people who are at risk will be helpful, rather than adding to the potential for problems. Ideally, training adds to participants' base of strengths, enhances their skills, and promotes their competence.

Social Work Highlights. The local affiliate of the National Center for the Prevention of Child Abuse and Neglect received funding to initiate a parent aid program. Participants in this volunteer-based program receive 30 hours of training. The training includes modules about child development, the dynamics of abuse and neglect, effective communication, active listening, and making referrals. The volunteer coordinator, Sarah Waverly, schedules a series of training workshops conducted by child welfare practitioners. Volunteer training and staff development are examples of the training role.

Macrolevel: Outreach Role

Through outreach, social workers educate citizens about social issues, injustice, and social services. They use community education strategies to spread information through various media and public relations activities.

Through their outreach role at the macrolevel, social workers help citizens broaden their knowledge about social problems and related social services. Community-based educational efforts can increase citizens' awareness of problems in a wide variety of areas, such as health care, disease, stress, indicators of the potential for suicide, substance abuse, child abuse and neglect, and other family-related issues. Informing the general public about public and private human service organizations makes more people aware of these resources and services and, thus, enhances their accessibility (Hepworth, Rooney, & Larsen, 1997). Providing information to the general public may encourage people to access informal and formal resources more quickly. Education through public information facilitates preventive actions.

Community education strategies include distributing posters and leaflets, conducting mass mailings, staffing information booths and programs, and arranging speaking engagements. Public service announcements, print media, films, and radio and television programming represent other ways to transmit educational information to the community members. To respect the unique needs of a broad spectrum of citizens, ethnically sensitive social workers provide multilingual, braille, large-print, signed, and culturally sensitive information.

Social Work Highlights. "How did you learn about OPTIONS?" This question on OPTIONS's client-satisfaction survey assesses the outreach efforts of this case management agency for older adults. Janice Steine, a social worker at OPTIONS, is responsible for analyzing the survey's results. The clients' responses were fairly evenly split among learning about OPTIONS's services from friends, clergy, physicians, and television spots. Many clients reported that they had friends who had found the OPTIONS staff helpful. Others indicated that they received brochures from doctors or ministers. A significant number called the agency after seeing public service announcements on television. Janice concludes that the survey results support continuing the multimethod approach to the agency's outreach efforts.

Professional System: Researcher and Scholar Roles

As researchers and scholars, social workers add to social work's base of theory and evaluate practice and program outcomes. These activities link social work practice and theory through knowledge-development strategies.

Research is a method of systematic investigation or experimentation, the aim of which is the discovery or interpretation of facts, the development of knowledge, and the practical application of new or revised theories. For social workers, research means building theories, designing practice strategies, and measuring outcomes. Professional scholarship that contributes to the professional knowledge base is an obligation shared by all social workers. Therefore, preparation for social work practice necessarily includes a strong research component.

The NASW (1999a) *Code of Ethics* describes standards for social workers' roles as researchers and scholars. The basis for ethical practice is theory supported by research. Social workers read professional journals and research literature to keep abreast of emerging knowledge in the field. In turn, social workers have a professional obligation to contribute to that knowledge base by conducting their own research and sharing their findings with colleagues.

Research builds a theoretical base that informs social workers' understanding of human behavior and the social environment. Social workers use this broad base of research to enhance social service programs, develop equitable social welfare policies, and improve social work practice methods. In addition, social workers use research methods to evaluate their practice, assess program effectiveness, and analyze social policies. Social workers integrate research and practice as consumers of research and as active researchers.

A variety of activities reflect social workers' involvement in conducting and using practice research (Kirk & Rosenblatt, 1983). As *research consumers,* social workers use research findings to guide practice. Practitioners read studies and apply these research findings to their practice. *Research practitioners* use research methods as a practice strategy. They evaluate their practice through case-by-case practice evaluation using single-system designs. Additionally, social workers can use research methods as intervention techniques by involving clients in monitoring their own behavior. Having clients keep records of their own behaviors can motivate change. As *clinical scientists,* social workers continuously and vigorously evaluate their own practice effectiveness. Finally, *research specialists* focus their practice primarily on research activities and develop proficiency in design, measurement, and statistical analysis.

Social Work Highlights. A research project sponsored by a state department of family services is studying the viability of using intensive in-home services to prevent out-of-home placements of children. Families referred to the research project had been extensively involved with multiple social service providers. Families randomly assigned to the experimental group received intensive in-home services provided by a trained family systems specialist. These family specialists were available to clients as needed 24 hours a day. The families in the control group continued to receive traditional services. The research hypothesis postulates that intensive crisis intervention reduces the likelihood that children will need to be removed from their own homes. Family policy advocates are monitoring the outcomes of this research closely as they consider innovative models for the prevention of child abuse and neglect.

Integrating Practice, Policy, and Research

The organization of social work functions into consultancy, resource management, and education incorporates the practice, policy, and research components of social work (Table 9.3). Social workers assume the described roles as they work with clients at all system levels in direct practice, policy analysis and formulation, and research and evaluation.

TABLE 9.3 Social Work Functions and Practice, Policy, and Research

	Practice	Policy	Research
Consultancy	Practitioners confer with consumer systems to resolve problems in social functioning. Social workers draw upon the personal, organizational, or community life experiences of the client systems.	Social workers are involved in identifying areas that require change and creating policy that has an impact at the practitioner, agency, and societal level.	Practice wisdom and empirically based research inform the practitioner in solving problems at all system levels.
Resource management	Client systems are linked with resources that support adaptive social functioning, meet needs, or resolve problematic situations.	Policy strategies for utilization and development of resources are integral for creating social change and achieving equity in the allocation of resources.	Research findings are utilized to address gaps and barriers in the health and human services delivery system and to locate and coordinate available services.
Education	In practice, information is vital for resolving issues, learning skills, preventing problems, and creating social change.	Knowledge is critical for informed decision making and policy development. Information is gathered, analyzed, and communicated throughout the process of formulating and implementing social policy.	Social work practice involves imparting information, knowledge, and skills for personal, institutional, and professional growth. The utility, validity, and reliability of the information imparted are essential.

Looking Forward

The paradigm presented in this chapter conceptualizes social work practice as a way of understanding the generalist perspective and the nature of the information exchange with consumers, as well as a way of doing. That is, social work practice can be seen as system-level intervention through the application of roles, strategies, and activities. The information-based social work practice framework reflects the idea that accessing, processing, communicating, and utilizing information are critical to survival today and, notably, into the twenty-first century. In a postindustrial society, the strategic resource is information. Information thus has become a product that helps clients locate tangible material, economic resources, and the personal social services designed to enhance interpersonal relationships. Professionals, including social workers, are frequently termed *information workers*. The practice activities of the social work profession are grouped around the related functions of consultancy for problem solving, resource management, and education, all of which focus on information exchange. The purpose of social work practice is embodied in the empowerment of clients through the selection and presentation of information that promotes the concept of health and wholeness, with an emphasis on partnerships, choice, and personal dignity.

CHAPTER

10 Social Work and Social Policy

Empowerment-oriented social workers argue that empowerment hinges on people's ability to obtain personal, organizational, and community resources (Breton, 1994, 2002; Gutiérrez, 1990, 1994; Hasenfeld, 1987; Simon, 1990). Social and economic development affects people's ability to access resources and achieve an optimal level of social functioning. Social policy initiatives can create macrolevel changes that expand people's access to society's opportunity structures, heighten the availability of resources, and create conditions favorable to personal growth and well-being.

This chapter explores the empowerment dimensions of social policy by considering the following topics:

- Social policy as both a process and a product
- Social policy and political ideologies
- Social work and social policy
- Street-level services
- Public welfare policies in the twentieth century
- Current public welfare programs

Social Policy

Social policy reflects a society's agenda for enhancing the well-being of societal members. As such, it reflects societal members' shared values, beliefs, and attitudes about how the society should care for its members and how it should achieve this mission. Social policy directs the formulation of social welfare laws and shapes the design of social service programs. This section defines social policy and describes the formulation, implementation, and analysis of social policy.

What Is Social Policy?

Social policies are principles and courses of action that influence the overall quality of life as well as the circumstances of individuals in groups and their intrasocial relationships (Gilbert & Terrell, 2001). Typically, social policy is identified with governmental or public policies that redress inequities in social institutions, improve the quality of life of people who are disadvantaged, and provide assistance to people in need. In addition, social policies influence private-sector services—including nonprofit social service agencies and for-profit businesses—as they construct administrative policies to guide their day-to-day procedures and operations.

Some define social policy variously as a guide, a directive, a standing plan, a set of principles, a collective strategy, and a plan of action. Others describe policies as rational, deliberate, explicit, and implicit goals that people pursue. Social policy is both a process and a product (Gilbert & Terrell, 2001). As a process, social policy consists of sequential steps to be followed in problem solving. As products, social policies are laws, programs, judicial decisions, and administrative directives. Social workers must evaluate both the process and the products of social policy in order to enhance its effectiveness.

Social Policy as Process: Policy Formulation

Policy formulation involves a series of tasks ranging from information gathering to implementing social policy. As professionals, social workers are involved at all stages of social welfare policy formulation. Formulating policy involves 10 steps:

1. Identify problems that affect social functioning.
2. Define the problem as a public issue.
3. Analyze findings and confirm evidence.
4. Provide the information to the public.
5. Study alternative solutions.
6. Prepare an initial policy statement that identifies goals.
7. Develop supportive organizational structures and political relationships.
8. Legitimize policy efforts through public support.
9. Construct the policy and/or program design.
10. Implement and assess the social policy.

Formulating social policy involves gathering a broad base of information from a variety of constituents and special-interest groups. The relationships among the actors in policy decisions affect the outcome of the policy at every stage of the way.

Social Policy as a Product: Policy Implementation

As a product, social policy includes legislation and executive orders, congressional actions, judiciary interpretations, administrative decisions, and actual programs and services. Social policy can result in a *law*—for example, mandatory reporting of child abuse by health care professionals, social workers, teachers, and day care providers. The social policy product can be a *program,* such as a congregate meal site that offers older people nutritious meals and socialization. Or the product can be a *court decision,* such as one that upholds the protection of a special population from overt discriminatory practices. As *administrative policy,* a social policy might prescribe an employment classification system or specify qualifications for professional staff in agencies.

Social policy products require more specific plans for implementation. After a social policy is in place and funds for its programmatic implementation become available, social workers make decisions about how to deliver services. They design programs to carry out the policy's goal of reaching a specified population to effect some desired change. They develop administrative policies that clearly define roles and tasks and direct the work of agency personnel. Finally, they write policy and procedure manuals to communicate expectations, responsibilities, and outcome measures. Implementing a social policy in one social system necessitates administering and implementing related policy decisions in other systems as well.

Examining Social Policy: Policy Analysis

According to Eveline Burns, a noted economist and social work educator, social policy analysis is "the study of the organized efforts of society to meet identifiable personal needs of, or social problems presented by, groups or individuals, evaluating them by reference to their adequacy and effectiveness in attaining certain goals, their economy in the use of scarce resources and their consistency with accepted social values" (Shlakman, 1969, p. 3). Throughout the process of formulating and implementing a policy, social workers analyze that policy to understand its intent and impact.

Social workers continuously monitor legislation and the development of other types of policy as well as evaluate related programs and services in order to assess the policy's effectiveness and demonstrate accountability. To analyze a policy, they examine how well it reaches the target population, measure to what degree it achieves its goals, evaluate its cost-effectiveness, and determine whether it produced any negative consequences. Policy analysis "becomes the basis for legislative advocacy or simply for organizational reform" (Figueira-McDonough, 1993, p. 185).

A policy's specifications or design for program implementation often builds on methods for evaluation. Responsibility for evaluation may be delegated to evaluators not directly associated with the agency, assigned by funding bodies, or initiated by accrediting and standard-setting organizations.

A framework for policy analysis presented by Miley, O'Melia, and DuBois (2004) includes a consideration of the specifications, feasibility, and merits of a policy:

Part I Policy Specifications

1. Detail the history of the policy under study and related policies
2. Describe the problems that the policy will redress
3. Identify the social values and ideological beliefs embedded in the policy
4. State the goals of the policy
5. Summarize the details of the policy regarding implementation, funding, eligibility criteria, and other stipulations

Part II Policy Feasibility

1. Identify projected outcomes of the policy
2. Discuss the political and economic feasibility of the policy
3. Characterize the support or dissent for the policy
4. Assess the ramifications of the policy for the existing health and human service delivery structures

Part III Policy Merits

1. Assess the effectiveness and efficiency of the implementation of the policy
2. Weigh the social costs and consequences of the policy
3. Evaluate the differential effects of the policy on diverse population groups
4. Judge the merits of the policy (p. 391)

Analyzing a social policy as it is being formulated is essential for determining its potential effects. Examining a policy after its implementation is critical for assessing its actual impact.

Legislative Analysis and Action. Social workers analyze social welfare legislation to determine a bill's intent, assess the potential effects on constituent groups, determine a position of support or opposition, and mobilize forces to endorse or reject passage of the bill. Effecting

Clients offer valuable insights by testifying at public hearings.

political change through legislative action is one of the primary ways to meet the profession's social policy objectives, such as creating humane and responsive institutions. Social work must "go back to its roots and rediscover effective political action" (Stuart, 1994, p. 8).

Since the political axiom "union gives strength" is paramount, legislative action frequently calls for activities of collective bodies, such as organizations, coalitions, and alliances. However, when social workers are involved in legislative activities, social worker–lobbyists often lay the groundwork. Tasks for lobbyists include the following:

- Identify what you want from the target of your lobbying and, likewise, what the target wants from you
- Develop alliances and coalitions to broaden the base of your power
- Prepare carefully, including gathering information about the advocacy issue for which you are lobbying, the person or group you intend to approach, and your opponents
- Tailor-make your presentation featuring the issues your target identifies as most significant
- Attend to creating positive first impressions
- Follow-up your contacts with thank-you notes
- Inform your legislative contacts and allies about your advocacy efforts with appointed officials (Richan, 1996)

BOX 10.1
Social Work Profile

Lobbying

My career path to becoming a social work lobbyist has led me through many fields of practice. Initially, my work in mental health made me think that one-on-one practice would be my career track. As I gained more experience and worked in management positions, I realized that I could influence social policies more directly by working at the macrolevel. When the state chapter of NASW advertised for a lobbyist, my social work colleagues encouraged me to apply for the position. Personally, I was pleased to learn that the state chapter was looking for a social worker willing to learn to be a lobbyist rather than wanting to hire a lobbyist who would need to be educated about social work.

Lobbying is a dynamic role for social workers; it is, at the same time, both exciting and frustrating. No one day is the same as the previous. With a hundred windmills to fight, I work with a variety of people on a variety of issues, creating networks and coalitions to influence policy development and policy change. Even though others might not know of the behind-the-scenes work of lobbyists, our efforts in shaping public policy can impact the lives of thousands of people. Social work lobbyists go to the mat on issues and, at times, need to be a bit scrappy—foregoing the nice gentle social worker persona. However, while lobbying requires persistence and strong advocacy, lobbyists should not ignite fires that burn bridges that might be needed for building coalitions in the future. In my opinion, the social work position will take on heightened importance as we deal with two critical issues—health policy and budget deficits. The movement toward universal health care coverage is gaining public support and has importance for all fields of social work practice. Continued budget deficits dominate with their ripple effect on hiring freezes, funding reductions for social programs, and service disentitlements.

My roles as a social work lobbyist include both advocate and educator. I am involved in advocacy for just social policy and in educating the public on policy issues and client needs. Productive social work lobbying is founded on the knowledge, values, and skills of generalist social work. For example, effective one-on-one communication skills are essential. Work in the macrosystem arena requires an understanding of social systems, including the human services delivery system and the many fields of social work practice. Communication with frontline workers in the field is essential for understanding the public issues that are inherent in private troubles and the personal difficulties that are a direct result of problems created by ineffective public policies. All social workers should be honest in their dealings with colleagues and clients, but lobbyists—their reputations are on the line—because their given word is absolutely gold. For example, in my lobbying work, I must ensure that the facts I present to legislators and other stakeholders in support of a policy position are accurate and up-to-date.

I believe that there is nothing more important than being a contributing member of our profession. Most direct-service social workers rely on the professional organization to attend to public policy issues that impinge on their day-to-day practice. I encourage joining professional organizations, because organizations like the NASW have the strength of collective voice and can work in coalition with other stakeholder organizations to influence state and federal policies. In addition to dealing with constituent issues, the NASW also engages in efforts to ensure the credibility of the social work profession and to educate the public that social workers are trained professionals with unique qualifications and credentials.

Members of social work organizations can provide support through their personal contacts with legislators, phone calls, letters, e-mails, and other grassroots community organizing efforts. Social workers who have expert knowledge in particular fields may be called upon to document the need for legislative action, draft legislation, and develop policy briefs that analyze the implications of legislation. Social workers' testimony at public hearings provides the occasion to spotlight issues, solicit public interest, publicize testimony, inform legislators, and offer officials opportunities to make public their positions on social concerns. Legislative advocacy gains momentum as social work practitioners recognize their impact on social welfare legislation through various political endeavors.

As advocates for social action, social workers may have opportunities to mobilize constituencies and/or clients to effect political change through legislative activities at the state and local levels (McNutt, 2002; Schneider, 2002). For example, state legislation to address the needs of Hispanic women, such as job training, bicultural resources, information and referral, and information about health care, public assistance, and child care, was the direct result of the lobbying efforts of the Hispanic Women's Task Force in New Jersey (Bonilla-Santiago, 1989).

The Influence of Values

Conflicting points of view about predominant social values, the definition of social problems, the distribution of resources, and the sources of solutions complicate the policymaking process. "The particular forms that the social policy response will take, as [Eveline] Burns emphasizes, must finally be mediated through conflicting values that political solutions will inevitably reflect. For values set limits to the use of particular social policy instruments" (Shlakman, 1969, p. 8). Societal values reflected in political ideologies ultimately influence the formulation of social policies and the administration of these policies at the direct service level.

Social Policy and Political Ideologies

Political ideologies influence our perceptions of problems and needs as either public issues or private troubles, assign responsibility and blame for social conditions, and give direction for solutions. Social welfare policies result from deliberations among various factions that represent divergent political perspectives, including liberalism, neoliberalism, conservativism, neoconservativism, and radicalism.

Liberalism

Liberals champion social policies that uphold fundamental human rights and social equality. They concern themselves with protecting citizens' political and civil liberties by ensuring economic freedom and promoting democratic participation. Liberals view social welfare as a legitimate function of government, and welfare provisions as citizens' rights. They promote governmental solutions to social problems and uphold the notion of public responsibility for creating conditions that favor citizens' well-being. Although, in the liberal view, ideally government programs address root causes so as to prevent problems from occurring, realistically, government programs also redress adverse social conditions.

With the call to cut public welfare expenses, *neoliberal* politicians soundly defeated liberals in the 1970s and 1980s. This view backs reductions in government spending and encourages partnerships between government and business to address issues related to citizens' welfare (Karger & Stoesz, 2002). Advocates of neoliberalism maintain that businesses and corporations administer welfare dollars more effectively than the government.

Conservativism

The *conservative* position promotes a capitalistic free-market economy and emphasizes traditional values, rugged individualism, competition, localism, and the work ethic. Conservative social policies tend to resist social change and strengthen existing social structures. Since conservatives believe that personal inadequacies cause problems, they conclude that government should limit its involvement in welfare. Ideally, from a conservative view, public welfare is only a temporary measure, as conservatives believe that welfare—particularly publicly supported assistance for the poor—destroys individual initiative. Conservatives advocate privatizing social welfare services through voluntary charities, self-help organizations, and business ventures.

Neoconservatives favor overturning liberal welfare programs and reforming welfare policies (Karger & Stoesz, 2002). The neoconservative position on welfare reflects a needs-based approach, establishes "workfare" requirements, enforces familial responsibility for dependents, and supports devolution, that is, a shift of responsibility for welfare from the federal level to states and localities. Neoconservatives advocate containing the growth of government programs and increasing the private sector's responsibility to address the social welfare problems. Neoconservatives blame megastructures—big government, big business, and big labor—for the problems in U.S. society. They identify mediating structures such as neighborhoods, voluntary associations, and churches as sources of empowerment and change (Berger & Neuhaus, 1977).

Radicalism

In sharp contrast to the conservative and neoconservative positions, *radicalism* acknowledges societal responsibility for inequities and advocates revolutionary social change. Because radicals blame institutional structures rather than individuals for creating problems in living, they favor macrostructural reform to eliminate the sources of social problems. Their chief public policy strategy—the redistribution of power and wealth—centers on removing economic inequities and class privilege and achieving political democracy and equality by establishing a welfare state. In their view, traditional public social welfare is an oppressive, stigmatizing program that regulates the poor (Piven & Cloward, 1971). Radicals promote sweeping changes to create a noncapitalistic welfare state in which all citizens share societal benefits equally.

Social Work and Political Ideologies

While many conclude that the liberal ideology is social work's primary perspective, the other positions influence social work as well (Macht & Quam, 1986). Ironically, conservatives criticize liberal social welfare policies, and services that social workers often support, for creating dependency. Radicals blame these same liberal policies for oppressing the disenfranchised and the poor. However, Siporin (1980) says that social workers "need to understand and utilize both control and reform types of strategies, principles, and procedures, as they are appropriate in helping situations. Social work practice needs both conservative and radical contributions" (p. 524). The interactive mix of various ideological perspectives generates a creative tension that invigorates and renews the profession.

The actual practice of social work reflects these diverse ideologies as well (Macht & Quam, 1986). Practice methodologies reflect different schools of thought, use distinctive strategies, and encounter acceptance by some people and rejection by others during particular periods of history. Charity Organization Society relief programs, traditional psychoanalysis and behaviorism, remedial group work, and social planning all represent conservative ideology. Liberal movements in social work include the settlement house movement, social group work's reciprocal and social goals models, and community organization's locality development strategies. Examples of radical social work practice include feminist therapy, consciousness-raising groups, and social action models of community organizing. The various methodologies are all equally viable alternatives, but not necessarily equally preferred in all situations. In fact, a dogmatic adherence to one approach denies the possibilities of other alternatives and limits innovative uses of resources.

Social Work and Social Policy

Policy implications are evident in professional practice at all social system levels. Systemically, decisions are made that affect empowerment in both the subsystem structures and the suprasystem structures. This reciprocity means that social workers influence welfare policies and, in turn, public social policies influence social workers' practice of their profession (Figure 10.1).

Social workers make policy decisions at the microlevel that determine the quality of their interactions with clients. For example, decisions about which methods and strategies to use with a given client are really policy decisions. Selecting clientele—that is, including some and excluding others—also involves making policy decisions. Typically, social workers practice within the context of agencies or social welfare organizations. Here too, policy decisions affect practice. For example, policy decisions determine which programs and services agencies support.

The various fields of social work, such as child welfare, family services, corrections, and income maintenance, provide settings for a multitude of public and private social service agencies and organizations. Social policy in each practice field establishes priorities, identifies target population groups, stipulates funding parameters, and specifies jurisdictional boundaries that direct each agency's programs and services.

The social service system comprises all fields of social work practice, including public and private service sectors, professional associations, accrediting organizations, funding bodies, and citizen interest groups. Special interests or qualifying criteria promoted by these systems shape the actual services offered and legitimize the delivery of those services.

The social service system is one component of the social welfare institution—the societal structure that is responsible for promoting the quality of life in the areas of health, education, and welfare for all citizens. The policy of the social welfare institution primarily

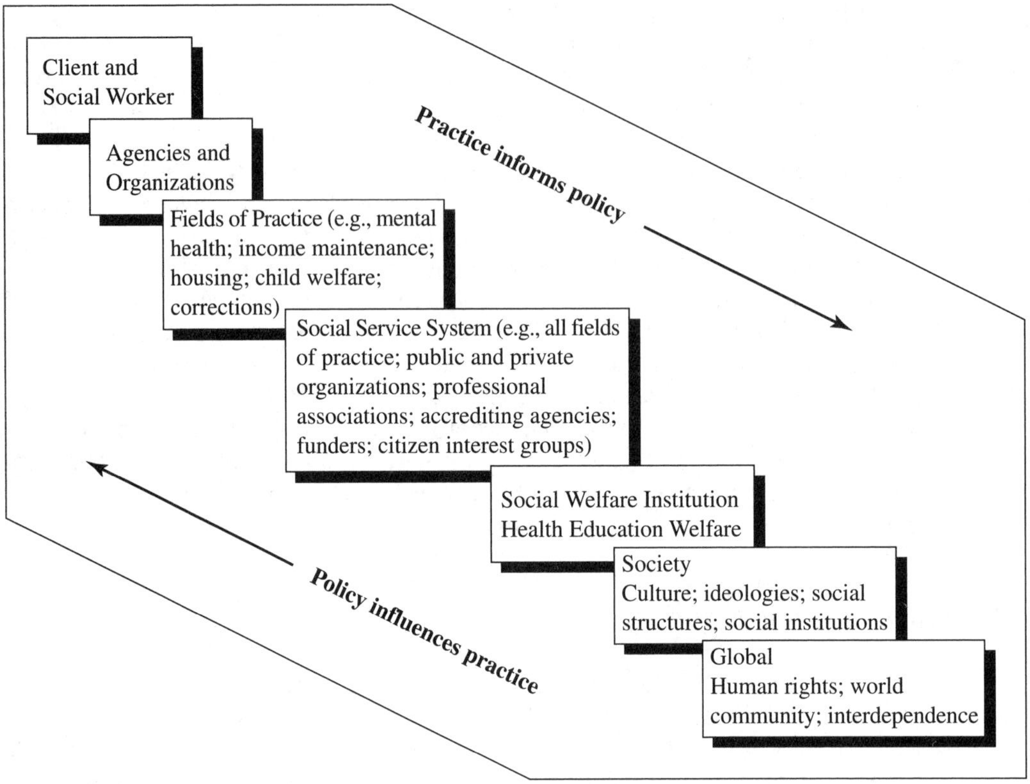

FIGURE 10.1 Integrating Social Work Practice and Policy

reflects the intent of social welfare legislation, laws, and judicial interpretations. Through practice research, lobbying, and expert testimony, social workers inform public policy-making bodies. Thus even direct-service workers shape the character of the social welfare institution.

The culture, the predominant ideologies and values, and the institutional structures of society influence social policy. The societal ethos is the context for policy decisions in such areas as standards of living, citizen entitlements, civil rights and civil liberties, and social justice directives. A society's ideologies influence whether it believes that social problems are public problems and how it responds through its social welfare policies. Factors that influence whether society defines a problem as a public issue include the drama of the situation, the pervasiveness of the problem, and its economic and political impact (Hilgartner & Bosk, 1988).

Finally, the global society becomes the ultimate context for social policies. International policies concern world hunger, natural resources, environmental protection, and peace initiatives, to name a few. Policies at this most encompassing macrolevel reflect international welfare arrangements, human rights agreements, and the societal interdependence of the world community.

At all system levels, there are significant political, social, and economic factors that affect social welfare policy decisions such as those related to social insurance, income maintenance, personal social services, housing, and health and nutrition programs. Social workers must follow closely activities in the broader areas of public and economic policymaking. Public policy at all governmental levels and in the private sector affects the lives of individuals and families. For example, legislation on environmental quality has implications for human development and quality of life. Setting priorities in the governmental budget process determines the amount of funding allocated for social service programs that serve all citizens, not just those eligible for categorical assistance programs.

Robert Morris (1986), in *Rethinking Social Welfare: Why Care for the Stranger?,* suggests that, as a society, we must come to some agreement about governmental responsibility for meeting human needs. Morris proposes that a desirable core program take national responsibility for work and income and include a national health care system. He reminds us that "broader concepts of social justice, other actions by government to create a more equitable and cohesive society can be dreamed of and planned for, but they are unlikely to be realized unless the foundation is securely in place" (p. 241).

Social Workers as Policy Practitioners

Social workers play a vital role in the domain of public policy. First, social workers can and should be committed to promoting citizen entitlements that empower social structures, enhance social functioning, and ensure social justice at the state and national level. Policy practice is integral to all aspects of social work. Second, direct-service workers are policymakers. In fact, policymaking is not an offhand addendum to direct service. Selecting who receives services and choosing the type and duration of intervention are "street-level" policy-based choices.

Street-Level Services

A cadre of civil servants employed in the public service arena provides government-sponsored services. Civil servants such as public school teachers, law enforcement and court officers, social workers, public health workers, and other public employees provide direct services to citizens. Government service workers educate the citizenry, protect the safety of the populace, and promote the health and social functioning of societal members. Most public service workers or street-level bureaucrats have the power to make discretionary decisions in the day-to-day performance of their jobs. They decide who qualifies for governmental programs, what benefits they receive, and on whom to enforce sanctions (Lipsky, 1980). Lipsky calls the public agencies and organizations that employ public service workers *street-level bureaucracies.*

Street-Level Bureaucracies

The governmental service sector of the social service delivery network includes services provided by schools, public health clinics, law enforcement agencies, public welfare agencies, local court jurisdictions, and legal organizations. Society often relegates the street-level workers in these systems to the role of low-level service provider, performing the "dirty work" of society:

> They socialize citizens to expectations of government services and a place in the political community. They determine the eligibility of citizens for government benefits and sanctions. They oversee the treatment (the service) citizens receive in those programs. Thus, in a sense, street-level bureaucrats implicitly mediate aspects of the constitutional relationship of citizens to the state. In short, they hold the keys to a dimension of citizenship. (Lipsky, 1980, p. 4)

The social welfare system includes publicly supported service provisions in the areas of income maintenance, unemployment, child protection, elderly services, rehabilitation, mental health, and criminal justice. The Social Security Act of 1935 and its subsequent amendments are a major source of public welfare policy for people who are poor or unemployed, older adults, people with disabilities, and children and families. Other laws and acts deal with specific groups, such as adult and juvenile offenders, victims of crime, children in need of protection, and persons with mental illness.

Street-Level Bureaucrats

Government service workers are, for the most part, the allocators of welfare and the protectors of public safety. Line workers have considerable influence on the interpretation of public policy through their decisions and actions in those services identified as street-level bureaucracies. The translation of legislative and administrative social welfare policies into procedures often overrides, and in some cases actually misrepresents, the original intent of the policy. Lipsky (1980) argues that, in some ways, the interpretive decisions and procedural actions of street-level bureaucrats become the public policies they implement through their positions.

Bureaucratic constraints in the public welfare sector foster certain behaviors in workers that seem antithetical to the service ideal of social work. Individualization is often lost as workers, including educators, police officers, and human service workers, find ways to deal with the masses impersonally (Lipsky, 1980). Perhaps there is a tendency, or even a preoccupation, to develop rules and regulations for dealing with the exception which, in turn, may encumber the typical situation. Workers in public agencies often find themselves reinforcing status quo procedural patterns rather than reforming the system. Consumers of public services may resign themselves to accepting the benefits provided rather than seeking those to which they are fully entitled.

Street-Level Clients

Labeling, which occurs in this system, has a detrimental and, as often noted, self-fulfilling quality. Stigmatizing labels are pervasive in the public arena, with clients referred to as "welfare mothers," "ex-cons," "juvenile delinquents," or "slow learners." Perpetuated by street-level workers, these labels become integrated into the identity of clients. Lipsky (1980) describes the process of "social construction of a client":

> People come to street-level bureaucracies as unique individuals with different life experiences, personalities, and current circumstances. In their encounters with bureaucracies they are transformed into clients, identifiably located in a very small number of categories,

> treated as if, and treating themselves as if, they fit standardized definitions of units consigned to specific bureaucratic slots. The processing of *people* into *clients,* assigning them to categories for treatment by bureaucrats, and treating them in terms of those categories, is a social process. Client characteristics do not exist outside of the process that gives rise to them. An important part of this process is the way people learn to treat themselves as if they were categorical entities. (p. 59)

Street-level bureaucrats exercise a tremendous amount of influence and control over clients in public welfare. These workers control clients' access to the opportunity structures of society, and their decisions have life-changing effects on their clientele.

Public Welfare Policy in the Twentieth Century

Adverse social conditions that resulted from rapid population growth, industrialization, and the economic depressions experienced in the United States in the late 1800s and the early 1900s led to the formulation of significant public welfare policies. Policymakers enacted legislation to deal with issues of public health, child and family welfare, and unemployment (Table 10.1).

TABLE 10.1 Social Welfare History

1921	Sheppard-Towner Act (An Act for the Promotion of Welfare and Hygiene of Maternity and Infancy)
1933	Federal Emergency Relief Act (FERA)
1935	Social Security Act
1941	Executive Order 8802 by President Franklin Roosevelt barring racial discrimination in defense industries and establishing a Federal Fair Employment Practices Committee
1944	Servicemen's Readjustment Act (G.I. Bill of Rights)
1950	Amendments to the Social Security Act for Aid to the Permanently and Totally Disabled
1962	Amendments to the Social Security Act for Social Service Provisions
1964	Civil Rights Act
1964	Economic Opportunity Act
1964	Food Stamp Act
1965	Amendments to the Social Security Act for Medicare and Medicaid
1971	Talmadge Amendments to the Social Security Act for the Work Incentive Program II
1972	Supplemental Security Income Program (SSI) replaced state programs for Aid to the Aged, Blind, and Disabled
1975	Title XX Amendments to Social Security Act for Social Services
1981	Omnibus Reconciliation Act
1988	Family Support Act
1990	Americans with Disabilities Act
1993	Family and Medical Leave Act
1996	Personal Responsibility and Work Opportunity Reconciliation Act

Genesis of Reform: Early-Twentieth-Century Legislation

In the late nineteenth century, the United States experienced tumultuous changes. Immigration, industrialization, and urbanization changed the pattern in the fabric of U.S. society. European immigrants entered the country in quest of the "American dream," bringing with them their own cultural ethos and life-styles. Concurrently, the nation was changing from an agrarian society characterized by self-sufficiency to an industrialized economy characterized by dependency on market wages.

As hubs of industry, urban centers experienced a burgeoning expansion of their population. The demographic shift of workers and immigrants to these centers brought displaced families to the cities. Overcrowded conditions, inadequate public sanitation and other public health issues, housing shortages, increased crime, and unsafe work conditions were typical urban concerns. These emerging public issues required new solutions.

Organized Ways of Helping

From colonial times, social welfare consisted chiefly of individually oriented assistance to the needy and worthy poor. Local communities cared for their needy and dependent members. By the turn of the century, however, organized ways of helping, precipitated by large-scale immigration, industrialization, and urbanization, began to emerge through the efforts of the Charity Organization Societies and the settlement house movement.

Charity Organization Society members worked with individuals to reform the character of the poor, reflecting societal attitudes toward the populations affected by social change. Charity workers offered encouragement through "friendly visiting" and casework services to help individuals and families with their shortcomings. During this same period, settlement house workers were highly visible in the movement to develop social policies to improve working conditions, deal with unemployment and workplace exploitation, redress public health problems, and provide for humane treatment of the mentally ill and criminals. Jane Addams directed her "war on poverty" at addressing the roots of problems through education and social reform.

Paving the Way for Public Services. For the most part, during this era political leaders believed that social welfare provisions were the responsibility of private agencies, the state government, and local communities. However, a number of legislative initiatives at the state level paved the way for public-domain health services and for human services at the national level. In 1899, the Illinois legislature enacted the first *law establishing a juvenile court* separate from the adult judicial process—An Act to Regulate the Treatment and Control of Dependent, Neglected, and Delinquent Children.

Labor laws were enacted to protect women and children from abuse in industry. Lillian Wald of the Henry Street Settlement House and Florence Kelly of the Hull House Settlement were board members on the National Child Labor Committee. *Public health,* including sanitation and public utilities, also gained attention at the turn of the twentieth century.

The first White House conference on children's problems and needs (1909) spearheaded progressive *reforms in child and family welfare.* Julia Lathrop and later Grace Abbott, both social activists associated with Hull House, directed the Children's Bureau, established in 1912. The Children's Bureau became the national focus of child welfare policy, dealing with child labor, maternal and infant health, and other aspects of child welfare, including delinquency (Parker, 1994). State health departments administered provisions for infant and maternal health in the Sheppard-Towner Act of 1921. All of these progressive ideologies and legislative actions set the stage for further social reform (Davis, 1967).

The Emergence of Public Welfare: The New Deal Programs

The Great Depression caused people to notice the institutional or structural breakdown of the economy. Massive unemployment, homelessness, abject poverty, and exhausted state and local resources characterized the period following the market collapse. Those people affected by the economic catastrophe of the depression could not be held personally responsible for the nation's plight. This set the direction for government intervention at the federal level to restabilize the economy.

The Hoover Administration. In spite of this argument, the Hoover administration continued to espouse the belief that "recovery was just around the corner." Hoover, himself a "self-made man" in the tradition of rugged individualism, directed his efforts to deal with the depression toward stimulating businesses to promote work. He believed that business would pull the country out of the depression as it had in the past (Platt & Drummond, 1967).

Hoover also believed in self-help as a moral duty. This position caused him to remain optimistic about the strength of the nation's economic life and to reject the idea of federal aid. He considered federal aid the equivalent of "government mastery" over the unemployed and needy (Trattner, 1999).

In accordance with the belief in governmental support for business, national legislation created the Reconstruction Finance Corporation to make loans to banks, agricultural credit corporations, life insurance companies, and other financial organizations. The public buildings program was expected to take up the slack of unemployment, and the Home Loan Bank Act of 1932 established federal home loan banks to aid homeowners who were about to lose their homes (Platt & Drummond, 1967). However, credit to homeowners did not relieve the plight of the growing numbers of unemployed or of the homeless who lived in "Hooverville" shacks (Hicks, Mowry, & Burke, 1970).

The pressure created by the unemployment of at least 10 million people in 1932 caused the nation to reexamine its position on direct federal aid for the poor (Rauch, 1944). Because Hoover opposed direct aid to citizens or outright grants to states, legislation that would have provided relief was either voted down by Congress or vetoed by Hoover (Hicks, Mowry, & Burke, 1970; Piven & Cloward, 1971).

Ironically, Hoover approved a congressional appropriation for government loans to farmers for feeding livestock, although he opposed additional grants for feeding farm families themselves (Trattner, 1999). When senators reasoned that hungry farmers could not feed livestock without first being fed themselves, the administration argued that it was not the federal government's responsibility to relieve human suffering through the "gift" of direct assistance. Hoover was nicknamed "Hardhearted Herb" for his opposition to direct relief (Platt & Drummond, 1967).

***Roosevelt's Administration*.** Whereas Hoover favored loans to businesses and opposed direct aid to the poor, the jobless, and the homeless, the administration of Franklin D. Roosevelt immediately set out to distribute as much money as possible to as many people as possible as quickly as possible. The Roosevelt administration changed the focus of direct aid from "a private to public responsibility and from a local to a federal function" (Mencher, 1967). Roosevelt believed in the responsibility of mankind for the well-being of others. He argued that the provision of public assistance was a matter of justice, not a matter of charity. As such, members of a society had a right to a minimum standard of living and that the existence of a democratic society depended on the well-being of its citizens (Trattner, 1999).

This humanitarian approach protected the dignity and worth of individuals by shifting responsibility for their condition from the poor themselves to society. President Roosevelt's message to Congress in 1934 provided the rationale for governmental responsibility to its citizenry, a political philosophy that undergirded his administration's New Deal programs. Roosevelt emphasized:

> Among our objectives I place the security of the men, women and children of the Nation first. This security for the individual and for the family concerns itself primarily with three factors. People want decent homes to live in; they want to locate them where they can engage in productive work; and they want some safeguard against misfortunes which cannot be wholly eliminated in this man-made world of ours. (Mencher, 1967, pp. 332–333)

This attitudinal change reflected a humanitarian emphasis on the quality of life, replacing the paternalism of Hoover's policy with objectivity, impartiality, and justice (Mencher, 1967). The public-policy focus of the 1930s emphasized the right of the poor to secure employment and had as its goal providing jobs for all.

***From Charity to Welfare*.** An elaborate system of social service programs, funded and administered through governmental agencies, emerged as the focus of social welfare shifted from the private auspices of charity and corrections to the domain of public welfare. Legislation created the public welfare system as a system of citizen entitlements to provide for the general welfare of societal members. Entitlements include the provision of social benefits offered through governmental programs and services to protect the interest of all citizens. Requirements such as income means tests for receiving public assistance and contribution formulas for obtaining social insurance stipulate eligibility for entitlement programs. Public services often restrict eligibility to those people who are unable to access or purchase services from the private-services sector. For example, public health services, special education, welfare provisions, and publicly supported legal services and housing assistance are available to people who qualify.

***New Deal Programs*.** Hastily conceived legislation to address the crying needs of the nation emerged in the famous "hundred day" period. For example, the *Agricultural Adjustment Act of 1933* established direct subsidies and price supports for farmers. The *Federal Emergency Relief Administration* (FERA) dispensed grants to states to make cash payments to the unemployed. The *Civilian Conservation Corps* (CCC), established in the first phase of the New Deal, provided work to unemployed young men in constructing public buildings, paving roads and bridges, clearing forests, developing flood controls, and improving national parks and beaches (Hicks, Mowry, & Burke, 1970).

Later, in 1935, legislation created the *Works Progress Administration* (WPA) to match the unemployed with jobs specific to their unique talents. Roosevelt appointed Harry Hopkins, a social worker who administered FERA, to oversee the WPA. The intent of this new program was to transfer the unemployed from direct relief rolls to WPA projects (Piven & Cloward, 1971).

The Social Security Act of 1935. Although Roosevelt introduced a "social security" bill on January 17, 1935, the Social Security Act did not emerge in isolation. Existing federal and state statutes and provisions in state widows' aid and old-age pension laws formed the basis for a national policy of social security. The proposal provided unemployment insurance; old-age insurance; and direct aid to people who were unemployed, old, blind, and orphans through state welfare systems.

The Need for Economic Security. The Social Security Act of 1935 was the first federal aid program to address the economic security of American citizens comprehensively. A variety of factors affect the way a society constructs measures for economic security:

> As Eveline Burns (1956) pointed out in her definitive work, *Social Security and Public Policy,* a variety of features also apply to social service delivery. Included are the general level of productivity of the country, national perception of an appropriate standard of living, available technology, level of employment, demographic characteristics of the population, changing roles of the family system, and technical and administrative inventiveness. (Jenkins, 1983, p. 816)

These factors presume governmental responsibility for taking the necessary steps to avoid economic breakdown and for making corrective action during times of economic stress.

Mencher (1967) describes "the evolution of direct money benefits from public charity to social security [as] one of the most striking features of economic security policy" (p. 388). The Social Security Act made a significant contribution in realigning public responsibility and gave birth to the welfare state. As a national policy, the federal government, through the passage of the Social Security Act, acknowledged citizen entitlement to welfare and assumed major funding responsibility for the welfare of U.S. citizens. Social workers, especially Harry Hopkins and Secretary of Labor Frances Perkins, played a key role in the development of this legislation.

Provisions for Economic and Social Security

Public measures to reduce economic insecurity include the provision of social security and other programs to ensure that there is opportunity for employment. Economic and social security provisions include social insurance, public assistance, income-conditioned pensions, and statutory payments (Burns, 1956). Ideally, social security systems ensure a minimum standard of living for all citizens.

The social insurance legislation of the 1930s insured the unemployed against those times that threatened their economic security. Since the source of unemployment compensation funds is a federal tax on employers' payrolls, the general public views unemployment insurance as a right. This spares unemployed workers from the demeaning experience of receiving "unearned" public aid. Likewise, since taxes on employees and employers fund the social security retirement supplement program, beneficiaries don't consider it charity. The 1939 amendments to the Social Security Act introduced family protection into the social insurance program by providing family entitlements to older adults as well as to employed workers' survivors and dependents (Bandler, 1989).

Legislators proposed categorical assistance programs, or programs created for certain categories of people—Old Age Assistance (OAA), Aid to the Blind (AB), and Aid to Dependent Children (ADC)—as citizens' rights for those populations who could not support themselves financially. Legislation added Aid to the Permanently and Totally Disabled (APTD) to the social security measures in 1950.

Criticisms of the Social Security Act of 1935. Proponents and opponents of national economic security measures compromised in the formulation of the Social Security Act of 1935. Resolution of issues about how to fund the program and criteria for who was eligible for benefits met with a great deal of criticism. Since taxation of wages was the principal source of funding, the poor literally had to pay for services for the poor. Employers were likely to pass their social security tax cost on to consumers. Benefits were based on earnings, not needs. Unemployment compensation, while helpful, was short-term and excluded many population groups touched by unemployment, including farm laborers, migrant workers, domestics, and workers' dependents (Trattner, 1999). And, for many, the most serious fault was the omission of health insurance provisions.

Opponents today argue that social insurance is too costly and that it creates dependency. Nonetheless, Census reports indicate that social insurance, in particular social security programs, is the most effective policy strategy for reducing poverty. For example, poverty among the elderly has been reduced from 35 percent at the poverty line or below to 13 percent over the last 35 years (Sasser, 1994). Said another way, were it not for Social Security benefits, nearly half of the population 65 and older would have incomes that fall below the official poverty level (Table 10.2).

Worthy and Unworthy Poor. The general public tends to judge the worthiness of the recipients of categorical programs. Beneficiaries of social insurance programs such as Social Security are not stigmatized because their benefits are seen as an entitlement based on their contributions. Few question the need to provide assistance to the "worthy poor"—people who are frail, elderly, or disabled. However, people still criticize the cost and administration of these services.

In contrast, recipients of public assistance programs do feel the scorn of others who view them as being "on the dole." The public tends to censure programs that aid the "unworthy poor" or people whom they judge able to work. For example, adults in families receiving public assistance are frequent targets of criticism. Public welfare critics contend that public assistance fosters dependency and stigmatizes recipients for their participation in programs. This position ignores the fact that every taxpayer is a potential welfare recipient and every welfare recipient is a potential taxpayer.

TABLE 10.2 Public Assistance and Social Insurance Compared

	Public Assistance	Social Insurance
Policy intent	Income supports for people meeting eligibility guidelines	Supplementary coverage for contributors
Examples	TANF, SSI, food stamps	OASDI
Auspices and administration	Federal and state	Federal
Eligibility	Needs-based: Participants must meet test of income and assets	Contributions: Eligibility based on credits achieved
Benefits	Variable amount, differs among states; principle of lesser eligibility applies	Fixed benefits based on coverage
Related medical	Medicaid	Medicare
Relatives' responsibility	Applied to legally defined dependents	None
Public's perception	Stigmatizing for "the poor"	Viewed as a right

The Great Society Programs: A Welfare Rights Initiative

The affluence of the decades preceding the 1960s hid from the nation a growing number of people in the "other America" (Harrington, 1962). Public officials, for the most part, ignored the social and economic plight of these people; however, political and social unrest marked the 1960s. Tumultuous conditions in urban areas punctuated by street rioting in many major cities brought the issues of the "other America" to public attention.

Policymakers identified several social problems as the root causes of poverty. Social welfare responses through the War on Poverty programs of the Kennedy administration and the Great Society programs of the Johnson administration attempted to get at the root causes of poverty, including racial discrimination, inadequate education, poor health, unemployment, and the erosion of civil rights.

Welfare Rights. The major theme of the 1960s welfare reform was welfare rights, an issue driven by concerned persons and organizations for the poor, as well as by the federal government. Initiatives included the following:

- The establishment of new services, both public and private, that offered the poor information about welfare entitlement and the assistance of experts in obtaining benefits.
- The initiation of litigation to challenge a host of local laws and policies that kept people off the welfare rolls.
- The support of new organizations of the poor which informed people of their entitlement to public welfare and mounted pressure on officials to approve their applications for assistance. (Piven & Cloward, 1971, p. 250)

The major result of this activity was a welfare explosion. However, this increase in the welfare rolls did not necessarily indicate that the number of poor was increasing. Rather,

BOX 10.2
Reflections on Diversity

International Policy Issues

The United Nations Millennium Summit, which met in September 2000, involved 147 world leaders to address ways in which their respective nations could contribute to strengthening global efforts for "peace, human rights, democracy, strong governance, environmental sustainability and poverty eradication, and to promoting principles of human dignity, equality, and equity" (United Nations Development Program [UNDP], 2003a, p. 27). Subsequently, 189 countries adopted the Millennium Declaration and agreed to a global compact, "The Millennium Development Goals." The Millennium Declaration emphasizes collective responsibility for social issues.

> We recognize that, in addition to our separate responsibilities to our individual societies, we have a collective responsibility to uphold the principles of human dignity, equality and equity at the global level. As leaders we have a duty therefore to all the world's people, especially the most vulnerable and, in particular, the children of the world, to whom the future belongs. (p. 27)

The Millennium Development Goals serve as benchmarks for progress in enhancing capabilities and improving conditions for human development. The goals "place human well-being and poverty reduction at the centre of global development objectives" (p. 27). Each goal supports key capabilities for human development including living a long and healthy life, being educated, having a decent standard of living, and enjoying political and civil freedoms. In addition, the goals correspond to essential contextual conditions in which human development takes place, including environmental sustainability, equity, and a global economic environment. Specifically, the Millennium Development Goals are as follows:

Goal 1: Eradicate extreme poverty and hunger
Goal 2: Achieve universal primary education
Goal 3: Promote gender equality and empower women
Goal 4: Reduce child mortality
Goal 5: Improve maternal health
Goal 6: Combat HIV/AIDs, malaria, and other diseases
Goal 7: Ensure environmental sustainability
Goal 8: Develop a global partnership for development (UNDP, 2003b)

These goals support the work of social workers in many countries and the efforts of international professional social work organizations. In addition to being familiar with the work of the United Nations in addressing social problems and injustices throughout the world, social workers should also be familiar with the policy positions and activities of international social work organizations. The International Federation of Social Workers offers practical and philosophical guidelines for social workers on a number of policy issues including human rights, migration, refugees, and peace and social justice. The Council on Social Work Education (2001), which accredits baccalaureate and master's degree social work programs, includes accreditation standards related to international social work, thereby recognizing the importance of understanding the global context of social work and having skills to analyze international social policy issues.

it suggested that those who were already poor were learning about existing programs and benefits and exercising their right to access these provisions.

Office of Economic Opportunity. As a response to the urban crisis and the political climate of the times, the Great Society initiative fostered a distinctive social service delivery system. In a controversial move to strengthen the urban connection, the Office of Economic Opportunity (OEO) developed a unique administrative arrangement. This structure bypassed state and local governments to initiate a relationship between the national government and the poor themselves. Piven and Cloward (1971) assert that *"the hallmark of the Great Society programs was the direct relationship between the national government and the ghettoes, a relationship in which both state and local governments were undercut"* (p. 261; authors' italics).

To promote self-direction, this legislation stressed involving local grassroots leadership in community planning and implementation of services. Local groups designed storefront programs for education, employment, legal services, information and referral services, and community action. The tenet of *maximum feasible participation* was a driving force of this legislation: To receive funds through the Economic Opportunity Act, programs had to involve consumers in planning, developing, and implementing the programs.

As a result of the OEO's community action component, many social workers reexamined the social justice position of the social work profession. They shifted their focus from therapy to reform, from psychoanalysis to the social sciences (Axinn & Stern, 2001).

Movement toward New Federalism

The liberal programs of the 1960s were short-lived. Conservatism in social welfare social policies, programming, and expenditures emerged with the election of President Richard M. Nixon and continued through the presidency of Ronald Reagan. Economic recession, inflation, and high unemployment rates characterized the economy in the 1970s and early 1980s. As a result, the number of people living in poverty increased dramatically. The federal government began distributing general revenue funds directly to the states through federalized block grants and turned over the administration of many welfare programs to the states as well. Additionally, public assistance programs increasingly incorporated workfare and job training elements.

Presidents Nixon and Carter both proposed similar guaranteed annual income plans which would provide a federal minimum income guarantee, work incentives, job training programs, and day care arrangements. President Nixon's Family Assistance Plan (FAP) was proposed as a replacement for AFDC and unemployment insurance for families with children. President Carter proposed a negative income tax that would apply to all people who were poor, regardless of family status: The Better Jobs and Income Proposal would have consolidated AFDC, SSI, and food stamps. Neither Nixon's Family Assistance Plan nor Carter's Better Jobs and Income Proposal gained Congressional approval.

President Reagan's election ushered in an era of ultraconservative ideological beliefs. Fueled by a belief in supply-side economics and the notion of a "trickle-down economy," New Federalism under the Reagan administration, and later under President Bush, emphasized privatization of services by charitable social service organizations and shifting responsibility for welfare assistance programs—AFDC, SSI, and food stamps—to state governments. Congressional legislation, including the Omnibus Reconciliation Act of 1981

(P.L. 97-35), the Gramm-Rudman-Hollings Act of 1985 (P.L. 101-508), and the Family Support Act of 1988 (P.L. 100-485), resulted in budget reductions, budget caps, and stricter eligibility requirements for entitlement programs.

Welfare Reform in the 1990s

Health care reform, welfare reform, and the passage of a crime bill were given a high priority on the Clinton administration's agenda. The crime bill received bipartisan support and quickly passed; the national health insurance bill for health care reform met resistance from the private insurance lobbies and political opponents, among others; the welfare reform act, called the Personal Responsibility and Work Opportunity Reconciliation Act of 1996 (P.L. 104-193), passed after much debate.

This welfare reform legislation, described by President Clinton as "ending welfare as we know it," transformed federal public welfare assistance programs (AFDC, SSI, and food stamps) into state-based programs with decreased federal fiscal support. The Temporary Assistance for Needy Families (TANF) program replaces Aid to Families with Dependent Children (AFDC) and provides states with greater latitude in designing their public assistance programs within specific federal guidelines.

Current Public Welfare Programs

Amendments to the Social Security Act over the last 50 years have expanded the population groups eligible for coverage and added new antipoverty strategies. Many programs have emerged to meet the income maintenance, social service, health, and nutritional needs of the poor. Among these programs are Old-Age Survivors Disability Insurance (OASDI), Temporary Assistance for Needy Families (TANF), Supplementary Security Income (SSI), Medicare and Medicaid, General Assistance (GA), Food Stamps, and Title XX Social Service Provisions.

OASDI

The federal government developed four social insurance programs to provide for the economic security of older adults, disabled workers, and survivors of workers. The Old-Age Survivors Disability Insurance (OASDI) program is made up of the following programs:

1. Old-Age and Survivors Insurance (OASI) was first established under the Social Security Act of 1935 as insurance for retired workers and expanded in 1939 to include survivors. It provides cash benefits for retired workers and their eligible family members and for survivors of insured workers.
2. Disability Insurance (DI), enacted through the 1956 amendments, provides cash benefits for disabled workers and their eligible family members.
3. Medicare, established in 1965, helps pay for the cost of hospital and medical for eligible elderly and disabled people. (Tracy & Ozawa, 1995, p. 2136)

Persons eligible for retirement benefits through OASDI have been "insured" by earning work credits for quarters of employment. Through a payroll deduction or self-employment tax, employees contribute to the Social Security fund. Benefits are calculated based on salary history. Eligibility depends on the claimant's age and the number of work credits needed for retirement benefits. Surviving spouses of deceased insured workers receive their spouses' full benefits. Cost of living adjustments increase the amount of benefits each year.

Social Security plays a significant role in reducing poverty rates among older adults. Ninety-one percent of people over age 65 receive OASDI benefits. The benefits represent a major source of income for 65 percent of the beneficiaries and the only source of income for 18 percent. The current poverty rate for Social Security beneficiaries is 10 percent; without these benefits, the poverty rate would be about 48 percent (Hungerford et al., 2001/2002; Social Security Administration, 2000a).

Eligibility for disability benefits under the social security program requires both a fully insured status and a medical or mental impairment that prohibits substantial gainful activity and that is expected to last for at least 12 months or result in death. The applicant for disability benefits must have had a minimum number of quarters in covered employment before the onset of the disability. Continued coverage depends on beneficiaries' participation, if possible, in state-sponsored rehabilitation services. In 2001, about 6.9 million persons, or 15 percent of those receiving OASDI payments, were workers with disabilities or their spouses and children ("Highlights and Trends," 2002).

Beneficiaries of OASDI are also eligible for Hospital Insurance (HI) provisions through Medicare and may enroll in Supplementary Medical Insurance (SMI) by paying a monthly premium. HI covers hospitalization and services and supplies required for inpatient care, skilled nursing care, home health services, and hospice care. SMI helps pay for physicians' fees, office visits, and medications. Retirees start receiving Medicare benefits on their qualifying birthday. Disabled beneficiaries experience a 24-month waiting period before their coverage begins.

Temporary Assistance for Needy Families (TANF)

With the passage of the Personal Responsibility and Work Opportunity Reconciliation Act of 1996 (PRWORA), block grants for Temporary Assistance for Needy Families (TANF) replaced Aid to Families with Dependent Children (AFDC), Emergency Assistance to Families with Children (EA), and the Job Opportunities and Basic Skills Training Program (JOBS).

AFDC: Predecessor of TANF. The AFDC program was designed to fulfill government's responsibility to needy dependent children. Under the governance of federal regulations, states administered the program and received public tax-fund money based on a state–federal matching formula. A 1961 law permitted states to provide aid to families with an unemployed father in the home.

While AFDC was criticized by some, others argue that it made a positive contribution as a social assistance program (Dear, 1989). As a national family allowance program, AFDC provided direct cash and noncash benefits to those families and children with the highest risk of poverty. This publicly sponsored and financed income-transfer program enhanced the well-being of millions of low-income people. In addition to income benefits, AFDC recipients received noncash benefits such as medical care, food supplements, housing subsidies, and social services. Dear concluded that in accordance with its original intent, this program assisted low-income families to remain intact.

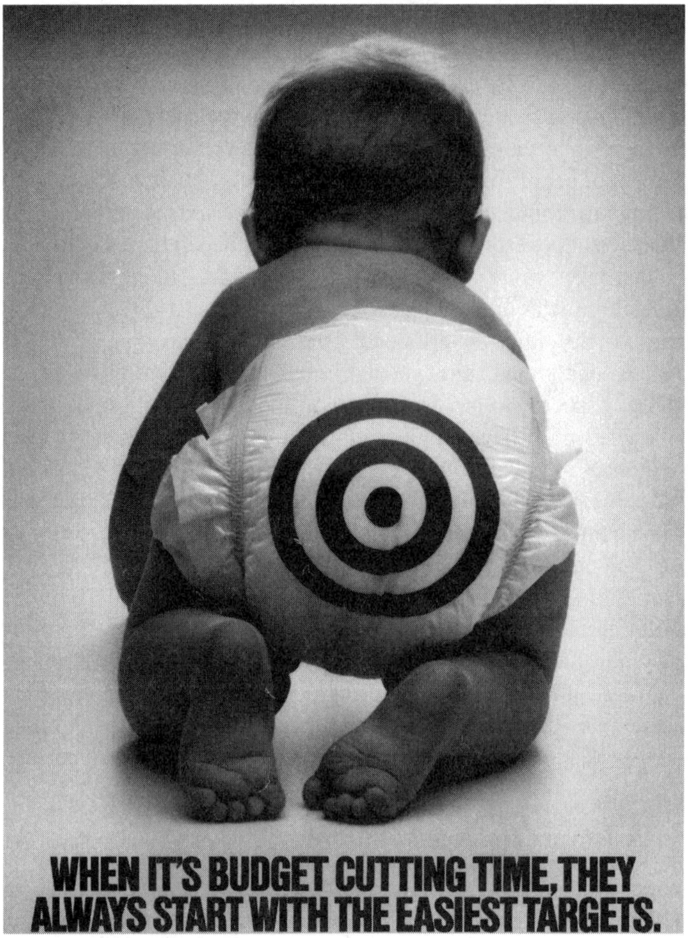

Children can't stand up for themselves. Which makes them an easy mark for politicians when they're cutting back. Give children a voice. Yours. Kids can't vote, but you can. The Children's Defense Fund

Purpose of TANF. The express purpose of TANF is to provide assistance to needy families with children so that the children can be cared for in their own homes, and to reduce dependency by promoting job preparation, work, and marriage. TANF's emphasis on the personal rather than the structural dimensions of poverty is evident even in the name of the legislation that creates this program—"The Personal Responsibility and Work Opportunity Reconciliation Act."

Stipulations for Funding. While the TANF legislation gives the states considerable latitude in designing state-based public assistance programs, it stipulates the parameters within which TANF programs must fall in order to qualify for block grant funding and imposes monetary penalties on state programs that do not comply. State responsibilities include the following:

- Determining eligibility requirements
- Establishing benefit levels
- Managing the block grant money according to federal stipulations
- Deciding on options such as whether to require personal responsibility contracts and whether to grant assistance to additional children born or conceived while the parent is receiving assistance or to unmarried teen parents and their children
- Filing their plan for TANF with the federal government every two years

Conditions of the TANF legislation include state performance bonuses and penalties, definitive work and community service requirements, and time limits for receiving TANF funds. Many states have already adopted more stringent guidelines than the law itself provides. Some examples of TANF stipulations encompass regulations such as the following:

- Limitations on benefits to families to no more than 60 months—in other words, a lifetime limit of five years—although states may expend their own funds to families who require assistance beyond the five-year lifetime limit
- Allowances for exemptions of up to 20 percent of a state's average monthly number of recipients for "hardships" such as domestic violence
- Work requirements, reductions of assistance to families where adults are not working the minimum number of hours per week (for fiscal years 1997 and 1998, 20 hours; for fiscal year 1999, 25 hours; and for fiscal years 2000 and beyond, 30 hours) after receiving TANF assistance for a two-year period, and penalties for state programs that fail to fulfill the work requirement mandates
- Performance bonuses for states meeting program goals in the fiscal years 1998 to 2002
- Awards to the five states with the greatest success in reducing out-of-wedlock births without increasing the state abortion rate
- Allowances for states to reduce grants to families by up to 25 percent when a parent fails to cooperate in establishing paternity or in matters related to support orders
- A permanent ban on cash assistance or food stamp benefits for persons with felony convictions for drug dealing, possession, or use
- Denials of assistance to teen parents who are not living at home or in approved, adult-supervised settings

The emphasis on work requirements for people receiving public assistance presupposes the employability of TANF recipients. However, data on these recipients' characteristics show that many have health- and mental health–related problems, educational deficits and learning disabilities, housing instability, domestic violence issues, and child care responsibilities that hamper their employability (Olson & Pavetti, 1996; Zedlewski, 2003). Moreover, most work-assistance programs provide only short-term interventions, such as a job search, whereas welfare-dependent people require more comprehensive programming. The work requirement also presumes that employment leads to self-sufficiency; however, when wages are low, workers' economic status remains marginal. One labor union official commented that this legislation is "an impetus toward a sub-minimum wage" (Levy, 1996). Finally, welfare-to-work stipulations presume the availability of jobs, but conditions in many communities require a parallel effort directed at economic development.

BOX 10.3

Reflections on Empowerment

Welfare Dependency or Welfare Dependability?

The question as to whether or not public welfare assistance programs promote dependency rather than self-sufficiency has been the subject of debate in recent years. National political campaigns shouted, "Empowerment, not entitlement!" However, persons familiar with the purpose of public welfare recognize this slogan as second generation rhetoric for "Workfare, not welfare!" Empowering social workers know that the solution is not one or the other. Ultimately, empowerment, entitlement, workfare, and welfare suggest the same end for persons who utilize public assistance on their road to self-sufficiency.

Public welfare recipients, for the most part, are not so much "dependent" on aid, as they do, however, find it "dependable" as an ongoing, secure source of income. The purpose of public assistance is in fact empowering. The public welfare system is an opportunity structure for individuals and families who lack the necessary income to fare well in an industrialized society. Entitlement programs suggest that services are offered as citizens' rights. Society benefits when all persons share a minimum level of economic security. Workfare requirements, supplemented by training and employment opportunities, benefit clients in their quest for self-sufficiency.

On the plus side, the debate has given rise to a whole cadre of supportive and supplemental services for persons who receive income maintenance through Temporary Assistance for Needy Families (TANF) program. Success in moving families enrolled in TANF from welfare to work is in great part attributed to strategies designed to maximize the " 'fit' between the demands of work and the family's abilities to meet those demands and the fit between the family's needs and the supplies available from work to meet those needs" (DeBord, Canu, & Kerpelman, 2000, p. 313). For low-income single parents, low-wage jobs, the high cost of child care, and the lack of reliable transportation create barriers to a successful work-family connection. Many states now offer incentives or "investments" including income exemptions, continued medical coverage, child care benefits, and transportation assistance for recipients who are pursuing an educational or employment plan. These supports are empowering. However, many states also link continued eligibility for assistance with clients' strident progress in their plans for self-sufficiency. This is potentially disempowering, particularly for clients who have histories of failure and low self-esteem, whose capabilities do not fit within predetermined timeframes for expected progress, whose life situations present many possibilities for disrupting their plans, and who may not readily find a place in the job market even though their training is complete.

States need to consider these individual factors in "empowering for self-sufficiency" as well as address structural factors in their economy. States themselves need to make strident progress in statewide job development and economic growth so that when TANF recipients are at the point of joining the workforce, there's a workforce for them to join that pays a living wage.

Lengthy debate has slowed the process of reauthorization of the PRWORA. Among the recommendations made by the NASW (2002c) are the following:

- Require development of individual self-sufficiency plans, intensive case management, and improved sanction procedures for families with multiple barriers to employment.

- Expand allowable work activities to include treatment and counseling for mental illness, substance abuse, and domestic violence.
- Extend time limits and exemptions for those who are actively participating in activities to overcome one or more barriers to self-sufficiency.
- Fund training programs for frontline staff on identifying the basic signs and symptoms of the more common mental health disorders, substance abuse problems, and signs of domestic violence. (pp. 2–3)

Supplemental Security Income

In 1974, legislation federalized several of the original state-based programs—Old Age Assistance (OAA), Aid to the Blind (AB), and Aid to the Permanently and Totally Disabled (APTD)—as the Supplemental Security Income (SSI) program, under the Social Security Administration. Eligible individuals receive monthly cash payments. To qualify for SSI, a person must be over age 65, be visually impaired, or have a physical or mental impairment that prohibits him or her from employment. With the enactment of the PRWORA, drug addiction and alcoholism are no longer considered qualifying disabilities.

Children under age 18 with a disability may qualify for SSI benefits; however, the PRWORA limits eligibility for SSI payments to those children who have a medically proven medical condition resulting in marked and severe functional limitations that is expected to last at least 12 months or result in death (Social Security Administration, 1997) and excludes conditions related to maladaptive behaviors.

Criteria for eligibility also include limited financial status and citizenship. When qualified applicants have other cash incomes, SSI payments supplement their earnings to bring their income to the level established for basic needs.

General Assistance

General Assistance (GA) programs provide limited in-kind or cash benefits to persons who need emergency relief, but do not qualify for cash-benefit programs, such as SSI or TANF. States, counties, or localities finance and administer GA. Actual programs and benefit structures vary widely from state to state, including types and levels of benefits, eligibility criteria, and rules about time limits. In the past, GA has included direct cash grants and voucher systems; however, now most programs severely limit or exclude cash grants (Gallagher, 1999; Uccello & Gallagher, 1997).

Most recipients of GA do not meet the eligibility requirements for any of the relevant categorical assistance programs. While GA clientele are already those individuals who have no other sources of income, many states have restricted or completely eliminated their GA programs in an effort to trim their budgets. For example, traditionally, GA has been the only program providing cash assistance for able-bodied adults without dependent children. Today, most states or localities that have GA programs exclude these individuals from eligibility. Some contend that misconceptions—that most GA recipients are able to work, that they remain on GA for extended periods of time, and that full-time, minimum-wage jobs raise living standards above the poverty level—about GA recipients form the basis for these restrictions (Halter, 1994).

Medicare and Medicaid

Social Security Act amendments added two health maintenance programs—Medicare (Title XVIII) and Medicaid (Title XIX)—in 1965. As a social insurance program, the intent of Medicare is to meet the health needs of people who are 65 years of age or older, some people under 65 with disabilities, and people with end stage renal disease. People who qualify for Social Security payments qualify for Medicare. People often cover the difference between the actual Medicare payment and medical costs with their own supplemental "medigap" insurance. However, the Medicare program underwrites health care costs substantially.

Medicaid is a medical assistance program for qualifying low-income families. In general, Medicaid, jointly financed by the federal and state governments, provides medical and hospital benefits for people who qualify for categorical assistance programs, including TANF and SSI, and provides transitional benefits for families no longer eligible for cash assistance programs; however, the PRWORA grants states the authority to develop specific eligibility criteria. This legislation essentially "decouples" welfare and Medicaid eligibility. Depending on the state guidelines, Medicaid covers medical costs, including inpatient hospitalization, nonelective surgical procedures, doctors' office fees, dental expenses, nursing home care, and prescription drugs. Many Medicaid participants have difficulty locating vendors of medical services (hospitals, physicians, and so forth) who will accept Medicaid payments. Funding cutbacks have affected eligibility for Medicaid coverage and redefined qualifications for being considered medically indigent. Medicaid rules exclude persons with marginal incomes, many of whom have no private health insurance. In general, the number of people with unmet medical needs has increased since the advent of welfare reform under TANF.

Food Stamps

The food stamp program, established by the Food Stamp Act of 1964, supplements the nutritional needs of people whose income falls below a specified level. The federal government funds the program under the direction of the U.S. Department of Agriculture (USDA). States administer the food stamp program, often in conjunction with categorical assistance programs.

The food stamp program is a major initiative for addressing the hunger problem in the United States and, in the long term, eliminating hunger and malnutrition (USDA, 2003). The administrative agency issues food stamps redeemable for food purchases only to unemployed or employed persons with low incomes who meet the program's income guidelines. P. L. 104-193 reduced the allocations for food stamps and limited food stamp provisions to childless, nondisabled persons ages 18 to 50 unless they are working or participating in some type of a workfare program. Recently, the numbers of participants in the Food Stamp Program have increased (Food Research Action Center, 2003). Statistics for October 2002 indicated more than 20.1 million people participate in the food stamp program, 1.8 million more than a year earlier. In spite of this increase, participation is 700,000 less than in 1997. At present, only about 60 percent of those eligible for food stamps enroll in the program.

Social Service Provisions of Title XX

In 1975, Congress approved the Title XX amendment of the Social Security Act. A major provision for social services, the original version of Title XX consisted of block grants to states for social services for families receiving AFDC or SSI, or who met specified income guidelines, targeted toward four broad service goals:

- Enhance economic self-support by preventing, reducing, or eliminating dependency
- Promote self-sufficiency
- Prevent inappropriate institutional care through the provision of community-based services
- Ensure appropriate institutional care and services for those who need them (Catalog of Federal Domestic Assistance, n.d.)

The 1981 Omnibus Budget Reconciliation Act (P.L. 97-35) changed Title XX to eliminate state matching funds and to remove the mandates to expend funds for public assistance recipients and target the original five service goals (Everett, 1995). Among the types of programs for which Title XX provides funds are those providing services such as information and referral, family planning, counseling, child day care, child protection, case management, homemakers and home health aides, education, and training. Title XX is a major source of funding for child welfare services.

Title XX also includes provisions for state governmental agencies to contract for the services of private social service vendors. This stipulation that government contract for services stimulated the growth of private social service agencies. Currently, the trend is toward reducing allocations of funding to Title XX block grants.

Looking Forward

The social work profession must change both societal attitudes toward clients and the public welfare system of service delivery. Social workers can contribute relevant professional values and working principles that will empower the largest segment of social welfare consumers—the disenfranchised. Thus, social workers must play a more visible, active role in the provision of public welfare services. It is important for social workers to provide these services. Social welfare policy must embody empowerment, and the delivery of public welfare services must reflect an intent to empower the individual.

PART FOUR

Contemporary Issues in Fields of Practice

Social workers are employed in broad fields of practice such as public welfare, corrections, health systems, and family services. Service provisions, generally clustered into each field of practice, are designed to respond to the unique needs presented by various population groups. Among social work's clientele, many—such as those affected negatively by the economic structure, those who have committed crimes, and people who have physical and mental disabilities—have experienced social rejection and oppression. Other consumers include families troubled by conflict and change and individuals touched by disruptions in the normal course of the life cycle.

Part Four emphasizes the practice issues that emerge in social work with particular populations. Featured are social work services to people who are poor, homeless, unemployed, or criminal offenders; people who have physical, developmental, and mental disabilities; people who are chemically dependent; and diverse families, youths, and aging adults.

CHAPTER 11 Social Work in the Public Domain

The social work profession has a long history of concern about the well-being of population groups that are considered disenfranchised. The disenfranchised groups in U.S. society have not changed over many decades. They continue to be the poor, the homeless, and the unemployed—societal groups that have a history of dependency on private and public support for their well-being. Certainly, it is the disenfranchised citizens who are in most need of social work services. Minorities, older adults, women, and dependent children are represented in disproportionate numbers among the ranks of those touched by poverty. Indeed, these are the groups toward whom the social justice mandate of the profession is directed. This chapter examines four areas of concern in the public domain:

- Poverty
- Homelessness
- Unemployment
- Criminal Justice

Social Work and Poverty

In spite of a decline in the overall rate of poverty in the United States to 11.7 percent in 2001, Census Bureau data indicate a trend toward greater income inequality (U.S. Census Bureau, 2002a). The wealthiest fifth of all families received nearly half of the national income while the poorest fifth received less than five percent (DeNavas-Walt & Cleveland, 2002). Moreover, income inequality is an ongoing social welfare problem in the world community. The daily income of one-sixth of the world's population represents 80 percent of the total daily world income (World Bank, 2003). A World Bank (2003) report on poverty indicates that worldwide, about 56 percent of the population, or almost 3 billion people subsist on less than the equivalent of two dollars a day. Of these people, about 1.2 billion live in abject poverty on less than one dollar a day. To clarify issues related to poverty, this section presents Harrington's concept of the "Other America," addresses the question, "Who are the poor?" by examining several commonly held stereotypes, contrasts relative and absolute poverty, and delineates several perspectives.

The Other America

Many credit Michael Harrington (1962), author of *The Other America: Poverty in the United States,* with sparking the War on Poverty during the Kennedy administration. Harrington asserts, "Poverty should be defined in terms of those who are denied the minimal levels of health, housing, food, and education that our present stage of scientific knowledge specifies as necessary for life as it is now lived in the United States" (p. 175). Harrington also called for a definition of poverty that addresses its psychological issues and absolute effects: A thorough definition of poverty examines the feelings of pessimism and defeat of those persons who experience poverty as well as the potential loss to societal members and society itself that results from poverty.

More than 40 years after Harrington's challenge, we are still trying to define poverty. Today, people tend to describe poverty in terms of its social consequences and impact on tax withholdings, without accounting for the human costs and human misery associated with impoverishment. They may deal with poverty coldly as a social condition, creating an emotional distance between the poor and the affluent. We need to reexamine the population groups affected by poverty, who, 40 years ago, Harrington proclaimed were living in the "other America." Now, as before, poverty creates a class of people who are poor. Those who are poor do not choose to be poor; they simply are poor. Children, the group that has a higher rate of poverty—16.3 percent—than any other age group, poignantly exemplify this fact. Children are at greater risk in some localities. For example, in 2000, the highest rates of child poverty are found in the District of Columbia (32 percent), Mississippi (27 percent), Louisiana (27 percent), New Mexico (25 percent), and West Virginia (24 percent) (Children's Defense Fund, 2003). In sum, children represent 35.7 percent of those who are poor, whereas they make up only about 25 percent of the population (Proctor & Dalaker, 2002).

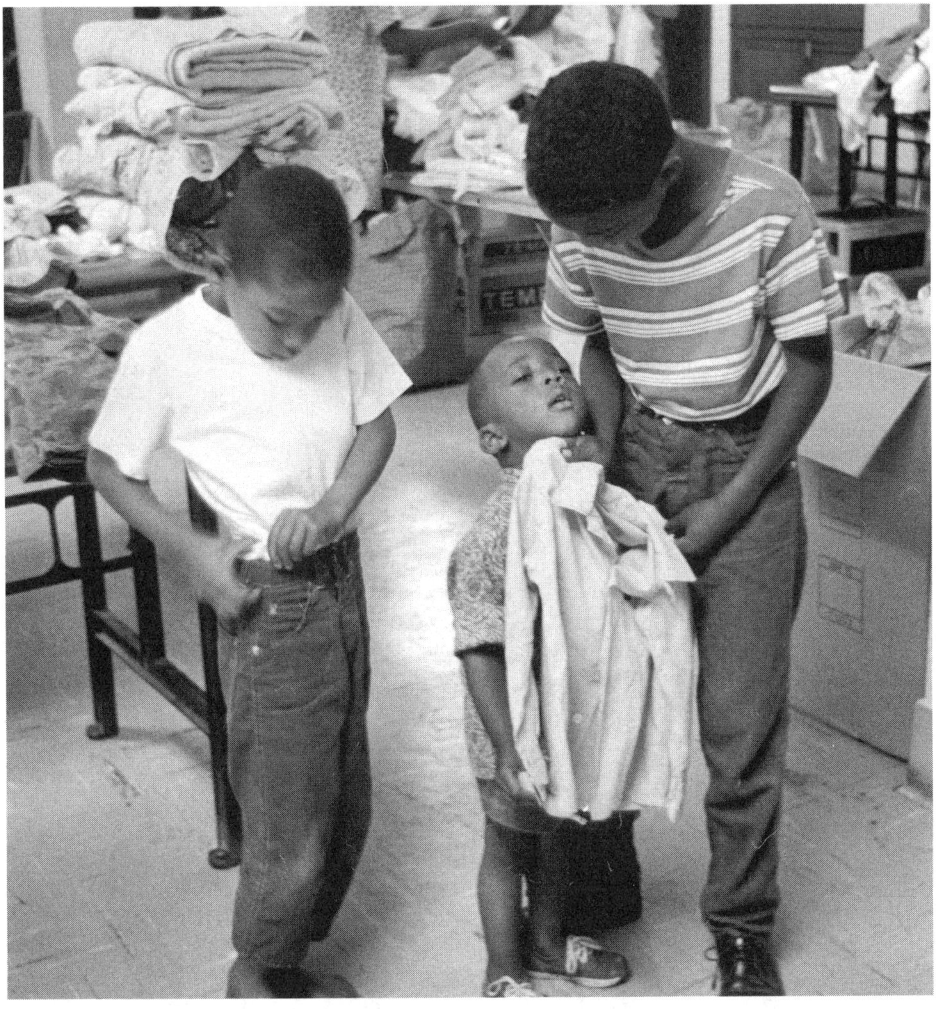

The rate of poverty for Black children in the United States is nearly 30 percent.

Who Are the Poor?

When you ask the question, Who are the poor? you're likely to elicite a wide range of responses. Some are accurate, and some reflect commonly held misperceptions about people who are poor. People often identify being poor with racial minorities. An initial examination of data on poverty in the United States does not support this view, as 47 percent of persons who are poor are non-Hispanic Whites (Proctor & Dalaker, 2002). However, this conclusion is misleading. In absolute numbers, there are more poor Whites than Blacks or Hispanics; however, a comparison of poverty rates reveals the disproportionate occurrence of poverty among minorities: 22.7 percent for Blacks, 21.4 percent for Hispanics of any race, and 10.2 percent for Asian and Pacific Islanders in contrast to 7.8 percent for non-Hispanic Whites.

A commonly held stereotype is that families that are poor are large; however, the size of families with incomes below the poverty line is not appreciably different from the overall average family size in the United States. It is true, however, that the risk of falling below the poverty line is greater for larger families. Some types of families are more at risk then others. For example, the rate of poverty for a family with a husband and wife present is 4.9 percent. With a purely male-headed household (no wife), the rate is 13.1 percent. For a purely female-headed household (no husband), the rate is 26.4 percent (Proctor & Dalaker, 2002).

Even the phrase *feminization of poverty,* which implies that adult women are now a more predominant group among those who are poor, is somewhat misleading. Currently, women and children do make up a large portion of those who are poor, but they also made up a large proportion of the poor in the early 1960s.

Statistical data highlight the risk of poverty for non-White female-headed households: 35 percent for Black female-headed households, 15 percent for Asian Americans and Pacific Islanders, and 37 percent for Hispanic origin female-headed households as compared to 19 percent for non-Hispanic White female-headed households (McKinnon, 2003; Proctor & Dalaker, 2002; Reeves & Bennett, 2003). Underlying this trend is the difficulty families face in today's economy when they must rely on a single income for their support. Complications to achieving self-sufficiency include the facts that women typically earn less than men, even for similar positions, and that child care expenses even when subsidized, drain financial resources. Statistics reveal the magnitude of these risks for children. About one-fourth of all children under 18 live in female-headed households. Of these children, about 40 percent live in poverty (Fields, 2003).

Even though the number of children in poverty in the United States has declined recently from 20 percent to 16.5 percent, recent studies underscore the alarming rate of poverty for all children under 18 (Mather & Rivers, 2003). A comparison of the rates of poverty in 22 countries found that of the countries studied, only Mexico had a higher child poverty rate than the United States. A recent United Nations study concluded that, among industrialized countries, the only country with a higher child poverty rate than the United States was Russia. The child poverty rate in the United States is substantially higher than in Scandinavian countries like Sweden where the child poverty rate is less than 3 percent (Adamson, Micklewright, & Wright, 2000). Specifically, in the United States, the rate of poverty for children under 18 is 30 percent for Black children and 28 percent for Hispanic children as compared with 10 percent for non-Hispanic White children (McKinnon, 2003; Ramirez & de la Cruz, 2003).

The general public often characterizes people who are poor as people who are really able to work; however, facts refute this misconception. Numerous people who receive welfare assistance merely supplement their wages. Furthermore, a large percentage of individuals with incomes below poverty level are employed full-time. For example, there is a working adult in 74 percent of the families of children who are poor (Children's Defense Fund, 2000a). In light of today's standards, a full-time job paying only minimum wage generates an income level well below the current poverty guidelines. By all reports, the working poor comprise a fast-growing segment of those who are poor.

Classifications of the Poor. Segalman and Basu (1981) characterize the poor along a continuum that includes the transitional poor, the marginal poor, and the residual poor. For the *transitional poor,* poverty is a temporary, short-term phenomenon experienced under conditions of change. People who are unemployed for short periods of time, immigrants, and even college students fall into this category. As a result of underemployment, the *marginal poor* earn just barely enough to meet their basic needs. For these people, the ability to secure self-sufficiency often depends on national economic and employment trends. While some who are marginally poor enjoy upward mobility, many are at risk of becoming entrenched in poverty. The *residual poor* remain in poverty over long periods of time, even from one generation to the next (i.e., transgenerationally or intergenerationally). Welfare grants frequently subsidize people who experience residual poverty over extended periods of time.

Many people believe that most people who are poor fall into the residual category; however, an analysis of the average length of stay on welfare assistance refutes this notion. Long-term welfare recipients "do, in fact, exist, but they are the exception, not the rule" (Pavetti, 1997). The patterns of welfare use differ for those persons who use welfare for a short duration and never return, for those who use welfare intermittently in recurrent economic or family crises, and for those who receive welfare continuously for long periods of time. For this reason, it is difficult to determine an average length of stay on the welfare rolls.

Past records indicate that, of those women who *ever* receive welfare, about half leave welfare within a year and almost three-fourths within two years (Pavetti, 1997). Unfortunately, although many women access welfare assistance for relatively short periods of time, they are also likely to return for additional assistance sometime within a five-year period. Recent studies of participation in TANF show similar patterns of participation, with more long-term assistance for those families facing more difficult challenges to economic self-sufficiency such as addiction, mental illness, illiteracy, and providing care for children with developmental disabilities.

Relative and Absolute Poverty

Sociologists measure poverty in absolute and relative terms. *Absolute measures* of poverty determine the level of income required for basic essentials; by definition, poverty occurs when incomes fall below this absolute level. A government-established index, the poverty line, is one such absolute measure. The poverty line is based on the current cost of a nutritional diet multiplied by an index number. This present-day replication of the English poor law bread scale barely, if at all, meets families' basic needs. By the 2003 U.S. Department of Health and Human Services poverty guidelines, a family of four in the contiguous states

TABLE 11.1 HHS Poverty Guidelines for 2003

Size of Family Unit	48 Contiguous States and D.C.	Alaska	Hawaii
1	$ 8,980	$11,210	$10,330
2	12,120	15,140	13,940
3	15,260	19,070	17,550
4	18,400	23,000	21,160
5	21,540	26,930	24,770
6	24,680	30,860	28,380
7	27,820	34,790	31,990
8	30,960	38,720	35,600
For each additional person, add	3,140	3,930	3,610

Source: Federal Register, Vol. 68, No. 26, February 7, 2003, pp. 6456–6458.

and Washington, DC is poor if its income falls below $18,400, $21,160 in Hawaii, and $18,400 in Alaska (U.S. Department of Health and Human Services [HHS], 2003a). By absolute measures, the incomes of about 11.7 percent of the total population of the United States, or about 32.9 million people, fall below the poverty line (U.S. Census Bureau, 2002a). See Table 11.1.

Actual income is only one part of the picture: A family's standard of living relative to that of other community members measures the family's *relative deprivation* (Williams, 1975). In other words, relative deprivation refers to perceptions of being poor in relation to others at the same time and place. So, to contrast the "wealth" of the poor in the United States with the abject poverty experienced by people in other nations does not make people who are poor in the United States less poor in relation to other U.S. citizens.

Why Are People Poor?

Two contrasting attitudes reveal the ways in which people who are poor have been regarded in U.S. history. One attitude places the blame on individuals, while the other places responsibility on society for allowing the conditions that create poverty. The attitude that holds the individual responsible points to character defects as the root cause of poverty. People who hold this view believe that changes in individuals will reduce the overall incidence of poverty. The attitude that places responsibility on society recognizes the role of structural problems in poverty. People who adopt the structural view see social reform as the key to eradicating poverty.

Shifts in attitudes tend to reflect prevailing economic trends, political ideologies, social conditions, and religious beliefs. In times of political, social, and religious conservatism, the social welfare provisions tend to be more punitive, constricting services through strict income guidelines and stigma. During times of political and social unrest, societal responses to poverty incline toward humanitarian aid. Social welfare provisions attempt to meet individual needs while trying to alleviate the social and environmental causes of poverty, such as inadequate education, poor health, unemployment, discrimination, and the erosion of civil rights.

Perceptions of People Who Are Poor. When people locate the cause of poverty in individuals, they frequently cite characteristics such as innate qualities, behavioral traits, and cultural considerations as factors that contribute to poverty (Popple & Leighninger, 2002). Some even believe that genetic inferiority, including limited intellectual capacity (or IQ), causes poverty. Stereotypes have made ethnic and racial groups particularly vulnerable to being labeled socially inferior and intellectually limited. However, contemporary research discredits theories that propose relationships between racial heritage and intelligence (Myers, 2004).

Many believe that behavioral qualities such as motivation—or, more specifically, lack of motivation and the absence of a work ethic—characterize people who are poor. However, factual evidence refutes this widely held misconception. Many people who are poor are underemployed; they hold low-paying jobs generally without medical or retirement benefits. It is ironic that so many of the working poor cling to jobs that provide incomes that are below poverty level because of their strong work ethic, the stigma associated with receiving welfare benefits, or even the lack of relevant assistance programs. On the other hand, to conclude that families receiving welfare assistance do not desire employment with adequate wages is a misconception.

Some believe that cultural differences make people functionally inferior and thus poor. For example, cultural deprivation is associated with low educational achievement and limited opportunities for people to change their circumstances. A *culture of poverty* develops that creates a unique subculture among those who are poor, differentiated by culturally transmitted values, belief systems, and behavior patterns (Cattell-Gordon, 1990; Lewis, 1969).

Social Work Highlights. Consider Nancy O'Rourke's response as she applies for public assistance: Nancy feels uncomfortable as she walks into the waiting room at the public aid office. The sheer number of applicants overwhelms her, and she is embarrassed to be among them. Nancy surveys the reception area and discovers several lines of people registering for different state aid programs. She braces herself as she gives her name to the receptionist and indicates in a lowered voice that she needs to apply for Temporary Assistance for Needy Families. Feeling that she needs to apologize, Nancy explains that she doesn't really want to apply for assistance, but her ex-husband hasn't sent child support for over two months. Recalling her friend's reassurance, "You're entitled to these benefits; after all, you paid taxes, unlike those other deadbeats," does nothing to lessen Nancy's discomfort.

Nancy completes the application forms and gives them to the receptionist. In return, the receptionist hands Nancy a card with a number on it and tells her to sit down and wait until a caseworker calls her number. Nancy spots an empty chair beside a middle-aged woman. Thinking she knows about "generational welfare families," Nancy presumes, with some indignation, that the woman is there with her pregnant daughter.

As Nancy sits down, the woman nods pleasantly and says, "Seems pretty busy today." Nancy, quickly and perhaps too loudly, asserts, "I've never been here before!" The woman lowers her head and confides, "Neither have I. It's humiliating, isn't it?" and goes on to explain tearfully, "My husband has Alzheimer's disease and is in a nursing home. I don't know how I'm going to pay the bills."

Notice the ramifications of the misconceptions, depreciating attitudes, and individualized notions about why people must seek public assistance for Nancy and the other clients waiting in the public aid office.

A Structural Perspective. From a structural perspective, inadequacies in the institutional fabric of society create the conditions that produce poverty. Beeghley (1983) offers a sociological analysis of such inadequacies:

1. The way in which the correlates of poverty create a vicious circle that often traps the poor and prevents them from changing their situation
2. The way the class system reproduces itself over time
3. The organization of the economy
4. The continuation of institutionalized discrimination against blacks and women. (p. 133)

The poverty treadmill creates a stressful cycle that limits opportunities for employment and educational advancement. Once a person becomes poor and lacks resources, many additional barriers emerge that prevent the person from escaping or breaking out of the cycle of poverty. Welfare services, designed to break the cycle, often further entrap recipients in poverty. For example, eligibility requirements insist that people literally exhaust all personal resources before they can receive even limited public assistance. Rules penalize individuals further by considering educational grants as available income, denying Medicaid benefits to the working poor, and, in many states, prohibiting welfare benefits to two-parent families. Liberals and radicals criticize the social welfare system for oppressing the very people it intends to help.

Beeghley (1983) contends that social stratification and a class system make it unlikely that children born into socially disadvantaged strata will ever escape poverty through social mobility. Furthermore, some even argue that a lack of social mobility creates a caste system of inherited or generational poverty.

The organization of the economic institutions of society also contributes to poverty (Beeghley, 1983). The nature of the jobs available to the poor, the unskilled, and the undereducated limit their opportunities. The low wages, lack of health and retirement benefits, and tenuous job security associated with marginal, part-time, and seasonal jobs contribute to the cycle of poverty. Finally, Beeghley asserts that discrimination against minorities and women accounts for the large proportion of these populations among the poor. Discriminatory practices give advantage to White males in employment, award custody of children to mothers without adequate child support, and create dependency roles for women through societally promoted child-rearing patterns. Beeghley's four-point analysis demonstrates that "most impoverished people live poorly for structural reasons, very few of which have to do with their motivations, skills, or other personal traits" (p. 133).

Service Responses to Poverty

Many programs have emerged to address the root causes of poverty in the areas of education, economic stability, and work participation. Three examples of model services include Project Head Start, low interest loan programs, and an empowerment-oriented program to support women making the transition from welfare to work.

Project Head Start. Project Head Start was established in 1965 as a part of the Great Society programs designed to address various aspects of poverty. Specifically, Project Head Start was seen as a way to boost the academic performance of children whose families had incomes below the poverty level by improving their access to quality early childhood education and "to support the families of these children with a wide variety of Head Start–sponsored programs, including a case management system" (Frankel, 1997, p. 172). Over the course of its existence, Head Start programs have provided educational and family support services to over 25 million children; 912,345 children were enrolled in 2002 (Administration for Children and Families [ACF], 2003). Head Start Bureau data indicate that 13 percent of the children enrolled had some type of disability. A recent addition, Early Head Start, a program for low-income families with infants and toddlers that provides information about child development and family support services, serves more than 62,000 young children under the age of three each year. Since it began in 1965, Project Head Start has served more than 21 million children. In spite of its excellent record and high name recognition, Head Start only enrolls about 60 percent of all eligible preschool children. Early Head Start is only able to serve about 3 percent of the infants and toddlers who are eligible (Children's Defense Fund, 2003).

Head Start has been highly successful in terms of its long-term positive influence on participants, and family involvement has been identified as a key component of its success (Children's Defense Fund, n.d.; Frankel, 1997).

All Head Start programs include social service components staffed by family service workers, often paraprofessionals with on-the-job training to prepare them for their work. Family service workers carry out tasks very similar to those of case managers (Frankel, 1997). They focus on such issues as employment, housing, parenting, access to health services, questions about child development, mental health difficulties, and drug and alcohol addictions. Family service workers also ensure linkages among families, Head Start teachers and other staff, and the communities. Frankel observes that a goal is to add more professional social workers to the ranks of program staff. In fact, "the Head Start Bureau indicated that it wants its workers to be more like social workers and that it wishes to incorporate social work values and roles" (p. 181). This area of practice certainly holds a great deal of potential for those social workers wanting to work collaboratively with families of young children.

Low-Interest Loan Programs. Increasing numbers of people who are poor are working full-time, but still find themselves vulnerable to financial disasters. For example, given their marginal incomes, they don't have extra money for auto repairs. One low-interest loan program, the Lutheran Social Service (LSS) Loan Fund in Duluth, Minnesota, was established to help city residents who were among the "working poor" to avert financial disasters (Raschick, 1997). The results of a program effectiveness study that evaluated the impact of the loan program on a random sample of 20 former program participants indicate that one of the advantages of this program was that "loan recipients are treated as banking customers and not as human service clients" (p. 30). Respondents' comments point to the program's contributions to their self-sufficiency. One person indicates, "Without the car, I wouldn't have been able to go to work because I started work at 4:30 A.M. and buses weren't running and I couldn't walk since it was a two-to-three hour walk" (p. 32). Another said, "I got a car with it and went to school and now I'm working. If it weren't for the car, I wouldn't have been able to finish school and if I hadn't finished school I couldn't have gotten a job" (p. 32). A benefit of the partnership between the social service agency and the bank was that it created an opportunity for "empowering the beneficiaries of government services to become true consumer*s* with meaningful market choices" (p. 34).

Other Empowerment-Oriented Projects. Project WISE, an initiative for women with low incomes in Denver, Colorado, incorporates elements of personal, interpersonal, and political empowerment, leading to personal and social change (East, 1999a; 1999b). The mission of this program is to help women sustain empowerment as they transition from welfare to economic self-sufficiency. The program provides affordable individual counseling, group experiences, and community advocacy opportunities to help women to realize both their personal and family goals and to participate fully in their communities.

The program addresses issues faced by women that go beyond job training and placement to include the effects of disempowerment and oppression that often malign women who are welfare recipients—issues such as low self-esteem, histories of physical or sexual abuse, domestic violence, and depression or other mental health difficulties. Personal counseling is augmented with support, educational groups, and opportunities for community involvement and leadership development. The voices of several women involved in this project illustrate the potential for change and success afforded through participation in this program:

> Today Eva is working and has maintained a job for over nine months. She says Project WISE gave her a safe place to tell her story where she was believed and promoted the confidence she needed to reenter the world. The welcoming atmosphere and the groups, along with individual counseling, were particularly helpful. Elizabeth is living on her own and completing her AA degree. She is still active with Project WISE as it has become an important place for support. Sarah is working, albeit at a low-wage job. She is very proud that she is no longer in transitional housing and is renting her own place with a housing subsidy. Joan is successful in continuing her education and is no longer moving from place to place. She thanks Project WISE for helping her and for believing in her abilities. Maria is working and feels she has more endurance in dealing with the stress in her life. She stated in a follow-up interview, "Project WISE helped me know where I am coming from and change the way I think and problem solve."
>
> None of these women are completely economically self-sufficient, as are few of us; they depend on public assistance and other forms of support for child care, medical care, and housing. At the same time, each of these women now describes having a greater sense of self-confidence and self-esteem and as being less subject to depression or anxiety. As Eva recently stated, "I'm still quiet, but I'm not afraid or ashamed." For each of the women, and the many others like them, it is important that her life story be placed in the context of welfare reform. Social workers can be catalysts for the voices of women to be expressed and heard and for innovative responses to be tried. In the quest for economic self-sufficiency, the hidden barriers can be just as important to overcome as the obvious barriers. (East, 1999a, p. 302)

Social Work and Homelessness

While homelessness is a prominent contemporary social problem, it is not a new phenomenon (Hopper & Baumohl, 1996). Historically, homelessness—represented by the "vagrants" of the mid-eighteenth century, the "tramps" of the turn of the century, and the "victims" of the depression—has been related to economic decline. The current crisis of homelessness was precipitated by economic recession in the early 1980s and magnified by a lack of affordable rental housing, larger numbers of persons with poverty and near poverty income levels (including many who work full-time), increased incidence of domestic violence, and reductions in federally funded programs (National Coalition for the Homeless [NCH], 2002a). These cutbacks embrace both lower levels of funding for programs—such as public assistance, housing supports, food stamps, and Medicaid—and stricter eligibility requirements for these categorical programs. Experts predict that the decreased availability of public assistance for families and the virtual elimination of other safety net programs such as General Assistance will lead to even greater levels of homelessness (NCH, 2002a).

Misconceptions about Homelessness

A number of misconceptions prevail in the general public's understanding of homelessness. For example, many believe that the majority of persons who are homeless have personal problems like mental illness or drug abuse. One recent study found that 90.8 percent of those surveyed in 1500 random telephone interviews believed that drug and alcohol abuse was a main contributing cause of homelessness (Link et al., 1996). In fact, homelessness is more likely to be precipitated by economic and social forces than by personal problems. Economically stressed families with children account for about 40 percent of the population who will become homeless (NCH, 2002b). Only 5 percent of those people with serious mental illnesses are homeless (NCH, 1999a). While there are a disproportionate number of people who have addictions who are homeless, the vast majority of people with addictions never become homeless (NCH, 1999b). The escalation of homelessness is clearly linked to socioeconomic factors such as an insufficient supply of suitable, affordable housing; an expansion of poverty in both urban and rural areas; and declining buying power—lower wages in the face of increasing prices.

A second misconception is that shelter space is available to relieve the problem of homelessness across the country. As a matter of fact, there is a disparity between the number of people who are homeless and the available shelter beds in almost every major urban area. Results of a recent study of 27 cities in the United States indicate that 37 percent of the requests for emergency shelter were unmet because of resource limitations (NCH, 2002c). Moreover, shelter space may be underutilized because of potential users' concerns about personal safety, rather than empty beds being indicative of an overabundance of beds. As for rural areas, very few shelters are even available.

A third misconception is that people who are homeless are unemployed. Data indicate that about 40 percent of those who are homeless are employed; however, there is certainly a link between being homeless and being poor. "Being poor can mean that one is an illness, an accident, or a paycheck away from homelessness" (NCH, 2003, p. 1). The recent economic recession has increased the instability of the job market, exacerbating the already precarious position of people who are poor. "In every state, no one earning minimum wage can afford a one- or two-bedroom apartment at Fair Market Rent" (p. 1).

A fourth misconception is that government initiatives are meeting both the crisis and long-term needs related to people who are homeless. Instead, experts on homelessness portray the government response at all levels as a reluctant, gradual, and only partial response to the growing crisis of homelessness and lack of housing. In fact, government spending on housing was reduced dramatically in the 1980s after President Carter left office: Funding for subsidized housing programs was cut by 81 percent and rental assistance programs by 72 percent (First, Rife, & Toomey, 1995). Some estimates indicate that as few as one-third of those qualifying for housing assistance actually receive it (NCH, 2002a). Although recently the U.S. Department of Housing and Urban Development (HUD) has made a commitment to deal with housing issues, very few initiatives are fully funded. Applicants may have to wait almost three years for an apartment in public housing and over two years for Section 8 rental assistance vouchers. HUD estimates indicate that about 5 million low-income households that qualify do not as yet receive housing assistance of any kind.

Incidence of Homelessness

It's difficult to determine exactly how many people are homeless. In part, this question is difficult to answer because "homelessness is a temporary circumstance—not a permanent condition" (NCH, 2002c); "point in time" counts, thus, are likely to underestimate the number of people who have experienced homelessness. It is also difficult to answer because many people who are homeless live in locations researchers might miss—in automobiles, in campgrounds, or with friends and relatives.

Given these constraints, there are some differences in opinion as to how many people in the United States are homeless. The first U.S. Census Bureau count in 1990 concluded that there were 178,828 people in shelters and 49,793 people living on the streets during a designated 24-hour period (U.S. Department of Commerce, 1990). Most homeless advocates criticized these figures as being gross underestimates because of large numbers of people missed by Census employees and because of the underlying false assumption that a "point in time" count would reveal the pervasiveness of homelessness as a social problem.

In contrast, in that same year, researchers conducted anonymous telephone surveys of a random sample of 1500 people in the 20 largest metropolitan areas in the United States (Link, Phelan, & Bresnahan, 1995). Respondents were asked if they had ever considered themselves homeless, including times they may have doubled up with friends or relatives. Study results indicate that 14 percent of those surveyed had been homeless at some time, and 4 percent indicated that they had been homeless at some time during the past 5 years. A 1994 follow-up study with the same respondents defined homelessness more precisely. When doubling up was included, the lifetime rate of homelessness was 15 percent, and the rate for the last 5 years was 3.6 percent. More explicitly, the researchers estimated that 6.5 percent had been literally homeless at some point in their lives. Of this subgroup, people were homeless for an average of 80 days, during which time 66 percent spent nights in cars and 25 percent spent nights in tents, boxes, or other makeshift housing. Alarmingly, 41 percent reported being hungry and 42 percent reported being assaulted or robbed. Based on their studies, these researchers estimate that 12 million people in the United States have experienced homelessness at some time in their lives. Their estimate is a staggering 18 million when doubling up is taken into consideration. Certainly, there are limitations to this study, including its sampling base and sample size, and the fact that it excludes rural areas from its purview. One can safely conclude that the 1990 Census Bureau study underestimates the extent of homelessness and that the social problem of homelessness is more pervasive than most realize.

Homelessness and Families. Families may well be the fastest-growing segment of the people who are homeless, constituting about 40 percent of those who become homeless (NCH, 2001). "For families, homelessness often means a weary progression from one place to another: living with relatives or friends for short periods of time, moving to shelters for 30 days, and then moving again" (First, Rife, & Toomey, 1995, p. 1333).

Typically, whether receiving public assistance or working full-time, families who are homeless are unable to afford housing because of their marginal financial circumstances. Domestic violence also contributes to homelessness among women and children. Some studies indicate that as many as 35 to 50 percent of the women who live in shelters have fled abusive situations (NCH, 1999c). Finally, homelessness itself contributed to the breakup of families. For example, some family shelters have policies that prohibit men and older boys from living at the shelter, and some parents may place their children in foster care or leave them with friends or relatives to avoid the insecurity of being without a home (Shinn & Weitzman, 1996).

Homelessness is particularly disorganizing for children. A review of research shows that homeless children experience poor nutrition, developmental delays, poor health, physical disabilities, educational underachievement, and psychological and behavioral problems (Rafferty & Shinn, 1994). Shinn and Weitzman (1996) report that "data from the National Health Interview Survey show that children who have moved three or more times are more likely to have emotional and behavioral problems, to repeat a grade, and to be suspended or expelled from school" (p. 118). Multiple school transfers, prolonged absence from school, lack of quiet space for homework, or the chaos of living on the streets further impedes learning.

Homelessness among Veterans. About 40 percent of the men who are homeless are veterans (NCH, 1999d). While many are Vietnam-era veterans, recent trends show an increase in homelessness among veterans with no combat experience but with an increased presence of risk factors such as mental illness and substance abuse. The results of one exploratory study on problems confronting veterans who are homeless indicate three major sources of difficulties: problems in the areas of health and mental health; problems related to resources, such as lack of employment opportunities, housing, and transportation; and problems in the general public's attitude toward them, such as rejection, prejudice, lack of respect, and fearfulness (Applewhite, 1997).

Military service has the reputation of providing numerous benefits, including education and job training, preferential consideration for civil service positions, and entitlements such as health care, low-cost home loans, and retirement pensions. In reality, high unemployment and limited education among veterans contribute to their problem with homelessness.

Homelessness in Rural Areas. A 1990 statewide survey of rural and nonurban homelessness found that people who are homeless in rural areas are "younger, are more likely to be single women or mothers with children, are more highly educated, and are less likely to be

BOX 11.1
Social Work Profile

Homeless and Housing Services

It all began when an undergraduate social work project transported me from a rural area to an inner-city church that worked closely with residents of a nearby public housing project. I lived with a family in public housing during the month-long field experience. For me, it was a time of self-discovery through my experiences within that community of families. The immersion into the day-to-day life of poverty left me with a deep respect for people who are poor and a commitment to social justice that continues to influence my work as a social worker today.

Prior to my present position with a large agency that focuses its work on homelessness and housing development, I worked in a variety of child welfare settings—a residential group home for teenage girls, public child welfare, and a nonprofit family service agency. These positions taught me a lot about social work—working in a bureaucracy, balancing the demands of many systems, and seeing firsthand the pervasive influence of the socio-political-cultural context on human behavior and organizational decision-making.

Looking back, I realize that my approach to working with people has changed. There was a time early in my career that I just wanted to be able to "fix things" for people, and the truth be told, "fix the people," themselves. When I think back on my work, I can hear myself saying, "You must do this" and "You will do that." I guess I really thought I knew what was best for the families with whom I worked. How naïve I was to think my directives could lead to successful outcomes or lasting changes in behavior. Now my practice strategy is to "walk with" others—offering ideas, options, resources, and possibilities to clients. Today, I affirm that the choices made and directions taken are theirs. Timing is everything, as not everyone moves along at the same pace. The option that someone refuses today may become the perfect opportunity tomorrow.

My understanding of people's reactions and behaviors has shifted too. When I worked in child welfare, I distinctly remember reacting to the anger directed at me or at "the system." As a result, I characterized parents as unmotivated, uncooperative, obstinate, indolent, or obstructive. Had I listened more carefully to my clients, I think I would have discovered that underneath their anger was a pervasive sense of grief over the multitude of losses they had experienced—the loss of their children, their privacy, their sense of control, their hope for the future. Even today in working with people who are homeless, I recognize that they also experience a deep sense of loss—loss of pride, loss of dignity, loss of identity, loss of their past as well as the future, and sometimes alienation from family members and friends.

Our guests at the homeless shelter and participants in other agency programs come from all walks of life. They are doctors, managers, factory workers, college graduates and high school dropouts. Some struggle with addiction, others with chronic mental illness. Some have worked all of their lives; others have a history of multigenerational poverty. All of them share a common characteristic—that is strength in surviving adversity, a desire for jobs so they can pay their rent, affordable housing, and safe places for their children. This field of practice reinforces the professional ideal of justice for all and the recognition that all persons should be afforded the same rights and opportunities. My policy advocate role includes educating local politicians about needs and influencing policy formulation through linkages with state and national organizations.

---

disabled" (First, Rife, & Toomey, 1994, p. 104). Of the groups identified in the survey, 26.8 percent were young families and 31.2 percent were people who were employed full- or part-time. Further exploration of these data demonstrates differences between rural and urban homelessness. In sharp contrast to urban areas, "are the extensive presence of social supports for rural women and minimal roles that mental illness and substance abuse play in the homeless episodes of rural women" (Cummins, First, & Toomey, 1998, Discussion section, ¶ 1). However, family conflict and dissolution are likely to precipitate homelessness in both areas. The researchers conclude that a depressed rural economy, skyrocketing unemployment, gender inequality manifested in low wages for women, and a greater demand for low-cost housing contribute to the crisis of homelessness in the rural areas of the United States.

The Federal Response to Homelessness

The major federal legislation that addresses homelessness is the Stewart B. McKinney Homeless Assistance Act of 1987 (P.L. 100-77), now known as the McKinney-Vento Homeless Assistance Act. This act provides the mechanism for a federal response to the crisis of homelessness. It established programs such as rehabilitation of SRO (single-room occupancy) housing; transitional housing; housing programs for persons with disabilities who are homeless; health care provisions; food assistance; veterans' provisions; emergency food and shelter programs; and education, training, and community services programs. Unfortunately, appropriations have not matched authorizations, resulting in the underfunding of programs. Additionally, programs are fragmented among numerous federal agencies, including the Department of Health and Human Services (DHHS), the Department of Housing and Urban Development (HUD), the Department of Education, the Department of Agriculture, the Department of Veterans Affairs, the Department of Labor, the Department of Transportation, the General Services Administration, and the Federal Emergency Management Agency (FEMA).

In order to organize services to people who are homeless within communities more effectively, the McKinney Act requires communities applying for funds to develop a cooperative Comprehensive Housing Affordability Strategy (CHAS) that describes both the emergency and the long-term needs of people in the community who are homeless, as well as their agreed-upon strategies for meeting these identified short- and long-term needs. "CHAS is important because it signifies the first time the federal government has officially recognized the relationship between the shortage of affordable housing and the crisis of contemporary homelessness" (Johnson, 1995, p. 1343).

Social Work's Response to Homelessness

Social workers need to develop innovative programs to address the root causes as well as the personal effects of homelessness. First, Rife, and Toomey (1995) propose multifaceted social work strategies that include life-sustaining services, rehabilitative services, and policy and program advocacy. *Life-sustaining programs* meet the day-to-day needs of persons who are homeless, such as access to emergency food and shelter, transitional housing, and social services. Case management is playing an increasingly prominent role in these types of programs and services. Research findings indicate that providing subsidies for rent is a critical component of successful transitional programs (Shlay, 1994). *Rehabilitative services* go beyond meeting basic needs. They include programs such as education, job training, addiction treatment programs, and domestic violence services "to help prepare families for self-sufficiency" (First, Rife, & Toomey, p. 1335). Finally, *policy and program advocacy* is essential for strengthening local, state, and federal responses to homelessness, and ensuring that social policies consider the realities of situations faced by people who are homeless. Long-term solutions necessarily encompass social and economic development initiatives and redress inequalities and discrimination that create obstacles in the road to self-sufficiency. Furthermore, people who are homeless experience empowerment through their own direct involvement in social action and advocacy efforts to counteract the effects of oppression, alienation, and hopelessness.

Social Work Highlights. One community agency that deals with issues of homelessness has among its services a transitional housing program and two shelters—one for single women and one for families. The program director shared two success stories in a recent newsletter (*Homeless Services News,* 1997):

> A woman and her four children entered into the Transitional Housing Program from the agency's family shelter with goals to obtain her GED, pay off her debts, and obtain permanent housing. Obstacles she had to overcome were domestic violence, transportation problems, and a backlog of community service hours for Project Head Start. While in the program, she paid her program fees promptly, paid her utility bill on time, and attended groups and other transitional program activities regularly. Within only six months time, she took and passed three of the six tests required for her GED, paid off many of her debts, and obtained permanent housing. Through her successful participation in the transitional program she has demonstrated a genuine desire and ability to change her life and give her children a better future.
>
> About a month ago a woman and her two children came to the agency looking for shelter. All of the other shelters in the area were full, but we were able to make room for them in our family shelter. The mother was very anxious; she really didn't know what to do first to deal with the many problems holding her back from becoming independent. Among the obstacles she faced were a $1,000 utility bill, no income, at least a month's delay before she would receive public assistance, and difficulties with arranging child care that prevented her from finding employment. Despite all of this, she got up early every morning to put in job applications and to locate houses to clean. She knew that she had to clear up her utility bill before she could get into housing and that she would need rent and deposit money as well. With determination she demanded money from her husband for utilities, and made up the difference with a utility grant and a lot of hard work. She has located a suitable, affordable apartment, takes her children along with her to clean houses, and hopes to locate reliable child care so that she can obtain stable employment.

The case manager with the program says this about her experiences at the shelter: "What I like most about my job is working one-on-one with the clients. When they first come in, they have a feeling of hopelessness. By the time they leave the shelter program, they've achieved goals they never thought possible."

Social Work and Unemployment

Fluctuations in the economy present structural problems that directly affect the workforce. Policymakers consider unemployment, at least at certain levels, tolerable and normal. However, social workers regard joblessness as a social welfare issue that has dramatic effects. "Access to employment opportunities remains the cornerstone of individual economic security; poverty and inequality of income are primarily a function of the labor market"

(Root, 1993, p. 334). The absence of equitable allocations of employment opportunities exacts human costs.

The Economy and Unemployment

Reports indicate that, in 2003, about 9 million persons or about 6 percent of the workers in the United States experienced job loss as compared to the mid-1990s when the rate of unemployment was about 5 percent (Bureau of Labor Statistics [BLS], 2003a). These figures are deceptive, however, as some population groups and areas of the country have been much harder hit by unemployment. For example, unemployment rates are lowest in South Dakota (3.3 percent) and highest in Louisiana (7.4 percent), Michigan (7.4 percent), Washington (7.5 percent), Alaska (7.9 percent), and Oregon (8.1 percent) (BLS, 2003b). Metropolitan areas have suffered even higher levels of job loss. Data from June 2003 indicate that "fourteen metropolitan areas registered unemployment rates of at least 10.0 percent, seven of which were located in California and five in Texas" (BLS, 2003c, p. 1). Furthermore, note the differences in the July 2003 unemployment rate among the White (5.5 percent), Black (11.1 percent), and Hispanic (8.2 percent) civilian labor force (BLS, 2003a).

In addition to unemployment, causes of changes in economic status include decreases in hours or pay; the increase in jobs in the service sector along with the decrease in higher-paying jobs in manufacturing and technology; the rapid expansion of part-time and casual positions with neither medical benefits nor retirement packages; and family-related events such as separation, divorce, or desertion. Single-parent families often lose the safety net of a second income, leading to an increased likelihood of economic instability.

Calculating Unemployment Rates. In the United States, economists base unemployment figures on monthly surveys of a random sample of households. They figure jobless rates as a ratio of unemployed persons to the total labor force. These rates probably underestimate unemployment because they exclude those who are not actively seeking employment. Moreover, the static jobless rate is portraying a dynamic condition: Some people are returning to work, while yet others are becoming unemployed.

Types of Unemployment. Root (1993) identifies several different types of joblessness:

- *Cyclical unemployment* results from recessions or economic fluctuations in the demand for workers.
- *Seasonal joblessness* is caused by periodic fluctuations in weather-dependent industries such as fishing, farming, and construction.
- *Frictional unemployment* is the unemployment suffered by people who are temporarily out of work because they are changing jobs.
- *Structural unemployment* occurs when people's skills fall short of new requirements or when discrimination occurs in employment practices.

Structural factors contribute to disproportionate unemployment rates among ethnic minorities and other oppressed populations. Distinguished by race, age, disability, sexual affiliation, and class, oppressed groups "must deal with discrimination, job rationing, and the consequences of exclusion and labor market disadvantage that undercut their ability to care for themselves and their dependents and forces some into a life of chronic unemployment, underemployment, poverty, and in some cases, institutionalization" (Briar, 1988, p. 6).

The Consequences of Unemployment

Unemployment leads to a number of challenges for individuals, families, and communities (Root, 1993). For individuals and families, psychological, social, and financial resources are stressed. Since work is fundamental to an adult's sense of competence, self-esteem typically plummets with job termination (Berk, 2004). People who are unemployed experience multiple losses, such as losses of family, self-esteem, social identity, and work-related friendships and social support (Root, 1993). Direct and indirect consequences of unemployment include depression, suicide, mental illness, spouse and child abuse, familial conflict, divorce, substance abuse, delinquency and crime rate increase, eating and sleeping disorders, and somatic complaints such as stress-related illness. Unemployment affects life expectations, feelings of well-being, and even life expectancy. Effects of unemployment may even be multigenerational. The unemployed status of parents can affect children's behavior, school achievement, and attitude toward work. Factors such as increases in marginal employment, decreases in standard of living, and lengthy bouts of joblessness all exacerbate the consequences of unemployment (Hooper-Briar & Seck, 1995).

Communities also bear the collective effects of unemployment. Waves of unemployment can mean bankruptcy, business failure, lost tax revenues, and resultant cutbacks in services. Ironically, in the face of cutbacks, unemployment increases demands for social services.

Ultimately, unemployment must be understood in the context of the world community. The economic interdependence of globalization suggests that both the effects of and solutions for unemployment are global challenges. Where unemployment is pervasive and oppression enduring, adaptations to the crisis of unemployment can become ingrained in the culture. Cultural traits such as a persistent sense of resignation, entrenched depression, and unsettled relationships, generated as a consequence of chronic unemployment, represent "the presence of a culturally transmitted traumatic stress syndrome that is induced by exploitation" (Cattell-Gordon, 1990, p. 41).

Unemployment Benefits

Provisions under two social insurance programs secure sources of income for people who are temporarily unemployed or have work-related injuries. *Unemployment compensation* originated in the Social Security Act of 1935. A combined state–federal venture, unemployment compensation provides temporary compensation in the form of partial wage replacement for people who have lost their jobs. *Workers' compensation* benefits cover individuals who cannot work because of work-related diseases or injuries. States fund and direct this program. Benefits and compensation for both unemployment and workers' compensation vary widely from state to state. Neither program is means tested. While social work plays a minimal role in these programs, people enrolled in these programs could benefit from direct social work involvement, particularly counseling to address unemployment and work-related health issues (Jones, 1995).

Over the years, policymakers have debated whether people are entitled to employment. Legislation—particularly the Employment Act of 1946 (P.L. 304)—affirmed opportunities for employment rather than guaranteeing jobs. Likewise, the programs of the War on Poverty in the 1960s followed the same principle of providing opportunities, and delineated governmental responsibilities for providing job training and education. The Manpower Development and Training Act (P.L. 87-415), which provided training for the poor and institutionalized, codified this responsibility.

Services for People Who Are Unemployed

Social workers can bring a holistic approach to unemployment problems (Briar, 1988). There is a critical need to confront the bias in the commonly held belief that the unemployed are jobless because something is wrong with them. Among the ranks of the unemployed are workers who are dislocated from jobs because of layoffs and industrial plant closings. These displaced workers join the ranks of those trying to find new positions in a technological society that demands education and skills on the part of those who acquire higher-paying jobs. Lower-wage service occupations create a class of underemployed. Quite often practitioners, concerned with the effects of unemployment, work in employee assistance programs. The stresses of unemployment may also be present as an overt or underlying factor in the problems brought to family agencies and mental health centers.

A framework for occupational problem solving places the job search in the person: situation context (Briar, 1988). The job search process provides an opportunity for self-examination in relation to the job market. A review of transferable skills develops a sense of competence about one's abilities which, in itself, is empowering. Two parallel processes deal with confronting the issues of job loss and job acquisition.

The Assessment and Stabilization of Symptoms

1. Assessing and addressing symptoms.
2. Normalizing the symptoms of job problems.
3. Assessing and addressing loss.
4. Assessing strengths and social supports.
5. Developing an interim stabilization plan.

Acquisition of a Job

1. Promoting self-assessment for short- and long-term job goals.
2. Promoting an assessment of the labor market.
3. Capacity building for self-promotion. (p. 52)

In addition to problem solving, occupational social workers may assist clients directly in securing entitlements. Social work activities in this resource management function include, at the microlevel, providing educational materials to workers; at the midlevel, building coalitions to promote occupational safety in the workplace; and at the macrolevel, providing public hearing testimony about unemployment (Shanker, 1983).

Social Work Highlights. Employee assistance programs (EAPs) have their roots in occupational social work. A business or industry may offer its own EAP or contract for this employee benefit with social service agencies or medical providers. Frequently located at the workplace site, EAPs provide an array of services that have advantages for both employers and employees. The primary focus of the EAP is to foster employee retention and prevent job loss. Employers benefit from programs that ultimately reduce employee absenteeism, increase employee productivity, and provide a drug-free work environment.

Among the services provided are personal and family counseling for stress, mental health issues, and chemical dependency. In the event of a plant closing or other reductions in force, EAP personnel can play an integral role in job loss and transition services. One client who will benefit from such EAP services is Mike Smith. When he calls his family together for a conference, Mike is still wondering how he will find the words to break the news that he has lost his job. "There's no easy way to say this," he begins. "I got a layoff notice today. I hope I won't be out of work too long. Your mom still has her job, but money will be tight."

His children respond with a lot of questions: Will they have to move? Are jobs available? What is going to happen to them? They also volunteer ways they can help. Later in the evening, Mike and his wife Rita consider their options. Mike resolves to take his supervisor's suggestion and make an appointment with the social worker in the company's employee assistance program. He wants information about unemployment benefit programs, job placement services, and retraining options, and he needs to sort out his feelings about his pending job loss so that he can deal effectively with the crisis it is precipitating.

EAP social workers provide services related to unemployment that encompass counseling with workers who are identified for layoff, consulting with managers and union representatives for planned organizational supports, and representing the interests of the unemployed in the community.

Social Work in Criminal Justice

The criminal justice system is an expanding arena for social work. Historically, the field of criminal justice was built on a law enforcement foundation, emphasizing punishment for criminal behavior. Although social workers acquired legitimacy in juvenile services early in the twentieth century, they have played a limited role in adult corrections. Criminal justice personnel often regarded social workers, because of their value orientation about people, as unwelcome professionals, considering them too soft to work in corrections. Some residual bias against social workers in law enforcement and criminal justice persists today. However, recently, social workers have expanded their roles to provide the following services:

- Community-based rehabilitation services
- Diversionary programs
- Supports for convicts' reintegration into their communities
- Counseling for prison inmates
- Social services for families of criminals
- Advocacy for victims of crime

To achieve credibility in the public criminal justice system, social workers must be educationally prepared to understand crime and delinquency, the nuances of working with involuntary clients, judicial processes and court procedures, and the roles of various professionals in this interdisciplinary field.

Crime and Delinquency

Simply put, crime comprises acts or behaviors that are contrary to the law. In other words, criminal activity violates public laws and moral codes. Criminals may have committed crimes against persons, property, or the state. A compilation of annual crime statistics, the *Uniform Crime Reports* (UCR), determines crime trends based on felony index crimes, including violent crimes of murder and nonnegligent manslaughter, forcible rape, robbery, and aggravated assault, and the property crimes of burglary, larceny-theft, motor vehicle theft, and arson. It also includes indexes of misdemeanors or lesser offenses. Preliminary data for 2002 show a 0.2 percent decrease in the National Crime Index as compared to data in 2001 and significantly lower than in the early 1990s (U.S. Department of Justice [DOJ], 2003a).

Delinquency. Juvenile criminal offenders are classified as delinquent or as minors in need of assistance. Delinquent behavior ranges from status offenses, or misconduct particular to juveniles such as running away and curfew violations, to criminal violations of the law. Most referrals to juvenile court—45 percent—are for property crimes. Crimes against persons, the most serious charge, represent 23 percent of the delinquency cases, public

BOX 11.2
Reflections on Empowerment

Delinquency Prevention Programs

Delinquency prevention efforts in many communities begin with elementary-school-age children. For example, Donna Banks coordinates the EMPOWER Program in the Hudson School District. Professional staff from the Court Services Delinquency Prevention Program, the local family service agency, and the school district, along with leadership from the parent–school organization, designed the curriculum for the EMPOWER program.

Five participating elementary schools set aside an hour each week to implement the EMPOWER curriculum at all grade levels. The curriculum features monthly themes such as "Let's Be Friends," "Let's Work Together," "Let's Make a Difference," and "Let's Learn about Our World." Activities during each month include rallies, poster contests, community service projects, essays, field trips, and discussion groups. Donna recruits parents and community volunteers to assist with program activities.

The direct influence on delinquency prevention is difficult to measure. However, since implementing the EMPOWER program, the schools have noted reduced truancy, higher involvement of parents in school programming, and an increase in students' participation in extracurricular activities. Through school-based, empowerment-oriented prevention programs, children develop positive feelings about themselves, have opportunities to play and work cooperatively, resolve disputes with other children in productive ways, and learn the difference between right and wrong.

Social workers also recognize the importance of community-based delinquency prevention activities such as youth clubs, structured recreational programs, organized sports, and youth volunteer programs. All of these programs provide purposeful activities for community youth. Without exception, prevention-oriented programs for youth set goals related to enhancing decision making, fostering good citizenship, and promoting healthy peer relationships. These goals foster empowerment.

order offenses account for 21 percent, drug offenses account for 11 percent (Sickmund, 2003). The juvenile court load is four times greater now than in 1960. Sixty-four percent of all delinquency cases involve youths 15 years old or younger.

The age at which jurisdiction can be transferred to criminal courts and the circumstances allowing these waivers vary from state-to-state; however, the trend is toward making it easier for juveniles to be tried as adults. Most stipulate multiple ways to impose adult sanctions on juveniles (Sickmund, 2003). Twenty-three states and the District of Columbia stipulate at least one condition for which no minimum age is specified for transfer to the criminal courts (Sickmund, 2003). Alarmingly, nearly 20,000 youths are housed in adult prisons, including about 3,500 youths sharing living spaces with adult prisoners (Juvenile Court Centennial Initiative, n.d.). This failure to separate youths places them at risk for sexual assault, suicide, and recidivism. A recent report, *And Justice for Some,* describes the racial disparities present in the juvenile justice system: Three out of four youths imprisoned are minority youths; youths waived to criminal courts are more likely minority youths; and imprisonment rather than community-based services or parole is the most likely course of action for minority youths (Poe-Yamagata & Jones, 2000). As many as 20 percent of the youths in prison have serious mental disorders, between 20 and 50 percent have attention deficit hyperactivity disorder, 12 percent have mental retardation, and more than 30 percent have learning disabilities (Aron & Mears, 2003).

In many states, juveniles are accountable for misbehavior that would not be considered criminal if they were adults. These status offenses are noncriminal behaviors classified as delinquent. Status offenses include running away, truancy, incorrigible behavior, curfew violations, and liquor violations. Law enforcement officials refer fewer than half of all status offenders to the court system (Sickmund, 2003).

Juvenile justice encompasses activities in both the criminal justice system and the child welfare system. Consequently, social workers have been influential in the development of juvenile justice. Today, social workers are more likely to be involved in juvenile than in adult corrections.

Crime and Punishment

A number of theories seek to explain criminal behavior. Early works, such as those of Cesare Lombroso and William Sheldon, supported a relationship between physical features and criminality. Lombroso identified physical and facial features characteristic of early forms of evolutionary development. He linked these subhuman features to criminal tendencies. Sheldon identified distinctive body types that predicted personality and temperament that predisposed people to criminal behavior. These early theories are dismissed today.

The early-twentieth-century physical and biological explanations of criminal behavior were replaced as support for social and psychological explanations gained acceptance. Psychological theories and social control theories present the genesis of criminal behavior as mental disorders or antisocial acts.

Punishment or Rehabilitation? Although there is no consensus about how to deal with crime, the position we take influences how we regard criminal behavior and how we treat offenders and their victims. Prominent positions in the history of corrections in the United States include retribution, deterrence, rehabilitation, reintegration, and control (Champion, 2001).

Retribution is probably the oldest goal of correction systems. A revenge motive or an "eye-for-an-eye" doctrine uses punishment to get even. Retribution is a factor in the current justice or "just-deserts" model. This model equates the penalty with the severity of the crime to provide a fair punishment for the criminal and a protection for society.

Ideally, *deterrence* is a strategy for preventing criminal behavior. To accomplish this, lawmakers establish the severity of punishments according to the seriousness of a crime. Administering punishments employs the principle of distributive justice. This philosophy promotes the establishment of criminal sanctions for all offenses, sentencing guidelines to which the courts must adhere.

As a goal of corrections, *rehabilitation* emerged from the reformatory movement of the late nineteenth century. Zebulon Reed Brockway, the first warden of the Elmira State Reformatory in New York, was a correctional reformer who believed in rehabilitation rather than punishment. Brockway advocated educational and vocational training, indeterminate sentencing, and parole (Champion, 2001; Quam, 1995).

Offenders are incarcerated or confined in a prison setting to restrict their liberty and reform their behavior. Rehabilitation emphasizes education to develop vocational skills. Programs designed to achieve the *reintegration* goal of corrections assist offenders, upon their release from prison, to adapt and then reestablish themselves in the community. Halfway houses and other service centers aid transition of prisoners into community life. Finally, community-based programs that provide intensive supervision and monitoring of offenders' whereabouts and behavior *control* offenders who remain in their communities.

The Criminal Justice System

There are three major components of the criminal justice system: law enforcement, the courts, and corrections (Figure 11.1). *Law enforcement officials* serve various jurisdictions (e.g., city police officers, county sheriffs, state patrols, FBI agents, and other investigative personnel). Law enforcement officials investigate reports of crime and apprehend, arrest, and book suspects. Persons who allegedly violate the law enter the *court system* for preliminary hearings, arraignments, and trials. Personnel in the court system include prosecution and defense attorneys and judiciary officials. Judges sentence those found guilty. Sentencing options include incarceration, fines, court supervision, and/or community service. Finally, *correctional institutions* include jails, prisons, reformatories, state and federal facilities, and penitentiaries.

Decisions and Dispositions. There are more felonies committed than reports made, more reports of crime than actual arrests, and of those arrested, not all are convicted, placed on probation, or sentenced to serve time in jail. However, in spite of a declining rate of crime, more adults than ever are in prison. At midyear in 2002, 1,426,118 prisoners were incarcerated in federal and state facilities, an increase under federal jurisdiction of 5.8 percent and under state jurisdiction of 0.9 percent (Harrison & Karberg, 2003). Local

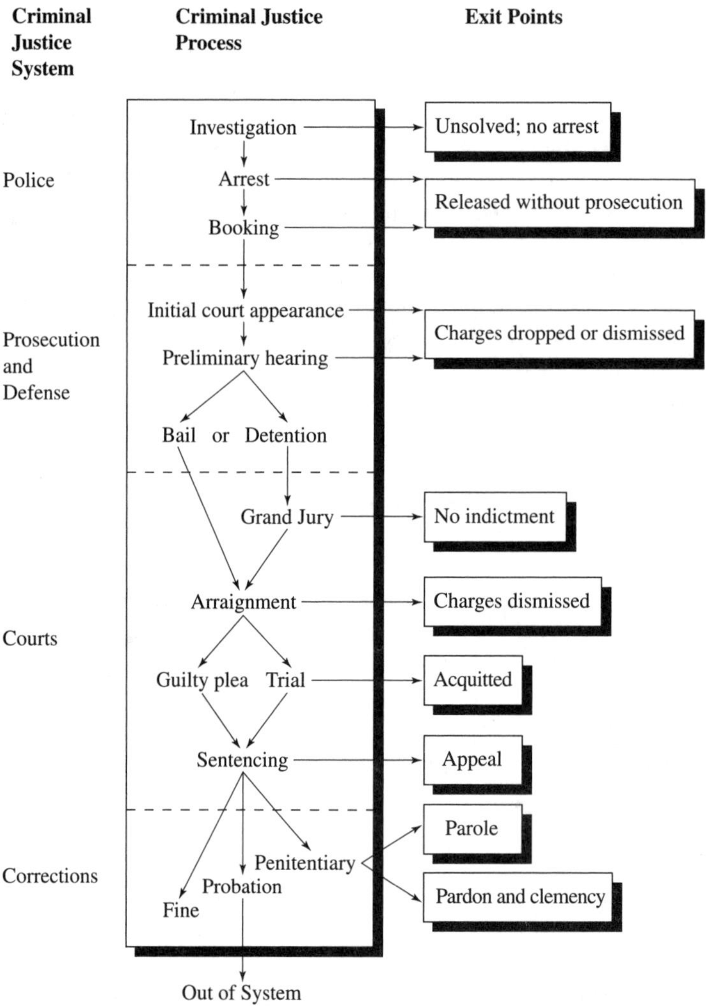

FIGURE 11.1 Flowchart of the Criminal Justice System

authorities held or supervised 737,912 offenders. The U.S. Department of Justice reported that, in 2001:

- The Nation's prison and jail population exceeded 2 million inmates for the first time.
- State and Federal correctional authorities held 88,776 noncitizens, up from 87,917 (1.0%) at midyear 2001.
- An estimated 12% of black males, 4% of Hispanic males, and 1.6% of white males in their twenties and early thirties were in prison or jail. (p. 1)

With respect to the likelihood of being incarcerated in a state or federal prison:

- Lifetime chances of a person going to prison are higher for men (11.3%) than for women (1.8%) [and for] blacks (18.6%) and Hispanics (10%) than for whites (3.4%)
- Based on current rates of first incarceration, an estimated 32% of black males will enter State or Federal prison during their lifetime, compared to 17% of Hispanic males and 5.9% of white males. (DOJ, 2003b, Lifetime likelihood section)

Special Problems. Several special problems confront the criminal justice system: drug or alcohol dependence, mental illness, mental retardation, HIV/AIDS, sex offenders, and an aging inmate population (Champion, 2001). There is a high correlation between crime and drug and alcohol abuse. Offenders who are chemically dependent often commit crimes while under the influence of drugs, continue to use drugs even when they are in jail, and experience a higher rate of failure with respect to probation and parole. In addition

> the "revolving door" alcoholic, the person repeatedly arrested for assault or drunken driving, is not reformed or cured by being jailed nor is he or she a deterrent to other drinkers, yet the public (and, indirectly, the legislature, judges and juries) continues to call for tougher laws with longer jail sentences rather than detoxification centers. (Hunter & Pudim, 1985, pp. 82–83)

Prisons also lack specialized programs and trained staff to deal with the unique needs of people with mental illnesses or developmental disabilities. The inability to provide proper mental health care in the criminal justice system results in a perpetuation of mental disorders and unusual discipline problems. Professionals generally agree that people who commit sex offenses (for example, rape, prostitution, child sexual molestation, voyeurism, and exhibitionism) need some form of intensive counseling or therapeutic intervention. In addition, older offenders have special needs for health care and environmental adaptations. Community reintegration is particularly challenging when members of older offenders' potential support systems are also elderly (Edwards, 1983).

Social Work Role in Criminal Justice

Social work can trace its nineteenth-century social science roots to the National Conference of Charities and Correction and, thus, to concerns with criminal justice (Miller, 1995). While the early-twentieth-century emphasis of the profession turned away from the field of adult corrections, early social work leaders, such as Jane Addams and Sophonisba Breckenridge, spearheaded the move to separate juveniles from the adult court system. Their efforts led to the establishment of the Illinois juvenile court system, the first juvenile court in the United States.

This legislation articulated three distinctive features of the juvenile court movement:

> 1. the creation of a separate court of justice for children because children are different,
> 2. the recognition that juvenile court is not a criminal court, but a civil court, emphasizing the rehabilitation and treatment of children, and
> 3. the creation of a system of probation. (Lathrop, 1917 as cited in Roush, 1996)

Social work professionals work in each area of the criminal justice system. *Police social workers* often work with law enforcement officers in situations involving domestic

BOX 11.3
Reflections on Diversity

Hate Crimes

Based on several legislative actions, the federal government defines hate crimes as "the violence of intolerance and bigotry, intended to hurt and intimidate someone because of their race, ethnicity, national origin, religion, sexual orientation, or disability" (DOJ, Community Relations Service, 2001, Hate Crime Section, ¶ 1). Enacted in 1990, the Hate Crime Statistics Act directed the Justice Department to collect data on crimes that "manifest prejudice based on race, religion, sexual orientation, or ethnicity" from local law enforcement agencies (National Criminal Justice Reference Service [NCJRS], n.d. a, ¶ 4). The Hate Crimes Sentencing Enhancement Act, a provision of the Violent Crime Control and Law Enforcement Act of 1994, further specifies that a hate crime is a crime against a person or property motivated by "the actual or perceived race, color, religion, national origin, ethnicity, gender, disability, or sexual orientation of any person" (¶ 3). State laws vary considerably in how they define protected statuses and hate crimes (Boeckmann & Turpin-Petrosino, 2002).

The Federal Bureau of Investigation (NCJRS, n.d. b) indicates that, during 2001, it received reports of 9,721 single-bias incidents, including 4,367 related to racial bias (44.9 percent), 2,098 related to ethnicity or national origin bias (21.6 percent), 1,828 related to religious intolerance (18.8 percent), 1,393 related to sexual orientation bias (14.3 percent), and 35 related to disability bias (0.4 percent). Over 12,000 people were victimized by these acts of violence against persons (64.6 percent) and property (34.7 percent). Among the locations for hate crime incidents are residences (30.9 percent); highways, roads, alleys, or streets (18.3 percent); and schools or colleges (10.1 percent).

The impact of hate crime is pervasive. Those personally victimized by hate crimes suffer the psychological consequences of oppression, marginalization, and fear, as do the members of groups to which those targeted by hate crimes belong (Humphreys, 2003). Research exploring the consequences of hate violence concluded that victims of such violence, like victims of assault and rape, felt powerless and found themselves more suspicious of others (Barnes & Ephross, 1994). Furthermore, "hate crimes often lead to retaliation and counterretaliation, which can lead to large-scale social unrest and even civil war" (Humphreys, p. 71). By definition, hate crimes represent significant violations of human rights.

Social workers can respond to hate violence in several ways, including working with those who have been victimized as well as those who have perpetrated hate violence; working with organizations, schools, and communities to promote acceptance of diversity and prevent hate violence; and promoting social policy that protects citizens against hate crimes (Humphreys, 2003; Swigonski, 2000).

---

violence, child abuse, and other types of victimization. As forensic social workers or specialists in other fields of practice, social workers are called on to provide court testimony. As *juvenile court officers,* social workers supervise delinquents, arrange for placements, and work in diversion programs. In adult courts, social workers who are *probation and parole officers* monitor the activities of offenders and prepare reports for the court on their rehabilitation. Finally, *social workers in correctional institutions* direct treatment groups with prisoners and provide family services and referrals.

Police Social Work. The police are often called on to respond to social service-type problems such as family disputes, domestic violence situations (child, partner, and elder abuse), sexual assault, and other types of victimization. Social workers employed by police departments work in tandem with law enforcement officials in situations requiring interprofessional cooperation. As members of a law enforcement team, social workers receive referrals for family-related problems. Typical reasons for referrals of juveniles include runaway behavior, vandalism, truancy, drug possession, theft, and problems at home. Referrals also include parental requests for help with their children's behavior, conflict with neighbors, domestic disputes, and suspected child abuse and elder abuse (Treger, 1995). The authority of the law enforcement agency can indeed be helpful in expediting referrals to community agencies. Typical responsibilities of police social workers include the following:

1. to establish solid working relationships with agencies providing emergency medical, psychiatric, and social work services in the community;
2. to provide the initial diagnostic assessment of clients referred to them by police officers, make appropriate referrals to local agencies, and follow-up to ensure that service was rendered;
3. to provide police officers with in-service training in crisis intervention techniques; and
4. to be on the job twenty-four-hours-a-day to serve as a back up resource for the policemen and policewomen on patrol. (Roberts, 1983, p. 101)

Cooperation with social service personnel enables police departments to provide crisis-oriented early intervention services, to offer police officers alternatives for dealing with socially oriented problems, to receive immediate social service consultation and assessment, to establish effective relationships between law enforcement and the social service system, and to provide referrals to appropriate community-based services (Corcoran, Stephenson, Perryman, & Allen, 2001; Dean et al., 2000; Treger, 1995).

Court Testimony and Forensic Social Work. Whether working in criminal justice or other fields of practice, social workers may be called upon to provide court testimony. To prepare themselves for their interactions with court systems, social workers need to "know more about how laws are made, changed, and enforced" (Barker & Branson, 2000, p. 12). They also need to understand the basis of court procedures, roles of various court-related personnel, rules for admissibility of evidence, and legal requirements regarding their relationships with and obligations to their clients.

As court witnesses, social workers must provide accurate information based on their personal knowledge. Effective testimony presents the facts clearly and avoids the use of jargon. Accurate records are important and may sometimes be entered as evidence. For example, child protective cases are heard through the juvenile court and family court. Child welfare workers provide testimony in matters regarding abuse, neglect, termination of parental rights, and permanency planning. To prepare for court appearances, social workers must collect documentation of their case activity, case history records, assessment materials, and, for credibility as expert witnesses, their own resume of professional experiences.

Forensic social workers specialize in working in the legal system. Specifically, their activities include "providing expert testimony in courts of law, investigating cases of possible criminal conduct, assisting the legal system in such issues as child custody disputes, divorce, nonsupport, delinquency, spouse or child abuse, mental hospital commitment, and relative's responsibility" (Barker & Branson, 2000, p. 1).

Juvenile Court Services. A number of major policy issues surface in juvenile justice, particularly with respect to formal court processing. Among these issues are court diversion programs to prevent further involvement in the criminal justice system, the implications of juvenile detention and institutionalization, the noncriminal nature of status offenses, the legal sanction of treatment alternatives, and the protection of due process (McNeece, 1983).

Critics of the juvenile justice system argue from two different points of view. Some argue that juvenile courts coddle young criminals, while other opponents argue that court jurisdiction over juveniles stigmatizes youths and encourages criminal behavior. Proponents suggest that help can and should be the domain of the juvenile court.

Social work practitioners employed in juvenile justice settings make treatment decisions, handle noncriminal status offenses and family-related problems, advocate the legal rights of the juvenile, and create a humane and equitable juvenile justice system (McNeece, 1983). Juveniles can benefit from diversionary programs to reform their behavior and prevent formal court involvement. Social workers provide supervision for youths in diversion and detention programs, interface with the child welfare system, schools, and families, and counsel youths.

Social workers are active in the prevention of delinquency through a variety of community-based efforts. The *National Center for the Assessment of Delinquent Behavior and Its Prevention* identifies a number of approaches to delinquency prevention. These strategies include correcting or controlling biological conditions and maladaptive psychological states, altering environmental conditions, developing social networks, reducing a delinquent's association with criminals, empowering youths for more socially acceptable problem solving, enhancing legitimate roles, providing positive recreational activity outlets, enhancing education and skill development, identifying consistent social expectations, providing sufficient economic resources, deterring youths from committing delinquent acts, and removing unnecessary labeling of youths as delinquents (Castelle, 1987).

Probation and Parole. *Probation* is a sentencing option that defers imprisonment. It specifies a period of time during which individuals under supervision can demonstrate appropriate behavior. The judge suspends imprisonment on the condition that individuals fulfill their terms of probation, including periodic visits to their court-designated probation officer (Barker, 2003).

Probation originated in Boston in the mid-1800s through the pioneering efforts of John Augustus and other social reformers and philanthropists. The volunteer probation program that rehabilitated petty thieves and drunkards was replaced in 1878 with a statute authorizing the mayor of Boston to set up a probation program and hire probation officers (Champion, 2001).

Court officers who supervise probationers and parolees are often social workers. Currently, probation officers, whether working with juveniles or adults, prepare social history information to aid in official decision making. They also provide supervision and casework services to offenders who are on probation.

Parole is a program granting early release from prison before offenders complete their full sentences. Judges base their decisions for parole on evidence of good conduct and rehabilitation. Court officers supervise parolees to ascertain that they follow the stipulations of their parole agreements.

Probation and parole officers must deal with their dual function of enforcing laws and providing casework services. They perform as agents of social control to resocialize offenders through their provision of services. In fact, many debate whether these social workers have the right to do anything beyond control and surveillance because of offenders' civil rights (Cunningham, 1983).

Social workers who work in probation and parole positions can facilitate solutions, link clients with appropriate community resources, and teach them acceptable behaviors for law-abiding community adjustment. Working as a court officer requires working within strict court-determined timeframes, preparing legal documents, refining teamwork skills, and often orchestrating various components in the court services system. Ethical issues emerge around limited confidentiality, nonjudgmentalism (particularly when the client behavior is repugnant or the crimes committed are heinous), and the locus of primary responsibility—clients and/or society (Scheurell, 1983).

Social Work in Correctional Facilities. Social workers in correctional facilities provide two types of services: supportive services within the institution and connections to resources in the community (Ivanoff, Smyth, & Finnegan, 1993). Within correctional facilities, social work services might be utilized in the areas of mental health, substance abuse, education, and vocational rehabilitation. Case coordination skills are also important because of the multifaceted nature of the problems, requiring numerous services. Social workers may work with inmates individually and in small groups to assist them in making behavioral changes and adapting to prison life by coping with an array of prison problems such as violence, sexual assault, psychological victimization, protection rackets, homosexuality, racial strife, and chemical dependence. As a source of empowerment, the interactions among women in groups have the potential for reversing negativity, discovering strengths, and identifying resources that will benefit women in and outside of prison (O'Brien, 2001). Furthermore, "anyone who is doing in-prison work needs to understand the context of women's incarceration and the disproportionate number of African-American and, in some states, Latina women who are incarcerated" (p. 48).

Social workers also provide services in the areas of "advocacy, brokerage, and linkage between incarcerated individuals and their community ties" (Ivanoff, Smyth, & Finnegan, 1993, p. 140). These networking services may be for the benefit of the prisoners themselves or their families. Additionally, "the social worker's input may influence decisions regarding a resident's movement within and between facilities as well as decisions made by parole boards and in competency hearings" (p. 140).

Social Work with Families of Prisoners. Social workers may be involved with families of prisoners as family members deal with the consequences of imprisonment. In 1999, 1.5 million children in the United States had a parent who was incarcerated (Mumole, 2000). Families may experience crisis at the point of arrest and arraignment, where notification may be delayed, visitation restricted, and procedures unclear. At sentencing, families must confront the realities of impending incarceration and the need to plan for the absence of a parent or other family member. During the term of imprisonment, the family must redefine

The majority of women in prison have dependent children.

the roles of its members, and at the same time struggle with the prison bureaucracy. Release of the family member precipitates a fourth crisis—how to deal with the reentry of the former prisoner into the family's daily life. Social workers and other human service workers can be instrumental in intervening with families at these times of crisis by offering positive support, providing concrete information, and planfully anticipating events (Carlson & Cervera, 1991).

Women in Prison. Women in prison face a unique set of problems (Singer, Bussey, Song, & Lunghofer, 1995). Many lack employment skills; have a history of sexual and physical victimization as well as problems with mental illness and substance abuse; and have an array of health complications, including AIDS, venereal disease, and pregnancy. Additionally, many female prisoners face separation from or the loss of custody of their children. In fact, recent data suggest that the majority of women in prisons have children (Mumole, 2000). Among the issues encountered are the effects of parent–child separations, stigma related to having a parent in prison, difficulties arranging for phone contacts and/or visitation, and problems resuming parenting roles after release from prison (Young & Smith, 2000). Research findings suggest that positive relationships with children and strengthened parenting skills result from family-oriented programming for mothers serving time in prison. One initiative sponsors a weeklong summer visitation program that houses children with host families in a community close to the prison. During the day, the children spend time with their mothers at the prison facility and engage in supervised parent–child activities.

Based on their survey of women in prison, Singer, Bussey, Song, and Lunghofer (1995) recommend improving conditions for women in prison by providing drug and alcohol screening; mental health services; confidential testing for and educational programs about sexually transmitted diseases and AIDS; medical services sensitive to women's issues, particularly pregnancy; parenting education; and regular supervised visits with children. They recommend working with women who are about to be discharged to develop links to supportive networks and community resources. Among the services women themselves identified as crucial upon release are housing, drug counseling, mental health counseling, financial aid, alcohol counseling, and education and training.

Victim Assistance Programs. A relatively new area of practice, social work with persons who have been victimized by crime, parallels social workers' involvement in criminal justice processes (Roberts, 1995). All 50 states, the District of Columbia, U.S. Virgin Islands, Guam, and Puerto Rico have compensation and assistance programs for victims and survivors of domestic violence, sexual assault, child abuse, drunk driving, homicide, and other crimes. Serving more than 5.6 million victims of crime a year, the funds for these services are distributed to states through the Office of Victims of Crime (OVC) of the U.S. Department of Justice (2002). The Crime Victims Fund was established by the 1984 Victims of Crime Act (VOCA) and collects its funds from fines, penalty assessments, and bond forfeitures from convicted federal offenders. In addition to providing compensation awards to individual crime victims, VOCA funds support community-based organizations that service crime victims, including domestic violence shelters, child abuse programs, hospitals, and victim service units in law enforcement agencies.

Victim assistance programs focus on developing services to address the aftermath of sexual assault or domestic violence as well as advocating the causes of persons who are victims of crimes with respect to developing restitution programs and creating changes in parole practices. These programs address the needs of clients, their families, or significant others; help persons in the legal process by monitoring the status of their cases, arranging court appearances, and assisting the client or survivors to deal with the details of victim compensation and restitution; and include prevention measures such as developing public awareness programs, setting up educational workshops, and providing in-service training for criminal justice personnel.

Mediation Programs. Mediation for victims and offenders is a relatively new area of social work practice (Umbreit, 1993). Mediation programs are often under the auspices of private agencies; however, there are an increasing number associated with public adult and juvenile criminal justice programs. "Victim–offender mediation provides an opportunity for crime victims to meet the offender, talk about the offense, express concerns, and negotiate a mutually agreeable restitution agreement" (p. 69). As mediators, social workers facilitate all phases of the process, including intake proceedings, separate preparation with the offender and with the person who was victimized, mediation, and follow-up.

Victim Witness Programs. Often based in the office of the prosecuting attorney, victim witness programs support the prosecution of offenders and assist those who have been victimized by crimes and the witnesses to the crimes. Social workers employed in victim witness program advocate the rights of persons victimized by crime, mediate between those victimized and the criminal justice system, and educate their clients about criminal justice systems and members of criminal justice systems about the dynamics of victimization (Gandy, 1983). Child and youth victim service programs are increasing in number. One example is centers that provide safe places for children to play while their parents are in court. Another program involves child advocacy services. Child advocates familiarize children with court procedures, accompany them to court, offer counseling and support around court-related issues, and link children and their families to appropriate social services.

Concluding Remarks

One would expect social workers to be integrally involved in delivering public services. Yet, during periods of its history as a developing profession, social work has disassociated itself from hands-on work in the provision of public welfare. In a quest for identity and elevated status as professionals, social workers often sought respectability and, accordingly, sought out a respectable clientele. Because, typically, the general public does not accord respectability to public services and their disenfranchised clientele, professionally educated social workers did not consider public services as part of their domain. Interestingly, however, despite the profession's attempt to remove itself from the provision of public services, most human service workers in this field are referred to as "social workers," regardless of their educational background. However, professional social workers have long been integrally involved in the public welfare domain at the policymaking level. Laudable attempts to eradicate social problems that affect the lives of the poor, the homeless, the unemployed, criminals, and otherwise disenfranchised persons have been made by social workers through their development and implementation of social welfare policy.

To achieve the social functioning and social justice mandates of the profession, social workers today must assert professional "ownership" of service delivery in public services. The contemporary challenge is for professional social workers themselves to be the connecting link at both the policy level and the level of direct implementation. Gone are the days when social workers could ignore the public domain and abdicate to nonprofessionals the social work mandate to work in partnership with the poor and the disenfranchised. If social workers are to make a difference in social welfare, they must be employed in public services.

CHAPTER

12 Social Work in Health, Rehabilitation, and Mental Health

Health is the cornerstone of human well-being and undergirds the quality of life. Broadly defined, a health problem is a condition or situation that results in disease, disability, death, or degradation. Maintaining health, recovering from illness, and overcoming disabilities depend upon people's ability to use resources in the physical and social environment. Inaccessible or inadequate health care compromises health, and social issues such as poverty, unemployment, stress, geographic isolation, and lack of social support networks exacerbate health problems. When people experience problems with health, challenges in social functioning often ensue.

Five basic premises reflect the close relationship between health and social functioning (Bracht, 1978). First, illness often disrupts people's equilibrium and capacity to cope. Institutionalization heightens the psychosocial effects of all types of illnesses, whether acute, chronic, or terminal. Second, social, cultural, and economic conditions influence people's ability to recover from illness, maintain health, and prevent disease. Third, social support and counseling complement medical treatment. Fourth, problems related to people's ability to access services often require community action. Finally, collaborative efforts of multiprofessional teams maximize health professionals' abilities to address the psychosocial and environmental complexities of medical problems.

Because health is central to effective social functioning, all social workers must consider the physical and social aspects of health. Moreover, many social workers work directly in health care services. This chapter examines the general implications of health care for social work and the specific applications of

- Social work in health systems
- Social work and AIDS
- Social work and physical disabilities
- Social work and mental health
- Social work and chemical dependency

Social Work in Health Systems

Virtually every specialty area in the health system—including emergency room services, oncology, pediatrics, general medicine and surgery, intensive care, rehabilitation, substance abuse programs, public health, and mental health—employs social workers. With the increased emphasis on cost-containment, health system planners are placing more emphasis on primary community-based and home health care (Keigher, 2000). The Bureau of Labor Statistics estimates that 30.22 percent of all social workers in the United States will be employed in health services in the year 2005 (Ginsberg, 1995). More specifically, a recent NASW membership survey indicates that 33.5 percent of the members who responded identified their area of practice as mental health, 12.7 percent as medical clinics, and 4.4 percent as substance abuse. This section explores the role of social work in health care by considering the system of health care as well as the various facets of the health care system that utilize social work services.

The System of Health Care

The health care system is a complex, comprehensive, interdisciplinary network of services comprising diagnosis, treatment, rehabilitation, health maintenance, and prevention activities for people of all ages and circumstances. Of specific interest to social work are those people who seek additional social supports when confronting issues of health, illness, and disability—the frail elderly; pregnant women; people with physical or mental disabilities or addictions; and people who are chronically ill, poor, homeless, or medically uninsured. Social workers are employed in a variety of health systems including public health, hospitals, medical clinics, health maintenance organizations, home health agencies, nursing homes, mental health clinics, and rehabilitation services.

Social Work's Contribution to Health Care

Social work services enable people who are ill or have a disability "to maintain, attain, or regain a mode of living that is satisfactory to them and helps them make a socially positive contribution to the human groups and communities of which they are a part" (Carlton, 1984, p. 8). The purposes of health care social work include

> to assist individuals, their families, and significant others to function when illness, disease, or disability results in changes in their physical state, mental state, or social roles; to prevent social and emotional problems from interfering with physical and mental health or with needed treatment; and to identify gaps in community services and to work with community-based agencies and institutions to expand the capacity of the community to provide adequate supports. (NASW, 1999d, pp. 168–169)

To accomplish these purposes, practitioners work directly with individuals, families, and groups. With respect to community-oriented services, health care social workers consult with communities around health care issues, assist in program planning, ensure outreach services for those community members at risk of developing health problems, and conduct health education and wellness training programs (Dziegielewski, 1998). Additionally, they participate in forming institutional, community, state, and federal health policies; plan and administer health care services; and conduct research.

Social Work in Public Health

In general public health "is primarily concerned with the promotion of health and the prevention of illness and other disabling conditions" (Moroney, 1995, p. 1967). To this end, public health initiatives often focus on promoting social justice and eliminating poverty (Berliner, 2002). As members of interdiscipinary teams, which include doctors, nurses, engineers, educators, business administrators, and lawyers, social workers focus on the social aspects of health and address social conditions in health and wellness. Public health settings include maternal and child health clinics, health planning agencies, the National Institutes of Health, and, at the international level, the World Health Organization (WHO).

Social workers cooperate with interdisciplinary colleagues to identify and modify social, psychological, and environmental factors that contribute to health problems or that influence

BOX **12.1**

Reflections on Empowerment

Empowering Communities by Planning for Public Health

Healthy People 2010 is a federal, state, and local community partnership project that focuses on health promotion and disease prevention (HHS, 2000b). Building on the results of the last decade, the federal public health service has developed several hundred national objectives in 28 focus areas to address health care concerns in the United States. In cooperation with the Centers for Disease Control, the National Health Services established an interactive data base to track progress on the objectives nationwide. As a strategic management tool, Healthy People 2010 expects states, local communities, and public and private sector partners to tailor their efforts to identified local health care issues. The two overarching goals of Healthy People 2010 are as follows:

- The first goal of Healthy People 2010 is to help individuals of all ages increase life expectancy *and* improve their quality of life (p. 8).
- The second goal of Healthy People 2010 is to eliminate health disparities among segments of the population, including differences that occur by gender, race or ethnicity, education or income, disability, geographic location, or sexual orientation (p. 11).

The Healthy People 2010 initiative emphasizes the relationship between individual health and the health of the larger community through its vision of "Healthy People through Healthy Communities." Local communities, guided by national standards and their own state's goals, participate in setting objectives specific to their communities. In most instances, community public health agencies or county boards of health sponsor the local planning initiatives. Communities engage a representative constituency to profile the community, considering geographical, cultural, and social factors; conduct health needs assessments; prioritize health objectives; and implement and evaluate health action plans.

Communities engage in change to benefit their members. And the results of efforts to enhance the health and well-being of community members are empowering for the community as a whole. Quality public health services that address emerging health-related issues and respond to adverse conditions are measures of a community's competence. The Healthy People 2010 initiative is the prevention agenda for the nation.

the use of health services. The exact emphasis of social work in public health depends on the particular nature of the agency's mission and the press of community health needs. Among the current social health concerns are teenage pregnancy, mental illness, particularly the increased incidence of depression, violence, hunger and malnourishment; issues associated with the aging world population; and the spread of HIV/AIDS. However, in general, public health social work is on the cutting edge of prevention and health promotion (Moroney, 1995).

Social Work Highlights. Social work practitioners who work in public health settings provide a variety of services. For example, consider the job descriptions of Pam Currior and Jeremy Powers, both social workers at the County Board of Health. Pam works primarily in direct services to individuals and families, while Jeremy, as a health planner, provides indirect services. Pam delivers outreach services in maternal and child health, family planning, and early screening for developmental disabilities. She also coordinates the home health care that the agency offers to individuals and families. Pam routinely presents health education programs and activities. She is a valued consultant about the psychosocial and community factors that affect clients and their utilization of health care services.

Jeremy engages in advocacy and planning activities associated with community health projects. Jeremy's responsibilities at the county board of health include conducting social and health needs assessments in the community, developing policy and procedures for new programs, and participating in research and evaluation of the health care delivery system in the community. Jeremy is the lead worker in organizing training and staff development activities for the County Board of Health and other health care providers.

Social Work in Primary Health Care

Primary health care deals with "common problems that are treated in community settings including prevention" (Oktay, 1995, p. 1887). Social work practitioners work in a variety of primary care health agencies, such as prepaid family medical plans, community and neighborhood health centers, clinics, medical practices, and HMOs. Many consider these settings less stigmatizing than mental health centers or even family service agencies.

Although social workers' involvement in primary health care services is somewhat limited, professionals working in this setting are often the first to identify personal and social problems (Cowles, 2000). For example, social workers with one clinic program identify clients' needs to access community-based services and their anxiety about health as the two most likely reasons physicians refer them for clinic-based social services (Wilson & Setturlund, 1986). Typically, social work services include individual and family counseling and group work with people experiencing challenges such as parent–child conflicts, obesity, bereavement, or problems with aging parents. Prevention activities include consulting with self-help groups, screening persons they identify to be at risk for health problems, and providing community education.

Social Work Highlights. Social workers practicing in primary care settings encounter a variety of challenges facing their clients, including such issues as abuse, psychiatric conditions, substance abuse, family problems, parenting issues, life transitions, loneliness, and stress (Oktay, 1995; Lesser, 2000). This vignette about family caregiving illustrates issues with which a social worker in primary health care might deal:

> A family sought help from the physician for an elderly member diagnosed with Alzheimer's disease. The family needed help in selecting and coordinating care because it was becoming too difficult to take care of their elderly relative at home. The doctor introduced the family to the social worker as part of the comprehensive care offered in the family practice office. The social worker worked briefly with the elderly person to help her understand what was taking place. She counseled the family as they coped with the loss of their parent as they knew her and some feelings about not being able to continue to care for their mother at home. The

social worker recommended that the family attend a community support group for caregivers of Alzheimer's disease patients and provided information and assistance in selecting a nursing home. (Lesser, 2000, p. 122)

Hospital-Based Services

Hospital-based social work began with the work of Ida Cannon at Massachusetts General Hospital in the early part of the twentieth century. Based on her experience as Chief of Social Services, she developed principles of medical social work that addressed the interrelationships between the social and physical dimensions of medical conditions. For Cannon, medical social work treated the social complications of disease by drawing on information about the patient's medical diagnosis, the patient's social situation, and principles of sociology (Lieberman, 1986).

The nature of social work in acute care hospitals has changed drastically in the face of managed care pressures for cost-containment and drastic reductions in both the number of people admitted for in-patient care and the lengths of their hospitalizations (Dziegielewski, 1998). Hospital-based social workers are redefining their fast-paced roles in light of these policy and organizational changes. Services still encompass a continuum of activities, including:

- *Referrals*—providing information on community resources and facilitating referrals
- *Pre-admission and discharge planning*—conferring with patients and families about problems associated with hospital admissions and posthospital care
- *Case finding or social risk screening*—offering services to patients and families at risk of experiencing difficulties because of medical conditions
- *Counseling patients and families*—helping clients deal with issues related to health and medical care and providing concrete assistance, such as financial help, bus passes, and adaptive devices
- *Psychosocial evaluations*—assessing psychological and social factors related to illness and recovery
- *Health education and other community service activities*
- *Case consultation with hospital staff and community agencies*—offering specialized knowledge about psychosocial problems, procedures, or social services
- *Program consultation with hospital staff*—recommending changes in policies and procedures to meet the needs of patients and their families more effectively and to ensure their rights
- *Planning activities*—participating in organizational planning to enhance hospital programs and community resources
- *Research*—utilizing research methodologies for client outcome assessment and program evaluation (Krell & Rosenberg, 1990)

Small hospitals often employ a single social worker, who is then responsible for all aspects of social services. Large hospitals usually employ several social workers, who specialize in fields such as pediatrics, trauma centers, orthopedic rehabilitation, renal (kidney) dialysis, neonatal intensive care, oncology, women's health, and emergency room services. As examples of social work in hospital-based settings, we shall consider two of these specializations—work in oncology and in emergency rooms.

Social Work and Oncology. Cancer affects the lives of many people. At any stage, it may disrupt developmental processes and challenge normal, everyday functioning. Some social work practitioners help people deal with the crisis of cancer by facilitating orientation groups for families at the time of their loved one's admission to the hospital (Parsonnet & O'Hare, 1990). These groups, co-led by a social worker and a volunteer who has recovered from cancer, familiarize families with the routines of the facility, educate them about cancer and its treatment, and provide emotional support. Increased family support cushions the effects of stress, and information about resources assists families in coping more effectively. Data gleaned from group participation alert staff to families who are at risk, such as those who are extremely disorganized, have a history of emotional problems, or state that they do not want their loved one to be told about the cancer. The orientation group empowers families at a time when family involvement is paramount.

Although both men and women are at risk of developing cancer, women are especially vulnerable to breast cancer, as women now have a lifetime risk rate for breast cancer of 1 in 8 (National Cancer Institute, 2002). Mastectomy, or surgical removal of the affected breast, has numerous psychosocial implications, including a perceived loss of femininity and self-esteem, the impact on significant others, and ramifications for sexual relationships. Social workers offer support and counseling to mastectomy patients and their families during treatment and recovery.

Social Work in Emergency Rooms. In many hospitals, social work practitioners are an integral part of the emergency room team. People who are treated in an emergency room are generally in a state of crisis. By employing crisis intervention techniques, social workers help people draw on their own personal resources as well as on resources in their social environments.

Those requiring emergency room services include people with acute illnesses or injuries; chronic illnesses exacerbated beyond toleration; or trauma resulting from rape, abuse, other criminal violence, or disasters. Others who are likely to use emergency room services are people who have attempted suicide; who have experienced acute or chronic mental illness; or who suffer from the effects of poverty, homelessness, substance abuse, or even loneliness. Individuals who cannot afford a personal physician or who cannot locate a physician who will accept a medical card frequently must rely on emergency room services to resolve both their emergency and nonemergency medical problems.

Social work services in emergency rooms include providing support and counseling to patients and their families, functioning as a member of an interdisciplinary team, and promoting communication by articulating the patient's problem to medical personnel or, conversely, the medical plan to the patient. Emergency room social workers often offer concrete assistance, such as helping clients obtain transportation vouchers, food, clothing, and prescriptions. They also expedite referrals to community agencies, advocate workable procedures and policies, and keep accurate records.

Social Work Highlights. The enthusiasm one emergency room social worker, Joe Ramos, shows when he talks about his job is contagious. Joe says:

> *On this job, no two days are the same. Keeping up with the fast pace keeps me busy, but that's what I like! For example, yesterday my day included doing crisis*

intervention work with the relatives of a teenager who had been seriously injured in an auto accident and locating community resources for an elderly man whose physical condition is becoming more frail but who wants to continue to live independently, the family of an injured child who turned out to be homeless, and a woman who was assaulted by her spouse. And that was all before lunch! In the afternoon, I led a staff development workshop on the protocol for reporting child abuse and neglect, worked with a few more families in the ER, filled out paperwork, and represented the hospital at a coalition that's putting together a community response to violence as a public health concern. Actually, what I like about this job, even more than its variety, is that it draws on my skills as a generalist social worker and gives me an opportunity to make a significant contribution to people who are in crisis and to the general well-being of our community.

Social Work in Long-Term Care

Long-term care (LTC) is the provision of continuous or intermittent health care, personal care, and social services over an extended period of time to people who are in some way limited in their ability to care for themselves (Garner, 1995). Among these limitations are any combination of physical, cognitive, emotional, and social factors that require the restoration of certain capabilities, the treatment of a condition, or the modification of the environment. Most people with these limitations are elderly, although people may experience them at any age. Population projections indicate that the number of people age 85 and older—the age group that is most vulnerable to disabilities and activity limitations—is expected to increase from an estimated 1.3 percent of the population in 2005 to an estimated 5 percent of the population in 2050 (U.S. Census Bureau, 2000a; 2000b).

Long-term care encompasses a continuum of services such as home health care, adult day care settings, nursing homes, and hospice programs. Most people who require LTC services receive these services in their own homes. Social work practitioners work in every aspect of long-term care. Their duties include direct case services and case management as well as the planning, development, evaluation, and regulation of programs (Garner, 1995).

Social Work in Home Health Care. The purpose of home health care is to sustain people with chronic physical, social, or emotional disabilities in their own homes. Among the problems these people encounter are problems with self-care, family relationships, adjustment to illness, personal adjustment, handicaps, and nutrition. Home health care is the fastest-growing health care service, more than doubling since 1988 (Goode, 2000). Currently, over 11,000 home health agencies provide services to almost 8 million clients annually. Of this number, 44 percent are proprietary agencies (U.S. Census Bureau, 2003). Total expenditures for home health care were over $41 billion in 2001, with Medicare the single largest source of funding. Rates of usage increase with age; the rate of usage for enrollees 85 and older is 6 times higher than that for enrollees ages 65 to 74 (Federal Interagency Forum on Aging-Related Statistics, 2000). Approximately 9,000 social workers are

BOX 12.2
Social Work Profile

Health Care Social Work

I believe that I have the best social work job ever! My social work position at a community-based, university-affiliated family practice residency program combines my interests in health and wellness, my early career work with children and adults who have disabilities, and my past experiences as a hospital-based social worker. In the family practice residency program, I provide the behavioral science perspective to the residency experience of physicians pursuing a family practice specialty. I spend approximately two-thirds of my time teaching the third-year residents about building relationships with their patients and honing their interviewing and listening skills; conducting group conferences related to a behavioral science topic; facilitating a support group for the resident "docs"; and engaging in administrative duties that include evaluating residents and attending hospital and community rotation conferences. The remainder of my work focuses on direct social work practice with patients referred by the family practice doctors. In this role, I provide individual and family counseling, make referrals for community services, and deal with a variety of mental health–related issues, such as anxiety and post-traumatic stress syndrome. I work with patients of all ages, from children to older adults, and help them work through some of the emotional traumas related to physical illnesses. I believe that listening is a strength that I bring to interactions with patients and colleagues. Even though listening comes naturally to me, it is not a skill that I take for granted. I didn't have to learn how to be quiet, but rather how in that quietness I could have presence in conversation.

I believe that social workers are well-respected professionals in the medical field. That respect comes from our abilities to use effective communication skills on physician-nurse-social worker teams. The social work perspective complements those of others on the medical team. Social workers have expertise about the social, behavioral, and psychological factors of health and illness and possess unique skills that contribute positively to patient care. I am gratified to observe that the family practice physicians with whom I've worked recognize the contributions that social workers, as members of the health care team, make to support patient health and are, thus, more likely to utilize community or hospital social workers in their practice.

I define my policy practice as my direct practice work with patients in the context of the health care delivery system. For example, using the DSM-IV is a practice policy decision at the micropractice level. I understand the content of the DSM-IV is essential to my work with individuals and families; however, I believe it is more important to know how to use it as a guide than to apply it as a prescription. Although understanding the intricacies of financing and funding may not be a top priority of practitioners, we do need to know the parameters of payment reimbursement systems such as Medicaid, Medicare, private insurance, and managed care. At the more macrosystem level, I have a keen interest in the potential of a universal health care policy for providing better access to health care for everyone, particularly the underinsured.

Health care social workers are in a unique position to identify patterns of incidence that reveal potential public health concerns. Medical social workers work closely with other health care advocates to address public health issues, such as contagious diseases, environmental safety, disaster response, maternal and child health, immunizations, water and air quality, lead poisoning, and cultural disparity in access to health care and mental health services. Although my own career path has not led into social work practice in public health, I believe this is an important arena for health care social workers now and in the future.

employed in home health service agencies nationwide (National Association of Home Care [NAHC], 2001). Social work services in home health care often includes the following:

- Developing plans that identify resources to sustain persons in their own homes
- Linking clients with resources
- Advocating availability and accessibility of community resources
- Providing short-term counseling on health-related issues
- Collaborating with other agencies
- Promoting wellness and health education
- Working with families with respect to caregiver issues
- Lobbying for more adequate home health care policy (Cowles, 2000; Egan & Kadushin, 1999)

Addressing issues of chronic illness actually constitutes a significant proportion of health services and costs. Home health care is promoted as a cheap solution; however, home health care may have hidden costs resulting from underpaid employees providing services for vulnerable groups (Kane, 1989). Frequently sustaining the quality of community-based care requires a variety of programs, including respite services and day care. Effective use of respite services requires using strategies and educating caregivers in such a manner that they will give themselves permission to use these services (Gonyea, Seltzer, Gerstein, & Young, 1988).

Case management organizes and arranges services and strives to contain costs. Optimal services focus on basic strategies for daily living and require close coordination of medical care, social services, support networks, and the promotion of health. Black, Dornan, and Allegrante (1986) suggest a multidisciplinary model for the delivery of services that emphasizes empowering people with chronic illness through the promotion of health. They advocate

> helping individuals maintain or improve functioning through enhancing their capacities to understand, manage, and cope successfully with the acute episodes and lasting impairments of their illnesses. In addition, [social work intervention] recognizes the need for health promotion to empower those who are chronically ill by strengthening their capacities to exert social, economic, and political influence for improving their life opportunities and fostering changes in the chronic-care service system. (p. 289)

Social Work in Hospice Programs. *Hospice* is a medieval term for a "house of rest." Today, hospices provide comprehensive programs of inpatient, outpatient, and bereavement services for persons with end-stage terminal illnesses. A report from the National Hospice and Palliative Care Organization [NHPCO] (2003) estimates hospice programs served 775,000 clients in 2001. With the advent of Medicare reimbursement for hospice services, fewer than half of the hospice programs are independent community-based organizations (41 percent); the majority are associated with hospitals (32 percent), skilled nursing facilities (1 percent), and home health agencies (22 percent) (National Association of Home Care [NAHC], 2001). Most hospice programs are nonprofit (72 percent); nearly all are Medicare-certified (92 percent) (NHPCO, 2003). Over 80 percent of all hospice clients in 2001 were over age 65. Typically, interdisciplinary teams—including physicians, nurses, home health aides, social workers, clergy, and volunteers—staff hospice programs. Over 4,000 master's level social workers were employed in Medicare-certified hospice programs in 2001 (NAHC, 2001).

The philosophy of hospice programs reflects values similar to the social work values of promoting self-determination, communicating respect, and upholding the dignity and worth of individuals. The overall goal is comfort and pain control, rather than cure. Hospice programs emphasize death with dignity through social, psychological, and spiritual support. They seek to make the experience of death as enriching as possible for dying people and their family members (Cowles, 2000). Other key features of hospice care include the following:

- The patient as the central focus of care
- A full range of programs and services that focus holistically on physical, psychosocial, spiritual dimensions
- Creative use of professional, volunteer, familial, and community-based resources
- Collaborative decision making rather than professional control of medical decisions
- Open communication among patients, their families, and health care staff (NASW, 2002d)

A recent study of individuals on dialysis indicates that from their perspective "quality end-of-life care includes 5 domains: receiving adequate pain and symptom management, avoiding inappropriate prolongation of dying, achieving a sense of control, relieving burden, and strengthening relationships with loved ones" (Singer, Martin, & Kelner, 1999). Because of the philosophy of hospice programs, these programs seem to be the service of choice for end-of-life care.

Social work roles in hospice work include direct services such as facilitating plans for adapting to the illness, assessing family and environmental resources, linking people with appropriate community-based resources, facilitating family communication, counseling, arranging for discharge, extending crisis services, and advocating access to health care resources (Fish, 1992). Indirect services include developing programs, providing staff support, and coordinating community resources. Part of the social work task is to assess the needs of caregivers and provide assistance prior to and after the death of the loved one. Considerations include support systems, relationships between caregivers and clients, communication processes, perception of the caregiver role, and families' past experiences with loss (Cowles, 2000).

Social workers face several challenges in hospice work. They must avoid emotional detachment and intellectualization as well as exaggerated compassion and pity. Above all, professionals must deal with their own anxiety about death.

Social Work and Genetics

The field of genetic services is expanding rapidly with the completion of the human genome project to identify all of the genes on human chromosomes and the promise of advances in the technology necessary for treating genetic disorders. A recent random sample survey of social workers conducted by the Human Genome Education Model project found that, although only 13 percent of the social workers surveyed had had a course in genetics, 78 percent discuss genetics with their clients, 27 percent refer clients to genetic counselors, 20 percent refer clients for genetic testing, and 52 percent provide some type of genetic counseling (Lapham, Weiss, & Allen, 2000).

To work effectively in this field, social workers must understand the basics of genetic inheritance and types of genetic conditions (NASW, 1999d; 2000b). Practice activities that are particularly relevant include case-finding and assessment, crisis intervention and supportive counseling, advocacy, education, liaison with self-help groups, and other supportive services (Rauch & Black 1995; Taylor-Brown & Johnson 1998). Basic competencies include such factors as the following:

- Having basic knowledge of genetics and related ethical, legal, and social issues
- Understanding the importance of privacy and confidentiality of genetic information, including their own records
- Understanding the influence of ethnicity, culture, health beliefs, and economics in clients' abilities to utilize genetic information and services
- Making appropriate referrals to genetics professionals and genetic support groups
- Helping clients cope with the psychosocial impact of genetic diagnoses
- Assisting clients in decision making about genetic testing, research, and treatments
- Maintaining awareness of new information, recognizing one's own limitations and need for constant updating
- Supporting client-focused policies (Lapham, Weiss, & Allen, 2000, p. 4)

Genetics issues extend into many fields of social work practice. Social workers in adoption services include genetic information in social histories and evaluations and provide genetic counseling for adoptive parents. Child protection workers may need to deal with genetic issues such as prenatal abuse, an issue that is beginning to be defined by legislation and the courts. Community organizers and occupational social workers may take on advocacy roles to protect unborn children from health and reproductive problems related to toxins in the environment and the workplace.

Furthermore, public knowledge about genetics and related ethical issues will likely increase the demand for genetic counseling. Clients may have questions about their family histories concerning birth defects, drug and alcohol use, or mental disorders (Rauch, 1990). As a specialized service, genetic counseling is often available only in large medical centers. Families may work with practitioners closer to home for follow-up services, support, counseling, and case coordination.

Ethical Issues

Ethical dilemmas are inherent in social work services related to any aspect of procreation. For instance, working with prospective parents in the prenatal period may raise ethical questions about creating life through in vitro fertilization or about terminating pregnancy through abortion. In each of these situations, there is no singular ethical position. Reamer (1986) raises several pertinent questions:

> Are social workers obliged to present themselves as neutral, value-free messengers, or are they entitled to persuade prospective parents to make a particular decision about the options available to them? Are social workers who have deep-seated and heartfelt beliefs about the morality of abortion obliged to keep them in their back pockets when working with clients, or is it permissible for practitioners to share their opinions? (p. 470)

Among the questions the Human Genome Project identifies are the following:

- Who should have access to personal genetic information, and how will it be used?
- Who owns and controls genetic information?
- How does personal genetic information affect an individual and society's perceptions of that individual?
- Do health care personnel properly counsel parents about the risks and limitations of genetic technology?
- How will genetic tests be evaluated and regulated for accuracy, reliability, and utility?
- Should testing be performed when no treatment is available? (Human Genome Project, 2003, Societal Concerns Arising from the New Genetics section)

Ethical issues abound in the field of genetic services. For clients, issues revolve around the implications of testing for themselves and their families. Genetics testing raises questions about the limits of confidentiality and the importance of privacy, and underlines the complexities of informed consent. Other issues include "discrimination, self-determination, and the immediate benefits of genetic test results" (NASW, 2000c). Social workers need to play a key role in addressing these issues within their agencies and in ensuring that future social policy legislation is responsive to clients' situations.

Social Work and AIDS

"The human immunodeficiency virus (HIV) is a sexually transmitted and blood-borne retrovirus that undermines and ultimately destroys the immune system" (Lloyd, 1995, p. 1257). HIV causes AIDS, which medical professionals now identify as the end stage of HIV disease. People with HIV disease are vulnerable to malignancies and other viral, parasitic, or bacterial infections, which, given the erosion of their immune systems, are often life-threatening. "HIV has not been cured, but the hope is offered that it is becoming a manageable (albeit complex) chronic disease" (Linsk & Keigher, 1997, p. 71) as a result of discoveries about how to prevent and treat the opportunistic illnesses associated with HIV/AIDS and about how to combine antiviral drugs to reduce the replication of the virus itself.

Prevalence

Many identify HIV/AIDS as the foremost contemporary global health concern. The United Nations reports indicate that 3.1 million people died from AIDS and 5 million people were newly infected with HIV in 2002 (Joint United Nations Programme on HIV/AIDS [UNAIDS], 2002a). Based on these figures, throughout the world *every day* about 8,600 people die from AIDS and about 14,000 more adults and children are infected with HIV. Nearly 25 million people have died from AIDS since the beginning of the epidemic. Data indicate that, currently, 42 million people are living with HIV/AIDS; of those infected, about 19.2 million are women and 3.2 million are children under 15 (UNAIDS, 2002b). At present, about 13.4 million children worldwide are orphans because of parental deaths from AIDS; estimates indicate that, by 2010, 25 million children will have lost one or both parents to AIDS (United Nations International Children's Fund [UNICEF], 2002). No part of the world is left untouched, although sub-Saharan regions in Africa have been hardest hit to date; the numbers of children orphaned because of AIDS in South and South-East Asia and Latin America are rapidly increasing. Statistics on the incidence of HIV/AIDS in southern African countries is alarming. More than one-third of all adults is infected with HIV in Botswana (38.8 percent), Lesotho (31 percent), Swaziland (33.4 percent), and Zimbabwe (33.7 percent) (UNAIDS, 2002a). Additionally, HIV/AIDS is spreading rapidly in Eastern Europe and the Central Asian Republics (UNAIDS, 2002c).

In the United States, estimates from 34 reporting regions indicate that, at the end of 2001, over 360,000 children and adults are living with HIV/AIDS. Cumulative records through December 2001 show that more than 800,000 people have contracted HIV/AIDS since the beginning of the epidemic and that over 460,000 people in the United States have died as the result of AIDS (Centers for Disease Control and Prevention [CDC], 2003a). In 2001, HIV/AIDS ranked as the leading cause of death among African American women ages 25 to 44 and African American men ages 35 to 44 and among the three leading causes of death for African American women ages 35 to 44 and African American men ages 25 to 34 (CDC, 2003b).

Data indicate there are nearly 4,000 children in the United States with HIV/AIDS. Of the 175 new cases of AIDS in children reported in 2001, 86 percent of the children acquired the disease prenatally (CDC, 2002a). Perinatal transmission of HIV is actually declining as a result of voluntary prenatal testing for HIV and follow-up treatments for those women found to be infected (CDC, 1999). As a result of advances in antiretroviral medication and obstetrical procedures, pregnant women with HIV who are aware of their HIV status and receive prenatal treatment for the disease can reduce the risk of transmitting HIV to their unborn child to less than 2 percent (Allen et al., 2001).

Minority population groups are disproportionately affected by HIV/AIDS; the spread of HIV has been widespread among African Americans and Hispanics. Of the adults and adolescents reported by the Centers for Disease Control and Prevention to have AIDS, about 54 percent are Black and 20 percent are Hispanic (CDC, 2003b). About three-fifths of all women reported with HIV/AIDS are African American and one-fifth is Hispanic.

Issues Facing Persons with HIV/AIDS

People who have a chronic illness such as HIV/AIDS face a number of issues. Their developmental stage and sociocultural circumstances, as well as the characteristics of the illness itself, influence the exact nature of these issues. Initially, people must deal with the crisis of the announcement of the illness. Then they must adapt to living in the context of chronic illness, and, finally, they must deal with their own impending death. In particular, the issues they confront include dealing with stigma, continuing their everyday lives, coping with loss, and making plans for their survivors. While these issues are difficult for everyone facing HIV/AIDS, women are often singled out as facing unique challenges.

Dealing with Stigma. People with HIV/AIDS must deal with public fear, isolation, victimization, and ostracism. Feelings of powerlessness, profound immobilization, and loss of control often engulf them (Poindexter & Linsk, 1999; Stephenson, 2000). The general public's identification of HIV/AIDS as a disease of marginalized populations further complicates the lives of persons with HIV/AIDS. African American women with HIV/AIDS face a triple oppression—the effects of race, gender, and the stigma of the chronic disease. A qualitative research study on the difficulties faced by parents caring for adult children with HIV/AIDS reveals the pervasive effects of stigma in rural areas (McGinn, 1996). Results indicated that this stigma limited access to health services; cut people with HIV/AIDS off from their extended families and friends; and ostracized them in their communities, places of employment, and churches.

Continuing Their Everyday Lives. People with HIV/AIDS face numerous difficulties in their everyday lives including living with uncertainty, reconstructing their future, all the while maintaining a sense of hope (Rose, 1998; Shernoff, 1998). These difficulties are compounded by the unpredictable nature of the disease. Challenges in continuing employment for persons with HIV/AIDS include maintaining interpersonal relationships and work activities while they and their colleagues deal with the chronic and, finally, terminal nature of the disease. Although people with HIV/AIDS are protected under the Americans with Disabilities Act, continuing to work is dependent on the person's physical stamina as well as the demands of the job. With respect to interpersonal relationships, family and friends may react with overprotection or even make unrealistic demands. However, being able to deal with fears and communicate openly are essential for ensuring a sense of dignity and self-worth. Finally, people with HIV/AIDS, like people with other terminal illnesses, face existential or spiritual issues that involve dealing with finding meaning in their lives and searching for value and meaning in their suffering and death. They must find ways to live satisfactorily in the context of dying.

Dealing with Losses. People with HIV disease often must cope with an overpowering, cumulative sense of loss that is not typical of their developmental stage. This loss includes the "loss of health, jobs, health insurance, housing, and other people with AIDS" (Taylor-Brown, 1995, p. 1298). Other losses are related to disfigurement, physical limitations, and self-esteem. Physical changes often precipitate a mourning process to deal with the loss of attractiveness and social desirability. As a result of losses of interpersonal relationships due to the deaths of partners, friends, and family members or to the withdrawal of significant people from social support networks, people with HIV disease must also cope with loneliness and isolation.

Planning for Survivors. People with HIV/AIDS often find a sense of continuity and resolution in planning for their survivors. Being involved in a planning process for the future of their survivors gives them an opportunity to come to terms with the contingencies of their own impending death. These tasks may be very concrete, such as making a will, planning the funeral, and contacting family and friends, or may involve subjective, interpersonal issues such as preparing a power of attorney, advanced directives, and a living will; working out financial arrangements; drawing up a will; planning the funeral; and contacting family and friends. Preparations also involve subjective, interpersonal issues such as mending broken relationships and working out details for the care of dependents.

Special Issues for Women. In the United States and throughout the world, the incidence of HIV/AIDS has increased dramatically among women, and yet the effect on women has remained largely invisible (Peterson, 1995; Tangenberg, 2000). Among the factors that contribute to this invisibility are racism, gender inequality, poverty, and powerlessness, as well as the discriminatory medical specifications of HIV/AIDS, which exclude many women who actually have contracted HIV/AIDS from the diagnostic category of HIV disease, and, thus, from treatment regimes. Complicating their situations, many women with HIV disease must deal with their disease in the context of caregiving responsibilities—caregiving for their partners with end-stage AIDS and parenting of children, some of whom may also have been infected (Van Loon, 2000). When children are involved, women often bear the responsibility for making guardianship and custody arrangements (Taylor-Brown, 1998).

A recent small-scale qualitative study of eight women with HIV/AIDS reveals several major concerns, including the women's worries about stigma and rejection, caregiving in the face of their own grief and the complexities of the illness, their need for social support while at the same time fearing ostracism if they disclosed their illness to others, despair about their own deaths, and their need for accurate information (Hackl, Somlai, Kelly, & Kalichman, 1997).

The Social Work Response to HIV/AIDS

The NASW (1999e) policy statement on HIV/AIDS supports service delivery that includes comprehensive health care services, access to a full complement of medical care and social and psychological services, advocacy to ensure human and civil rights, and education and prevention programs. Also it holds the profession accountable for disseminating information about HIV/AIDS and promoting culturally competent, sensitive practice through educational curricula and continuing education opportunities. Furthermore, the policy statement urges social workers' participation in political action and lobbying.

Continuum of Programs and Services. The effects of HIV/AIDS require a broad continuum of health-related services, including public health initiatives for education and prevention, primary care, hospital care, home health care, case management, foster care for children with HIV/AIDS, work-related services through employee assistance organizations, rehabilitation, hospice programs, correctional facilities, aging services, and education and prevention activities. Social workers, as part of interdisciplinary health teams and as core providers of services, work in any or all of these settings (Anderson, 1998; Babcock, 1998; Battjes & Delany, 1998; Brennan, 1998; Goicoechea-Balbona, 1998; Martin, 1998; Pomeroy, Kiam, & Abel, 1999).

In inpatient care settings, social workers play a pivotal role in working with people with HIV/AIDS and with their loved ones and families. Through daily sessions, social workers identify the psychosocial needs of persons affected by HIV/AIDS. Practitioners provide information and education about HIV/AIDS and form support groups to reduce isolation, expand networks of social and emotional support, and increase members' sense of control over their lives (Aronstein, 1998; Edell, 1999). Practitioners also arrange referrals to appropriate community resources and financial assistance programs, prepare appropriate discharge plans, and support advocacy efforts in HIV/AIDS-related policy. Empowerment strategies can counteract stigma by providing support and care, instilling hope, reconnecting clients with the future, and increasing clients' personal control.

Families, partners, and confidants of people with HIV/AIDS benefit from participating in support groups to deal with the losses they feel as well as their isolation, conflict, anger, emotional exhaustion, and physical fatigue (Jankowski, Videka-Sherman, & Laquidara-Dickinson, 1996; Tolliver, 2001). "Support groups may be useful for forums for sharing care-giving strategies and coping with the emotional demands of informal care" (Taylor-Brown, 1995, p. 1300).

Advocacy. The kinds of issues associated with HIV/AIDS call for using a variety of advocacy strategies. For example, social workers can advocate funding for programs and services to ensure quality of life for people with HIV/AIDS and for laws to protect their civil liberties (NASW, 1999f). For people with HIV/AIDS, misunderstanding, stigma, and the complexities of HIV disease complicate their dealings with the bureaucracies of health care, medical insurance, income maintenance, social security, and other community-based resources. A social worker may sometimes approach these systems directly to appeal a client's cause or may suggest ways in which clients can successfully speak out on their own behalf. Directed at creating macrolevel change, cause advocacy presses "for adequate funding of research on all aspects of HIV/AIDS, including prevention, clinical intervention, and vaccine development" (p. 182).

Ethical and Legal Issues. A plethora of value, ethical, and legal issues emerge. Ethical dilemmas revolve around conflicts between personal values and clients' values; conflicts with other professionals whose personal biases and unresolved personal issues are barriers to the delivery of services; concerns about the "right to know" which clients are HIV-infected conflicting with the clients' rights to privacy; the dilemma of whether to reveal a client's HIV status to sexual partners when the client refuses to disclose this information; and various legal issues involving mandatory testing, the duty to treat, confidentiality, discrimination, and personal rights (Patania, 1998; Reamer, 1993). The fact that laws regarding confidentiality and HIV/AIDS vary from state to state further complicates these issues.

When working with people with HIV/AIDS, social workers must deal with their fears of contagion; denial; discomfort with talking about sex, sexuality, and changes in sexual behavior; feelings of helplessness, hopelessness, anger, and victim blaming; and concerns about being inadequate. Research by Gillman (1991) and by Riley and Greene (1993) on the effects of training programs indicates that having an accurate base of information about HIV/AIDS reduces practitioners' fears and increases their willingness to work with people with HIV/AIDS. Support groups for professionals working with people with HIV/AIDS assist them in dealing with stress, reduce their feelings of isolation, and provide opportunities for them to share their feelings about the many issues that surface when working in emotionally laden situations (Schoen, 1998; Warren, 1998).

Social Work Highlights. Illustrative examples selected from a retrospective case analysis based on case management services at the Little Sisters of the Assumption Family Health Service (LSA), located in New York City in East Harlem, reveal the types of services provided as well as the concerns facing one family in dealing with HIV/AIDS (Indyk et al., 1993). The case presented is that of Maria, a 27-year-old woman from Puerto Rico living in New York City, who had a 6-year-old son and a 4-year-old daughter. Maria's husband, an IV drug user with AIDS, had committed suicide. Maria herself had only discovered that she, too, had contracted AIDS when she was referred to LSA. Her father was her only source of family support; however, her communication with him was limited.

> As her medical and social needs increased and hospitalizations became more frequent, a social worker and nurse from LSA became the intermediaries for orchestrating Maria's hospital management in lieu of family members. Staff from LSA visited regularly and communicated with Maria's friends, encouraging them to visit and to keep in touch with her. Visits by LSA nurses were reassuring to Maria, especially in light of the often fragmented inpatient care. During the last phase of Maria's life, LSA was providing daily visits for support and advocacy. . . .
>
> Counseling by LSA's social worker helped Maria resolve issues around her husband's AIDS-related suicide. A trusting relationship with the LSA staff enabled Maria to deal with issues of death and dying and to develop permanent plans for her children. Religious counseling from the pentecostal ministry complemented LSA's professional psychosocial counseling, which allowed Maria to take stock of her life and helped her family to achieve partial acceptance of her imminent death. . . .
>
> LSA also arranged for entitlements for income maintenance and new housing to accommodate Maria's deteriorating health status and increasing disability. LSA assumed responsibility for the development of viable plans for Maria's children and provided legal advocacy that resulted in a will drawn up by the Gay Men's Health Crisis and administered by a private lawyer in Maria's home. . . .
>
> LSA provided opportunities for the family to celebrate life and enjoy collective experiences that the children will remember. Maria and her children participated in a variety of LSA-sponsored activities, such as day trips and extended excursions to the countryside, woods, and beaches, as well as holiday dinners and other parties at the LSA center. (pp. 382–384)

These examples illustrate community-based case management as a social work strategy that can "effectively address some of the diverse and changing needs of AIDS patients and their families, such as bridging service gaps and fortifying patient and system strengths while minimizing their weaknesses" (Indyk et al., 1993, p. 380). Case managers coordinate medical care to ensure continuity, provide counseling services and advocacy, arrange for personal care and homemaking services, organize group activities for children and family events, and facilitate planning for children.

Social Work and Physical Disabilities

When people incur disabilities as the result of accidents, illnesses, or congenital defects, they experience unique challenges and interruptions in accomplishing their life tasks. Based on the mandate for social justice, social workers insist that people with disabilities have a right to the same opportunities to participate in community life and access services that are available to other citizens as well as specialized services necessitated by their specific disabilities (NASW, 1999g).

Settings

Social work practitioners work with people with physical and developmental disabilities in numerous settings. *School social workers* respond to the Education for All Handicapped Children's Act of 1975. This act establishes the right of all children to education; mandates an integrated, mainstreamed program for children with special needs; and dictates developing individualized educational plans. School social workers often function as members of an interdisciplinary educational team working with children with special needs and their families. *Medical social workers* provide counseling and rehabilitation support to individuals and their families. They play key roles in planning clients' discharge from medical facilities and coordinating appropriate community resources. Some social workers find work in rehabilitation counseling programs, although this role is underrealized.

Demographic Data

Statistics indicate that there are more than 50 million citizens in the United States who experience activity limitations as a result of chronic health problems (McNeil, 2001); this means that about 1 in 5 have a disability. Of these persons, about half have disabilities classified as severe. Projections indicate that the prevalence of disability will increase because of increases in life expectancy and the proportion of people over 65. Overall, persons with limitations are more likely than those without physical limitations to be high school drop-outs, experience unemployment, or hold lower paying jobs (National Organization on Disability, 2002).

Data show a greater frequency of disability among older adults and people who have low levels of income and education (Asch & Mudrick, 1995), population groups that are likely to be served by social workers. Thus, professional concern with disability should be integral to preparation for social work practice.

Unique Challenges

Unique challenges confront people with physical disabilities. Persons with stroke-related or other paralysis and spinal cord injuries often experience feelings of dependency when their conditions require assistance or total care in activities of daily living such as feeding, bathing, and toileting. Architectural and transportation barriers further limit people with mobility impairments. Communication disorders, such as stroke-related aphasia, result in difficulties in processing verbal or nonverbal information and/or expressing a response. Hearing and visual losses create unique challenges in communication and mobility, respectively. However, in the view of the social model of disability championed by the Disability Rights Movement, social workers must recognize that "for many disabled people the physical and attitudinal barriers to employment, mobility and other life activities may be more persistently problematic than their impairments in and of themselves" (Beaulaurier & Taylor, 1999, p. 169).

Self-Image and Social Relations. Persons with disabilities may experience disruptions in social relationships as a result of being ignored, rejected, or more subtly evaded by their peers who do not have disabilities. Patronizing sympathy, diverted stares, artificial levity, and awkward silences create strained social interactions. In fact, interpersonal relations between people with and without disabilities tend to follow a superior-inferior model of social interaction. Clearly, people with disabilities are relegated to "stigmatized social positions" and subjected to prejudicial attitudes, discriminatory practices, and negative stereotyping (Scotch, 2000).

Social workers must recognize the social marginality and stigma that people with disabilities feel in order to orient those people to the problems they face in social interaction with families and the community. Rehabilitation programs need to discuss the impact of stigma, enable clients to deal with their feelings, and work out effective methods of confronting and countering the effects of stigma.

Empowering Relationships

Practitioners' attitudes that devalue clients create conditions that undermine empowerment. Limiting our expectations for persons who have disabilities actually magnifies their negative self-identity and depreciates their sense of personal control. Exploratory research that focused on consumers' perspectives on their relationships with social workers demonstrated this by identifying several key issues in social workers' relationships with consumers with disabilities, including

- Prejudgment of consumers based on their disabilities
- Disregard for the uniqueness of each consumer
- Presumption of familiarity of consumers' situations based on their records rather than their revelations
- Rejection of the notion of consumer capability
- Failure to draw on the consumers' expertise (Gilson, Bricout, & Baskind, 1998)

Clients' impressions of the interpersonal encounter are especially important in developing professional relationships with persons who have disabilities. Empowering relationships enhance persons with disabilities' competence and social functioning. Collaborative, strengths-focused approaches recognize people first and rely on the expertise of consumers to define their own situations, including their needs, priorities, and hopes for the future (Gilson, Bricout, & Baskind, 1998; Russo, 1999). "Social workers must begin to re-focus their activities to begin the transition toward empowerment objectives: to maximize and expand the range of life choices of clients with disabilities, to assist and facilitate client decision-making with regard to life choices, and to bolster and promote achievement of life choices" (Beaulaurier & Taylor 1999, p. 173). Fundamentally, our words reveal our attitudes and influence our understanding of people and their situations. "Person first language" communicates respect (Blaska, 1993). See Table 12.1.

Vocational Rehabilitation

The main goal of vocational rehabilitation is to enhance clients' employability, emphasizing the importance of employment for self-sufficiency and independence. Effective rehabilitation planning encourages clients' participation in all aspects of decision making and provides opportunities for clients to assert increased autonomy and independence.

Candidates for rehabilitation may express their need for employment by stating, "I need help finding a job," or they may internalize their need as a problem, stating, for example, "I can't find a job because I'm disabled." In these instances, the practitioner and client must determine the reasons for the client's unemployment: Is it due to the client's functional limitations or to social constraints such as discrimination?

The limitations presented by disabilities may necessitate being selective about job placements. Rehabilitation planners must consider clients' transferable job skills and their capacity for conducting successful job searches. Rehabilitation planners assess factors such

TABLE 12.1 Words with Dignity

The following words have strong negative connotations.	The following words are more affirmative and reflect a more positive attitude.
Do Not Use:	**Words with Dignity:**
handicap the handicapped crippled with victim spastic patient (except in hospital) invalid paralytic stricken with	physically disabled person with a disability person who has multiple sclerosis person who has muscular dystrophy paraplegic (person with limited or no use of lower limbs) quadriplegic (person with limited or no use of all four limbs) person who has cerebral palsy person who had polio person with mental retardation person with mental disability person who is blind person who is visually impaired person who has a speech impairment person with a learning disability
birth defect inflicted	caused by "__________________"
afflicted/afflicted by deformed/deformed by	disabled since birth
incapacitated poor unfortunate	born with "__________________"
deaf and dumb deaf mute	deaf person pre-lingually (deaf at birth) deaf post-lingually (deaf after birth) deaf deaf/profoundly deaf (no hearing capability) hearing-impaired (some hearing capability)
confined to a wheelchair restricted to a wheelchair wheelchair bound	person in a wheelchair person who uses a wheelchair person who walks with crutches
Explanation: Crutches, walkers, and wheelchairs are mobility aids. Without the use of these mobility aids, the person is restricted from participation in the community.	
normal (acceptable only for quoting statistics)	non-disabled (referring to non-disabled persons as normal insinuates that disabled persons are abnormal)

Basic Guidelines

Make reference to the person first, then the disability, i.e.: "A person with a disability" rather than a "disabled person." However the latter is acceptable in the interest of conserving print space or saving announcing time.

Use an adjective as a description, not a category or priority, i.e.: "The architect in a wheelchair" rather than "the wheelchair architect."

AVOID NEGATIVE CONNOTATIONS OR ATTITUDES

Source: Commission of Persons with Disabilities, Iowa Department of Human Rights. Used with permission.

as the climate in their community for employing people with disabilities as well as the availability of accessible transportation.

Criteria of Effective Plans. Effective rehabilitation plans include a combination of services that target the removal of specific barriers to employability. For example, clients may agree that they need counseling and guidance to establish realistic vocational goals and acquire suitable employment. In other situations, people may need services that reduce disability-related limitations. Or, to qualify for entry-level positions, clients who lack transferable vocational skills may need training in sheltered workshops or job coaching in supportive employment settings.

An individualized rehabilitation plan outlines clients' long-range goals and identifies services that can assist them in achieving their goals. Access to services may be restricted by eligibility requirements, and practitioners may be forced by policy constraints to consider the most cost-effective or time-efficient alternatives. The plan, with any amendments, will identify timeframes for implementing and completing services, specify the source of payment, and delineate clients' and practitioners' roles in monitoring, follow-up, and evaluation.

Social Work Highlights. Given the multidimensional nature of recovery from a life-changing trauma, social workers often participate on the interdisciplinary team that provides rehabilitation services. According to the Centers for Disease Control and Prevention (2002b), accidents are the leading source of death and disability for adults ages 25 through 44. Estimates indicate that 5.3 million live with a traumatic brain injury disability (Thurman et al., 1999). Individuals face a variety of challenges in their recovery from major accidents including isolation, financial crises, depression and hopelessness, anger, and the need to locate sufficient social support. One example of an effective initiative is hospital-based trauma support group called REBUILD (Bradford, 1999). REBUILD provides a venue for peer support. Extending its function beyond meeting the needs of group members, REBUILD members now provide in-service education for paramedics, rescue workers, emergency room personnel, social work students, and other professionals. Their social action and community education activities have played a vital role in recovery. One group member shares the personal impact of these activities:

> Visiting patients, sharing my experiences with the other group members, and the "public appearances" allow me to take the worst event of my entire life and use it for something positive. I have believed that I not only survived the accident but recovered as well as I did for a reason. Whether it is to provide encouragement to someone else in a similar situation or to give insight to a caregiver so that the next patient receives better care—I feel like my accident and recovery is serving a purpose. (Development of REBUILD's Outreach Efforts section, ¶ 7)

Environmental Modifications

When professionals focus solely on microissues, they may underestimate the impact of the social construction of disability and overlook environmental influences in rehabilitation. When social workers emphasize changing personal behavior and making adjustments, they may miss the significance of the social, psychological, legal, and economic aspects of dis-

BOX 12.3

Reflections on Diversity

Working with People Who Are Deaf or Hard of Hearing

There are 28 million people in the United States who are deaf or hard of hearing. In general, a greater proportion of those over 65 experience some level of hearing loss (Desselle & Proctor, 2000). People who are deaf or hard of hearing experience the same issues facing others, such as difficulties with health, mental health, addictions, family violence, unemployment, and poverty. These issues are complicated by a lack of understanding of deaf culture, prejudicial attitudes, and communication barriers that reduce access to programs and services. People who are deaf or hard of hearing are particularly vulnerable to discrimination in educational and workplace settings. To them, deafness is not a disability, although some may use the term *disability* to increase their political leverage.

Deaf culture is extensive, although often unknown to people who are not deaf or hard of hearing. Deaf culture is distinguished by its unique language, theater, literature, poetry, humor, organized groups, and residential schools, including Gallaudet University, which is the only deaf college in the United States. Historically, American Sign Language (ASL) evolved in Martha's Vineyard, "the island that spoke by hand" to enhance communication for the large number of people living in the area who were born deaf (Kageleiry, 1999). ASL, the third most prevalent language in the United States, relies on a distinct grammar based on the visual cues of facial expressions and body movements. Associations, social clubs, and informal social networks strengthen the sense of the deaf community. Formal national and state organizations, such as the national Association for the Deaf, support various consumer advocacy efforts, particularly those related to education and employment.

Professionals who have expertise in working with people who are deaf and hard of hearing suggest some basic considerations for communicating effectively:

- Secure a quiet location, free from background noise
- Gain the individual's attention by tapping his or her shoulder or waving your hand
- Face the individual when you are speaking
- Speak clearly using a normal tone
- Remember that not all people who are deaf read lips
- Recognize that people who wear hearing aids may still have difficulties understanding speech (Williams, Clemmey, & Fuerst, 2000)

Resources that facilitate reasonable access include telecommunication devices for the deaf (TTD), assistive listening devices, and interpreter services. If the person indicates that he or she prefers using an interpreter, social workers need to identify the language through which the person communicates, as not everyone uses ASL. The Americans with Disabilities Act (ADA) requires agencies to secure, arrange, and pay for qualified interpreters. In no circumstance is it appropriate to engage a family member or friend to act as the interpreter for a client. Considering these identified needs and legal rights to reasonable accommodation under the ADA, social workers need to understand deaf culture, develop basic strategies for communicating appropriately, and identify resources that will ensure reasonable accommodation, and therefore, facilitate access to culturally appropriate services. According to Halpern (1996), the role of professionals is "not to give Deaf people a voice; it is to make sure that the voice already present is heard. And we can do that. We can teach other hearing people to listen."

The Americans with Disabilities Act of 1990 affirms the rights of persons with disabilities to participate in all aspects of society.

ability. Successful adjustment to disabilities requires dealing effectively with the realities of the social and occupational world. Thus, social workers who promote clients' competence consider the interactions between clients and their social and physical environments.

Any consideration of disability must take into account its social context. Not only do individuals endure the physical limitations imposed by conditions that are disabling, but also they suffer social alienation imposed by degrading stereotypes and a disabling environment. The social and psychological impact of a disability is as important for achieving optimal social functioning as is the nature of the disability itself. Although rehabilitation services focus primarily on personal adjustment, rehabilitation must also address societal factors in order to confront social devaluation, stigma, social marginality, and environmental press, all of which exacerbate the consequences of disabilities. In short, disability is partly a social problem that requires socially constructed solutions.

Rehabilitation programs in schools and the workplace should be directed at overcoming prejudicial attitudes and discriminatory practices. Successful integration and mainstreaming of students and employees incorporates a combination of information about disabilities and contact with people who are disabled. Research suggests that to effect sufficient, significant, and consistent changes of attitudes toward those who have disabilities and to create opportunities for employment requires "substantial employer education in the successful accommodation of qualified workers with disabilities" (Bricout & Bentley, 2000).

Social Work and Developmental Disabilities

As defined by law, *developmental disability* is a nondiagnostic term referring to the criteria that determine a person's eligibility for relevant federally funded programs (DeWeaver, 1995). At present, there are almost 4 million persons in the United States with developmental disabilities (Administration on Developmental Disabilities, 2002). Developmental disability includes mental retardation, cerebral palsy, epilepsy, autism, and other organic impairments. The Developmental Disabilities Assistance and Bill of Rights Act of 1990 (P.L. 101-496) indicates that the term *developmental disability* denotes a severe, chronic disability of a person 5 years of age or older that

- is attributable to a mental or physical impairment or combination of mental and physical impairments
- is manifested before the person attains age 22
- is likely to continue indefinitely
- results in substantial functional limitations in three or more of the following areas of major life activity: self-care, receptive and expressive language, learning, mobility, self-direction, capacity for independent living, and economic self-sufficiency
- reflects the person's need for a combination and sequence of special, interdisciplinary, or generic care, treatment, or other services that are of lifelong or extended duration and are individually planned and coordinated; except that such term, when applied to infants and young children means individuals from birth to age 5, inclusive, who have substantial developmental delay or specific congenital or acquired conditions with a high probability of resulting in developmental disabilities if services are not provided.

Types of Developmental Disabilities

One primary type of developmental disability is mental retardation. According to the American Association on Mental Retardation ([AAMR] 2002), mental retardation is a disability characterized by significant limitations both in intellectual functioning and in adaptive behavior as expressed in conceptual, social, and practical adaptive skills. This disability originates before age 18 (The AAMR section, ¶ 1). The assumptions essential to applications of this definition include the following:

- Limitations in present functioning must be considered within the context of community environments typical of the individual's age peers and culture.
- Valid assessment considers cultural and linguistic diversity as well as differences in communication, sensory, motor, and behavioral factors.
- Within an individual, limitations often coexist with strengths.
- An important purpose of describing limitations is to develop a profile of needed supports.
- With appropriate personalized supports over a sustained period, the life functioning of the person with mental retardation generally will improve. (The AAMR section, ¶ 3)

By way of clarification, *developmental disability* is a global category that includes mental retardation among other disabilities. Thus, all people who have a mental retardation have a developmental disability; however, not all those who have a developmental disability have a mental retardation. Estimates indicate that the prevalence rate for developmental disabilities is 11.28 per 1,000 people in the United States (Larson et al., 2000).

Cerebral palsy, autism, orthopedic problems, hearing loss, epilepsy, and learning disorders are other subcategories of developmental disability. *Cerebral palsy* is a condition caused by damage to the muscle control centers of the brain before or after birth. People with cerebral palsy manifest varying degrees of difficulty in motor functioning, including problems with balance, walking, facial control, and speech. Although retardation may complicate the effects of cerebral palsy, retardation is by no means a necessary component.

Autism is a rare disorder given public attention by the movie *Rainman.* Autism involves distortion of cognitive functioning, motor development, and sensory perceptions, as well as language delays and inappropriate expression of emotion. Often children with autistic behavior are at risk for institutional placement. *Orthopedic problems,* or problems involving bones, muscles, and joints, exemplified by disorders such as spina bifida and congenital hip dislocations, are considered developmental disabilities only if the problems are present from birth and the condition disrupts children's functioning in at least three of the areas of life activity detailed in the Developmental Disabilities Act. A *hearing problem* that is present at birth or that develops in childhood is a developmental disability because of its potentially disruptive nature, particularly as it affects speech and language. Finally, developmental disabilities such as *epilepsy,* including grand and petit mal seizures, and *specific learning disabilities* may be present in an individual. By definition, learning disabilities exclude retardation and emotional disturbances, as well as vision, hearing, and motor disorders. Learning disabilities interfere with activities such as writing, spelling, reading, and math calculations (DeWeaver, 1995).

Legislative Mandates

Legislative mandates determine the definition of developmental disability and provide the framework for comprehensive services for people who have a developmental disability. Federal funds underwrite services such as institutional and other residential programs; income maintenance—SSI, OASDI, Medicaid, food stamps, and Title XX—to support people living in their own homes, in adult foster care, and in group homes; community-based support services, including day activity programs, case management, respite care, family support, planning, and advocacy; and preventive programs such as screening for at-risk disorders (e.g., lead poisoning and PKU or phenokytenuria, a genetic disorder the effects of which are preventable if detected in early infancy) and services for children with physical impairments. Legislated provisions include social work activities in areas such as case management, child development education, alternative community living arrangements, and nonvocational social development services.

Institutional versus Community-Based Services

Institutional placement of children with a mental retardation was the typical response of human service professionals well into the 1960s. Founded in 1950, the National Association of Retarded Children, now the National Association of Retarded Citizens, supported diverse programs such as shelter workshops, activity centers, and residential alternatives, and advocated legislative reforms (The ARC of the United States, 2001).

Legislative actions in the 1960s and 1970s gave further protection to the rights of people with developmental disabilities including public education, individualized educational programming, and vocational rehabilitation. The enormous costs and the press to ensure the civil rights of persons with disabilities prompted deinstitutionalization and the subsequent development of community-based services.

Least Restrictive Alternatives. Community residential services, educational opportunities, and supportive employment programs maintain people who are mentally retarded in communities in as normal a life-style as possible. In keeping with these new service mandates, programming emphases turned to mainstreaming, normalization, and deinstitutionalization. All these efforts—mainstreaming, normalization, and deinsitutionalization—focus on providing the least restrictive alternatives in education, employment, and housing.

In educational settings, *mainstreaming* encourages enrollment of children who have developmental disabilities in regular classrooms. Schools provide the specialized supports and resources necessary for successful integration and educational achievement.

The principle of *normalization* means that people with developmental disabilities participate in age-appropriate activities of everyday living in the same way as others. Proponents of normalization favor "normal and similar" activities in education, employment, and recreation rather than "separate and special" activities.

The goal of *deinstitutionalization* is to provide care in less restrictive community-based services rather than in institutions. Smaller, neighborhood-based, independent residential settings replace the larger institutional settings that previously segregated people with developmental disabilities. Social rehabilitation theories, community care options, and the civil rights movement influenced the deinstitutionalization movement in the field of developmental disabilities.

Social Service Delivery Issues

Social work contributes to the provision of services for persons with developmental disabilities. Social work activities include offering counseling services for individuals and families, preparing functional assessment and evaluations, arranging housing, supporting employment activities, accessing community resources, and advocating clients' rights in the policy milieu. Services are available to people with developmental disabilities to enhance their development throughout their lives, from infancy to later adulthood. Objectives include promoting personal competence, establishing self-respect, acquiring life skills, and fostering independence. To address the unique needs and potentialities of each person, social workers and clients develop individualized, flexible plans of action. These plans consider clients' growth potential and provide assistance appropriate to their level of competence.

Throughout the life span, a variety of service arrangements offer individualized supports, ranging from total assistance to intermittent assistance to independent living. These services touch on many domains of living—housing, employment, education, health, family, and community. Social workers validate clients' capacities to grow and affirm their accomplishments and progress. Effective services enhance clients' potential for growth and their full participation in community life and their maximum contribution to society. In addition, "social work interventions and social policies need to refocus on the transactions and goodness-of-fit between the person with a disability and the physical, social and political environment" (Kropf & DeWeaver, 1996, p. 179).

Ethical Issues. The NASW statement, "People with Disabilities" (1999g), clearly delineates the position of the social work profession "to take action with people who have disabilities in advocating for their rights to participate fully and equitably in society" and to work with people with disabilities from a strengths perspective (p. 273). Moreover the statement defines the ethical responsibilities of social workers as professionals and members of society:

> NASW recognizes the right to self-determination and maintains that all people, with or without disabilities, have a right to control their own destinies. NASW is committed to the implementation of full participation of people with disabilities and advocates for their inclusion in decision making in all of the arenas of social work practice, policy, and planning. NASW will work to ensure that society continues to work toward equal opportunity in society, in independent living, and in self-sufficiency for people with disabilities. (p. 273)

To this end, NASW supports independent living, housing, and transportation; accessible community resources and public services; education; employment opportunities; adequate income; and affordable and accessible health care. "Full inclusion of individuals with disabilities includes involvement in the planning of services, training in self-advocacy, and looking beyond limitations to strengths" (pp. 274–275). Ethical professional practice supports self-determination and social inclusion for people with disabilities.

A climate of progress and change results as people with disabilities, advocates, and social work practitioners question the effectiveness of services, raise issues regarding quality of life and human rights, promote principles of normalization and self-determination, and engage in social action. Long concerned with human rights issues, social workers support social changes that accord people with developmental disabilities their rightful dignity. To ensure the empowerment of people with disabilities, social workers promote independent living, social action, and legislative reform, and involve people with developmental disabilities in advocacy efforts.

Services for Families. Historically, services were provided through partnerships between the public and private sectors that allocated public money to community service providers for programs and services. Missing from this partnership of experts were the *real* experts—the people with disabilities and their families (Bradley, 2000). Too often in the past, professionals acted as if they were in a better position to make life-changing decisions on behalf of people with disabilities. However, directly involving persons with disabilities in developing comprehensive service plans and selecting service providers is a core theme of disability rights. This requires that people with disabilities have real power and control over their own decision making. It mandates that, when brokering services and arranging informal supports, professionals serve the best interests of the consumer rather than the vested interests of agencies. Social workers grapple with difficult questions:

- Who is the client? Persons with disabilities or their families?
- How does one balance self-determination and concerns for individuals' safety?
- How do professionals ensure personal choice in the face of shortages of services and funding and the press for cost containment?

In their qualitative study, Freedman and Boyer (2000), identified flexible funding, proactive and preventive supports, resource information, targeted outreach, interagency collaboration, and greater range of coverage by health insurance as examples of services appreciated by families caring for individuals with developmental disabilities. The findings of this study underscore the significance of choice, flexibility, and individualization in service delivery.

Emphasizing self-determination changes the power imbalance "by placing the choices, preferences, and individual gifts of people with developmental disabilities at the center of the system and encouraging a range of traditional and nontraditional providers to compete for the opportunity to supply needed supports" (Bradley, 2000, p. 192). As support brokers, social workers assist people with disabilities in developing their individualized plans, budgets, and arrangements for required services in the networks of formal and informal supports. Challenges include waiting lists, pressure to contain costs, and ensuring clients' participation in evaluating outcomes and agencies' governing structures.

Social Work Highlights. Family members of children who have a retardation benefit from sharing their experiences in support groups. What they learn is that their child's disability is secondary to the child's personhood.

> At an early-intervention group meeting, the speaker, a parent of a twenty-four-year-old severely retarded young woman, brought pictures of her daughter to show to the group. She described her daughter as similar in many ways to other people in her family, having beautiful curly hair, wanting to listen to Elvis Presley all day, always knowing where other family members had left their keys or glasses, and enjoying being helpful around the house. The daughter also was stubborn and opinionated at times, and usually, but not always, able to make her wants known. The other parents at the meeting were then asked to talk about their own children, how they were similar to other members of their family, how they were unique, what they looked like. Some parents went on to share funny things that their child had done or said. Some parents found it difficult to describe their child. Many parents realized that for the first time they were not thinking of their child as a handicapped child, but as a *child.* (Greenbaum & Markel, 1990, p. 379)

Social Work and Mental Health

The concept of *mental health* is difficult to describe in concrete terms because it is a broad, culturally based concept. It encompasses a number of factors valued by society as signs of effective personal and social functioning. The factors contributing to mental health in Western culture are a sense of physical well-being; constructive interaction with others; and personal competence, including self-worth, self-reliance, and morale. More specifically,

> mental health is a state of successful performance of mental function resulting in productive activities fulfilling relationships with other people, and the ability to adapt to change and to

> cope with adversity. Mental health is indispensable to personal well-being, family and interpersonal relationships, and contribution to community or society. . . . Mental health is the springboard of thinking and communication skills, learning, emotional growth, resilience, and self-esteem. These are the ingredients of each individual's successful contribution to community and society. (HHS, 1999, pp. 4–5)

People often recognize mental health more by its absence than by its presence. The absence of mental health shows up in people's daily lives in two ways—as interferences with personal adjustment or as interruptions in social relations. Affected individuals or others in their social networks note behavioral signs or verbal signals that indicate that something is not quite right.

DSM IV-TR

The *Diagnostic and Statistical Manual of Mental Disorders* (4th edition)—called the DSM IV-TR—is an important tool for assessing behavioral characteristics and interactions with the environment and diagnosing mental disorders (American Psychiatric Association, 2000). This guide closely parallels the classification system of the World Health Organization.

The DSM IV-TR includes broad categories of mental disorders for psychological syndromes, personality disorders, mental retardation or developmental disabilities, and alcohol and drug addictions. The types and severities of problems range from brief interferences with social functioning to long-term disruptions, from acute crisis experiences to chronic limitations, and from mild stressors to severe strains. The manual organizes behavior in relation to five different axes (Table 12.2). Within these axes, behaviors, circumstances, and thought patterns associated with specific mental disorders are detailed. The DSM IV-TR allows professionals from various disciplines and with various theoretical orientations to share a common diagnostic language and thus communicate more effectively.

Prevalence of Mental Disorders

Recent epidemiological studies indicate that about 22.1 percent of the population in the United States 18 years of age or older, or about 44.3 million people, are affected by mental disorders in any given year (National Institute of Mental Health [NIMH], 2003). In any given year, about 7.3 percent of adults experience a *serious* mental illness, such as schizophrenia (1.1 percent), bipolar disorder (1.2 percent), and severe forms of depression (5.0 percent). Worldwide, depression is the leading cause of disability (NIMH, 2001).

Theories of Mental Illness and Intervention

The theoretical base of social work practice in the mental health field draws upon psychological, organic, and sociocultural theories. These theories help practitioners understand mental illness and suggest intervention methods. Often, practitioners combine various theories into an eclectic understanding of human behavior.

Psychological Theories. Among the major theoretical perspectives in psychology are the psychoanalytic, behavioristic, cognitive, and humanistic schools of thought. *Psychoanalytic*

TABLE 12.2 Multiaxial Assessment of Mental Disorders

The DSM IV-TR provides a framework for making systematic, comprehensive, multiaxial assessments that take into consideration a variety of circumstances surrounding the problematic behavior. The five axes and selected examples include the following:

Axis I: Clinical Disorders
- Mood disorders such as depression
- Anxiety disorders such as phobias and posttraumatic stress
- Schizophrenia and other psychotic disorders
- Substance-related disorders

Axis II: Personality Disorders and Mental Retardation
- Personality disorders such as paranoid personality disorder and antisocial personality disorder
- Mental retardation

Axis III: General Medical Conditions
- Presence of chronic or acute illness
- Diseases of the body

Axis IV: Psychosocial and Environmental Problems
- Occupational problems
- Economic problems
- Problems with health care systems
- Death of family member or friend

Axis V: Global Assessment of Functioning
- Overall level of functioning during the last year

theories, spawned by Sigmund Freud, emphasize the impact of early childhood, familial relationships, and unconscious conflicts on personality structure. Psychoanalytic therapies provide insight-oriented analysis, which enhances clients' awareness of underlying unconscious dynamics and helps them work through their conflicts. *Behaviorist theories* generally support the premise that all behavior is learned. Interventions extinguish clients' maladaptive behaviors and promote their learning of more adaptive patterns. The *cognitive perspective* examines the effect of information processing on behavior or how thinking affects behavior. With respect to interventions, changes in thinking lead to changes in behavior. Cognitive developmental theories provide a framework for adapting intervention to the developmental level of the client (Rosen, 1985). Finally, the *humanistic perspective* focuses on individuals' capacities and potential for growth. Humanistic, person-centered clinicians assume that clients are experts on their own situations and have the capacity for working out their own solutions.

Organic Theories. Recent research suggests that organic factors underlie a number of mental disorders. Researchers are examining factors such as hormones, biochemical balance, neurotransmitters, genetics, and even sunlight for their effects on psychological functioning. Certain types of mood disorders (i.e., depression and bipolar disorders) and schizophrenia demonstrate definite physiological origins. When clients have physiologically based mental disorders, psychiatrists or medical doctors direct their medical treatment. The discovery of psychotropic medications that calm anxiety, lift depression, and control psychotic symptoms such as hallucinations and delusions transformed the treatment of mental illness substantially and reduced institutionalization dramatically. Treatment plans usually combine medical interventions with individual or group therapy or other supportive services for clients and their families.

Sociocultural Theories. Sociocultural perspectives on mental health emphasize the influence of social and cultural contexts on human behavior. In other words, maladaptive behavior results from interaction between individuals and their environments. Thomas Szasz (1960) argues that mental illnesses do not, in fact, exist; rather, the social and psychological manifestations to which we attach the label "mental illness" result in *problems in living.* According to Szasz, mental illness is a myth:

> The notion of mental illness thus serves mainly to obscure the everyday fact that life for most people is a continuous struggle, not for biological survival, but for a "place in the sun," "peace of mind," or some other human value. . . . Sustained adherence to the myth of mental illness allows people to avoid facing this problem, believing that mental health, conceived as the absence of mental illness, automatically insures the making of right and safe choices in one's conduct of life. But the facts are all the other way. It is the making of good choices in life that others regard, retrospectively, as good mental health! . . . The myth of mental illness encourages us, moreover, to believe in its logical corollary: that social intercourse would be harmonious, satisfying, and the secure basis of a "good life" were it not for the disrupting influences of mental illness or "psychopathology." . . . Our adversaries are not demons, witches, fate, or mental illness. We have no enemy whom we can fight, exorcise, or dispel by "cure." What we do have are *problems in living*—whether those be biologic, economic, political, or sociopsychological. . . . My argument was limited to the proposition that mental illness is a myth, whose function it is to disguise and thus render more palatable the bitter pill of moral conflicts in human relations. (p. 118)

Szasz's argument points out the inherent problem with applying the term *mental illness.* People often label others who engage in behavior that violates social norms as mentally ill.

Sociologists also suggest that labeling people as mentally ill typecasts them and limits their ability to obtain other roles. Once applied, the label "mental illness" is difficult to remove (Rosenhan, 1975). Labeling theory further suggests that when we categorize people as "mentally ill," that label shapes their perceptions of themselves and limits others' understanding of their capabilities. Labels create expectancies for behavior and elicit stereotypic responses from people so labeled. Thus, diagnostic labels can become lenses for viewing behavior rather than tools for understanding behavior. Labels denoting pathology are stigmatizing; they focus on deficits and deviance rather than on competence and strengths.

Service Delivery

Historically, social work became involved in mental health through Ida Cannon's work at Massachusetts General Hospital in 1906 and through Mary Jarrett's program in 1913 at

Boston Psychiatric, where psychiatric social work was established as a specialty. Also, the Veterans Administration, through its psychiatric social work services, has provided leadership in the mental health field over the years. Today, social workers are among the main providers of mental health inpatient and outpatient services for individuals who evidence acute or chronic mental disorders. Almost 40 percent of all NASW members identify mental health as their primary area of practice (Gibelman & Schervish, 1997).

Public and Private Programs. Various types of public and private programs offer inpatient and outpatient mental health services, including community mental health centers, Veterans Administration hospitals and clinics, state and county mental hospitals, private psychiatric hospitals, psychiatric units in general hospitals and medical centers, and outpatient facilities (Lin, 1995), as well as residential treatment centers, private practice, correctional facilities, schools, and employee assistance programs. Federal, state, or local funding bodies underwrite public mental health facilities and programs. Private agencies and clinics generally rely on fees and insurance reimbursements for their revenue. Mental health advocates express concern that a two-tier system of services emerges—comprehensive services for the medically insured and limited services for others.

The most frequent primary diagnosis for admission to state and county mental hospitals is schizophrenia; that for private psychiatric hospitals is affective (mood) disorders. Government-sponsored facilities often carry the financial burden for persons with chronic mental illness who require extended hospitalizations, and for veterans who have addictions and are without private insurance coverage.

Outpatient Services. Psychology clinics, community mental health facilities, day treatment centers, and social service agencies provide outpatient services. In addition, specialized mental health program components are found in hospices, employee assistance programs, self-help groups, and research facilities, to name a few areas. Community support services for people with chronic mental illness offer outpatient programming involving independent living, supportive employment, and activity centers for socialization, recreation, and treatment.

The current practice of outpatient care is consistent with the plans of the Joint Commission on Mental Illness and Health (1961) and the legislation that followed:

> The objective of modern treatment of persons with major mental illness is to enable the patient to maintain himself in the community in a normal manner. To do so, it is necessary (1) to save the patient from the debilitating effects of institutionalism as much as possible, (2) if the patient requires hospitalization, to return him to home and community life as soon as possible, and (3) thereafter to maintain him in the community as long as possible. Therefore, aftercare and rehabilitation are essential parts of all service to mental patients, and the various methods of achieving rehabilitation should be integrated in all forms of services, among them day hospitals, night hospitals, aftercare clinics, public health nursing services, foster family care, convalescent nursing homes, rehabilitation centers, work services, and ex-patient groups. We recommend that demonstration programs for day and night hospitals and the more flexible use of mental hospital facilities, in the treatment of both the acute and the chronic patient, be encouraged and augmented through institutional, program, and project grants. (p. xviii)

Multidisciplinary Teams. Because the problems of mental illness are multifaceted and affect all aspects of people's lives, multidisciplinary teams often provide services. Teams include psychiatrists, clinical psychologists, social workers, psychiatric nurses, rehabilitation specialists, occupational therapists, and perhaps pharmacists and dieticians. Each team member possesses specialized knowledge, expertise, and a professional orientation that brings breadth to the team in understanding problems, assessing behavior, and proposing treatment plans. Typically, a case manager coordinates the team's plan. The case manager acts as the liaison between the client, the team, and other providers of services.

Deinstitutionalization

The most noteworthy change in mental health services during the last 30 years is the decrease in long-term hospitalization and the increase in community-based mental health services. Deinstitutionalization resulted in dramatic reductions in the resident populations of state and county mental hospitals and the closure of many of these facilities. The number of people institutionalized declined from 560,000 in 1955 to 125,000 in 1981. During this time, community-based mental health centers began to serve clients in their own communities, a trend that continues today. State and county mental hospitals are no longer the major providers for persons with chronic mental illness (CMI). For those clients who need inpatient care, privately operated nursing homes and board and care facilities provide those services, often supported by Medicaid reimbursement. Two questions about deinstitutionalization linger: Do community-based mental health systems adequately serve people who have persistent or long-term mental illnesses? Has deinstitutionalization resulted in a significant homeless population of people who have mental illnesses?

Impetus for Deinstitutionalization. The impetus for deinstitutionalization derived from many sources, including the press for economic efficiency, humanitarian concerns about the effects of institutionalization, and the refinement of psychotropic drugs. Either short- or long-term hospitalization is expensive. As individual states were carrying the financial burden for institutional programs, they pressed to use the more economical, federally subsidized, community-based approach. Interestingly, the status of a large number of people who had not been considered for community placement before deinstitutionalization directives changed to take advantage of community-based services.

Reform-minded individuals and mental health advocates were concerned about the dehumanizing effects of institutionalization, including loss of personal identity and depletion of motivational energy. Institutionalized individuals became apathetic, lost initiative, and felt devoid of hope. Community-based treatment offered a more normal environment. Psychoactive drug therapy provided a means of controlling such symptoms of mental illness as hallucinations, delusions, and other idiosyncratic behavior. These medications gave family and community providers more confidence in their ability to care for persons with serious mental illness.

Social Work Highlights. J. Doe was admitted to the psychiatric unit of the local hospital following a serious suicide attempt. During therapy, J. revealed a history of severe physical, emotional, and sexual abuse inflicted by her parents. When she was 10, her father had sexually assaulted her. Placed in a long-term foster home throughout her adolescent years, J.

discovered the meaning of emotional attachment. Marrying in her mid-20s, she discovered love that she had not experienced as a young child. At least during the early years of their marriage, J.'s husband was loving, kind, and honest and provided the emotional support that his wife so desperately needed.

J. and her husband raised several children. As a parent, she gave her children attention, love, security, self-confidence, and a strong sense of belonging to the family unit, pieces that were missing from her own family experience. As the children grew older, J. and her husband experienced serious marital difficulties. At that time, J. sought personal counseling at a family service agency. She reluctantly disclosed that her husband had abused alcohol during most of their marriage, and she painfully admitted that her husband had physically abused her for the past several years. J. reasoned that her husband was abusive because she was unable to satisfy him sexually and that somehow she deserved to be punished. She often alluded to events from her past that haunted her, but she could not bring herself to talk about them. J. was caught between the anguish of experiencing emotional pain and the fear of disclosing her childhood trauma. Unable to confront her past and deal with the marital dysfunction, she attempted suicide.

Upon admission to a psychiatric unit, she was diagnosed with severe depression. After several weeks of inpatient hospitalization and therapy, J. revealed her history of childhood abuse and was subsequently diagnosed as having posttraumatic stress syndrome. As is typical of children from severely abusive homes, J. had emotionally repressed the severe trauma and pain of her childhood. When the repressed emotions surfaced, the empathic response of the social worker gave J. permission to experience them, work through the deep-seated feelings of anger and rage, and develop a more integrated sense of self-identity.

Social Work in Mental Health

Mental health specialists, like the social worker who counseled J. Doe, provide individual and group therapy, case management, advocacy, resources, community organization, planning, and preventive education. They need a variety of specialized knowledge:

- Diagnostic assessment using the *Diagnostic and Statistical Manual* (DSM IV-TR)
- The law and due process regarding voluntary and involuntary commitment
- Ethical and legal issues, such as confidentiality and duty to warn
- Procedures for dealing with crises such as suicide, psychotic behavior, and violent aggression

Social work practice in the field of mental health must and should support the development of policies and programs that promote mental health for all people and that create health-producing environments. Services should be affordable, humanely implemented, and accessible via a comprehensive network.

Social Work and Chemical Dependency

Drug or alcohol use in and of itself is not a disorder; however, its use can lead to psychological or physical dependencies that are problematic. Drug and alcohol abuse interferes with people's judgment and their abilities to carry out their social roles and obligations. People who are dependent on drugs often deny the implications of their addiction, disregard the negative consequences of their behavior, and develop a tolerance to the drug. Although specialized treatment services are available for helping persons deal with chemical dependency issues, problems associated with drug abuse and drug addiction cross all fields of practice.

Alcohol and Drug Dependence

Psychoactive drugs alter the normal functioning of the brain. Depressants such as alcohol, barbiturates, and heroin diminish responses. Alcohol is the most commonly used depressant drug. Furthermore, alcohol has a particularly strong potential for addiction. Research suggests that some people are vulnerable to alcohol addiction because of their genetic makeup. In contrast to depressants, stimulants intensify reactions. Stimulants such as amphetamines and cocaine are highly addictive. The use of methamphetamine, a designer drug, and crack cocaine, the smoking form of cocaine, is prevalent. Use of stimulants can cause hallucinations, delusions, and other symptoms of paranoid schizophrenia, a serious mental disorder. A third type of psychoactive drug, hallucinogens—including, marijuana, and lysergic acid diethylamide (LSD)—alter consciousness and interfere with information-processing mechanisms. Finally, chemical dependency can also result from the misuse of over-the-counter nonprescription drugs. Habit-forming sleeping aids, diet pills, nasal sprays, and cold medications can lead to "drugstore addiction," a hidden form of drug abuse.

Substance Dependence. The DSM IV establishes criteria for determining whether a person is substance-dependent. According to the DSM IV-TR, substance dependence is indicated when at least three of the following criteria occur at any time in the same 12-month period:

- Tolerance develops with continued use
- Withdrawal symptoms experienced when usage is reduced or discontinued
- Usage in larger amounts over a longer period of time than originally intended
- Persistent desire and inability to control substance use
- Daily activities center on procuring, using, and recovering from effects of substance use
- Substance consumption activities replace expected social, occupational, or recreational activities
- Continued usage despite knowledge of physical and psychological impairments (American Psychiatric Association, 2000)

Substance Abuse. Substance abuse excludes characteristics of substance dependence as defined by the DSM IV-TR. It is associated with recurrent substance use that results in one or more of the following behaviors: role difficulties at work, school, or home, such as absenteeism or child neglect; driving while impaired; disorderly conduct; and argumentativeness and other interpersonal problems (American Psychiatric Association, 2000).

Consequences of Substance Dependence and Abuse. When people are psychologically dependent on a drug or alcohol, they use the substance as a way to endure everyday stress. When people become addicted or physically dependent on drugs or alcohol, their bodies develop a tolerance for the substance. They require higher and higher doses to achieve the effect. When they stop using the substance, they suffer withdrawal symptoms. The World Health Organization (WHO) subdivides alcohol-related disabilities into three types of problems in functioning: (1) physical problems, such as liver disease, (2) psychological problems, such as anxiety or intellectual impairments, and (3) social problems, such as crime, distressed relationships, or problems at work.

Prevalence of Substance Abuse

The National Household Survey on Drug Abuse (NHSDA), a project of the Substance Abuse and Mental Health Services Administration (SAMHSA), reports the prevalence and incidence of illicit drug and alcohol use among the U.S. population ages 12 and older. According to 2000 survey results, an estimated 15.9 million citizens used illicit drugs during the survey period. The rate of illicit drug use among major racial and ethnic groups "among blacks was 7.4 percent, whites 7.2 percent, and Hispanics, 6.4 percent. Current use was highest among American Indians and Alaska Native population (9.9 percent)" and among persons reporting multiple race (12.6 percent) (SAMHSA, 2002a).

About 48.3 percent of persons ages 12 and older reported drinking alcohol during the survey period (SAMHSA, 2002a). Of that subgroup of the sample, approximately one-fifth participated in binge drinking—five or more drinks on the same occasion (SAMHSA, 2002b). With a prevalence rate of 67.5 percent, age 21 is the peak age for current alcohol use, binge drinking, and heavy alcohol use (recurrent binge drinking). Rates for binge drinking any heavy alcohol use were slightly higher among unemployed persons than for their fully employed counterparts. Experts generally concur that about 10 percent of the population that consumes alcohol in the United States are alcoholic. Grant (2000) reports that approximately one in four (28.6 percent) children are exposed at some time to alcohol dependence (alcoholism) or alcohol abuse within their immediate families.

Alcohol and drug dependence has profound implications for both individuals and society. Substance abuse is associated with significant physical and mental health problems, family disruption, crime, and delinquency. Furthermore, research studies implicate alcohol abuse in domestic violence, mental health problems, family difficulties, child abuse and neglect, crime, and delinquency (Barnes, Welt, & Hoffman, 2002; Caetano, Craig, Field, & Nelson, 2003; Johnson, Brems, & Burke, 2002; Schumacher, Fals-Stewart, & Leonard, 2003; Thompson, 2003).

Special Populations and Alcohol Abuse

Alcohol and drug use affects people from all walks of life; however, Anderson (1995) distinguishes several subgroups with particular vulnerabilities, including teens, older adults, women, lesbians and gay men, and ethnic minorities. Since adolescents often experiment with alcohol, intervention efforts need to be directed at reducing their use of alcohol. Those who develop dependencies tend to have problems in school, associate with friends who use drugs, and come from families with histories of substance abuse.

Although older adults are less likely to experience addictions, studies indicate that 10 percent of those over age 65 are problem drinkers, and about 8 percent are alcohol dependent (Vinton & Wambach, 1998). Their problems with alcohol tend to be either lifelong or a reaction to the stress and losses associated with aging. In either case, alcohol dependence complicates physical and psychosocial functioning.

For women, alcoholism is associated with life stress and depression, its onset is later in life, and treatment is sought earlier. Of particular concern is the large number of women of childbearing age who consume alcohol and the potential for their babies to develop fetal alcohol syndrome. Recent research suggests that frequent drinking among pregnant women has increased dramatically (Centers for Disease Control and Prevention, 2003c).

The life stress experienced by lesbians and gay men is thought to increase their vulnerability to alcoholism. Furthermore, recovery may be complicated by the dearth of intervention programs designed for lesbian and gay alcoholics. Their reluctance to reveal personal issues regarding their sexual orientation during the course of treatment for chemical dependency may further complicate their recovery.

Differences also emerge in relation to ethnic minority status. Native Americans are perhaps most seriously affected by alcoholism. Estimates indicate that the rate of alcoholism among Native Americans is much higher than the rate for the general population (Beauvais, 1998). For all ethnic and racial minorities, ethnically sensitive social workers develop culturally appropriate intervention programs.

Delivery of Services

Historically, beginning with the work of Mary Richmond, social workers have been involved in the treatment of addictions. More recently, social workers' presence is more prominent in the arenas of practice research and policy development (Straussner, 2001). Several factors make the "profession extremely well suited to the ever changing field of addictions" (p. 8), such as the profession's biopsychosocial perspective, adaptability, and broad foundation that incorporates multiple fields of practice, including mental health and child welfare.

Established in 1973 as an agency of the U.S. Department of Health and Human Services, the National Institute on Drug Abuse ([NIDA], 2003) provides funds for research on alcohol and drug abuse and substance abuse prevention, and sponsors numerous information exhibits, town meetings, and programs. Treatment for drug dependencies has expanded to include methadone maintenance programs, therapeutic communities or residential self-help programs, after-care programs, detoxification, inpatient and outpatient counseling, and drug education.

Drug and alcohol treatment may be provided by an agency or organization whose mission or single purpose relates to chemical dependency. These single-purpose agencies often provide a range of services, from prevention and treatment to policy development.

By contrast, other organizations, such as child welfare, mental health, employee assistance, criminal justice, medical, and family service agencies, may intervene in cases of alcohol and drug dependency if this is one of several problems that clients present. Unfortunately, because of the multiproblem nature of chemical dependencies, professionals frequently overlook addictions.

Services range from residential or inpatient detoxification and follow-up treatment to community-based social services. Intervention modalities with individuals, families, or small groups are frequently combined with clients' participation in self-help groups such as Alcoholics Anonymous.

Mandatory Treatment. Mandatory alcohol and drug treatment targets certain groups, such as employees, criminal offenders, and families involved in child protection programs. Employee assistance programs (EAPs) often deal with alcoholism and drug dependency because of the frequent work-related problems associated with chemical dependency and the press for a drug-free workplace (Kurzman & Akabas, 1993). Interestingly, recovery rates cited for EAPs are high—up to 87 percent (National Institute on Alcohol Abuse and Alcoholism, 1999b), suggesting that job retention may be a powerful incentive. Education programs inform employees about substance abuse and train supervisors and managers to identify addiction problems and make appropriate referrals.

The criminal justice system frequently orders individuals to receive treatment. For example, law enforcement codes often stipulate that people arrested while under the influence of alcohol or drugs must participate in an educational treatment program. Subsequent violations can result in the loss of their driving privileges. Additionally, as a condition of probation or parole, court orders may stipulate criminal offenders' participation in drug treatment and periodic drug testing.

Finally, in the field of child welfare, substance abuse is now implicated in the majority of substantiated cases of child abuse and neglect and the out-of-home placement of children (Azzi-Lessing & Olsen, 1996). Family members, as a part of family reunification or family preservation plans, may be required to enter programs to treat their chemical dependency.

Substance Abuse Prevention Programs

Prevention programming focuses on strengthening individuals and families and enhancing community norms against drug use. Prevention programs also emphasize "protective factors" and reverse or reduce known risk factors (NIDA, 2000). A resilience paradigm for prevention of adolescent substance abuse emphasizes a strengths-oriented approach in contrast the traditional risk-factor interventions. In their review of the literature on the resilience model, Kaplan and Turner (1996) identify personal, familial, school, and community factors associated with individual resilience:

Individual Attributes

- Easygoing temperament
- Intellectual capabilities
- Self-efficacy
- Realistic appraisal of the social environment
- Problem-solving skills for social relationships
- Sense of direction
- Understand and respond to the feelings of others
- Humor
- Adaptive distancing from troubled caretakers

Family Protective Factors

- Positive relationships with a caring adult
- Positive family environment
- Realistic parental expectations

- Responsibilities within the household
- Effective parental modeling of resilience
- Extended support networks

School Protective Factors

- Involvement in school decision-making
- Realistically high student performance expectations
- Supportive climate

Community Protective Factors

- Positive community norms
- Adequate community resources for children and families

Social Work Highlights. Three categories of prevention programs describe the audiences that the programs target. Universal programs reach the general population; selective programs target "at-risk" subsets of the population; and indicated programs focus on persons already experimenting with drugs. The National Institute on Drug Abuse describes one model, the Adolescent Transitions program (ATP), which integrates all these approaches to prevention.

> The ATP is a school-based program that focuses on parenting practices and integrates the universal, selective, and indicated approaches for middle and junior high school interventions within a comprehensive framework. The *universal* level of the ATP strategy, directed to the parents of all students in a school, establishes a Family Resource Room. The goal, through collaboration with the school staff, is to engage parents, establish norms for parenting practices, and disseminate information about risks for problem behavior and substance use. The videotape "Parenting in the Teenage Years" helps parents identify observable risk factors and focuses on the use of effective and ineffective family management skills, including positive reinforcement, monitoring, limit-setting, and relationship skills to facilitate evaluation of levels and areas of risk.
>
> The *selective* level of intervention, the Family Check-Up, offers family assessment and professional support to identify those families at risk for problem behavior and substance use. The *indicated* level, the Parent Focus curriculum, provides direct professional support to parents for making the changes indicated by the Family Check-Up. Services may include behavioral family therapy, parenting groups, or case management services. Following this tiered strategy, a family in the indicated parenting intervention would have participated in a Family Check-Up and received information from the school's Family Resource Room about risk factors for early substance use and parenting practices that reduce the risk of drug use for their children.
>
> This program is based on a series of intervention trials, which comprise the Parent Focus curriculum and other intervention strategies, including working with high-risk teens in groups (Teen Focus curriculum) and using directed strategies involving videotapes and newsletters. The findings from these studies indicate that parent interventions are needed for youth at high risk to reduce escalation of drug use, and repeated booster sessions are needed throughout the period of risk. These interventions were especially important because it was found that youth at high risk should not be placed together in groups because it can worsen problem behaviors, including those related to school and drug use. (Sloboda & David, n.d., Adolescents Transition Program section, ¶ 1–3)

Social Work Roles

Employed in a variety of substance abuse settings, social workers provide individual and family counseling as well as referrals to services in occupational, educational, legal, and health systems. Drug treatment agencies are now more likely to employ social workers because of more stringent licensure and regulation, the stipulations of insurance funding for health care, and the press for upgrading with certified professionals.

Requisites for Working with Addictions. There are several requisites for working with people who are chemically dependent. First, there must be a commitment to self-determination and treatment modalities that enhance the client's right to make choices. Probing for underlying causes must be abandoned, as it only serves to block change. Guidelines for practice in addictions include:

- Understand the biological, psychological, and social factors associated with addiction
- Recognize the twofold treatment goal to stop using drugs and alcohol and to restore productive functioning in the family, workplace, and community
- Use an ecological approach to assessment and treatment planning that considers such factors as sociocultural influences, race and ethnicity, age, gender, and availability of social supports
- Promote strategies to enhance personal motivation and social support in order to retain clients through completion of treatment programs
- Ensure effective transitions to continuing or aftercare programs following initial treatment
- Accept the fact that persons with addictions often require multiple and episodic treatment experiences in their recovery process

From the Client's Perspective. A qualitative child welfare study explored clients' perspectives on "both impediments and contributions to effective recovery [from addictions] and family reunification in order to learn from the voice of experience" (Akin & Gregoire, 1997, p. 394). Note the clients' emphasis on respectfulness, strengths, and nonjudgmentalism in their summary of recommendations:

- Be open and honest with clients in delineating mutual expectations.
- Use language that clients can understand.
- Demonstrate support and care through behaviors. Actions speak to these clients louder than words.
- Help clients get the resources they need, such as housing, child care, and transportation.
- Listen to parents' stories, opinions, and aspirations. From these narratives emerged the resources clients used to survive as well as clues about their hopes for the future. Knowing clients' hopes and dreams directs the helping process toward goals that are important to them.
- Maintain a hopeful and nonjudgmental attitude. Parents want to know the worker believes in their ability to change their lives. Workers can instill hope by not judging the parent, by providing praise and positive feedback for small victories, and by being patient during times of slow progress.
- Share power and provide clients with choices.

- Help clients set incremental goals. When clients are full participants in the goal-setting process, they are more vested in the work required for making significant changes in their lives.
- Find ways to understand the nature of addiction and to know the parent as a unique individual. (p. 401)

Social Work Highlights. One day treatment center incorporated parenting groups as a part of its program for recovering addicts (Plasse, 1995). Many of the participants became involved in these parenting groups as a step toward reunification with their children, who had been removed from their homes. Activities included keeping a journal, role plays, and other skill development activities.

One client in this program is L, who is the 23-year-old mother of three children—a 7-year-old girl and 3-year-old twin boys. The children were removed from L's custody as a result of her addiction and her mother's complaint to a child protection worker. At the time she began the treatment program, L was living in a women's shelter and was quite upset about being separated from her children.

L revealed to group members that she feared she was repeating the pattern of her own mother's verbally and physically abusive behavior. She recognized similarities to her mother in her own behavior swings between explosive anger and depression. She believed that her addiction was the direct result of her low self-esteem, which had its roots in her childhood experiences.

Given her anger with her mother, L refused contact with her mother. As a result, she saw her children less frequently, and her sadness intensified. Discussions with other group members, role playing, journal assignments, and activities for enhancing communication skills all helped L begin to confront her anger with her mother and reestablish communication with her mother and her children. "During the 30 weeks of the parenting group, L obtained an apartment and took custody of her daughter. She reported to the group that she posted some of the group handouts about discipline and anger on the walls of her new apartment" (Plasse, 1995, p. 71).

Numerous positive changes resulted from the reunification of L and her daughter. She was able to recognize her daughter's need for regular contact with her grandmother and her brothers. L arranged for the boys to spend weekends and holidays at her new apartment. L enjoyed the support of other women at the center with whom she had developed friendships, and they joined her on a number of outings with the children. L had made great strides during her time at the center. She remained free from drugs, and had made measurable progress in reuniting her family. Her ability to realistically assess her situation was evidenced by the worker's closing remarks: "Although L had increased the visiting time with the twins by the end of the parenting group, she realized that she needed more time before she could raise them on a full time basis" (Plasse, 1995, p. 71).

Concluding Remarks

Social work has a commitment to health care because, to reach their maximum potential, all people need a supportive social environment. All people have a right to good health and should have access to higher-quality health care services. Social work can contribute to the health care field through setting practice standards: providing social services in health care systems so that persons may function adequately in their social roles; supporting a policy that creates a healthy environment and services that promote health for all people; and advocating adequate health care programs and services. Indeed, the NASW (1999c) supports policy that promotes health care that is affordable, humane, accessible, coordinated, and comprehensive. This policy directive charges social workers to advocate legislation and practices that promote quality health care delivery and services to all persons, especially vulnerable populations.

Social workers must be radically involved in health and mental health to prevent the development of a two-tier system of health services. Although the wealthy and the medically insured have access to health care providers, the poor and underinsured are often restricted or transferred to public health care facilities amidst charges of patient dumping. Severe cutbacks in the government-sponsored medical insurance programs Medicaid and Medicare, as well as cost-containment measures promoted by the corporate health care system, deny access to particular types of services, limit the utilization of service provisions, and promote early release. Social workers must challenge inequities and inadequacies of health care provision and must advocate health policies that benefit all societal members.

CHAPTER

13 Social Work with Families and Youths

The family photograph albums of the 2000s are certainly different from the family photograph albums of the 1900s. In the new albums we can see changes in family structure and size, as well as advances in the technology of photography itself. Over the course of the last century, sweeping changes in the economy and the labor force brought on by industrialization and urbanization altered the structure of the family. For example, today many women work outside the home, the number of single-parent families has increased dramatically, and the composition of families is no longer the traditional nuclear family. However, one feature has not changed: The primary relationships in families continue to provide the foundation for the well-being of humankind. Families nurture and socialize children. Indeed, families are integral to the development of all people, the functioning of other social institutions, and society as a whole. To describe social work's role with respect to families, this chapter presents information about

- The contemporary family, including its forms, roles, and family-centered services
- Child maltreatment
- Various types of child welfare services
- School social work
- Services for adolescent youths

The Contemporary Family

The concept of a family has changed from that of a basic kinship grouping of husband, wife, and children, or a constellation of persons related by blood, marriage, or adoption, to a concept that is more inclusive. Currently, the term *family* encompasses those constellations of two or more persons who regard their relationship as family and assume the responsibilities and obligations associated with family membership (NASW, 1999h). Thus, a family may be a group of nonrelated people who, nonetheless, define themselves as a family because of their emotional bonds. Exploring changes in family forms, functions, roles, and the family life cycle helps us understand the issues contemporary families present.

Variations in Family Form

Most people view the traditional nuclear family composition of a father and mother and their children as the "normal" structure for families. However, U.S. Census Bureau figures indicate that 82 percent of men and 67 percent of women ages 20 to 24 have never been married and 29 percent of men and 19 percent of women ages 30 to 34 have never been married (Kreider & Fields, 2001). Current data indicate that about 50 percent of all marriages end in divorce; many of those couples who are married are deciding not to have children. Cohabitation is also changing family life (Scommegna, 2002). "An estimated 40 percent [of children in the United States] live with their unmarried mother and her boyfriend some time before their 16th birthday" (p. 1). Divorce and remarriage significantly change family structures. Families now embrace a variety of forms, including blended families, single-parent families, gay and lesbian families, and multigenerational families.

Single-Parent Families. The U.S. Census Bureau reports that, in 2000, about 16.8 million or 23.3 percent of all children under 18 lived in families headed by persons who are single (Mather & Rivers, 2003). Census data indicate that the majority of single-parent families are headed by women.

Statistics show that the number of children living in single-parent families is increasing, while the number of children living in two-parent families is decreasing. Seventy-seven percent of children in the United States lived with two parents in 1980 as compared with 69 percent in 2002 (Children's Defense Fund, 2002a; Fields, 2003). In 2001, "78 percent of white, non-Hispanic children lived with two parents, compared with 38 percent of black children and 65 percent of children of Hispanic origin" (Federal Interagency Forum on Child and Family Statistics, 2002a, p. 7). "One-third of all births, including 4 in 10 first births, were to unmarried women in 2000. Nearly two-thirds of women under age 25 having their first child were not married" (p. 9). Furthermore, the State of America's Children Yearbook predicts that 50 percent of all children will reside in a single-parent family at some point before their eighteenth birthday (Children's Defense Fund, 2002b). One factor influencing this change is the increase in births to unmarried mothers. In fact, the "never married" category is a fast growing subtype of the single-parent family.

Typically, single-parent families are less prosperous. In 2000, 40 percent of all female-headed single-parent families had incomes below the poverty line (Federal Interagency Forum on Child and Family Statistics, 2002b). The U.S. Census Bureau reports that, in 2002, family income for 51.7 percent of children raised in mother-only families was below the poverty level, as compared to 5.2 percent of children raised in father-only families and 31.8 percent of children raised in two-parent families (Fields, 2003). In fact, the phrase, "the feminization of poverty" captures the link between female-headed families and poverty.

Social Work and Single-Parent Families. Social work services with single-parent families focus on both the broader social issues affecting these families and interpersonal issues presented by the families themselves (Strand, 1995). The social work profession pays particular attention to developing social policies that seek to ameliorate the poverty of single-parent families through income supports. Notable social welfare policies relevant to families include employment, housing, health care, child care, child support, food stamps, TANF, family medical leave, and domestic violence legislation.

While macrolevel interventions address these policy issues, microlevel interventions seek to lessen the emotional consequences of being a single parent. In essence, one parent must fulfill all of the adult roles in the family if the family is to function effectively. Often by default, children assume responsibilities for preparing meals, caring for younger siblings, and being a companion and listener to the parent. The needs of single-parent families engender a large part of the demand for child welfare services.

Empowerment-based social work practice builds on the strengths of successful single parents. Seven themes accentuate single parents' competency:

- Accepting challenges
- Making parenting tasks a priority
- Disciplining children consistently with nonpunitive actions
- Developing open patterns of communication within their families

- Fostering individuality
- Finding time for themselves
- Creating distinctive family rituals and traditions (Olson & Haynes, 1993)

Blended Families. The changing patterns of marriage, divorce, and remarriage in the United States significantly affect family life. Whereas first marriages join two families, second marriages often involve the interweaving of three or more family units. A blended family—sometimes called a reconstituted or remarried family or a stepfamily—is a family grouping consisting of a biological parent, his or her offspring, and a spouse, who may also bring children into the relationship. The blend expands further when children are born in the new marriage. The blended family includes stepparents, stepsiblings, step-grandparents, and a myriad of aunts, uncles, and family members from all of the former marriages. Subsequent remarriages compound the complexity of relationships geometrically.

Social Work and Blended Families. Research suggests that "blended families are not necessarily problematic, that they are different from biological families in ways that need to be recognized and accepted" (Kelly, 1992, p. 586). Family strengths that promote rebuilding and renewal within blended families include caring, communication, pride, unity, and ties with their communities and their extended families (Duncan & Brown, 1992).

Death, divorce, and remarriage interrupt family functioning. In these times of crisis and change, families may seek social work services. Difficulties in readjustment, relating to both current situations and complexities of past history, affect marital and parent–child relationships. In remarriages, family members bring emotional baggage from their families of origin, from their first marriages, and from the processes of separation or divorce (McGoldrick & Carter, 1989; Whitsett & Land, 1992a; 1992b). In order for remarried families to perform the roles expected of them and restabilize the lives of their members, each family member must deal with the past:

> There are at least three key emotional attitudes that permit transition through the developmental steps involved in the formation and stabilization process for remarried families: resolution of the emotional attachment to the ex-spouse(s); giving up attachment to the ideal of first-family structure and accepting a different conceptual model of family; and accepting the time, space, ambivalence, and difficulty of all family members in moving toward stepfamily organization. (McGoldrick & Carter, p. 414)

Children also feel the impact of remarriage (Visher & Visher, 1996). Major issues for children include dealing with the losses caused by the breakup of their first family, divided loyalties, questions of belonging, membership in two households, unreasonable expectations of steprelations, fantasies of the reunification of their natural parents, guilt over causing the divorce, and, for adolescents in particular, problems with identity and sexuality. Children must regain equilibrium in their lives by coping with the initial disruptions and adapting to their families' reorganization.

Gay and Lesbian Families. A growing proportion of families involve partners of the same sex. While census data are not available, other estimates speculate that there are between 1.5 million and 3 million gay and lesbian families raising between 8 and 10 million children (Laird, 1996). Family structures are varied and include adoptive and biological children, blended families, and shared custody arrangements. Gay and lesbian families function no differently from traditional family relationships. Parents love and care about their children and provide for their children's needs, and, in turn, their children love them. Gay and lesbian families display "unique strengths, courage, and resilience" (Okun, 1998) in the context of heterosexist, homophobic society.

The attitudes, stigma, and homophobia directed at homosexuality compound the problems gay and lesbian families experience with developmental transitions, family life-cycle issues, and environmental stresses (Hare, 1994; Laird, 1994; Levy, 1992). Gay and lesbian families often confront additional external sources of stress: an overzealous child welfare system, custodial problems with the other biological parent and with relatives, and ostracism by some members of the gay and lesbian community because of their previous heterosexual unions. Gay men and lesbian women have joined together to confront discriminatory practices and prejudicial attitudes. The gay rights movement is instrumental in addressing issues of civil rights for gay and lesbian parents. Some court decisions support custodial rights, and sociopolitical organizations work to reduce discriminatory practices.

Social Work and Gay and Lesbian Families. Laird (1996) points out that "gay couples and families rarely seek help for issues concerning sexual orientation" (p. 565). Rather, their concerns are very similar to those of other families—"life-cycle transitions or crises, situations of physical or mental illness, parent-child or couple relationships problems, [and] the need for additional resources" (p. 565).

Multigenerational Families. Intergenerational characteristics and biological lineage distinguish multigenerational families from other family groups. Frequently this family form involves three or more generations of a family occupying the same household. Data on the extent of multigenerational families are limited. However, studies indicate that increasing numbers of families accommodate the needs of their dependent elderly parents and grandparents. Also, the numbers of adult children and their offspring who return to their family of origin are increasing (Berk, 2004).

"Sandwich generation" adults, caring simultaneously for their children and their aging parents, face special challenges. For one thing, the role relationships between aging parents and their adult children must adapt, particularly in those instances in which older parents are dependent on their adult children. Also, parents must redefine their roles in the context of their children's adult status if their nest is "refeathered" by returning children and grandchildren. Family-systems intervention takes into account intergenerational dynamics and may involve multiple generations concurrently.

Although multigenerational, extended kin networks exist for all families, this has particular significance among ethnic and minority families. For Hispanic Americans, a multigenerational, extended family network is integral to family life. The preservation of family unity, respect, and loyalty characterizes Hispanic families (Williams & Diaz, 1987). Asian American families reflect their cultural tradition of respecting elders, a strong family orientation, and family loyalty. The extended kin structure is particularly dominant in the social relations of traditional Native American families. In other Native American family types, such as bicultural and neotraditional families, a modified kin system is influential. Grandparents take a major role in rearing children, giving advice, and establishing norms for the family

(Red Horse, Lewis, Feit, & Decker, 1978). Ethnically sensitive social workers translate their understanding of cultural diversity into their practice with various types of families.

Grandparent-Headed Families. The family form, grandparent-headed families, is the fastest growing form of families in the United States. These grandparents may not fit our image of "traditional grandparent." They "may be younger, still employed, and caring for their own elderly parents, and may even have children or adult offspring still living at home" (Okun, 1998, pp. 320–321). They are pressed into parenting their grandchildren because of the major life problems experienced by the children's parents—alcohol and drug abuse, HIV/AIDS, incarceration, and founded cases of child maltreatment forcing the removal of children from their parental homes. In any event, these grandparents must integrate life-changing circumstances into their own plans for the future. Among the stresses these grandparents experience are changes in role relationships with their own adult child who is the parent of the child in their care, loss of freedom, isolation from age peers, financial strain, health insurance, day care, and their worries about the future (Fuller-Thompson & Minkler, 2000; Goldberg-Glen, Sands, Cole, & Cristofalo, 1998; Okun, 1998; Whitley, White, Kelly, & Yorke, 1999; American Association of Retired Persons, 2000). Social workers focus on such services as providing information about health, legal, and social services; facilitating role adaptations and mediating intergenerational conflicts through counseling; linking grandparents with needed resources; and leading grandparent support groups (Burnette, 1997).

Social Work Highlights. The story of Carolee and Don illustrates the challenges and the possibilities (Okun, 1998). Carolee, age 61, and Don, age 62, were planning their retirement when the call came about the death of their daughter Liza and the plight of their 4-year-old grandson, Will. Will was in foster care when the family gathered for Liza's funeral in the community where Liza and Will had lived. The family began to discuss their options to care for Will:

> "There was never any question in my mind, I knew I had to take him. I wasn't going to let him go to strangers, and I understood why the other kids couldn't take him, although I must admit, that would have been the best solution," said Carolee. Don resisted at first, but when it became clear that Carolee was determined, he acquiesced. "She's not that well. I don't want her to have to keep on working so hard. We had such plans," admitted Don. The family agreed that Carolee and Don would become custodial guardians, but that the boy would alternate between his three sets of uncles and aunts during the summer. (p. 322)

The first months were difficult. They all grieved the loss of Liza, and Will had to adapt to living in an entirely new community with people who were virtually "strangers." Tensions were apparent as Will's behaviors became increasingly difficult to handle. The support Carolee and Don found at a local family service agency and a grandparents support group helped them deal with their situation more effectively. Carolee's comments at the end of the first year testify to these changes:

> We share the same meaning in our lives now. It's no longer him and his work and me and the kids. This time despite the fact that we're always tired and there's never a day when we don't feel as if a knife has gone through our hearts thinking about Liza, we are really together, like partners. Will is a challenge, but he's also a gift and we've learned that we can learn and manage. (p. 323)

Family Functions

Although single-parent, blended, gay and lesbian, and multigenerational families differ from traditional nuclear families, they are nonetheless viable alternatives for meeting the role requirements and functional expectations of families. While the forms of families are changing, their functions and roles remain relatively constant.

Families are the basic units of society that carry out functional responsibilities in economic production, childbearing, child rearing, education, and socialization. More than two centuries ago, the shift from a basically agrarian society to a market-driven economy resulted in families becoming wage-earning consumers. Economic dependency on employment in the workplace, subject to the ups and downs of the marketplace, replaced economic self-sufficiency. Although societal institutions have assumed more and more responsibility for education, maintenance of health, and the distribution of goods and services, the family system remains central to societal organization.

Although public schooling now serves the education function, early socialization of children continues to be a function of families. The family is the primary social context for developing personality, learning prosocial behavior, refining relationship skills, and establishing communication patterns. Today, families continue to provide a supportive and safe environment to ensure the physical and emotional well-being of all of their members. Optimally, families serve as buffers between their members and society, a safe retreat where family members can regroup and reenergize.

Family Roles

All family members must fulfill certain roles to ensure the effective functioning of their families. Family members' roles define the behavior patterns necessary for competent family interactions. The allocation of roles to particular family members depends on cultural variables, the type of family constellation, and the family's position in its life cycle. Families may access social service supports when, for whatever reasons, they are unable to fulfill their respective role requirements (Kadushin & Martin, 1988).

Parents, children, and communities each have distinct roles and obligations in the family network. In general, the parental role requires parents to provide for the basic needs of their children, including food, shelter, health care, and safety as well as emotional needs. Parents should stimulate their children's intellectual, social, and spiritual development. Parents also socialize their children by providing appropriate family interaction and discipline.

Children play a role in their own socialization. Children have an obligation to learn attitudes and values, to develop acceptable behavior, and to cooperate with their parents and other family members:

> When the child's capacity permits this, parents, not unreasonably, expect some developing reciprocal responses from children that provide affection, pleasure, and comfort to parents. Children who consistently refrain from, or are incapable of, responding with feeling toward parental displays of affection incur the danger of growing parental dissatisfaction in the relationship. (Kadushin & Martin, 1988, p. 14)

The community's role is one of *parens patriae,* or representing the interests of children. Community obligations take the form of protecting children through such actions as regulating and licensing day care and prohibiting child abuse and child labor. The community provides resources for children through programs such as social insurance, various forms of public assistance, health care, schools, and recreation programs. When communities fail to meet these obligations, social action is required (Kadushin & Martin, 1988).

Family Role Inadequacies. Family members' failure to meet their role requirements may lead to breakdowns in family functioning. Kadushin and Martin (1988) identify eight types of problems that can precipitate the need for child welfare services:

- *Parental role unoccupied.* The absence of one parent, whether temporary or permanent, leaves a vacancy in the parental role. The absence of a parent affects a family's ability to function without adapting its parent–child system. Unoccupied roles can result from the death of a parent, hospitalization, incarceration, migratory work, military service, divorce, or illegitimacy.

- *Parental incapacity.* Parents may be unable to implement their parental role adequately because of physical, mental, or emotional incapacities. These include emotional immaturity, illness, physical handicaps, retardation, chemical dependency, and lack of adequate information about child care. Parents who are incapable of providing adequate care for children may benefit from remedial, educational, and supplemental resources.

- *Role rejection.* Outright rejection of the parental role, either with forethought or through passive abdication, is likely to occur when parents feel overwhelmed or burdened by child-rearing tasks. The result is indifference, neglect, abuse, abandonment, and desertion.

- *Intrarole conflict.* Intrarole conflicts result from disagreements between mothers and fathers over responsibility for child care and conflicting expectations about parenting style. Some examples of these conflicts are the caregiver versus breadwinner debate, the love–discipline dilemma, and the child need–parental energy balance.

- *Interrole conflict.* Sometimes people experience conflict between parental roles and their other occupational or social roles. Workplace demands, social obligations, and intergenerational care expectations may conflict with the duties and obligations of parenting.

- *Role-transition problems.* Transitions that parents encounter affect their performance of parental roles. Changes in marital status, employment, the family constellation, or living arrangements all present adaptive challenges that can lead to role disruptions.

- *Child incapacity or handicap.* Children with special needs, such as children with a physical illness, mental retardation, emotional disturbance, or other condition that involves intensive care, place extraordinary role demands on family members. "Such a child imposes on its parents a burden of care, of specialized knowledge, of patience and control beyond that which any society can normally expect of them, and the possibility of adequately meeting the needs of such a child is reduced" (p. 22). Children may also be the source of family problems when they reject their roles or otherwise experience role conflicts—for example, between the demands of their parents and those of their peers.

- *Deficiency of community resources.* Community conditions and environmental stresses such as inadequate housing, unemployment, poverty, discrimination, inaccessible health and human services can adversely affect families' ability to function.

Family-centered services support effective parenting.

Family-Centered Services

Family service agencies encompass a broad spectrum of programs and services that reflect their family-centered mission. Family services include counseling for families, individuals, and groups; family life education; financial assistance; employee assistance programs; and advocacy for families and social change. The concerns addressed by family services include domestic violence, the feminization of poverty; addiction; the effects of alternative family structures, including single-parent and blended families; the effects of stress on the family; and maladaptive communication patterns. People interested in working in family services need specialized knowledge about family systems and communication processes, the impact of alternative structures on the functioning of families, and the effects of transitions in family life.

Historical Perspective. Social workers trace their involvement in family services to the Charity Organization Societies' emphasis on family welfare. In her book *Social Diagnosis,* Mary Richmond (1917) underscores the significance of the family. For Richmond, "case" and "family" were synonymous. She suggested that individual treatment would crumble away if families were not the basis of casework. Richmond and Francis McLean, both leaders in the Charity Organization Society movement, were instrumental in founding the

National Association of Societies for Organizing Charity, formerly known as Family Service America and now, the Alliance for Children and Families. The mission of the Alliance for Children and Families includes strengthening "members' capacity to serve and advocate for children, families, and communities" (Alliance for Children and Families, 2003).

Over the years, the Alliance for Children and Families and its predecessor organization, Family Service America have developed a nationwide network of family service agencies. Today, changing social conditions and needs of families have renewed professionals' interest in family advocacy. The redesign of the journal *Social Casework* and its renaming as *Families in Society* reflects this emphasis on family-oriented practice. Also, child protective services emphasize family preservation and family strengths.

Types of Family Services. Family services address the needs of families that experience stress as a result of life transitions, inadequate role performance, or the effects of societal conditions. A broad range of agencies—public and private, sectarian and nonsectarian, for-profit and nonprofit—offer family services. Some of these agencies, such as family service or public child welfare agencies, may have family intervention as their primary objective. Others, such as employee assistance programs, community mental health centers, or elderly service agencies, intervene with families as one of several agency functions. Families may seek services voluntarily, or court officials may require them to seek treatment because of evidence of child abuse or the delinquency of their children.

The problems that precipitate families' needs for social services may vary considerably. Some families experience only transient difficulties that are easily resolved. These families often participate in classes for parenting or conflict management or short-term counseling to resolve their difficulties. Other families require more intensive interventions to address chronic problems and ongoing stress.

Social Work Highlights. The juvenile division of the Freemont Police Department referred 14-year-old C. J. Watson to the youth service agency as a result of a shoplifting offense. This was his third encounter with the police. At age 9, he stole a neighbor's bicycle, and at age 12, C. J. and several of his friends harassed very young children on Halloween, knocking them down and stealing their bags of treats. In each of these incidents, the courts directed C. J.'s mother, Sally Watson, age 30, to assume responsibility for supervising and disciplining him. According to C. J., being grounded doesn't mean anything because his mother works evening hours and he does as he pleases.

At present, C. J. lives at the Freemont Apartments with his mother and his sister, Heather, age 12. C. J. was born when his mother was 16. They lived with his grandmother while his mother attended high school. He doesn't know the identity of his biological father. When his mother got pregnant again before graduating, she married Henry Watson. Mr. Watson adopted C. J. when Heather was born; however, the Watsons divorced after five years. To support her family, Sally took a job as a sales clerk at a discount department store. She has now worked there for six years, earning an annual income of $9,638. Mr. Watson is currently delinquent in his child support payments.

The social worker observes that C. J. looks unkempt. His shoulder-length hair is unwashed. He's wearing neon-colored sunglasses, ragged jeans, and a faded black tee shirt and has a pack of cigarettes in his pocket. According to C. J., this is what he always wears,

"Except on Sundays, when my mom makes me go to church." The only time C. J. bathes is on Sunday morning. The social worker found it difficult to talk with C. J. about the police referral, as he offered few responses other than "I don't know" and "I don't care."

Sally states that she has neither the time nor the money to be hassled by the antics of a 14-year-old boy who gets into trouble. She claims that the latest stealing incident was the first time that his behavior caused serious intervention by outside authorities. She says she repeatedly tells C. J. that if he ever gets into trouble with the law, she will not be responsible. "A couple of days in juvenile detention would teach him a lesson," she said. Sally's mother, Mrs. Gamble, also present at the interview, agreed. Sally says that in the past, neighbors often complained about C. J.'s mischief. He apparently had cut down a neighbor's rosebush, taken lunch money from neighborhood kids, and thrown mud at houses and people's laundry. Sally always paid for the damages, often borrowing money from her mother. She repeated that she was tired of being held responsible for his behavior, and sighed, "I just don't know where *he* went wrong."

Sally says that C. J. had a typical childhood. He had a few friends at church and at school and had done well academically until junior high. At present, he is in the 10th grade at Freemont High School and is failing most of his classes. His school attendance record shows a high number of absences due to health problems. According to Sally, she doesn't make him go to school when he has headaches or an upset stomach. When the social worker asks if C. J. has been seen by a physician, Sally says that it wasn't really serious enough to spend money on—that she could take care of it with a couple of aspirins.

Sally doesn't like C. J.'s friends. She believes that they have been a bad influence on C. J. and holds them responsible for his current predicament. She claims that they were the ones who talked C. J. into shoplifting. She describes C. J. as a follower, doing what his friends tell him to do in order to be accepted by them. She insists, "He would never shoplift on his own!"

This case example raises a number of questions: Who is the client system? From a family-centered perspective, what are the problems and needs? Upon what resources and strengths can the family draw? What needs to change? What commitments do the family members need to make to each other? What environmental structures require modification for the family's well-being? How do empowerment principles apply?

Sometimes social workers examine problems looking for a single cause and seeking a single solution. In working with families, this tendency results in one family member's behavior being identified as *the problem.* In the case of C. J., it would be easy to identify either C. J. or his mother as the problem. This viewpoint overlooks the influences of the family system and its environment. Family-centered practice considers the contextual and transactional nature of the relationships among social systems. Practitioners and families frame problems not as the dysfunctional behavior of a single family member but, rather, as family problems that require family-based solutions.

A Family Systems Perspective

Intervention with family systems focuses on families as units. The systems approach considers the dynamics of relationships among family members and between family members and their environment. Stress arises when an individual family member experiences difficulty, when family members have trouble coping with one another, or when the family or one of its members has problems stemming from the environment. Ideally, families provide a balance between stress on the one hand and the ability of family members to adapt on the other.

Family-based social workers consider the interactions between families and their environments (Pecora, Whittaker, & Maluccio, 2000). Social workers and clients identify environmental systems that affect families and assess the transactions between families and their environments in terms of relationships, needs, and resources. Ultimately, the purpose of intervention is to develop mutually agreed-upon goals in order to improve the fit between families and their environments. This is possible through developing families' resources and increasing their competence in utilizing resources.

When considering *intergenerational family systems,* social workers explore the ways in which intergenerational forces shape families' interactions. Such exploration involves studying influences on relationships and behaviors and may involve a plan to differentiate the generations from each other more sharply.

The aim of this approach is to understand the structural relationship of the family as a unit and communication patterns among family members. Structural dynamics in the family include the roles each family member performs, the rules governing the general functioning of the family, and the family's communication networks.

A complicated set of interpersonal relationships is inherent in family systems. *Role boundaries* define the specific and expected behaviors of each family member. Family problems arise when these boundaries are either unclear or constructed too tightly. Sex, age, and generation often define how families assign roles. For example, locating nurturing parental functions solely with the mother creates family friction when she seeks out-of-home employment or education. Likewise, members of dual-career families may need to redefine their parental wage-earner role and its corollary expectations. Other families may be underorganized with respect to roles. For example, when families fail to assume or lack clearly understood roles for caretaking, children may go unsupervised or even experience neglect.

Family rules provide the parameters for behavior among family members and in the community. When such rules are absent, anomie or confusion results. On the other hand, when family members rigidly enforce rules, anger and hostility may erupt. Family rules specify behavioral expectations; they should not be used to forcibly control family members.

Effective communication in families results from open and flexible lines of communication among all family members. Closed communication, such as the silent treatment, one-way directives, or circular messages, is ineffective. In their efforts to enhance communication, families and practitioners may target for change the covert communication patterns that foster coalitions and alliances, triangular relationships, and hidden agendas. In a family treatment approach, interventions realign family structures, create more effective communication patterns, and establish realistic structural boundaries. Ultimately, the purpose of family treatment is to achieve family unity.

Ecological Principles. In family-centered practice, a number of ecological principles guide social workers' and clients' work together. Social workers view the problems experienced by families as difficulties in transactions among social systems, or as interruptions of development:

- Intervention moves beyond a simplistic single-cause, single-solution model to a feedback model of change.

- Life experiences and families' natural helping networks are integral to the process of change. Strategies of intervention should acknowledge families as resources and utilize family members' active participation to enhance families' level of competent functioning.
- The ecosystems perspective holds that changes in a family's environment or in a family member's behavior may result in significant changes in the family system as a whole.
- In selecting strategies or methodologies of intervention, it is important to recognize the principle of equifinality, which suggests that there are multiple pathways that lead to the same result. (Hartman & Laird, 1983)

In accordance with these ecological principles, family-centered social work practice envisions change in the functioning of families or their members, in the social structures on which families depend for resources and opportunities to grow, and in the transactional relationships among various social systems.

Social Work's Support of Families

The NASW advocates the following policies that provide support to families:

- Full and equitable employment
- Early childhood and family life education
- Provisions for quality care for children and older family members
- Accessible and affordable housing
- Paid family medical leave
- Comprehensive health care services
- Gender-equitable income supports and tax credits
- Family-centered prevention and treatment-oriented services to address issues related to abuse and neglect (NASW, 1999h)

As Briar-Lawson (1998) asserts, "when systems designed to serve families fail, families cannot succeed" (p. 540). Families need both social and economic safety nets; therefore, social workers must be in the forefront of advocacy for family-responsive public policies.

Social work's family-support policy is built on a number of principles concerning the relationship between families and societal institutions. Fundamental supports for families include economic and social entitlements such as income supports, employment, education, and health care. Access to services must be provided without bias or violation of civil rights, thereby affirming cultural pluralism. In order to address the complex nature of families and family needs, systems need competent professionals in the public and private sectors to deliver services in partnership with families. Services must include a broad number of readily accessible options. Above all, family welfare should be a central focus of all societal institutions, including schools, workplaces, medical facilities, churches, and the media.

Child Maltreatment

Only recently has child maltreatment received recognition as a social problem, although the history of child abuse and neglect is long-standing. Child maltreatment cuts across all racial, ethnic, and religious groups and is found in all strata of society. Statistics on the incidence of child maltreatment are staggering, yet not surprising, considering the pervasiveness of violence in our society. Where once families may have insulated their members from societal violence, today violence pervades family relationships and erodes the safe haven of the family for children.

Historical Perspective

Statutes to protect children from assault and neglect date back to early U.S. history, when abused children were placed in almshouses or indentured for their protection. However, although children were legally protected from cruelty and neglect, there was scant outreach or enforcement.

The Case of Mary Ellen. One well-publicized case of maltreatment in 1874 involved a child, Mary Ellen Wilson, who was turned away by the police and charity agencies alike (Watkins, 1990). The diminutive child was brought into the courtroom wrapped in a horse blanket. She was bruised and had a gash across her face where she had been cut with a pair of scissors. Mary Ellen's parents were deceased, and she had lived with Mrs. Connolly for as long as she could remember. Her court testimony revealed that she had been beaten or whipped for unknown reasons almost every day. She was isolated, never allowed to interact with others or go beyond the yard, and Mrs. Connolly even locked her in the bedroom when she was away. Mary Ellen slept on a small piece of rug on the floor and had no clothes except those she wore. Other witnesses, including neighbors, a welfare worker, and an investigator from the Society for the Prevention of Cruelty to Animals (not in an official capacity, but as a humane citizen) corroborated Mary Ellen's testimony. Mary Ellen was removed from the custody of Mrs. Connolly, and Mrs. Connolly was indicted for assault.

The public response to this case of child maltreatment led to the foundation of the Society for the Prevention of Cruelty to Children, a private-sector child-protection organization. The Society "established the law enforcement approach to child rescue, which emphasized the removal of children from their homes and prosecution of their neglectful and abusive parents" (Watkins, 1990, p. 501).

Public interest in child welfare issues in the United States was evident in the early part of the twentieth century, particularly in the 1909 White House Conference on Dependent Children and in the establishment of the Children's Bureau in 1912 to direct the federal response to issues related to the welfare of children. Child protection came under the purview of public agencies in 1935 with the passage of the Social Security Act. The Children's Bureau, through the provisions of Title V, extended grants to states for "the protection and care of homeless, dependent, and neglected children, as well as children in danger of becoming delinquent" (Cohen, 1992, p. 23).

Increased Concern. Public and professional concern about child maltreatment has increased sharply over the past 25 years (Wells, 1995). Child maltreatment was rediscovered by the medical profession in the early 1960s, when the phrase *battered child syndrome* was devised by C. Henry Kempe and his associates in 1962 to describe the medical condition resulting from severe physical abuse of young children. The self-help organization Parents Anonymous was founded shortly thereafter. By the mid-1960s, every state had passed legislation mandating the reporting of child abuse.

The Child Abuse Prevention and Treatment Act of 1974 (P.L. 93-247) included provisions for the following:

- Establishing a clearinghouse for information, distributing training materials, and conducting research
- Overseeing grant funding for demonstration projects aimed at preventing, identifying, and treating child abuse and neglect
- Studying the effectiveness of reporting laws
- Requiring states to develop specific procedures for preventing, identifying, and treating child abuse and neglect (Tower, 1996)

Legal Definition of Child Abuse and Neglect

The Child Abuse Prevention and Treatment Act (P.L. 104-235), as amended and reauthorized in October 1996, defines child abuse and neglect as an act or failure to act:

- Resulting in imminent risk of serious harm, death, serious physical or emotional harm, sexual abuse, or exploitation
- Of a child (a person under the age of 18, unless the child protection law of the state in which the child resides specifies a younger age for cases not involving sexual abuse)
- By a parent or caretaker (including any employee of a residential facility or any staff person providing out-of-home care) who is responsible for the child's welfare (National Clearinghouse on Child Abuse and Neglect, 1997)

State laws render the legal definitions of child abuse and neglect. Civil laws "describe the circumstances and conditions that obligate mandated reporters to report known or suspected cases of abuse, and they provide definitions necessary for juvenile/family courts to take custody of a child alleged to have been maltreated" (National Clearinghouse on Child Abuse and Neglect, 1997). *Criminal laws* stipulate the circumstances under which child maltreatment results in action in the criminal courts.

Reporting Laws. All 50 states and the District of Columbia have enacted reporting laws that define child abuse, indicate what must be reported, and detail the reporting procedures. Although laws concerning child abuse and neglect vary from state to state, these laws all require social workers and other professionals to report suspected child abuse or neglect to the proper authority. Social workers must be aware of both their legal obligations and potential ethical dilemmas involved in reporting child abuse. For example, some statutes mandate reporting of "reasonable cause to believe" or "reasonable suspicion"; whereas other statutes only require the person reporting "to know or suspect" (Smith, 2002). Furthermore, there are legal consequences for failing to report: "Most states have criminalized the failure to report child abuse and to a lesser degree, some states have also allowed civil suits based on an individual's failure to report" (McLeod & Polowy, 2000, p. 12). Among the practical steps social workers can take to prepare themselves for practice are the following:

- Identifying the state-specific legal requirements that apply
- Knowing the indicators of child abuse and neglect
- Understanding reporting processes and procedures

- Keeping detailed, accurate records
- Identifying agency procedures, supervisory consultants, and legal counsel resources (McLeod & Polowy)

Types of Child Abuse and Neglect

Child abuse and neglect is the maltreatment of children by primary parental caretakers. Child maltreatment typically falls into the categories of physical abuse, emotional abuse, physical neglect, and emotional neglect.

- *Physical abuse* involves a willful or nonaccidental injury resulting from the harmful action of a parent or caretaker, such as punching, beating, shaking, kicking, burning, or biting. Indicators of parental physical abuse include a story about the injury that does not fit the facts, delays in seeking treatment, and evidence of multiple injuries in various stages of healing.

- *Emotional abuse* is parental or caregiver behavior that consciously intends to harm children emotionally. Among such behavior is rejecting, terrorizing, ignoring, scapegoating, isolating, or corrupting children.

- *Child neglect* is a failure to provide for children's basic needs or a lack of supervision to an extent that compromises children's health or safety. Neglect categories include physical neglect (for example, abandonment or failure to provide for health care), educational neglect (for example, permitting chronic truancy or failure to enroll a child in school), and emotional neglect (for example, failure to provide adequate nurturance and affection or allowing a child to witness spousal abuse). Neglect may lead to stunted growth, learning disabilities, developmental lags, failure to thrive, and a variety of medical problems.

- *Sexual abuse,* often silenced by the adult offender's intimidating threats and exertion of power over the child, includes a variety of sexual acts, including fondling, intercourse, incest, rape, sodomy, and child pornography.

Incidence

According to recent statistics released by the Children's Bureau, an estimated 3 million referrals on approximately 5 million children as alleged victims of child maltreatment were made to child protective agencies (U.S. Department of Health and Human Services, Administration on Children, Youth and Families [HHS/ACYF], 2003). Of those referrals, 903,000 were founded—in other words, showed substantiated evidence of abuse or neglect. The incidence rate of child abuse and neglect in 2001 was 12.4 cases per 1,000 children, a figure statistically similar to the rate of 12.2 in the prior year.

The 2001 figures collected by the National Child Abuse and Neglect Data System (NCANDS) indicate that neglect is the most common form of substantiated child maltreatment (59.2 percent), followed by physical abuse (18.6 percent), sexual abuse (9.6 percent), emotional maltreatment (6.8 percent) (HHS/ACYF, 2003). More than half the children were age 7 years or younger; 27.7 percent were in the age group of birth to 3 years of age; 24.1 percent were between the ages of 4 and 7, 22.8 percent between ages 8 and 11, and 19.5 percent were between ages 12 and 15, and 5.6 percent were youths ages 16 to 21.

Factors Contributing to Child Maltreatment

Ecological models consider a complex interaction of factors at various system levels (Bethea, 1999; Hansen, Sedlar, & Warner-Rogers, 1999; Wiehe, 1996). Parents' characteristics such as low self-esteem, limited tolerance for frustration, loneliness or isolation, inappropriate and often rigid expectations for children's behavior, beliefs with respect to punishment, lack of empathy for children, and inadequate knowledge about children's developmental levels also contribute to child abuse. Alcohol and drugs play a significant role in child maltreatment. Estimates indicate that "children whose parents abuse alcohol and drugs are almost three times more likely to be abused and more than four times more likely to be neglected than children of parents who do not abuse alcohol and drugs" (Child Welfare League of America, 2000). Alcohol consumption can lead parents to disregard behavioral norms and ignore their parental responsibilities.

Relationships and kinship networks are important resources for families. The strength of interpersonal relationships and social supports mitigates against abuse; the lack of social support increases stress and isolation, both factors that increase child maltreatment. Conflict over changing role expectations and particularly conflict about children seem to precipitate violence. Stress, unemployment, marital problems, social isolation, and a family history of violence also may play a role.

With respect to macrolevel influences, societal factors such as the quality of communities and neighborhoods, police departments, the criminal justice system, agencies in the social service delivery system, and the workplace all affect families. Research findings suggest that the stress of unemployment triggers abuse of all types. Communities inadvertently contribute to abuse when they respond ineffectively to the problem. Factors such as the high levels of violence in society, including domestic violence, likely contribute to child maltreatment. Poverty is cited as a problem second only to involvement with alcohol and drugs according to child welfare officials (Children's Defense Fund, 2000a). Furthermore, "the notion that parents have the right to rear children as they see fit, in the privacy of their home, is a deeply-rooted tradition in American history" (Vondra, 1990, p. 25).

Psychological Effects of Child Maltreatment

The psychological effects of abuse and neglect on children are pervasive (Lowenthal, 1999; Thomas, Leicht, Hughes, et al., 2003). For example, children who are abuse reactive may experience difficulty regulating and describing their emotions; avoid intimacy through withdrawal, avoiding eye contact, and hyperactive or inappropriate behaviors; and behave provocatively and aggressively. They may also experience disturbances of attachment and difficulties in learning. Children who have experienced maltreatment often think negatively of themselves as learners, experience low self-esteem, and manifest low levels of motivation for school achievement (Lowenthal).

Sexual Abuse of Children

Sexual abuse encompasses a wide range of sexual maltreatment and misuse by family members and strangers. Sexual abuse includes molestation, rape, child pornography, incest, and child prostitution. Through various international human rights laws, the world community now recognizes that all children have a fundamental right to protection from sexual abuse (Levesque, 1999).

In the United States, figures based on a nationwide 1995 Gallup survey of 1,000 parents "suggest that 1.1 million children per year were forced to have sex, had been sexually touched, or had been forced to sexually touch an adult or an older child" (American Medical Association, 1996). The American Academy of Pediatrics (2000) reports that "at least 1 out of 5 adult women and 1 out of 10 adult men report having been sexually abused in childhood" (What Is Child Abuse section, ¶ 1). Comparing these incidence projections with actual reporting rates suggests that only a small proportion of the sexual abuse of children is reported to authorities.

Child sexual abuse includes both coercive sexual behavior involving a child and sexual activity between a child and a person who is "much older" (i.e., five or more years) than the child for the sexual gratification of the older person (Browne & Finkelhor, 1986). Sexual behaviors may include sexual contact, oral-genital contact, and sexual intercourse. Incest, or intrafamilial abuse, refers to sexual contact when the people involved are related; sexual assault and extrafamilial abuse are terms used when the perpetrator is not related to the child. In cases of incest, compliance is usually the result of the "authority" of the adult involved (Damon & Card, 1999).

A number of risk factors have been identified as associated with child sexual abuse; however, "none of these factors bear a strong enough relationship to the occurrence of abuse that their presence could play a confirming or disconfirming role in the identification of actual cases" (Finkelhor, 1993, p. 67). Among these risk factors are the following:

- preadolescent age
- female
- presence of stepfather
- absence of natural parent(s)
- disability, illness, or employment of the mother
- poor parent and child-victim relationship
- parental conflict or violence (Finkelhor)

A review of research in the field shows that the initial effects of child sexual abuse may include feelings of fear, anger and hostility, and guilt and shame (Browne & Finkelhor, 1986; Graverholtz, 2000). Behavioral symptoms indicate anxiety and distress, and include inappropriate sexual behavior. Problems at school, truancy, running away, and delinquency often emerge as a reaction to sexual abuse. Likely responses include feelings of betrayal, stigmatization, and powerlessness. Long-term effects include depression, self-destructive behavior, suicide, anxiety, and lower self-esteem. Additionally, adults who have been sexually abused as children experience difficulties in interpersonal relationships with both men and women, trusting others, sexual intimacy, and parenting. They may be more vulnerable to further victimization in other relationships as well. Childhood experiences of sexual abuse increase the likelihood of involvement in prostitution and substance abuse.

Browne and Finkelhor's review (1986) also cites factors that contribute to children's responses to sexual abuse. Research shows that the impact is more detrimental if the perpetrator is the child's father or stepfather, if the relationship involves genital contact, if the perpetrator uses force or penetrates the child, and if the child protective system removes the child from his or her home.

Child Welfare Services

Broadly speaking, child welfare encompasses services that deal with all aspects of children's well-being, including protecting and promoting their health and social-psychological development, strengthening families, and addressing adverse social conditions that interfere with children's healthy development (Liederman, 1995). The social work profession predominates in this area of the social service delivery system. Social work practitioners who want to work in child welfare need specialized knowledge about normal and atypical child development as well as about contextual factors that influence development, how children respond to trauma and stress, and the legalities of child welfare.

Society preempts parental rights and authority in any situation where child maltreatment occurs. This societally sanctioned interference includes allocating resources for family-based service interventions, as well as curtailing or even terminating parents' rights to rear their children autonomously. Typically, services require the coordination of the juvenile court and the public social service department's protective service unit.

Child Welfare Legislation

The child welfare system is a network of public and private services influenced by federal and state child welfare laws. Direct services include counseling, protective and nonprotective day care, adoption services, child abuse investigation and protective services, residential or group home care, homemaker and home health aide services, foster family care, therapeutic foster care, residential treatment, teen parent programs, and family life education. Also, child welfare agencies address planning and program development and advocate social change that will enhance the healthy development of children. By tracing the changes over a 20-year period, we can identify significant changes in philosophy and legislative priorities.

The 1980 Adoption Assistance and Child Welfare Act. The 1980 Adoption Assistance and Child Welfare Act (P.L. 96-272) emphasizes permanency planning. The act redirected the nation's efforts toward strengthening families to care for their own children and developing appropriate permanent placements when that is not possible. This reform in child welfare led professionals to believe that no child is unadoptable, and efforts to find permanent homes for children with special needs have taken on new meaning in the delivery of services. The philosophy of P.L. 96-272 guided programming for services:

- Ideally, children should remain in their own homes with appropriate family service supports.
- If the safety of children requires temporary out-of-home placement, then service efforts should emphasize "reunification" of children with their families as soon as possible.
- Workers should proceed to terminate parental rights and devise permanent plans for children if family reunification efforts fail.

BOX **13.1**

Reflections on Empowerment

Child Protective Services and Empowerment

Protecting children from harm and empowering families to care adequately for their children are dual goals of state-sponsored child protective service agencies. Child protective service workers investigate reports of child maltreatment. When reports of child abuse and neglect are founded or indicated, in-home family-centered services are implemented to keep the family together and protect children from further harm. When children must be removed from families, all reasonable efforts must be made to reunify families. Tens of thousands of families benefit from family preservation and family reunification services every year. Yet, highly publicized cases of child abuse and neglect resulting in the maiming or death of children propel child advocacy groups to question the mandate of family preservation and family reuninification programs.

Thus, a central issue in child welfare involves child protection versus preservation of the family, or, put another way, from the conflict between the social control function and the helping function in this field of practice. Social work practice in child maltreatment is laden with value issues and ethical dilemmas. Questions arise such as:

- At what point should intrusive measures be taken in family life?
- How can social workers provide services that support family integrity and offer a safety net for at-risk children?
- How do practitioners deal with the life-changing decisions to remove children from their homes or terminate parental rights?
- How can practitioners uphold principles of nonjudgmentalism, individual dignity and worth, and self-determination, given the existence of battered children?

Child protective service agencies must respond to community expectations for accountability in protecting children. Competent communities, in turn, must offer resources for parents that reduce the risk for potential abuse.

P.L. 96-272 stipulates services to ensure the success of permanency planning efforts, including home-based services, adoption services, and foster care and institutional services.

Child Abuse Prevention and Treatment Act Amendments of 1996. Federal legislation on child abuse began with the authorization of the 1974 Child Abuse Prevention and Treatment Act (CAPTA) (P.L. 93-247). It has been revised and amended several times. The provisions in the 1996 amendments detail a comprehensive approach that

- Integrates the work of social service, legal, health, mental health, education, and substance abuse agencies and organizations
- Strengthens coordination among all levels of government and with private agencies; civic, religious, and professional organizations; and individual volunteers
- Emphasizes the need for abuse and neglect prevention, assessment, investigation, and treatment at the neighborhood level

- Ensures properly trained support staff with specialized knowledge to carry out their child protection duties
- Is sensitive to ethnic and cultural diversity (Administration for Children and Families, n.d.)

The Adoption and Safe Families Act of 1997. The Adoption and Safe Families Act of 1997 (ASFA) incorporates several key principles to guide reform in state-based child welfare services. In essence, the ASFA refocuses child welfare goals to emphasize safety, permanence, and well-being for children (Barbell & Wright, 1999; Tracy & Pine, 2000). To reduce long-term out-of-home placements and facilitate adoptions, this law establishes new timelines (and specifies exceptions) for steps such as holding permanency hearings within 12 months of a child's entrance into foster care and filing petitions for the termination of parental rights if a child has been in care 15 of the last 22 months. As a result, efforts must focus concurrently on family reunification and permanency planning. Workers are exempted from making reasonable efforts to return children to their own homes in circumstances such as chronic abuse or a history of termination of parental rights. If returning to their families jeopardizes children's safety, child welfare workers must make reasonable efforts for timely placement of children according to their established permanency plans. This legislation places considerable emphasis on adoption as the most viable plan for permanency.

Keeping Children and Families Safe Act of 2003. The Keeping Children and Families Safe Act of 2003 (P.L. 105-36) reauthorizes the CAPTA (P.L. 93-247). Stipulations of this legislation include provisions for improving child protective services; funding demonstration projects that link child protection agencies with agencies that focus on health, mental health, and developmental disabilities; enhancing prevention activities; and expanding entitlements to technical assistance to the for-profit sector of service delivery.

Supportive, Supplemental, and Substitutive Services

Kadushin and Martin (1988) organize this myriad of child welfare services into a framework of supportive, supplemental, and substitutive services (see Table 13.1).

Supportive services for families are first-line social service supports that address problems in the welfare of children. They enhance child–parent relationships and strengthen parents' abilities to provide for their children's needs. Family support programs incorporate efforts to preserve or strengthen families and maintain children in their own homes. Intact families access the supportive services of family counseling agencies, child guidance clinics, and community mental health services.

For families whose children have been removed from their homes, supportive services facilitate family reunification. The goal in these protective situations is to strengthen parental roles so that parents can care for their children in adequate, socially acceptable ways. Additional examples of supportive services are family life education and other services for adolescent parents that provide them with information to support their assumption of parental roles.

Supplementary services fulfill some missing part of the parental role. Supplementary services are "the second-line of defense, called upon when the parental role is inadequately covered but the family configuration is such that, with supplementation, the child can con-

TABLE 13.1 Family Services

Services	Purpose	Premise	Selected Examples
Services that preserve or strengthen families	To support parents in fulfilling parental roles	Families have a right to raise their own children	Home-based services: family counseling, parent education, respite care
Services that augment family functioning	To supplement parental roles when inadequacies exist	Children have a right to develop in a healthy family environment	Parent aides, homemaker services, day care, protective services, income maintenance
Services that provide temporary or permanent out-of-home placement for children	To substitute for parents when parents are unable to fulfill parental roles	Children have the right to adequate care and safe environments	Foster care, group care, shelter care, residential care, institutionalization, permanency planning

tinue to live at home without harm" (Kadushin, 1980, p. 27). For example, homemaker services, family preservation, and protective day care augment child care functions. Ideally, providers of supplementary services join with parents to enhance their abilities to parent. Financial maintenance programs, particularly TANF and social insurance programs, aid parents in their income-producing responsibilities.

Substitutive services replace parents' roles in the family. Substituting another family or living arrangement implies that "someone else takes over all aspects of the parental role" (Kadushin, 1980, p. 313). Substitute services often require a change in legal custody of the child, a change of guardianship, severance of parental responsibility, or termination of parental rights. Examples of substitutive services include out-of-home placements, foster care, adoption, and shelter or institutional placement services for children.

Primary Prevention

Prevention efforts in child welfare services gained prominence with the passage of the Child Abuse Prevention and Treatment Act (P.L. 93-247) in 1974. The act specifically called for a nationwide, coordinated effort to identify, treat, and prevent child maltreatment. It also stipulated policies for collecting data on the incidence of child maltreatment, created a clearinghouse for the dissemination of information about prevention and treatment of child abuse and neglect, and required training for child welfare personnel. The National Center on Child Abuse and Neglect was established to implement the legislative objectives, monitor the federal and state initiatives in this area, and support research and innovative primary prevention programs.

All families benefit from services directed at preventing family breakdown and child maltreatment and promoting healthy family functioning. Promotion models emphasize mastery and develop capabilities. "By building on strengths rather than rectifying deficits, people become more adaptive in not only dealing with difficult life events but in setting growth-oriented goals and achieving personal aspirations" (Dunst, Trivette, & Thompson, 1991, p. 31).

Primary prevention strengthens families' competencies, promotes positive child-rearing practices, and develops community resources to sustain healthy family functioning.

Children develop positive self-concepts through primary prevention programs.

Prevention of child abuse aims to reduce the prevalence of child maltreatment. Program areas that contribute to a sound prevention strategy are as follows:

- Support programs for new parents, providing education in child development, parent-and-child relationships, and adult relationships; information on community resources; and programs enhancing parent-and-child bonding and infant stimulation;
- Education for parents directed toward the creation of social networks and the continuation of instruction in childcare and child development, home-visitor services, and special education support programs;
- Early and regular child and family screening and treatment;
- Childcare opportunities, including emergency, respite, and crisis-oriented care;
- Life skills training for children and young adults in the areas of child development, family management, self-development, methods of seeking help, education in sexuality, family planning, and issues relating to parenting;
- Self-help groups and other neighborhood supports;
- Family support services, including crisis care programs, home-based programs, counseling services, community resource information, and health care;
- Community organization activities; and
- Public information and education on child abuse prevention. (Family Resource Coalition, n.d., Families and Child Abuse Prevention section, ¶ 4)

Social Work Highlights. Primary prevention programs strengthen families and foster children's well-being. Among the model programs highlighted by the Family Resource Coalition (n.d.) are those emphasizing family resources, family supports, and parent education.

Model: Family-Child Resources

Family-Child Resources, Inc., a private prevention and early intervention agency, offers services and support for children and their families in and around York, Pennsylvania. All services are family-centered and many are based in the home, school, or workplace. Family-Child Resources has forged strong partnerships with state and local organizations. Effective working relationships with medical and legal professionals, and with agency and school personnel, have enhanced the quality of services and have contributed to successful replication of the program in both urban and rural settings. Information and consulting services regarding program models, program development, funding, and materials are routinely provided.

Services include:

- Home-based assessment and intervention for high-risk families;
- Community-based prevention groups for children being affected by divorce or separation, substance abuse, and/or child abuse;
- Elementary school-based student support programs;
- Classes, study groups, and presentations to enhance parenting skills;
- Perinatal coaching to encourage healthy relationships between parents and their newborns;
- Counseling for adults and children;
- Custody workshops to assist divorcing parents in helping their children cope with divorce;
- Developmental assessment, specialized therapies, and play groups for children birth to three who have developmental delays; and
- Training and consultation for education, legal, medical, and human services professionals.

Family-Child Resources' active participation in committees of professional organizations and state and local policy-setting agencies creates partnerships and alliances and keeps the agency abreast of best practices, legislative changes, and funding sources. (Family Resource Coalition, Child Abuse Prevention Program Models section, ¶ 2)

Model: Friends of the Family

Friends of the Family, founded in 1972, is a non-profit community mental health and family support center in Van Nuys, California. Its mission is to foster strong families and the development of resilient children by providing quality mental health and human development programs to mainstream and underserved populations in the Los Angeles area. Friends of the Family's primary goals are to (1) improve family functioning, (2) decrease the incidence of child abuse and neglect, (3) encourage positive parent development, and (4) ameliorate costly social problems through primary prevention. Friends of the Family's programs include:

- Community mental health programs, offering group counseling;
- Comprehensive services to adolescent parents;
- Domestic violence prevention and treatment program; and
- Cultural Connections, a program to increase access to counseling by African American and Latino families.

Throughout its history of providing family support services, Friends of the Family has been known for its flexibility and responsiveness. The organization designs and facilitates the development of programs that are community-based, consumer-driven, and designed for universal access, and that emphasize primary and secondary prevention and health promotion. (Family Resource Coalition, Child Abuse Prevention Program Models section, ¶ 3)

Model: Wisconsin Family Resource Programs

A large interdisciplinary committee of educators, health and human services providers, parents, legislators, and state agency representatives developed a legislative proposal for parenting education and support programs that would be universally available to all Wisconsin parents. Wisconsin lawmakers first appropriated funds in the 1989–1991 biennium. Three key features of the programs are especially notable: (1) they are available to all families within their communities, (2) they emphasize prevention-oriented services, and (3) they maintain independent parent advisory boards that actively participate in the development, operation, and governance of services.

Wisconsin's Family Resource Programs are administered by the Children's Trust Fund, a state agency with a 10-year history of successful administration of grants to family resource and child abuse and neglect prevention programs.

Wisconsin's Family Resource Programs provide prevention services and support systems that build on and emphasize family strengths. Programs are collaborative and community- and neighborhood-based, and emphasize services for families with children three years of age or younger. The Programs select and administer strengths-based outcome evaluations.

Parent education and support are provided through a combination of center- and home-based services, which include: group and family-based parent education, workshops, support groups, drop-in programs, outreach, and referrals. The Programs' "one-stop-shop" approach creates continuity among services for families and provides linkages to other community programs. Many of Wisconsin's Family Resource Programs are also directly providing economic self-sufficiency programs, such as job training and GED courses. Each center adapts its programs to meet the needs of families in its community. (Family Resource Coalition, Child Abuse Prevention Program Models section, ¶ 4)

Family Support and Family Preservation Services

The purposes of federal grants for family support and family preservation services are twofold—to strengthen families and to prevent child abuse. Family support services are proactive, community-based services designed to reduce stress and help parents care for their children before crises occur. These preventive services range from respite care to health education to developmental screening to other programs that can assist parents with child-rearing activities. Family preservation services are time-limited, family-centered, home-based services that help families cope with crises or problems that interfere with parents' abilities to deal with their children effectively. Their intent is to prevent out-of-home placement of children by ensuring the safety of children within their own families (Roditti, 1995; Tracy, 1995).

Based on a perspective that is both strengths-oriented and family-focused, the Children's Bureau delineates principles for family support and family preservation initiatives:

- The welfare and safety of children and of all family members must be maintained while strengthening and preserving the family whenever possible. Supporting families is the best way of promoting children's healthy development.

BOX 13.2
Social Work Profile

Child Welfare

I believe that public child welfare services provide a safety for children and families at risk. The clients we serve through the state agency, for the most part, have been mandated to participate in court-ordered services. Child protective service workers investigate reported incidents of child abuse and neglect, complete risk assessments, provide an array of case management services, monitor case plans, and provide specialized treatment services. We work collaboratively with private sector child welfare, substance abuse, and mental health providers through purchase of service contractual arrangements.

I can honestly say that child welfare case management was the hardest job I ever had, as the problems associated with child maltreatment are emotion-laden and the workloads are heavy. As a child welfare professional, I constantly struggle to define who the client is, as child welfare is about both protecting children *and* helping families. Although child safety is paramount, there is a true need to promote family relationships.

My 20 some years of experience in the field of child welfare tells me that family involvement is requisite to the success of maintaining children in their own homes or reunifying families after a separation. Because of the nature of child maltreatment, practitioners can lose trust in families' abilities to make good decisions or they may even have a tendency to suspect parents' intentions. Workers are often challenged to find potential in family functioning and to value family involvement throughout the intervention process. When I facilitate a case review after a recommendation is made to remove children from their family, the first question I ask is whether the parents were provided with opportunities to fully participate in the case plan.

As a child welfare administrator and supervisor, I'm concerned about the ethical bind that direct service case managers face between implementing a philosophy of family-focused services and meeting the billing requirements of a child-focused funding stream. On the one hand, service supervisors tell their line workers to focus on strengthening family relationships. On the other hand, Medicaid payment reimbursement requires documentation of rehabilitation treatment services that are child-focused. This bind is further complicated by the large caseload of child welfare case managers, which restricts the time they have available to match family needs with community resources and to locate the informal social supports needed to sustain families.

I see two trends that the local child welfare service community will need to confront. The first relates to the fact that many states are redesigning organizational structures to streamline child welfare and juvenile court services, as legislators press the system to become more efficient and get documented results. The second trend is the consideration of performance-based payment models. I believe the recent emphasis on outcomes and results-oriented practice will likely raise the consideration of performance-based to purchase-of-service contracts. Traditionally, the public child welfare agency has purchased services from private sector family service agencies for the majority of the treatment services. Performance-based contracts will likely be more complex in that they will be predicated on achieving client outcomes rather than tallying service units.

The empowerment philosophy and value base of social work ground child welfare practitioners in making ethical decisions and choices that often involve major life changes for children and families.

- Services focus on the family as a whole, looking toward identifying, enhancing, and respecting family strengths as opposed to focusing on family deficits or dysfunctions.

Service providers work with families as partners in identifying and meeting individual and family needs.

- Services are easily accessible (often delivered in the home or in community-based settings, using schedules convenient to parents) and are delivered in a manner that respects cultural and community differences.
- Services are flexible and responsive to real family needs. Linkages to a wide variety of supports and services outside the child welfare system (e.g., housing, substance abuse treatment, mental health, health, job training, child care) are generally crucial to meeting families' and children's needs.
- Services are community-based and involve community organizations and residents (including parents) in their design and delivery.
- Services are intensive enough to meet family needs and keep children safe. The level of intensity necessary to achieve these goals may vary greatly between preventive (family support) and crisis services. (Roditti, 1995, pp. 1048–1049)

Family preservation programs vary greatly; however, most include provisions for short-term, intensive work with families as well as small caseloads, 24-hour availability, and a range of services that includes education, counseling, advocacy, skills training, and referrals to other community resources. Some programs use a team approach, uniting the expertise of social work professionals, paraprofessionals, and the families.

Homemaker–Home Health Aide Services. Family preservation plans may draw on the resources of homemakers and home health aides to provide support to families when caretakers are unable to provide for their families adequately. Although homemaker–home health aide programs were primarily designed for older adults through the Medicare amendments of the Social Security Act (Title XVIII), an increasing number of services are available to families with children.

As child welfare paraprofessionals, homemakers and home health aides provide in-home services that augment professional social work services. They perform housekeeping chores and provide personal care when parents have a physical or mental illness or when children have disabling conditions requiring additional assistance. In instances of child abuse and neglect, court directives may place an aide with a family to work on developing parenting skills as well as to observe family dynamics or facilitate children's out-of-home placements.

As home management specialists, homemakers and home health aides provide interactions, often daily, with families to maintain them as intact units. In addition to helping with cleaning and preparing meals, homemakers teach family members home management skills and act as role models for effective adult–child interactions. Working collaboratively with families and drawing on their strengths is an important dimension of their work.

Social Work Highlights. The case example that follows (Downs, Costin, & McFadden, 1996) describes a social worker's family preservation activities with Amy, a 23-year-old mother of three children: Jeremy, age 6; Tiffany, age 4; and Ashley, her baby, whose health is medically fragile as a result of Amy's use of crack during her pregnancy. Jimmy, the father of the two oldest children, visits occasionally; however, his behavior is abusive when he has been drinking. Amy's life has been on a roller coaster for the last few years. After being evicted twice for nonpayment of rent, she and her children drifted from shelter to shelter until Amy's cousin agreed to Amy's living with her. Amy's mother and Jimmy have threatened to "call the state" several times to have the children removed from Amy's custody because of their concern about the children's safety and their exposure to their mother's involvement in the drug scene.

> Her nerves are frayed from the children's constant fighting and whining and Ashley's irritable fretful crying. She tries to keep the children quiet because they annoy her cousin, who threatens to kick her out. She needs a drink or a joint to tolerate the children when they get out of control. Amy is frightened because she has been hitting the children too hard in futile discipline attempts. She left bruises on Jeremy's back and arms after hitting him with a belt to show him that he couldn't hit his sister. When she took Ashley to the emergency room because the infant seemed very congested, a nurse noticed Jeremy's bruises and was concerned about Ashley's nutrition, as she was below the twentieth percentile. The hospital called children's protective services.
>
> Ten years ago the children might have been placed in foster care. After a careful assessment of risk, the CPS worker refers Amy to a program that offers intensive, comprehensive family-based services designed to preserve the family unit, protect the children, and keep the children out of care.
>
> Carolyn, the family-based services worker, carries a beeper so that she is available to Amy and the children around the clock, if needed. Because her caseload is limited to two or three families, she has the time during the next 6 weeks to work intensively with the family. She will attempt to keep the family together by identifying and supporting their strengths, bringing in resources, teaching them problem-solving skills, and providing hope. She will engage Amy by helping her to locate housing and furniture, working with her household tasks, and being an understanding and caring constant figure in her life. Carolyn will use a wide range of techniques and strategies, drawn from family therapy and social learning sources, to enable Amy to face and solve the problems that have led to the threat of child placement. She will also begin to put into place a safety net of ongoing community resources that will meet the children's developmental needs, and Amy's needs during a long recovery process. (p. 226)

Day Care

Day care requires fewer adjustments in children's daily life and is an integral part of both family support and family preservation (Roditti, 1995). Day care services for children may be either *protective*—to provide care for children who have been abused or neglected—or *nonprotective*—to provide care for children of working parents or as a respite from parenting responsibilities. Day care includes a range of programs, including provisions for children of working parents; for supports during normal life transitions; for additional resources and supports, such as parenting programs and respite care; for specialized assistance, including family-focused services, programs for teen parents, and crisis nurseries; and for supplemental services in the context of family preservation and child protection activities. Services may be offered at day care centers, at licensed or approved private family homes, or in group homes. Day treatment is a special type of day care that provides intensive therapy for specific targeted populations, such as children with behavioral problems and mental disorders.

Crisis nurseries maintain a 24-hour capacity to respond to the crisis or respite needs of families to prevent child maltreatment. Crisis nurseries give parents an opportunity to leave their children in a safe place during short-term crises. Such nurseries serve as nonpunitive community resources that prevent the incidence of child abuse and neglect in times of overwhelming stress.

Family Group Conferencing

Family group conferencing is a relatively new initiative in child welfare that emphasizes establishing partnerships with families. The first model for the family group conference (FGC) was developed in New Zealand in 1989 in response to child welfare legislation—The Child, Young Persons, and Their Families Act. This Act specifically "enables and empowers families to make and implement decisions in cases of abuse, neglect, and delinquency" (Sieppert, Hudson, & Unrau, 2000). FGCs have been incorporated into child welfare practices in various locations in the United States, the United Kingdom, Australia, British Columbia, Israel, Norway, Sweden, and South Africa.

Originally based on the traditional processes for decision making in Maori culture (aboriginal people in New Zealand), the FGC places families in a central role in child protection (Lupton, 1998; Mitchell & Kitson, 1997). It provides "an opportunity for the family, including the extended family, to hear the concerns and contribute to the decisions-making process with respect to the child" (Connolly & McKenzie, 1999, p. 23). The three phases of the FGC process include sharing information, deliberating privately among family members, and reaching an agreement. Social workers continue to ensure children's safety; however, their roles also shift to facilitate family participation. The FGC moves away from the attitude that says "welfare knows best" to "a concrete means of empowering families to make their own decisions and find their own solutions" (Connolly, 1994, pp. 99–100). "Experience has also shown that families and professionals can work in partnership and that sharing child protection responsibility can have the effect of increasing the safety net for children at risk" (Connolly & McKenzie, p. 33).

One example of FGC is the experience of the Williams family (Connolly & McKenzie, 1999). Mr. Williams's alleged abuse of 12-year-old Janice, the oldest of three children, was brought to the attention the child protection agency. After admitting that he abused Janice, he moved away from the family home. Janice was frightened of her father and was very concerned that he would return home. Janice's mother was having difficulty coping. Although she was supportive of Janice, she also "wanted things back the way they had been" (p. 29). The FGC coordinator worked with the Williams family to set up a conference and commit to a plan of support for Janice. Although all grandparents were deceased, the Williams family had a fairly extensive network of family members and friends.

> All but one member of the maternal side of the family attended the FGC. Encouraged by the coordinator, the uncle who was unable to attend wrote a letter to the meeting expressing his views. Both of Mr. Williams's sisters attended the meeting. In addition to the family, there were a number of quasi-family members, friends who had known the family for many years and were present by family request. Because of Janice's fear and distress at the prospect of meeting her father so soon after the abuse, the coordinator exercised her statutory authority and excluded him from the meeting. As required by the legislation, Mr. Williams's views were recorded and were presented to the family group as part of the information-sharing phase of the meeting.
>
> Prior to the FGC, members of the extended family had largely lost touch with each other, and the meeting provided the opportunity to renew lost links. Family members were supportive of one another at the meeting, and the decisions reflected their desire to reestablish contact. With this in mind, regular contact visits were arranged and child care assistance was offered and subsequently provided by the family. Although the family acknowledged the fact that Mr. Williams wanted to return home, they also discussed at length the importance of Janice feeling safe. They also recognized Mrs. Williams support needs and the con-

flicting nature of competing needs within the family. Finally, the family group decided that the daughter needed the security of a court restraining order with respect to Mr. Williams, and the paternal aunts undertook to provide him with support in terms of dealing with the decision. Financial assistance for the family was provided by the welfare agency together with ongoing support and supervision. (pp. 19–20)

Foster Care

The placement of children in foster homes and other types of out-of-home care such as group homes and small residential facilities is a *temporary* substitute care option. Foster homes provide short-term living arrangements for children in a family home setting when children cannot safely remain with their own families.

Historical Perspective. Since colonial times, communities have made provision for the care of dependent and destitute children. Children who were abandoned or orphaned were often placed in almshouses, apprenticed, or indentured. Grounded in English law and tradition, indenturing afforded males the opportunity to become self-sufficient by developing a trade and enabled females to acquire domestic skills (Wiltse, 1985).

Charles Loring Brace originated the substitute family practices that have become so much a part of modern foster care. As secretary of the New York Children's Aid Society in 1853, Brace envisioned family life for destitute children in the idealized environment of the family and small town communities. This vision of permanency was guided by the good intention of Christian charity; however, in retrospect, the child rescue movement did

Volunteers in the Foster Grandparents Program spend quality time playing with young children.

not recognize the inherent abuses of orphan trains, cheap farm labor, and the separation of children from familiar environments.

At the turn of the century, Charles Birtwell of the Boston Children's Aid Society recognized the preeminence of children's needs. Considering the best interest of children, Birtwell advocated children's remaining with or returning quickly to their biological families. To this end, Birtwell viewed foster care as temporary and suggested providing services for biological families.

The first White House Conference on Dependent Children was held in 1909 under Theodore Roosevelt's administration. The U.S. Children's Bureau was created in 1912 as a direct result of the conference's support for the idea of a federal bureau to address children's issues (Parker, 1994). The conference also addressed the child dependency issue and advocated a national system of financial aid to mothers. A landmark social welfare resolution was passed, stating "that no child should be removed from its home for reasons of poverty alone" (Cohen, 1992, p. 23). The intent of this resolution was to eliminate family separations and child placements based solely on families' financial inability to care for their children.

Further studies of the foster care system, notably a 1959 report by Maas and Engler, *Children in Need of Parents,* challenged the premise that the placement of children in foster care was, in fact, temporary. This research found that children placed in foster care arrangements were not likely to return to their biological families. For the next decade, child welfare professionals examined the inconsistencies between their philosophy of foster care and the reality of foster care practices.

Permanency planning emerged from the Oregon Project as a model that child welfare workers implemented nationwide in the 1970s. The purpose of permanency planning is to reduce lengths of stay in temporary substitutive care arrangements, provide services to reunify families, and eliminate obstacles or barriers to child placement by courts and agencies. The ultimate goal of permanency planning is to ensure stability in children's living arrangements. Often this means employing more aggressive attempts to free children legally from their biological families. Amendments to P.L. 105-89, the Adoption and Safe Families Act of 1997, allow a redirection of the reasonable efforts requirement away from children's reunification with their biological parent or parents to finalizing their permanency placement plan (Hollingsworth, 2000).

Foster Care Placements. Although the current philosophical emphasis in child welfare is on maintaining children in their own homes, placement services continue to be a major part of the child welfare delivery system. Types of foster care placement include shelter homes offering temporary shelter for children requiring short-term care; long-term foster homes for children in need of a permanent plan who are unlikely to return to their own homes or be adopter; specialized foster homes for children with special needs, such as developmental disabilities; and therapeutic foster care, in which specially trained foster parents provide intensive treatment services (Downs, Costin, & McFadden, 1996).

Estimates provided by the Adoption and Foster Care Analysis and Reporting System (AFCARS) indicate that, in September 2001, 542,000 children were in foster care (Children's Bureau, 2003). For those children placed in foster care, the average length of stay is two years and nine months. Placement occurs in a variety of settings, including foster family care, formal kinship care, group homes, supervised independent living situations, and pre-adoptive homes. More than half of all children placed in foster care remain in foster families more than 18 months. AFCARS also reports that 263,000 children left the foster care system in 2001. Of these children, 57 percent were reunified with their families (148,606), 18 percent were adopted (46,668), and 7 percent were emancipated (19,008).

Placement of children in living arrangements outside their family home occurs for a number of reasons, including the following:

- Parents' inability or unwillingness to continue their caretaking responsibilities
- Child endangerment that results from abuse or neglect
- Parents' absence through death, abandonment, or incarceration
- Parents' serious physical or mental illness
- Parental difficulties with alcohol and drug problems
- Children's behavioral, personality, or physical problems

Regardless of the problem that precipitates foster care placement, children experience confusion and trauma when they are separated from their natural families. Foster care services provide a temporary safety net for abused and neglected children as their families work toward reunification.

Any substitute care that more closely approximates a family life environment is preferable to group homes or institutionalization. In fact, foster family care has typically been the treatment of choice for "normal" children, with group living and residential programs reserved for children with special needs, particularly those who were troubled or severely disturbed. Locating foster family homes for children with special needs has been coupled with supportive services to their foster families, such as respite care, family counseling, medical assistance, and intensive individual therapy. Recent efforts at implementing a privatized foster care system in Kansas suggest the need for ongoing evaluation and outcomes assessment to determine whether permanency goals for children can be realized under privatized managed care approaches (Petr & Johnson, 1999).

Social Work Highlights. Speaking from her experiences as a foster parent, Chubbuck (1998) relates stories of children in foster care and their permanency plans:

> On December 22nd three children came to live with us because Mom was arrested for drug and weapon charges. They came with only the clothes on their backs. At the last minute, we scrambled to make Christmas for them. My community, my church, my family and my friends came together to make Santa come alive right before their eyes. Later, after opening presents of new clothes and toys, I was tucking in the oldest boy. As we talked, he had tears in his eyes. I asked, "It's pretty hard being here without your Mom on Christmas, isn't it?" He said, "No, not really, she usually didn't make Christmas day anyway." I asked, "Are you sick?" He said, "No." He went on to say that this was the first time Santa ever spelled his name right and he couldn't understand why all those strangers would do this for his brother, sister and him. With tears in my eyes, I said, "Because you are all so special and it's our way to say thanks for you just being with us to love." That kindness changed him like the tiny mustard seed blooming. Their permanency plan was to live with their grandmother since their mother was sentenced to fourteen years. When I talk with the grandmother, she says that young man is always wanting to help someone. What better gift could anybody be given or receive than this kind of display of compassion and love? (¶ 10)

Formal Kinship Care. One type of foster placement called formal kinship care, or placing children with relatives, is being used with an increasing number of children whose circumstances require out-of-home placements. "Recognition of extended family networks as a resource has brought kinship care to the forefront as an option for children who must live apart from their biological parents" (Ingram, 1996). About one-fourth of all children in foster care in the United States were placed in the care of relatives in 2001 (Children's Bureau, 2003). The kinship placement rates in California, Illinois, and New York are even more dramatic. In California, about half of all foster placements are with relatives; in Illinois and New York, more than half of all placements are in some form of kinship care (Child Welfare League of America, 2003). Kinship care "is now recognized as the fastest growing sector of out-of-home placement" (Leslie, Landsverk, Horton, Ganger, & Newton, 2000, p. 315).

Factors influencing the growth of formal kinship care include decreasing availability of nonkinship foster parents and legislative initiatives such as the Personal Responsibility and Work Opportunity Act of 1996, which emphasize preserving families and family ties through placements with adult relatives. Additionally, the Child Welfare League of America (n.d.) suggests factors such as increased incidence of child maltreatment, poverty, HIV/AIDS, family violence, parental incarceration also contribute to rising rates of children in kinship care.

"Recognition of extended family networks as a resource has brought kinship care to the forefront as an option for children who must live apart from their biological parents" (Ingram, 1996). Formal kinship placements do, however, raise concerns about financial support for relatives, ensuring the success of permanency planning efforts, and providing for the protection and safety of children (Everett, 1995; Ingram, 1996; Testa, Shook, Cohen, & Woods, 1996). In general, permanency plans for children in formal kinship care are most likely ongoing placements with their relatives rather than reunification with their families (U.S. Department of Health and Human Services, 2000a).

Social Work Highlights. The following example demonstrates both the benefits of kinship care and the problems that occur when the press for permanency planning creates dilemmas for grandparents who do not wish to assume the legal role of parent:

> Wayne and Aaron have been with their parental grandparents since 1991. The children have been [wards of the state] since 1993 due to the voluntary surrender by both parents.
>
> The grandparents have contributed immensely to the children's sense of security and stability. Bonding and attachment are well established. Both the foster care and adoption worker agree that it is in the best interests of the children to remain with the grandparents. They are aware, however, that current policy prohibits such an arrangement unless the grandparents proceed with adoption.
>
> The grandparents have vacillated about adopting. To keep from losing the children, the grandmother decided that she wants to adopt. The grandfather does not. He is willing to keep the children in his home but he wants to remain the grandfather. He does not want to become the father. He states that he is reluctant to accept the responsibility that is his son's. The grandmother cannot adopt if her spouse disagrees and she has threatened to divorce him.
>
> ***Outcomes***
>
> The children are thriving in the custody and care of their paternal grandparents. Since they have been [wards of the state] for more than six months, they have been listed in MARE [a list of children available for adoption]. The grandparents are willing to continue to provide care but are unable to agree about adoption. (Mills & Usher, 1996, pp. 612–613)

Independent Living Services. Originally authorized under Title IV-E of the Social Security Act, independent living services provided programming for older youths in foster care that eased their transition to independent adulthood (Children's Bureau, 1999). The Foster Care Independence Act of 1999 (P.L. 106-169) reauthorizes funding to states to help children who are "aging out" of foster care at age 18 to find work or to continue their education; extends Medicaid coverage to 18-, 19-, and 20-year-olds who have left foster care; stipulates funding for housing assistance; and increases the amount of monetary resources allowed in determining eligibility (National Foster Care Awareness Project, 2000). Estimates indicate that nearly 20,000 youths "age out" of foster care annually (Children's Bureau, 2003). Emphasizing empowerment, the Foster Care Independence Program assists older youths in foster care in their transition to adulthood by providing a variety of services, including life skills training, mentoring, support groups, and supervised apartment living. Research on the views of youths who had participated in an independent living program found that participants identified a number of aspects of the program as helpful, including the instruction about finances and skills building (McMillen, Rideout, Fisher, & Tucker, 1997). As one participant said, "They don't do things for you. They tell you how to get them done . . . right, exactly . . . 'cause a lot of people in the system they will go and do it for you. [The independent-living specialist] will be the first one to tell you. 'I will not do anything for you. I will let you know a way you can get it done but I will not do it for you'" (p. 477).

Residential Group Homes and Institutional Care

Social workers arrange alternatives to family foster care when the needs of children require specialized care offered only through out-of-home services. "Group care services are provided under public, voluntary nonprofit, and proprietary auspices, in child welfare, child mental health, and juvenile justice systems, often to the same population of youth" (Whittaker, 2000). The Child Welfare League of America (1981) describes three different types of group care for children: institutional care, residential treatment, and group home services.

Institutional care for children includes treatment in large, total-care facilities for children exhibiting severe behavioral and emotional problems. Typically, these institutions are state-operated juvenile correctional and child mental health facilities. Serving an entire state population, these facilities care for large numbers of children in a central location. Institutional programs intervene in all aspects of daily living, provide care and treatment, work with parents during placement, and offer postplacement activities to assist children in their successful return to their families and communities.

Residential treatment provides a therapeutic group environment for children with emotional disturbances that cannot be dealt with effectively in less intensive substitute family arrangements. Typically, residential treatment facilities are located within local communities. Nonprofit voluntary agencies sponsor many of these programs. As out-of-home arrangements, residential treatment facilities offer community-based residential programming to youths and their families.

Finally, *group care* is offered under the auspices of group home services. Many group homes provide a homelike environment in remodeled houses located in residential neighborhoods. Each group home serves a relatively small number of children or adolescents. For whatever reason, family foster care is not appropriate for these children. Because of their needs, this youth population benefits from a combination of group living and specialized services.

Adoption

The Child Welfare League of America asserts that adoption is a means of finding families for children, not finding children for families (Cole, 1985). Children are eligible for adoption when their biological parents, for whatever reason, voluntarily relinquish their rights or when court actions terminate their parental rights. Biological relatives adopt a large proportion of children who qualify for adoption. Intermediaries, such as licensed agencies, arrange children's placements and adoption. Legitimate intermediaries all have nonprofit status. In fact, for-profit adoptions are illegal in all jurisdictions in the United States.

Recent child welfare legislation, the Adoption and Safe Families Act of 1997, promotes the adoption of children in out-of-home placements by authorizing adoption incentive payments to states. The Adoption and Foster Care Analysis and Reporting System indicates that, in 2001, of the 176,000 children available for adoption in the public child welfare system, 50,000 children were adopted (Children's Bureau, 2003). This legislation also supports initiatives that provide technical assistance to increase adoptions (Hollingsworth, 2000). Some suggest this legislation makes adoption the "new panacea" for resolving the many problems associated with foster care (McGowan & Walsh, 2000).

The number of children, particularly infants, available for adoption has declined. No longer feeling that a stigma is attached to out-of-wedlock births, many women choose to rear their children rather than place them for adoption. Emphasis on parents' rights to child welfare services supports their efforts to provide for their children themselves.

Currently, the main type of adoption in which agency-based social work professionals are involved is special needs adoption. Federal law defines special needs adoption

> as indicating that the child cannot or should not be returned to the home of his or her birth parents and that the child has a specific factor or conditions (such as ethnic background; age; membership in a minority or sibling group; or the presence of a physical, mental, or emotional handicap) that make it reasonable to conclude that the child cannot be placed with adoptive parents without providing adoption assistance or medical assistance. (Barth, 1995, p. 49)

The Adoption and Safe Families Act, like the Adoption Assistance and Child Welfare Act, provides for federal payments for programs that subsidize costs incurred by adoptive parents of children with special needs. The financial guidelines for participating in these adoption assistance programs vary considerably from state to state.

Basically, adoption involves eight steps:

- Identifying a suitable adoptable child
- Legally freeing the child for adoption
- Making preparations for adoption
- Selecting the adoptive family
- Placing the child
- Providing postplacement service supports
- Legally finalizing the adoption
- Providing postadoption services to the adoptive child (Cole, 1985)

Previously, professionals believed that their role ended with the legal consummation of the adoption; however, currently, many are exploring post-legal adoption services as a way to

Large numbers of children with special needs, older children, and sibling groups await adoption in foster family care.

meet the ongoing needs of adoptive families (Watson, 1992). Post-legal adoption services include working with families during the initial transitional period or if subsequent difficulties arise, offering services that anticipate adoptive children's developmental needs at key points in their lives, and providing assistance if persons who are adopted wish to locate their biological parents. Formal and informal social supports appear to play a key role in successful adoptions (Groze, 1996).

Child Welfare Services Continuum

The continuum of family service options ranges from community education efforts that reach all families to specialized placement services for children with exceptional needs (Laird & Hartman, 1985). The continuum includes primary prevention programs that benefit all families, early intervention services for at-risk families, protective services for children who are abused and neglected, and temporary and permanent out-of-home placements for children who require substitute care. To preserve and reunify families, social workers need to employ less intrusive interventions and utilize the least restrictive placement environments.

Studies indicate that minorities are overrepresented in child welfare services (Chand, 2000). Racism and discrimination deny minorities access to community resources and societal opportunities that would enhance their abilities to meet the needs of their families.

BOX 13.3

Reflections on Diversity

Adoptive Families for Special Needs Kids

No one in social services questions that the purpose of adoption is to find families for children, not to find children for families. Children who are readily available for adoption include, among others, children with special needs. The special needs classification includes older children, sibling groups, children with emotional or behavioral problems, children with disabilities, and racial and ethnic minorities. Children with special needs need families with special qualities.

Successful adoptions hinge on making a good match between these children and loving and caring families. Agencies screen potential adoptive parents for their motivation, capability, and commitment to extending their families to include children with special needs. The central question is: What is the best family for this child?

Although families may have room in their hearts and homes for special needs children, their own resources may limit which child they can adopt. Agencies often offer assistance for adoptive families to supplement the care for children with disabilities or behavioral disorders. Adoptive children with extraordinary medical and psychological needs are often eligible for medical assistance. Families may also receive financial supplements, counseling services, and respite care.

Child welfare practitioners advocate keeping siblings together. Again, financial assistance and counseling services, particularly for children who are abuse-reactive, help adoptive families meet the extra demands imposed by their instantly larger family.

Many social workers oppose transracial adoptions. Issues related to preserving racial and cultural identity and survival in a racist society are raised by the Association of Black Social Workers in adopting children of color. Likewise, tribal approval is required before adopting Native American children outside of the tribe. When a transracial adoption is made, families benefit from community services that help bridge the racial and cultural gap.

Because of the disproportionate number of African American children in the child welfare system, Morton (1999) suggests a potential disparate impact in using assessment scales and indexes to make treatment or placement decisions for children and families of different racial and gender groups. In addition, African American children disproportionately receive involuntary intervention in child maltreatment cases, resulting in longer terms of intervention and separation of family members.

Racial and ethnic minority families are often labeled in ways that insinuate psychopathology, deviance, lack of motivation, and subnormal intelligence. In contrast, competence-centered social work practice with minorities focuses on personal and family strengths rather than deficiencies:

> It is the task of the Child Welfare system to recognize and build on those strengths and to offer support and preventive intervention in areas of vulnerability. What is quite clear at this point is that ethnicity has great impact on family organization and functioning and needs to be looked at, not from a "cultural deviant" or "deficit" perspective as it often has been in the past, but from a "cultural variant" or "nondeficit" approach. (Allen, 1985, p. 177)

Families have much to gain from a family service system that focuses on competence and strength.

Family-Centered Approach to Child Welfare

Currently, child welfare services reflect a family-centered approach to practice. Founded on a belief in family strengths, the family-centered approach focuses on both preserving families and protecting children. Because family life is so important for children, child welfare efforts emphasize maintaining children in their own families rather than recommending alternative living arrangements that separate family members. Principles for family-centered practice in child welfare include

- Focusing attention on family units
- Strengthening families' capacities to function effectively
- Involving families in developing family-centered policies, services, and evaluating programs
- Linking families with various community-based networks of supports and services (National Child Welfare Resource Center, 2000)

Within this context, family services provide a *safety net* for children when childrearing practices are inadequate or dangerous. When circumstances warrant the temporary or permanent placement of children outside of their homes, family service workers need to provide a sense of permanency in living arrangements, as well as continuity in relationships with foster parents and other child care providers. The premise of child welfare is that all children deserve nurturing family relationships.

Social Work in the Schools

Working collaboratively with classroom teachers and support staff, school social workers provide supportive services for children and their families in the context of school settings. School social workers may be employed by educational cooperatives composed of a number of school districts and work in one or more of those districts, or they may be hired directly by a single district to work at one or more district sites.

Requirements for school social worker positions vary from state to state. Some states require a B.S.W. degree, others an M.S.W., and yet others an M.S.W. degree that includes specialized school social work courses and passing scores on credentialing examinations. School social workers need specialized knowledge about

- Developmental psychology
- Social psychology of learning
- Behavior modification applications and techniques
- Family systems
- Organizational culture, communication, and change
- Local school policies and relevant state and federal legislation, such as the Family Education Rights and Privacy Act of 1974 (P.L. 93-385), Education for All Handicapped Children Act of 1975 (P.L. 94-142), Education for All Handicapped Children Act of 1986 (P.L. 99-457), and Individuals with Disabilities Education Act of 1990 (P.L. 101-475).

School social work has changed from a clinical-casework approach to an approach that reflects home-school-community liaisons (Allen-Meares, Washington, & Welsh, 1996; Schrenzel, 1994). This more ecologically based approach underscores the importance of partnerships between schools, families, and communities and emphasizes the role of social workers as collaborative partners.

Types of Programs and Services

School social workers offer a myriad of programs and services (Alameda-Lawson & Lawson, 2002; Allen-Meares, Washington, & Welsh, 1996; Altshuler, 2003; Freeman, 1995). They often work with children who are having difficulties with life transitions or who are delinquent, abused, neglected, or sexually abused. They deal with educational issues, such as low achievement motivation, underachievement, nonattendance, learned helplessness, and burnout. They work with children who have special education needs or problems with chemical dependency, or who face multiple stressors that affect their educational achievements. They also address factors in children's social context that affect their performance in school, such as poverty, homelessness, discrimination, sexual harassment, mobility, teen pregnancy, child abuse and domestic violence, youth-gang violence, and health issues including HIV/AIDS.

Social Work Highlights. Allen-Meares, Washington, and Welsh (1996) offer the following example illustrating one school social worker's use of environmental modification techniques:

> In ten elementary school referrals received in the fall, the boys, all from different classrooms, were described by the referring teachers as "having acting-out behavior with poor attention-span in the morning." Further investigation of this pattern of behavior showed that all ten were assigned to the same school bus. Riding on the bus with the children one morning, the school social worker observed arguing and name calling resulting in a fight while the frustrated bus driver shouted for the students to behave themselves "or else." As the students left the bus, many still quite agitated, they were greeted in the halls with further threats and reprimands by various staff members. In each of the classrooms, teachers were drawn into the combative behavior and further threats were made. The behavior of the boys tended to escalate. The social worker discussed his observations with the principal. Together they developed a three-pronged plan consisting of an in-service program for bus drivers for handling behavior on the bus, a change of bus routes designed to break up the student grouping on the bus, and a request for the teachers to meet the students at the classroom doors in the morning and greet them cheerfully with words of encouragement. Three weeks later the social worker and principal watched in the hall as students entered the building. A change had taken place. Teachers and students were working together to "have a good day." On the daily bulletin to the teachers, the last sentence read, "Congratulations! We did it." (p. 235)

Children with Special Educational Needs

Social workers in schools often work with children who have special educational needs, such as learning disabilities, attention deficit disorders, problematic behavior and immature social skills, speech therapy needs, and mental retardation. Examples of school social work services related to the provisions of the Education for All Handicapped Children Act of 1975 (P.L. 94-142) include the following:

- Developing community-based referral procedures to locate children who qualify for educational services
- Preparing assessments based on observations and interviews with family members
- Participating in multidisciplinary staff conferences at which staff members prepare an Individual Educational Program (IEP) for each child involved in a special education program
- Monitoring progress to ensure that IEPs remain current and reflect planning that results in the least restrictive environment possible
- Ensuring that parents understand their rights and mediating conflicts that might develop between parents and school personnel
- Encouraging parents' participation in placement and programming decisions
- Working collaboratively with multidisciplinary team members to evaluate and modify programs and services

Social Work Highlights. Parental involvement in school programming is essential to the overall educational plan for children with special needs. One competence-promoting program addresses the parental investment in school programs for children with behavioral disorders (Nystrom, 1989). Teachers complained that parents didn't cooperate with them and seemed to lack investment in their children's educational plans. The social worker initiated a parent-teacher discussion group that enabled parents and teachers to share common concerns. Interestingly, as a result of these discussions, the teachers themselves became more empathetic with families' parenting issues and frustrations. Participants' heightened awareness of common issues allowed parents and teachers to understand each others' positions.

Early Developmental Screening

A number of physical, cognitive, and psychosocial developmental markers indicate developmental progress. Pediatricians routinely monitor children's physical growth, neurological development, and nutrition. Special education districts or public health facilities such as well-baby clinics and maternal-child health centers offer screening for hearing, vision, motor skills, and speech and language development. Preschool screening may indicate the need for further diagnostic testing for childhood diseases, mental retardation, behavioral disorders, developmental disabilities, or developmental delays.

Social workers practice in many settings that offer prescreening for developmental problems, including medical settings, well-baby clinics, and schools. Common to each setting is the role of working with parents as they deal with the results of the screening and linking parents with resources for special education, speech therapy, and support groups for parents, to name a few. Social workers offer information and education to parents to enhance parenting skills and enrich children's early learning environments.

Social Work Highlights. Joanie Peters, a social worker with the Harper School District, greeted several parents and their children who gathered at the Harper-Collins Neighborhood Center. Children between the ages of 3 to 5 are participating in the early childhood screening project. A team comprising a psychologist, nurse, speech and language clinician, and social worker was conducting the district's annual community-based early childhood screening project. Their combined assessments identify special developmental and learning needs of preschool children and initiate referrals to the New Start Program.

New Start offers several different types of programs for children, depending on the nature of their developmental difficulties. Some children enroll in special education preschool classes, while others enter a "readiness class" to aid their transition to kindergarten.

Joanie co-leads the "Morning Out" program, an educational discussion group for parents of children in the kindergarten readiness class. Through group activities, parents learn more about child development, games for family fun, and age-appropriate activities for children. Joanie recalls that research data from the first half of the three-year project indicate that parents who participate in "Morning Out" are more likely to be involved in their children's school activities, readily contact team members about their questions or concerns, and view themselves as integral members of the educational team.

Developmental Transitions

School social workers are keenly aware of the impact of developmental transitions on both the well-being and the academic performance of school-age youth. Long-standing research indicates that transitions during early adolescence are particularly challenging for middle school girls. Among the factors influencing girls' transitions are the timing of puberty in relation to educational transitions, differences in educational expectations and opportunities as compared with their male counterparts, low self-esteem, and underachievement, particularly in the areas of math and science (Muno & Keenan, 2000).

Social Work Highlights. Interdisciplinary professionals in one school district in the northwestern region of the United States designed an initiative, the After School Girls Leadership (ASGL) program, targeting self-esteem issues in middle school girls (Muno & Keenan, 2000). Carefully developed so as to create a base of support within the school district, the design also included an extensive plan for assessing the outcomes of the program. Program participants met two afternoons a week for twelve weeks. The initial focus was on establishing positive group norms through activities, such as making body maps and community maps. These maps facilitated the participants' reflections on themselves and their community. Subsequently, participants were involved in a process of inquiry that began with generating and reviewing questions, proceeded to identifying themes and a project, and culminated in sponsoring an event. The following case example about one participant's experience in this empowerment-oriented venture illustrates the potential of this approach:

> Krissa J, an eighth-grade program member, walks purposefully into our downstairs classroom. As on other days, her tall figure arrives just minutes after the regular school day has ended. Her arms are loaded down with a stuffed green backpack and a French horn. Immediately she asks, "Are we going to play that game today, the one where we get to say what we have in common?" "Maybe later," I tell her. "Are you willing to lead it?" I ask, realizing this is probably why she's asked to play it.
>
> Krissa blossoms in the program. This is somewhat surprising to me, because at first her behavior is problematic. She acts childishly and disrupts the group by casting criticisms and acting bossy. Yet as our group progresses, so does Krissa. When we invite girls to a mid-program pizza party and performance evaluation, it is Krissa who flawlessly demonstrates

the critical-thinking steps from the ASGL flowchart. As she asks whether others agree with her ideas, she sorts through question cards, picks up ones others have put down, and works diligently. She says how long it takes to do the question sorting—"days and days"—and that it's boring at times. In light of these complaints, her perseverence is impressive.

As a program instructor and evaluator, I suspect that for Krissa the program is a rare chance to be cast in a leading role. Her regular school day does not appear to invite this. Program experiences such as creating body and community maps and leading games and projects are opportunities for self-expression. She seems to feel safe in taking risks as a thinker. Krissa's challenges—being a "young" eighth-grader, inconsistent teacher expectations, negative attitudes about self—appear similar to the challenges described in the literature. Program activities feel different to her, and she takes well to them.

By the end of the school year, others also note a change in Krissa. She is perceived more as a decision maker. One of her teachers remarks, "She is Miss Straightforward, focused businesswoman, goal-oriented, 'A' student." Her mom writes that "now she listens to other views, if they differ from hers, and then makes her decision instead of just saying they are wrong and she's right." Krissa initially writes that a leader is "a person who is not bossy, can share their power, listens to everyone in the group, and is a good, loud speaker." Over the weeks of the program, Krissa clearly demonstrates these behaviors and tells us she plans to "be a coleader next time." (Muno & Keenan, 2000, Case Study section, ¶ 1–4)

Specialized Services for Adolescents

Adolescent youths in the United States are at-risk. These risks result from issues such as poverty, lack of access to health care, child abuse and neglect, sexual exploitation, teen pregnancy, alcohol and drug abuse, crime, violence, gang involvement, and academic failure (McWhirter, McWhirter, McWhirter, & McWhirter, 1998; Splittgerber & Allen, 1996; Stephens, 1997). A recent study by the Carnegie Council on Adolescent Development indicates the magnitude of youths at risk in the United States. The findings suggest that

> approximately 7 million of the 28 million young people enrolled in middle or junior high schools are considered at high risk of failing in school and participating in such harmful behaviors as alcohol and drug abuse and premature and unprotected sexual activity. Additionally, many young people were likely to be involved in violent behavior, either as victims or perpetrators. Many also have little access to needed health service. Another 7 million young people may be at moderate risk; they constitute a subgroup with serious academic, social, and personal problems. (Splittgerber & Allen, 1996)

Youths "lose hope for the future. They turn to peers for attention; they turn to guns for protection, security and status; and they turn to sex and drugs for comfort and relief of boredom. The gang too often becomes their 'family'—the only place where they receive attention and approval" (Stephens, 1997, p. 1).

Factors Enhancing Resiliency and Promoting Competence

Youths' exposure to risk factors, alone, does not predict outcomes. Factors that enhance resiliency and promote competence appear to offer important sources of protection and resources for ensuring opportunities for positive life choices. A profile of resiliency includes characteristics of youths themselves as well as their social environments, including their families, schools, and communities (Bernard, 1992; McWhirter, McWhirter, McWhirter, & McWhirter, 1998).

Personal characteristics of resilient youths include those related to social competence, problem-solving skills, autonomy, and a sense of purpose and future (Bernard, 1992). Youths' *social competence* involves their abilities to relate to and communicate with others effectively. It oftentimes includes such qualities as "responsiveness, flexibility, empathy and caring, communication skills, a sense of humor, and any other prosocial behavior" (p. 3). Additionally, youths who are more flexible and adaptive, and who have a sense of humor "tend to establish more positive relationships with others, including friendships with their peers" (p. 3). *Problem-solving skills* include youths' abilities to solve social and cognitive problems by thinking "abstractly, reflectively, and flexibly" (p. 4) and a willingness and capacity for exploring alternative solutions. *Autonomy* refers to youths' sense of "identity and an ability to act independently and exert some control over [their] environment" (p. 4). Finally, a *sense of purpose and future* includes "healthy expectancies, goal-directedness, success orientation, achievement motivation, educational aspirations, persistence, hopefulness, hardiness, belief in a bright future, a sense of anticipation, a sense of a compelling future, and a sense of coherence" (p. 4). A sense of purpose and the future is the "most powerful predictor of positive outcome" (p. 4).

Families of resilient youths exhibit distinct qualities. First, they offer a climate of caring and support; resilient youths are likely to report having a close bond with at least one person in their families. Second, family members communicate their high expectations for youths' behavior and achievement—"You have everything you need to be successful—and you can do it!" (Bernard, 1992, p. 6). Families of resilient youths go beyond providing simple votes of confidence. They communicate to youths a perspective that difficulties can be worked out; validate youths' worth; provide structure for youthful family members through clear expectations and predictable rules and regulations; and anchor youths with a sense of life's meaning and purpose. Finally, families of resilient youths encourage youths' participation in and contribution to family life.

Schools that foster resiliency in youths exhibit similar characteristics. First, these schools demonstrate their caring and support for students, knowing that this climate enhances youths' motivation to achieve. Second, they communicate their high expectations for student achievement as evidenced by their "academic emphasis, teachers' clear expectations and regulations, high level of student participation, many, varied, alternative resources" (Bernard, 1992, p. 8). Recent "research on successful programs for youth at risk of academic failure has clearly demonstrated that a school-wide climate of high expectations is a critical factor in reducing academic failure and increasing the number of college-bound youth" (p. 8). Finally, schools that foster resiliency emphasize youth participation and involvement, by "providing them with the opportunities to participate and be meaningfully involved and have roles of responsibility within the school environment" (p. 9).

Communities also influence the resilience of youth. The characteristics of competent communities parallel those of competent families and schools that promote resiliency (Bernard, 1992). First, competent communities manifest caring and support for community members, including young people. They contain social networks to "promote and sustain social cohesion" (p. 10), have available and accessible resources for community members, and find ways to build social networks that are responsive to the varying needs of community members. Second, they demonstrate high expectations for youths. Interestingly, "in cultures that have as a norm the valuing of youth as resources as opposed to problems, youth tend to be less involved in all problem behaviors" (p. 11). More specifically with respect to alcohol abuse, "countries in which drunkenness is more socially acceptable tend to have higher rates of alcohol abuse" (p. 11). Finally, competent communities create "opportunities [for youths] to participate in the life of the community" (p. 11).

Model Programs

Knowing factors that enhance resiliency and promote competence for youths and their social environments provides an orientation for programs and services for community youths. "If we can determine the personal and environmental sources of social competence and wellness, we can better plan preventive interventions focused on creating and enhancing the personal and environmental attributes that serve as the key to healthy development" (Bernard, 1992, p. 3). Successful prevention programs "focus on enhancing and creating positive environmental contexts—families, schools, and communities that, in turn, reinforce positive behaviors" (p. 3). Including prevention as a key component of effective juvenile justice systems is an absolute necessity (Bilchik, 1998).

There are numerous examples of programs and services for youths that focus on resiliency and competence. Stephens (1997) suggests a broad spectrum of services for youths at risk including positive reinforcement; parent education that provide parents with opportunities to learn effective parenting techniques; healthy start programs that address mother–infant relationships; mentoring programs that provide positive adult role models; programs that teach skills for resolving conflicts nonviolently; community–school partnerships; character education to promote universal values such as truthfulness, fairness, tolerance, and responsibility; youth-oriented community service programs; community policing and restorative justice programs. Davis (1994) presents a program model focusing on youth at risk of substance abuse. Schroeder (1995) highlights use of anger management and conflict resolution programs. Furstenberg and Hughes (1995) report the results of their longitudinal study of 252 children of teen moms to explore factors that influence the youths' abilities for overcoming social disadvantage—with a specific focus on the roles of family-based and community-based social capital. They found that the "degree to which the parents and children were embedded in a protective social network and were themselves a closely bonded unit with mutual expectations, trust, and loyalty" was related to successful outcomes in young adulthood.

Bowen and Chapman (1996) report findings from their study of students participating in a school-based program designed to increase retention. Their findings indicate that social support, particularly parental support, plays a particularly crucial role in adolescents' development and adaptation. Support from teachers and neighbors were other factors that predicted individual adaptation and played a more significant role than support from peers. Subjects were participating in an at-risk program designed to increase school retention. Splittgerber and Allen (1996) also report on the outcomes of a school-based mentoring program. "The Partnership for School Success" is a school dropout prevention program in Minneapolis, Minnesota. One program component involves mentors who meet with youths at least once a week to establish a friendship and talk with youths about school issues. "The project extends traditional mentoring to include checking on students' behaviors consistently over time and immediately connecting students with pertinent interventions." For Splittgerber and Allen, "the great challenge facing educators, parents, and community leaders is to translate this out of school time into constructive experiences that promote healthy personal and social development."

Teen Pregnancy

Even though the teen birth rate in the United States has been declining, it still exceeds the rate in other developed countries (Annie E. Casey Foundation, 2003a). Research comparing adolescents in the United States and Europe found virtually no difference in teens' levels of sexual activities, but identified a considerable difference in their use of contraception. For example, 20 percent of the sexually active teens in the United States report not using birth control in contrast to only 4 percent in Great Britain. The most recent figures indicate that the "teen birth rate fell from 37 births per 1,000 females ages 15 to 17 in 1990 to 27 births per 1,000 in 2000" (p. 46). Although overall teen birth rates are declining, there are considerable differences among states and large urban areas. New Hampshire and Vermont have the lowest rate—10 per 1,000 females ages 15 to 17; Mississippi has the highest—44 per 1,000. Among large metropolitan areas, Miami's rate of 174 per 1,000 is highest, and San Francisco and Seattle have the lowest rate—20 per 1,000. "Slightly more than half (51 percent) of the fathers of children born to girls under age 18 were in their 20s" (p. 44).

Teenage pregnancy is a critical social problem. Statistics suggest that the babies born to teenagers are at risk. They are more likely to drop out of high school, less likely to find employment, and more likely to have babies themselves before age 20. Furthermore, births to teens—particularly young teens—are associated with risks to the teenagers' health and psychosocial well-being.

Often, unplanned and unwanted pregnancies disrupt adolescents' educational and career plans, increase health risks, and precipitate economic stress (Berk, 2004). In addition to the loss of educational opportunities, pregnant adolescents frequently must deal with losses in social relationships and identity, particularly their physical appearance. Among the health risks are pregnancy complications, giving birth to babies with low birth weights, and infant mortality (Combs-Orme, 1993).

Teen parents often present multiple needs and require services from a variety of agencies. Public social services that target adolescent pregnant females include the Department of Health and Human Services; maternal and child health clinics; public assistance; Medicaid; community health centers; food stamps; Women, Infants and Children (WIC) food supplement program; and job training services. Among the services in the voluntary sector are supportive counseling for young parents, including fathers, educational programs for new parents, and adoption services. Exemplary programs for adolescent parents emphasize interdisciplinary cooperation, prevention of additional pregnancies, and expansive services that extend into early infancy. "Longer term goals for the adolescent, such as return to school, preparation for employment, economic self-sufficiency, and enhanced parent–child interaction are now considered as important for the mother as good prenatal care and obstetrical outcomes" (Vecchiolla & Maza, 1989, p. 3).

Prevention efforts need to be comprehensive (Franklin & Corcoran, 2000). Effective prevention programs address motivational issues and provide hope, opportunity, information, and skills. Such efforts should include opportunities for experiencing success in academic and nonacademic areas to build adolescents' self-esteem. Additionally, prevention programs can develop employment-related skills and provide family life education and comprehensive adolescent health services, including assistance in family planning and sex education.

Social Work Highlights. The "Peer Companionship Project" provides peer counseling support for socially isolated, young adolescent parents. Social workers train teen parents as peer counselors to interact with young parents (Rubenstein, Panzarine, & Lanning, 1990). As program employees, the peer counselors attend weekly training groups and receive professional supervision and support. The peer counselors offer positive role modeling and provide emotional support to program participants. The project encourages teens to avoid subsequent pregnancies and encourages them to complete high school.

Adolescent Suicide

Suicide is the third leading cause of death among youths ages 15 to 24, a rate of 11.1 deaths by suicide per 1,000 youths. Suicide represents 13.5 percent of the deaths for this age group (Centers for Disease Control and Prevention, 2002b; 2002c). Even the statistics mask the actual problem, in that for every death by suicide, estimates indicate there are 50 to 150 suicide attempts. Unsettling reports indicate that one-third of U.S. teenagers say they have considered suicide, 15 percent have thought seriously about it, and 6 percent have actually attempted suicide (McGeady, 1991). Studies indicate the rate of suicide is even higher among gay and bisexual males (2 to 3 in 10) as compared to the rate among heterosexual males (1 in 10) (Dempsey, 1994; Proctor & Groze, 1994).

Related factors include depression; stress, especially stress related to school failure or drastic life changes; and family disruptions, discord, and disintegration. Other factors include concerns over sexual identity, previous suicidal behavior, hopelessness, and drug and alcohol abuse (Garland & Zigler, 1993). Such variables as the sociocultural context, familial influences, and developmental levels are also important considerations (Zayas, Kaplan, Turner, Romano, & Gonzalez-Ramos, 2000).

Studies indicate that young teens want to learn about indicators of suicide, so prevention efforts need to be integrated with educational efforts. Other important factors include dealing with teens' feelings of helplessness, hopelessness, and low self-esteem. Prevention efforts employ problem-solving and skill-building techniques to enhance adolescents' coping skills, use family interventions to improve communication and conflict resolution skills, and improve peer relationships by working on teenagers' interpersonal skills and self-images (Ciffone, 1993).

Runaway Youths

While getting an accurate count of runaway youths is difficult, estimates report about a million youths in the United States as runaways (National Runaway Switchboard, 2003). About half of that number run away to escape abusive situations (Vissing & Diament, 1997). The bulk of runaways run away once and return home within a week. Adolescents who run away repeatedly are a small minority, whereas "throwaway" children represent a large proportion of the total number of runaway youths.

Adolescents who run away identify running as their only alternative to family situations they perceive as intolerable. Many stable or "normal" youths run away and return home with a new appreciation for their parents. Other runaways, whose background reflects rejection, may run to a shelter or to the home of a friend or relative or involve themselves in the street culture. Becoming involved in the street culture increases alienation from families and reduces the possibility of returning home. Children on the run are at risk of being physically assaulted, sexually exploited, or raped; using drugs; and engaging in criminal activity and prostitution.

Eating Disorders

Given the societal obsession with thinness and adolescent self-consciousness about body image, it is not surprising that eating disorders are more prevalent in adolescence than at any other age. Once thought to be predominantly a problem among females, current studies indicate that eating disorders are more frequent among males than was previously assumed. Persons with *anorexia nervosa* restrict their intake of food severely, resulting in a loss of at least 15 to 25 percent of their ideal body weight. "Anorexia almost always begins with a deliberate desire to be thin and consequent dieting, and it ends in a condition in which the [adolescent] seems unwilling or unable to eat normally" (Lefrancois, 1995, p. 513). More common than anorexia, *bulimia* involves episodes of binge eating, sometimes followed by purging. While not life-threatening, bulimia does involve serious physiological and emotional consequences (Kuntz, Groze, & Yates, 1992). Considering the serious, sometimes life-threatening nature of the problem, intervention with people who have eating disorders often occurs in mental health settings and involves individual or group treatment, family therapy, and carefully coordinated interdisciplinary planning (Van Bulow, 1991).

Adolescent Youths as Resources for Building Competent Communities

Viewing youths as individuals with strengths and resources for building competent communities is quite different from the view of youths as problem-ridden or victims of risk-filled circumstances (Checkoway, Finn, & Pothukuchi, 1995; Finn & Checkoway, 1998). Youth participation is "a process through which young people solve problems and carry out plans that provide tangible benefits and increase their involvement in the community" (Checkoway, Finn, & Pothukuchi, 1995, p. 190). To facilitate this process, professionals work *with* youths to encourage activities involving reflection and action leading to community change. Among the activities youths plan and implement are social action strategies, community planning, advocacy, public education initiatives, and extensions of community-based services. Youths comment positively about the benefits of their participation: "Because of the center I have been able to accomplish many things and have been part of many leadership activities which have helped me be a better leader, listener, and friend" (p. 194). Roles for workers emphasize viewing youths as having strengths, working collaboratively with youths as full partners and building capacities.

Social Work Highlights. A recent pilot study of community-based youth initiatives identified a number of model programs that involved youths focused on capacity building, promoted working as collaborative partners, and emphasized cultural competence (Finn & Checkoway, 1998). One example, the Youth Action Program (YAP) of East Harlem, New York, illustrates these principles in action:

> This program was founded by a group of teachers and students in East Harlem schools who began by asking young people what they wanted to change in the community and starting several projects that reflected these priorities. One of the first projects was to rehabilitate an abandoned city-owned building and donate it to homeless youths. Today this program involves 60 low-income young people who rehabilitate buildings and provide housing for the homeless while also completing their education and preparing for employment.
>
> Young people, many of whom are teenage parents, products of the foster care or welfare system, or on parole from earlier trouble with the law, receive work-site training in construction skills, high school equivalency education, social services, and counseling to meet personal goals and to make subsequent employment decisions. When construction is complete, the building becomes permanent housing for homeless youths and their families, in a model which became a prototype for the national YouthBuild USA program supported by the federal government.
>
> YAP has also established the Young People's East Harlem Resource Center, a comprehensive multiservice facility for young people of East 103rd Street in East Harlem. The center is a safe haven for neighborhood youths. It offers personal guidance, academic assistance, and advocacy assistance in negotiating social services systems and helping youths develop their own projects.
>
> Youth participation is central to the governance of the program. A policy committee has a majority of young people and makes major governance decisions. Committee members make policy and program decisions, consult with membership through advisory councils, and conduct meetings for organizational leaders and general members. As one young person interviewed by one of the authors in 1991 concluded, "Working with YAP we learned from the meetings, the discussions, the decisions we had to make. We learned group dynamics, how to deal with people and problems. We were empowered, because the program was based on our ideas. We got a sense of pride, of importance, something teenagers in East Harlem don't get anywhere else." (pp. 339–340)

Concluding Remarks

Family, in all of its forms and variations, is the foundational unit of society. The family rears and socializes children, provides a base of support and identity throughout the life span, and shapes future generations. For these reasons, society must be committed to the family and must provide the resources required for maintaining the family's integrity and well-being. Through the child welfare system, society demonstrates this commitment by supporting prevention and intervention services directed at decreasing the evidence of family breakdown and increasing family stability.

The social work profession, recognizing the centrality of the family unit, works toward the preservation and strengthening of families. To embrace a philosophy of empowerment, social workers must recognize families' competency and capacity for change. But families cannot provide for their members without access to resources. Empowerment-based social work redresses social issues affecting families—poverty, discrimination, homelessness, unemployment, and access to health care, among others.

CHAPTER

14 Adult and Aging Services

Adulthood spans nearly half a century. The service needs during these decades relate to family needs as well as life transitions. Adults access social services from a wide range of settings and in virtually every field of practice—family services, medical social work, occupational social work, addictions, and mental health. Focusing on services for adults, this chapter details the following:

- Specialized services for adults, such as occupational social work
- Intimate partner violence
- Elder abuse
- Programs and services for older adults, including gerontological social work

Services for Adults

We have already considered many of the difficulties encountered by adults—poverty, discrimination, homelessness, domestic violence, health and rehabilitation challenges, mental illness, addictions, and family problems and parenting. This section explores some additional issues, including infertility, financial stress, providing care for aging parents, and bereavement. Given the centrality of the workplace in the world of adults, the chapter also presents occupational social work as an important field of practice in the arena of services for adults.

Infertility Counseling

The American Society for Reproductive Medicine reports that about 9 percent of those who are reproductive age in the United States, or about 5.3 million people, are infertile (National Women's Health Information Center, 1998). Because people presume that they will have the capacity for reproduction, their discovery of infertility is a personal and medical emergency. Reactions vary and may include such disruptions as depression, preoccupation with infertility, loss of interest in relationships, and marital difficulties. More specifically, a study of involuntarily childless women, indicates that they

1. defined infertility as negative or stigmatizing,
2. showed a strong personal commitment to motherhood,
3. strongly identified motherhood as important to the role of women in Western society,
4. showed strong support for the continued availability of artificial insemination donor and surrogate motherhood,
5. expressed deep satisfaction with adoption but ongoing regret about infertility and the "need" to experience pregnancy and childbirth or to produce a biologically related child, and
6. experienced discomfort regarding the notion of birth reunions while supporting the need for adoption registries. (Miall, 1989, p. 49)

Today, reproductive technology provides many people with the hope of producing a biologically related child. *In vitro* fertilization, a procedure whereby the sperm and ovum are joined in the laboratory and the embryo is then transferred to the biological mother's uterus, is one viable option among many for infertile couples who desire children.

Social work practitioners working with infertility issues are likely to be employed by medical centers with in vitro fertilization programs. Social work roles include participating in patient orientation programs; preparing psychosocial evaluations; providing supportive counseling for couples in the program; presenting alternatives, such as adoption, when procedures are unsuccessful; facilitating support groups; and assisting with insurance issues (Needleman, 1992). Group work is particularly successful for increasing couples' understanding of infertility, dealing with the depression frequently associated with infertility, and reducing isolation (Goodman & Rothman, 1986).

A key issue is dealing with the pain and stigma associated with infertility and reproductive technology (Schaffer & Diamond, 1993). Perspective parents may devalue adoption as a second-best, last-choice alternative. Accordingly, social workers must "confront the larger issues concerning infertility, adoption, and the new reproductive technologies, allowing infertile couples to lead social supported, meaningful lives regardless of the choices they make" (Miall, 1989, p. 50).

Financial Stress

Financial problems are often among the issues that confront families who consult social workers (Chatterjee & Farkas, 1992). Some agencies now hire financial counselors to provide consultation for clients with serious money problems (Wollan & Bauer, 1990). Among the economic services offered to clients are the following:

- Developing budgeting skills and wise use of credit
- Providing information about monetary and in-kind resources
- Linking clients with appropriate resources
- Conferring with clients to develop viable debt repayment plans
- Assisting with the resolution of problems with employers, housing, and banks

Research into these services has some interesting implications for practice (Wollan & Bauer, 1990). Linking families with additional external resources is associated with positive financial counseling outcomes. These resources include financial assistance programs, such as public assistance; unemployment compensation; in-kind assistance, such as the provision of food stamps, food pantries, transportation, and energy cost supplements; and other types of grants and loans. Research findings point to the need for early identification and referral of persons with financial difficulties: Those with severe problems were less likely to improve.

Providing Care for Aging Parents

With life expectancy lengthening and the probability of chronic illness increasing with age, it becomes more and more likely that middle-age adults will have to deal with the changing needs of their aging parents. Although some middle-age adults live a long distance away from their parents, it is more likely that aging parents have at least one adult child living close by. A recent nationwide telephone survey of a random sample of households in the

"Parent-caring" is a significant issue for adult children.

United States found that members of nearly one in four households provided care to a relative or friend 50 years of age or older at some time during the last 12 months (National Alliance for Caregiving, 1997). This means that more than 22.4 million households are involved in family caregiving tasks annually. About 5 million households provide care for persons with dementia-related problems. Rough estimates place the 1997 value of informal caregiving at $196 billion (Arno, Levine, & Memmott, 1999). The nationwide study also found that 64 percent of the caregivers were employed, about half, full-time. Inevitably, caregivers must juggle the demands of providing care with the obligations of their jobs. A small-scale qualitative study found that costs to caregivers included lost wealth, limited opportunities for continuing education and promotion, and lowered on-the-job productivity (Mature Market Institute, 1999). Aggregate costs in lost productivity to business is $11.4

billion per year (MetLife, 1997). Interestingly, only a small proportion of family caregivers report using formal services (Tennstedt, 1999). They are more likely to access formal services when caregiving needs increase beyond their abilities to provide care (Ory, Yee, Tennstedt, & Schultz, 2000).

Changing conditions such as having fewer children, increased mobility of family members, preponderance of single-parent families, and increased longevity of those who receive care affect family members' abilities to provide care for their aging parents (Giarrusso, Silverstein, & Bengston, 1996). "The pool of family caregivers is dwindling. In 1990 there were 11 potential caregivers for each person needing care. In 2050 that ratio will be 4:1" (National Family Caregivers Association, 2002).

Next to spousal caregivers, the "kin-keepers" are most likely to be daughters or daughters-in-law; however, everyone involved may feel stress and strain, including other family members and the aging parents themselves. Concerns range from strained personal relations, fatigue brought on by attempting to fulfill too many role demands, inadequate community support, and lack of information about the aging process. A qualitative study identifies caregivers' perceived control of their situations—including utilizing their own internal strengths, drawing on the resources of others when they needed help, and anticipating future requirements—as a significant protective factor (Szabo & Strang, 1999).

Many different situations may press families into caregiving roles, including their loved one's failing health, mobility issues, functional disabilities, and cognitive frailty associated with Alzheimer's disease. About 4 million older adults have developed senile dementia associated with Alzheimer's disease (HHS, 2003b). However, the risk of developing Alzheimer's disease increases with age: less than 3 percent of those between ages 65 to 74, whereas nearly half of those 85 and older may develop the disease. Moreover, "the prevalence, incidence, and cumulative risk of Alzheimer's disease appears to be much higher in African-American than in non-Hispanic whites" (Alzheimer's Association, n.d., What the Research Shows section, ¶ 1). At present, about 70 percent of those with Alzheimer's disease live at home; family and friends provide about 75 percent of all home care (Alzheimer's Association, 2003). Alzheimer's disease is a progressive disease that causes changes in personality, forgetfulness, and impaired physical and social functioning. As people with Alzheimer's degenerate further into wandering behavior, communication deficits, and agitation or hostility, they become dependent on others for assistance with their activities of daily living. Their needs for support from families, friends, and the formal social service delivery system increase dramatically with the advancement of the disease (Carpentier & Ducharme, 2003; Martindale-Adams et al., 2002; Mittelman, 2002; Morhardt, Sherrell, & Gross, 2003; Toseland et al., 2003).

Social workers provide multiple services to family caregivers that support their efforts to continue to care for their aging parents at home. Social workers link families to community resources for home health care and household services, coordinate respite services, offer counseling and emotional support, and sometimes mediate between elders and their families. They work in partnership with family members on case management activities to enhance the delivery of services to frail elders (Mayer et al., 1990). Caregiver support groups are effective in providing support, reducing isolation, educating caregivers about aging processes, and discovering creative solutions to the various problems with which caregivers must deal (Bass et al., 1998; Sherrell & Newton, 1996; Toseland, 1995).

Bereavement Counseling

Because of their place in the life cycle, adults often deal with loss and grief. For example, middle-age adults often experience the death of their parents or the untimely death of their spouse, partners, or peers. People often draw on the resources of existing social support networks or supplement these resources with the support of mutual aid groups, such as the Compassionate Friends, widow-to-widow programs, and neonatal death support groups.

People who are mourning the loss of a loved one must accept the reality of the loss. They may feel numb from the loss, encounter "pangs of grief," experience disorganization and despair, and eventually reorganize and redirect their emotional energy into other relationships (Parkes, 1998). Typically, people encounter both physical and psychological effects of loss over an extended period of time. The sociocultural context—including spiritual dimensions, economic and social circumstances, cultural influences, and the marginalizing effects of oppression and discrimination—also influences grieving processes (Berzoff, 2003).

Kübler-Ross (1969) identifies five emotional responses often experienced in the grieving process: denial, bargaining, anger, depression, and, finally, acceptance. Factors such as their developmental level, the circumstances of the loss, and the personal meaning of the loss influence how people in mourning work through their grief. Additional complications include the following:

- Sudden untimely deaths, such as suicide, murder, catastrophic circumstances, and stigmatized deaths
- Multiple losses leading to grief overload
- Perceived lack of social support (Berk, 2004)

Cultural Differences and Grief. Studies indicate striking similarities in the way people from different cultures deal with grief; however, there are also marked differences. For example, differences occur from culture to culture in the degree of openness about expressing grief. Understanding cultural differences helps to prevent ethnocentric assumptions that one's own experience with grief provides a valid baseline for understanding the experience of another. What one culture considers normal other cultures may regard as deviant.

Social Work Highlights. Social workers in many different settings, such as family service agencies, employee assistance programs, mental health centers, and medical facilities, provide bereavement counseling and play a vital role in working through issues related to death and dying (Hobart, 2001; Zilberfein & Hurwitz, 2003). The following example relates one client's experience in working with a strengths-focused practitioner on issues of grief (Mass, 1990).

> Margie had been married only eight years when her twenty-seven-year old husband, Mickey, died from an insidious form of lung cancer that had been diagnosed only two months earlier. The social worker had contact with both Margie and Mickey; however, because of Mickey's weak condition, the practitioner's work with Margie was more intensive. During the two months before Mickey's death, the social worker encouraged Margie to talk about her life with Mickey—that they had been childhood sweethearts, graduating from high school together, getting married, working hard to buy their home, making plans for the future. Margie loved being a homemaker, leaving financial matters and other details to Mickey.

Margie continued to meet with the social worker after Mickey died. Her emotions varied from anger and guilt to extreme sadness, feelings of abandonment, and even denial. She longed so to be with Mickey again that she believed she saw him in stores or walking on the street. She was relieved to learn that many people who suffered the loss of a loved one had these experiences, as she thought she was losing her mind. In an effort to build her self-esteem and sense of mastery, the social worker and Margie determined tasks that Margie could work on—learning to balance her checkbook, making decisions, and assuming more responsibility for herself.

The social worker hears from Margie occasionally since their work together concluded. After her father died, Margie wrote to say, "'You would have been proud of me—the way I could be there for my mother and brother while handling my own grief.' In a recent note, she indicated that she was happily married and had a child. Thus Margie was able to reconnect with others, refocus on the present, and once again look to the future." (Mass, 1990, p. 287)

Occupational Social Work

Many challenges that adults face show up at the workplace and, furthermore, issues related to jobs may create additional problems or tension in their lives. For example, addictions, family crises, domestic abuse, and dependent care issues are all likely to influence productivity and job-related stress, and the presence or absence of family-friendly work policies are likely to affect family life. Because of the significance of work in adults' lives, businesses and industries often respond to their employees' needs through employee assistance programs. Employers are taking more responsibility for the well-being of employees through their support of employee assistance programs.

Occupational social work plays a key role in employee assistance programs. It is the *"field of practice in which social workers attend to the human and social needs of employees in the work milieu by designing and executing appropriate interventions to ensure healthier individuals and environments"* (Googins & Godfrey, 1985, p. 396). Concerns of occupational social workers move beyond concerns of individuals' problem behaviors to concerns "with organizational and environmental change to foster healthier and more healthful organizations and communities" (Smith & Gould, 1993, p. 9). To function effectively, occupational social workers need specialized knowledge about

- The psychological meaning of work
- Work-related stress and burnout
- The effects of organizational structure and programs on social functioning
- Addictions in the workplace and substance abuse counseling
- Retirement and retirement planning
- The psychosocial implications of reduction in the workforce or unemployment
- Work-related legislation, such as the Civil Rights Act of 1964, the Age Discrimination in Employment Act of 1967, the Americans with Disabilities Act of 1990, the Family and Medical Leave Act of 1993, and the Violence Against Women Act, reauthorized in 2000

Origins of Occupational Social Work. Historically, the tie between social work and labor began with the activity of medieval guilds, which provided shelter and support for those members of the guild who were in need. Settlement house workers were well known for their advo-

BOX **14.1**

Reflections on Diversity

Diversity in the Workplace—The ADA

People with disabilities are a diverse population group. What they have in common is discrimination based on their disability or handicap. The Americans with Disabilities Act (ADA), signed into law by President George Bush in July 1990, seeks to alleviate discrimination against people with disabilities in employment and public accommodations.

The law bars all forms of employment discrimination that adversely affect the employment opportunities or work status of people with disabilities. The law also prohibits denying people with disabilities access to public services because of architectural and communication barriers. In general, the law required that employers, government agencies, public transportation systems, and places of public accommodation meet the ADA requirements by January 1992.

The ADA represents the most significant expansion of the civil rights laws in over 25 years. It provides protection from discrimination for people with disabilities in much the same way that the Civil Rights Act of 1964 provided protection to racial minorities. The antidiscrimination provisions of both acts are enforced by the Equal Employment Opportunity Commission (EEOC).

People with disabilities are entitled to the full and equal enjoyment of employment and access to public accommodations. The ADA requires that work sites and public places make reasonable accommodations in order to be accessible to persons with disabilities. Accommodations include making existing facilities easily accessible, restructuring jobs, altering work schedules, acquiring adaptive devices or equipment, modifying examinations and training materials, and providing readers or interpreters.

---

cacy for workers' rights and workplace safety. "Mary Parker Follet [an early social work leader] pioneered workplace reforms [in the 1920s] and to this day is quoted in business schools for her creative work in bringing union and management perspectives into a new dialectic of 'coactive power'" (Briar-Lawson, 1998, p. 540). The prominence of industrial social work reemerged in World War II when unions employed social workers as advocates. Also, the military became a major industrial employer of social workers during times of war. Internationally, government-supported industrial social work has existed for many years in countries such as Belgium, Brazil, France, Germany, India, Peru, Poland, and Zambia (Kurzman, 1987).

Programs and Services. Currently many corporations, government agencies, labor unions, and not-for-profit organizations employ occupational social workers. Typically, programs in the workplace are called employee assistance programs (EAPs), whereas union programs are called membership assistance programs (MAPs). These programs and services are available either to all participants in the workforce or to union members and their families. They may be run "in-house," or the organization may contract for services from family service agencies or hospital-based programs. About 80 percent of all large U.S. firms have EAPs. This translates to EAP coverage for 31 percent of all employees (National Clearinghouse for Alcohol and Drug Information, 1997a). About 90 percent of the Fortune 500 companies now host employee assistance programs. The Department of Labor indicates that companies save from 5 to 16 dollars for every dollar they invest in EAPs.

Occupational social workers facilitate change in both employees and workplace organizations and address a wide range of personal and social needs that benefit people of all ages. Services include providing resources and referrals to community-based services; working to make drug-free workplaces a reality; and providing personal and family counseling, interpersonal communication training, parenting education, and pre- and postretirement planning services. Other occupational social work interest areas include affirmative action, sexual harassment, disabilities, burnout, stress management, conflict mediation, care arrangements for children and dependent elders, unemployment, and health and wellness promotion programs (Kurzmann & Akabas, 1993). Occupational social workers are also in pivotal positions to provide supports to individuals who, in returning to work through welfare-to-work initiatives, face numerous difficulties in their quest for self-sufficiency (DeBord, Canu, & Kerpelman, 2000; Iverson, 1998).

Because of their relatively broad knowledge base, social workers contribute in other ways as well. As charitable allocations analysts, urban affairs advisors, or community services coordinators, social workers may be employed by corporations and businesses to "manage corporate contributions to civic and humanitarian concerns" (Smith & Gould, 1993, p. 14). Activities may include such areas as organizational planning and development, community service initiatives, and implementation of work-related policies, such as the ADA, nondiscrimination and affirmative action laws, or the Family Medical Leave Act. For example, occupational social workers may consult with management to develop organizational policies and procedures for dealing with relocation, sexual harassment and affirmative action issues, responses to HIV/AIDS, retirement planning, employee schedules, equality in benefit packages for domestic partners, and provisions for day care facilities.

In sum, several challenges face occupational social workers as they plan for their future work roles in business and industry, including to

- Improve the fit between the needs of individuals and their families, work organizations, and communities
- Help people in need of employment transition into jobs and become gainfully employed
- Introduce to the workplace social work values and principles, such as valuing diversity and balancing family needs with work demands
- Generate knowledge in the area of social work and the world of work that will inform practice and policy (Barak & Bargal, 2000, p. 4)

Social Work Highlights. Joseph Kohl is an employee assistance program social worker in the Human Resources Department of Millwork Industries. Joe draws on the systems approach suggested by Balgopal (1989) in working with employees who are injured on the job. Balgopal presents interventions at the micro-, mid-, and macrolevels. At the *microlevel,* intervention might involve counseling to deal with the effects of job disruption, family stress, problems with the provision of benefits, arrangements for retraining, and even reactions to loss of work. *Midlevel* advocacy with insurance companies to ensure appropriate and timely payments or with other bureaucratic structures to secure disability payments or rehabilitation services may be required. *Macrolevel* interventions address safety issues through improving hazardous work environments, lobbying for work-safety legislation, and influencing management to address procedures that menace workers' well-being.

Workplace Issues and Sexual Minorities. Through their roles in employee assistance organizations, occupational social workers can assist in ensuring that workplaces support a culture of acceptance and that managers deal directly with prejudicial attitudes and discriminatory actions that create hostile working conditions for sexual minorities (Poverny, 2000). Laws and company policies are forging the way for such actions. For example, an amendment to Executive Order 11478 signed into law in 1998 offers protection to federal employees against discrimination based on sexual orientation. By recent count, eight states offer some form of benefits to domestic partners, and numerous cities and other municipalities have passed laws that prohibit discrimination based on sexual orientation (National Gay and Lesbian Task Force, 2000; Van der Meide, 2000). Additionally, "many of the Fortune 500 companies have led the way toward workplace inclusion by establishing non-discrimination policies and practices" (Poverny, p. 75). The fact that sexual harassment can include same-sex interactions mandates proactive social work interventions. An emerging advocacy issue for social workers is the apparent lack of legal and workplace policy support for transgendered individuals. Among the leadership activities for occupational social workers Poverny suggests are facilitating education and training programs for managers and employees, organizing and promoting participation in support groups, and supporting "coming out" for employees who make this choice.

Preretirement Planning. A number of factors affect adults' successful transition to retirement. These factors include emotional and financial preparation for retirement, the voluntary or involuntary nature of the decision, and personal coping capacities (Berk, 2004). Persons who plan for and anticipate challenges of retirement are more likely to make optimal transitions to retirement. However, in spite of the benefits accrued from planning for retirement, relatively few employees actually make retirement plans.

Social workers employed in business and industry educate workers about retirement and retirement planning, develop support networks, and provide retirement counseling services. Many preretirement programs include activities that enable group participants to describe their own preretirement plans, relate problems they anticipate, identify their competencies, and set priorities and objectives (Monk, 1990).

Social policies that strengthen the economic well-being of retired people and direct services that create new opportunities support people who are retired. Among the issues relating to retirement are equitable retirement policies, adequate housing, appropriate recreational and educational programming, sufficient opportunities for volunteer work, and vocational guidance and retraining for those who wish to pursue different careers.

Intimate Partner Violence

Child maltreatment confers a legacy of violence on children. However, it is not the only kind of violence among family members that surfaces: Intimate partner violence is also part of the fabric of family violence. The case study that follows illuminates many of the key issues related to intimate partner violence.

Social Work Highlights. I bent over my desk, bleary eyed from fatigue but determined to catch up on a large stack of paperwork that had been seriously neglected over the past week.

It was 3:30 A.M. and the sudden shrill of the doorbell in the stillness of the night startled me. I recall thinking, "Please, not another one!" As I opened the door to my late-night caller, I found, not to my surprise, a uniformed police officer. While the officer spoke, my attention was drawn to the sobbing little girl who stood directly behind her mother. And even through the shadows of the porch, the woman looked bewildered and frightened.

It was not until I stood aside to allow Susan and her small daughter entry into the shelter for abused women that the gravity of her situation became evident. Susan's face was bruised; her eyes were swollen and discolored. Her condition left little need for an immediate explanation. After establishing that Susan had received emergency medical treatment for her injuries, we began the intake process. I documented only the necessary information and left the majority of questions for the following day. I hoped that perhaps, after a little rest, Susan would be able to discuss her circumstances more fully.

Susan's childhood history included accounts of her own experiences of sexual abuse and her mother's experiences of spousal abuse. She married at age 16, hoping to leave violence behind. However, within a year of her marriage, Susan, who was pregnant, found herself once again the victim of physical, psychological, and sexual violence from the very person who had promised to love and protect her. She endured this violence for four years, but this current incident seemed particularly out of control.

During the next few days, the shelter staff worked with Susan to locate affordable and appropriate housing, establish her eligibility for public assistance, obtain an order of protection through legal services, and network a variety of community resources that would assist her in rebuilding a life for herself and her daughter, Christi. Susan showed signs of taking charge of the direction of her life by becoming actively involved in the decision-making process.

I was all too familiar with the number of women who left the shelter to return home to their abusive spouses. Therefore, my face registered no noticeable surprise when Susan informed me that she had made contact with her spouse and had decided to return home that very evening. She felt certain that he was truly sorry for his violent behavior and stated that he had promised that he would change. I gently reminded Susan that this was a promise that he had made several times over the past four years, and yet her circumstance worsened with each successive beating. Susan replied that she believed that he really meant it this time. She was equally certain that she could not make it on her own. "He loves me and Christi," she said (Morris, 1990).

Incidence

Susan's story is not uncommon, and neither is its outcome. Based on a national survey on crime victimization, Bureau of Justice estimates indicate that, in the United States in 2001, approximately 700,000 violent crimes were committed against intimate partners (Rennison, 2003). About 85 percent of those victimizations reported involved women as victims. Unreported instances cause the figures to surge to a much higher level. A recent large-scale, nationwide survey indicated that almost 25 percent of the women surveyed and 7 percent of the men report having been raped and/or physically assaulted by a current or former spouse or partner (Tjaden & Thoennes, 2000). Women were more likely than men to experience chronic abuse and injurious physical assault. Findings suggest that emotional and verbal abuse and controlling behaviors often accompany physical abuse. Domestic violence is a major health issue for women.

It also contributes to homelessness, alcohol addiction, mental health problems, and suicide (Easton, Swan, & Sinha, 2000; Hutchison, 1999; Morella, 1993; Slaughter, 1993). Ironically, of those who experience intimate partner violence, many return to live with their partner.

International Dimensions

Worldwide the rates of violence against women are staggering, as reports indicate that "at least one woman in every three has been beaten, coerced into sex, or otherwise abused in her lifetime" (Heise, Ellsberg, & Gottemoeller, 1999, p. 1). As a testimony to the international recognition that violence against women is discriminatory and violates their human rights, the United Nations adopted the *Declaration on the Elimination of Violence against Women.* The *Optional Protocol* to this convention, adopted in 1999, confers on women "the right to seek redress for violations of their human rights, including gender-based violence" (United Nations, 2000, Response by the International Community Section, ¶ 2). According to Kofi Annan, the Secretary General of the United Nations, "violence against women is perhaps the most shameful human rights violation. It knows no boundaries of geography, culture or wealth. As long as it continues, we cannot claim to be making real progress towards equality, development, and peace" (¶ 1). Intimate partner violence represents a serious human rights issue.

Dynamics of Intimate Partner Violence

In domestic situations, it is more common for men to abuse their female partners than to be abused. In fact, current data indicate that 85 percent of those victimized by intimate partner violence are women. In 1999, the rates per 1,000 women and men were 7.7 and 1.5, respectively (Rennison & Welchans, 2000).

Research shows that both men and women in marital and premarital relationships engage in violent behavior, but the motivations are different for each. For women, the use of violence most often occurs in acts of self-defense, reactions to violent situations, or retaliations for abuse perpetrated against them (Flynn, 1990). Males, on the other hand, are more likely to inflict violence to intimidate their partners or exercise control over them. The World Health Organization (2002) reports that the triggers of violence in intimate relationships are similar in all parts of the world. Trigger events include such things as "disobeying or arguing with the man, questioning him about money or girlfriends, not having food ready on time, not caring adequately for the children or the home, refusing to have sex, and the man suspecting the woman of infidelity" (p. 15).

Violence is a means to acquire power and control (Figure 14.1). Perpetrators draw on strategies of intimidation, humiliation, isolation, guilt, economic dependency, coercion, and threats to magnify their own power and control and to diminish their partners' power and control.

Cycle of Domestic Violence. Spousal violence often unfolds in a predictable cycle (Walker, 1984). "Violence between intimate partners always gets worse although there may be plateaus and even temporary reversals during periods of legal or extralegal and psychological intervention" (Walker, 1989, p. 697). Initially, there is a period of rising tensions, a time when women think they have some control over the abuse. They believe that by catering to their partners

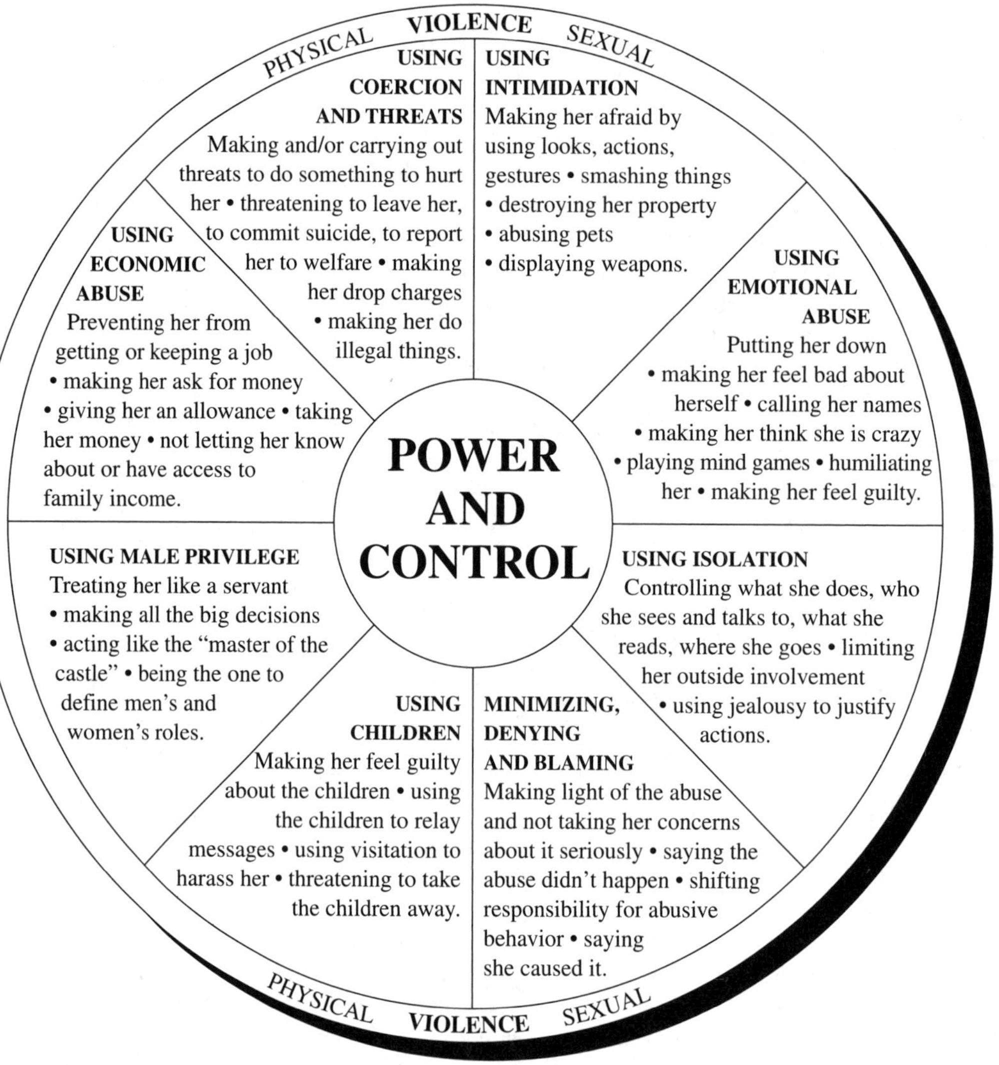

FIGURE 14.1 Power and Control Wheel

Source: Reprinted by permission of Minnesota Program Development, Inc., Domestic Abuse Intervention Project, Duluth, Minnesota.

they can slow down abusive incidents, whereas refusing to meet their partners' demands precipitates abuse. Inevitably, the abuse occurs in an explosion of violence or an acute incident of battering. Although this phase is short, the physical violence is likely to be intense.

A reduction of tension following the outburst of violence reinforces the physically abusive behavior. Loving contrition or simply a time of no tension characterizes the third phase. Either factor reinforces women's remaining in violent relationships. Learned helplessness, powerlessness, and low self-esteem decrease the likelihood that women will leave their spouses.

Typically, women develop skills that minimize their pain: Denial, dissociation, and splitting enable them to remain and survive. For many women, services from systems they perceive as nonresponsive and critical do not offer viable alternatives for changing their situations.

The Violence Against Women Act

In 2000, President Clinton signed the reauthorization of the landmark legislation, the Violence Against Women Act. This legislation takes a comprehensive approach to legal issues surrounding domestic violence and sexual assault. The reauthorization includes such features as increases in funding for emergency shelters and transitional housing, funds for civil and legal services to women who are victims of domestic and sexual violence, protection for immigrant women who are battered, services to women with disabilities who experience domestic violence, and training for child protective service workers and judges (Family Violence Prevention Fund, 2003). The original act established a nationwide enforcement of protection of abuse orders, a toll-free National Domestic Violence hotline, and a Violence Against Women Office at the Department of Justice (U.S. Department of Justice, n.d.).

TANF Exceptions and Domestic Violence

Intimate partner violence occurs in all socioeconomic strata; however, incidence is higher among those who receive public assistance benefits (Sachs, 1999; Tolman & Raphael, 2000). Recent research suggests that the incidence may be as high as 20 to 30 percent for welfare recipients (Raphael & Haennicke, 1999). A provision in the TANF legislation, the Wellstone/Murray amendment, creates the Family Violence Option (FVO), allowing "states to waive work requirements and time limits, and increase services to victims of domestic violence and their families without being penalized financially" (Sachs, p. 1). The temporary waivers provide flexibility in the work and job training requirements and allow exceptions to identifying fathers when such revelations would endanger women and their children. Additionally, the FVO "enables states to keep women safe through the welfare-to-work process by giving them the opportunity to obtain access to domestic violence counseling, safety planning, and other needed services before seeking work" (Raphael & Haennicke, p. 4). Most states have adopted the FVO provisions; however, states vary in their policies and procedures for screening for domestic violence and implementing waivers. "If the FVO can be the vehicle for delivery of preventive and interventive services, it may be a useful tool in increasing women's safety and long-term well-being by preventing premature job placement, increasing supports for safety during employment, and maintaining a viable safety net if abuse continues" (Tolman & Raphael, 2000, p. 24).

Service Responses to Intimate Partner Violence

Media attention to the crisis of domestic violence heightens public awareness and intensifies professional responses. Communities are likely to offer services, such as multidisciplinary and law enforcement crisis response teams, emergency shelters, programs for battered women and their children, and counseling for abusive partners. The multidimensional issues of intimate partner violence warrant a multidisciplinary approach to intervention. Often clients require a combination of medical, legal, financial, educational, and social services.

Transitional Services. Emergency and transitional services are often the first point of entry into the service delivery system for women who have been abused. They include such points of contact as the following:

- Information and referral
- Hospital emergency room personnel
- Police departments
- Clergy, family doctors, dentists, or attorneys
- Hotlines and crisis intervention services
- Victim assistance programs
- Supervisors at work or EAP personnel

Shelters. Typically, the main sources of referrals to crisis shelters for women who have been abused are police officers or domestic violence hot-line staff. Shelters offer safe, supportive environments for women who have been abused and their children. Shelter staff offer support services, such as counseling and group treatment. They often refer participants to other community services for their legal and medical needs and for employment, housing, day care, and ongoing counseling services (Roberts & Roberts, 1990). Clearly, few would dispute the importance of shelters. As protective measures, they offer emergency housing and access to financial assistance, education and job training, and legal services.

Advocacy. Many domestic violence initiatives include advocacy in the continuum of services they offer. Although the exact roles of advocates vary from program to program, typically advocates are involved in outreach services, community education, and follow-up with services for women after interventions by police officers. In the context of supportive services, they furnish information about the legal system, offer additional counseling and advocacy services, assist women in obtaining orders of protection, and go with them to various court proceedings (Weisz, 1999). "Having someone with them physically or emotionally can help survivors accept and act on information that is provided. Because of this support, some women follow through with legal actions, such as getting protective orders and testifying in the prosecution of batterers" (p. 140). An assessment of one advocacy program notes that "advocates lent a supportive empathic presence and possessed valuable information. Advocates' relationships with survivors enabled them to take further legal actions against batterers" (p. 138). Clearly, women using these advocacy services experience empowerment through informative relationships.

Counseling Services. Empowerment-oriented goals of working with persons who are victims of intimate partner violence include reinstating feelings of personal worth and a sense of control and, at a more macrolevel, creating opportunities for influencing community and social change. Empowerment-oriented social workers avoid a deficit or blame-finding approach to intervention as this revictimizes those who have experienced abuse. A focus on clients' strengths, competence, and involvement in all aspects of the process counteracts the effects of the prodigious victimization associated with intimate partner violence.

Four basic principles help persons who have been victimized by abuse experience empowerment (Kopp, 1989). Clients must perceive themselves as causal agents in achieving a solution to problems. Clients must perceive social workers as possessing helpful knowledge and skills. The problem solving effort must be a partnership between practitioners and clients. And clients must draw on a number of influential power structures (family networks, support networks, personal networks, and so on) to achieve a redistribution of power.

Support groups provide opportunities for persons who have been victimized by intimate partner violence to disclose their personal feelings, consider alternative choices, and evaluate decisions. Group sessions often enable participants to explore issues regarding their own perspectives and ways of relating to others. Support groups offer a forum for dealing with stress and anger and resolving relationship problems. They provide a platform for promoting community and social change.

In applying an empowerment model to their work with women who had experienced domestic violence, Nosko and Breton (1997–1998) found that demonstrating respect, self-determination, and individualization were related to key elements of group work practice. For example, with respect to planning, social workers adopting an empowerment perspective "no longer assume that the onus is on them to 'figure out' what is needed in the group, now they directly ask the group members" (p. 46). In essence, they lead by following the leads of their clients. With an empowerment-orientation, power shifts to clients. For example, Nosko and Breton indicate they "look to the women to learn about abuse rather than presenting themselves as the experts because they know the theories about abuse" (p. 62). They also assert that "a paradigm in which victimhood is the core construct is paternalistic, presumes fundamental weakness in the women, and fails to acknowledge their strengths, competence, and power" (p. 63).

Violence among Sexual Minorities

Very few prevalence studies have been conducted focusing on the incidence of abusive relationships among gay, lesbian, bisexual, and transgendered people. Those that exist are small-scale exploratory studies that rely on nonrandom samples. As a group, however, these studies suggest prevalence rates of between 25 and 33 percent, rates very similar to rates of intimate partner violence in the heterosexual population (National Coalition of Anti-Violence Programs [NCAVP], 2003). One study of an ethnically diverse sample of 500 gay men, lesbians, bisexuals, and transgendered people indicates 9 percent of the sample reported violence in their current relationships, 32 percent reported violence in past relationships, and 83 percent of the respondents indicated experiencing emotional abuse (Turell, 2000). A prevalence study by the National Coalition of Anti-Violence Programs (NCAVP) documented about 5,000 reports of abuse in the 11 regions providing data (NCAVP, 2003). The report concluded that domestic violence among lesbian, gay, bisexual, and transgendered people is extensively underreported.

The same range of violent behaviors is present in same-sex and heterosexual relationships—physical, emotional, psychological, and sexual abuse (Elliott, 1996). However psychological abuse can be made even more intimidating in same-sex relationships with the additional threat "of 'outing' to family, landlords, employers, or others. This 'blackmail' potential for same-sex abusers often isolates gay and lesbian victims to a greater extent than their heterosexual female counterparts" (p. 4). Same-sex violence demonstrates "that routine, intentional intimidation through abusive acts and words is not a gender issue, but a power issue" (p. 3).

For those lesbian, gay, bisexual, and transgendered people who risk reporting abusive situations, most will have difficulty locating appropriate services in their own communities, as services for lesbian, gay, bisexual, and transgendered people are scarce, even in large urban communities (NCAVP, 2003; Renzetti, 1996; Waldron, 1996). If they seek traditional services through the police, women's shelters, medical personnel, clergy, or family members and friends, they will often encounter misunderstanding, discrimination, prejudicial attitudes fed by homophobia, biphobia, and transphobia and heterosexist programs and services. If they seek orders of protection, the most widely used legal option, they will likely discover that domestic protective orders are marginally available to sexual minorities: Domestic protective orders are clearly unavailable in 6 states, arguably unavailable in 1 state, neutrally available in 39 states and the District of Columbia, and affirmatively available in only 6 states (Hawaii, Illinois, Kentucky, New Jersey, Ohio, and Pennsylvania) (NCAVP, 2002). As the NCAVP (1999) points out:

> Gendered notions of social roles are part of our national consciousness, and they are intricately woven into the web of the law as heterosexual paradigms. Coupled with heterosexist and homophobic laws which regulate or prohibit adult sexual and marital relationships, these heterosexual paradigms are a powerful barrier to equitable applications of domestic violence laws which might otherwise be used for protection by victims of non-heterosexual relationship abuse. (Availability of Domestic Violence Protective Orders, Implications Section, ¶ 2)

Initiatives to develop and expand community-based services, conduct outreach and community education, lobby for legislative change, and train judicial and criminal justice personnel will begin to redress these issues and broaden the scope of services for lesbian, gay, bisexual, and transgendered persons who are in abusive relationships. The present dearth of services calls for multilevel efforts, including ascertaining the incidence of same-sex violence in communities, establishing networks of appropriate services, advocating changes in state and federal laws and the criminal justice system's policies, and educating social service professionals about same-sex violence (Hamberger, 1996).

Children's Reactions to Domestic Violence

Recent estimates suggest that, in the United States alone, about 3.3 million children are exposed to domestic violence annually (Fantuzzo & Mohr, 1999). Certainly not all children who experience violence in their families develop behavioral or emotional disturbances, nor do they automatically become adults who abuse others. However, violence in families has far-reaching effects.

Some consider children's exposure to domestic violence a form of psychological maltreatment. For example, children of women who experience abuse have a greater chance of being abused themselves. And children who are both witnesses to and victims of abuse have the greatest psychological difficulties. Research indicates that even infants experience distress, including crying, irritability, sleep disturbances, emotional distress, and attachment issues when they are exposed to violence in their homes (Edleson, 1999; Osofsky, 1999). When older children are exposed to such violence, they may develop a number of patterns of problematic behaviors, including anxiety, depression, low self-esteem, low levels of empathy, and aggressive behaviors (Carter, Weithorn, & Behrman, 1999; Osofsky, 1999). They are also likely to experience negative effects in their peer relationships and school performance.

Not all children respond negatively as several factors mediate the effects of witnessing violence. These include the presence of an adult who cares, "safe havens" in the community, someone to intervene on their behalf, and individual characteristics, such as emotional resilience and personal feelings of mastery and competence.

Services for Children. Comprehensive domestic violence services include programming for children, who represent half of all shelter residents (Carter, Weithorn, & Behrman, 1999). Programs include such initiatives as individual and group counseling. Associated activities help children develop adaptive responses, learn effective and safe problem-solving techniques, examine their attitudes toward relationships, take responsibility for their own behavior, work on issues related to anger, explore the negative consequences of violence in resolving conflicts, and develop more positive self-esteem. Child advocacy is a more recent addition to shelter programs. Child advocates "help child residents access the benefits and services they need, ensure that legal protections are in place for the children, and provide training to shelter staff on child development and the impact of domestic violence on children" (p. 7).

Social Work Highlights. One program works with young children, ages 5 to 7, who have witnessed violence in their families (Tutty & Wagner, 1994). The group, the Storybook Club, is one of several ongoing programs at the Calgary YWCA Support Center: Alternatives to Domestic Violence. Each session centers around reading a story that deals with a particular theme, such as divorce, anger, fear, fighting, and personal safety. The children discuss the story and videotape their story. They watch and discuss their video over a snack. Discussion time as well as the "cuts" in action afford opportunities to develop alternative strategies for resolving conflicts and dealing with feelings.

Community prevention strategies can play a key role in addressing the interrelated issues of child abuse and domestic violence (Carter & Schechter, 1997). Community-based prevention activities address directly the silence in our society that often surrounds family violence—"the belief that family violence is a private matter; the reluctance of friends, neighbors, and relatives to reach out to troubled families; and the lack of information available on how to have healthy, nonviolent family relationships" (p. 13). One such program involves peer educators who

> serve as community organizers who work with neighborhood residents to mobilize them into action aimed at preventing domestic violence and child abuse. A variety of organizing

strategies could be employed by peer educators to reach deep into the community. For example, a small group of young parents—both men and women trained as peer educators, from various ethnic and racial groups in a community—could do regular work with the naturally occurring support networks within neighborhoods to encourage conversations about healthy relationships and family violence in their ongoing activities. Possible sites for these discussions include housing projects, beauty shops, schools, churches, neighborhood block clubs, parent groups, social clubs, and organized athletic events. (p. 13)

Elder Abuse

Abuse occurs throughout the life cycle; however, the problem of elder abuse has only recently been acknowledged. The federal definition of elder abuse first appeared in the 1987 amendments to the Older Americans Act. All 50 states have now enacted legislation that authorizes adult protective services (APS) to address the abuse of adults who are vulnerable or who have disabilities. These state statutes vary considerably in terms of defining elder abuse, determining eligibility for protective services, and delineating provisions for mandatory reporting (National Center on Elder Abuse [NCEA], 2003a). Although the majority of states do make reporting elder abuse mandatory, only some have specific penalties for noncompliance. Types of agencies designated by state laws as receiving and investigating reports of elder abuse include adult protective service units of state-level human service agencies, local social service agencies with a protective service component, and law enforcement officials.

Recent national survey figures indicate 472,813 reports of elder abuse in 2000, representing a significant increase from the 1986 baseline of 117,000 reports (Teaster, 2001). Of these reports, 396,398 were investigated, and 166,019 were substantiated, although the actual substantiation rate is not available because of reporting differences among the states. Experts believe that the actual reports of elder abuse represent only the "tip of the iceberg."

Types of Elder Abuse

Various definitions of elder abuse are found in federal legislation, such as the 1987 Amendments to the Older Americans Act, state laws, and the National Center for Elder Abuse (NCEA). "*Elder abuse* is an all-inclusive term representing all types of mistreatment or abusive behavior toward older adults," including abusive, neglectful, or exploitative behaviors (Wolf, 2000). Types of elder abuse include the following:

- *Neglect* is refusing or failing to meet one's obligations or duties to a dependent or older adult.
- *Psychological abuse* inflicts harm, emotional anguish, or pain through verbal and/or nonverbal actions.
- *Physical abuse* involves assault or physical force that results in physical harm, pain, or impairment.
- *Sexual abuse* occurs when older or dependent adults are forced into sexual contact of any kind.
- *Financial exploitation* includes illegal or improper appropriations of an older or dependent adult's assets, investments, or property.

- *Abandonment* results when the person assuming responsibility for the care of an older adult deserts that individual.
- *Self-neglect* occurs when the actions of an older adult threaten his or her safety or well-being. (NCEA, 2003b)

The 2000 Survey of State Adult Protective Services (Teaster, 2001) examined data from all states and jurisdictions. Findings indicate the most commonly reported types of elder abuse were self-neglect (42 percent), physical abuse (20 percent), and caregiver neglect/abandonment (13 percent). The majority of those victimized by elder abuse are women (56 percent), White (66 percent), and 80 years of age and older (45 percent, excluding self-neglect).

Dynamics of Elder Abuse

Elders are abused by family caregivers, paid caretakers, family members, and their life partners. Studies on reports of elder abuse conducted in 1996 by the National Center on Elder Abuse (2003) found adult children the most likely perpetrators (47.3 percent), followed by spouses (19.3 percent) and other family members (8.8 percent). Other research challenges the predominant image of elder abuse, that of adult children abusing their parents. Findings from Pillemer and Finkelhor's (1988) large-scale study—a community-based self-report survey of persons over age 65—indicate that perpetrators are primarily spouses (58 percent) as opposed to children (24 percent). A more recent 50-state survey of adult protective services also found that the majority of perpetrators were family members—either spouses/intimate partners (30 percent) or adult children (18 percent) (Teaster, 2001). These results suggest that elder abuse is an extension of domestic violence. These results suggest that elder abuse is also an extension of spousal abuse.

Family members who are primary care providers may inflict harm on their elderly charges as a result of stress and frustration. They may feel overburdened by caregiving responsibilities that they neither wanted nor expected. Although caregiver stress may play some role in elder abuse, the dynamics, like other forms of family violence, are often rooted in a need to gain and maintain control over the older or dependent adult (Brandl, 2000).

Frail and dependent elderly adults are vulnerable to abuse by family and nonfamily members who have behavioral problems or mental disorders. For example, persons with alcohol and drug addictions or mental instability may perpetrate various types of elder abuse (Kosberg, 1990).

Elder abuse occurs in long-term care facilities, such as nursing homes, board-and-care-homes, and other institutions as well. Contributing factors to elder abuse in these settings include untrained personnel, understaffing, and, simply, misunderstanding of the needs and behaviors of elders.

Identification of Elder Abuse

Several factors may complicate the identification of elder abuse. Frail elders tend to be homebound, rather than out in the community under more public scrutiny. Moreover, dependent elderly persons are often reluctant to bring charges against abusive caregivers. They may tolerate abuse to avoid what they consider to be an untenable alternative, such as a nursing home placement, or even assume that they themselves are to blame for the abusive behavior.

Practitioners who are more alert to indicators of elder abuse and neglect are better able to detect maltreatment by caregivers. Among the clues they look for are the following:

- The caregiver does not provide an opportunity for the elderly person to speak to or be alone with the practitioner.
- The caregiver is indifferent toward or angry at the elder.
- The caregiver does not provide appropriate assistance or adaptive devices for the frail elder.
- Explanations of recurrent injuries are inconsistent.
- The caregiver does not reveal injuries that become apparent upon physical evaluation.
- The caregiver or client frequently changes doctors or medical providers.
- The time between the onset of illness and the seeking of medical care is atypically long.
- The caregiver is emotionally cold toward or threatens the elder.
- The account of the injury is implausible.
- Flirtatious interactions between the elder and the caregiver may suggest a sexual relationship. (Quinn & Tomita, 1986)

Ethical Issues

Social workers in adult protective services experience competing values and ethical problems in investigating and following up on reports of elder abuse. Older adults may be reluctant to acknowledge the abuse, confront the abuser, or press charges against caregivers. Social workers must balance the client's right to autonomy in decision making with their professional obligation to protect the client's well-being. Whether or not the social worker takes preemptive actions hinges on a legal determination of the client's competence. "Laws governing protective services attempt to safeguard those people who are unable to look after themselves while upholding the rights of individuals who have the capacity to make decisions, however 'inappropriate' or unpopular" (Atkinson & Nelson, 1995, p. 217). Some agencies have established formal ethics committees to review complex situations. The membership of these committees typically includes attorneys, mental health practitioners, law enforcement personnel, ethicists, and agency staff.

Social Service Responses

The reauthorization of the Older Americans Act (1987) required prevention programs, public education, outreach, and information and referral services to address the problems of elder abuse. Federal activities have resulted in the following outcomes: "(1) the 1990 congressional appropriation of funding for the federal elder abuse prevention program, (2) the 1990 formation of a departmental task force on elder abuse in the U.S. Department of Health and Human Services (DHHS), and (3) federal support of the creation and operation of two national resource centers on elder abuse" (Tatara, 1995, p. 838). The multifaceted nature of elder abuse requires multidimensional solutions. Advocacy efforts and protective services are needed as well as a continuum of programs and services, including

- Public education and professional training for community professionals, including clergy; promotion of intergenerational understanding
- Provision of a continuum of services with coordinated components, such as community-based in-home care, support groups for caregivers, and adult day care
- Formation of multidisciplinary service teams
- Focus of services on the family

An empowerment model provides a sense of hope, restores power and control to the persons who have been victimized, and focuses on their strengths and resourcefulness (Brandl, 2000). Moreover, to ensure an empowering approach, older adults need to be involved in developing policies and planning and evaluating programs focused on preventing and responding to issues of elder abuse (Harbison, 1999; Slater, 2000).

Social Work Highlights. An 89-year-old woman was financially and physically abused by her grandnephew, who had lived with her for about 14 years. The grandnephew was unemployed and relied solely on his aunt's savings for his personal support. Alerted by delinquent property taxes, the court appointed a conservator, who prevented further financial misappropriation by the grandnephew.

Professional practitioners involved in the case were suspicious of physical abuse when explanations for a serious eye injury seemed implausible. Although the grandnephew admitted to striking his aunt to "shut her up," he reported that her eye injury had resulted from a fall. According to the woman, her eye was injured by "something that flew through the window." During her hospitalization, the grandnephew did not visit his aunt, nor did he want her to return to her own home.

The woman was ultimately discharged from the hospital with a plan for home-based services. However, the home health providers were unable to make contact with her. After a week, concerned practitioners gained entry into her house when she did not answer phone calls or respond to her doorbell. They found the woman in poor condition, lying in human excrement. Her grandnephew provided no care and denied entry to the in-home attendants. After another brief hospitalization, the woman transferred to a board-and-care home (Quinn & Tomita, 1986). The woman in this case example experienced several different types of elder abuse, including physical abuse, active neglect, and financial exploitation. It also raises numerous ethical issues in relation to social workers' potential responses to this particular situation.

Services for Older Adults

Older adults are becoming increasingly prominent by their sheer number. As the baby boomers grow older, we will, indeed, experience a "graying of America." In 2002, 12.4 percent of the population in the United States was 65 years of age or older. By 2030, 20 percent of the population will be age 65 and older (Administration on Aging [AoA], 2002). Even more dramatic increases will be seen in the number of those over 85, currently the fastest growing segment of those older than 65. Projections indicate there will be almost 18.9 million people 85 years or older by 2050, a cumulative increase of over 400 percent. Furthermore, the number of centenarians (people 100 years of age and older) has nearly doubled in the last decade.

The population group over 65 is also becoming more diverse. The percentage of older adults who are members of minority population groups is expected to rise from 16.4 percent in 2000 to 25.4 percent in 2030—an 81 percent increase among older Whites and a 219 percent increase among older minority groups (AoA, 2002). Demographers anticipate the fastest rate of growth among Hispanic Americans; projections suggest a 328 percent increase in the numbers of Hispanic Americans over 65 by 2030.

Similar trends in population aging are occurring worldwide (United Nations, Population Division, 2003). Estimates indicate there were 606 million adults over age 60 in 2000. Projections suggest this number will increase to about 1.9 billion by 2050. At that time, experts expect the world population over 60 will be about equal to the number of children. The implications of the aging of the world population become clearer when we review additional population projections. Worldwide, the number of centenarians will rise from about 167,000 in 2000 to 3.4 million in 2050. Of those who are 100 years of age or older in 2050, 471,000 will live in the United States. Additionally, by 2050, at least 10 percent of the population in approximately 21 countries is expected to be 80 years of age or older. Mirkin and Weinberger (2000) conclude "there can be little doubt that changes in age distribution have complex social and economic implications at the societal and individual levels" (p. 4).

Setting the Record Straight about Aging

At one time, the popular notion of appropriate aging was a picture of an elderly person in a rocking chair. People believed that old age resulted in a disengagement between elders and society. However, the activities of most older adults today contradict this portrait of aging. For these older adults, this time of their lives has come to mean a time of opportunities, such as travel and recreational activity and a time to pursue hobbies, personal interests, education, volunteer work, and even a new career! Contrast the usual visual image of aging as one of steady decline with an aging process marked by continued health and well-being. Gerontologists point to the need to increase the "health span" so that the health span is equal to the life span. For many, later adulthood is a time for embracing new possibilities.

Realistically, sensory loss and changes in mobility are often associated with increased age; however, these changes do not necessarily diminish older adults' sense of personal competence. In fact, the productive period of the life span is extending well into the ninth decade. Both personal and environmental adaptations promote competence in social functioning. Research indicates that "many of the physical and mental problems of older Americans—once inaccurately blamed on aging—are, in fact, due to disease" (Pryor, 1994, p. 12). However, ageism lumps all older people into one stereotypic category, "the old folks," leading to a lowered sense of self-esteem and diminished sense of personal control among older adults. It may well be that, if our society maintains its ageist bias, it will overlook the valuable contributions and resources of older adults (Woolf, n.d.).

Successful Aging

According to Rowe and Kahn (1998), "gerontologists of the new millennium will increasingly focus on how to promote *successful aging,* or how older adults can retain the ability to function in their environments as they age" (p. xiii). Based on the results of the MacArthur Foundation study of aging, they concluded that three key features characterize successful aging:

- Avoiding disease and disability
- Continuing engagement with life, including both social relationships and productive activity
- Maintaining mental and physical functioning (p. 49)

Older individuals who are aging successfully take steps proactively to prevent declines and find ways to adapt creatively to changes that may occur so as to minimize their impact on their lives.

The findings of the MacArthur Foundation study of aging (Rowe & Kahn, 1998) provide data that confronts a number of negative misconceptions about aging, including the following:

- "*To be Old is to be Sick*" (p. 13): Older adults are healthier than those in past generations. At 65, most women will live another 20 years, and men, another 15. Furthermore, most older adults can expect to remain active and productive throughout their lives.
- "*You Can't Teach an Old Dog New Tricks*" (p. 19): Long-held stereotypes of older adults suggest that they are incapable of learning, and, more to the point, are likely to experience grave declines in memory. The actual rate of degenerative illnesses such as Alzheimer's disease suggests that less than 10 percent of persons over age 65 are afflicted with this disorder. Research indicates that people of any age, given opportunities, can learn new skills. Factors that help people maintain mental functioning include regular physical activity, social support networks, and beliefs in one's capabilities.
- *The Horse is Out of the Barn* (p. 22): Many people believe that, when they are older, making health-related life-style changes will not make a difference to their well-being. In actuality, it is never too late to make life-style changes to reduce health risks and improve the quality of life.
- *The Secret to Successful Aging is to Choose Your Parents Wisely* (p. 28): Genetics may play a role in longevity; however, research suggests that life-style and environmental factors play a more important role than genetic factors.
- *The Lights may be on, but the Voltage is Low* (p. 31): Although sexual activity may decline with age, people have needs for intimacy and remain sexual throughout their lives.
- *The Elderly Don't Pull Their own Weight* (p. 33): Equating being older with being unproductive is totally inaccurate. Interestingly, almost one-third of all older adults are employed full- or part-time. Furthermore, although paid employment may not be a part of the daily routines of many older adults, this does not mean their lives are empty. More than likely, their days are filled with meaningful activities, such as volunteer work, caregiving, and work in their own homes.

The picture of successful aging offers us a more optimistic view of older adults. One study illustrates key ingredients that contribute to this end (Fisher & Specht, 1999).

Activity and health status, not numeric age, differentiate the young-old from the old-old.

Respondents identified such factors as having positive interactions with others, opportunities for growth, sense of purpose, and independence. This study also found a relationship between creativity and successful aging. As one 69-year-old woman remarked, "If you're going to age successfully, you're coping. Creativity involves everything you do—an emotional or mental coping. Life itself is a matter of creativity especially when you're older because you have the time to think about the challenges and come up with solutions." Or, according to a 78-year-old woman, "It gives you an interest, something to look forward to, something to fill your mind and days. I think you have to have an interest. There's nothing more exciting than having a new project." Clearly, social workers can play a role in prevention activities that promote successful aging.

Fostering Resiliency. Gutheil and Congress (2000) caution that overemphasizing successful aging may cause us to evaluate those older adults with disabilities and cognitive frailties negatively. It may well be that individuals demonstrate considerable strength, adaptability, and resilience in the face of these difficulties. "Resilience in old age may be best thought of as the ability to survive and overcome numerous major stressors, including disease, disability, and a range of other major losses" (p. 42). Factors that contribute to resiliency include coping strategies that manage the meaning of stress, sense of mastery, flexibility, and access to social support. Numerous studies indicate that sense of personal control rather than health per se plays a significant role in promoting a positive sense of psychological well-being (Smith et al., 2000). "Resilience is fostered by interdependence with others and grounded in the ability to adapt to changing demands" (Gutheil & Congress, p. 44). Modifying environments to fit the needs of individuals also plays a role in fostering resiliency. Practice principles that promote resilience include the following:

- Identify indicators of strengths and resilience in the client.
- Involve the client in identifying areas of resilience.
- Help the client to identify what areas he or she can still control.
- Assist the client in letting go of what he or she cannot control.
- Identify and encourage informal and formal supports that foster resiliency.
- Identify new, untapped areas of strength and emerging resiliencies.
- Identify and work to enhance or alter aspects of the physical environment that either support or undermine resilience.
- Identify and work to enhance or alter aspects of the physical environment that either support or undermine resilience.
- Reevaluate resiliency based on changing levels of capability. (p. 45)

An empowerment orientation to social work presses us to look beyond the surface when we interact with older adults whose functional capabilities might suggest that they have not been "successful" in their aging processes. Only when we explore further will we discover that there are many varieties of "success." Resilience reveals the courageous abilities of many to manage in very difficult situations. Even for those older adults who seem to have given up in the face of adversity, discovering their strengths and capabilities and fostering resiliency may well be the catalyst that will make a difference in their lives.

Gerontological Social Work

Gerontological social work, or social work with older adults, is a rapidly expanding field of practice. One study found that about 5 percent of NASW members work in the field of aging (Gibelman & Schervish, 1997), although other studies indicate that older adults are a major part of most practitioners' client loads (Peterson & Wendt, 1990). Practitioners who work with older adults need specialized knowledge about social conditions that confront older adults, including health care issues, poverty, employment, housing, and mental health, as well as knowledge about the normal aging process and atypical changes such as Alzheimer's disease. They also need to be familiar with the details of Social Security (OASI), SSI, Medicare, Medicaid, and the programs and services available through the national network of the Area Agencies on Aging.

Issues in Working with Older Adults

Practitioners who work with older adults must examine their own attitudes about aging, illness, and death. This is particularly challenging, as the issues of older adulthood are outside the life experiences of most professional social workers. "In working with the elderly, social workers must confront personal issues of aging, disability, and death in ways that few others must. If social workers have their own unresolved issues about death, disability, or aging, they impede progress and work" (Barry, 1988, p. 451). Frequently, people influenced by ageism presume that older individuals are incapable of change; however, this notion is

BOX 14.2
Social Work Profile

Aging Services

There was no real "lightening bolt" that jolted me toward a social work career. An introductory social work class sounded interesting to me, so I enrolled; I enjoyed the class, and the rest is history. I discovered that I loved working with older adults during my practicum experiences.

Finding ways to support independent living for older adults has been a consistent driving force in my career. However, the field of aging services is constantly evolving—constantly shifting to address current trends, emerging issues, and demographic changes. For example, services for older adults will increase in the future, as the needs of aging "baby boomers" will need to be addressed and the role of family caregivers is likely to expand. One significant policy change necessitated by these trends will be for Medicaid to fund assisted-living programs—programs that provide care representing the step between living in one's own home and in a nursing home.

When I started, the agency's focus was on facilitating comprehensive needs assessments and linking clients with services. Over time, the agency services have expanded in terms of the variety of programs the agency offers, the geographic area it covers, and receiving referrals of complicated cases requiring more intense involvement. Because the nature of our work with a vulnerable population raises ethical dilemmas, our agency formed an ethics committee comprised of persons from a number of disciplines, including mental health practitioners, police officers, attorneys, and ethicists. The ethics committee, through their consultation and review of cases, offers valuable assistance to case managers in balancing what workers believe to be in the best interests of clients and the clients' rights to self-determination. The tendency to convince frail, elderly clients to take a particular course of action or to impose services on them is the point where good intentions can go awry. Because our case managers now have a clearer understanding of client autonomy and are less likely to act with paternalism or maternalism, the role of the ethics committee has shifted to looking at more complicated cases involving guardianship petitions.

Informed by a philosophy that promotes independence, preserves dignity, and provides for choices, the agency mission directs us into three service arenas—to protect, to advocate, and to support. Programs include case management, a telephone reassurance initiative staffed by volunteers, elder abuse prevention and protective services, ombudsmen services in area nursing homes, money management, and caregiver support. Participants in the caregiver support groups are likely to join the group initially because they want information. Then, they discover that just the process of telling their story lightens their emotional load. Our follow-up evaluations often include comments like, "Just knowing that I'm not alone has been extraordinarily helpful to me," and "I've been able to meet others who are experiencing similar situations; they know what I'm going through." Another venue for information and support is the new Senior Center in one of the rural communities in our catchment area. The Senior Center provides more than a meal and an afternoon of bingo. Instead, it hosts a wide variety of activities, classes, and concerts that correspond with the interests of the participants. With programs that serve as gathering places, build networks of social support, and emphasize health and wellness activities, the Senior Center makes a significant contribution to the successful aging of the now healthy aging adults that program serves.

---

dispelled by a competence perspective that suggests that all people have the capacity for change throughout the life cycle (Berk, 2004). Social workers can take steps to increase their effectiveness and heighten their sensitivity to the diversity of aging:

- Modify stereotypes and negative images.
- Be aware of the effects of membership in a particular cohort.
- Recognize the tremendous variability among elderly individuals.
- Learn how gender and ethnic minority status affect the aging experience. (Toseland, 1995, pp. 153–154)

Competence-based practitioners work collaboratively with older clients, rather than simply providing concrete resources that address narrowly defined, specific problems. Using positive language in framing conversations with older clients promotes competence and emphasizes strengths (Chapin & Cox, 2001; Cox, 2002; Kivnick & Murray, 2001; Miley, 2002; Thompson & Thompson, 2001). One example is "asking a client to talk about the ways they have managed specific life situations instead of asking them to identify symptoms or problems they experience could convey our positive expectations about their abilities and our willingness to collaborate with them to change things for the better" (Lewis, 1996, p. 109).

Continuum of Services

Basically, formal services for older adults fall into three categories: social supports for those who are healthy, community services for those in frail health, and institutional long-term care for people who are no longer able to live independently even with the support of family members and community-based services (Tobin & Toseland, 1990). See Table 14.1. The long-term care needs of people who are frail, have functional disabilities, and need assistance with daily living require either community-based or institutional services that address a broad range of health care, personal, and social needs.

Bringing together a variety of services, such as financial assistance, transportation, housing, home energy assistance, information and referral, rehabilitation, telephone assurance networks, and counseling, under both public and private agencies requires fine-tuned coordination of programs and social policies. That services for older adults fall under the auspices of a variety of legal statutes, sources of funding, and administrative agencies further complicates service delivery.

Social workers are often employed in those settings supplying services that case managers draw upon—home health services presented in Chapter 12, adult protective services and programs for family caregivers presented earlier in this chapter, family service agencies, support groups, congregate living facilities and other types of senior housing programs, adult day care and respite services, nursing homes, and multipurpose service senior centers, to name a few.

Case Management Services for Older Adults

A case manager is a professional who collaborates with clients to assess their needs, locate and link them to appropriate programs and services, and evaluate the outcomes (Rose & Moore, 1995). Case managers coordinate and sustain networks of formal and informal resources "to optimize the functioning and well-being of people with multiple needs" (Moxley, 1989, p. 21). Case management services are particularly appropriate when clients' situations require multiple services. As advocates, case managers are in a position to ensure that clients have access to the programs and services to which they are entitled and to redress

TABLE 14.1 Resources for Older Adults

Income support	Income maintenance (SSI) Social insurance (OASDHI)
Health Care	Medicare Medicaid Home health/homemaker aides
Nutrition	Food stamps Food commodity programs (USDA) Congregate and homebound meals
Housing	Public subsidized housing Tax postponement options for homeowners Housing rehabilitation plans
Transportation	Reduced bus fares Dial-a-ride services Specially equipped vans
Socialization	Multipurpose senior centers Adult day care Telephone reassurance programs Volunteer programs Adult education programs
Legal services	Legal aide Legal issues: guardianships, trusteeships, and living wills

issues related to fragmented social service delivery networks (Sunley, 1997). Case management is the wave of the future in many fields of practice given the climate of fiscal conservatism and bureaucratically managed access to services (Austin & McClelland, 1996). For older adults, case management services play a particularly critical role in linking older clients and their families with networks of community-based support, thereby reducing the likelihood of premature placements in nursing home facilities.

Within the field of services for people who are aging, case managers are found in public, private not-for-profit, and private for-profit agencies. "Frail elderly often have multiple health problems, functional disabilities, and social losses—complex situations that require comprehensive multidimensional assessment for effective care planning and services" (Austin, 1996, p. 76). In addition to work with individual clients, case managers are in a pivotal position "to identify and document service delivery effects, barriers, and obstacles originating at the system level, especially in fiscal and operational policies" (Austin, 1993, p. 457). Client-oriented and system-oriented objectives for case management services in long-term care specify the purpose of case management:

Client-Oriented Objectives

- To secure appropriate services
- To monitor the client's situation to ensure appropriate ongoing services

- To enhance access to the full continuum of long-term care services
- To provide supports for caregivers
- To serve as a connecting link between community-based and institutional programs and services

System-Oriented Objectives

- To prompt the development of a full complement of community-based services
- To ensure quality in accessible, efficient services
- To strengthen the coordinated delivery of long-term care services
- To avert inappropriate institutionalization through targeting efforts with those most at risk of placement
- To implement plans that control costs (Austin, 1996)

Prominent functions in case management with individual clients include outreach, assessment, case planning, accessing resources, advocacy, monitoring, and evaluation (Abramson & Rosenthal, 1995; Austin & McClelland, 1996; Greene, 1992; Nelson, 1995). Case managers link clients with resources and coordinate services to develop plans that incorporate the least restrictive alternatives possible. In this frontline service, social workers provide information to older adults and their families about the continuum of services that are available for supportive or supplemental assistance. Social workers match individuals' circumstances with resources they need, such as meal services, transportation, housing, telephone reassurance programs, support groups, adult day care, respite care, and senior center activities.

Meal Services. Maintaining a nutritionally balanced diet is important for older people's continued health. Malnutrition and dietary deficiencies may result in a number of health problems, including diabetes, coronary disease, osteoporosis, certain cancers, and confusion and memory loss. To achieve adequate nutrition, older adults may need dietary consultation, help in deferring grocery costs, or assistance in preparing meals. Other programs that reduce food costs or provide meals are available.

Food Stamps. The food stamp program, sponsored by the U.S. Department of Agriculture (USDA) since the 1960s, allows people with low incomes to reduce their food bills by purchasing food stamps at a lower dollar value to exchange for groceries. Regrettably, older people underutilize the food stamp program because their pride reacts to the stigma attached to government assistance. The USDA surplus commodities program is another way the government distributes food to eligible low-income older adults. Local officials or service organizations usually coordinate the distribution, which consists primarily of cheese and other dairy products.

Congregate and Home-Delivered Meals. The Title III nutrition program subsidizes congregate meals. These programs offer low-cost, nutritionally balanced meals at centrally located or convenient, handicap-accessible sites, such as churches, senior centers, service clubs, and settlement or neighborhood centers. Congregate meal programs often encourage socialization through recreational events and activity programs.

In some communities, home-delivered meals are available to people who are homebound. When neighborhood volunteers deliver these meals, they often serve as friendly visitors. Contact with volunteers reduces the social isolation of homebound adults and may even assist them in accessing other social services.

Transportation. For older adults, access to transportation is essential for maintaining independence. However, even for healthy older adults, public transit systems present barriers. Public transportation has fixed routes and predetermined schedules, and passengers must often deal with lengthy walks, poor crowd-flow design, insufficient seating, stairways, and inconvenient transfers and connections. The Urban Mass Transportation Act and particularly the Biaggi amendments mandate special efforts to address the public transportation needs of persons with disabilities. These efforts have resulted in reduced fares for elderly passengers, dial-a-ride or call-ahead services, and specialized vehicle design. Social workers often help older clients identify and access local transportation services.

Housing. Where people live is important to their general well-being and self-esteem. The ability to live independently in the community is strongly correlated with self-efficacy, even among the oldest old (Rodin, 1989). Moreover, people need to decide for themselves where to live. Thus, older people should have a choice of housing options and sufficient information for making their decisions.

Regarding housing needs, a balance must be established between the individual's requirements and the available environmental supports. Assessing older adults' needs for housing involves more than considering domiciles alone. Attention must be given to the total living environment, including transportation, shopping, recreation, medical services, and social opportunities (Cox, 1994). Increasing individuals' capabilities through adaptive devices in combination with lowering environmental demands maximizes choices in living arrangements and housing options.

Continuing to maintain homestead property or other private dwellings affords older adults satisfaction and a sense of accomplishment. Familiar surroundings, personal belongings, and the memories attached to long-time residences provide security, a sense of personal stability, and access to neighborhood social networks. However, maintaining private dwellings can be a financial burden for older adults on fixed retirement incomes, particularly in relation to upkeep and the structural changes needed to accommodate motor and sensory changes. Additionally, financial circumstances force some older adults to live in substandard housing units (owner-occupied or rental) located in deteriorating neighborhoods in inner cities or isolated rural areas (Sherman, 1990).

Numerous programs provide financial support for housing rehabilitation and home weatherization, energy subsidies, and tax relief. Social workers employed in senior advocacy services, community action programs, and senior centers help older citizens to access appropriate housing services and benefits through community education and outreach. Social workers involved in urban and rural community planning activities must continue to address the housing needs of this growing constituency through community action, legislative reforms, and the development of programs to provide a range of housing options.

Many older people choose to live in congregate arrangements, such as age-segregated apartment complexes, retirement communities, mobile home parks, condominiums, and shared housing arrangements. Another option is a "buy-in," sponsored by fraternal organizations, private corporations, and sectarian agencies. For a fee, life-care facilities offer a graduated housing plan for people of retirement age. In this arrangement, a variety of housing is available, from independent living quarters and supervised apartments to nursing homes. Facilitating clients' choices of the most appropriate housing arrangement for their particular circumstances is a key case management task.

Empowerment Orientation to Case Management. Adopting "management" tactics in case management activities oversteps the boundaries of client self-determination (Dinerman, 1992). When working with older adults who are frail, confused, or dependent, case managers' actions may be controlling disguised as caring, "not from malevolence but simply from the dynamic of powerful and resourceful professionals interacting with vulnerable and resource-weak clients. . . . Precisely when care is beneficent, intrusions upon autonomy can go unchecked, unscrutinized, even unobserved behind the curtain of good intentions" (Collopy, 1992, p. 56). On the other hand, "case managers who 'overrespect' an individual's autonomy run the risk of engaging in benign neglect and underserving the client" (Austin, 1996, p. 93). The collaborative planning characteristic of empowerment-based case management must strike a balance between the press for autonomous decision making and the imperative of providing a "safety net" of services.

A Swedish study of the daily life of the older adults who were among the noninstitutionalized "oldest old" underlines the significance of clients' involvement in decision making (Carlsson-Ågren, Berg, & Wenestam, 1992). Researchers found that those who were better adjusted controlled their own daily schedules. On the other hand, the daily schedules of those who were not as well adjusted were controlled by external conditions rather than their own personal preferences. The researchers concluded that caregiving interventions need to consider the personal timetables of participants to ensure that participants remain in charge of their lives. Empowerment-oriented case management can play a significant role in preserving the health and well-being of older adults.

Social Work Highlights. The example of the social work practitioner's work with Mr. S. illustrates the multifaceted nature of case management strategies:

> Mr. S. is a 70-year-old man who is recovering from a recent stroke. His family contacts the public services social worker to ask about getting him assistance with personal care needs, activities, and transportation to medical services. The social worker visits Mr. S. in his home to perform the comprehensive functional assessment, which suggests that he is experiencing significant depression resulting from the loss of positive self-image and functioning associated with the stroke.
>
> In working with the client and his family, the social worker provides them with information regarding the effects of the stroke, in particular, that it can cause depression. As a broker of services, the social worker may help them purchase or arrange for home health services that might help the client not only compensate for his ADL [activities of daily living] impairment but also regain through physical and speech therapy as much functioning as possible. If the client is willing, the social worker might also refer him to a mental health professional for treatment of depression. In securing transportation services for the client, the social worker may have to advocate on his behalf with a provider who does not believe Mr. S. qualifies for the agency's services. The social worker also may encounter conflict within the family about Mr. S.'s perceived abilities, the likelihood of his regaining his independence, and the options available if he does not. The social worker may mediate this conflict by providing information, acting as a referee in discussions, and modeling appropriate listening and communication skills. As facilitator, the worker's practice should be an active

> demonstration of problem-solving skills and planning techniques that the client and family can use for themselves in the future. Finally, if the social worker discovers that a number of the other adult services clients and families could benefit from a stroke support group, he or she might join with others in the community to develop one. (Nelson, 1995, p. 97)

Adult Day Care and Respite Services

Adult day care and respite services are relatively new options for older adults. These arrangements provide health and social services for older residents of a community over long periods of time (Rathbone-McCuan, 1990; Streets, 1995). Older adults who utilize adult day care centers may have physical and mental limitations that require a "safe environment" as well as assistance and supervision for all or part of a day. Some adult day centers provide specialized programs for persons with Alzheimer's disease, AIDS, or severe mental illness (Gordon, 1995). Adult day care provides a less expensive alternative to individual care along with more expansive possibilities for socialization, rehabilitation, and activities.

Adult day care centers not only serve as alternatives to the institutional placement of adults in frail health, but also provide respite or supportive services for family caregivers. These services allow family caregivers some relief from the daily stresses of caregiving. Some communities provide respite services on an individual basis, allowing family caregivers time off from their duties. Other respite alternatives include temporary placement in foster care, a group home, or a nursing home.

Adult day centers typically incorporate a social service component (Gordon, 1995). Social workers are involved in adult day care settings in a variety of ways, including administering programs, coordinating home-based services, counseling, facilitating caregiver support groups, and providing in-service training and community education. As an integral member of the day center team, a social worker is often involved with adult day care participants from the initiation of their application for services, monitoring care plans and providing support for participants and their families, individually and in small groups.

Social Work in Nursing Homes

When we hear the term *nursing homes,* we often think of older adults. Actually, any adult with a functional impairment may live in a nursing home. About 1.6 million people live in nursing homes; about 50 percent of those living in nursing homes are age 85 and older (U.S. Census Bureau, 2002b). Currently, less than 4.5 percent of all adults 65 and older reside in nursing homes. However, this statistic is somewhat deceiving as 18.2 percent of those 85 and older reside in nursing homes (AoA, 2002). In actuality, older adults have a one in two chance of living in a nursing home at some time during their lives and a one in four chance of spending more than a year in a nursing home. Risk factors that increase the likelihood of institutionalization include chronic disability, cognitive impairments, advanced age, and hospitalization. Of these, low cognitive functioning is a major risk factor (Federal Interagency Forum on Aging-Related Statistics, 2000). There are approximately 15,000 Medicare and Medicaid certified nursing homes in the United States (U.S. Census Bureau, 2002b). Qualified nursing homes may designate some rooms for "skilled care" services that fill the gap between discharge from hospitals and returning home.

BOX 14.3
Reflections on Empowerment

Gay and Lesbian Aging

Although there are few references to gay and lesbian aging in the professional literature, estimates indicate that there are between 1.75 and 3.5 million older gay men and lesbian women in the United States (Woolf, 1998). Gay men and lesbian women who were 65 and older in the year 2000 were born in 1935 or earlier. The timing of their births places their adult experiences either in the sociocultural context that treated homosexuality as a crime or a mental illness, or in the midst of the gay rights movement and other discourse on homosexuality during the later part of the twentieth century. Their issues regarding a homosexual identity are likely to be influenced by the historical experiences of their cohort group (Langley, 2001; Rosenfeld, 1999). These factors add further challenges to the aging processes.

It may well be that living with stigma and discrimination may prepare gay men and lesbian women for aging. Throughout their lives, older gays and lesbians have encountered discrimination, prejudicial attitudes, and negative stereotyping. Research suggests that dealing with these issues successfully in earlier years provides a base of resources for dealing with the stigma associated with aging (Woolf, 1998). Complicating issues of aging is the fact that many older gay men and lesbian women have never identified themselves as gay or lesbian (Quam, 1993).

Additionally, many lesbian women and gay men socialize in diverse networks of friends (Woolf, 1998). They look to their friends for social and emotional support. Since these support networks involve community—rather than employment-based friendships, they are likely to continue to be sources of support after retirement. Woolf suggests that retirement may actually have a hidden bonus for gay men and lesbian women. If they had not "come out" in the workplace, retired gay men and lesbians no longer worry that their sexual orientation would be revealed to their colleagues at work. Since they no longer need to be concerned about threats to their financial stability, many older gay men and lesbian women feel free to be involved in social groups and to participate in political activities.

Because so little is publically known about older gay men and lesbian women and because their cohort experience affects how they view themselves, social workers face challenges in their work with this population. Issues range from agencies' failure to consider sexual diversity among older adults to the policy implications of benefits that more often than not exclude domestic partnerships from consideration. For example, Quam (1993) relates the concerns of two gay men in their seventies who had carefully planned for old age. These men had concerns about how they might be treated by health care providers. How would staff in a hospital or long-term care facility treat their 30-year relationship? Would they be able to make critical health care decisions for one another should that need arise? Such legal issues as planning for retirement, durable powers of attorney for financial and health care, advanced care directives, guardianships and conservatorships, trusts, and other types of estate planning require careful planning and consultation with attorneys who understand the implications for gay men and lesbian women (Dubois, 1999). One social service organization that addresses the range of issues facing lesbian, gay, bisexual, and trangender senior citizens is Senior Action in a Gay Environment (SAGE).

Empowerment-oriented social workers direct their attention to macro- as well as microlevel challenges facing older gay men and lesbian women. Increasing one's awareness of issues related to aging and sexual diversity is an important starting point. Ensuring that programs and services for older adults are inclusive builds on this awareness. Advocating inclusive health care and retirement benefits and organization and agency policies that are responsive to diversity requires priority actions.

Ethnically diverse older adults face special challenges when they enter the dominant culture's long-term care institutions because of the potential loss of connections to their families, culture, and communities. Social workers may employ advocacy strategies to mediate the cultural differences. Language and cultural differences require adaptations to facilitate communication among staff and residents.

Most nursing homes are for-profit facilities, although some are nonprofit facilities sponsored by sectarian agencies, fraternal organizations, or the government. State and federal guidelines regulate nursing homes strictly. Regulations require nursing homes certified for Medicare and Medicaid to employ a social worker or a "social service designee" along with a professionally certified social work consultant who supervises the paraprofessional and provides staff-development training. Major functions of social workers in nursing homes include the following:

- Facilitate the admissions process
- Develop individualized plans of care
- Enhance the social and psychological well-being of nursing home residents and their families
- Involve the entire facility in meeting psychosocial needs
- Plan discharges to ensure appropriateness and continuity of care for transfers within and discharges from the nursing home (NASW, 1993)

Social Work Highlights. Ruth Stein is a social worker at Golden Acres Nursing Home. Although Ruth serves on Golden Acres's planning team and conducts staff development training, most of her time is spent in direct-service activities with residents and their families. She often confers with prospective residents and their family members when they apply for admission, during the waiting period, at the time of relocation, and as they adjust to their new home.

Ruth helps residents and their families deal with numerous issues, such as the transitions involved in moving into the nursing home. Mr. Olsen wept as he met with Ruth. Helen, his wife of 60 years, has been at the nursing home three weeks now. He feels exhausted and, in his opinion, has no viable options. He feels as though he has "given up" now that Helen lives at the nursing home even though he knows that Helen's forgetfulness, disorientation, and wandering are stressful for him to handle.

Mr. Olsen finds it difficult to leave Helen after his daily visits. He feels lonely without her and believes she, too, misses him. He has heard that Helen wanders aimlessly, looking for him in the hallways and calling his name, after he leaves. But deciding to leave his centennial farm is not easy, even though his health is failing, too. Mr. Olsen is pleased when Ruth tells him that he and his wife can share a suite and furnish it with some of their personal belongings, including their treasured antique oak bed.

Ruth knows that many social and psychological factors influence residents' adjustments to nursing homes. People bring with them their own histories and identities, complete with personal preferences and idiosyncrasies. Finding ways to preserve the unique identity of residents is vital for their well-being in congregate living arrangements. Ruth believes that residents benefit from participating fully in their plans for admission and care, and from making decisions throughout their residency at the nursing home. Her practice reflects an empowerment-oriented approach to social work in long-term care that "seeks to engage participants in the process of increasing their knowledge and skills relative to their efforts to meet their own needs and those of others" (Cox, 2002, p. 27).

Multipurpose Senior Centers

Numbering over 29,000, multipurpose senior centers are the hub of the community service network for more than 10 million older adults (AoA, 2003a). Senior centers provide programming primarily for healthy older adults.

Senior centers provide a combination of direct and indirect services, including recreational programs, adult day care, counseling and support groups, volunteer programming, learning forums, information and referral, outreach, and advocacy. Some centers host congregate meal programs and sponsor senior citizen clubs and organizations. Satellite offices for a number of public and private social services for older adults may offer their programs at senior centers. This arrangement centralizes and coordinates service delivery.

Social workers who are on staff at multipurpose senior centers design and administer programs, offer counseling services, and work in prevention and education. Leading social, recreational, and educational groups may be included in the social worker's responsibilities. Toseland (1995) suggests that these types of groups "provide members with an opportunity to become actively engaged with peers in activities that enhance enjoyment, stimulate learning, and promote healthy growth and development" (p. 184). Interestingly, participating in group activities helps prevent, or at least slows, physical and cognitive declines. Group activities also are excellent resources for "building social support, camaraderie, and a spirit of community" (p. 185). Program activities in social, recreational, and educational groups may include discussions; reminiscence; educational programming; physical activities; special events; and expressive programs such as art, music, drama, and dancing (Toseland, 1995).

A brief excerpt from a group meeting transcript demonstrates the significance of participating in discussions and activities with a group of peers:

> MS. W.: I wanted to say before we start that I've really been enjoying these meetings. I'm not a joiner. But since my husband died, I've been lonely, and needed to do something besides sit at home and think about him. I wasn't so sure I'd like this when I started. But I really look forward to coming and I've made a number of friends here. In fact, I had lunch with Sadie [a group member] on Monday. I really enjoyed it. It's the first time I've been out to lunch in quite a while.
>
> MS. L. [SADIE]: I really enjoyed it too!
>
> MS. A.: Well I'm so glad to hear that. I think the group is turning out really well, and each of you are responsible for that. [pause] Okay, who's going to start sharing about what was the best time of their life? (Toseland, 1995, p. 205)

Senior Volunteers

Of the 59 million persons in the United States who volunteer, 15 million are older adults, representing nearly one-half of those citizens over 65 years of age (AoA, 2003b; BLS,

2002d). Older adults meet the qualifications for volunteer positions for one basic reason: If they are retired, they have time to commit to volunteer activities. Coordinators make a successful match between volunteers' capabilities on the one hand and the service needs of organizations and communities on the other. Empowerment-oriented volunteer services build on the resources, strengths, and skills of volunteers.

Older adults interested in volunteering can find opportunities to do so in a variety of venues—formal and informal, as well as locally sponsored and nationally based programs. Informally, many older adults volunteer their services to transport friends to meetings, ap-

Participating in volunteer activities contributes to successful aging.

pointments, and the grocery store; babysit, and assist others with home chores and caregiving activities (Soo & Gong-Soog, 1998). Additionally, older adults may find opportunities for volunteer work in formally organized activities. Local churches and synagogues often rely on volunteers to staff programs, fold bulletins, organize bulk mailings, and visit members who are homebound or having difficulties. Museums, hospitals, nursing homes, libraries, literacy projects, social service agencies, and schools are examples of other local organizations that routinely solicit volunteers.

Senior volunteers are also involved in such federally supported initiatives as the Administration on Aging (AoA), the Corporation for National and Community Service, and SCORE—Older Americans Helping Young Businesses to Grow. The Administration on Aging uses over 500,000 volunteers in its 57 state and territorial units on aging, their 655 Area Agencies on Aging, and 221 tribal organizations (Administration on Aging, 2003b). Volunteers serve in programs designed for active seniors as well as outreach programs to older adults whose activities are limited by physical or cognitive frailty. Examples of volunteer activities include the following:

- Assisting at group meal sites and "meals on wheels" programs
- Accompanying individuals needing assistance to health care services
- Visiting with individuals who are homebound
- Completing home repair and weatherizing projects
- Providing counseling services on such topics as health promotion, nutrition, and financial matters
- Serving as ombudsmen to residents in nursing homes to ensure their well-being
- Assisting in programs such as senior centers and adult day care programs (Administration on Aging, 2003b)

As a part of the Corporation for National and Community Service, Senior Corps assists people who are 55 years of age and older locate volunteer opportunities in their own communities. Some of the innovative programs developed under this auspice are the Foster Grandparent Program (linking older adults with foster children), the Senior Companion Program (providing supports for older adults who are living independently), and the Retired Senior Volunteer Program (offering a variety of opportunities, including volunteer work in court-related services and nursing homes). Finally, retired executives and small business owners can lend their expertise to new business entrepreneurs as SCORE volunteers.

Research indicates that a number of factors influence older adults to volunteer (Soo & Gong-Soog, 1998). For one, there is a greater proportion of younger seniors volunteering. Education seems to play a role: Individuals who have completed higher levels of education are more likely to participate in volunteer activities. Economics may also influence individuals' volunteer activities. The monetary costs incurred in volunteering, such as "out-of-pocket" costs for materials or transportation, may create barriers for those who have limited discretionary income. This research suggests that social workers involved in planning volunteer activities need to incorporate outreach efforts to involve those older adults who are not currently part of the volunteer corps. It also suggests that "economic incentives such as free meals, tax credits, refreshments, transportation assistance, or reimbursement for transportation or meals may facilitate volunteer participation among low-income older people.

Modest payments may also motivate volunteer efforts, as demonstrated by the Senior Companion Program and the Foster Grandparent Program."

Volunteerism promotes seniors' active involvement in their communities. The perspectives and base of experiences of older volunteers enrich communities. In turn, volunteering itself contributes to the health and psychological well-being of the older adults who volunteer (Soo & Gong-Song, 1998).

Challenge to Social Workers

Social workers practicing in the area of services for people who are aging face interesting challenges. They must prepare themselves and the service delivery system for increased numbers of older adults who are likely to require social work services. They must also embrace a more positive view of aging and challenge others in society to do the same (Hinterlong, Rozario, Morrow-Howell, & Sherraden, 2000). According to Morrow-Howell (2000):

> We are in the midst of a longevity revolution. How we will spend time in these extended years is not fully determined and the possibilities are numerous. Hopefully, we can be purposeful in the roles and expectations that we create for this new "third age" of human life. We need to define the possibilities and create the opportunities based on knowledge about what improves society and what improves the health, mental health, and life satisfaction of our large older population. Our 21st century society may seek the involvement of its older citizenry in work, volunteer, and caregiving roles, and the baby boomers and subsequent generations may seek increased involvement. How we shape and support these roles and how we match opportunity to capacity and preference may influence the impact of these activities on older adults' well-being. Let us proceed with as much knowledge about the effects of productive engagement as possible. (p. 12)

Concluding Remarks

Much of social work intervention focuses on the transitions and crises associated with development throughout the life span. This chapter has presented a sampling of the many developmental issues and events in the lives of adults that are of concern to social workers. The challenge is to understand the impact of the environment on people and to devise solutions that address the multifaceted dimensions of all developmental problems, issues, and needs.

EPILOGUE

Early in the text, we proposed a number of professional tenets that embody the purpose of contemporary social work. The tenets, which reflect our vision for social work, are rooted in the tradition of social work pioneers and informed by the contemporary perspectives of competence and empowerment. As you consider a career in social work, consider these themes and their implications for your practice activities:

- Empower people, individually and collectively, to utilize their own problem-solving and coping capabilities more effectively.
- Support a proactive position in regard to social and economic policy development to prevent problems of individuals and society.
- Uphold the integrity of the profession in all aspects of social work practice.
- Establish linkages between people and societal resources to further social functioning and enhance the quality of life.
- Develop cooperative networks within the institutional resource system.
- Facilitate the responsiveness of the institutional resource systems to meet health and human service needs.
- Promote social justice and equality of all people in regard to full participation in society.
- Contribute to the development of knowledge for the social work profession through research and evaluation.
- Encourage an information exchange in those institutional systems in which both problems and resource opportunities are produced.
- Enhance communication effectiveness through an appreciation of diversity and in ethnically sensitive, nonsexist social work practice.
- Employ educational strategies for the prevention and resolution of problems.
- Embrace a worldview of human issues and problem solutions.

Social work is a profession filled with many challenges and opportunities. Practitioners are challenged to deal creatively with problems presented by those who are disenfranchised and oppressed and by those who are facing life transitions and crises. Opportunities exist for social work practice in a wide array of fields, including family services, child welfare, health, mental health, rehabilitation, public welfare, housing, criminal justice, community development, schools, and business and industry. Social workers can make a unique contribution to change processes in these fields of practice through their use of empowerment strategies.

Social work is an empowering profession. The process of social work is empowering, and the product of professional activities is empowerment. Social workers work with clients in partnerships that affirm clients' strengths and competencies. The professional activities of practitioners, reflected in the dual purpose of social work, are directed at empowering consumers in all social systems to realize their own potential and create responsive social structures.

Empowerment is achieved to the extent that people gain mastery over their lives and to the extent that institutional structures respond humanely and equitably to human needs.

Social work is both a way of thinking and a way of doing. To develop an understanding of social work, it is essential to view the profession from the broadest possible perspective. In other words, social workers must have a conceptual understanding of the interplay of human behavior, practice, and policy. A generalist orientation to social work offers a framework for viewing problems with a wide-angle lens, recognizing the dynamics of the person:environment interaction, analyzing the context of all human situations, and developing interventions that address problems, issues, and needs at all systems levels. The themes discussed and integrated throughout this book—strengths, empowerment, diversity, and social justice—are the filters through which knowledge and values are understood, and they provide the foundation for intervention skills. These same themes will continue to be prominent in your education for professional social work practice.

APPENDIX A

Code of Ethics of the National Association of Social Workers

Preamble

The primary mission of the social work profession is to enhance human well-being and help meet the basic human needs of all people, with particular attention to the needs and empowerment of people who are vulnerable, oppressed, and living in poverty. A historic and defining feature of social work is the profession's focus on individual well-being in a social context and the well-being of society. Fundamental to social work is attention to the environmental forces that create, contribute to, and address problems in living.

Social workers promote social justice and social change with and on behalf of clients. "Clients" is used inclusively to refer to individuals, families, groups, organizations, and communities. Social workers are sensitive to cultural and ethnic diversity and strive to end discrimination, oppression, poverty, and other forms of social injustice. These activities may be in the form of direct practice, community organizing, supervision, consultation, administration, advocacy, social and political action, policy development and implementation, education, and research and evaluation. Social workers seek to enhance the capacity of people to address their own needs. Social workers also seek to promote the responsiveness of organizations, communities, and other social institutions to individuals' needs and social problems.

The mission of the social work profession is rooted in a set of core values. These core values, embraced by social workers throughout the profession's history, are the foundation of social work's unique purpose and perspective:

- service
- social justice
- dignity and worth of the person
- importance of human relationships
- integrity
- competence

This constellation of core values reflects what is unique to the social work profession. Core values, and the principles that flow from them, must be balanced within the context and complexity of the human experience.

Purpose of the *NASW Code of Ethics*

Professional ethics are at the core of social work. The profession has an obligation to articulate its basic values, ethical principles, and ethical standards. The *NASW Code of Ethics* sets forth these values, principles, and standards to guide social workers' conduct. The *Code* is relevant to all social workers and social work students, regardless of their professional functions, the settings in which they work, or the populations they serve.

The *NASW Code of Ethics* serves six purposes:

1. The *Code* identifies core values on which social work's mission is based.
2. The *Code* summarizes broad ethical principles that reflect the profession's core values and establishes a set of specific ethical standards that should be used to guide social work practice.
3. The *Code* is designed to help social workers identify relevant considerations when professional obligations conflict or ethical uncertainties arise.
4. The *Code* provides ethical standards to which the general public can hold the social work profession accountable.
5. The *Code* socializes practitioners new to the field to social work's mission, values, ethical principles, and ethical standards.
6. The *Code* articulates standards that the social work profession itself can use to assess whether social workers have engaged in unethical conduct. NASW has formal procedures to adjudicate ethics complaints filed against its members. In subscribing to this *Code,* social workers are required to cooperate in its implementation, participate in NASW adjudication proceedings, and abide by any NASW disciplinary rulings or sanctions based on it.

The *Code* offers a set of values, principles, and standards to guide decision making and conduct when ethical issues arise. It does not provide a set of rules that prescribe how social workers should act in all situations. Specific applications of the *Code* must take into account the context in which it is being considered and the possibility of conflicts among the *Code*'s values, principles, and standards. Ethical responsibilities flow from all human relationships, from the personal and familial to the social and professional.

Further, the *NASW Code of Ethics* does not specify which values, principles, and standards are most important and ought to outweigh others in instances when they conflict. Reasonable differences of opinion can and do exist among social workers with respect to the ways in which values, ethical principles, and ethical standards should be rank ordered when they conflict. Ethical decision making in a given situation must apply the informed judgment of the individual social worker and should also consider how the issues would be judged in a peer review process where the ethical standards of the profession would be applied.

Ethical decision making is a process. There are many instances in social work where simple answers are not available to resolve complex ethical issues. Social workers should take into consideration all the values, principles, and standards in this *Code* that are relevant to any situation in which ethical judgment is warranted. Social workers' decisions and actions should be consistent with the spirit as well as the letter of this *Code.*

In addition to this *Code,* there are many other sources of information about ethical thinking that may be useful. Social workers should consider ethical theory and principles generally, social work theory and research, laws, regulations, agency policies, and other relevant codes of ethics, recognizing that among codes of ethics social workers should consider the *NASW Code of Ethics* as their primary source. Social workers also should be aware of the impact on ethical decision making of their clients' and their own personal values and cultural and religious beliefs and practices. They should be aware of any conflicts between personal and professional values and deal with them responsibly. For additional guidance social workers should consult the relevant literature on professional ethics and ethical decision making and seek appropriate consultation when faced with ethical dilemmas. This may involve consultation with an agency-based or social work organization's ethics committee, a regulatory body, knowledgeable colleagues, supervisors, or legal counsel.

Instances may arise when social workers' ethical obligations conflict with agency policies or relevant laws or regulations. When such conflicts occur, social workers must make a responsible effort to resolve the conflict in a manner that is consistent with the values, principles, and standards expressed in this *Code.* If a reasonable resolution of the conflict does not appear possible, social workers should seek proper consultation before making a decision.

The *NASW Code of Ethics* is to be used by NASW and by individuals, agencies, organizations, and bodies (such as licensing and regulatory boards, professional liability insurance providers, courts of law, agency boards of directors, government agencies, and other professional groups) that choose to adopt it or use it as a frame of reference. Violation of standards in this *Code* does not automatically imply legal liability or violation of the law. Such determination can only be made in the context of legal and judicial proceedings. Alleged violations of the *Code* would be subject to a peer review process. Such processes are generally separate from legal or administrative procedures and insulated from legal review or proceedings to allow the profession to counsel and discipline its own members.

A code of ethics cannot guarantee ethical behavior. Moreover, a code of ethics cannot resolve all ethical issues or disputes or capture the richness and complexity involved in striving to make responsible choices within a moral community. Rather, a code of ethics sets forth values, ethical principles, and ethical standards to which professionals aspire and by which their actions can be judged. Social workers' ethical behavior should result from their personal commitment to engage in ethical practice. The *NASW Code of Ethics* reflects the commitment of all social workers to uphold the profession's values and to act ethically. Principles and standards must be applied by individuals of good character who discern moral questions and, in good faith, seek to make reliable ethical judgments.

Ethical Principles

The following broad ethical principles are based on social work's core values of service, social justice, dignity and worth of the person, importance of human relationships, integrity, and competence. These principles set forth ideals to which all social workers should aspire.

Value: *Service*

Ethical Principle: *Social workers' primary goal is to help people in need and to address social problems.*

Social workers elevate service to others above self-interest. Social workers draw on their knowledge, values, and skills to help people in need and to address social problems. Social workers are encouraged to volunteer some portion of their professional skills with no expectation of significant financial return (pro bono service).

Value: *Social Justice*

Ethical Principle: *Social workers challenge social injustice.*

Social workers pursue social change, particularly with and on behalf of vulnerable and oppressed individuals and groups of people. Social workers' social change efforts are focused primarily on issues of poverty, unemployment, discrimination, and other forms of social injustice. These activities seek to promote sensitivity to and knowledge about oppression and cultural and ethnic diversity. Social workers strive to ensure access to needed information, services, and resources; equality of opportunity; and meaningful participation in decision making for all people.

Value: *Dignity and Worth of the Person*

Ethical Principle: *Social workers respect the inherent dignity and worth of the person.*

Social workers treat each person in a caring and respectful fashion, mindful of individual differences and cultural and ethnic diversity. Social workers promote clients' socially responsible self-determination. Social workers seek to enhance clients' capacity and opportunity to change and to address their own needs. Social workers are cognizant of their dual responsibility to clients and to the broader society. They seek to resolve conflicts between clients' interests and the broader society's interests in a socially responsible manner consistent with the values, ethical principles, and ethical standards of the profession.

Value: *Importance of Human Relationships*

Ethical Principle: *Social workers recognize the central importance of human relationships.*

Social workers understand that relationships between and among people are an important vehicle for change. Social workers engage people as partners in the helping process. Social workers seek to strengthen relationships among people in a purposeful effort to promote, restore, maintain, and enhance the well-being of individuals, families, social groups, organizations, and communities.

Value: *Integrity*

Ethical Principle: *Social workers behave in a trustworthy manner.*

Social workers are continually aware of the profession's mission, values, ethical principles, and ethical standards and practice in a manner consistent with them. Social workers act honestly and responsibly and promote ethical practices on the part of the organizations with which they are affiliated.

Value: *Competence*

Ethical Principle: *Social workers practice within their areas of competence and develop and enhance their professional expertise.*

Social workers continually strive to increase their professional knowledge and skills and to apply them in practice. Social workers should aspire to contribute to the knowledge base of the profession.

Ethical Standards

The following ethical standards are relevant to the professional activities of all social workers. These standards concern (1) social workers' ethical responsibilities to clients, (2) social workers' ethical responsibilities to colleagues, (3) social workers' ethical responsibilities in practice settings, (4) social workers' ethical responsibilities as professionals, (5) social workers' ethical responsibilities to the social work profession, and (6) social workers' ethical responsibilities to the broader society.

Some of the standards that follow are enforceable guidelines for professional conduct, and some are aspirational. The extent to which each standard is enforceable is a matter of professional judgment to be exercised by those responsible for reviewing alleged violations of ethical standards.

1. Social Workers' Ethical Responsibilities to Clients

1.01 Commitment to Clients

Social workers' primary responsibility is to promote the well-being of clients. In general, clients' interests are primary. However, social workers' responsibility to the larger society or specific legal obligations may on limited occasions supersede the loyalty owed clients, and clients should be so advised. (Examples include when a social worker is required by law to report that a client has abused a child or has threatened to harm self or others.)

1.02 Self-Determination

Social workers respect and promote the right of clients to self-determination and assist clients in their efforts to identify and clarify their goals. Social workers may limit clients' right to self-determination when, in the social workers' professional judgment, clients' actions or potential actions pose a serious, foreseeable, and imminent risk to themselves or others.

1.03 Informed Consent

(a) Social workers should provide services to clients only in the context of a professional relationship based, when appropriate, on valid informed consent. Social workers should use clear and understandable language to inform clients of the purpose of the services, risks related to the services, limits to services because of the requirements of a third-party payer, relevant costs, reasonable alternatives, clients' right to refuse or withdraw consent, and the time frame covered by the consent. Social workers should provide clients with an opportunity to ask questions.

(b) In instances when clients are not literate or have difficulty understanding the primary language used in the practice setting, social workers should take steps to ensure clients' comprehension. This may include providing clients with a detailed verbal explanation or arranging for a qualified interpreter or translator whenever possible.

(c) In instances when clients lack the capacity to provide informed consent, social workers should protect clients' interests by seeking permission from an appropriate third party, informing clients consistent with the clients' level of understanding. In such instances social workers should seek to ensure that the third party acts in a manner consistent with clients' wishes and interests. Social workers should take reasonable steps to enhance such clients' ability to give informed consent.

(d) In instances when clients are receiving services involuntarily, social workers should provide information about the nature and extent of services and about the extent of clients' right to refuse service.

(e) Social workers who provide services via electronic media (such as computer, telephone, radio, and television) should inform recipients of the limitations and risks associated with such services.

(f) Social workers should obtain clients' informed consent before audiotaping or videotaping clients or permitting observation of services to clients by a third party.

1.04 Competence

(a) Social workers should provide services and represent themselves as competent only within the boundaries of their education, training, license, certification, consultation received, supervised experience, or other relevant professional experience.

(b) Social workers should provide services in substantive areas or use intervention techniques or approaches that are new to them only after engaging in appropriate study, training, consultation, and supervision from people who are competent in those interventions or techniques.

(c) When generally recognized standards do not exist with respect to an emerging area of practice, social workers should exercise careful judgment and take responsible steps (including appropriate education, research, training, consultation, and supervision) to ensure the competence of their work and to protect clients from harm.

1.05 Cultural Competence and Social Diversity

(a) Social workers should understand culture and its function in human behavior and society, recognizing the strengths that exist in all cultures.

(b) Social workers should have a knowledge base of their clients' cultures and be able to demonstrate competence in the provision of services that are sensitive to clients' cultures and to differences among people and cultural groups.

(c) Social workers should obtain education about and seek to understand the nature of social diversity and oppression with respect to race, ethnicity, national origin, color, sex, sexual orientation, age, marital status, political belief, religion, and mental or physical disability.

1.06 Conflicts of Interest

(a) Social workers should be alert to and avoid conflicts of interest that interfere with the exercise of professional discretion and impartial judgment. Social workers should inform clients when a real or potential conflict of interest arises and take reasonable steps to resolve the issue in a manner that makes the clients' interests primary and protects clients' interests to the greatest extent possible. In some cases, protecting clients' interests may require termination of the professional relationship with proper referral of the client.

(b) Social workers should not take unfair advantage of any professional relationship or exploit others to further their personal, religious, political, or business interests.

(c) Social workers should not engage in dual or multiple relationships with clients or former clients in which there is a risk of exploitation or potential harm to the client. In instances when dual or multiple relationships are unavoidable, social workers should take steps to protect clients and are responsible for setting clear, appropriate, and culturally sensitive boundaries. (Dual or multiple relationships occur when social workers relate to clients in more than one relationship, whether professional, social, or business. Dual or multiple relationships can occur simultaneously or consecutively.)

(d) When social workers provide services to two or more people who have a relationship with each other (for example, couples, family members), social workers should clarify with all parties which individuals will be considered clients and the nature of social workers' professional obligations to the various individuals who are receiving services. Social workers who anticipate a conflict of interest among the individuals receiving services or who anticipate having to perform in potentially conflicting roles (for example, when a social worker is asked to testify in a child custody dispute or divorce proceedings involving clients) should clarify their role with the parties involved and take appropriate action to minimize any conflict of interest.

1.07 Privacy and Confidentiality

(a) Social workers should respect clients' right to privacy. Social workers should not solicit private information from clients unless it is essential to providing services or conducting social work evaluation or research. Once private information is shared, standards of confidentiality apply.

(b) Social workers may disclose confidential information when appropriate with valid consent from a client or a person legally authorized to consent on behalf of a client.

(c) Social workers should protect the confidentiality of all information obtained in the course of professional service, except for compelling professional reasons. The general expectation that social workers will keep information confidential does not apply when disclosure is necessary to prevent serious, foreseeable, and imminent harm to a client or other identifiable person. In all instances, social workers should disclose the least amount of confidential information necessary to achieve the desired purpose; only information that is directly relevant to the purpose for which the disclosure is made should be revealed.

(d) Social workers should inform clients, to the extent possible, about the disclosure of confidential information and the potential consequences, when feasible before the disclosure is made. This applies whether social workers disclose confidential information on the basis of a legal requirement or client consent.

(e) Social workers should discuss with clients and other interested parties the nature of confidentiality and limitations of clients' right to confidentiality. Social workers should review with clients circumstances where confidential information may be requested and where disclosure of confidential information may be legally required. This discussion should occur as soon as possible in the social worker–client relationship and as needed throughout the course of the relationship.

(f) When social workers provide counseling services to families, couples, or groups, social workers should seek agreement among the parties involved concerning each individual's right to confidentiality and obligation to preserve the confidentiality of information shared by others. Social workers should inform participants in family, couples, or group counseling that social workers cannot guarantee that all participants will honor such agreements.

(g) Social workers should inform clients involved in family, couples, marital, or group counseling of the social worker's, employer's, and agency's policy concerning the social worker's disclosure of confidential information among the parties involved in the counseling.

(h) Social workers should not disclose confidential information to third-party payers unless clients have authorized such disclosure.

(i) Social workers should not discuss confidential information in any setting unless privacy can be ensured. Social workers should not discuss confidential information in public or semipublic areas such as hallways, waiting rooms, elevators, and restaurants.

(j) Social workers should protect the confidentiality of clients during legal proceedings to the extent permitted by law. When a court of law or other legally authorized body orders social workers to disclose confidential or privileged information without a client's consent and such disclosure could cause harm to the client, social workers should request that the court withdraw the order or limit the order as narrowly as possible or maintain the records under seal, unavailable for public inspection.

(k) Social workers should protect the confidentiality of clients when responding to requests from members of the media.

(l) Social workers should protect the confidentiality of clients' written and electronic records and other sensitive information. Social workers should take reasonable steps to ensure that clients' records are stored in a secure location and that clients' records are not available to others who are not authorized to have access.

(m) Social workers should take precautions to ensure and maintain the confidentiality of information transmitted to other parties through the use of computers, electronic mail, facsimile machines, telephones and telephone answering machines, and other electronic or computer technology. Disclosure of identifying information should be avoided whenever possible.

(n) Social workers should transfer or dispose of clients' records in a manner that protects clients' confidentiality and is consistent with state statutes governing records and social work licensure.

(o) Social workers should take reasonable precautions to protect client confidentiality in the event of the social worker's termination of practice, incapacitation, or death.

(p) Social workers should not disclose identifying information when discussing clients for teaching or training purposes unless the client has consented to disclosure of confidential information.

(q) Social workers should not disclose identifying information when discussing clients with consultants unless the client has consented to disclosure of confidential information or there is a compelling need for such disclosure.

(r) Social workers should protect the confidentiality of deceased clients consistent with the preceding standards.

1.08 Access to Records

(a) Social workers should provide clients with reasonable access to records concerning the clients. Social workers who are concerned that clients' access to their records could cause serious misunderstanding or harm to the client should provide assistance in interpreting the records and consultation with the client regarding the records. Social workers should limit clients' access to their records, or portions of their records, only in exceptional circumstances when there is compelling evidence that such access would cause serious harm to the client. Both clients' requests and the rationale for withholding some or all of the record should be documented in clients' files.

(b) When providing clients with access to their records, social workers should take steps to protect the confidentiality of other individuals identified or discussed in such records.

1.09 Sexual Relationships

(a) Social workers should under no circumstances engage in sexual activities or sexual contact with current clients, whether such contact is consensual or forced.

(b) Social workers should not engage in sexual activities or sexual contact with clients' relatives or other individuals with whom clients maintain a close personal relationship when there is a risk of exploitation or potential harm to the client. Sexual activity or sexual contact with clients' relatives or other individuals with whom clients maintain a personal relationship has the potential to be harmful to the client and may make it difficult for the social worker and client to maintain appropriate professional boundaries. Social workers—not their clients, their clients' relatives, or other individuals with whom the client maintains a personal relationship—assume the full burden for setting clear, appropriate, and culturally sensitive boundaries.

(c) Social workers should not engage in sexual activities or sexual contact with former clients because of the potential for harm to the client. If social workers engage in conduct contrary to this prohibition or claim that an exception to this prohibition is warranted because of extraordinary circumstances, it is social workers—not their clients—who assume the full burden of demonstrating that the former client has not been exploited, coerced, or manipulated, intentionally or unintentionally.

(d) Social workers should not provide clinical services to individuals with whom they have had a prior sexual relationship. Providing clinical services to a former sexual partner has the potential to be harmful to the individual and is likely to make it difficult for the social worker and individual to maintain appropriate professional boundaries.

1.10 Physical Contact

Social workers should not engage in physical contact with clients when there is a possibility of psychological harm to the client as a result of the contact (such as cradling or caressing clients). Social workers who engage in appropriate physical contact with clients are responsible for setting clear, appropriate, and culturally sensitive boundaries that govern such physical contact.

1.11 Sexual Harassment

Social workers should not sexually harass clients. Sexual harassment includes sexual advances, sexual solicitation, requests for sexual favors, and other verbal or physical conduct of a sexual nature.

1.12 Derogatory Language

Social workers should not use derogatory language in their written or verbal communications to or about clients. Social workers should use accurate and respectful language in all communications to and about clients.

1.13 Payment for Services

(a) When setting fees, social workers should ensure that the fees are fair, reasonable, and commensurate with the services performed. Consideration should be given to clients' ability to pay.

(b) Social workers should avoid accepting goods or services from clients as payment for professional services. Bartering arrangements, particularly involving services, create the potential for conflicts of interest, exploitation, and inappropriate boundaries in social workers' relationships with clients. Social workers should explore and may participate in bartering only in very limited circumstances when it can be demonstrated that such arrangements are an accepted practice among professionals in the local community, considered to be essential for the provision of services, negotiated without coercion, and entered into at the client's initiative and with the client's informed consent. Social workers who accept goods or services from clients as payment for professional services assume the full burden of demonstrating that this arrangement will not be detrimental to the client or the professional relationship.

(c) Social workers should not solicit a private fee or other remuneration for providing services to clients who are entitled to such available services through the social workers' employer or agency.

1.14 Clients Who Lack Decision-Making Capacity

When social workers act on behalf of clients who lack the capacity to make informed decisions, social workers should take reasonable steps to safeguard the interests and rights of those clients.

1.15 Interruption of Services

Social workers should make reasonable efforts to ensure continuity of services in the event that services are interrupted by factors such as unavailability, relocation, illness, disability, or death.

1.16 Termination of Services

(a) Social workers should terminate services to clients and professional relationships with them when such services and relationships are no longer required or no longer serve the clients' needs or interests.

(b) Social workers should take reasonable steps to avoid abandoning clients who are still in need of services. Social workers should withdraw services precipitously only under unusual circumstances, giving careful consideration to all factors in the situation and taking care to minimize possible adverse effects. Social workers should assist in making appropriate arrangements for continuation of services when necessary.

(c) Social workers in fee-for-service settings may terminate services to clients who are not paying an overdue balance if the financial contractual arrangements have been made clear to the client, if the client does not pose an imminent danger to self or others, and if the clinical and other consequences of the current nonpayment have been addressed and discussed with the client.

(d) Social workers should not terminate services to pursue a social, financial, or sexual relationship with a client.

(e) Social workers who anticipate the termination or interruption of services to clients should notify clients promptly and seek the transfer, referral, or continuation of services in relation to the clients' needs and preferences.

(f) Social workers who are leaving an employment setting should inform clients of appropriate options for the continuation of services and of the benefits and risks of the options.

2. Social Workers' Ethical Responsibilities to Colleagues

2.01 Respect

(a) Social workers should treat colleagues with respect and should represent accurately and fairly the qualifications, views, and obligations of colleagues.

(b) Social workers should avoid unwarranted negative criticism of colleagues in communications with clients or with other professionals. Unwarranted negative criticism may include demeaning comments that refer to colleagues' level of competence or to individuals' attributes such as race, ethnicity, national origin, color, sex, sexual orientation, age, marital status, political belief, religion, and mental or physical disability.

(c) Social workers should cooperate with social work colleagues and with colleagues of other professions when such cooperation serves the well-being of clients.

2.02 Confidentiality

Social workers should respect confidential information shared by colleagues in the course of their professional relationships and transactions. Social workers should ensure that such colleagues understand social workers' obligation to respect confidentiality and any exceptions related to it.

2.03 Interdisciplinary Collaboration

(a) Social workers who are members of an interdisciplinary team should participate in and contribute to decisions that affect the well-being of clients by drawing on the perspectives, values, and experiences of the social work profession. Professional and ethical obligations of the interdisciplinary team as a whole and of its individual members should be clearly established.

(b) Social workers for whom a team decision raises ethical concerns should attempt to resolve the disagreement through appropriate channels. If the disagreement cannot be resolved, social workers should pursue other avenues to address their concerns consistent with client well-being.

2.04 Disputes Involving Colleagues

(a) Social workers should not take advantage of a dispute between a colleague and an employer to obtain a position or otherwise advance the social workers' own interests.

(b) Social workers should not exploit clients in disputes with colleagues or engage clients in any inappropriate discussion of conflicts between social workers and their colleagues.

2.05 Consultation

(a) Social workers should seek the advice and counsel of colleagues whenever such consultation is in the best interests of clients.

(b) Social workers should keep themselves informed about colleagues' areas of expertise and competencies. Social workers should seek consultation only from colleagues who have demonstrated knowledge, expertise, and competence related to the subject of the consultation.

(c) When consulting with colleagues about clients, social workers should disclose the least amount of information necessary to achieve the purposes of the consultation.

2.06 Referral for Services

(a) Social workers should refer clients to other professionals when the other professionals' specialized knowledge or expertise is needed to serve clients fully or when social workers believe that they are not being effective or making reasonable progress with clients and that additional service is required.

(b) Social workers who refer clients to other professionals should take appropriate steps to facilitate an orderly transfer of responsibility. Social workers who refer clients to other professionals should disclose, with clients' consent, all pertinent information to the new service providers.

(c) Social workers are prohibited from giving or receiving payment for a referral when no professional service is provided by the referring social worker.

2.07 Sexual Relationships

(a) Social workers who function as supervisors or educators should not engage in sexual activities or contact with supervisees, students, trainees, or other colleagues over whom they exercise professional authority.

(b) Social workers should avoid engaging in sexual relationships with colleagues when there is potential for a conflict of interest. Social workers who become involved in, or anticipate becoming involved in, a sexual relationship with a colleague have a duty to transfer professional responsibilities, when necessary, to avoid a conflict of interest.

2.08 Sexual Harassment

Social workers should not sexually harass supervisees, students, trainees, or colleagues. Sexual harassment includes sexual advances, sexual solicitation, requests for sexual favors, and other verbal or physical conduct of a sexual nature.

2.09 Impairment of Colleagues

(a) Social workers who have direct knowledge of a social work colleague's impairment that is due to personal problems, psychosocial distress, substance abuse, or mental health difficulties and that interferes with practice effectiveness should consult with that colleague when feasible and assist the colleague in taking remedial action.

(b) Social workers who believe that a social work colleague's impairment interferes with practice effectiveness and that the colleague has not taken adequate steps to address the impairment should take action through appropriate channels established by employers, agencies, NASW, licensing and regulatory bodies, and other professional organizations.

2.10 Incompetence of Colleagues

(a) Social workers who have direct knowledge of a social work colleague's incompetence should consult with that colleague when feasible and assist the colleague in taking remedial action.

(b) Social workers who believe that a social work colleague is incompetent and has not taken adequate steps to address the incompetence should take action through appropriate channels established by employers, agencies, NASW, licensing and regulatory bodies, and other professional organizations.

2.11 Unethical Conduct of Colleagues

(a) Social workers should take adequate measures to discourage, prevent, expose, and correct the unethical conduct of colleagues.

(b) Social workers should be knowledgeable about established policies and procedures for handling concerns about colleagues' unethical behavior. Social workers should be familiar with national, state, and local procedures for handling ethics complaints. These include policies and procedures created by NASW, licensing and regulatory bodies, employers, agencies, and other professional organizations.

(c) Social workers who believe that a colleague has acted unethically should seek resolution by discussing their concerns with the colleague when feasible and when such discussion is likely to be productive.

(d) When necessary, social workers who believe that a colleague has acted unethically should take action through appropriate formal channels (such as contacting a state licensing board or regulatory body, an NASW committee on inquiry, or other professional ethics committees).

(e) Social workers should defend and assist colleagues who are unjustly charged with unethical conduct.

3. Social Workers' Ethical Responsibilities in Practice Settings

3.01 Supervision and Consultation

(a) Social workers who provide supervision or consultation should have the necessary knowledge and skill to supervise or consult appropriately and should do so only within their areas of knowledge and competence.

(b) Social workers who provide supervision or consultation are responsible for setting clear, appropriate, and culturally sensitive boundaries.

(c) Social workers should not engage in any dual or multiple relationships with supervisees in which there is a risk of exploitation of or potential harm to the supervisee.

(d) Social workers who provide supervision should evaluate supervisees' performance in a manner that is fair and respectful.

3.02 Education and Training

(a) Social workers who function as educators, field instructors for students, or trainers should provide instruction only within their areas of knowledge and competence and should provide instruction based on the most current information and knowledge available in the profession.

(b) Social workers who function as educators or field instructors for students should evaluate students' performance in a manner that is fair and respectful.

(c) Social workers who function as educators or field instructors for students should take reasonable steps to ensure that clients are routinely informed when services are being provided by students.

(d) Social workers who function as educators or field instructors for students should not engage in any dual or multiple relationships with students in which there is a risk of exploitation or potential harm to the student. Social work educators and field instructors are responsible for setting clear, appropriate, and culturally sensitive boundaries.

3.03 Performance Evaluation

Social workers who have responsibility for evaluating the performance of others should fulfill such responsibility in a fair and considerate manner and on the basis of clearly stated criteria.

3.04 Client Records

(a) Social workers should take reasonable steps to ensure that documentation in records is accurate and reflects the services provided.

(b) Social workers should include sufficient and timely documentation in records to facilitate the delivery of services and to ensure continuity of services provided to clients in the future.

(c) Social workers' documentation should protect clients' privacy to the extent that is possible and appropriate and should include only information that is directly relevant to the delivery of services.

(d) Social workers should store records following the termination of services to ensure reasonable future access. Records should be maintained for the number of years required by state statutes or relevant contracts.

3.05 Billing

Social workers should establish and maintain billing practices that accurately reflect the nature and extent of services provided and that identify who provided the service in the practice setting.

3.06 Client Transfer

(a) When an individual who is receiving services from another agency or colleague contacts a social worker for services, the social worker should carefully consider the client's needs before agreeing to provide services. To minimize possible confusion and conflict, social workers should discuss with potential clients the nature of the clients' current relationship with other service providers and the implications, including possible benefits or risks, of entering into a relationship with a new service provider.

(b) If a new client has been served by another agency or colleague, social workers should discuss with the client whether consultation with the previous service provider is in the client's best interest.

3.07 Administration

(a) Social work administrators should advocate within and outside their agencies for adequate resources to meet clients' needs.

(b) Social workers should advocate for resource allocation procedures that are open and fair. When not all clients' needs can be met, an allocation procedure should be developed that is nondiscriminatory and based on appropriate and consistently applied principles.

(c) Social workers who are administrators should take reasonable steps to ensure that adequate agency or organizational resources are available to provide appropriate staff supervision.

(d) Social work administrators should take reasonable steps to ensure that the working environment for which they are responsible is consistent with and encourages compliance with the *NASW Code of Ethics.* Social work administrators should take reasonable steps to eliminate any conditions in their organizations that violate, interfere with, or discourage compliance with the *Code.*

3.08 Continuing Education and Staff Development

Social work administrators and supervisors should take reasonable steps to provide or arrange for continuing education and staff development for all staff for whom they are responsible. Continuing education and staff development should address current knowledge and emerging developments related to social work practice and ethics.

3.09 Commitments to Employers

(a) Social workers generally should adhere to commitments made to employers and employing organizations.

(b) Social workers should work to improve employing agencies' policies and procedures and the efficiency and effectiveness of their services.

(c) Social workers should take reasonable steps to ensure that employers are aware of social workers' ethical obligations as set forth in the *NASW Code of Ethics* and of the implications of those obligations for social work practice.

(d) Social workers should not allow an employing organization's policies, procedures, regulations, or administrative orders to interfere with their ethical practice of social work. Social workers should take reasonable steps to ensure that their employing organizations' practices are consistent with the *NASW Code of Ethics.*

(e) Social workers should act to prevent and eliminate discrimination in the employing organization's work assignments and in its employment policies and practices.

(f) Social workers should accept employment or arrange student field placements only in organizations that exercise fair personnel practices.

(g) Social workers should be diligent stewards of the resources of their employing organizations, wisely conserving funds where appropriate and never misappropriating funds or using them for unintended purposes.

3.10 Labor-Management Disputes

(a) Social workers may engage in organized action, including the formation of and participation in labor unions, to improve services to clients and working conditions.

(b) The actions of social workers who are involved in labor-management disputes, job actions, or labor strikes should be guided by the profession's values, ethical principles, and ethical standards. Reasonable differences of opinion exist among social workers concerning their primary obligation as professionals during an actual or threatened labor strike or job action. Social workers should carefully examine relevant issues and their possible impact on clients before deciding on a course of action.

4. Social Workers' Ethical Responsibilities as Professionals

4.01 Competence

(a) Social workers should accept responsibility or employment only on the basis of existing competence or the intention to acquire the necessary competence.

(b) Social workers should strive to become and remain proficient in professional practice and the performance of professional functions. Social workers should critically examine and keep current with emerging knowledge relevant to social work. Social workers should routinely review the professional literature and participate in continuing education relevant to social work practice and social work ethics.

(c) Social workers should base practice on recognized knowledge, including empirically based knowledge, relevant to social work and social work ethics.

4.02 Discrimination

Social workers should not practice, condone, facilitate, or collaborate with any form of discrimination on the basis of race, ethnicity, national origin, color, sex, sexual orientation, age, marital status, political belief, religion, or mental or physical disability.

4.03 Private Conduct

Social workers should not permit their private conduct to interfere with their ability to fulfill their professional responsibilities.

4.04 Dishonesty, Fraud, and Deception

Social workers should not participate in, condone, or be associated with dishonesty, fraud, or deception.

4.05 Impairment

(a) Social workers should not allow their own personal problems, psychosocial distress, legal problems, substance abuse, or mental health difficulties to interfere with their professional judgment and performance or to jeopardize the best interests of people for whom they have a professional responsibility.

(b) Social workers whose personal problems, psychosocial distress, legal problems, substance abuse, or mental health difficulties interfere with their professional judgment and performance should immediately seek consultation and take appropriate remedial action by seeking professional help, making adjustments in workload, terminating practice, or taking any other steps necessary to protect clients and others.

4.06 Misrepresentation

(a) Social workers should make clear distinctions between statements made and actions engaged in as a private individual and as a representative of the social work profession, a professional social work organization, or the social worker's employing agency.

(b) Social workers who speak on behalf of professional social work organizations should accurately represent the official and authorized positions of the organizations.

(c) Social workers should ensure that their representations to clients, agencies, and the public of professional qualifications, credentials, education, competence, affiliations, services provided, or results to be achieved are accurate. Social workers should claim only those relevant professional credentials they actually possess and take steps to correct any inaccuracies or misrepresentations of their credentials by others.

4.07 Solicitations

(a) Social workers should not engage in uninvited solicitation of potential clients who, because of their circumstances, are vulnerable to undue influence, manipulation, or coercion.

(b) Social workers should not engage in solicitation of testimonial endorsements (including solicitation of consent to use a client's prior statement as a testimonial endorsement) from current clients or from other people who, because of their particular circumstances, are vulnerable to undue influence.

4.08 Acknowledging Credit

(a) Social workers should take responsibility and credit, including authorship credit, only for work they have actually performed and to which they have contributed.

(b) Social workers should honestly acknowledge the work of and the contributions made by others.

5. Social Workers' Ethical Responsibilities to the Social Work Profession

5.01 Integrity of the Profession

(a) Social workers should work toward the maintenance and promotion of high standards of practice.

(b) Social workers should uphold and advance the values, ethics, knowledge, and mission of the profession. Social workers should protect, enhance, and improve the integrity of the profession through appropriate study and research, active discussion, and responsible criticism of the profession.

(c) Social workers should contribute time and professional expertise to activities that promote respect for the value, integrity, and competence of the social work profession. These activities may include teaching, research, consultation, service, legislative testimony, presentations in the community, and participation in their professional organizations.

(d) Social workers should contribute to the knowledge base of social work and share with colleagues their knowledge related to practice, research, and ethics. Social workers should seek to contribute to the profession's literature and to share their knowledge at professional meetings and conferences.

(e) Social workers should act to prevent the unauthorized and unqualified practice of social work.

5.02 Evaluation and Research

(a) Social workers should monitor and evaluate policies, the implementation of programs, and practice interventions.

(b) Social workers should promote and facilitate evaluation and research to contribute to the development of knowledge.

(c) Social workers should critically examine and keep current with emerging knowledge relevant to social work and fully use evaluation and research evidence in their professional practice.

(d) Social workers engaged in evaluation or research should carefully consider possible consequences and should follow guidelines developed for the protection of evaluation and research participants. Appropriate institutional review boards should be consulted.

(e) Social workers engaged in evaluation or research should obtain voluntary and written informed consent from participants, when appropriate, without any implied or actual deprivation or penalty for refusal to participate; without undue inducement to participate; and with due regard for participants' well-being, privacy, and dignity. Informed consent should include information about the nature, extent, and duration of the participation requested and disclosure of the risks and benefits of participation in the research.

(f) When evaluation or research participants are incapable of giving informed consent, social workers should provide an appropriate explanation to the participants, obtain the participants' assent to the extent they are able, and obtain written consent from an appropriate proxy.

(g) Social workers should never design or conduct evaluation or research that does not use consent procedures, such as certain forms of naturalistic observation and archival research, unless rigorous and responsible review of the research has found it to be justified because of its prospective scientific, educational, or applied value and unless equally effective alternative procedures that do not involve waiver of consent are not feasible.

(h) Social workers should inform participants of their right to withdraw from evaluation and research at any time without penalty.

(i) Social workers should take appropriate steps to ensure that participants in evaluation and research have access to appropriate supportive services.

(j) Social workers engaged in evaluation or research should protect participants from unwarranted physical or mental distress, harm, danger, or deprivation.

(k) Social workers engaged in the evaluation of services should discuss collected information only for professional purposes and only with people professionally concerned with this information.

(l) Social workers engaged in evaluation or research should ensure the anonymity or confidentiality of participants and of the data obtained from them. Social workers should inform participants of any limits of confidentiality, the measures that will be taken to ensure confidentiality, and when any records containing research data will be destroyed.

(m) Social workers who report evaluation and research results should protect participants' confidentiality by omitting identifying information unless proper consent has been obtained authorizing disclosure.

(n) Social workers should report evaluation and research findings accurately. They should not fabricate or falsify results and should take steps to correct any errors later found in published data using standard publication methods.

(o) Social workers engaged in evaluation or research should be alert to and avoid conflicts of interest and dual relationships with participants, should inform participants when a real or potential conflict of interest arises, and should take steps to resolve the issue in a manner that makes participants' interests primary.

(p) Social workers should educate themselves, their students, and their colleagues about responsible research practices.

6. Social Workers' Ethical Responsibilities to the Broader Society

6.01 Social Welfare

Social workers should promote the general welfare of society, from local to global levels, and the development of people, their communities, and their environments. Social workers should advocate for living conditions conducive to the fulfillment of basic human needs and should promote social, economic, political, and cultural values and institutions that are compatible with the realization of social justice.

6.02 Public Participation

Social workers should facilitate informed participation by the public in shaping social policies and institutions.

6.03 Public Emergencies

Social workers should provide appropriate professional services in public emergencies to the greatest extent possible.

6.04 Social and Political Action

(a) Social workers should engage in social and political action that seeks to ensure that all people have equal access to the resources, employment, services, and opportunities they require to meet their basic human needs and to develop fully. Social workers should be aware of the impact of the political arena on practice and should advocate for changes in policy and legislation to improve social conditions in order to meet basic human needs and promote social justice.

(b) Social workers should act to expand choice and opportunity for all people, with special regard for vulnerable, disadvantaged, oppressed, and exploited people and groups.

(c) Social workers should promote conditions that encourage respect for cultural and social diversity within the United States and globally. Social workers should promote policies and practices that demonstrate respect for difference, support the expansion of cultural knowledge and resources, advocate for programs and institutions that demonstrate cultural competence, and promote policies that safeguard the rights of and confirm equity and social justice for all people.

(d) Social workers should act to prevent and eliminate domination of, exploitation of, and discrimination against any person, group, or class on the basis of race, ethnicity, national origin, color, sex, sexual orientation, age, marital status, political belief, religion, or mental or physical disability.

APPENDIX B

Code of Ethics of the International Federation of Social Workers

The Ethics of Social Work—Principles and Standards

Adopted by the IFSW General Meeting, Colombo, Sri Lanka, July 6–8, 1994

1. Background

Ethical awareness is a necessary part of the professional practice of any social worker. His or her ability to act ethically is an essential aspect of the quality of the service offered to clients.

The purpose of IFSW's work on ethics is to promote ethical debate and reflection in the member associations and among the providers of social work in member countries.

The basis for the further development of IFSW's work on ethics is to be found in "Ethics of Social Work—Principles and Standards" which consists of two documents, **International Declaration of Ethical Principles of Social Work,** and **International Ethical Standards for Social Workers.** These documents present the basic ethical principles of the social work profession, recommend procedure when the work presents ethical dilemmas, and deal with the profession's and the individual social worker's relation to clients, colleagues, and others in the field. The documents are components in a continuing process of use, review and revision.

2. International Declaration of Ethical Principles of Social Work

2.1 Introduction

The IFSW recognises the need for a declaration of ethical principles for guidance in dealing with ethical problems in social work.

The purposes of the *International Declaration of Ethical Principles* are:

1. to formulate a set of basic principles for social work, which can be adapted to cultural and social settings.
2. to identify ethical problem areas in the practice of social work (below referred to as 'problem areas'), and
3. to provide guidance as to the choice of methods for dealing with ethical issues/problems (below referred to as 'methods for addressing ethical issues/problems').

Compliance

The International Declaration of Ethical Principles assumes that both member associations of the IFSW and their constituent members adhere to the principles formulated therein. The IFSW expects each member association to assist its members in identifying and dealing with ethical issues/problems in the practice of their profession.

Member associations of the IFSW and individual members of these can report any member association to the Executive Committee of the IFSW should it neglect to adhere to these principles. National Associations who experience difficulties adopting these principles should notify the Executive Committee of IFSW. The Executive Committee may impose the stipulations and intentions of the Declaration of Ethical Principles on an association which neglects to comply. Should this not be sufficient the Executive Committee can, as a following measure, suggest suspension or exclusion of the association.

The International Declaration of Ethical Principles should be made publicly known. This would enable clients, employers, professionals from other disciplines, and the general public to have expectations in accordance with the ethical foundations of social work.

We acknowledge that a detailed set of ethical standards for the member associations would be unrealistic due to legal, cultural and governmental differences among the member countries.

2.2 The Principles

Social workers serve the development of human beings through adherence to the following basic principles:

2.2.1. Every human being has a unique value, which justifies moral consideration for that person.

2.2.2. Each individual has the right to self-fulfilment to the extent that it does not encroach upon the same right of others, and has an obligation to contribute to the well-being of society.

2.2.3. Each society, regardless of its form, should function to provide the maximum benefits for all of its members.

2.2.4. Social workers have a commitment to principles of social justice.

2.2.5. Social workers have the responsibility to devote objective and disciplined knowledge and skill to aid individuals, groups, communities, and societies in their development and resolution of personal-societal conflicts and their consequences.

2.2.6. Social workers are expected to provide the best possible assistance to anybody seeking their help and advice, without unfair discrimination on the basis of gender, age, disability, colour, social class, race, religion, language, political beliefs, or sexual orientation.

2.2.7. Social workers respect the basic human rights of individuals and groups as expressed in the United Nations Universal Declaration of Human Rights and other international conventions derived from that Declaration.

2.2.8. Social workers pay regard to the principles of privacy, confidentiality, and responsible use of information in their professional work. Social workers respect justified confidentiality even when their country's legislation is in conflict with this demand.

2.2.9. Social workers are expected to work in full collaboration with their clients, working for the best interests of the clients but paying due regard to the interests of others involved. Clients are encouraged to participate as much as possible, and should be informed of the risks and likely benefits of proposed courses of action.

2.2.10. Social workers generally expect clients to take responsibility, in collaboration with them, for determining courses of action affecting their lives. Compulsion which might be necessary to solve one party's problems at the expense of the interests of others involved should only take place after careful explicit evaluation of the claims of the conflicting parties. Social workers should minimise the use of legal compulsion.

2.2.11. Social work is inconsistent with direct or indirect support of individuals, groups, political forces or power-structures suppressing their fellow human beings by employing terrorism, torture or similar brutal means.

2.2.12. Social workers make ethically justified decisions, and stand by them, paying due regard to the IFSW International Declaration of Ethical Principles, and to the **International Ethical Standards for Social Workers** adopted by their national professional association.

2.3 Problem Areas

2.3.1. The problem areas raising ethical issues directly are not necessarily universal due to cultural and governmental differences. Each national association is encouraged to promote discussion and clarification of important issues and problems particularly relevant to its country. The following problem areas are, however, widely recognized:

1. **when the loyalty of the social worker is in the middle of conflicting interests**
   - between those of the social workers own and the clients
   - between conflicting interests of individual clients and other individuals
   - between the conflicting interests of groups of clients
   - between groups of clients and the rest of the population
   - between systems/institution and groups of clients
   - between system/institution/employer and social workers
   - between different groups of professionals
2. **the fact that the social worker functions both as a helper and controller**
   The relation between these two opposite aspects of social work demands a clarification based on an explicit choice of values in order to avoid a mixing-up of motives or the lack of clarity in motives, actions and consequences of actions. When social workers are expected to play a role in the state control of citizens they are obliged to clarify the ethical implications of this role and to what extent this role is acceptable in relation to the basic ethical principles of social work.
3. **the duty of the social worker to protect the interests of the client will easily come into conflict with demands for efficiency and utility**
   This problem is becoming important with the introduction and use of information technology within the fields of social work.

2.3.2. The principles declared in section 2.2 should always be at the base of any consideration given or choice made by social workers in dealing with issues/problems within these areas.

2.4 Methods for the Solution of Issues/Problems

2.4.1. The various national associations of social workers are obliged to treat matters in such a way that ethical issues/problems may be considered and tried to be solved in collective forums within the organization. Such forums should enable the individual social worker to discuss, analyse and consider ethical issues/problems in collaboration with colleagues, other expert groups and/parties affected by the matter under discussion. In addition such forums should give the social worker opportunity to receive advice from colleagues and others. Ethical analysis and discussion should always seek to create possibilities and options.

2.4.2. The member associations are required to produce and/or adapt ethical standards for the different fields of work, especially for those fields where there are complicated ethical issues/problems as well as areas where the ethical principles of social work may come into conflict with the respective country's legal system or the policy of the authorities.

2.4.3. When ethical foundations are laid down as guidelines for actions within the practice of social work, it is the duty of the associations to aid the individual social worker in analysing and considering ethical issues/problems on the basis of:

1. The basic **principles** of the Declaration (section 2.2)
2. The ethical/moral and political **context** of the actions, i.e., an analysis of the values and forces constituting the framing conditions of the action.
3. The **motives** of the action, i.e., to advocate a higher level of consciousness of the aims and intentions the individual social worker might have regarding a course of action.
4. The **nature** of the action, i.e., help in providing an analysis of the moral content of the action, e.g., the use of compulsion as opposed to voluntary co-operation, guardianship vs participation, etc.
5. The **consequences** the action might have for different groups, i.e., an analysis of the consequences of different ways of action for all involved parties in both the short and long term.

2.4.4. The member associations are responsible for promoting debate, education and research regarding ethical questions.

3. International Ethical Standards for Social Workers

(This section is based on the "International Code of Ethics for the Professional Social Worker" adopted by the IFSW in 1976, but does not include ethical principles since these are now contained in the new separate **International Declaration of Ethical Principles of Social Work** in section 2.2 of the present document.)

3.1 Preamble

Social work originates variously from humanitarian, religious and democratic ideals and philosophies and has universal application to meet human needs arising from personal-societal interactions and to develop human potential. Professional social workers are dedicated to service for the welfare and self-fulfilment of human beings; to the development and disciplined use of validated knowledge regarding human and societal behaviour; to the development of resources to meet individual, group, national and international needs and aspirations; and to the achievement of social justice. On the basis of the **International Declaration of Ethical Principles of Social Work,** the social worker is obliged to recognize these standards of ethical conduct.

3.2 General Standards of Ethical Conduct

3.2.1. Seek to understand each individual client and the client system, and the elements which affect behaviour and the service required.

3.2.2. Uphold and advance the values, knowledge and methodology of the profession, refraining from any behaviour which damages the functioning of the profession.

3.2.3. Recognise professional and personal limitations.

3.2.4. Encourage the utilisation of all relevant knowledge and skills.

3.2.5. Apply relevant methods in the development and validation of knowledge.

3.2.6. Contribute professional expertise to the development of policies and programs which improve the quality of life in society.

3.2.7. Identify and interpret social needs.

3.2.8. Identify and interpret the basis and nature of individual, group, community, national, and international social problems.

3.2.9. Identify and interpret the work of the social work profession.

3.2.10. Clarify whether public statements are made or actions performed on an individual basis or as representative of a professional association, agency or organization, or other group.

3.3 Social Work Standards Relative to Clients

3.3.1. Accept primary responsibility to identified clients, but within limitations set by the ethical claims of others.

3.3.2. Maintain the client's right to a relationship of trust, to privacy and confidentiality, and to responsible use of information. The collection and sharing of information or data is related to the professional service function with the client informed as to its necessity and use. No information is released without prior knowledge and informed consent of the client, except where the client cannot be responsible or others may be seriously jeopardized. A client has access to social work records concerning them.

3.3.3. Recognize and respect the individual goals, responsibilities, and differences of clients. Within the scope of the agency and the client's social milieu, the professional service shall assist clients to take responsibility for personal actions and help all clients with equal willingness. Where the professional service cannot be provided under such conditions the clients shall be so informed in such a way as to leave the clients free to act.

3.3.4. Help the client—individual, group, community, or society—to achieve self-fulfilment and maximum potential within the limits of the respective rights of others. The service shall be based upon helping the client to understand and use the professional relationship, in furtherance of the client's legitimate desires and interests.

3.4 Social Work Standards Relative to Agencies and Organizations

3.4.1. Work and/or cooperate with those agencies and organizations whose policies, procedures, and operations are directed toward adequate service delivery and encouragement of professional practice consistent with the ethical principles of the IFSW.

3.4.2. Responsibly execute the stated aims and functions of the agency or organizations, contributing to the development of sound policies, procedures, and practice in order to obtain the best possible standards or practice.

3.4.3. Sustain ultimate responsibility to the client, initiating desirable alterations of policies, procedures, and practice, through appropriate agency and organization channels. If necessary remedies are not achieved after channels have been exhausted, initiate appropriate appeals to higher authorities or the wider community of interest.

3.4.4. Ensure professional accountability to client and community for efficiency and effectiveness through periodic review of the process of service provision.

3.4.5. Use all possible ethical means to bring unethical practice to an end when policies, procedures and practices are in direct conflict with the ethical principles of social work.

3.5 Social Work Standards Relative to Colleagues

3.5.1. Acknowledge the education, training and performance of social work colleagues and professionals from other disciplines, extending all necessary cooperation that will enhance effective services.

3.5.2. Recognise differences of opinion and practice of social work colleagues and other professionals, expressing criticism through channels in a responsible manner.

3.5.3. Promote and share opportunities for knowledge, experience, and ideas with all social work colleagues, professionals from other disciplines and volunteers for the purpose of mutual improvement.

3.5.4. Bring any violations of professionals ethics and standards to the attention of the appropriate bodies inside and outside the profession, and ensure that relevant clients are properly involved.

3.5.5. Defend colleagues against unjust actions.

3.6 Standards Relative to the Profession

3.6.1. Maintain the values, ethical principles, knowledge and methodology of the profession and contribute to their clarification and improvement.

3.6.2. Uphold the professional standards of practice and work for their advancement.

3.6.3. Defend the profession against unjust criticism and work to increase confidence in the necessity for professional practice.

3.6.4. Present constructive criticism of the profession, its theories, methods and practices.

3.6.5. Encourage new approaches and methodologies needed to meet new and existing needs.

REFERENCES

Abbott, E. (1919). The social caseworker and the enforcement of industrial legislation. In *Proceedings of the National Conference of Social Work, 1918 Kansas City* (pp. 312–317). Chicago: Rogers & Hall Co., Printers.

Abramson, J. S., & Rosenthal, B. B. (1995). Interdisciplinary and interorganizational collaboration. In R. L. Edwards (Ed.), *Encyclopedia of social work: Vol. 2* (19th ed.) (pp. 1479–1489). Washington, DC: NASW Press.

Acker, G. M. (1999). The impact of clients' mental illness on social workers' job satisfaction and burnout. *Health and Social Work, 24*(12), 112–199. Retrieved September 17, 2003, from EBSCOhost Academic Search Elite database.

Adam, C. T. (1981). A descriptive definition of primary prevention. *Journal of Primary Prevention, 2,* 67–79.

Adamson, D., Micklewright, J., & Wright, A. (2000). *Innocenti report card: A League table of child poverty in rich nations. Florence, Italy: UNICEF Innocenti Research Centre.* Retrieved August 26, 2000, from www.unicef-icdc.org/pdf/poverty.pdf

Administration for Children and Families. (n.d.). *Child Abuse Prevention and Treatment Act.* Retrieved October 9, 2000, from www.asf.dhhs.gov/programs/cb/policy/capta.htm

Administration for Children and Families. (1998). *Program instructions.* Retrieved September 25, 2000, from www.acf.dhhs.gov/programs/cb/policy/pi9802/htm

Administration for Children and Families. (2003). *Head Start program fact sheet: Fiscal year 2002.* Retrieved June 27, 2003, from www.acf.hhs.gov/programs/hsb/research/2003.htm

Administration on Aging. (2002). *A profile of older Americans 2002.* Retrieved August 29, 2003, from www.aoa.dhhs.gov/prof/Statistics/profile/2002profile.pdf

Administration on Aging. (2003a). *Multipurpose senior centers—Bridging the gap.* Retrieved August 29, 2003, from www.aoa.gov/press/oam/May_2003/media/fact_sheets/MultiPurpose%20Senior%20Centers.pdf

Administration on Aging. (2003b). *Volunteer opportunities.* Retrieved August 29, 2003, from www.aoa.dhhs.gov/eldfam/ Volunteer_Opps/Volunteer_Opps_pf.asp

Administration on Developmental Disabilities. (2002). *ADD Fact sheet: Developmental disabilities programs.* Retrieved June 28, 2003, from www.acf.dhhs.gov/programs/add/Factsheet.htm

Akin, B. A., & Gregoire, T. K. (1997). Parents' views on child welfare's response to addiction. *Families in Society, 78,* 393–404.

Alameda-Lawson, T., & Lawson, M. A. (2002). Building community collaboratives. In M. O'Melia & K. K. Miley (Eds.), *Pathways to power: Readings in contextual social work practice* (pp. 108–127). Boston: Allyn & Bacon.

Allen, D., Ammann, A., Bailey, H., Baker, C., Berger, R., Guthrie, B., et al. (2001). Revised recommendations for HIV screening of pregnant women. *Morbidity and Mortality Weekly Report, 50*(19), 59–86. Retrieved June 29, 2003, from www.cdc.gov/mmwr/

Allen, J. A. (1985). Understanding the family: A central concern in child welfare. In J. Laird & A. Hartman (Eds.), *A handbook of child welfare: Context, knowledge and practice* (pp. 149–177). New York: The Free Press.

Allen, J. P., & Turner, E. (1990). Where diversity reigns. *American Demographics, 12*(8), 34–38.

Allen-Meares, P., Washington, R. O., & Welsh, B. L. (1996). *Social work services in schools* (2nd ed.). Boston: Allyn & Bacon.

Alliance for Children and Families. (2003). *About the Alliance.* Retrieved August 31, 2003, from www.alliance.org/

Altshuler, S. J. (2003). From barriers to successful collaboration: Public schools and child welfare working together. *Social Work, 48*(1), 52–63.

Alzheimer's Association. (n.d.). *African-Americans and Alzheimer's disease: The silent epidemic.* Retrieved September 22, 2003, from www.alz.org/ResourceCenter/Diversity/downloads/AA_EDU-SilentEpidemic.pdf

Alzheimer's Association. (2003). *Statistics: About Alzheimer's disease.* Retrieved August 25, 2003, from www.alz.org/ResourceCenter/FactSheets/FSAlzheimerStats.pdf

American Academy of Pediatrics. (2000). *Sexual abuse.* Retrieved June 30, 2003, from www.medem.com/MedLB/article_detaillb.cfm?article_ID=ZZZ1LW3YA7C&sub_cat=355

American Association of Social Workers. (1929). *Social casework: Generic and specific: A report of the Milford Conference* (reprinted 1974). Washington, DC: National Association of Social Workers.

American Association on Mental Retardation. (2002). *Definition of mental retardation.* Retrieved September 28, 2003, from www.aamr.org/Policies/faq_mental_retardation.shtml

American Medical Association. (1996). *Advocacy & communications: Facts about family violence.* Retrieved August 27, 1997, from www.ama-assn.org/ad-com/releases/1996/fvfact.htm

American Psychiatric Association. (2000). *Diagnostic and statistical manual of mental disorders-TR* (4th ed.). Washington, DC: Author.

American Public Welfare Association. (1996). *The Personal Responsibility and Work Opportunity Reconciliation Act of 1996.* Retrieved April 10, 1997, from www.apwa.org/reform/analysis.htm

Anderson, G. (1998). Providing services to elderly people with HIV. In D. M. Aronstein & B. J. Thompson (Eds.), *HIV and social work* (pp. 443–450). New York: Haworth Press.

Anderson, J. D. (1979). Social work with groups in the generic base of social work practice. *Social Work with Groups, 2,* 281–293.

Anderson, J. D. (March, 1990). *Preparing students for family-centered practice in the 1990's: A multicultural perspective.* Paper presented at the annual program meeting of the Council on Social Work Education, Reno, NV.

Anderson, J. D. (February, 1992). *Between individual and community: Small group empowerment practice in a generalist perspective.* Paper presented at the annual program meeting of the Council on Social Work Education, Kansas City, MO.

Anderson, R. E., Carter, I., & Lowe, G. (1999). *Human behavior in the social environment: A social systems approach* (5th ed.). New York: Aldine De Gruyter.

Anderson, S. C. (1995). Alcohol abuse. In R. L. Edwards (Ed.), *Encyclopedia of social work: Vol. 1* (19th ed.) (pp. 203–215). Washington, DC: NASW Press.

Annie E. Casey Foundation. (2003a). *KIDS COUNT 2003 data book online: Summary and findings.* Retrieved August 31, 2003, from www.aecf.org/kidscount/databook/pdfs/e_sum_findings.pdf

Annie E. Casey Foundation. (2003b). *Summary and findings: Percent of children in poverty.* Retrieved August 11, 2003, from www.aecf.org/kidscount/databook/summary/summary11.htm

Applewhite, S. L. (1997). Homeless veterans: Perspectives on social services use. *Social Work, 42,* 19–30.

Arno, P., Levine, C., & Memmott, M. (1999). *The economic value of informal caregiving.* Retrieved October 14, 2000, from www.aoa.dhhs.gov/

Aron, L. Y., & Mears, D. P. (2003). *Disability law and juvenile justice.* The Urban Institute. Retrieved July 3, 2003, from www.urban.org/urlprint.cfm?ID=8411

Aronstein, D. M. (1998). Organizing support groups for people affected by HIV. In D. M. Aronstein & B. J. Thompson (Eds.), *HIV and social work* (pp. 293–299). New York: Haworth Press.

Asch, A., & Mudrick, N. R. (1995). Disability. In R. L. Edwards (Ed.), *Encyclopedia of social work: Vol. 1* (19th ed.) (pp. 752–761). Washington, DC: NASW Press.

Atkinson, V. I., & Nelson, G. M. (1995). Adult protective services. In G. M. Nelson, A. C. Eller, D. W. Streets, & M. L. Morse (Eds.), *The field of adult services: Social work practice and administration* (pp. 215–230). Washington, DC: NASW Press.

Austin, C. D. (1993). Case management: A systems perspective. *Families in Society, 74,* 451–458.

Austin, C. D. (1996). Aging and long term care. In C. D. Austin & R. W. McClelland (Eds.), *Perspectives on case management practice* (pp. 73–98). Milwaukee, WI: Families International.

Austin, C. D., & McClelland, R. W. (1996). Introduction: Case management—Everybody's doing it. In C. D. Austin & R. W. McClelland (Eds.), *Perspectives on case management practice* (pp. 1–16). Milwaukee, WI: Families International.

Austin, D. M. (1983). The Flexner myth and the history of social work. *Social Service Review, 57,* 357–376.

Austin, D. M. (1985). Historical perspectives on contemporary social work. *Urban and Social Change Review, 18*(2), 16–18.

Axinn, J., & Stern, M. J. (2001). *Social welfare: A history of the American response to need* (5th ed.). Boston: Allyn & Bacon.

Azzi-Lessing, L., & Olsen, L. (1996). Substance abuse-affected families in the child welfare system: New challenges, new alliances. *Social Work, 41,* 15–23.

Babcock, J. H. (1998). Involving family and significant others in acute care. In D. M. Aronstein & B. J. Thompson (Eds.), *HIV and social work* (pp. 101–108). New York: Haworth Press.

Balgopal, P. R. (1989). Occupational social work: An expanded clinical perspective. *Social Work, 34,* 437–442.

Balgopal, P. R. (1995). Asian Americans overview. In R. L. Edwards (Ed.), *Encyclopedia of social work: Vol. 1* (19th ed.) (pp. 231–238). Washington, DC: NASW Press.

Balgopal, P. R. (2000a). Social work practice with immigrants and refugees: An overview. In P. R. Balgopal (Ed.), *Social work practice with immigrants and refugees* (pp. 1–29). New York: Columbia University Press.

Balgopal, P. R. (2000b). Conclusion. In P. R. Balgopal (Ed.), *Social work practice with immigrants and refugees* (pp. 229–240). New York: Columbia University Press.

Bandler, J. T. D. (1989). Family protection women's issues in Social Security. *Social Work, 34,* 307–311.

Bandura, A., & Cervone, D. (1983). Self-evaluative and self-efficacy mechanisms governing the motivational effects of goals systems. *Journal of Personality and Social Psychology, 45,* 1017–1028.

Barak, M. E., & Bargal, D. (2000). Human services in the context of work: Evolving and innovative roles for occupational social work. *Administration in Social Work, 23*(3/4), 1–11.

Barbarin, O. A. (1983). Coping with ecological transitions by black families: A psychosocial model. *Journal of Community Psychology, 11,* 308–322.

Barbell, K., & Wright, L. (1999). Family foster care in the next century. *Child Welfare, 78*(1), 3–14.

Barker, R. L. (1991). *Social work in private practice* (2nd ed.). Washington, DC: NASW Press.

Barker, R. L. (2003). *The social work dictionary* (5th ed.). Washington, DC: NASW Press.

Barker, R. L., & Branson, D. M. (2000). *Forensic social work: Legal aspects of professional practice* (2nd ed.). New York: Haworth Press.

Barna, G. (2003). *America's faith* is *changing—but beneath the surface.* Retrieved August 23, 2003, from www.barna.org/cgi-bin/PagePressRelease.asp?PressReleaseID=135&Reference=B

Barnes, A., & Ephross, P. H. (1994). The impact of hate violence on victims. *Social Work, 39,* 247–251.

Barnes, G. M., Welt, J. W., & Hoffman, J. H. (2002). Relationship of alcohol use to delinquency and illicit drug use in adolescents: Gender, age, and racial/ethnic differences. *Journal of Drug Issues, 32*(1), 153–178.

Barnes, M., & Bennett, G. (1998). Frail bodies, courageous voices: Older people influencing community care. *Health and Social Care in the Community, 6*(2), 102–111.

Barnes, M., & Shardlow, P. (1997). From passive recipient to active citizen: Participation in mental health user groups. *Journal of Mental Health, 6*(3), 289–300.

Barry, J. (1988). Autobiographical writing: An effective tool for practice with the oldest old. *Social Work, 33,* 449–451.

Barth, R. P. (1995). Adoption. In R. L. Edwards (Ed.), *Encyclopedia of social work: Vol. 1* (19th ed.) (pp. 48–59). Washington, DC: NASW Press.

Bartlett, H. M. (1961). *Analyzing social work practice by fields.* Silver Spring, MD: National Association of Social Workers.

Bartlett, H. M. (1970). *The common base of social work practice.* New York: National Association of Social Workers.

Bass, D. M., et al. (1998). The buffering effects of a computer support network on caregiver strain. *Journal of Aging and Health, 10*(1), 20–43.

Battjes, R. J., & Delany, P. J. (1998). Services in correctional facilities: Negotiating a complex environment. In D. M. Aronstein & B. J. Thompson (Eds.), *HIV and social work* (pp. 469–482). New York: Haworth Press.

Beaulaurier, R., & Taylor, S. H. (1999). Self-determination and consumer control: Guiding principles in the empowerment model as utilized by the Disability Rights Movement. In W. Shera & L. Wells (Eds.), *Empowerment practice in social work: Developing richer conceptual foundations* (pp. 159–177). Toronto, Canada: Canadian Scholars Press.

Beauvais, F. (1998). Spotlight on special populations: American Indians and alcohol. *Alcohol Health and Research World, 22*(4), 253–259. Retrieved September, 13, 2003, from www.niaaa.nih.gov/publications/arh22-4/253.pdf

Bednar, S. G. (2003). Elements of satisfying organizational climates in child welfare agencies. *Families in Society, 84*(1), 7–12.

Beeghley, L. (1983). *Living poorly in America.* New York: Praeger Press.

Beless, D. W. (1995). Council on Social Work Education. In R. L. Edwards (Ed.), *Encyclopedia of social work: Vol. 1* (19th ed.) (pp. 632–636). Washington, DC: NASW Press.

Ben-Ari, A. T. (2002). Dimensions and predictions of professional involvement in self-help groups: A view from within. *Health and Social Work, 27*(2), 95–130.

Beresford, P. (1999). Towards an empowering social work practice: Learning from service users and their movements. In W. Shera & L. Wells (Eds.), *Empowerment practice in social work: Developing richer conceptual foundations* (pp. 259–277). Toronto, Canada: Canadian Scholars Press.

Beresford, P., & Evans, C. (1999). Research note: Research and empowerment. *British Journal of Social Work, 29*(5), 671–677.

Berger, P., & Neuhaus, J. R. (1977). *To empower people: The role of mediating structures in public policy.* Washington, DC: American Enterprise Institute.

Berger, R. M. (1983). What is a homosexual? A definitional model. *Social Work, 28*(2), 132–136.

Berger, R. M. (1986). Gay men. In H. L. Gochros, J. S. Gochros, & J. Fischer (Eds.), *Counseling the sexually oppressed* (pp. 162–180). Englewood Cliffs, NJ: Prentice-Hall.

Berger, R. M., & Kelly, J. J. (1995). Gay men overview. In R. L. Edwards (Ed.), *Encyclopedia of social work: Vol. 2* (19th ed.) (pp. 1064–1075). Washington, DC: NASW Press.

Berk, L. E. (2004). *Development through the lifespan* (4th ed.). Boston: Allyn & Bacon.

Berkman, C. S., & Zinberg, G. (1997). Homophobia and heterosexism in social workers. *Social Work, 42*(4), 319–332.

Berliner, H. S. (2002). Public health and social justice. *Society, 39*(4), 25–27.

Berman-Rossi, T., & Miller, I. (1994). African-Americans and the settlements during the late nineteenth and early twentieth centuries. *Social Work with Groups, 17*(3), 77–95.

Bernard, B. (1992). Fostering resiliency in kids: Protective factors in the family, school, and community. *Illinois Prevention Resource Center: Prevention Forum, 12*(3), pp. 1–16.

Bernard, V. W., Ottenberg, P., & Redl, F. (1971). Dehumanization. In W. E. Henry & N. Sanford (Eds.), *Sanctions for evil* (pp. 102–124). San Francisco: Jossey-Bass.

Berzoff, J. (2003). Introduction: Special issue on end-of-life care. *Smith College Studies in Social Work, 73*(3), 259–271.

Bethea, L. (1999). Primary prevention of child abuse. *American Family Physician, 59*(6), 1577–1586. Retrieved September 17, 2003, from EBSCOhost Academic Search Elite database.

Biestek, F. P. (1957). *The casework relationship.* Chicago: Loyola University Press.

Biggerstaff, M. A. (1995). Licensing, regulation, and certification. In R. L. Edwards (Ed.), *Encyclopedia of social work: Vol. 2* (19th ed.) (pp. 1616–1624). Washington, DC: NASW Press.

Bilchik, S. (1998). A juvenile justice system for the 21st century. *Crime & Delinquency, 44*(1), 89–101.

Black, R. B., Dornan, D. H., & Allegrante, J. P. (1986). Challenges in developing health promotion services for the chronically ill. *Social Work, 31,* 287–293.

Blaska, J. (1993). The power of language: Speak and write using "person first." In M. Nagler (Ed.), *Perspectives on disability: Text and readings on disability* (pp. 25–32). Palo Alto, CA: Health Markets Research.

Bloom, M. (1995). Primary prevention overview. In R. L. Edwards (Ed.), *Encyclopedia of social work: Vol. 2* (19th ed.) (pp. 1895–1905). Washington, DC: NASW Press.

Bodily, C. L. (1991). "I have no opinions. I'm 73 years old!": Rethinking ageism. *Journal of Aging Studies, 5*(3), 245–264.

Boeckmann, R. J., & Turpin-Petrosino, C. (2002). Understanding the harm of hate crime. *Journal of Social Issues, 58*(2), 207–225.

Bonilla-Santiago, G. (1989). Legislating progress for Hispanic women in New Jersey. *Social Work, 34,* 270–272.

Book, H. E. (1988). Empathy: Misconceptions and misuses in psychotherapy. *American Journal of Psychiatry, 145*(4), 420–424.

Booth, R. (1990). Sexual orientation: Overview and implications for social work practice. Unpublished manuscript. Black Hawk College, Moline, IL.

Boushey, H. (2001). *The effects of the Personal Responsibility and Work Opportunity Reconciliation Act on working families.* Economic Policy Institute. Retrieved August 23, 2003, from www.epinet.org/content.cfm/webfeatures_viewpoints_tanf_testimony

Bowen, G. L., & Chapman, M. V. (1996). Poverty, neighborhood danger, social support, and the individual adaptation among at-risk youth. *Journal of Family Issues, 17*(5), 641–666.

Boyd-Franklin, N. (2003). *Black families in therapy: A multisystems approach.* New York: Guilford Press.

Bracht, N. F. (1978). *Social work in health care: A guide to professional practice.* New York: Haworth Press.

Bradford, A. (1999). REBUILD: An orthopedic trauma support group and community outreach program. *Health and Social Work, 24*(4), 307+. Retrieved September 17, 2003, from InfoTrac Expanded Academic ASAP database.

Bradley, V. J. (2000). Changes in services and supports for people with developmental disabilities: New challenges to established practice. *Health and Social Work, 25*(3), 191–200.

Brandl, B. (2000). Power and control: Understanding domestic abuse in later life. *Generations, 24*(11), 39–45.

Breckinridge, S. (1936). Tenement-house legislation in Chicago. In E. Abbott (Ed.), *The tenements of Chicago 1908–1935* (pp. 34–71). Chicago: University of Chicago Press.

Bremer, W. W. (1986). Hopkins, Harry Lloyd. In W. I. Trattner (Ed.), *Biographical dictionary of social welfare in America* (pp. 399–402). New York: Greenwood Press.

Brennan, D. J. (1998). Bereavement work in hospice and home care. In D. M. Aronstein & B. J. Thompson (Eds.), *HIV and social work* (pp. 135–144). New York: Haworth Press.

Breton, M. (1993). Relating competence promotion and empowerment. *Journal of Progressive Human Services, 5*(1), 27–44.

Breton, M. (1994). On the meaning of empowerment and empowerment-oriented social work practice. *Social Work with Groups, 17*(3), 23–37.

Breton, M. (2002). Empowerment practice in Canada and the United States: Restoring policy issues at the center of social work. *The Social Policy Journal, 1*(1), 19–34.

Briar, K. H. (1988). *Social work and the unemployed.* Silver Spring, MD: National Association of Social Workers.

Briar-Lawson, K. (1998). Capacity building for integrated family-centered practice. *Social Work, 43*(6), 539–550.

Bricker-Jenkins, M. (1990). Another approach to practice and training: Clients must be considered the primary experts. *Public Welfare, 48*(2), 11–16.

Bricout, J. C., & Bentley, K. J. (2000). Disability status and perceptions of employability by employers. *Social Work Research, 24*(3), 87–95. Retrieved September 17, 2003, from EBSCOhost Academic Search Elite database.

Brieland, D. (1995). Social work practice: History and evolution. In R. L. Edwards (Ed.), *Encyclopedia of social work: Vol. 3* (19th ed.) (pp. 2247–2258). Washington, DC: NASW Press.

Brill, N. I. (1998). *Working with people: The helping process* (6th ed.). New York: Longman.

Brill, N. I., & Levine, J. (2002). *Working with people: The helping process* (7th ed.). Boston: Allyn & Bacon.

Brody, E. (1976, May). *Environmental factors in dependency.* Paper presented for the National Academy of Sciences, Washington, DC.

Brooklyn Association for Improving the Condition of the Poor. (1878). *The annual report of the Brooklyn Association for Improving the Condition of the Poor, 1878.* Brooklyn, NY: Eagle Job and Book Printing Department.

Brooklyn Association for Improving the Condition of the Poor. (1885). *The annual report of the Brooklyn Association for Improving the Condition of the Poor, 1885.* Brooklyn, NY: Eagle Job and Book Printing Department.

Brotheridge, C. M., & Lee, R. T. (2002). Testing a conservation of resources model of the dynamics of emotional labor. *Journal of Occupational Health Psychology, 7*(1), 57–67.

Brown, J. C. (1933). *The rural community and social work.* New York: Family Welfare Association of America.

Brown, P. A. (1994). Participatory research: A new paradigm for social work. In L. Gutiérrez & P. Nurius (Eds.), *Education and research for empowerment practice* (pp. 293–303). Seattle, WA: University of Washington, Center for Policy and Practice Research, School of Social Work.

Browne, A., & Finkelhor, D. (1986). Impact of child sexual abuse: A review of the research. In S. Chess, A. Thomas, & M. Hertzig (Eds.), *Annual progress in child psychiatry and child development* (pp. 555–584). New York: Brunner/Mazel.

Bureau of Labor Statistics. (2002a). *Occupational outlook handbook: Social workers.* Retrieved June 23, 2003, from www.bls.gov/oco/ocos060.htm

Bureau of Labor Statistics. (2002b). *Career guide to industries: Social services, except childcare.* Retrieved June 23, 2003, from www.bls.gov/oco/cg/cgs040.htm

Bureau of Labor Statistics. (2002c). *Occupational outlook handbook: Social and human service assistants.* Retrieved June 23, 2003, from www.bls.gov/oco/ocos059.htm

Bureau of Labor Statistics. (2002d). *Volunteering in the United States.* Retrieved August 30, 2003, from www.bls.gov/news.release/volun.nr0.htm

Bureau of Labor Statistics. (2003a). *Labor force statistics from the current population survey.* Retrieved August 24, 2003, from http://data.bls.gov/cgi-bin/surveymost?ln

Bureau of Labor Statistics. (2003b). *Unemployment rates for states.* Retrieved August 24, 2003, from www.bls.gov/web/laumstrk.htm

Bureau of Labor Statistics. (2003c). *News: Metropolitan area employment and unemployment: June 2003.* Retrieved August 24, 2003, from www.bls.gov/news.release/archives/metro_07302003.pdf

Burnette, D. (1997). Grandparents raising grandchildren in the inner city. *Families in Society, 78*(5), 489–499.

Burns, E. (1956). *Social security and public policy.* New York: McGraw-Hill.

Butler, R. N. (1969). Age-ism: Another form of bigotry. *The Gerontologist, 9* (Part I).

Caetano, R., Craig A., Field, C. A., & Nelson, S. (2003). Association between childhood physical abuse, exposure to parental violence, and alcohol problems in adulthood. *Journal of Interpersonal Violence, 18*(3), 240–257.

Cahill, S. (2000). Preface. In P. Currah & S. Minter. *Transgender equality: A handbook for activists and policymakers* (pp. iii–iv). The Policy Institute of the National Gay and Lesbian Task Force. Retrieved September 13, 2003, from www.ngltf.org/downloads/transeq.pdf

Canda, E. R. (1988). Spirituality, religious diversity, and social work practice. *Social Casework, 69,* 238–247.

Canda, E. R. (1989). Religious content in social work education: A comparative approach. *Journal of Social Work Education, 25,* 36–45.

Canda, E. R., & Furman, L. D. (1999). *Spiritual diversity in social work practice: The heart of helping.* New York: Columbia University Press.

Caplan, G. (1964). *Principles of preventive psychiatry.* New York: Basic Books.

Carlson, B. E., & Cervera, N. J. (1991). Incarceration, coping, and support. *Social Work, 36,* 279–285.

Carlsson-Ågren, M., Berg, S., & Wenestam, C. G. (1992). Daily life of the oldest old. *Journal of Sociology and Social Welfare, 19*(2), 109–124.

Carlton, T. O. (1984). *Clinical social work in health settings.* New York: Springer.

Carlton-LeNey, I., & Alexander, S. C. (2001). Early African American social welfare pioneer women: Working to empower the race and the community. *Journal of Ethnic and Cultural Diversity, 10*(2), 67–84.

Carpentier, N., & Ducharme, F. (2003). Care-giver network transformations: The need for an integrated perspective. *Aging and Society, 23*(4), 507–525.

Carter, J., & Schechter, S. (1997). *Child abuse and domestic violence: Creating community partnerships for safe families: Suggested components of an effective child welfare response to domestic violence.* Retrieved September 14, 2003, from www.mincava.umn.edu/link/documents/fvpf1/fvpf1.shtml

Carter, L. S., Weithorn, L. A., & Behrman, R. E. (1999). Domestic violence and children: Analysis and recommendations. *The Future of Children, 9*(3), 4–20. Retrieved September 14, 2003, from www.futureofchildren.org/usr_doc/vol9no3Art1%2Epdf

Castelle, G. (1987). Juvenile offender institutions. In A. Minahan (Ed.), *Encyclopedia of social work: Vol. 2* (18th ed.) (pp. 15–21). Silver Spring, MD: National Association of Social Workers.

Castex, G. M. (1994). Providing services to Hispanic/Latino populations: Profiles in diversity. *Social Work, 39,* 288–295.

Catalog of Federal Domestic Assistance. (n.d.). *93.667 Social Services Block Grant.* Retrieved December 16, 2003, from www.cfda.gov/public/viewprog.asp?progid=1311

Cattell-Gordon, D. (1990). The Appalachian inheritance: A culturally transmitted traumatic stress syndrome? *Journal of Progressive Human Services, 1*(1), 41–57.

Centers for Disease Control & Prevention. (1999). *Status of perinatal HIV prevention: U.S. declines continue.* Retrieved June 29, 2003, from www.cdc.gov/hiv/pubs/facts/perinatl.pdf

Centers for Disease Control & Prevention. (2002a). *HIV/AIDS surveillance report, 13*(2). Retrieved June 28, 2003, from www.cdc.gov/hiv/stats/hasr1302.pdf

Centers for Disease Control & Prevention. (2002b). *Table 33: Leading causes of death and numbers of deaths, according to age: United States. Health United States, 2002.* Retrieved August 31, 2003 from www.cdc.gov/nchs/data/hus/tables/2002/02hus033.pdf

Centers for Disease Control & Prevention. (2002c). *Table 47: Death rates for suicide, according to sex, race, Hispanic origin, and age: United States, selected years 1950–2000. Health United States, 2002.* Retrieved August 31, 2003 from www.cdc.gov/nchs/data/hus/tables/2002/02hus047.pdf

Centers for Disease Control & Prevention. (2003a). *Basic statistics.* Retrieved June 28, 2003, from www.cdc.gov/hiv/stats.htm

Centers for Disease Control & Prevention. (2003b). *HIV/AIDS among African Americans: Key facts.* Retrieved June 28, 2003, from www.cdc.gov/hiv/pubs/Facts/afam.pdf

Centers for Disease Control & Prevention. (2003c). *Fetal alcohol information.* Retrieved September 14, 2003, from www.cdc.gov/ncbddd/fas/fasask.htm

Champion, D. J. (2001). *Corrections in the United States: A contemporary perspective* (3rd ed.). Upper Saddle River, NJ: Prentice-Hall.

Chand, A. (2000). The over-representation of black children in the child protection system: Possible causes, consequence, and solutions. *Child and Family Social Work, 51,* 66–77.

Chapin, R., & Cox, E. (2001). Changing the paradigm: Strengths-based and empowerment-oriented social work with frail elders. *Journal of Gerontological Social Work, 36*(3/4), 165–179.

Charlton, J. I. (1998). *Nothing about us without us: Disability, oppression and empowerment.* Berkeley, CA: University of California Press.

Chatterjee, P., & Farkas, K. J. (1992). Spending behaviors: Implications for human service practitioners. *Families in Society, 73,* 613–621.

Chau, K. L. (1989). Sociocultural dissonance among ethnic minority populations. *Social Casework, 70,* 224–239.

Checkoway, B., Finn, J., & Pothukuchi, K. (1995). Young people as community resources: New forms of participation. In P. Adams & K. Nelson (Eds.), *Reinventing human services: Community- and family-centered practice* (pp. 189–202). New York: Aldine De Gruyter.

Chenoweth, L. (2002). Social work, stress, and burnout: A review. *Journal of Mental Health, 11*(3), 255–265.

Chestang, L. (1976). Environmental influences on social functioning: The Black experience. In P. J. Cafferty & L. Chestang (Eds.), *The diverse society: Implications for social policy* (pp. 59–74). Washington, DC: National Association of Social Workers.

Child Welfare League of America. (n.d.). *Summary of The Adoption and Safe Families Act of 1997 (P.L. 105-89).* Retrieved September 14, 2003, from www.cwla.org/advocacy/asfapl105-89summary.htm

Child Welfare League of America. (1981). *Directory of member agencies.* New York: Author.

Child Welfare League of America. (2001). *Fact sheet: The Child Protection/Alcohol and Drug Partnership Act (S.484/H.R. 1901) will help keep children safe and in permanent families.* Retrieved December 30, 2003, from www.cwla.org/cwla/advocacy/aodfactsheet.htm

Child Welfare League of America. (2003). *Kinship care: Fact sheet.* Retrieved December 30, 2003, from www.cwla.org/programs/kinship/factsheet.htm

Children's Bureau. (1999). *Title IV-E Independent Living Programs: A decade in review.* U.S. Department of Health and Human Services, Administration for Children and Families, Administration on Children, Youth and Families. Retrieved August 31, 2003, from www.calib.com/nccanch/pubs/otherpubs/il/ILPrept.pdf

Children's Bureau. (2003). *AFCARS report: Preliminary FY 2001 estimates as of March 2003.* U.S. Department of Health and Human Services, Administration for Children and Families, Administration on Children, Youth and Families. Retrieved August 31, 2003, from www.acf.hhs.gov/programs/cb/publications/afcars/report8.pdf

Children's Defense Fund. (n.d.). *Issue basics: Increase investments in Head Start.* Retrieved October 18, 2000, from www.cdfactioncouncil.org/Head%20Start%20Basics.htm

Children's Defense Fund. (2000a). *Child abuse and neglect fact sheet.* Retrieved September 30, 2000, from www.childrensdefense.org/ss_child_abuse.html

Children's Defense Fund. (2000b). *Issue basics: Child abuse and neglect basics.* Retrieved September 25, 2000, from www.cdfactioncouncil.org/Child%20Abuse.htm

Children's Defense Fund. (2000c). *Issue basics: Adoption and Safe families Act (ASFA).* Retrieved December 30, 2003, from www.cdfactioncouncil.org/ASFA.htm

Children's Defense Fund. (2002a). *The state of children in America's union: A 2002 action guide to leave no child behind.* Retrieved June 29, 2003, from www.childrensdefense.org/pdf/minigreenbook.pdf

Children's Defense Fund. (2002b). *25 key facts about America's children.* Retrieved June 29, 2003, from www.childrensdefense.org/keyfacts.htm

Children's Defense Fund. (2003). *2003 child care and Head Start organizer's kit.* Retrieved September 27, 2003, from www.cdfactioncouncil.org/childcare_toolkit_2003.pdf

Chubbuck, P. (1998). Outcomes and accountability: Through the eyes of a foster parent. *The Prevention Report,* (1). Retrieved October 2, 2003, from www.uiowa.edu/~nrcfcp/services/publication/spring98.htm#outcomes

Chung, D. K. (1992). Asian cultural commonalities: A comparison with mainstream American culture. In S. M. Faruto, R. Biswas, D. K. Chung, K. Murase, & F. Rose-Sheriff (Eds.), *Social work practice with Asian Americans* (pp. 27–44). Newbury Park, CA: Sage.

Ciffone, J. (1993). Suicide prevention: A classroom presentation to adolescents. *Social Work, 38,* 197–203.

Clark, E. J. (2003). The future of social work practice. In R. A. English (Ed.), *Encyclopedia of social work: 2003 supplement* (pp. 61–70). Washington, DC: NASW Press.

Cnaan, R., Wineburg, R. J., & Boddie, S. G. (1999). *The newer deal: Social work and religion in partnership.* New York: Columbia University Press.

Cohen, N. (1992). *Child welfare: A multicultural focus.* Boston: Allyn & Bacon.

Cohen, N. E. (1958). *Social work in the American tradition.* New York: Holt, Rinehart, and Winston.

Cohen, W. J. (1986). Perkins, Frances. In W. I. Trattner (Ed.), *Biographical dictionary of social welfare in America* (pp. 589–591). New York: Greenwood Press.

Cole, E. S. (1985). Adoption: History, policy, and program. In J. Laird & A. Hartman (Eds.), *A hand-book of child welfare: Context, knowledge, and practice* (pp. 638–666). New York: The Free Press.

Collopy, B. J. (1992). Autonomy in long term care: Some crucial distinctions. In S. M. Rose (Ed.), *Case management and social work practice* (pp. 56-76). New York: Longman.

Combs-Orme, T. (1993). Health effects of adolescent pregnancy: Implications for social work. *Families in Society, 74,* 344–354.

Compton, B., & Galaway, B. (1999). *Social work processes* (6th ed.). Pacific Grove, CA: Brooks/Cole Publishing Company.

Conceptual frameworks II: Second special issue on conceptual frameworks. (1981). *Social Work, 26*(1).

Congress, E. (1990, March). *Educating social work students in the utilization of a crisis intervention model with Hispanic clients.* Paper presented at the annual program meeting of the Council on Social Work Education, Reno, NV.

Congress, E. (1994). The use of culturalgrams to assess and empower culturally diverse families. *Families in Society, 75,* 531–540.

Connaway, R., & Gentry, M. (1988). *Social work practice.* Englewood Cliffs, NJ: Prentice-Hall.

Connolly, M. (1994). An art of empowerment: The Children, Young Persons, and Their Families Act (1989). *British Journal of Social Work, 24*(1), 87–100.

Connolly, M., & McKenzie, M. (1999). *Effective participatory practice: Family group conferencing in child protection.* New York: Aldine De Gruyter.

Conrad, A. P. (1988). Ethical considerations in the psychosocial process. *Social Casework, 69,* 603–610.

Cooper, S. (2000). Consumer/survivor voice: Rural recovery. *Rural Mental Health, 25*(4), Retrieved September 14, 2003, from www.narmh.org/pages/c_sframe.html

Corcoran, J., Stephenson, M., Perryman, D., & Allen, S. (2001). Perceptions and utilization of a police-social work crisis intervention approach to domestic violence. *Families in Society, 82*(4), 393–398.

Costin, L. B. (1983). Edith Abbott and the Chicago influence on social work education. *Social Service Review, 57,* 94–110.

Council of Economic Advisors for President's Initiative on Race. (1998). *Changing America: Indicators of social and economic well-being by race and Hispanic origin.* Washington, DC: U.S. Government Printing Office. Retrieved December 30, 2003, from http://w3.access.gpo.gov/eop/ca/pdfs/ca.pdf

Council on Social Work Education. (2001). *Educational policy and accreditation standards.* Alexandria, VA: Author.

Cowger, C. D. (1977). Alternative stances on the relationship of social work to society. *Journal of Education for Social Work, 13*(3), 25–29.

Cowger, C. D., & Snively, C. A. (2002). Assessing client strengths: Individual, family, and community empowerment. In D. Saleebey (Ed.), *The strengths perspective in social work practice* (3rd ed.) (pp. 106–123). Boston: Allyn & Bacon.

Cowles, L. A. (2000). *Social work in the health field: A care perspective.* New York: Haworth Press.

Cox, E. O. (2002). Empowerment-oriented practice applied to long-term care. *Journal of Social Work in Long-Term Care, 1*(2), 27–46.

Cox, H. G. (1994). *Later life* (3rd ed.). Englewood Cliffs, NJ: Prentice-Hall.

Crystal, D. (1989). Asian Americans and the myth of the model minority. *Social Casework, 70,* 405–413.

Cummins, L. K., First, R. J., & Toomey, B. G. (1998). Comparisons of rural and urban homeless women. *Affilia, 13*(4), 435–453. Retrieved September 17, 2003, from InfoTrac Expanded Academic ASAP database.

Cunningham, G. (1983). Social work and criminal justice: New dimensions in practice. In A. R. Roberts (Ed.), *Social work in juvenile and criminal justice settings* (pp. 231–240). Springfield, IL: Charles C Thomas.

Curiel, H. (1995). Hispanics: Mexican Americans. In R. L. Edwards (Ed.), *Encyclopedia of social work: Vol. 2* (19th ed.) (pp. 1233–1244). Washington, DC: NASW Press.

Damon, L. L., & Card, J. A. (1999). Incest in young children. In R. T. Ammerman & M. Hersen (Eds.), *Assessment of family violence: A clinical and legal sourcebook* (pp. 184–209). New York: John Wiley & Sons.

Davenport, J., & Davenport, J. A. (1986). Lindeman, Eduard Christian. In W. I. Trattner (Ed.), *Biographical dictionary of social welfare in America* (pp. 498–500). New York: Greenwood Press.

Davenport, J. A., & Davenport, J. (1995). Rural social work overview. In R. L. Edwards (Ed.), *Encyclopedia of social work: Vol. 3* (19th ed.) (pp. 2076–2085). Washington, DC: NASW Press.

Davis, A. F. (1967). *Spearheads for reform: The social settlements and the Progressive movement, 1890–1914.* New York: Oxford University Press.

Davis, R. B. (1994). Intervening with high risk youth: A program model. *Adolescence, 29*(116), 763–774.

Day, P. J. (2003). *A new history of social welfare* (4th ed.). Boston: Allyn & Bacon.

De Hoyos, G., De Hoyos, A., & Anderson, C. B. (1986). Sociocultural dislocation: Beyond the dual perspective. *Social Work, 31,* 61–67.

de Schweinitz, K. (1961). *England's road to social security.* New York: A. S. Barnes and Company.

Dean, C. W. et al. (2000). *Social work and law enforcement partnerships: A summons to the village—Strategies and effective practices.* The Department of Criminal Justice, The University of North Carolina at Charlotte. Retrieved August 23, 2003, from www.gcc.state.nc.us/pubs/SWAPP.pdf

Dear, R. B. (1989). What's right with welfare? The other face of AFDC. *Journal of Sociology and Social Welfare, 16*(2), 5–43.

DeBord, K., Canu, R. F., & Kerpelman, J. (2000). Understanding a work-family fit for single parents moving from welfare to work. *Social Work, 45*(4), 313–324.

Deglau, E. (1985). A critique of social welfare theories: The culture of poverty and learned helplessness. *Catalyst, 6*(19), 31–55.

DeLois, K. A. (1998). Empowerment practice with lesbians and gays. In L. M. Gutierrez, R. J. Parsons, & E. O. Cox (Eds.), *Empowerment in social work practice: A sourcebook* (pp. 65–71). Pacific Grove, CA: Brooks/Cole.

Demone, H. W. (1998). The political future of privatization. In M. Gibelman & H. W. Demone (Eds.), *The privatization of human services: Policy and practice issues: Vol. 1* (pp. 205–244). New York: Springer.

Dempsey, C. L. (1994). Health and social issues of gay, lesbian, and bisexual adolescents. *Families in Society, 75,* 160–167.

DeNavas-Walt, C., & Cleveland, R. (2002). Money income in the United States: 2001 U.S. Census Bureau, *Current Population Reports, P60-218.* Washington, DC: U.S. Government Printing Office. Retrieved September 1, 2003, from www.census.gov/prod/2002pubs/p60-218.pdf

DePoy, E., Hartman, A., & Haslett, D. (1999). Critical action research: A model for social work knowing. *Social Work, 44*(6), 560–570.

Desselle, D. D., & Proctor, T. K. (2000). Advocating for the elderly hard-of-hearing population: The deaf people we ignore. *Social Work, 45*(3), 277–281.

Devore, W., & Schlesinger, E. G. (1999). *Ethnic-sensitive social work practice* (5th ed.). Boston: Allyn & Bacon.

DeVos, G. (1971). Conflict, dominance, and exploitation. In W. E. Henry & N. Sanford (Eds.), *Sanctions for evil* (pp. 155–173). San Francisco: Jossey-Bass.

DeWeaver, K. L. (1995). Developmental disabilities: Definitions and policies. In R. L. Edwards (Ed.),

Encyclopedia of social work: Vol. 1 (19th ed.) (pp. 712–720). Washington, DC: NASW Press.

Dinerman, M. (1992). Managing the maze: Case management and service delivery. *Administration in Social Work, 16*(1), 1–9.

Dobrec, A. (1990, October). *Effective models of family-based practice.* Paper presented at the Family Empowerment Conference: University of Iowa, School of Social Work, Iowa City, IA.

Dodd, P., & Gutiérrez, L. (1990). Preparing students for the future: A power perspective on community practice. *Administration in Social Work, 14*(2), 63–78.

Downs, S. W., Costin, L. B., & McFadden, E. J. (1996). *Child welfare and family services: Policies and practices.* White Plains, NY: Longman Publishers USA.

Dressel, P. (1992). Patriarchy and social welfare work. In Y. Hasenfeld (Ed.), *Human services as complex organizations* (pp. 205–223). Newbury Park, CA: Sage.

Dubois, M. R. (1999). Legal planning for gay, lesbian, and non-traditional elders. *Albany Law Review, 63*(1), 263+. Retrieved September 17, 2003, from InfoTrac Expanded Academic ASAP database.

Dulaney, D. D., & Kelly, J. (1982). Improving services to gay and lesbian clients. *Social Work, 27,* 178–183.

Duncan, S. F., & Brown, G. (1992). RENEW: A program for building remarried family strengths. *Families in Society, 73,* 149–158.

Dunham, A. (1970). *The new community organization.* New York: Thomas Y Crowell.

Dunst, C. J., Trivette, C. M., & Thompson, R. B. (1991). Supporting and strengthening family functioning: Toward a congruence between principles and practice. *Prevention in Human Services, 9*(1), 19–43.

Dziegielewski, S. F. (1998). *The changing face of health care social work: Professional practice in the era of managed care.* New York: Springer.

East, J. F. (1999a). Hidden barriers to success for women in welfare reform. *Families in Society, 80*(3), 295–304.

East, J. F. (1999b). An empowerment model for low-income women. In W. Shera & L. Wells (Eds.), *Empowerment practice in social work: Developing richer conceptual foundations* (pp. 142–158). Toronto, Canada: Canadian Scholars' Press.

Easton, C. J., Swan, S., & Sinha, R. (2000). Prevalence of family violence in clients entering substance abuse treatment. *Journal of Substance Abuse Treatment, 18*(1), 23–28.

Edell, M. (1999). Replacing community: Establishing linkages for women living with HIV/AIDS—A group work approach. *Social Work with Groups, 21*(3), 49–62.

Edleson, J. L. (1999). *Problems associated with children's witnessing of domestic violence.* Retrieved September 14, 2003, from www.vaw.umn.edu/documents/vawnet/witness/witness.html

Edwards, D. W. (1983). Special problem offenders. In A. R. Roberts (Ed.), *Social work in juvenile and criminal justice settings* (pp. 349–361). Springfield, IL: Charles C Thomas.

Egan, M., & Kadushin, G. (1999). The social worker in the emerging field of home care: Professional activities and ethical concerns. *Health and Social Work, 24*(1), 43+. Retrieved September 17, 2003, from InfoTrac Expanded Academic ASAP database.

Ekman, P., & Friesen, W. V. (1975). *Unmasking the face.* Englewood Cliffs, NJ: Prentice-Hall.

Elkind, D. (1984). *All grown up and no place to go.* Reading, MA: Addison-Wesley.

Elkind, D. (1988). *The hurried child: Growing up too fast too soon* (Rev. ed.). Reading, MA: Addison-Wesley.

Elliott, P. (1996). Shattering illusions: Same-sex domestic violence. In C. M. Renzetti & C. H. Miley (Eds.), *Violence in gay and lesbian domestic partnerships* (pp. 1–8). New York: Harrington Park Press.

Erikson, E. H. (1963). *Childhood and society* (2nd ed.). New York: Norton.

Evans, C., & Fisher, M. (1999). User controlled research and empowerment. In W. Shera & L. Wells (Eds.), *Empowerment practice in social work: Developing richer conceptual foundations* (pp. 348–369). Toronto, Canada: Canadian Scholars' Press.

Everett, J. E. (1995). Child foster care. In R. L. Edwards (Ed.), *Encyclopedia of social work: Vol. 1* (19th ed.) (pp. 375–389). Washington, DC: NASW Press.

Family Resource Coalition. (n.d.). *Family support programs and the prevention of child abuse: Overview of family support programs.* Retrieved August 31, 2003, from www.fww.org/articles/misc/frc.htm

Family Violence Prevention Fund. (2003). *The Violence Against Women Act: History of the Violence Against Women Act (VAWA).* Retrieved September 14, 2003, from http://endabuse.org/programs/display.php3?DocID=126

Fantuzzo, J. W., & Mohr, W. K. (1999). Prevalence and effects of child exposure to domestic violence. *The Future of Children, 9*(3), 21–32. Retrieved August 25, 2003, from www.futureofchildren.org/usr_doc/vol9no3Art2.pdf

Federal Interagency Forum on Aging-Related Statistics. (2000). *Older Americans 2000: Key indicators of well-being—Health care.* Retrieved December 30, 2003, from www.agingstats.gov/chartbook2000/healthcare.html

Federal Interagency Forum on Child and Family Statistics. (2002a). *America's children: Key national indicators of well-being, 2002: Population and family characteristics.* Retrieved June 29, 2003, from www.childstats.gov/ac2002/pdf/pop.pdf

Federal Interagency Forum on Child and Family Statistics. (2002b). *America's children: Key national indicators of well-being, 2002: Economic indicators.* Retrieved June 29, 2003, www.childstats.gov/ac2002/pdf/econ.pdf

Fields, J. (2003). Children's living arrangements and characteristics: March 2002. *Current Population Reports, P20-547.* Washington, DC: U.S. Census Bureau. Retrieved June 29, 2003, from www.census.gov/prod/2003pubs/p20-547.pdf

Figueira-McDonough, J. (1993). Policy practice: The neglected side of social work intervention. *Social Work, 38,* 179–188.

Fine, M., & Asch, A. (1988). Disability beyond stigma: Social interaction, discrimination, and activism. *Journal of Social Issues, 44,* 3–21.

Finkelhor, D. (1993). Epidemiological factors in the clinical identification of child sexual abuse. *Child Abuse and Neglect, 17,* 67–70.

Finn, J. (2000). An exploration of helping processes in an online self-help group focusing on issues of disability. *Health and Social Work, 24*(3), 220+. Retrieved September 17, 2003, from InfoTrac Expanded Academic ASAP database.

Finn, J., & Checkoway, B. (1998). Young people as competent community builders: A challenge to social work. *Social Work, 43*(4), 335–345.

Finn, J., & Lavitt, M. (1994). Computer-based self-help groups for sexual abuse survivors. *Social Work with Groups, 17*(1/2), 21–46.

First, R. J., Rife, J. C., & Toomey, B. G. (1994). Homelessness in rural areas: Causes, patterns, and trends. *Social Work, 39,* 97–108.

First, R. J., Rife, J. C., & Toomey, B. G. (1995). Homeless families. In R. L. Edwards (Ed.), *Encyclopedia of social work: Vol. 2* (19th ed.) (pp. 1330–1337). Washington, DC: NASW Press.

Fischer, J. (1978). *Effective casework practice: An eclectic approach.* New York: McGraw-Hill.

Fish, N. M. (1992). Social work practice in hospice care. In M. J. Holosko & P. A. Taylor (Eds.), *Social work practice in health care settings* (2nd ed.) (pp. 403–418). Toronto, Canada: Canadian Scholars' Press.

Fisher, B. J., & Specht, D. K. (1999). Successful aging and creativity in later life. *Journal of Aging Studies, 13*(4), 457+. Retrieved September 17, 2003, from InfoTrac Expanded Academic ASAP database.

Fisher, M. (1994). Partnership practice and empowerment. In L. Gutiérrez & P. Nurius (Eds.), *Education and research for empowerment practice* (pp. 275–291). Seattle, WA: University of Washington, Center for Policy and Practice Research, School of Social Work.

Fleming, J. & Ward, D. (1999). Research as empowerment: The social action approach. In W. Shera & L. Wells (Eds.), *Empowerment practice in social work: Developing richer conceptual foundations* (pp. 370–389). Toronto, Canada: Canadian Scholars' Press.

Flexner, A. (1916). Is social work a profession? In *Proceedings of the National Conference of Charities and Correction, 1915* (pp. 576–590). Chicago: The Hildmann Printing Co.

Flynn, C. P. (1990). Relationship violence by women: Issues and implications. *Family Relations, 39*(2), 194–198.

Fong, R. (1994). Family preservation: Making it work for Asians. *Child Welfare, 73*(4), 331–341.

Food Research Action Center. (2003). *Food Stamp participation jumped by 332,700 persons in October 2002; Level topped 20.1 million persons.* Retrieved June 26, 2003, from www.frac.org/html/news/fsp/02oct.html

Frank, G. (1988). Beyond stigma: Visibility and self-empowerment of persons with congenital limb deficiencies. *Journal of Social Issues, 44,* 95–115.

Frankel, A. L. (1997). Head Start and social work. *Families in Society, 78*(2), 172–183.

Franklin, C., & Corcoran, J. (2000). Preventing adolescent pregnancy: A review of programs and practices. *Social Work, 45*(1), 40–52.

Franklin, D. L. (1986). Mary Richmond and Jane Addams: From moral certainty to rational inquiry in social work practice. *Social Service Review, 60,* 504–523.

Freedberg, S. M., & Goldstein, J. L. (1986). Reynolds, Bertha Capen. In W. I. Trattner (Ed.), *Biographical dictionary of social welfare in America* (pp. 616–619). New York: Greenwood Press.

Freedman, R. I., & Boyer, N. C. (2000). The power to choose: Supports for families caring for individuals with developmental disabilities. *Health and Social Work, 25*(1), 59+. Retrieved September 17, 2003, from InfoTrac Expanded Academic ASAP database.

Freeman, E. M. (1995). School social work overview. In R. L. Edwards (Ed.), *Encyclopedia of social work: Vol. 3* (19th ed.) (pp. 2087–2099). Washington, DC: NASW Press.

Freire, P. (1990). *Pedagogy of the oppressed.* New York: Continuum.

Freud, S. (1987). Social workers as community educators: A new identity for the profession. *Journal of Teaching in Social Work, 1,* 111–126.

Freud, S., & Krug, S. (2002). Beyond the code of ethics, Part 1: Complexities of ethical decision making in social work practice. *Families in Society, 83*(5/6), 474–482.

Fuller-Thompson, E., & Minkler, M. (2000). African American grandparents raising grandchildren: A national profile of demographic and health characteristics. *Health and Social Work, 25*(2), 109+. Retrieved September 17, 2003, from InfoTrac Expanded Academic ASAP database.

Furstenberg, F. F., & Hughes, M. E. (1995). Social capital and successful development among at risk youth. *Journal of Marriage and the Family, 57*(3), 580–592.

Gabassi, P. G., Cervai, S., Rozbowsky, P., Semeraro, A., & Gregori, D. (2002). Burnout syndrome in the helping professions. *Psychological Reports, 90*(1), 309–314.

Gallagher, L. J. (1999). A shrinking portion of the safety net: General Assistance from 1989 to 1998. *The Urban Institute: Series A, No. A-36.* Retrieved August 23, 2003, from www.urban.org/UploadedPDF/anf_a36.pdf

Galper, J. (1975). *The politics of social services.* Englewood Cliffs, NJ: Prentice-Hall.

Gandy, J. T. (1983). Social work and victim assistance programs. In A. R. Roberts (Ed.), *Social work in juvenile and criminal justice settings* (pp. 121–136). Springfield, IL: Charles C Thomas.

Gans, H. (1972). The positive functions of poverty. *American Journal of Sociology, 78,* 275–289.

Garbarino, J. (1983). An ecological approach to child maltreatment. In L. H. Peltond (Ed.), *The social context of child abuse and neglect* (pp. 228–267). New York: Human Sciences Press.

Garland, A. F., & Zigler, E. (1993). Adolescent suicide prevention: Current research and social policy implications. *American Psychologist, 48,* 169–182.

Garner, J. D. (1995). Long-term care. In R. L. Edwards (Ed.), *Encyclopedia of social work: Vol. 2* (19th ed.) (pp. 1625–1634). Washington, DC: NASW Press.

General Services Administration. (2002). Social services block grant. *Catalog of Federal Domestic Assistance.* Retrieved August 23, 2003, from www.cfda.gov/public/viewprog.asp?progid=1311

Germain, C. (1979). *Social work practice: People and environments.* New York: Columbia University Press.

Germain, C. (1981). The physical environment and social work practice. In A. N. Maluccio (Ed.), *Promoting competence in clients: A new/old approach to social work practice* (pp. 103–124). New York: The Free Press.

Germain, C. B. (1983). Using social and physical environments. In A. Rosenblatt & D. Waldfogel (Eds.), *Handbook of clinical social work* (pp. 110–133). San Francisco: Jossey-Bass.

Germain, C. B., & Gitterman, A. (1980). *The life model of social work practice.* New York: Columbia University Press.

Germain, C. B., & Gitterman, A. (1987). Ecological perspective. In A. Minahan (Ed.), *Encyclopedia of social work: Vol. 1* (18th ed.) (pp. 488–489). Silver Spring, MD: National Association of Social Workers.

Germain, C., & Gitterman, A. (1995). Ecological perspective. In R. L. Edwards (Ed.), *Encyclopedia of social work: Vol. 1* (19th ed.) (pp. 816–824). Washington, DC: NASW Press.

Germain, C. B., & Gitterman, A. (1996). *The life model of social work practice: Advances in theory and practice* (2nd ed.). New York: Columbia University Press.

Gesten, E. L., & Jason, L. A. (1987). Social and community intervention. *Annual Review of Psychology, 38,* 427–460.

Giarrusso, R., Silverstein, M., & Bengston, V. L. (1996). Family complexity and the grandparent role. *Generations, 20*(1), 17–23.

Gibelman, M. (1995). Purchasing social services. In R. L. Edwards (Ed.), *Encyclopedia of social work: Vol. 3* (19th ed.) (pp. 1998–2007). Washington, DC: NASW Press.

Gibelman, M. (1998). Theory, practice, and experience in the purchase of services. In M. Gibelman & H. W. Demone (Eds.), *The privatization of human services: Policy and practice issues: Vol. 1* (pp. 1–51). New York: Springer.

Gibelman, M., & Schervish, P. H. (1997). *Who we are: A second look.* Washington, DC: NASW Press.

Gil, D. G. (1994). Confronting social injustice and oppression. In F. G. Reamer (Ed.), *Foundation of social work knowledge* (pp. 231–263). New York: Columbia University Press.

Gil, D. G. (2002). Challenging injustice and oppression. In M. O'Melia & K. K. Miley (Eds.), *Pathways to power: Readings in contextual social work practice* (pp. 35–54). Boston: Allyn & Bacon.

Gilbert, M. C. (2000). Spirituality in social work groups: Practitioners speak out. *Social Work with Groups, 22*(4), 67–84.

Gilbert, N., & Terrell, P. (2001). *Dimensions of social welfare policy.* Englewood Cliffs, NJ: Prentice-Hall.

Gilligan, C. (1982). *In a different voice: Psychological theory and women's development.* Cambridge, MA: Harvard University Press.

Gillman, R. (1991). From resistance to rewards: Social workers' experiences and attitudes toward AIDS. *Families in Society, 72,* 593–601.

Gilson, S. F., Bricout, J. C., & Baskind, F. R. (1998). Listening to the voices of individuals with disabilities. *Families in Society, 79*(2), 188–196.

Ginsberg, L. (1976). *Social work in rural communities: A book of readings.* New York: Council on Social Work Education.

Ginsberg, L. (1993). *Social work in rural communities: A book of readings.* Alexandria, VA: Council on Social Work Education.

Ginsberg, L. (1995). *The social work almanac* (2nd ed.). Washington, DC: NASW Press.

Gochros, H. L., Gochros, J. S., & Fischer, J. (1986). *Counseling the sexually oppressed.* Englewood Cliffs, NJ: Prentice-Hall.

Goicoechea-Balbona, A. M. (1998). Children with HIV/AIDS and their families: A successful social work intervention based on the culturally specific health care model. *Health and Social Work, 23*(1), 61+. Retrieved September 17, 2003, from InfoTrac Expanded Academic ASAP database.

Goldberg-Glen, R., Sands, R. G., Cole, R. D., & Cristofalo, C. (1998). Multigeneratonal patterns and internal structures in families in which grandparents raise grandchildren. *Families in Society, 79*(5), 477–489.

Goldstein, H. (1973). *Social work practice: A unitary approach.* Columbia, SC: University of South Carolina Press.

Goldstein, H. (1987). The neglected moral link in social work practice. *Social Work, 32,* 181–186.

Goldstein, H. (1990). The knowledge base of social work practice: Theory, wisdom, analogue, or art? *Families in Society, 71,* 32–43.

Gonyea, J. G., Seltzer, G. B., Gerstein, C., & Young, M. (1988). Acceptance of hospital-based respite care by families and elders. *Health and Social Work, 13,* 201–208.

Goode, R. A. (2000). *Social work practice in home health care.* New York: Haworth Press.

Goodman, K., & Rothman, B. (1986). Group work in infertility treatment. In M. Parnes (Ed.), *Innovations in social group work: Feedback from practice to theory* (pp. 75–94). New York: Haworth Press.

Googins, B., & Godfrey, J. (1985). The evolution of occupational social work. *Social Work, 30,* 396–402.

Gordon, N. (1995). Adult day care. In R. L. Edwards (Ed.), *Encyclopedia of social work: Vol. 1* (19th ed.) (pp. 74–82). Washington, DC: NASW Press.

Gordon, W. E. (1969). Basic constructs for an integrative and generative conception of social work. In G. Hearn (Ed.), *The general systems approach: Contributions toward an holistic conception of social work* (pp. 5–11). New York: Council on Social Work Education.

Gotterer, R. (2001). The spiritual dimension in clinical social work practice: A client perspective. *Families in Society, 82*(2), 187–193.

Gottlieb, B. H. (1985). Assessing and strengthening the impact of social support on mental health. *Social Work, 30,* 293–300.

Gramick, J. (1983). Homophobia: A new challenge. *Social Work, 28,* 137–141.

Grant, B. F. (2000). Estimates of U.S. children exposed to alcohol abuse and dependence in the family. *American Journal of Public Health, 90*(1), 112–115. Retrieved June 29 2003, from EBSCOhost Academic Search Elite.

Graverholtz, L. (2000). An ecological approach to understanding sexual revictimization: Linking personal, interpersonal, and sociocultural factors and processes. *Child Maltreatment, 5*(1), 5–17.

Green, J. (2000). Introduction. In P. Currah & S. Minter (Eds.), *Transgender equality: A handbook for activists and policymakers* (pp. 2–12). The Policy Institute of the National Gay and Lesbian Task Force. Retrieved September 13, 2003, from www.ngltf.org/downloads/transeq.pdf

Green, J. W. (1999). *Cultural awareness in the human services: A multi-ethnic approach* (3rd ed.). Boston: Allyn & Bacon.

Green, J. W., & Leigh, J. W. (1985, November). *The ethnographic interview: A contribution to the skill of ethnic competent practice.* Paper presented at the NASW Professional Symposium, Chicago, IL.

Greenbaum, J., & Markel, G. (1990). Crisis prevention for parents of children with handicapping conditions. In H. J. Parad & L. G. Parad (Eds.), *Crisis intervention book 2: The practitioners' source book for brief therapy* (pp. 359–385). Milwaukee, WI: Family Service America.

Greene, R. R. (1992). Case management: An arena for social work practice. In B. S. Vourlekis & R. R. Greene (Eds.), *Social work case management* (pp. 11–25). New York: Aldine de Gruyter.

Greene, R. R. (1999). *Human behavior theory and social work practice.* New York: Aldine de Gruyter.

Greenwood, E. (1957). Attributes of a profession. *Social Work, 2,* 45–55.

Greif, G. L. (1986). The ecosystems perspective "Meets the press." *Social Work, 31,* 225–226.

Grier, W. H., & Cobbs, P. M. (1968). *Black rage.* New York: Basic Books.

Grinnell, R. M. (1973). Environmental modification: Casework's concern or casework's neglect. *Social Service Review, 47,* 208–220.

Grinnell, R. M., Kyte, N. S., & Bostwick, G. J. (1981). Environmental modification. In A. N. Maluccio (Ed.), *Promoting competence in clients: A new/old approach to social work practice* (pp. 152–184). New York: The Free Press.

Groze, V. (1996). *Successful adoptive families: A longitudinal study of special needs adoption.* Westport, CT: Praeger.

Gullotta, T. P. (1987). Prevention's technology. *Journal of Primary Prevention, 8,* 4–23.

Gumpert, J., Saltman, J. E., & Sauer-Jones, D. (2000). Toward identifying the unique characteristics of social work practice in rural areas: From the voices of practitioners. *Journal of Baccalaureate Social Work, 6*(1), 19–35.

Gurteen, S. H. (1882). *Handbook of charity organization.* Buffalo: The Currior Company.

Gutheil, I. A., & Congress, E. (2000). Resiliency in older people: A paradigm for practice. In E. Norman (Ed.), *Resiliency enhancement: Putting the strengths perspective into social work practice* (pp. 40–52). New York: Columbia University Press.

Gutiérrez, L. M. (1990). Working with women of color: An empowerment perspective. *Social Work, 35,* 149–153.

Gutiérrez, L. M. (1994). Beyond coping: An empowerment perspective on stressful life events. *Journal of Sociology and Social Welfare, 21,* 201–219.

Gutiérrez, L., & Lewis, E. (1999). *Empowering women of color.* New York: Columbia University Press.

Hackl, K. L., Somlai, A. M., Kelly, J. A., & Kalichman, S. C. (1997). Women living with HIV/ AIDS: The dual challenge of being a patient and caregiver. *Health and Social Work, 22*(5), 53–62.

Hall, A. S., & Torres, I. (2002). Partnerships in preventing adolescent stress: Increasing self-esteem, coping, and support through effective counseling. *Journal of Mental Health Counseling, 24*(2), 97–109.

Halpern, C. (1996). Listening in on deaf culture: Standards. *International Journal of Multicultural Studies, 5*(2). Retrieved September 14, 2003, from www.colorado.edu/journals/standards/V5N2/ AWARD/halpern2.html

Halter, A. P. (1994). Chipping away at General Assistance: A matter of economics or an attack on poor people? *Social Work, 39,* 705–709.

Hamberger, L. K. (1996). Intervention in gay male intimate violence requires coordinated efforts on multiple levels. In C. M. Renzetti & C. H. Miley (Eds.), *Violence in gay and lesbian domestic partnerships* (pp. 83–92). New York: Harrington Park Press.

Hansen, D. J., Sedlar, G., & Warner-Rogers, J. E. (1999). Child physical abuse. In R. T. Ammerman & M. Hersen (Eds.), *Assessment of family violence: A clinical and legal sourcebook* (pp. 127–156). New York: John Wiley & Sons.

Harbison, J. (1999). Models of intervention for "Elder Abuse and Neglect": A Canadian perspective on ageism, participation, and empowerment. *Journal of Elder Abuse & Neglect,* 10(3/4), 1–17.

Hare, J. (1994). Concerns and issues faced by families headed by a lesbian couple. *Families in Society, 75,* 27–35.

Harrington, M. (1962). *The other America: Poverty in the United States.* Baltimore: Penguin Books.

Harrison, P. M., & Karberg, J. C. (2003). Prison and jail inmates at midyear 2002. *Bureau of Justice Statistics Bulletin.* Retrieved August 23, 2003, from www.ojp.usdoj.gov/bjs/pub/pdf/pjim02.pdf

Hartman, A. (1986a). Jarrett, Mary Cromwell. In W. I. Trattner (Ed.), *Biographical dictionary of social welfare in America* (pp. 421–424). New York: Greenwood Press.

Hartman, A. (1986b). The life and work of Bertha Reynolds: Implications for education and practice today. *Smith College Studies in Social Work, 56*(2), 79–94.

Hartman, A. (1990, October). *Family-based strategies for empowering families.* Paper presented at the Family Empowerment Conference of the University of Iowa, School of Social Work, Iowa City, IA.

Hartman, A. (1993). The professional is political. *Social Work, 38,* 365–366, 504.

Hartman, A., & Laird, J. (1983). *Family-centered social work practice.* New York: The Free Press.

Hasenfeld, Y. (1987). Power in social work practice. *Social Service Review, 61,* 470–483.

Healy, K. (2001). Participatory action research and social work: A critical appraisal. *International Social Work, 44*(1), 93–105.

Hebert, L. E., Scherr, P. A., Bienias, J. L., Bennett, D. A., & Evans, D. A. (2003). Alzheimer disease in the U.S. population: Prevalence estimates using the 2000 census. *Archives of Neurology, 60*(8), 1119–1122.

Hearn, G. (1969). Introduction. In G. Hearn (Ed.), *The general systems approach: Contributions toward an holistic conception of social work* (pp. 1–4). New York: Council on Social Work Education.

Heise, L., Ellsberg, M., & Gottemoeller, M. (1999). Ending violence against women. *Population Reports, 27*(4), 4+. Retrieved August 20, 2000, from InfoTrac Expanded Academic ASAP database.

Henig, R. M., & Eastman, P. (1995). Combating Alzheimer's disease: Slowing down Alzheimer's. *AARP Bulletin, 36*(1), 18–20.

Hepworth, D., Rooney, R. H., & Larsen, J. A. (1997). *Direct social work practice* (5th ed.). Pacific Grove, CA: Brooks/Cole.

Herrerias, C. (1989). Prevention of child abuse and neglect in the Hispanic community: The MADRE parent education program. *Journal of Primary Prevention, 9,* 104–119.

Hersch, P. (1991). What is gay? What is straight? *The Family Therapy Networker, 15*(1), 40–41.

Hicks, J., Mowry, G. E., & Burke, R. E. (1970). *A history of American democracy.* New York: Houghton Mifflin.

Highlights and Trends: Social Security (OASDI). (2002). *Social Security Bulletin: Annual Statistical Supplement,* p. 1. Retrieved October 2, 2003, from www.ssa.gov/policy/docs/statcomps/supplement/2002/supp02.pdf

Hilgartner, S., & Bosk, C. L. (1988). The rise and fall of social problems: A public arenas model. *American Journal of Sociology, 94*(1), 53–78.

Hines, P. M., & Boyd-Franklin, N. (1996). African American families. In M. McGoldrick, J. Giordano, & J. K. Pearce (Eds.), *Ethnicity and family therapy* (2nd ed.) (pp. 66–84). New York: Guilford Press.

Hinterlong, J., Rozario, P. Morrow-Howell, N., & Sherraden, M. (2000, November). Productive aging: Individual and institutional challenges. Paper presented for NASW Social Work 2000 Conference, Baltimore, MD.

Ho, M. K. (1987). *Family therapy with ethnic minorities.* Newbury Park, CA: Sage.

Ho, M. K. (1989). Social work practice with Asian Americans. In A. Morales & B. Sheafor (Eds.), *Social work: A profession of many faces* (5th ed.) (pp. 521–541). Boston: Allyn & Bacon.

Hobart, K. R. (2001). Death and dying and the social work role. *Journal of Gerontological Social Work, 36*(3/4), 181–192.

Hodge, D. R. (2000). Spirituality: Towards a theoretical framework. *Social Thought, 19*(4), 1–20.

Hodson, W. (1925). Is social work professional? A reexamination of the question. In *Proceedings of the National Conference of Social Work, 1925, Denver* (pp. 629–636). Chicago: The University of Chicago Press.

Hofstadter, R. (1955). *Social Darwinism and American thought.* Boston: Beacon Press.

Hogan, P. T., & Siu, S. F. (1988). Minority children and the child welfare system: An historical perspective. *Social Work, 33,* 493–498.

Holahan, C. J., Wilcox, B. L., Spearly, J. L., & Campbell, M. D. (1979). The ecological perspective in community mental health. *Community Mental Health Review, 4*(2), 1–9.

Hollingsworth, L. D. (2000). Adoption policy in the United States: A word of caution. *Social Work, 45*(2), 183–186.

Hollis, E. V., & Taylor, A. L. (1951). *Social work education in the United States.* New York: Columbia University Press.

Hollis, F. (1964). *Casework: A psychosocial therapy.* New York: Random House.

Hollis, F. (1967). Principles and assumptions underlying casework principles. In E. Younghusband (Ed.), *Social work and social values* (pp. 22–38). London: George Allen & Unwin Ltd.

Holmes, G. E., & Saleebey, D. (1993). Empowerment, the medical model and the politics of clienthood. *Journal of Progressive Human Services, 4*(1), 61–78.

Homeless Services News (1997). Project NOW Community Action Agency, Rock Island, IL.

Hooper-Briar, K., & Seck, E. T. (1995). Jobs and earnings. In R. L. Edwards (Ed.), *Encyclopedia of social work: Vol. 2* (19th ed.) (pp. 1539–1545). Washington, DC: NASW Press.

Hoover, D. W. (1986). Addams, Jane. In W. I. Trattner (Ed.), *Biographical dictionary of social welfare in America* (pp. 13–15). New York: Greenwood Press.

Hopper, K., & Baumohl, J. (1996). Redefining the cursed word: A historical interpretation of American homelessness. In J. Baumohl (Ed.), *Homelessness in America* (pp. 3–14). Phoenix, AZ: The Oryz Press.

Hopps, J. G. (1982). Oppression based on color. *Social Work, 27,* 3–5.

Hughes, M., & Demo, D. H. (1989). Self-perceptions of Black Americans: Self-esteem and personal efficacy. *American Journal of Sociology, 95,* 132–159.

Human Genome Program. (2003). *Ethical, legal, and social issues.* Human Genome Project Information, U.S. Department of Energy Office of Science, Office of Biological and Environmental Research. Retrieved September 25, 2003, from www.ornl.gov/TechResources/Human_Genome/elsi/elsi.html

Humphreys, K., & Moos, R. H. (1996). Reduced substance-abuse-related health care costs among voluntary participants in alcoholics anonymous. *Psychiatric Services,* 47, 709–713.

Humphreys, N. A. (2003). Hate crimes. In R. A. English (Ed.), *Encyclopedia of social work: 2003 supplement* (pp. 71–81). Washington, DC: NASW Press.

Hungerford, T., Rossette, M., Iams, H., & Koenig, M. (2001/2002). Trends in the economic status of the elderly, 1976–2000. *Social Security Bulletin, 64*(3), 12–22.

Hunter, A. M., & Pudim, R. A. (1985). Addictive behavior and the justice system. In H. B. Milkman & H. J. Shaffer (Eds.), *The addictions: Multidisiciplinary perspectives and treatments* (pp. 75–84). Lexington, MA: D. C. Heath.

Hunter, J., & Schaecher, R. (1995). Gay and lesbian adolescents. In R. L. Edwards (Ed.), *Encyclopedia of social work: Vol. 2* (19th ed.) (pp. 1055–1063). Washington, DC: NASW Press.

Hunter, M. S., & Saleeby, D. (1977). Spirit and substance: Beginnings in the education of radical social workers. *Journal of Education for Social Workers, 13*(2), 60–67.

Hutchinson, I. W. (1999). Alcohol, fear, and woman abuse. *Sex roles: A Journal of Research, 40*(11), 893+. Retrieved September 23, 2003, from InfoTrac Expanded Academic ASAP database.

Hyslop, J. H. (1898). Causes of poverty. *The Charities Review, 7,* 383–389.

Ifill, D. (1989). Teaching minority practice for professional application. *Journal of Social Work Education, 25,* 29–35.

Indyk, D., Belville, R., Lachapelle, S., Gordon, G., & Dewart, T. (1993). A community-based approach to HIV case management: Systematizing the unmanageable. *Social Work, 38,* 380–387.

Ingalls, J. D. (1973). *A trainer's guide to andragogy* (United States Department of Health, Education and Welfare Publication No srs73–05031). Washington, DC: U.S. Government Printing Office.

Ingram, C. (1996). Kinship care: From last resort to first choice. *Child Welfare, 75*(5), 550–566.

International Federation of Social Workers. (1994). *The ethics of social work: Principles and standards.* Retrieved September 14, 2003, from www.ifsw.org/Publications/4.4.pub.html

International Federation of Social Workers. (1998). *IFSW policy papers: International policy on refugees.* Retrieved September 21, 2003, from www.ifsw.org/Publications/4.5.7.pub.htm

International Federation of Social Workers. (2000). *International Federation of Social Workers: Definition of social work.* Retrieved August 11, 2003, from www.ifsw.org/Publications/4.6e.pub.html

International Federation of Social Workers. (2003). *Welcome to IFSW.* Retrieved September 21, 2003, from www.ifsw.org/

Ivanoff, A., Smyth, N. J., & Finnigan, D. J. (1993). Social work behind bars: Preparation for fieldwork in correctional institutions. *Journal of Teaching in Social Work, 7*(1), 137–149.

Iverson, R. R. (1998). Occupational social work for the 21st century. *Social Work, 43*(6), 551–566.

Izard, C. (1977). *Human emotions.* New York: Plenum.

Janis, I., & Rodin, J. (1980). Attribution, control and decision making: Social psychology and health care. In G. Stone, F. Cohen, & N. Adler (Eds.), *Health Psychology* (pp. 487–521). San Francisco: Jossey-Bass.

Jankowski, S., Videka-Sherman, L., & Laquidara-Dickinson, K. (1996). Social support networks of confidants to people with AIDS. *Social Work, 41,* 206–213.

Jenkins, S. (1983). Social service priorities and resource allocation. In A. Rosenblatt & D. Waldfogel (Eds.), *Handbook of clinical social work* (pp. 814–825). San Francisco: Jossey-Bass.

Johnson, A. K. (1995). Homelessness. In R. L. Edwards (Ed.), *Encyclopedia of social work: Vol. 2* (19th ed.) (pp. 1338–1346). Washington, DC: NASW Press.

Johnson, L. C. (1998). *Social work practice: A generalist approach* (5th ed.). Boston: Allyn & Bacon.

Johnson, M. E., Brems, C., & Burke, S. (2002). Recognizing comorbidity among drug users in treatment. *American Journal of Drug and Alcohol Abuse, 28*(2), 243–262.

Joint Commission on Mental Illness and Health. (1961). *Action for mental health.* New York: Science Editions.

Joint United Nations Programme on HIV/AIDS. (2002a). *Global summary of the HIV/AIDS epidemic: December 2002.* Retrieved June 28, 2003, from www.unaids.org/worldaidsday/2002/press/update/epiupdate_en.pdf

Joint United Nations Programme on HIV/AIDS. (2002b). *The pandemic's toll on children.* Retrieved June 28, 2003, from www.unaids.org/barcelona/presskit/childrenonthebrink/pandemicsToll.pdf

Joint United Nations Programme on HIV/AIDS. (2002c). *Impact of AIDS worsens African famine—Epidemic spreading rapidly in new areas of the world, says new report.* Retrieved June 28, 2003, from www.unaids.org/worldaidsday/2002/press/WAD02EpiPR_en.docjournals/standards/V5N2/AWARD/halpern.html

Jones, L. W. R. (1995). Unemployment compensation and workers' compensation. In R. L. Edwards (Ed.), *Encyclopedia of social work: Vol. 3* (19th ed.) (pp. 2413–2417). Washington, DC: NASW Press.

Joseph, M. V. (1988). Religion and social work practice. *Social Casework, 69,* 443–452.

Juvenile Court Centennial Initiative. (n.d.). *Fact Sheets: Juvenile justice system: Children in adult jails.* Retrieved October 19, 2000, from www.ojjdp.ncjrs.org/jcci/fadultjail.html

Kadushin, A. (1980). *Child Welfare Services* (3rd ed.). New York: Macmillan.

Kadushin, A., & Martin, J. A. (1988). *Child welfare services* (4th ed.). New York: Macmillan.

Kageleiry, J. (1999). *Martha's Vineyard Chamber of Commerce: The island that spoke by hand.* Retrieved November 8, 2000, from www.mvy.com/spokehand.html

Kane, N. M. (1989). The home care crisis of the nineties. *The Gerontologist, 29,* 24–31.

Kane, R. A., & Caplan, A. L. (1992). *Ethical conflicts in the management of home care: The case manager's dilemma.* New York: Springer.

Kaplan, C. P., & Turner, S. (1996). Promoting resilience strategies: A modified consultation model. *Social Work in Education, 18*(3), 158–168.

Karger, H. J., & Stoesz, D. (2002). *American social welfare policy: A pluralist approach* (4th ed.). New York: Longman.

Keigher, S. M. (2000). Knowledge development in health & social work. *Health and Social Work 25*(1), 3+. Retrieved September 23, 2003, from InfoTrac Expanded Academic ASAP database.

Keith-Lucas, A. (1972). *The giving and taking of help.* Chapel Hill, NC: University of North Carolina Press.

Kelly, P. (1992). Healthy stepfamily functioning. *Families in Society, 72,* 579–587.

Kemp, S. P. (2001). Environment through a gendered lens: From person-in-environment to woman-in-environment. *Affilia, 16*(1), 7+. Retrieved October 7, 2002, from EBSCOhost Academic Search Elite database.

Kemp, S. P., Whittaker, J. K., & Tracy, E. M. (1997). *Person-environment practice: The social ecology of interpersonal helping.* New York: Aldine De Gruyter.

Kemp, S. P., Whittaker, J. K., & Tracy, E. M. (2002). Contextual social work practice. In M. O'Melia & K. K. Miley (Eds.), *Pathways to power: Readings in contextual social work practice* (pp. 15–34). Boston: Allyn & Bacon.

Kessler, R. C., Mickelson, K. D., & Zhao, S. (1997). Patterns and correlates of self-help group membership in the United States. *Social Policy, 27*(3), 27+. Retrieved September 17, 2003, from InfoTrac Expanded Academic ASAP database.

Kettner, P. M., & Martin, L. L. (1993). Performance, accountability, and purchase of service contracting. *Administration in Social Work, 17*(1), 61–79.

Kettner, P. M., & Martin, L. L. (1994). Purchase of service at 20: Are we using it well? *Public Welfare, 52*(3), 14–20, 42.

Kettner, P. M., & Martin, L. L. (1996). The impact of declining resources and purchase of service contracting on private, nonprofit agencies. *Administration in Social Work, 20*(3), 21–38.

Kettner, P., & Martin, L. (1998). Accountability in purchase-of-service contracting. In M. Gibelman & H. W. Demone (Eds.), *The privatization of human services: Policy and practice issues: Vol. 1* (pp. 183–204). New York: Springer.

Khinduka, S. K. (1987). Social work and the human services. In A. Minahan (Ed.), *Encyclopedia of social work: Vol. 2* (18th ed.) (pp. 684–695). Silver Spring, MD: National Association of Social Workers.

Kieffer, C. (1984). Citizen empowerment: A developmental perspective. In J. Rappaport, C. Swift, & R. Hess (Eds.), *Studies in empowerment: Steps toward understanding and action* (pp. 9–36). New York: Haworth Press.

Kirk, S. A., & Rosenblatt, A. (1983). New applications of research in clinical practice. In A. Rosenblatt & D. Waldfogel (Eds.), *Handbook of clinical work* (pp. 549–559). San Francisco: Jossey-Bass.

Kitano, H. H. (1987). Asian Americans. In A. Minahan (Ed.), *Encyclopedia of social work: Vol. 1* (18th ed.) (pp. 156–171). Silver Spring, MD: National Association of Social Workers.

Kivisto, P. (1995). *Americans all.* Belmont, CA: Wadsworth.

Kivnick, H. G., & Murray, S. V. (2001). Life strengths interview guide: Assessing elder clients' strengths. *Journal of Gerontological Social Work, 34*(4), 7–31.

Knowles, M. S. (1980). *The modern practice of adult education: From pedagogy to andragogy.* Chicago: Follett.

Kohlberg, L. (1973). Continuities and discontinuities in childhood and adult moral development revisited. In *Collected papers on moral development and moral education.* Cambridge, MA: Harvard University Moral Education Research Foundation.

Kopp, J. (1989). Self-observation: An empowerment strategy in assessment. *Social Casework, 60,* 276–281.

Kosberg, J. I. (1990). Assistance to victims of crime and abuse. In A. Monk (Ed.), *Handbook of gerontological services* (2nd ed.) (pp. 450–473). New York: Columbia University Press.

Kosmin, B. A., Mayer, E., & Keysar, A. (2001). *American religious identification survey 2001.* New York: The Graduate Center of the City University of New York. Retrieved August 23, 2003, from www.gc.cuny.edu/studies/aris.pdf

Kramer, R. M. (1994). Voluntary agencies and the contract culture: "Dream or nightmare?" *Social Service Review, 68,* 33–60.

Kreider, R. M., & Fields, J. M. (2001). Number, timing, and duration of marriages and divorces: Fall 1996. *Current Population Reports, P70-80.* U.S. Census Bureau, Washington, DC. Retrieved June 29, 2003, from www.census.gov/prod/2002pubs/p70-80.pdf

Krell, G. I., & Rosenberg, G. (1990). Predicting patterns of social work staffing in hospital settings. In K. W. Davidson & S. S. Clarke (Eds.), *Social work in health care: Part II* (pp. 617–640). New York: Haworth Press.

Krogsrud, K. (1965). *Social Darwinism and social welfare policy.* Unpublished manuscript. University of Chicago, Chicago, IL.

Kropf, N. P., & DeWeaver, K. L. (1996). Social work practice with persons with developmental disabilities. In D. F. Harrison, B. A. Thyer, & J. S. Wodarski (Eds.), *Cultural diversity and social work practice* (2nd ed.) (pp. 176–200). Springfield, IL: Charles C Thomas.

Kübler-Ross, E. (1969). *On death and dying.* New York: Macmillan.

Kuhn, M. (1987). Politics of aging: The Gray Panthers. In L. L. Carstensen & B. A. Edelstein (Eds.), *Handbook of clinical gerontology* (pp. 376–386). New York: Pergamon Press.

Kuntz, B., Groze, V., & Yates, W. R. (1992). Bulimia: A systemic family history perspective. *Families in Society, 73,* 604–612.

Kurzman, P. A. (1987). Industrial social work. In A. Minahan (Ed.), *Encyclopedia of social work: Vol. 1* (18th ed.) (pp. 899–910). Silver Spring, MD: National Association of Social Workers.

Kurzman, P. A., & Akabas, S. H. (1993). *Work and well-being: The occupational social work advantage.* Washington, DC: NASW Press.

Kyrouz, E. M., & Humphreys, K. (n.d.). *A review of research on the effectiveness of self-help mutual aid groups.* Retrieved September 14, 2003, from http://telosnet.com/review/selfres.html

Laird, J. (1994). Lesbian families: A cultural perspective. *Smith College Studies in Social Work, 64,* 263–296.

Laird, J. (1996). Family-centered practice with lesbian and gay families. *Families in Society, 77*(9), 559–572.

Laird, J., & Hartman, A. (1985). Keeping families together. In J. Laird & A. Hartman (Eds.), *A handbook of child welfare: Context, knowledge, and practice* (pp. 329–333). New York: The Free Press.

Langley, J. (2001). Developing anti-oppressive empowering social work practice with older lesbian women and gay men. *British Journal of Social Work, 31,* 917–932.

Lapham, E. V., Weiss, J. O., & Allen, L. (2000, November). Multicultural and social implications of the new genetics: Challenges for the 21st century. Paper presented for NASW Social Work 2000 Conference, Baltimore, MD.

Larson, S. et al. (2000). Prevalence of mental retardation or developmental disabilities. *MR/DD Data Brief, 2*(1). Retrieved August 24, 2003, from http://rtc.umn.edu/nhis/databrief2/dtbrf2.pdf

Lawton, M. P. (1980). *Environment and aging.* Monterey, CA: Brooks/Cole.

Lawton, M. P., & Nahemow, L. (1973). Ecology and the aging process. In C. Eisdorfer & M. P. Lawton (Eds.), *The psychology of adult development and aging* (pp. 619–675). Washington, DC: American Psychological Association.

Lee, J. A. B. (2001). *The empowerment approach to social work practice* (2nd ed.). New York: Columbia University Press.

Lefrancois, G. R. (1995). *Of children: An introduction to child development* (8th ed.). Belmont, CA: Wadsworth.

Leiby, J. (1984). Charity organization reconsidered. *Social Service Review, 58,* 523–53.

Lenrow, P. B., & Burch, R. W. (1981). Mutual aid and professional services. In B. H. Gottlieb (Ed.), *Social networks and social supports: Vol. 4, Sage Studies in Community Mental Health* (pp. 233–257). Beverly Hills, CA: Sage.

Leon, A. M., Altholz, A. S., & Dziegielewski, S. F. (1999). Compassion fatigue: Considerations for working with the elderly. *Journal of Gerontological Social Work, 32*(1), 43–61.

Leonard, P. (1976). The function of social work in society. In N. Timms & D. Watson (Eds.), *Talking about welfare: Readings in philosophy and social policy* (pp. 252–266). Boston: Routledge and Kegan Paul.

Lerner, M. J. (1965). Evaluation of performance as a function of performer's reward and attractiveness. *Journal of Personality and Social Psychology, 1,* 355–360.

Lerner, M. J., & Simmons, C. H. (1966). Observer's reaction to the "innocent victim": Compassion or rejection? *Journal of Personality and Social Psychology, 4,* 203–210.

Leslie, L. K., Landsverk, J., Horton, M. B., Ganger, W., & Newton, R. R. (2000). The heterogeneity of children and their experiences in kinship care. *Child Welfare, 79*(3), 315–334.

Lesser, J. G. (2000). Clinical social work and family medicine: A partnership in community services. *Health and Social Work, 25*(2), 19+. Retrieved September 23, 2003, from InfoTrac Expanded Academic ASAP database.

Leung, P., Cheung, K. M., & Stevenson, K. M. (1994). A strengths approach to ethnically sensitive practive for child protective service workers. *Child Welfare, 53,* 707–721.

Levesque, R. J. R. (1999). *Sexual abuse of children: A human rights perspective.* Bloomington, IN: Indiana University Press.

Levinson, D. J. (1978). *The seasons of a man's life.* New York: Alfred A. Knopf.

Levy, C. J. (1996, November 17). Welfare and the working poor. *New York Times.* Retrieved September 14, 2003, from http://civic.net/civic-values.archive/199611/msg 00162.html

Levy, C. S. (1973). The value base of social work. *Journal of Education for Social Work, 9,* 34–42.

Levy, C. S. (1976). *Social work ethics.* New York: Human Sciences Press.

Levy, E. F. (1992). Strengthening the coping resources of lesbian families. *Families in Society, 73,* 23–31.

Lewandowski, C. A., & Glenmaye, L. F. (2002). Teams in child welfare settings: Interprofessional and collaborative processes. *Families in Society, 83*(3), 245–254.

Lewis, J. S. (1996). Sense of coherence and the strengths perspective with older persons. *Journal of Gerontological Social Work, 26*(3/4), 99–112.

Lewis, O. (1969). The culture of poverty. In D. Moynihan (Ed.), *On understanding poverty.* New York: Basic Books.

Lewis, R. G., & Ho, M. (1975). Social work with Native Americans. *Social Work, 20,* 379–382.

Lewis, R. G., & Ho, M. (1989). Social work with Native Americans. In A. Morales & B. Sheafor (Eds.), *Social work: A profession of many faces* (5th ed.) (pp. 511–519). Boston: Allyn & Bacon.

Libassi, M. F., & Maluccio, A. N. (1986). Competence-centered social work: Prevention in action. *Journal of Primary Prevention, 6,* 168–180.

Licther, D. T., & Crowley, M. L. (2002). Poverty in America: Beyond welfare reform. *Population Bulletin, 57*(2). Retrieved August 30, 2003, from www.prb.org/Template.cfm?Section=Population_Bulletin1&template=/ContentManagement/ContentDisplay.cfm&ContentID=6084

Lieberman, A. A. (1986). Cannon, Ida Maud. In W. I. Trattner (Ed.), *Biographical dictionary of social welfare in America* (pp. 161–164). New York: Greenwood Press.

Liederman, D. S. (1995). Child welfare. In R. L. Edwards (Ed.), *Encyclopedia of social work: Vol. 1* (19th ed.) (pp. 424–433). Washington, DC: NASW Press.

Lin, A. M. (1995). Mental health overview. In R. L. Edwards (Ed.), *Encyclopedia of social work: Vol. 2* (19th ed.) (pp. 1705–1711). Washington, DC: NASW Press.

Link, B., Phelan, J., & Bresnahan, M. (1995). Lifetime and five-year prevalence of homelessness in the United States: New evidence on an old debate. *American Journal of Orthopsychiatry, 65,* 347–354.

Link, B. G., Phelan, J. C., Stueve, A., Moore, R. E., Bresnahan, M., & Struening, E. L. (1996). Public attitudes and beliefs about homeless people. In J. Baumohl (Ed.), *Homelessness in America* (pp. 144–148). Phoenix, AZ: Oryz Press.

Linsk, N. L., & Keigher, S. M. (1997). Of magic bullets and social justice: Emerging challenges of recent advances in AIDS treatment. *Health and Social Work, 22*(1), 70–74.

Linzer, N. (1999). *Resolving ethical dilemmas in social work practice.* Boston: Allyn & Bacon.

Lipsky, M. (1980). *Street-level bureaucracy: Dilemmas of the individual in public services.* New York: Russell Sage Foundation.

Lipsky, M. (1984). Bureaucratic disentitlement in social welfare programs. *Social Service Review, 58,* 3–27.

Lloyd, G. A. (1995). HIV/AIDS: An overview. In R. L. Edwards (Ed.), *Encyclopedia of social work: Vol. 2* (19th ed.) (pp. 1257–1290). Washington, DC: NASW Press.

Locke, B., Lohmann, R., & Meehan, K. (1985). A model for human services planning, present and future. In A. Summers, J. M. Schriver, P. Sundet, & R. Meinert (Eds.), *Social work in rural areas: Proceedings of the Tenth National Institute on Social Work in Rural Areas at Columbia, MO* (p. 77). Arkansas College.

Loewenberg, F. M. (1988). *Religion and social work practice in contemporary American society.* New York: Columbia University Press.

Loewenberg, F. M., & Dolgoff, R. (1992). *Ethical decisions for social work practice* (4th ed.). Itasca, IL: F. E. Peacock Publishers.

Loewenberg, F. M., Dolgoff, R., & Harrington, D. (2000). *Ethical decisions for social work practice* (6th ed.). Belmont, CA: Wadsworth.

Lowe, G., Zimmerman, L., & Reid, P. N. (1989, March). *How we see ourselves: A critical review of text versions of social work's professional evolution.* Paper presented at the annual program meeting of the Council on Social Work Education, Chicago, IL.

Lowenthal, B. (1999). Effects of maltreatment and ways to promote children's resiliency. *Childhood Education, 75*(4), 204–209. Retrieved September 17, 2003, from InfoTrac Expanded Academic ASAP database.

Lowy, L., Bloksberg, L. M., & Walberg, H. J. (1971). *Integrative learning and teaching in schools of social work.* New York: Association Press.

Lubove, R. (1965). *The professional altruist: The emergence of social work as a career, 1880–1930* (reprinted 1975). New York: Atheneum.

Lum, D. (1996). *Social work practice and people of color: A process stage approach* (3rd ed.). Pacific Grove, CA: Brooks/Cole.

Lum, D. (2004). *Social work practice and people of color: A process-stage approach.* Pacific Grove, CA: Brooks/Cole.

Lundblad, K. S. (1995). Jane Addams and social reform: A role model for the 1990s. *Social Work, 40,* 661–669.

Lupton, C. (1998). User empowerment or family self-reliance? The Family Group Conference model. *British Journal of Social Work, 28*(1), 107–128.

Maas, H., & Engler, R. (1959). *Children in need of parents.* New York: Columbia University Press.

Macht, M., & Quam, J. (1986). *Social work: An introduction.* Columbus, OH: Charles E. Merrill.

MacIver, R. M. (1964). *Power transformed.* New York: Macmillan.

Macrae, C. N., & Bodenhausen, G. V. (2000). Social cognition: Thinking categorically about others. *Annual Review of Psychology, 31*(1), 93–120. Retrieved September 17, 2003, from InfoTrac Expanded Academic ASAP database.

Malone, D., McKinsey, P. D., Thyer, B. A., & Straka, E. (2000). Social work early intervention for young children with developmental disabilities. *Health and Social Work, 25*(3), 169+. Retrieved September 23, 2003, from InfoTrac Expanded Academic ASAP database.

Maluccio, A. N. (1979). *Learning from clients: Interpersonal helping as viewed by clients and social workers.* New York: The Free Press.

Maluccio, A. N. (1981). Competence oriented social work practice: An ecological approach. In A. N. Maluccio (Ed.), *Promoting competence in clients: A new/old approach to social work practice* (pp. 1–24). New York: The Free Press.

Maluccio, A. N. (1983). Planned use of life experiences. In A. Rosenblatt & D. Waldfogel (Eds.), *Handbook of clinical social work* (pp. 134–154). San Francisco: Jossey-Bass.

Maluccio, A. N. (1999). Action as a vehicle for promoting competence. In B. R. Compton & B. Galaway (Eds.), *Social work processes* (6th ed.) (pp. 354–365). Pacific Grove, CA: Brooks/Cole.

Maluccio, A. N., & Whittaker, J. K. (1989). Therapeutic foster care: Implications for parental involvement. In R. P. Hawkins & J. Breiling (Eds.), *Therapeutic foster care: Critical issues* (pp. 161–181). Washington, DC: Child Welfare League of America.

Marden, C. F., Meyer, G., & Engel, M. H. (1992). *Minorities in American society* (6th ed.). New York: HarperCollins.

Markowitz, L. M. (1991). Homosexuality: Are we still in the dark? *The Family Therapy Networker, 15*(1), 27–35.

Markowitz, L. M. (1994). The cross-currents of multiculturalism. *The Family Therapy Networker, 18*(4), 18–27, 69.

Martin, S. M. (1998). Services to people with HIV in the workplace. In D. M. Aronstein & B. J. Thompson (Eds.), *HIV and social work* (pp. 403–410). New York: Haworth Press.

Martindale-Adams, J., Nichols, L. O., Burns, R., & Malone, C. (2002). Telephone support groups: A lifeline for isolated Alzheimer's disease caregivers. *Alzheimer's Care Quarterly, 3*(2), 181–189.

Martinez-Brawley, E. E. (1990). *Perspectives on the small community: Humanistic views for practitioners.* Washington, DC: NASW Press.

Martinez-Brawley, E. E. (1993). Community-oriented practice in rural social work. In L. Ginsberg (Ed.), *Social work in rural communities* (2nd ed.) (pp. 67–81). Alexandria, VA: Council on Social Work Education.

Marty, M. (1986). *Modern American religion, Vol. 1: The irony of it all, 1893–1919.* Chicago: The University of Chicago Press.

Maslach, C. (2003). Job burnout: New directions in research and intervention. *Current Directions in Psychological Science, 12*(5), 189–192.

Maslach, C., Schaufeli, W. B., & Leiter, M. P. (2001). Job burnout. *Annual Review of Psychology, 52*(1), 397–424. Retrieved November 29, 2002, from InfoTrac Expanded Academic ASAP database.

Maslow, A. H. (1970). *Motivation and personality.* New York: Harper & Row.

Mass, S. (1990). A crisis intervention model for dying patients and their families. In H. J. Parad & L. G. Parad (Eds.), *Crisis intervention book 2: The practitioner's source book for brief therapy* (pp. 275–290). Milwaukee: Family Service America.

Mather, M., & Rivers, K. (2003). *State profiles of child well-being: Results from the 2000 census.* The Annie E. Casey Foundation and the Population Reference Bureau. Retrieved August 30, 2003, from www.prb.org/Template.cfm?Section=PRB&template=/ContentManagement/ContentDisplay.cfm&ContentID=8459

Mathews T. J., Menacker F., & MacDorman M. F. (2003). Infant mortality statistics from the 2001 period linked birth/infant death data set. *National Vital Statistics Reports, 52*(2). Hyattsville, MD: National Center for Health Statistics. Retrieved September 21, 2003, from www.cdc.gov/nchs/data/nvsr/nvsr52/nvsr52_02.pdf

Maton, K. I., & Pargament, K. I. (1986). The roles of religion in prevention and promotion. *Prevention in Human Services, 5*(2), 161–205.

Maton, K. I., & Rappaport, J. (1984). Empowerment in a religious setting: A multivariate investigation. In J. Rappaport, C. Swift, & R. Hess (Eds.), *Studies in empowerment: Steps toward understanding and action* (pp. 37–72). New York: Haworth Press.

Mature Market Institute. (1999). *The MetLife juggling act study: Balancing caregiving with work and the costs involved.* Findings from a National Study by the National Alliance for Caregiving and the National Center on Women and Aging at Brandeis University. Retrieved September 15, 2003, from www.caregiving.org/JugglingStudy.pdf

Mayadas, N. S., & Segal, U. A. (2000). Refugees in the 1990s: A U.S. perspective. In P. R. Balgopal (Ed.), *Social work practice with immigrants and refugees* (pp. 198–228). New York: Columbia University Press.

Mayer, J. B., Kapust, L. R., Mulcahey, A. L., Helfand, L., Heinlein, A. N., Seltaer, M. M., Litchfield, L. C., & Levin, R. J. (1990). Empowering families of the chronically ill: A partnership experience in a hospital setting. *Social Work in Health Care, 14*(4), 73–90.

McCallion, P., & Toseland, R. W. (1995). Supportive group interventions with caregivers of frail older adults. *Social Work with Groups, 18*(1), 11–25.

McGeady, M. R. (1991). Disconnected kids: An American tragedy. *America, 164,* 639–645.

McGinn, F. (1996). The plight of rural parents caring for adult children with HIV. *Families in Society, 77*(5), 269–278.

McGoldrick, M. (1989). Women through the family life cycle. In M. McGoldrick, C. M. Anderson, & F. Walsh (Eds.), *Women in families: A framework for family therapy* (pp. 200–226). New York: W. W. Norton.

McGoldrick, M., & Carter, B. (1989). Forming a remarried family. In B. Carter & M. McGoldrick (Eds.), *The family life cycle: A framework for family therapy* (pp. 402–429). New York: Garder Press.

McGoldrick, M., Garcia-Preto, N., Hines, P. M., & Lee, E. (1989). Ethnicity and women. In M. McGoldrick, C. M. Anderson, & F. Walsh (Eds.), *Women in families: A framework for family therapy* (pp. 169–189). New York: W. W. Norton.

McGowan, B. G., & Walsh, E. M. (2000). Policy challenges for child welfare in the new century. *Child Welfare, 79*(1), 11–27.

McKinnon, J. (2003). The Black population in the United States: March 2002. *Current Population Reports, P20-541.* Washington, DC: U.S. Census Bureau. Retrieved June 30, 2003, from www.census.gov/prod/2003pubs/p20-541.pdf

McLeod, P., & Polowy, C. I. (2000). Social workers and child abuse reporting: A review of state mandatory reporting requirements. Washington, DC: National Association of Social Workers.

McMillen, J. C., Rideout, G. B., Fisher, R. H., & Tucker, J. (1997). Independent-living services: The views of former foster youth. *Families in Society, 78*(5), 471–479.

McNeece, C. A. (1983). Juvenile justice policy. In A. R. Roberts (Ed.), *Social work in juvenile and criminal justice settings* (pp. 19–43). Springfield, IL: Charles C Thomas.

McNeil, J. (2001). *Americans with disabilities: Household economic studies.* U.S. Census Bureau. Retrieved September 12, 2003, from www.census.gov/prod/2001pubs/p70-73.pdf

McNutt, J. G. (2002). New horizons in social work advocacy. *Electronic Journal of Social Work, 1*(1). Retrieved August 22, 2003, from www.ejsw.net/IssueView2.asp

McPheeters, H. L. (1971). *A core of competence for baccalaureate social welfare.* Atlanta, GA: The Undergraduate Social Welfare Manpower Project.

McWhirter, J. J., McWhirter, B. T., McWhirter, A. M., & McWhirter, E. H. (1998). *At-risk youth: A comprehensive response.* Pacific Grove, CA: Brooks/Cole.

Mehrabian, A. (1981). *Silent messages* (2nd ed.). Belmont, CA: Wadsworth.

Mencher, S. (1967). *Poor law to poverty program.* Pittsburgh: University of Pittsburgh Press.

Merton, R. K. (1949). Discrimination and the American creed. In R. M. MacIver (Ed.), *Discrimination and national welfare* (pp. 99–126). New York: Harper & Brothers.

MetLife. (1997). *The Metlife study of employer costs for working caregivers: Costs of caregiving to U.S. business.* Retrieved December 30, 2003, from http://w3.access.gpo.gov/eop/ca/pdfs/ca.pdf

Meyer, C. H. (1970). *Social work practice: A response to the urban crisis.* New York: The Free Press.

Meyer, C. H. (1983). *Clinical social work in an ecosystems perspective.* New York: Columbia University Press.

Meyer, C. H. (1987). Direct practice in social work: Overview. In A. Minahan (Ed.), *Encyclopedia of social work: Vol. 1* (18th ed.) (pp. 409–422). Silver Spring, MD: National Association of Social Workers.

Meyer, C. H. (1988). The eco-systems perspective. In R. A. Dorfman (Ed.), *Paradigms of clinical social work* (pp. 275–294). New York: Brunner/Mazel.

Miall, C. E. (1989). Reproductive technology vs. the stigma of involuntary childlessness. *Social Casework, 70,* 43–50.

Middleman, R., & Goldberg, G. (1974). *Social service delivery: A structural approach to social work practice.* New York: Columbia University Press.

Miley, K. K. (1992, April). *Religion and social work practice.* Paper presented at the Midwest Conference on Social Work Education, LaCrosse, WI.

Miley, K. K. (2002). Unacknowledged resources of aging: Empowerment for older adults. In M. O'Melia & K. K. Miley (Eds.), *Pathways to power: Readings in contextual social work practice* (pp. 230–246). Boston: Allyn & Bacon.

Miley, K., & DuBois, B. (1999). Empowering processes for social work practice. In W. Shera & L. Wells (Eds.), *Empowerment practice in social work: Developing richer conceptual foundations* (pp. 2–12). Toronto, Canada: Canadian Scholars' Press.

Miley, K., O'Melia, M., & DuBois, B. (2004). *Generalist social work practice: An empowering approach* (4th ed.). Boston: Allyn & Bacon.

Miller, C. T., & Kaiser, C. R. (2001). A theoretical perspective on coping with stigma. *Journal of Social Issues, 57*(1), 73–92.

Miller, J. G. (1995). Criminal justice: Social work roles. In R. L. Edwards (Ed.), *Encyclopedia of social work: Vol. 1* (19th ed.) (pp. 653–659). Washington, DC: NASW Press.

Miller, J. N. (1988). New management concepts in family and children's services. In P. R. Keys & L. H. Ginsberg (Eds.), *New management in human services* (pp.

212–234). Silver Spring, MD: National Association of Social Workers.

Mills, C. S., & Usher, D. (1996). A kinship care case management approach. *Child Welfare, 75*(5), 600–618.

Mills, C. W. (1959). *The sociological imagination.* New York: Oxford University Press.

Mirkin, B., & Weinberger, M. B. (2000). *The demography of population ageing.* United Nations Population Division. Retrieved August 30, 2003, from www.un.org/esa/population/\publications/bulletin42_43/weinbergermirkin.pdf

Mitchell, M. (1986). Utilizing volunteers to enhance informal social networks. *Social Casework, 67,* 290–298.

Mitchell, P., & Kitson, B. (1997). Family group conferences. *Representing Children, 10*(1), 20–28.

Mittelman, M. S. (2002). Family caregiving for people with Alzheimer's disease: Results of the NYU spouse caregiver intervention study. *Generations, 26*(1), 104–106.

Mokuau, N. (1987). Social workers' perceptions of counseling effectiveness for Asian American clients. *Social Work, 32,* 331–335.

Monahan, D. J. (2002). Teen pregnancy prevention outcomes: Implications for social work practice. *Families in Society, 83*(4), 431–439.

Monk, A. (1990). Pre-retirement planning programs. In A. Monk (Ed.), *Handbook of gerontological services* (2nd ed.) (pp. 400–419). New York: Columbia University Press.

Morales, S., & Reyes, M. (2000). Cultural and political realities for community social work practice with Puerto Ricans in the United States. In F. G. Rivera & J. L. Erlich (Eds.), *Community organization in a diverse society* (pp. 75–96). Boston: Allyn & Bacon.

Morella, C. A. (1993). Testimony at battered women and child custody litigation hearing for the United States House committee on the Judiciary, August 6, 1992. Washington, DC: U.S. Government Printing Office.

Morhardt, D., Sherrell, K., & Gross, B. (2003). Reflections of an early stage memory loss support group for persons with Alzheimer's and their family members. *Alzheimer's Care Quarterly, 4*(3), 185–188. Retrieved September 22, 2003, from InfoTrac Expanded Academic ASAP.

Moroney, R. M. (1995). Public health services. In R. L. Edwards (Ed.), *Encyclopedia of social work: Vol. 3* (19th ed.) (pp. 1967–1973). Washington, DC: NASW Press.

Morris, J. (1997). Care or empowerment? A disability rights perspective. *Social Policy and Administration, 31*(1), 45–53.

Morris, K. (1990). Domestic violence. Unpublished manuscript. Black Hawk College, Moline, IL.

Morris, R. (1986). *Rethinking social welfare: Why care for the stranger?* White Plains, NY: Longman, Inc.

Morrow-Howell, N. (2000). *Productive engagement of older adults: Effects on well-being.* St. Louis, MO: Washington University, Center for Social Development. Retrieved September 15, 2003, from gwbweb.wustl.edu/csd/Publications/2000/reportmhowell.pdf

Morton, T. D. (1999). The increasing colorization of America's child welfare system: The overrepresentation of African-American children. *Policy & Practice of Public Health Services, 57*(4), 23+. Retrieved September 17, 2003, from InfoTrac Expanded Academic ASAP database.

Moxley, D. P. (1989). *The practice of case management.* Newbury Park, CA: Sage.

Mumole, C. J. (2000). Incarcerated parents and their children. *Bureau of Justice Statistics Special Report.* Retrieved August 23, 2003, from www.ojp.usdoj.gov/bjs/pub/pdf/iptc.pdf

Muno, A., & Keenan, L. D. (2000). The after-school girls leadership program: Transforming the school environment for adolescent girls. *Social Work in Education, 22*(2), 116–128. Retrieved September 23, 2003, from EBSCO Academic Search Elite database.

Myers, D. G. (2004). *Psychology* (7th ed.). New York: Worth.

National Alliance for Caregiving and the American Association of Retired Persons. (1997). *Family Caregiving in the US: Findings from a national survey.* Retrieved September 15, 2003, from www.caregiving.org/finalreport.pdf

National Association of Home Care. (2001). *Basic statistics about home care.* Retrieved June 28, 2003, from www.nahc.org/Consumer/hcstats.html

National Association of Social Workers. (1981). *Standards for the classification of social work practice, policy statement 4.* Silver Spring, MD: Author.

National Association of Social Workers. (1993). *NASW clinical indicators for social work in psychosocial services in nursing homes.* Retrieved July 25, 2000, from www.naswdc.org/practice/standards/nursing.htm

National Association of Social Workers. (1999a). *Code of ethics.* Washington, DC: NASW Press.

National Association of Social Workers. (1999b). International policy on human rights. In author (2003), *Social work speaks: National Association of Social Workers policy statements 2003–2006* (6th ed.) (pp. 209–217). Washington, DC: NASW Press.

National Association of Social Workers. (1999c). Professional impairment. In author (2003), *Social work speaks: National Association of Social Workers policy statements 2003–2006* (6th ed.) (pp. 280–284). Washington, DC: NASW Press.

National Association of Social Workers. (1999d). Health care. In author (2003), *Social work speaks: National*

Association of Social Workers policy statements 2003–2006 (6th ed.) (pp. 167–175). Washington, DC: NASW Press.

National Association of Social Workers. (1999e). Genetics. In author (2003), *Social work speaks: National Association of Social Workers policy statements 2003–2006* (6th ed.) (pp. 161–166). Washington, DC: NASW Press.

National Association of Social Workers. (1999f). HIV and AIDS. In author (2003), *Social work speaks: National Association of Social Workers policy statements 2003–2006* (6th ed.) (pp. 176–184). Washington, DC: NASW Press.

National Association of Social Workers. (1999g). People with disabilities. In author (2003), *Social work speaks: National Association of Social Workers policy statements 2003–2006* (6th ed.) (pp. 270–275). Washington, DC: NASW Press.

National Association of Social Workers. (1999h). Family policy. In author (2003), *Social work speaks: National Association of Social Workers policy statements 2003–2006* (6th ed.) (pp. 132–137). Washington, DC: NASW Press.

National Association of Social Workers. (2000). *Social workers and genetics education important for the future.* Retrieved September 3, 2000, from www.socialworkers.org/NASW/press_release/genetics.htm

National Association of Social Workers. (2002a). Rural social work. In author (2003), *Social work speaks: National Association of Social Workers policy statements 2003–2006* (6th ed.) (pp. 298–303). Washington, DC: NASW Press.

National Association of Social Workers. (2002b). Social services. In author (2003), *Social work speaks: National Association of Social Workers policy statements 2003–2006* (6th ed.) (pp. 327–337). Washington, DC: NASW Press.

National Association of Social Workers. (2002c). *Reauthorization of the Personal Responsibility and Work Opportunity Reconciliation Act: Improving assistance to recipients with multiple barriers to self-sufficiency.* Retrieved August 23, 2003, from www.social workers.org/advocacy/welfare/factsheets/barriers.pdf

National Association of Social Workers. (2002d). Hospice care. In author (2003), *Social work speaks: National Association of Social Workers policy statements 2003–2006* (6th ed.) (pp. 189–194). Washington, DC: NASW Press.

National Association of Social Workers. (2003). *About NASW.* Retrieved July 2, 2003, from www.socialworkers.org/nasw/default.asp

National Cancer Institute. (2002). *Cancer facts: Lifetime probability of breast cancer in American women.* Retrieved June 28, 2003, from http://cis.nci.nih.gov/fact/5_6.htm

National Center on Elder Abuse. (2003a). *State elder abuse laws.* Retrieved August 25, 2003, from www.elderabusecenter.org/default.cfm?p=statelaws.cfm

National Center on Elder Abuse. (2003b). *The basics: Major types of elder abuse.* Retrieved August 25, 2003, from www.elderabusecenter.org/default.cfm?p=basics.cfm

National Child Welfare Resource Center for Family-Centered Practice. (2000). Can we put clothes on this emperor? *Best Practice Next Practice, 1*(1), 7–10.

National Clearinghouse for Alcohol and Drug Information. (1995). *Domestic violence & alcohol and other drugs.* Retrieved August 11, 1997, from www.health.org/pubs/makelink/ml-domvi.htm

National Clearinghouse for Alcohol and Drug Information. (1997a). *Employee assistance programs.* Retrieved August 11, 1997, from www.health.org/pubs/PRIMER/employee.htm

National Clearinghouse for Alcohol and Drug Information. (1997b). *Health care costs, the deficit, & alcohol, tobacco, and other drugs.* Retrieved August 11, 1997, from www.health.org/pubs/makelink/ml-hcare.htm

National Clearinghouse on Child Abuse and Neglect. (1997). *In fact: Answers to frequently asked questions on child abuse and neglect.* Retrieved August 26, 1997, from www.calib.com/nccanch/pubs/infact.htm

National Coalition for the Homeless. (1999a). *NCH fact sheet #5: Mental illness and homelessness.* Retrieved August 12, 2003, from www.nationalhomeless.org/mental.html

National Coalition for the Homeless. (1999b). *NCH fact sheet #6: Addiction disorders and homelessness.* Retrieved August 12, 2003, from www.nationalhomeless.org/addict.html

National Coalition for the Homeless. (1999c). *NCH fact sheet #8: Domestic violence and homelessness.* Retrieved August 12, 2003, from www.nationalhomeless.org/domestic.html

National Coalition for the Homeless. (1999d). *NCH fact sheet #9: Homeless veterans.* Retrieved August 12, 2003, from www.nationalhomeless.org/veterans.html

National Coalition for the Homeless. (2001). *NCH fact sheet #7: Homeless families with children.* Retrieved August 12, 2003, from www.nationalhomeless.org/families.html

National Coalition for the Homeless. (2002a). *NCH fact sheet #1: Why are people homeless?* Retrieved August 12, 2003, from www.nationalhomeless.org/why.pdf

National Coalition for the Homeless. (2002b). *NCH fact sheet #3: Who is homeless?* Retrieved August 12, 2003, from www.nationalhomeless.org/who.pdf

National Coalition for the Homeless. (2002c). *NCH fact sheet #2: How many people experience homelessness?* Retrieved August 12, 2003, from www.nationalhomeless.org/howmany.pdf

National Coalition for the Homeless. (2003). *People need livable incomes.* Retrieved August 12, 2003, from www.nationalhomeless.org/facts/income.pdf

National Coalition of Anti-Violence Programs. (1999). *Lesbian, gay, bisexual, and transgender domestic violence, 1998.* Retrieved August 25, 2003, from www.vaw.umn.edu/documents/glbtdv/glbtdv.html#id2635383

National Coalition of Anti-Violence Programs. (2002). *Lesbian, gay, bisexual, and transgender domestic violence, 2001.* Retrieved August 25, 2003, from www.avp.org/

National Coalition of Anti-Violence Programs. (2003). *Lesbian, gay, bisexual, and transgender domestic violence, 2002.* Retrieved August 25, 2003, from www.coavp.org/2003/ncavp_2002_dv_report.pdf

National Criminal Justice Reference Service. (n.d. a). *Hate crime resources—Legislation.* Retrieved August 24, 2003, from www.ncjrs.org/hate_crimes/legislation.html

National Criminal Justice Reference Service. (n.d. b). *Hate crime resources—Facts and figures.* Retrieved August 24, 2003, from www.ncjrs.org/hate_crimes/facts.html

National Family Caregivers Association. (2002). *Family caregiving statistics.* Retrieved December 30, 2003, from www.nfcacares.org/NFC2002_stats.html

National Foster Care Awareness Project. (2000). *Frequently asked questions about the Foster Care Independence Act of 1999 and the John H. Chafee Foster Care Independence Program.* Retrieved August 31, 2003, from www.childrensdefense.org/pdf/foster_faq.pdf

National Gay and Lesbian Task Force. (2000). Eight states now offer domestic partner benefits, NGLTF finds. Retrieved October 22, 2000, from www.ngltf.org/news/printed.cfm?releaseID=338

National Hospice and Palliative Care Organization. (2003). *NHPCO facts and figures.* Retrieved June 28, 2003, from www.nhpco.org/files/public/Facts_Figures_Jan_03.pdf

National Institute of Mental Health. (2001). *The impact of mental illness on society.* Retrieved June 29, 2003, from www.nimh.nih.gov/publicat/burden.pdf

National Institute of Mental Health. (2003). *The numbers count: Mental disorders in America.* Retrieved June 29, 2003, from www.nimh.nih.gov/publicat/numbers.pdf

National Institute on Alcohol Abuse and Alcoholism. (1999a). *One in four children exposed to family alcohol abuse or alcoholism. NIH news advisory December 30, 1999.* Retrieved September 15, 2003, from www.niaaa.nih.gov/press/1999/4children.htm

National Institute on Alcohol Abuse and Alcoholism. (1999b). *Alcohol alert 44.* Retrieved September 9, 2000, from http://silk.nih.gov/silk/niaaa1/publication/aa44.htm

National Institute on Drug Abuse. (2000). *Preventing drug use among children and adolescents: A research-based guide.* Retrieved September 15, 2003, from www.drugabuse.gov/Prevention/Prevopen.html

National Institute on Drug Abuse. (2003). *About NIDA.* Retrieved August 24, 2003, from www.drugabuse.gov/about/AboutNIDA.html

National Organization on Disability. (2002). *Key findings: 2000 N.O.D./Harris Survey of Americans with Disabilities.* Retrieved June 29, 2003, from www.nod.org/content.cfm?id=1077

National Runaway Switchboard. (2003). *Frequently asked questions.* Retrieved August 31, 2003, from www.nrscrisisline.org/faq.asp#many

National Study of Youth and Religion. (2002). *Do teens pray? How often?* Retrieved August 23, 2003, from www.youthandreligion.org/news/docs/8-FrequencyofPrayer.pdf

National Women's Health Information Center. (1998). *Infertility.* Retrieved October 14, 2000, from www.4woman.gov/faq/infertility.htm

NCADD. (1997). *Alcohol and other drugs in the workplace.* Retrieved August 11, 1997, from www.ncadd.org/workplac.html

Needleman, S. K. (1992). Social work practice with infertility. In M. J. Holosko & P. A. Taylor (Eds.), *Social work practice in health care settings* (2nd ed.) (pp. 63–82). Toronto, Canada: Canadian Scholars' Press.

Nelson, G. M. (1995). Case management. In G. M. Nelson, A. C. Eller, D. W. Streets, & M. L. Morse (Eds.), *The field of adult services: Social work practice and administration* (pp. 88–103). Washington, DC: NASW Press.

Nelson, J. (1993). Improvisational theater helps teen mothers raise sights. *Children Today, 22*(2), 24–27.

Newberger, C. M., & De Vos, E. (1988). Abuse and victimization: A life-span developmental perspective. *American Journal of Orthopsychiatry, 58,* 505–511.

Nosko, A., & Breton, M. (1997–1998). Applying a strengths, competence and empowerment model. *Groupwork, 10*(1), 55–69.

Nystrom, J. F. (1989). Empowerment model for delivery of social work services in public schools. *Social Work in Education, 11,* 160–170.

O'Brien, P. (2001). Claiming our soul: An empowerment group for African-American women in prison. *Journal of Progressive Human Services, 12*(1), 35–51.

O'Connell, B. (1978). From service to advocacy to empowerment. *Social Casework, 59,* 195–202.

Ogunwole, S. U. (2002). *The American Indian and Alaska Native population 2000.* U.S. Census Bureau. Retrieved September 21, 2003, from www.census.gov/prod/2002pubs/c2kbr01-15.pdf.

Oktay, J. S. (1995). Primary health care. In R. L. Edwards (Ed.), *Encyclopedia of social work: Vol. 3* (19th ed.) (pp. 1887–1894). Washington, DC: NASW Press.

Okun, B. F. (1998). *Understanding diverse families: What practitioners need to know.* New York: Guilford Press.

Oliver, M. (1997). The Disability Movement is a new social movement. *Community Development Journal, 32*(3), 244–251.

Olson, K., & Pavetti, L. (1996). *Personal and family challenges to the successful transition from welfare to work.* The Urban Institute. Retrieved September 30, 2003, from www.urban.org/url.cfm?ID=406850

Olson, M. R., & Haynes, J. A. (1993). Successful single parents. *Families in Society, 75,* 259–267.

Opton, E. M. (1971). It never happened and besides they deserved it. In W. E. Henry & N. Sanford (Eds.), *Sanctions for evil* (pp. 49–70). San Francisco: Jossey-Bass.

Ortiz, L., Villereal, S., & Engel, M. (2000). Culture and spirituality: A review of literature. *Social Thought, 19*(4), 21–36.

Ory, M. G., Yee, J. L., Tennstedt, S. L., & Schultz, R. (2000). *The extent and impact of dementia care: Unique challenges experienced by family caregivers.* Retrieved October 2, 2003, from www.aoa.gov/prof/research/The%20Extent%20and%20Impact%20of%20Dementia%20Care.pdf

Osofsky, J. D. (1999). The impact of violence on children. *The Future of Children, 9*(3), 33–49. Retrieved September 15, 2003, from www.futureofchildren.org/usr_doc/vol9no3Art3.pdf

Ostrander, S. A. (1985). Voluntary social service agencies in the United States. *Social Service Review, 59,* 435–454.

Parker, J. K. (1994). Women at the helm: Succession politics at the Children's Bureau, 1912–1968. *Social Work, 39,* 551–559.

Parkes, C. M. (1998). Bereavement in adult life. *British Medical Journal, 316*(7134), 856–859. Retrieved September 17, 2003, from InfoTrac Expanded Academic ASAP database.

Parsonnet, L., & O'Hare, J. (1990). Group orientation program for families of newly admitted cancer patients. *Social Work, 35,* 37–40.

Parsons, R., Hernández, S., & Jorgensen, J. D. (1988). Integrated practice: A framework for problem solving. *Social Work, 33,* 417–421.

Parsons, R. J., East, J. F., & Boesen, M. B. (1994). Empowerment: A case study with AFDC women. In L. Gutiérrez & P. Nurius (Eds.), *Education and research for empowerment practice* (pp. 259–274). Seattle, WA: University of Washington, Center for Policy and Practice Research, School of Social Work.

Patania, S. S. (1998). Ethical issues in clinical practice. In D. M. Aronstein & B. J. Thompson (Eds.), *HIV and social work* (pp. 247–267). New York: Haworth Press.

Patten, S., Gatz, Y. K., Jones, B., & Thomas, D. (1989). Posttraumatic stress disorder and the treatment of sexual abuse. *Social Work, 34,* 197–203.

Pavetti, L. A. (1997). *Time on welfare and welfare dependency.* The Urban Institute. Retrieved September 15, 2003, from www.urban.org/url.cfm?ID=900288

Pecora, P. J., Whittaker, J. K., & Maluccio, A. N. (2000). *The child welfare challenge: Policy, practice, and research.* Hawthorne, NY: Aldine deGruyter.

Peebles-Wilkins, W. (1989). Black women and American social welfare: The life of Federicka Douglass Sprague Perry. *Affilia, 4*(1), 33–44.

Peebles-Wilkins, W. (1995a). Fernandis, Sarah A. Collins (1863–1951). In R. L. Edwards (Ed.), *Encyclopedia of social work: Vol. 3* (19th ed.) (p. 2584). Washington, DC: NASW Press.

Peebles-Wilkins, W. (1995b). Young, Whitney Moore, Jr. (1921–1971). In R. L. Edwards (Ed.), *Encyclopedia of social work: Vol. 3* (19th ed.) (p. 2618). Washington, DC: NASW Press.

Pellew, H. E. (1878). Report on outdoor relief administration in New York City. *Proceedings of the Conference of Charities, 1878* (pp. 53–72). Boston: A. Williams and Company.

Perlman, H. H. (1957). *Social casework: A problem-solving process.* Chicago: University of Chicago Press.

Perlman, H. H. (1976). Believing and doing: Values in social work education. *Social Casework, 57,* 381–390.

Perlmutter, F. D., & Cnaan, R. A. (1993). Challenging human service organizations to redefine volunteer roles. *Administration in Social Work, 17*(4), 77–95.

Peterson, D. A., & Wendt, P. F. (1990). Employment in the field of aging: A survey of professionals in four fields. *The Gerontologist, 30,* 679–684.

Peterson, K. J. (1995). HIV/AIDS: Women. In R. L. Edwards (Ed.), *Encyclopedia of social work: Vol. 2* (19th ed.) (pp. 1325–1330). Washington, DC: NASW Press.

Petr, C. G. (1992). Adultcentrism in practice with children. *Families in Society, 73,* 408–416.

Petr, C. G., & Johnson, I. C. (1999). Privatization of foster care in Kansas: A cautionary tale. *Social Work, 43*(3), 263–267.

Pew Research Center. (2001). *Section IV. Religion in American Life.* Retrieved June 25, 2003, from http://people-press.org/reports/print.php3?PageID=115

Pierce, D. (1989). *Social work and society.* New York: Longman.

Pillemer, K., & Finkelhor, D. (1988). The prevalence of elder abuse: A random sample survey. *The Gerontologist, 28,* 51–57.

Pincus, A., & Minahan, A. (1973). *Social work practice model and method.* Itasca, IL: Peacock.

Pinderhughes, E. B. (1982). Afro-American families and the victim system. In M. McGoldrick, J. K. Pearce, & J. Giordano (Eds.), *Ethnicity and family therapy* (pp. 108–122). New York: Guilford Press.

Pinderhughes, E. B. (1983). Empowerment for our clients and for ourselves. *Social Casework, 64,* 331–338.

Pinderhughes, E. B. (1989). *Understanding race, ethnicity, and power.* New York: The Free Press.

Pinderhughes, E. (1995a). Direct practice overview. In R. L. Edwards (Ed.), *Encyclopedia of social work: Vol. 1* (19th ed.) (pp. 740–751). Washington, DC: NASW Press.

Pinderhughes, E. (1995b). Empowering diverse populations: Family practice in the 21st century. *Families in Society, 76,* 131–140.

Pinderhughes, E. B. (1997). The interaction of difference and power as a basic framework for understanding work with African Americans: Family theory, empowerment and educational approaches. *Smith College Studies in Social Work, 67*(3), 323–347.

Piven, F. F., & Cloward, R. A. (1971). *Regulating the poor: The functions of public welfare.* New York: Vintage Books.

Plant, R. (1970). *Social and moral theory in casework.* London: Routledge and Kegan Paul.

Plasse, B. R. (1995). Parenting group for recovering addicts in a day treatment center. *Social Work, 40,* 6574.

Platt, N., & Drummond, M. J. (1967). *Our nation from its creation.* Englewood Cliffs, NJ: Prentice-Hall.

Poe-Yamagata, E., & Jones, M. A. (2000). *And justice for some. Building Blacks for Youths.* Retrieved September 14, 2003, from www.buildingblocksforyouth.org/justiceforsome/jfs.pdf

Poindexter, C. C., & Linsk, N. L. (1999). HIV-related stigma in a sample of HIV-affected older female African American caregivers. *Social Work, 44*(1), 46–61.

Pollard, W. P. (1995). Civil rights. In R. L. Edwards (Ed.), *Encyclopedia of social work: Vol. 1* (19th ed.) (pp. 494–502). Washington, DC: NASW Press.

Pomeroy, E. C., Kiam, R., & Abel, E. M. (1999). The effectiveness of a psychoeducational group for HIV-infected/affected incarcerated women. *Research on Social Work Practice, 9*(2), 171–187.

Popple, P. R. (1985). The social work profession: A reconceptualization. *Social Service Review, 59,* 560–577.

Popple, P. R., & Leighninger, L. H. (2002). *Social work, social welfare, and American society* (3rd ed.). Boston: Allyn & Bacon.

Population Reference Bureau. (2003a). *The geography of diversity.* Ameristat 2001. Retrieved September 25, 2003, from www.prb.org/Template.cfm?Section=PRB&template=/ContentManagement/ContentDisplay.cfm&ContentID=8226

Population Reference Bureau. (2003b). *2003 world population data sheet of the Population Reference Bureau: Demographic data and estimates for the countries and regions of the world.* Retrieved August 30, 2003, from www.prb.org/pdf/WorldPopulationDS03_Eng.pdf

Poverny, L. M. (2000). Employee assistance practice with sexual minorities. *Administration in Social Work, 23*(3/4), 69–91.

Powell, T. J. (1995). Self-help groups. In R. L. Edwards (Ed.), *Encyclopedia of social work: Vol. 3* (19th ed.) (pp. 2116–2123). Washington, DC: NASW Press.

Proctor, B. D., & Dalaker, J. (2002). Poverty in the United States: 2001. U.S. Census Bureau, *Current Population Reports, P60-219.* Washington, DC: U.S. Government Printing Office. Retrieved August 25, 2003, from www.census.gov/prod/2002pubs/p60-219.pdf

Proctor, C., & Groze, V. (1994). Risk factors for suicide among gay, lesbian, and bisexual youths. *Social Work, 39,* 504–513.

Pryor, H. (1994, October). Theory into practice: Gerontologist Robert Butler shows how research into aging can work. *AARP Bulletin, 35*(9), p. 12.

Pumphrey, R. E., & Pumphrey, M. W. (1961). Education for the new profession. In R. Pumphrey & M. Pumphrey (Eds.), *The heritage of American social work: Readings in its philosophical and institutional development* (pp. 284–287). New York: Columbia University Press.

Puzzanchera, C. et al. (2000). *Juvenile court statistics 1997.* National Center for Juvenile Justice. Retrieved August 23, 2003, from www.ncjrs.org/pdffiles1/ojjdp/180864.pdf

Quam, J. K. (1993). Gay and lesbian aging. *SIECUS Report, 21*(5), 10–12. Retrieved September 15, 2003, from www.siecus.org/siecusreport/volume21/21-5.pdf

Quam, J. K. (1995). Brockway, Zebulon Reed. In R. L. Edwards (Ed.), *Encyclopedia of social work: Vol. 3* (19th ed.) (p. 2576). Washington, DC: NASW Press.

Quinn, M. J., & Tomita, S. K. (1986). *Elder abuse and neglect: Causes, diagnosis, and intervention strategies.* New York: Springer.

Rafferty, Y., & Shinn, M. (1994). The impact of homelessness on children. *American Psychologist, 46,* 1170–1179.

Ramirez, R. R., & de la Cruz, G. P. (2003). The Hispanic population in the United States: March 2002. *Cur-*

rent Population Reports, P20-540. Washington, DC: U.S. Census Bureau. Retrieved June 30, 2003, from www.census.gov/prod/2003pubs/p20-540.pdf

Ramos, J. (1995). Migrant workers. In R. L. Edwards (Ed.), *Encyclopedia of social work: Vol. 2* (19th ed.) (pp. 1720–1725). Washington, DC: NASW Press.

Raphael, J., & Haennicke, S. (1999). *Keeping battered women safe through the welfare-to-work journey: How are we doing? A report of the implementation of policies for battered women in state Temporary Assistance for Needy Families (TANF) programs.* Retrieved December 30, 2003, from www.ssw.umich.edu/trapped/pubs_fvo1999.pdf

Rappaport, J. (1981). In praise of paradox: A social policy of empowerment over prevention. *American Journal of Community Psychology, 9,* 1–25.

Rappaport, J. (1984). Studies in empowerment: Introduction to the issue. *Prevention in Human Services, 3,* 1–7.

Rappaport, J. (1985). The power of empowerment language. *Social Policy, 17,* 15–21.

Rappaport, J. (1987). Terms of empowerment/ exemplars of prevention: Toward a theory for community psychology. *American Journal of Community Psychology, 15*(2), 121–144.

Raschick, M. (1997). Helping working poor families with low-interest loans. *Families in Society, 78*(1), 26–35.

Rathbone-McCuan, E. (1990). Respite and adult day services. In A. Monk (Ed.), *Handbook of gerontological services* (2nd ed.) (pp. 546–567). New York: Columbia University Press.

Rauch, B. (1944). *The history of the New Deal 1933–1938.* New York: Creative Age Press.

Rauch, J. B. (1990). Genetic services for foster children: An unmet need? *Child Welfare, 19,* 341–355.

Rauch, J. B., & Black, R. B. (1995). Genetics. In R. L. Edwards (Ed.), *Encyclopedia of social work: Vol. 2* (19th ed.) (pp. 1108–1117). Washington, DC: NASW Press.

Reamer, F. G. (1986). The use of modern technology in social work: Ethical dilemmas. *Social Work, 31,* 469–472.

Reamer, F. G. (1990). *Ethical dilemmas in social services: A guide for social workers* (2nd ed.). New York: Columbia University Press.

Reamer, F. G. (1993). AIDS and social work: The ethics and civil liberties agenda. *Social Work, 38,* 412–419.

Reamer, F. G. (1994). Social work values and ethics. In F. G. Reamer (Ed.), *Foundation of social work knowledge* (pp. 195–230). New York: Columbia University Press.

Reamer, F. G. (1995). Ethics and values. In R. L. Edwards (Ed.), *Encyclopedia of social work: Vol. 1* (19th ed.) (pp. 893–902). Washington, DC: NASW Press.

Reamer, F. G. (1999). *Social work values and ethics.* New York: Columbia University Press.

Red Horse, J. G., Lewis, R., Feit, M., & Decker, J. (1978). Family behavior of urban American Indians. *Social Casework, 59,* 67–72.

Reeves, T., & Bennett, C. (2003). The Asian and Pacific Islander population in the United States: March 2002. *Current Population Reports, P20-540.* Washington, DC: U.S. Census Bureau. Retrieved June 30, 2003, from www.census.gov/prod/2003pubs/p20-540.pdf

Reid, K. E. (1986). Coyle, Grace L. (1986). In W. I. Trattner (Ed.), *Biographical dictionary of social welfare in America* (pp. 201–204). New York: Greenwood Press.

Reitsma-Street, M., & Brown, L. (2002). Community action research. In M. O'Melia & K. K. Miley (Eds.), *Pathways to power: Readings in contextual social work practice* (pp. 74–94). Boston: Allyn & Bacon.

Rennison, C. M. (2003). Intimate partner violence, 1993–2001. *Bureau of Justice Statistics—Crime data brief.* Retrieved August 29, 2003, from www.ojp.usdoj.gov/bjs/pub/pdf/ipv01.pdf

Renzetti, C. M. (1996). The poverty of services for battered lesbians. In C. M. Renzetti & C. H. Miley (Eds.), *Violence in gay and lesbian domestic partnerships* (pp. 1–8). New York: Harrington Park Press.

Reynolds, B. C. (1951). *Social work and social living.* New York: Citadel Press.

Richan, W. C. (1996). *Lobbying for social change* (2nd ed.). New York: Haworth Press.

Richmond, M. (1917). *Social diagnosis.* New York: Russell Sage Foundation.

Richmond, M. (1922). *What is social case work?* New York: Russell Sage Foundation.

Riley, J. L., & Greene, R. R. (1993). Influence of education on self-perceived attitudes about HIV/AIDS among human service providers. *Social Work, 38,* 396–401.

Roberts, A. R. (1983). The history and role of social work in law enforcement. In A. R. Roberts (Ed.), *Social work in juvenile and criminal justice settings* (pp. 91–103). Springfield, IL: Charles C Thomas.

Roberts, A. R. (1995). Victim services and victim/witness assistance programs. In R. L. Edwards (Ed.), *Encyclopedia of social work: Vol. 1* (19th ed.) (pp. 2440–2444). Washington, DC: NASW Press.

Roberts, A. R., & Roberts, B. S. (1990). A comprehensive model for crisis intervention with battered women and their children. In A. R. Roberts (Ed.), *Crisis intervention handbook: Assessment, treatment and research* (pp. 105–123). Belmont, CA: Wadsworth.

Rodin, J. (1989). Sense of control: Potentials for intervention. *The quality of aging: Strategies for intervention: Annals of the American Academy of Political and Social Science, 503,* 29–42.

Roditti, M. G. (1995). Child day care: A key building block of family support and family preservation programs. *Child Welfare, 74*(6), 1043–1068.

Rogers, C. (1961). *On becoming a person.* Boston: Houghton Mifflin.

Romanyshyn, J. M., & Romanyshyn, A. L. (1971). *Social welfare: Charity to justice.* New York: Random House.

Root, L. S. (1993). Unemployment and underemployment: A policy and program-development perspective. In P. A. Kurzman & S. H. Akabas (Eds.), *Work and well-being: The occupational social work advantage* (pp. 332–349). Washington, DC: NASW Press.

Rose, A. (1998). Back to the future: Survival, uncertainty, and hope. In D. M. Aronstein & B. J. Thompson (Eds.), *HIV and social work* (pp. 65–74). New York: Haworth Press.

Rose, S. M., & Moore, V. L (1995). Case management. In R. L. Edwards (Ed.), *Encyclopedia of social work: Vol. 1* (19th ed.) (pp. 335–340). Washington, DC: NASW Press.

Rosenfeld, D. (1999). Identity work among lesbian and gay elderly. *Journal of Aging Studies, 13*(2), 121+. Retrieved September 23, 2003, from InfoTrac Expanded Academic ASAP database.

Rosenhan, D. L. (1975). On being sane in insane places. In T. J. Scheff (Ed.), *Labeling madness* (pp. 54–74). Englewood Cliffs, NJ: Prentice-Hall.

Rosenthal, R., & Jacobson, L. (1968). *Pygmalion in the classroom.* New York: Holt, Rinehart & Winston.

Roth, W. (1987). Disabilities: Physical. In A. Minahan (Ed.), *Encylopedia of social work: Vol. 1* (18th ed.) (pp. 434–438). Silver Spring, MD: National Association of Social Workers.

Roush, D. W. (1996). *Desktop guide to good juvenile detention practice 1996.* U.S. Department of Justice. Retrieved September 15, 2003, from www.ncjrs.org/pdffiles/desktop.pdf

Rowe, J. W., & Kahn, R. L. (1998). *Successful aging.* New York: Panthenon Books.

Rubenstein, E., Panzarine, S., & Lanning, P. (1990). Peer counseling with adolescent mothers: A pilot program. *Families in Society, 71,* 136–141.

Rubin, Z., & Peplau, L. A. (1975). Who believes in a just world? *Journal of Social Issues, 31*(3), 65–89.

Ruch, G. (2002). From triangle to spiral: Reflective practice in social work education, practice and research. *Social Work Education, 21*(2), 199–216.

Russo, R. J. (1999). Applying a strengths-based practice approach in working with people with developmental disabilities and their families. *Families in Society, 80*(1), 25–33.

Ryan, W. (1976). *Blaming the victim* (Rev. ed.). New York: Vintage Books.

Sachs, H. (1999). Domestic violence as a barrier to women's economic self-sufficiency. *Welfare Information Notes, 3*(10). Retrieved September 25, 2003, from www.financeprojectinfo.org/Publications/domesticviolence.htm

Saleebey, D. (2003). Strengths-based practice. In R. A. English (Ed.), *Encyclopedia of social work: 2003 supplement* (pp. 150–162). Washington, DC: NASW Press.

Saltzman, A., & Furman, D. M. (1999). *Law in social work practice.* Chicago, IL: Nelson-Hall.

Sanders, D. S. (1975). Dynamics of ethnic and cultural pluralism: Implications for social work education and curriculum innovation. *Journal of Education for Social Work, 11*(3), 95–100.

Sasser, J. (1994, March 1). Balanced budget amendment. *Congressional Record* (daily ed.). pp. S2045–2081.

Schaefer, R. T. (1998). *Racial and ethnic groups* (7th ed.). New York: Longman.

Schaffer, J. A., & Diamond, R. (1993). Infertility: Private pain and secret stigma. In E. Imber-Black (Ed.), *Secrets in families and family therapy* (pp. 106–120). New York: W. W. Norton.

Schechter, S., & Gary, L. T. (1988). A framework for understanding and empowering women. In M. B. Straus (Ed.), *Abuse victimization across the life span* (pp. 240–253). Baltimore: Johns Hopkins University Press.

Scheer, J., & Groce, N. (1988). Impairment as a human constant: Cross cultural and historical perpectives on variation. *Journal of Social Issues, 44,* 23–37.

Scheurell, R. (1983). Social work ethics in probation and parole. In A. R. Roberts (Ed.), *Social work in juvenile and criminal justice settings* (pp. 241–251). Springfield, IL: Charles C Thomas.

Schneider, D. M., & Deutsch, A. (1941). *The history of public welfare in New York State, 1867–1940.* Chicago: University of Chicago Press.

Schneider, R. (2002). Influencing "state" policy: Social work arena for the 21st century. *The Social Policy Journal, 1*(1), 113–116.

Schoen, K. (1998). Caring for ourselves: Understanding and minimizing the stresses of HIV caregiving. In D. M. Aronstein & B. J. Thompson (Eds.), *HIV and social work* (pp. 527–536). New York: Haworth Press.

Schrenzel, J. (1994). The school-community partnership: Helping at-risk youth. *Smith College Studies in Social work, 64*(2), 181–191.

Schriver, J. M. (1987). Harry Lurie's critique: Person and environment and early casework practice. *Social Service Review, 61,* 514–532.

Schroeder, K. (1995). Antiviolence program. *Education Digest, 60*(6), 76.

Schroeder, O. C. (1987). Civil rights. In A. Minahan (Ed.), *Encyclopedia of social work: Vol. 1* (18th ed.) (pp.

280–287). Silver Spring, MD: National Association of Social Workers.

Schumacher, J. A., Fals-Stewart, W., & Leonard, K. E. (2003). Domestic violence treatment referrals for men seeking alcohol treatment. *Journal of Substance Abuse Treatment, 24*(3), 279–283.

Schwartz, W. (1969). Private troubles and public issues: One social work job or two? *The social welfare forum, 1969* (pp. 22–43). New York: Columbia University Press.

Scommegna, P. (2002). *Increased cohabitation changing children's family settings. Research on today's issues.* Demographic and Behavioral Sciences Branch, Center for Population research, National Institute of Child Health and Human Development. Retrieved August 30, 2003, from www.nichd.nih.gov/about/cpr/dbs/pubs/ti13.pdf

Scotch, R. K. (1988). Disability as the basis for a social movement: Advocacy and the politics of definition. *Journal of Social Issues, 44*(1), 159–172.

Scotch, R. K. (2000). Models of disability and the Americans with Disabilities Act. *Berkeley Journal of Employment and Labor Law, 21*(1), 213+. Retrieved September 17, 2003, from InfoTrac Expanded Academic ASAP database.

Segalman, R., & Basu, A. (1981). *Poverty in America: The welfare dilemma.* Westport, CT: Greenwood Press.

Seligman, M. E. (1975). *Helplessness.* San Francisco: W. H. Freeman.

Sennett, R., & Cobb, J. (1972). *The hidden injuries of class.* New York: Alfred A. Knopf.

Shafer, C. M. (1969). Teaching social work practice in an integated course: A general systems approach. In G. Hearn (Ed.), *The general systems approach: Contributions toward an holistic conception of social work* (pp. 26–36). New York: Council on Social Work Education.

Shanker, R. (1983). Occupational disease, worker's compensation, and the social work advocate. *Social Work, 28,* 24–27.

Shera, W., & Page, J. (1995). Creating more effective human service organizations through strategies of empowerment. *Administration in Social Work, 19*(4), 1–15.

Sherman, S. R. (1990). Housing. In A. Monk (Ed.), *Handbook of gerontological services* (2nd ed.) (pp. 477–507). New York: Columbia University Press.

Shernoff, M. (1995). Gay men: Direct practice. In R. L. Edwards (Ed.), *Encyclopedia of social work: Vol. 2* (19th ed.) (pp. 1075–1084). Washington, DC: NASW Press.

Shernoff, M. (1998). Getting started: basic skills for effective social work with people with HIV and AIDS. In D. M. Aronstein & B. J. Thompson (Eds.), *HIV and social work* (pp. 27–50). New York: Haworth Press.

Sherrell, K., & Newton, N. (1996). Parent care as a developmental task. *Families in Society, 77*(3), 174–181.

Shinn, M., & Weitzman, B. C. (1996). Homeless families are different. In J. Baumohl (Ed.), *Homelessness in America* (pp. 109–122). Phoenix, AZ: Oryz Press.

Shlakman, V. (1969). Eveline Burns: Social Economist. In S. Jenkins (Ed.), *Social security in international perspective* (pp. 3–25). New York: Columbia University Press.

Shlay, A. B. (1994). Running on empty: Monitoring the lives and circumstances of formerly homeless families with children. *Journal of Social Distress and the Homeless, 3*(2), 135–162.

Shupe, D. R. (1985). Perceived control, helplessness, and choice. In J. E. Birren & J. Livingston (Eds.), *Cognition, stress & aging* (pp. 174–197). Englewood Cliffs, NJ: Prentice-Hall.

Sickmund, M. (2003). Juveniles in court. Juvenile offenders and victims. *National Report Series Bulletin.* U.S. Department of Justice, Office of Justice Programs, Office of Juvenile Justice and Delinquency Prevention. Retrieved August 23, 2003 from www.ncjrs.org/pdffiles1/ojjdp/195420.pdf

Sieppert, J. D., Hudson, J., & Unrau, Y. (2000). Family group conferencing in child welfare: Lessons from a demonstration project. *Families in Society, 81*(4), 382–391.

Simon, B. L. (1990). Rethinking empowerment. *Journal of Progressive Human Services, 1,* 27–39.

Simon, B. L. (1994). *The empowerment tradition in American social work: A history.* New York: Columbia University Press.

Singer, M. I., Bussey, J., Song, L-Y., & Lunghofer, L. (1995). The psychosocial issues of women serving time in jail. *Social Work, 40,* 103–114.

Singer, P. A., Martin, D. K., & Kelner, M. (1999). Quality end-of-life-care: Patients' perspectives. *Journal of the American Medical Association, 281*(2), 163–168. Retrieved August 25, 2000, from http://jama.ama.org/issues/v281n2/full/jsc80231.html

Siporin, M. (1975). *Introduction to social work practice.* New York: Macmillan.

Siporin, M. (1980). Ecological system theory in social work. *Journal of Sociology and Social Welfare, 7,* 507–532.

Siporin, M. (1985). Current social work perspectives on clinical practice. *Clinical Social Work Journal, 13,* 198–217.

Slater, P. (2000). Elder abuse and user involvement: Strategic components. *Journal of Adult Protection, 2*(2), 18–28.

Slaughter, L. M. (1993, April 19). Domestic violence awareness month. *Congressional Record* (daily ed), p. E937.

Sloboda, Z., & David, S. L. (n.d.). *Some research-based drug abuse prevention programs. Preventing drug abuse among children & adolescents.* National Institute on Drug Abuse. Retrieved September 28, 2003, from http://165.112.78.61/Prevention/PROGRM.html

Smalley, R. E. (1967). *Theory for social work practice.* New York: Columbia University Press.

Smith, G. C. et al. (2000). The effects of interpersonal and personal agency on perceived control and psychological well-being in adulthood. *The Gerontologist, 40*(4), 458–468.

Smith, M. L., & Gould, G. M. (1993). A profession at the crossroads: Occupational social work— Present and future. In P. A. Kurzman & S. H. Akabas (Eds.), *Work and well-being: The occupational social work advantage.* Washington, DC: NASW Press.

Smith, S. K. (2002). *Mandatory reporting of child abuse and neglect.* Retrieved December 30, 2003, from www.smith-lawfirm.com/mandatory_reporting.htm

Social Security Administration. (1997). *Social Security: The definition of disability for children.* Retrieved August 23, 2003, from www.ssa.gov/pubs/11053.pdf

Social Security Administration. (2000a). *Facts and figures about Social Security 2000.* Retrieved October 2, 2000, from www.ssa.gov/statisticsfast_facts/2000/ff2000.pdf

Social Security Administration. (2000b). *Highlights of Social Security data, July 2000.* Retrieved October 2, 2000, from www.ssa.gov/policy/programs/ssd.html

Social Security Administration. (2003). *Facts and figures about Social Security.* Retrieved September 27, 2003, from www.ssa.gov/policy/docs/chartbooks/fast_facts/2003/ff2003.pdf

Sohng, S. S. L. (1999). Research as an empowerment strategy. In L. M. Gutiérrez, R. J. Parsons, & E. O. Parsons (Eds.), *Empowerment in social work practice: A sourcebook* (pp. 187–203). Pacific Grove, CA: Brooks/Cole.

Soifer, S. (1991). Infusing content about Jews and about anti-semitism into the curricula. *Journal of Social Work Education, 27,* 156–167.

Solomon, B. B. (1976). *Black empowerment: Social work in oppressed communities.* New York: Columbia University Press.

Solomon, B. B. (1983). Value issues in working with minority clients. In A. Rosenblatt & D. Waldfogel (Eds.), *Handbook of clinical social work* (pp. 866–887). San Francisco: Jossey-Bass.

Solomon, B. B. (1989). Social work with Afro-Americans. In A. Morales & B. Sheafor (Eds.), *Social work: A profession of many faces* (pp. 567–586). Boston: Allyn & Bacon.

Soo, Y. K., & Gong-Soog, H. (1998, December). Volunteer participation and time commitment by older Americans. *Family and Consumer Sciences Research Journal,* pp. 146+. Retrieved September 17, 2003, from InfoTrac Expanded Academic ASAP database.

Specht, H., & Courtney, M. E. (1994). *Unfaithful angels: How social work has abandoned its mission.* New York: The Free Press.

Special issue on conceptual frameworks. (1977). *Social Work, 22*(5).

Splittgerber, F. L., & Allen, H. A. (1996). Learning and caring communities: Meeting the challenge of at-risk youth. *Clearing House, 69*(4), 214–216.

Staub-Berasconi, S. (1991). Social action, empowerment and social work—An integrative theoretical framework for social work and social work with groups. *Social Work with Groups, 14*(3/4), 35–51.

Stephens, G. (1997). Youth at risk: Saving the world's most precious resource. *Futurist, 31*(2), 1–6.

Stephenson, J. (2000). Rural HIV/AIDS in the United States. *Journal of the American Medical Association, 284*(2), 167–168.

Strand, V. C. (1995). Single parents. In R. L. Edwards (Ed.), *Encyclopedia of social work: Vol. 3* (19th ed.) (pp. 2157–2164). Washington, DC: NASW Press.

Straussner, S. L. A. (2001). The role of social workers in the treatment of addictions: A brief history. *Journal of Social Work Practice in the Addictions, 1*(1), 3–9.

Streets, D. W. (1995). Adult day care. In G. M. Nelson, A. C. Eller, D. W. Streets, & M. L. Morse (Eds.), *The field of adult services: Social work practice and administration* (pp. 296–316). Washington, DC: NASW Press.

Stuart, P. H. (1994, November). *Political action in early social work practice theory: Lessons for the '90's.* Paper presented at the Association of Baccalaureate Program Directors, San Francisco, CA.

Substance Abuse and Mental Health Services Administration. (2002a). *National Household Survey on Drug Abuse 2001: Highlights.* Retrieved June 28, 2003 from www.samhsa.gov/oas/nhsda/2k1nhsda/PDF/cover.pdf

Substance Abuse and Mental Health Services Administration. (2002b). *National Household Survey on Drug Abuse 2001: Alcohol use* (Chapter 2). Retrieved June 29, 2003, from www.samhsa.gov/oas/nhsda/2k1nhsda/PDF/ch3.pdf

Sue, D. W., & Sue, D. (2002). *Counseling the culturally different: Theory and practice.* New York: John Wiley.

Sullivan, T. R. (1994). Obstacles to effective child welfare service with gay and lesbian youths. *Child Welfare, 73,* 291–304.

Sumner, W. G. (1887). The abolition of poverty. In A. G. Keller & M. Davie (1934), *Essays of William Graham Sumner, Vol. 1* (pp. 107–111). New Haven, CT: Yale University Press.

Sumner, W. G. (1903). *What social classes owe to each other.* New York: Harper and Brothers.

Sunley, R. (1997). Advocacy in the new world of managed care. *Families in Society, 78*(1), 84–94.

Sutton, C. T., & Broken Nose, M. A. (1996). American Indian families: An overview. In M. McGoldrick, J. Giordano, & J. K. Pearce (Eds.), *Ethnicity and family therapy* (2nd ed.) (pp. 31–44). New York: Guilford Press.

Swift, C. (1984). Empowerment: An antidote for folly. *Prevention in Human Services, 3,* xi–xv.

Swift, C., & Levin, G. (1987). Empowerment: An emerging mental health technology. *Journal of Primary Prevention, 8,* 71–94.

Swigonski, M. E. (2000, November). From hate crimes to human rights: Resources for LGBT empowerment. Paper presented for NASW Social Work 2000 Conference, Baltimore, MD.

Szabo, V., & Strang, V. R. (1999). Experiencing control in caregiving. *Journal of Nursing Scholarship, 31*(1), 71–75.

Szasz, T. S. (1960). The myth of mental illness. *American Psychologist, 15,* 113–118.

Tangenberg, K. (2000). Marginalized epistemologies: A feminist approach to understanding the experiences of mothers with HIV. *Affilia, 15*(1), 31–48.

Tatara, T. (1995). Elder abuse. In R. L. Edwards (Ed.), *Encyclopedia of social work: Vol. 1* (19th ed.) (pp. 843–842). Washington, DC: NASW Press.

Taylor-Brown, S. (1995). HIV/AIDS practice. In R. L. Edwards (Ed.), *Encyclopedia of social work: Vol. 2* (19th ed.) (pp. 1291–1305). Washington, DC: NASW Press.

Taylor-Brown, S. (1998). Talking with parents about permanency planning. In D. M. Aronstein & B. J. Thompson (Eds.), *HIV and social work* (pp. 349–360). New York: Haworth Press.

Taylor-Brown S., & Johnson, A. M. (1998). *Social work's role in genetic services. NASW social work practice update.* Retrieved March 14, 2001, from www.naswdc.org/practice/genetics.htm

Teare, R. J., & McPheeters, H. L. (1970). *Manpower utilization in social welfare: A report based on a symposium on manpower utilization in social welfare services.* Atlanta, GA: Southern Regional Education Board.

Teare, R. J., & McPheeters, H. L. (1982). A framework for practice in social welfare: Objectives and roles. In D. S. Sanders, O. Kurren, & J. Fischer (Eds.), *Fundamentals of social work practice* (pp. 56–72). Belmont, CA: Wadsworth.

Teaster, P. B. (2001). *A response to the abuse of vulnerable adults: The 2000 survey of state adult protective services.* National Center on Elder Abuse. Retrieved August 25, 2003, from www.elderabusecenter.org/pdf/research/apsreport030703.pdf

Telfair, J., & Gardner, M. M. (2000). Adolescents with sickle cell disease: Determinants of support, group attendance and satisfaction. *Health and Social Work, 25*(1), 43+. Retrieved September 23, 2002, from InfoTrac Expanded Academic ASAP database.

Tennstedt, S. (1999, March). *Family caregiving in an aging society.* Paper presented at the U.S. Administration on Aging Symposium. Longevity in the New American Century. Baltimore, MD. Retrieved September 15, 2003, from www.aoa.gov/prof/research/famcare.pdf

Terrell, P. (1974). The social worker as radical: Roles of advocacy. In P. E. Weinberger (Ed.), *Perspectives on social welfare* (2nd ed.) (pp. 331–338). New York: Macmillan.

Testa, M. F., Shook, K. L., Cohen, L. S., & Woods, M. C. (1996). Permanency planning options for children in formal kinship care. *Child Welfare, 75*(5), 451–470.

The ARC of the United States. (2001). *Introduction to the ARC.* Retrieved August 24, 2003, from www.thearc.org/about.htm

Thomas, D., Leicht, C., Hughes, C., Madigan, A., & Dowell, K. (2003). *Emerging practices in the prevention of child abuse and neglect.* U.S. Department of Health and Human Services, Office of Child Abuse and Neglect. Retrieved August 31, 2003, from www.calib.com/nccanch/prevention/emerging/report.pdf

Thompson, M. P. (2003). A comparison of risk factors for intimate partner violence-related injury across two national surveys on violence against women. *Violence Against Women, 9*(4), 438–457.

Thompson, N., & Thompson, S. (2001). Empowering older people: Beyond the care model. *Journal of Social Work, 1*(1), 61–76.

Thurman, D. J. et al. (1999). *Traumatic brain injury in the United States: A report to Congress.* Retrieved September 8, 2000, from www.cdc.gov/ncipc/pubres/tbicongress.htm

Tidwell, B. J. (1987). Racial discrimination and inequality. In A. Minahan (Ed.), *Encyclopedia of social work: Vol. 2* (18th ed.) (pp. 448–455). Silver Spring, MD: National Association of Social Workers.

Tillich, P. (1959). *Theology of culture.* New York: Oxford University Press.

Tillich, P. (1962). The philosophy of social work. *Social Service Review, 36*(1), 13–16.

Tjaden, P., & Thoennes, N. (2000). *Extent, nature, and consequences of intimate partner violence: Findings from the National Violence Against Women Survey.* National Institute of Justice and the Centers for Disease Control. Retrieved September 15, 2003, from www.ncjrs.org/pdffiles1/nij/181867.pdf

Tobin, S. S., & Toseland, R. W. (1990). Models of services for the elderly. In A. Monk (Ed.), *Handbook of gerontological services* (pp. 27–51). New York: Columbia University Press.

Tolliver, D. E. (2001). African American female caregivers of family members living with HIV/AIDS. *Families in Society, 82*(2), 145–156.

Tolman, R. M., & Raphael, J. (2000). *A review of research on welfare and domestic violence.* Retrieved September 15, 2003, from www.ssw.umich.edu/trapped/jsi_tolman_final.pdf

Toseland, R. W. (1995). *Group work with the elderly and family caregivers.* New York: Springer.

Toseland, R. W., McCallion, P., Gerber, T., & Banks, S. (2003). Predictors of health and human services use by persons with dementia and their family caregivers. *Social Science & Medicine, 55*(7), 1255–1266.

Tourse, R. W. (1995). Special-interest professional associations. In R. L. Edwards (Ed.), *Encyclopedia of social work: Vol. 3* (19th ed.) (pp. 2314–2319). Washington, DC: NASW Press.

Tower, C. C. (1996). *Understanding child abuse and neglect* (3rd ed.). Boston: Allyn & Bacon.

Towle, C. (1957). *Common human needs* (Rev. ed.). New York: National Association of Social Workers.

Tracy, B. (1990). *International social work.* Unpublished manuscript, Marycrest College, Davenport, IA.

Tracy, B., & DuBois, B. (1987, September). *Information model for generalist social work practice.* Paper presented at the Association of Baccalaureate Program Directors, Kansas City, KS.

Tracy, E. M. (1995). Family preservation and home-based services. In R. L. Edwards (Ed.), *Encyclopedia of social work: Vol. 2* (19th ed.) (pp. 973–983). Washington, DC: NASW Press.

Tracy, E. M., & Pine, B. A. (2000). Child welfare education and training: Future trends and influences. *Child Welfare, 79*(1), 93–113.

Tracy, M. B., & Ozawa, M. N. (1995). Social Security. In R. L. Edwards (Ed.), *Encyclopedia of social work: Vol. 3* (19th ed.) (pp. 2186–2195). Washington, DC: NASW Press.

Trattner, W. I. (1999). *From poor law to welfare state: A history of social welfare in America* (6th ed.). New York: The Free Press.

Treger, H. (1995). Police social work. In R. L. Edwards (Ed.), *Encyclopedia of social work: Vol. 3* (19th ed.) (pp. 1843–1855). Washington, DC: NASW Press.

Tully, C. T. (1995). Lesbians overview. In R. L. Edwards (Ed.), *Encyclopedia of social work: Vol. 2* (19th ed.) (pp. 1591–1596). Washington, DC: NASW Press.

Tully, C. T. (2000). *Lesbians, gays, & the empowerment perspective.* New York: Columbia University Press.

Tutty, L. M., & Wagner, S. (1994). The evolution of a group for young children who have witnessed family violence. *Social Work with Groups, 17* (1/2), 89–104.

Turell, S. C. (2000). A descriptive analysis of same-sex relationship violence for a diverse sample. *Journal of Family Violence, 15*(3), 281–293.

Uccello, C. E., & Gallagher, L. J. (1997). General Assistance programs: The state-based part of the safety net. *The Urban Institute: Series A, No. A-4.* Retrieved August 23, 2003, from www.urban.org/UploadedPDF/Anf_4.pdf

Umbreit, M. S. (1993). Crime victims and offenders in mediation: An emerging area of social work practice. *Social Work, 38,* 69–73.

United Nations. (1948). *Universal Declaration of Human Rights.* Retrieved December 30, 2003, from www.un.org/Overview/rights.html

United Nations. (1994). *Human rights and social work.* Geneva, Switzerland: Center for Human Rights.

United Nations. (2000). *Fact sheet: Violence against women.* Retrieved August 30, 2003, from www.eurowrc.org/13.institutions/5.un/un-en/04.un_en.htm

United Nations Development Programme (UNDP). (2003a). *Chapter 1: The millennium development goals.* New York: Oxford University Press. Retrieved September 21, 2003, from www.undp.org/hdr2003/pdf/hdr03_chapter_1.pdf

United Nations Development Programme (UNDP). (2003b). *Overview: Millennium development goals.* New York: Oxford University Press. Retrieved September 21, 2003, from www.undp.org/hdr2003/pdf/hdr03_overview.pdf

United Nations International Children's Fund (UNICEF). (2002). *Orphans and other children affected by HIV/AIDS.* Retrieved June 28, 2003, from www.unicef.org/pubsgen/hiv-orphansand/fact-sheet-orphan-en.pdf

United Nations Population Division. (2003). *World Population prospects: The 2002 revision, Highlights.* Retrieved August 30, 2003, from www.un.org/esa/population/publications/wpp2002/WPP2002-HIGHLIGHTSrev1.PDF

U.S. Census Bureau. (1997a). *Census brief: Disabilities affect one-fifth of all Americans.* Retrieved July 22, 2000, from www.census.gov/prod/www/abs/briefs.html

U.S. Census Bureau. (2000a). *Projections of the total resident population by 5-year age groups and sex with special age categories: Middle Series, 2001 to 2005.* Retrieved June 28, 2003, from www.census.gov/population/www/projections/natsum-T3.html

U.S. Census Bureau. (2000b). *Projections of the total resident population by 5-year age groups, race, and Hispanic origin with special age categories: Middle Series, 2050 to 2070.* Retrieved June 28, 2003, from www.census.gov/population/www/projections/natsum-T3.html

U.S. Census Bureau. (2002a). *Poverty: 2001 highlights.* Retrieved August 24, 2003, from www.census.gov/hhes/poverty/poverty01/pov01hi.html

U.S. Census Bureau. (2002b). *Statistical abstract of the United States 2002.* Washington, DC: U.S. Government Printing Office.

U.S. Census Bureau. (2002c). *Table 4: Poverty status status of families, by type of family, presence of related children, race, and Hispanic origin: 1959 to 2001.* U.S. Bureau of the Census, Current Population Survey, Annual Demographic Supplements. Poverty and Health Statistics Branch/HHES. Retrieved September 1, 2003, from www.census.gov/hhes/poverty/histpov/hstpov4.html

U.S. Census Bureau. (2002d, September 24). *Poverty rate rises, household income declines, Census Bureau reports.* Retrieved June 24, 2003, from www.census.gov/Press-Release/www/2002/cb02-124.html

U.S. Census Bureau. (2002e). *Facts and features: American Indian/Alaska Native heritage month,* November 2002. Retrieved September 21, 2003, from www.census.gov/Press-Release/www/2002/cb02017.html

U.S. Census Bureau. (2003). Table 1: Characteristics of the civilian noninstitutionalized population by age, disability status, and type of disability. *Disability status: 2000—Census 2000 brief.* Retrieved June 28, 2003, from www.census.gov/hhes/www/disable/disabstat2k/table1.html

U.S. Committee for Refugees. (2000). *News & Resources: 7 million people forced to flee last year; Refugee total rises for first time in 7 years.* Retrieved June 13, 2003, from www.refugees.org/news/press_releases/2000/061300a.htm

U.S. Committee for Refugees. (2003a). *Key statistics: World Refugee Survey 2003.* Retrieved September 19, 2003, www.refugees.org/downloads/wrs03/SSKeyStatistics.pdf

U.S. Committee for Refugees. (2003b). *Principal sources of refugees (as of December 31, 2002). World Refugee Survey, 2003.* Retrieved September 19, 2003, www.refugees.org/downloads/wrs03/SSTable5.pdf

U.S. Department of Agriculture. (2003). *Food stamp program.* Retrieved December 16, 2003, from www.fns.usda.gov/fsp/

U.S. Department of Commerce. (1990, April 12). *Bureau of census press release.* Washington, DC: author.

U.S. Department of Health and Human Services. (1999). Chapter 1: Introduction and themes. *Mental health: A report of the Surgeon General.* Retrieved September 28, 2003, from www.surgeongeneral.gov/library/mentalhealth/pdfs/C1.pdf

U.S. Department of Health and Human Services. (2000a). *Report to the Congress on kinship foster care.* Retrieved September 15, 2003, from http://aspe.hhs.gov/hsp/kinr2c00/full.pdf

U.S. Department of Health and Human Services. (2000b). *Healthy people 2010 (2nd ed.). With understanding and improving health and objectives for improving health* (2 vol.). Washington, DC: U.S. Government Printing Office. Retrieved September 22, 2003, from www.healthypeople.gov/Document/pdf/uih/uih.pdf

U.S. Department of Health and Human Services. (2003a, February 7). Annual update of the HHS poverty guidelines. *Federal Register Online, 68*(20), 6456–6458. Retrieved August 11, 2003, from http://a257.g.akamaitech.net/7/257/2422/14mar20010800/edocket.access.gpo.gov/2003/03-3018.htm

U.S. Department of Health and Human Services. (2003b). Alzheimer's disease fact sheet. *NIH Publication No. 03-3431.* Public Health Service, National Institutes of Health, National Institute on Aging. Retrieved September 22, 2003, from www.alzheimers.org/pubs/adfact.html

U.S. Department of Health and Human Services, Administration on Children, Youth and Families. (2003). *Child maltreatment 2001.* Washington, DC: U.S. Government Printing Office.

U.S. Department of Justice. (n.d.). *Summary of the criminal provisions of the Violence Against Women Act.* Retrieved September 13, 2003, from www.ojp.usdoj.gov/vawo/laws/vawa_summary.htm

U.S. Department of Justice. (2001). *Hate crime: The violence of intolerance.* Retrieved August 24, 2003, from www.usdoj.gov/crs/pubs/crs_pub_hate_crime_bulletin_1201.htm

U.S. Department of Justice. (2002). *OVC fact sheet: State crime victim compensation and assistance grant programs.* Office of Justice Programs, Office of Victims of Crime. Retrieved September 22, 2003, from www.ojp.usdoj.gov/ovc/publications/factshts/compandassist/fs000280.pdf

U.S. Department of Justice. (2003a). *Preliminary uniform crime report, 2002.* Retrieved June 30, 2003, from www.fbi.gov/pressrel/pressrel03/12month2002.htm

U.S. Department of Justice. (2003b). *Criminal offenders statistics.* Retrieved August 23, 2003, from www.ojp.usdoj.gov/bjs/crimoff.htm

United Way of America. (2001). *Impact report: Strengthening the home front, The 2001 United Way of America annual report.* Retrieved August 23, 2003, from http://national.unitedway.org/files/pdf/2001annualreport/2001annualreport.pdf

Van Bulow, B. (2001). Eating problems. In A. Gitterman (Ed.), *Handbook of social work practice with vulnerable populations* (pp. 205–233). New York: Columbia University Press.

Van der Meide, W. (2000). *Legislating equality: A review of laws affecting gay, lesbian, bisexual, and transgendered people in the United States.* The Policy Institute of the National Gay and Lesbian Task Force. Retrieved September 15, 2003, from www.ngltf.org/downloads/legeq99.pdf

Van Loon, R. A. (2000). Redefining motherhood: Adaptation to role change for women with AIDS. *Families in Society, 81*(2), 152+. Retrieved September 17, 2003, from InfoTrac Expanded Academic ASAP database.

Van Waters, M. (1931). Philosophical trends in modern social work. In *Proceedings of the National Conference of Social Work, 1930, Boston* (pp. 3–19). Chicago: The University of Chicago Press.

Vecchiolla, F. J., & Maza, P. L. (1989). *Pregnant and parenting adolescents: A study of services.* Washington, DC: Child Welfare League of America.

Vidaver, R. M. (1975). *Developments in human services education and manpower.* New York: Behavioral Publications.

Vinton, L., & Wambach, K. G. (1998). Alcohol and drug use among the elderly. In C. A. McNeece & D. M. DiNitto (Eds.) *Chemical dependency: A systems approach* (2nd ed.) (pp. 391–405). Boston: Allyn & Bacon.

Visher, E. B., & Visher, J. S. (1996). *Therapy with stepfamilies.* New York: Brunner/Mazel.

Vissing, T. M., & Diament, J. (1997). Housing distress among high school students. *Social Work, 42*(1), 31–41.

Vondra, J. I. (1990). The community context of child abuse and neglect. *Marriage and Family Review,* 15(1/2), 19–38.

Wade, C., & Cirese, S. (1991). *Human sexuality* (2nd ed.). San Diego, CA: Harcourt Brace Jovanovich.

Wagner, D. (1990). *The quest for a radical profession: Social service careers and political ideology.* Lanham, MD: University Press of America.

Wagstaff, G. F. (1983). Correlates of a just world in Britain. *The Journal of Social Psychology, 121,* 145–146.

Waldron, C. M. (1996). Lesbians of color and the domestic violence movement. In C. M. Renzetti & C. H. Miley (Eds.), *Violence in gay and lesbian domestic partnerships* (pp. 43–52). New York: Harrington Park Press.

Walker, L. E. A. (1984). Battered women, psychology and public policy. *American Psychologist, 39,* 1178–1182.

Walker, L. E. A. (1989). Psychology and violence against women. *American Psychologist, 44,* 695–702.

Wallace, M. E. (1982). Private practice: A nationwide study. *Social Work, 27,* 262–267.

Walsh, R. (1989). Toward a psychology of human survival: Psychological approaches to contemporary global threats. *American Journal of Psychotherapy, 43,* 158–180.

Warren, J. R. (1998). Meeting the emotional needs of health care providers. In D. M. Aronstein & B. J. Thompson (Eds.), *HIV and social work* (pp. 537–540). New York: Haworth Press.

Washington, R. O. (1982). Social development: A focus on practice and education. *Social Work, 27,* 104–109.

Watkins, S. A. (1990). The Mary Ellen myth: Correcting child welfare history. *Social Work, 35,* 500–503.

Watkins, T. R. (1983). Services to individuals. In J. W. Callicutt & P. J. Lecca (Eds.), *Social work and mental health* (pp. 45–58). New York: The Free Press.

Watson, K. W. (1992). Providing services after adoption: The public child welfare agency must take the lead to meet the lifelong needs of the adoption triangle. *Public Welfare, 50*(1), 4–13.

Wayland, H. I. (1894). A scientific basis of charity. *The Charities Review, 3,* 263–274.

Weaver, H. N. (1998). Indigenous people in a multicultural society: Unique issues for human services. *Social Work, 43*(3), 203–211.

Weaver, H. N. (1999). Indigenous people and the social work profession: Defining culturally competent services. *Social Work, 44*(3), 217–225. Retrieved September 18, 2003, from EBSCOhost Academic Search Elite database.

Wedel, K. A. (1995). Designing and implementing performance contracting. In R. L. Edwards & J. A. Yankey (Eds.), *Skills for effective human service management.* (pp. 335–351). Washington, DC: NASW Press.

Weick, A. (1999). Guilty knowledge. *Families in Society, 80*(4), 327–332.

Weick, A., Rapp, C., Sullivan, W. P., & Kisthardt, W. (1989). A strengths perspective for social work practice. *Social Work, 34,* 350–354.

Weil, M., & Karls, J. M. (1989). Historical origins and recent developments. In M. Weils & J. M. Karls (Eds.), *Case management in human service practice* (pp. 1–28). San Francisco: Jossey-Bass.

Weil, M. O. (1996). Community building, building community practice. *Social Work, 41*(5), 481–499.

Weisz, A. N. (1999). Legal advocacy for domestic violence survivors: The power of an informative relationship. *Families in Society, 80*(2), 138–147.

Wells, S. J. (1995). Child abuse and neglect overview. In R. L. Edwards (Ed.), *Encyclopedia of social work: Vol. 1* (19th ed.) (pp. 346–366). Washington, DC: NASW Press.

Wharton, A. S. (1999, January). The psychosocial consequences of emotional labor. *The Annals of the*

American Academy of Political and Social Science, pp. 158–167.

White, N. J., & Madara, E. J. (2002). *The self-help sourcebook: Your guide to community and online support groups* (7th ed.). Denville, NJ: American Self-Help Clearinghouse.

Whitley, D. M., White K. R., Kelly, S. J., & Yorke, B. (1999). Strengths-based case management: The application to grandparents raising grandchildren. *Families in Society, 80*(2), 110–119.

Whitsett, D., & Land, H. (1992a). Role strain, coping, and marital satisfaction of stepparents. *Families in Society, 73,* 79–92.

Whitsett, D., & Land, H. (1992b). The development of a role strain index for stepparents. *Families in Society, 73,* 14–22.

Whittaker, J. K. (2000). The future of residential group care. *Child Welfare, 79*(3), 59–74.

Wiehe, V. R. (1996). *Working with child abuse and neglect: A primer.* Thousand Oaks, CA: Sage.

Wilensky, H. L., & Lebeaux, C. N. (1965). *Industrial society and social welfare.* New York: The Free Press.

Williams, C. L., Clemmey, H., & Fuerst, S. (2000, November). *Do you read lips?* Mental health deaf and hard of hearing populations. Paper presented at the NASW Social Work 2000 Conference, Baltimore, MD.

Williams, L. F., & Diaz, C. (1987). Family: Multigenerational. In A. Minahan (Ed.), *Encyclopedia of social work: Vol. 1* (18th ed.) (pp. 529–540). Silver Spring, MD: National Association of Social Workers.

Williams, R. M. (1975). Relative deprivation. In L. A. Coser (Ed.), *The idea of social structure* (pp. 355–378). New York: Harcourt Brace Jovanovich.

Wilson, J., & Setturlund, D. (1986). Toward holistic social work practice in general medical settings. *Social Work in Health Care, 12*(2), 1–13.

Wiltse, K. T. (1985). Foster care: An overview. In J. Laird & A. Hartman (Eds.), *A handbook of child welfare: Context, knowledge, and practice* (pp. 565–616). New York: The Free Press.

Wolf, R. S. (2000). The nature and scope of elder abuse. *Generations, 24*(11), 6–13.

Wolk, J. L. (1994). Grant writing: Linking the social work program to the community. *Journal of Teaching in Social Work, 10*(1/2), 83–97.

Wollan, B. J., & Bauer, J. W. (1990). Correlates of financial counseling outcomes: Implications for practitioners. *Families in Society, 71,* 148–157.

Woolf, L. M. (1998). *Gay and lesbian aging.* Retrieved September 15, 2003, from www.webster.edu/~woolflm/oldergay.html

Woolf, L. M. (n.d.). *Effects of age and gender on perceptions of younger and older adults.* Retrieved September 15, 2003, from www.webster.edu/~woolflm/ageismwoolf.html

Working definition of social work practice. (1958). *Social Work, 3*(2), 5–9.

Working statement on the purpose of social work. (1981). *Social Work, 26,* 6.

World Bank. (2003). *Issue briefs: Poverty.* Retrieved August 24, 2003, from http://web.worldbank.org/WBSITE/EXTERNAL/NEWS/0,,contentMDK:20040961~menuPK:34480~pagePK:36694~piPK:116742~theSitePK:4607,00.html

World Health Organization. (2002). *World report on violence and health: Summary.* Retrieved August 30, 2003, from www.who.int/violence_injury_prevention/violence/world_report/en/Full%20WRVH%20summary.pdf

York, G. Y. (1987). Religious-based denial in the NICU: Implications for social work. *Social Work in Health, 12*(4), 31–45.

Young, D. S., & Smith, C. J. (2000). When moms are incarcerated: The needs of children, mothers, and caregivers. *Families in Society, 81*(2), 130–141.

Zayas, L. H., Kaplan, C., Turner, S., Romano, K., & Gonzalez-Ramos, G. (2000). Understanding suicide attempts by adolescent Hispanic females. *Social Work, 45*(1), 53–63.

Zedlewski, S. R. (2003). *Work and barriers to work among welfare recipients in 2002.* The Urban Institute. Retrieved October 2, 2003, from www.urban.org/url.cfm?ID=310836

Zilberfein, F., & Hurwitz, E. (2003). Clinical social work practice at the end of life. *Smith College Studies in Social Work, 73*(3), 299–324.

Zimmerman, M. A., & Rappaport, J. (1988). Citizen participation, perceived control, and psychological empowerment. *American Journal of Community Psychology, 16,* 725–750.

Zunz, S. J. (1998). Resiliency and burnout: Protective factors for human service managers. *Administration in Social Work, 22*(3), 39–54.

Zunz, S. J., & Chernesky, R. H. (2000). The workplace as a protective environment: Management strategies. In E. Norman (Ed.), *Resiliency enhancement: Putting the strengths perspective into social work practice* (pp. 157–176). New York: Columbia University Press.

NAME INDEX

SUBJECT INDEX